SOURCEBOOK ON TORTS

Graham Stephenson, LLM, Solicitor
Principal Lecturer in Law
University of Central Lancashire

Cavendish
Publishing
Limited

First published in Great Britain 1996 by Cavendish Publishing Limited, The Glass House, Wharton Street, London WC1X 9PX
Telephone: 0171-278 8000 Facsimile: 0171-278 8080

British Library Cataloguing-in Publication Data.

Stephenson, Graham 1947 –
Sourcebook on Torts
1 Torts – England
I Titles
344.2'063

ISBN 1 85941 049 9

Printed and bound in Great Britain

PREFACE

This is always the hardest part of the book, coming as it usually does immediately after finishing the proof reading and the last few checks on the sources of the materials. It is conventional to trot out at this stage the justifications for writing the book and collecting the materials together, but I can only say that I have put it together because I was asked by the publishers to do so.

I could say that the book is designed to introduce undergraduate students to some of the primary source materials that they ought to be reading in their tort course and should be particularly useful to those who are denied access or easy access to a law library or who find that the demand on materials is such that their library is overwhelmed by the number of students and consequently access to the materials is extremely difficult. Part time students might well be a readily identifiable class of persons falling into this category, to use a familiar phrase.

I have tried to cover the basic material I would expect a student to be referred to in their tort course, but I have found it necessary because of obvious space limitations to leave out a number of areas. These include actions for breach of statutory duty, deceit, trespass to land and goods, two of my especially favourite topics, and economic torts which I consider, probably without justification, as exceptionally turgid, though I expect somebody out there gets thoroughly excited by them.

Those who know me well acknowledge readily my incredible patience and realise that it is easy for me to recognise that virtue in others, such as family, close friends and the publishers during the last six months. I finished the draft of the book in early March of this year, but I should say that the law is as it was thought to be, by me at least, on 29 February 1996.

Graham Stephenson
Preston

ACKNOWLEDGMENTS

Grateful acknowledgment is made to the Controller of Her Majesty's Stationary Office for permission to reproduce Crown Copyright materials; to the Incorporated Council of Law Reporting for England and Wales for permission to reproduce extracts from the *Law Reports* and the *Weekly Law Reports*; to Butterworths for permission to reproduce extracts from the *All England Law Reports*; and to Sweet & Maxwell for permission to reproduce extracts from the *Criminal Appeal Reports*.

CONTENTS

TABLE OF CASES

W

TABLE OF STATUTES

CHAPTER 1

INTRODUCTION

Individuals, businesses and other organisations in a complex post-industrial society suffer losses of various kinds as a result of the activities of others. Tort law is one of the areas of law primarily concerned with the question of whether these losses are to be compensated for by the person responsible for the relevant activity, or whether the loss must lie where it falls, with the victim. The other major area dealing with similar issues is the law of contract.

Tort law is, to a lesser extent, also concerned with preventing or deterring certain types of conduct. An action in tort is a civil action, as opposed to a criminal prosecution, and is initiated by an individual, business or other organisation rather than by the state, as is usually the case in a criminal matter. An action, in normal circumstances, will be brought in tort to obtain damages, monetary compensation, for some loss sustained by the victim, eg personal injury, damage to or loss of property, damage to economic interests or loss of reputation.

The word 'tort' is French for 'wrong', and we can therefore say that a tort is a civil wrong. Tort law comprises the rules of liability which dictate whether the defendant's activity constitutes a civil wrong, thus enabling the court to grant a remedy, ie compensation, to the plaintiff victim. This seems straightforward enough but there are obvious difficulties with the explanation of what is tort law in view of the diverse nature of the causes of action which appear to fall within its scope.

It is common in an introduction of this kind to discuss the issue of whether there is a law of tort or torts. The search for some unifying factor underlying all causes of action in tort, thus enabling us to distinguish between tort actions and other types of action, eg actions for breach of contract, would appear to be a vain one. Indeed, the fragmentary nature of tort law would seem to militate strongly against discovery of any such principle.

It might, therefore, be more appropriate to talk of a law of torts, a rather loose collection of random causes of action, a residual category of civil wrongs falling outside and independent of the law of contract, the other major source of civil wrongs. If this view is taken, it must nonetheless be acknowledged that the major part of the area covered in this and other books on tort law is within the scope of one single tort, ie negligence, but by the same token, it has to be recognised that there are other causes of action, totally independent of negligence, with their own specialised rules of liability which clearly fall within the subject matter of tort law.

Attempts have conventionally been made to assimilate the various causes of action within the tort umbrella into groupings to provide some coherence or structure to the subject. For example, it is possible to arrange the subject in terms of the interests protected, eg personal safety, reputation, property and economic interests, and group those torts offering some protection in relation to that particular interest.

A number of torts protect the interest in personal safety, ie negligence, trespass to the person (assault and battery, and false imprisonment), public and, possibly, private nuisance, and, arguably, the tort known as the rule in *Rylands v Fletcher*. Property interests in goods are in the main protected by the torts of negligence and interference with goods, whereas interests in land are covered by the actions for trespass to land, under the rule in *Rylands v Fletcher* and in nuisance. Interests in reputation are protected by the defamation actions of libel and slander, whilst economic interests are within the scope of the so-called economic torts, deceit and, to a limited extent, the negligence action.

Alternatively, the grouping could be based on the level of the defendant's blameworthiness, namely, torts requiring proof of intention on the part of the defendant, those whose liability rules are founded on a lack of care established against the defendant, and those where liability is imposed irrespective of fault, namely the strict liability torts. The intentional torts would include trespass to the person and land, interference with goods and deceit by way of illustrations. Negligence would clearly constitute the paramount example of a tort based on the defendant's carelessness, and product liability, nuisance and the rule in *Rylands v Fletcher*, on the face of it at least, would be prime examples of strict liability torts. However, it must be pointed out that the former was originally based on common law negligence and the latter two have in modern times come under severe pressure from the all embracing negligence action as we shall see in the relevant chapters.

Neither of the two approaches is entirely satisfactory, but the latter has been adopted in the main in this book. It has to be borne in mind, however, that some torts will protect more than one interest and that the degree of protection offered may fluctuate, depending on for which interest protection is being sought. For example, in the earlier chapters we shall see the vast gap in protection afforded by the negligence action to the personal safety and property interests on the one hand, and the much less favoured economic interests on the other.

TORT AND OTHER TYPES OF LIABILITY

It is traditional at some point in an introduction of this nature to compare tort liability with the types of liability with which it has a close connection, with a view to marking out more clearly the territory of the subject. Tort law has more in common with the law of contract, but there are connections and overlaps with criminal law, actions for breach of trust and the more recently recognised law of restitution. We have already distinguished between civil wrongs, which are pursued at the initiative of an individual, and criminal matters, which are normally taken up by the state in the public interest. The function of the criminal law is usually stated as being the punishment of the offender by fine or imprisonment, whereas tort law is essentially concerned with compensating the victim of the tort by a damages award made against the perpetrator. Criminal law also seeks to affect the future behaviour of the transgressor, but also that of others with similar criminal tendencies.

Tort law may perform this function but, as we shall see, to a much lesser extent. Some tort actions will also constitute crimes, eg assault and battery, intentional damage to the property of others and public nuisance. In addition, criminal sanctions and a civil action may arise on the same facts in the context of a road traffic accident or an accident in the workplace. In some tort actions the court may award what are known as exemplary damages, which are clearly designed to punish the defendant, although, unlike a fine in a criminal matter being payable to the state, the exemplary award is controversially handed over to the victim over and above any damages designed as compensation. The incidence of such awards is, however, less frequent nowadays precisely for the reason that such payments blur the distinction, as far as the judiciary perceives it, between criminal and civil matters. The distinction is blurred in the eyes of the public in any event by the availability of compensation orders payable to the victims of crime in criminal cases under s 35 Powers of Criminal Courts Act 1973, although this power is rather restricted in practice.

As mentioned above, tort law is more akin to contract law than any other subject. It would be easy to say that contract law is really a specialised area of tort law because of the similar origin of the two types of action, but this would be to ignore the reality that contract has been treated historically as a separate subject from tort with its own independent cause of action. Indeed, there is little to choose between books on tort and contract in terms of depth, breadth and the numbers of them produced for the academic market.

Taken together, tort and contract form the basis of the English law of obligations, although it would be misleading not to acknowledge the contribution to such a classification of the law of restitution and that of the much ignored area of bailment. Traditionally, contract was seen to be based on consent and tort primarily was perceived as a series of primary duties imposed by society irrespective of the consent of those making up that society. This is an oversimplification, as it must be acknowledged that many contractual duties are implied into certain types of contract irrespective of the wishes of the parties to the contract in question. For example, the Sale of Goods Act 1979 (as amended) implies terms of satisfactory quality (s 14(2)), description (s 13) and fitness for particular purpose (s 14(3)) into sale of goods contracts. There are many other examples of this, and these make a significant inroad into the idea that contract is based solely on the agreement of the parties.

Likewise, it is inappropriate to say that all tort duties are imposed as a matter of law. Consent does play some part in the imposition of tort duties, eg in relation to liability for negligent mis-statement and occupier's liability. One of the major issues in recent years has been that of concurrent liability in contract and tort arising from the same facts. It now seems to be the case, after some deliberation, that its existence has been accepted.[1] Indeed, as Jones states:[2]

> Insisting on a contractual analysis to the exclusion of tortious obligations whenever the parties are in a contractual relationship would create an excess of formalism, and result in anomalies that would defy rational justification.

1 See Jones, *Textbook on Torts* (4th edn, 1993, Blackstones), p 6; Stanton, *The Modern Law of Tort* (1994, Sweet and Maxwell), pp 6–8.

2 Jones, see *supra* p 7.

The issue of the interplay between contractual and tortious liability will be returned to in Chapters 2 and, more particularly, 6, as the existence or non-existence of a contractual duty has been considered in some cases as a relevant factor in deciding whether the defendant is thought to owe a duty of care in the tort of negligence, more especially in the cases involving claims for damage to economic interests.

It has to be recognised, however, that there are some significant differences still between liability in contract and tort. One of the most significant departures between the two causes of action concerns the purpose of the award of damages in the respective actions. In contract the plaintiff is normally entitled to be placed in the position he should have been had the contract been properly performed.[3] In other words, the plaintiff is entitled to his expectation loss. In tort, the plaintiff is to be put in the position she was in before the tort was committed, sometimes crudely known as the 'out of pocket expenses' rule. Other differences include limitation periods and tests of remoteness of damage.

Actions for breach of trust and other equitable obligations are historically separate from tort law, as the principles were developed in the Chancery Court as opposed to the common law courts. Even where the claim for breach of any such obligation is met with an award of monetary compensation, it will nonetheless still be regarded as being outside the scope of tort law.

The law of restitution provides some remedies which enable a plaintiff to recoup money, eg money paid under a mistake of fact. This is normally regarded as being outside the subject of books on tort. The requirement to repay money in such circumstances does not come about as a result of the breach of a duty owed to the plaintiff, nor as a result of damage to the latter, but is based on the principle of unjust enrichment of the defendant.

The law of restitution has justifiably gained considerable momentum as a subject in its own right in recent years. There is on occasions an overlap between tort law and restitution, and the plaintiff may seek a restitutionary remedy instead of the normal damages claim. This area of liability is covered in the leading books on restitution.[4]

There have been suggestions in recent years that tort law is only a part of a larger area of law known as the law of obligations. Such an area would also take in contract, restitution and bailment. It would of necessity contain a vast amount of material and, from a purely pragmatic point of view, would be extremely difficult to teach or study as a single subject area. There are also theoretical obstacles in that, as observed above, it would still be necessary to distinguish certainly at least between contract and tort actions. It is probably only true to say that tort is a major but separate part of an overall and much looser classification of the law of obligations, despite the obvious similarities with contract.

---

3 In limited circumstances a plaintiff may choose reliance based damages in contract, see Burrows, *Remedies for Torts and Breach of Contract* (2nd edn, Butterworths), pp 248–56.

4 See Goff and Jones, *The Law of Restitution* (4th edn, 1993); Birks, *An Introduction to The Law of Restitution* (revsd edn, 1989); Burrows, *The Law of Restitution*.

FUNCTIONS OF TORT LAW

Rather than concentrating too much time and energy on searching for some spurious unifying principle which enables us to identify tort law from other types of civil liability, effort might be more usefully directed at an inquiry into the way in which tort law operates. Howarth prefers to look at this question from the converse angle by asking what we would miss if tort law did not exist and we were only left with contract law in the main. He answered thus:[5]

> ... it ought to be said that abolishing the law of torts may not make a great difference at all. In theory a great deal of it could be reinvented through implied terms in contracts, constructive (ie made-up) trusts and orders to restore the plaintiff's property. One might remark that in countries where attempts have been made greatly to restrict the scope of tort law, eg New Zealand and Sweden, such developments do not seem yet to have happened. But that might have as much to do with the legal limits of imagination and the will of the judiciary as with the theoretical possibilities.

It is normal to mention in this context several aims or objectives of tort law of which we would not feel the benefit if tort law no longer existed. Monetary compensation has already been identified as a primary function, but in any list of aims would come deterrence, appeasement or vindication of rights, justice, and 'to provide a public forum in which to discuss new forms of behaviour and the consequences of new technologies'.[6]

Appeasement and vindication of rights

It is fairly clear that these two aims only have a limited role to play in modern tort law and are therefore dealt with briefly and together. The idea of appeasement may have been a factor in the early days of the legal system, whereby allowing an individual the opportunity to make a claim in a civil court against the transgressor would prevent the victim from resorting to some form of self-redress which might result in a breakdown of law and order. The vindication of rights function is probably more important these days and there appears to have been a resurgence in its popularity as evidenced by recent litigation in respect of large scale disasters such as the Zeebrugge and *Piper Alpha* incidents. Victims or the families of deceased victims are often interviewed on television, saying that they are not really interested in compensation, rather supporting the idea of the deterrence function of the law by expressing the view that nobody else should have to undergo what they or their relatives have had to go through.

Of course, in relation to the civil liberties torts, eg assault, battery and, more particularly, false imprisonment, vindication of rights has a significant part to play, especially in relation to injured feelings and loss of dignity and respect, over and above any compensatory function. Such an analysis might also be applied to defamation actions. Despite this, if tort law ceased to exist, it is unlikely that, in relation to these two functions at least, much would be lost.

5 *Textbook on Tort* (1995, Butterworths), p 7.

6 Howarth, *op cit* p 13.

JUSTICE

Justice might be perceived as requiring that a defendant be made to pay for his wrongdoing by being ordered to compensate his victim. The defendant is forced to correct or rectify the situation which he has brought about. This might have some appeal as a valid argument in the context of torts which require the proof of some element of blameworthiness on the part of the defendant, eg trespass to the person, negligence, etc, but this analysis runs into difficulties with the torts which are categorised as strict liability in nature, where proof of fault is not an essential requirement. Of course, it might be argued that even though the defendant is not at fault in such instances, nonetheless it is his activity which has created the risk which has resulted in the harm to the plaintiff, but this is difficult to rationalise in terms of wrongdoing, involving as it must a moral dimension.

Justice may be more appropriately served by looking to the plaintiff's need for compensation rather than the defendant's moral turpitude. This, however, would take the debate into the different, and controversial, realm of distributive justice. There are serious doubts whether tort law is capable of social engineering in the redistribution of wealth in society.[7]

The arguments concerning the defendant having to pay for his wrongdoing or risk-creating are themselves weakened further by the fact that, in most types of accident, any compensation paid to the tort victim will come from an insurance company rather than the particular defendant's own pocket. Of course, the defendant may have paid something by way of premiums to the insurance company, but where the claim is for substantial damages, far exceeding the amount of those premiums, there is little scope for arguing that tort law is achieving the aim of corrective justice. As Jones observes[8] '[liability] insurance removes the connection between the wrongdoer and the plaintiff's compensation'. Howarth reinforces the point graphically:[9]

> There is a paradox that when insurance intervenes, the higher the sum claimed in relation to the premiums paid the less the requirements of rectificatory justice are fulfilled.

There seems to be considerable doubt as to whether tort does or can serve the cause of justice in the light of the above.

DETERRENCE

If taken in isolation, the liability rules in tort law clearly seem to have a deterrent function, whether the claim be for compensation or an injunction. However, in the areas most important in a quantitative sense, ie road and work accidents, the impact of liability insurance clouds the picture significantly. The threat of having to pay compensation to the victim of one's wrongful action

7 See Stanton, *op cit* p 16, Jones, *op cit* p 14; Atiyah, *Accidents, Compensation and The Law* (5th edn (ed Cane)), pp 158–59.

8 *Op cit* p 14.

9 *Op cit* p 13.

cannot be dismissed lightly and, in some torts, will still be a powerful deterrent to many. This is particularly the case in the realms of liability for defamation, assault and battery and the economic torts. The fear of having to pay substantial damages to a victim of a defamatory statement no doubt explains why publishers employ the services of expert libel lawyers to advise on material before it is published. The use of injunctions in this area to prevent publication of alleged defamatory material reinforces the deterrent aspect of this particular cause of action. The granting of the injunction works as a deterrent on the particular defendant but also provides a warning to others of a like mind that, in appropriate cases, the courts will not shrink from such orders.

It is, however, very difficult, in the absence of factual studies, to evaluate the precise effect of the fear of imposition of tort liability on the behaviour of potential defendants. In respect of road traffic accidents, it is suspected that other factors may be at play in deterring bad driving. Notions of self-preservation, safety of others, eg passengers, and fear of damage to one's own property are at least part of the picture, in addition to which one must also consider the vital impact of the criminal sanctions for poor driving. Insurance also plays its part in reducing the deterrent aspect of tort law, in that the transgressor is not the person paying the compensation and normally will only be out of pocket to the extent of any no-claims bonus on the insurance policy. A similar process is at work in the field of industrial accidents where liability insurance is also compulsory.

On the other hand, a finding of fault against a professional person, even if the damages award is met by an insurance company, may have a significant effect on the reputation of the defendant and must provide some measure of deterrence, although this must not be overstated. Disciplinary action by a professional body, if any, may concentrate the mind more closely than any concern about an award of damages. In the absence of a system of tort law, it might be surmised that there would, in some of these areas, be little difference in the preventative effect of the law.

There is another school of thought concerned with the deterrent aspect of tort law. In the interests of overall economic efficiency, it is argued that society should be moving towards a cost-justified level of accidents. This is known as the 'general deterrence' theory and is largely based on the work of Calabresi,[10] where the view is taken that there is a point at which the costs of prevention of accidents outweigh the savings made in the costs of the accidents. Once that point has been reached no further savings are possible and, indeed, more expenditure on prevention is wasted. This economic efficiency argument is not universally accepted.[11]

We have seen in this brief discussion that there are severe limits to the scope of tort law as an effective deterrent and that, certainly in some areas, if it did not exist it might not be missed too much.

10 *The Costs of Accidents*, 1970.

11 Atiyah, *op cit* pp 374–94.

PUBLIC FORUM FUNCTION

According to Howarth this function takes two forms. The first is that tort law performs a kind of ombudsman[12] function through the medium of the negligence action, investigating the causes of accidents and subjecting the defendant's activity to the scrutiny of reasonableness. Not all accidents are, or could be, subjected to such a process. It may only be purely random incidents which are placed under the judicial microscope and that those which might be considered more appropriate for full investigation are not pursued for all sorts of good reasons, or are settled before being the focus of the open court. This is the piecemeal nature of a system which depends in the main upon individual initiative to set the ball rolling. Public enquiries are generally thought to be a more successful way of launching investigations into major accidents.

The other form is best expressed in Howarth's own words:

> Another form of the idea is that tort law provides a way for the optimal regulation of new forms of behaviour and new technologies to be worked out on a case by case basis, so that the legislature has a pattern of thought and decision about a new problem to work on before plumping for a particular set of regulations.

It might be argued that this form of function is subject to the same criticism as the other, being dependent upon the accidents of litigation for it to be capable of making a contribution.

COMPENSATION FUNCTION

Finally, it is necessary to consider the primary function of tort law – namely, compensation. On the face of it, tort is a loss shifting device, whereby a person who has sustained a loss attempts to transfer that loss to the person who has apparently brought such loss into being. A plaintiff who succeeds in unlocking the door to the tort system, ie manages to establish liability against another under the rules of tort, wins the equivalent of the jackpot in the National Lottery if the injuries are severe.

However, the tort system operates against the backdrop of a well-established insurance market, in circumstances where the two most commonly successful types of claim, road and workplace accidents, are covered by compulsory insurance. Tort law is, therefore, in reality a loss spreading mechanism, distributing the loss amongst the relevant category of premium payers. Consequently, in the majority of cases the existence of insurance guarantees that the victim will get compensation, and in some cases the very fact of insurance may well influence the issue of imposition of liability in the first place. For example, in road traffic accidents it appears that the slightest momentary lapse of attention may found the basis of liability, the courts being readily influenced by the fact that the defendant will not be paying personally out of his own pocket for the damages.

It is worth considering what the position would be if tort law was abolished overnight. The victim's loss would have to lie where it fell, unless she had

12 See Linden, *Tort as Ombudsman* (1973) 51 Can Bar R 155.

adequate first party insurance covering the type of loss in question, or could unlock the door to some other compensation system. If the circumstances giving rise to the injury, though no longer a tort, were classified as constituting a crime of violence falling within the scope of the Criminal Injuries Compensation Scheme, the victim could obtain a reasonable level of compensation, although this may not be the case when the Criminal Injuries Compensation Act 1995 comes into force. Alternatively, the injured party might make use of the court's power to award compensation in criminal cases mentioned earlier in this chapter. Both these sources of compensation have serious limitations and would certainly not make up for the loss of the tort action in cases of severe injury in particular.

If the injury to the victim falls outside the scope of the above, it is necessary to consider what other forms of compensation might be available. A victim of a serious accident or chronic illness or disease not attributable to any breach of tortious duty, may well find that the only available source of compensation, short of falling upon charity, is the state benefits scheme. It is not proposed to go into any detail in relation to the benefits that might be available but merely to make some general observations about the relationship between compensation in the tort system and that in the state system.

Serious injury or disease, for which the victim manages to pin the blame on a defendant in the tort system, is generously compensatable, for as we shall see in Chapter 14, the principle underlying an award of damages in tort is that of full compensation. The plaintiff is entitled to be compensated under a number of different heads of damage in appropriate cases. In particular, s/he is paid damages for the non-pecuniary losses sustained as a result of the accident, as well as pecuniary losses, eg loss of earnings and medical expenses. Non-pecuniary losses include pain and suffering and loss of amenity. A substantial element in any claim where the injury or illness is severe will be a claim for future loss of earnings. As a consequence, particularly where the plaintiff was a top earner before the accident, a final award may be extremely high.

The state system is nowhere near as generous, as the general principle underlying this scheme is to replace lost income and not to compensate normally for the non-pecuniary loss favoured by the tort system. In addition, the state scheme falls far short of replacing all lost income, and those in the higher income bracket can certainly not expect generous treatment at the hands of the state benefits scheme. It is therefore without doubt the case that if tort law were to be abolished, in the absence of a replacement scheme, it would be sorely missed by those who might have been its beneficiaries.

It is likely that the abolition of the torts scheme will remain politically unacceptable. It is also unlikely that the present state benefits system would be enhanced in order to fill the gap. Consequently, it would be necessary to install a new system to compensate the long term injured or sick who would otherwise have succeeded under tort law. Some form of no-fault scheme might fit the bill, but suggestions for its introduction in this country remain unheeded and are likely to remain so for the foreseeable future.[13] Financing such a scheme will

13 See the Pearson Commission, 1978, Cmnd 7054; and, of course, Atiyah, *op cit* generally.

always be a major stumbling block, even though it may be the case that such a scheme would appear to be cheaper to run than the tort system, which is notoriously expensive, especially in comparison with the state benefits system in this country.[14] We can conclude, therefore, that the main function of tort law – namely, its compensation mechanism – would be sorely missed if the tort action was removed from the legal catalogue of actions and no substitute was put in place for it.

CONCLUSION

It is likely that tort law will be with us for some time to come more or less in its present form. The following chapters of this sourcebook will cover the liability rules of tort law together with materials on the available remedies as appropriate. As mentioned earlier in this introductory chapter, the book has been organised primarily on the basis that the torts can be grouped according to the extent of the blameworthiness of the potential defendant. This is a rough and ready classification which is not entirely satisfactory, but it should at least give some structure to the materials.

It is proposed to start with the tort of negligence, which is the tort wider in scope than all the others and of course forms the basis of accident compensation in the UK. The initial negligence chapters will look at the general principles, and will be followed by chapters dealing with areas of particular difficulty for the law of negligence, namely, liability for damage to financial interests, liability for psychiatric injury, and occupier's liability. It is then proposed to look at the materials making up the torts falling under the heading of trespass to the person as an illustration of an intentional tort. We shall then go on to consider the stricter liability torts, namely, nuisance, *Rylands v Fletcher*, product liability and liability relating to animals.

Defamation, sticking out like a sore thumb, has a chapter to itself, as it is difficult to categorise it satisfactorily in one of the previous groupings. The final chapters will consider vicarious liability and remedies. Defences will be dealt with in the context of the relevant torts in the main.

14 See Atiyah, *op cit*, Chapter 17.

CHAPTER 2

DUTY OF CARE

INTRODUCTION

The focus of this and the next six chapters will be the tort of negligence, the major tort of the 20th century. Discussion of this area of tort law tends to dominate most academic courses, and this is also reflected in the treatment in the textbooks on tort law. Negligence is the tort of all torts, arriving on the scene, in any organised form at least, late in our legal development, but immediately threatening to take a stranglehold on the law of civil obligations. It has been perceived as a danger to the neighbouring law of contract, the uneasy relationship between these two areas of law being a persistent theme in many of the cases, particularly those involving claims for financial harm.[1] Its impact on other torts cannot be ignored either, particularly in nuisance,[2] and the rule in *Rylands v Fletcher*.[3]

It should perhaps not be so surprising that the tort should have developed so rapidly in a post-industrial society where technological change itself has been rapid, throwing up new problems on a regular basis but at the same time massively increasing the numbers of older problems, particularly road and work-related accidents. As society becomes more complex and technologically oriented, product liability claims become not only more common but also more sophisticated. In addition, as society moves from a largely manufacturing-based economy to a services-dominated one, there is a consequential increase in problems arising from the provision of poor or inadequate services. The action based on the tort of negligence has been asked to deal with these types of issues more and more over recent years. It has so far had to bear the brunt of claims for accident compensation as outlined in Chapter 1, and perhaps it is not so surprising that it is groaning under the pressure.[4]

THE ELEMENTS OF NEGLIGENCE

In this chapter, we are concerned with negligence as an independent tort rather than negligence relating to the way or manner in which other legal duties may be broken, eg a negligent breach of contract or a negligent trespass to goods. In these instances negligence is a word being used to describe the conduct of the defendant, where it might be less confusing to use the word 'careless'. The tort of negligence involves more than just careless behaviour, having developed a conceptual apparatus all of its own to deal with problems of varying kinds. It is often said that negligence comprises three elements: duty, breach and damage. The damage aspect is sometimes broken down into the components of causation and remoteness.

---

1 See Chapter 6.

2 See Chapter 9.

3 See Chapter 10.

4 See Howarth, *Negligence after Murphy: Time to Rethink* (1991) CLJ 58.

It can safely be said that all these elements are interrelated and fused together at times and confusion is often the inevitable result as far as the student is concerned. Some of the confusion is, however, generated by the judiciary, a situation which is avoidable.[5] Judges are often found talking about issues of breach of duty or causation instead of duty, and *vice versa*. It is, however, convenient to attempt to discuss each of the elements in isolation from each other, but it has to be remembered that the plaintiff has to show that all three elements are present before succeeding in the tort of negligence.

It is proposed to deal with the duty issue first, although there is a school of thought which believes that the breach issue should be considered first. The reasoning behind this is that unless one understands the concept of fault, ie blameworthy conduct, then it is not very illuminating to consider theoretical notions about whether a duty is owed by a defendant. As we shall see, if the plaintiff fails to establish that he is owed a duty of care, it does not matter whether the defendant has been careless or not – there is no liability. Likewise, if there is no breach, there is no liability even if, as a matter of law, it is a duty situation. Similar arguments relate to the damage aspect; if there is no damage, there is no liability in negligence.

This does not really take us any further forward. The justification here for placing the duty issue first is that, in many cases, the duty issue is referred by the trial court to the appeal court for resolution before any evidence is heard. In these circumstances the court is being asked to assume that the facts as set out in the statement of claim are true and whether they disclose a cause of action known to law. If the answer to this question is in the negative, the case need not proceed any further. This is the procedure in Scotland and is often adopted in England.[6] If the answer is in the affirmative, the case should then be referred back to the trial court to hear the argument and evidence. However, once the decision on the duty issue has been resolved in favour of the plaintiff a settlement may follow, as this may have been the only substantial ground on which to defend the action. Even if it was not the only issue of substance, it is nonetheless one less obstacle for the plaintiff to face at trial and may persuade the defendant that it is in his interests to offer suitable terms for settlement.

The remainder of this chapter will consider this important duty issue. The two subsequent chapters will cover the other two no less important elements making up the tort of negligence.

DUTY OF CARE

The plaintiff has to show that s/he is owed a duty outside contract or other torts to take reasonable care for his/her safety or whatever other interest of his/hers has been damaged. If s/he fails to establish this, his/her case will be unsuccessful no matter how careless the defendant has been and irrespective of whether that carelessness has brought about the damage to the interest in

5 See Howarth, *op cit*.

6 *Donoghue v Stevenson* [1932] AC 562; *Anns v Merton London Borough Council* [1978] AC 728.

question. The duty concept is being used here to keep issues of liability firmly under control. It is a control mechanism enabling a court to say whether or not the damage claimed for is legally recognised. Another way of expressing it is in terms of immunity from suit. If there is no notional duty on a careless defendant, then he is immune from action, despite his lack of care. Immunities are granted for certain types of loss, subject to exceptions, eg damage to financial interests.

Liability for psychiatric harm is severely restricted, as we shall see, so it might be said that this is an area of partial immunity. Other types of immunity are based on the status of the defendant, eg public authorities, the police and legal personnel, namely judges, advocates, etc. Some in this category are considered absolute. There is general immunity in relation to the difficult area of omissions, otherwise known as misfeasance. On the other hand the law has selected certain plaintiffs as its favourite, the most obvious of these being the rescuer.[7]

Lying beneath these significant immunities are value judgments by the judiciary. The reasons for these particular choices are often obscured by notions such as reasonable foreseeability, proximity, and whether it is just and reasonable. However. it is more frequently the case that judges express their reasons for denying or imposing liability in particular instances, and many of these will be discussed in the cases extracted below.

The duty issue is dominated by the search for the Holy Grail, namely the desire to discover some general guiding principle which can be referred to in novel cases where there is no existing precedent on the issue of whether the situation in hand is a duty or not, and provide an answer one way or the other. It was fashionable 60 years ago to question whether such a quest was at all worthwhile. The experience of the last 20 years, chronicled below, may persuade some that it is worth reconsidering whether we need the cumbersome duty concept. After all, the French and Dutch have done without such a concept 'without any noticeable detriment either to the coherence of their law or to the well-being of their societies'.[8] Nonetheless, we are still left with the concept which seems to take up a disproportionate amount of time in the appellate courts, at the same time generating much bewilderment among students and academics alike.

We shall briefly look at the position before the landmark case of *Donoghue v Stevenson*,[9] and consider the development of the duty concept following that case until the early 1980s and then, finally, the current situation.

Pre-1932

Before 1932 all that can be said is that there were specific situations where it was recognised that some situations were duty situations and others were not. As Street observed:[10]

7 See Linden, *Rescuers and Good Samaritans* (1971) 34 MLR 241.

8 Howarth, *op cit*, p 157.

9 [1932] AC 562.

10 *Street on Torts* ((ed Brazier M), 9th edn, 1993, Butterworths), p 173.

> The law originally developed in an empirical manner by decisions that, in some particular circumstances there was a duty, and that in others there was none.

The first real attempt to discover the elusive general principle lying behind the various cases was made by Brett MR in *Heaven v Pender*:[11]

> The proposition which these recognised cases suggest, and which is therefore, to be deduced from them, is that whenever one person is by circumstances placed in such a position with regard to another that everyone of ordinary sense who did think would at once recognise that if he did not use ordinary care or skill in his own conduct with regard to those circumstances he would cause danger of injury to the person or property of the other, a duty arises to use ordinary care and skill to avoid such danger. Without displacing the other propositions to which allusion has been made as applicable to the particular circumstances in respect of which they have been enunciated, this proposition includes, I think, all the recognised cases of liability. It is the only proposition which covers them all.

This early attempt to formulate the general principle was not greeted with any especial enthusiasm.[12] The next opportunity to establish a general statement of this kind arose in the case of *Donoghue v Stevenson* itself. In this case the House of Lords decided by a majority of three to two that a manufacturer of a product owed a duty of care to the ultimate consumer of the product to take reasonable care in the preparation of the product to avoid injury to the consumer or damage to his property. The case concerned the sale of a bottle of ginger beer to the friend of the pursuer. The beer contained the remains of a decomposed snail, the existence of which did not become apparent until the pursuer had drunk some of the drink. The problem facing the pursuer was that she did not have a contract with either the retailer or the manufacturer. She was forced to pursue her action in negligence. We start with a brief extract from Lord Buckmaster's speech, one of the dissenting judges:

> I turn, therefore, to the decided cases to see if they can be construed so as to support the appellant's case. One of the earliest is the case of *Langridge v Levy*.[13] It is a case often quoted and variously explained. There a man sold a gun which he knew was dangerous for the purchaser's son. The gun exploded in the son's hands, and he was held to have a right of action in tort against the gun maker. How far it is from the present case can be seen from the judgment of Parke B, who, in delivering the judgment of the court, used these words: 'We should pause before we made a precedent by our decision which would be an authority for an action against vendors, even of such instruments and articles as are dangerous in themselves, at the suit of any person whomsoever into whose hands they might happen to pass, and who should be injured thereby'; and in *Longmeid v Holliday*[14] the same eminent judge points out that the earlier case was based on a fraudulent mis-statement, and he expressly repudiates the view that it has any wider application. The case of *Langridge v Levy*, therefore, can be dismissed from consideration with the comment that it is rather surprising it has so often been cited for a proposition it cannot support.

11 (1883) 11 QBD 503 at p 509.

12 See *Le Lievre v Gould* [1893] 1 QB 491 *per* AL Smith LJ at p 504.

13 (1837) 2 M & W 519; (1838) 4 M & W 337.

14 (1851) 6 Ex 761.

The case of *Winterbottom v Wright*[15] is, on the other hand, an authority that is closely applicable. Owing to negligence in the construction of a carriage it broke down, and a stranger to the manufacture and sale sought to recover damages for injuries which he alleged were due to negligence in the work, and it was held that he had no cause of action either in tort or arising out of contract. This case seems to me to show that the manufacturer of any article is not liable to a third party by negligent construction, for there can be nothing in the character of a coach to place it in a special category. It may be noted also, that in this case Alderson B said:[16] 'The only safe rule is to confine the right to recover to those who enter into the contract; if we go one step beyond that, there is no reason why we should not go 50.'

Longmeid v Holliday[17] was the case of a defective lamp sold to a man whose wife was injured by its explosion. The vendor of the lamp, against whom the action was brought, was not the manufacturer, so that the case was not exactly parallel to the present, but the statement of Parke B in his judgment covers the case of the manufacturer, for he said: 'It would be going much too far to say, that so much care is required in the ordinary intercourse of life between one individual and another, that, if a machine not in its nature dangerous, ... but which might become so by a latent defect entirely unknown although discoverable by the exercise of ordinary care, should be lent or given by one person, even by the person who manufactured it, to another, the former should be answerable to the latter for a subsequent damage accruing to the use of it.' It is true that he uses the words 'lent or given' and omits the word 'sold', but if the duty be entirely independent of contract and is a duty owed to a third person, it seems to me to be the same whether the article be originally given or sold. The fact in the present case that the ginger beer originally left the premises of the manufacturer on a purchase, as was probably the case, cannot add to his duty, if such existed, to take care in its preparation.

It has been suggested that the statement of Parke B does not cover the case of negligent construction, but the omission to exercise reasonable care in the discovery of a defect in the manufacture of an article where the duty of examination exists is just as negligent as the negligent construction itself.

The general principle of these cases is stated by Lord Sumner in the case of *Blacker v Lake & Elliott Ltd*[18] in these terms: 'The breach of the defendant's contract with A to use care and skill in or about the manufacture or repair of an article does not of itself give any cause of action to B when he is injured by reason of the article proving to be defective.'

From this general rule there are two well known exceptions:

(1) in the case of an article dangerous in itself; and

(2) where the article, not in itself dangerous, is in fact dangerous by reason of some defect or any other reason, and this is known to the manufacturer.

Until the case of *George v Skivington*[19] I know of no further modification of the general rule.

15 (1842) 10 M & W 109.

16 (1842) 10 M & W 115.

17 (1851) 6 Ex 761, 768.

18 (1912) 106 LT 533, 536.

19 (1869) LR 5 Ex 1.

As to (1), in the case of things dangerous in themselves, there is, in the words of Lord Dunedin, 'a peculiar duty to take precaution imposed upon those who send forth or install such articles when it is necessarily the case that other parties will come within their proximity': *Dominion Natural Gas Co Ltd v Collins & Perkins*.[20] And as to (2), this depends on the fact that the knowledge of the danger creates the obligation to warn, and its concealment is in the nature of fraud. In this case no one can suggest that ginger beer was an article dangerous in itself, and the words of Lord Dunedin show that the duty attaches only to such articles, for I read the words 'a peculiar duty' as meaning a duty peculiar to the special class of subject mentioned.

Of the remaining cases, *George v Skivington* is the one nearest to the present, and without that case, and the statement of Cleasby B in *Francis v Cockerell*[21] and the *dicta* of Brett MR in *Heaven v Pender*,[22] the appellant would be destitute of authority. *George v Skivington* related to the sale of a noxious hair wash, and a claim made by a person who had not bought it but who had suffered from its use, based on its having been negligently compounded, was allowed. It is remarkable that *Langridge v Levy* was used in support of the claim and influenced the judgment of all the parties to the decision. Both Kelly CB and B stressed the fact that the article had been purchased to the knowledge of the defendant for the use of the plaintiff, as in *Langridge v Levy*, and Cleasby B who, realising that *Langridge v Levy* was decided on the ground of fraud, said: 'Substitute the word "negligence" for "fraud" and the analogy between *Langridge v Levy* is complete.' It is unnecessary to point out too emphatically that such a substitution cannot possibly be made. No action based on fraud can be supported by mere proof of negligence.

I do not propose to follow the fortunes of *George v Skivington*; few cases can have lived so dangerously and lived so long. Lord Sumner, in the case of *Blacker v Lake & Elliot Ltd*[23] closely examines its history, and I agree with his analysis. He said that he could not presume to say that it was wrong, but he declined to follow it on the ground which is, I think, firm that it was in conflict with *Winterbottom v Wright*.

So far, therefore, as the case of *George v Skivington* and the *dicta* in *Heaven v Pender* are concerned, it is my opinion better that they should be buried so securely that their perturbed spirits shall no longer vex the law.

In my view, therefore, the authorities are against the appellant's contention, and apart from authority, it is difficult to see how any common law proposition can be formulated to support her claim.

The principle contended for must be this: that the manufacturer, or indeed the repairer, of any article, apart entirely from contract, owes a duty to any person by whom the article is lawfully used to see that it has been carefully constructed. All rights in contract must be excluded from consideration of this principle; such contractual rights as may exist in successive steps from the original manufacturer down to the ultimate purchaser are *ex hypothesis* immaterial. Nor can the doctrine be confined to cases where inspection is difficult or impossible to introduce. This conception is simply to misapply to tort doctrine applicable to sale and purchase.

20 [1909] AC 640, 646.

21 (1870) LR 5 QB 501, 515.

22 (1883) 11 QBD 503, 509 *et seq*.

23 (1912) 106 LT 533, 536.

> The principle of tort lies completely outside the region where such considerations apply, and the duty, if it exists, must extend to every person who, in lawful circumstances, uses the article made. There can be no special duty attaching to the manufacture of food apart from that implied by contract or imposed by statute. If such a duty exists, it seems to me it must cover the construction of every article, and I cannot see any reason why it should not apply to the construction of a house. If one step, why not 50? Yet if a house be, as it sometimes is, negligently built, and in the consequence of that negligence the ceiling falls and injures the occupier or anyone else, no action against the builder exists according to English law, although I believe such a right did exist according to the laws of Babylon.

Nearly all of Lord Buckmaster's speech is in a similar vein, paying close attention to the previous cases, dismissing contemptuously those which are against his view, supporting wholeheartedly those which would deny liability. This provides clear evidence of the piecemeal approach referred to by Street above. Only once does His Lordship refer, and then only briefly, to factors beyond the cases, when he asks the question: if one step, why not 50? This is a reference to what we would now call the floodgates argument, the fear that by allowing certain claims the courts will be inundated with litigants, a frequently exaggerated claim but to which we will have cause to return later.

Compare the extracts from Lord Buckmaster's speech with the celebrated comments of Lord Atkin, who admittedly deals with the precedents in similar fashion, but then goes on to widen the nature of the enquiry giving birth to the so-called 'neighbour' principle.

> My Lords, the sole question for determination in this case is legal. Do the arguments made by the pursuer in her pleading, if true, disclose a cause of action? I need not restate the particular facts. The question is whether the manufacturer of an article of drink sold by him to a distributor, in circumstances which prevent the distributor or the ultimate purchaser or consumer from discovering by inspection any defect, is under a legal duty to the ultimate or consumer to take reasonable care that the article is free from defect likely to cause injury to health. I do not think a more important problem has occupied your Lordships in your judicial capacity: important both because of its bearing on public health and because of the practical test which it applies to the system under which it arises. The case has to be determined in accordance with Scots law; but it has been a matter of agreement between the experienced counsel who argued this case, and it appears to be the basis of the judgments of the learned judges of the Court of Session, that for the purposes of determining this problem the laws of Scotland and England are the same.
>
> It is remarkable how difficult it is to find, in the English authorities, statements of general application defining the relations between parties that give rise to the duty. The courts are concerned with the particular relations which come before them in actual litigation, and it is sufficient to say whether the duty exists in those circumstances. The result is that the courts have been engaged upon an elaborate classification of duties as they exist in respect of property, whether real or personal, with further divisions as to ownership, occupation or control, and distinctions based on the particular relations of the one side or the other, whether manufacturer, salesman or landlord, customer, tenant, stranger, etc. In this way it can be ascertained at any time whether the law recognises a duty, but only where the case can be referred to some particular species which has been examined and classified. And yet the duty which is common to all the cases where liability is

> established must logically be based upon some element common to the cases where it is found to exist.
>
> To seek a complete logical definition of the general principle is probably to go beyond the function of the judge, for the more general the definition the more likely it is to omit essentials or to introduce non-essentials. The attempt was made by Brett MR in *Heaven v Pender*,[24] in a definition to which I will later refer. As framed, it was demonstrably too wide, though it appears to me, if properly limited, to be capable of affording a valuable practical guide.
>
> At present I content myself with pointing out that, in English law, there must be, and is, some general conception of relations giving rise to a duty of care, of which the particular cases found in the books are but instances. The liability for negligence, whether styled as such or treated as in other systems as a species of '*culpa*', is no doubt based upon a general public sentiment of moral wrongdoing for which the offender must pay. But acts or omissions which any moral code would censure cannot, in a practical world, be treated so as to give a right to every person injured by them to demand relief. In this way rules of law arise which limit the range of complainants and the extent of their remedy. The rule that you are to love your neighbour becomes, in law – you must not injure your neighbour; and the lawyer's question – who is my neighbour? – receives a restricted reply. You must take reasonable care to avoid acts or omissions which you can reasonably foresee would be likely to injure your neighbour. Who then, in law, is my neighbour? The answer seems to be – persons who are so closely and directly affected by my act that I ought reasonably to have them in contemplation as being so affected when I am directing my mind to the acts or omissions which are called into question.

After a thorough survey of the cases and indicating that he was favouring the imposition of liability, Lord Atkin continued:

> It is always a satisfaction to an English lawyer to be able to test his application of fundamental principles of the common law by the development of the same doctrines by the lawyers of the courts of the United States. In that country I find that the law appears to be well established in the sense in which I have indicated. The mouse had emerged from the ginger beer bottle in the United States before it appeared in Scotland, but there it brought a liability upon the manufacturer. I must not in this long judgment do more than refer to the illuminating judgment of Cardozo J in *Macpherson v Buick Motor Co* in the New York Court of Appeals,[25] in which he states the principles of law as I should desire to state them, and reviews the authorities in other states than his own. Whether the principle he affirms would apply to the particular facts of that case in this country would be a question for consideration if the case arose. It might be that the course of business, by giving opportunities of examination to the immediate purchaser or otherwise, prevented the relation between the manufacturer and the user of the car being so close as to create a duty. But the American decision would undoubtedly lead to a decision in favour of the pursuer in the present case.

24 (1883) 11 QBD 503, 509.

25 217 NY 382.

> My Lords, if your Lordships accept the view that this pleading discloses a relevant cause of action you will be affirming the proposition that by Scots and English law alike a manufacturer of products, which he sells in such a form as to show that he intends them to reach the ultimate consumer in the form in which they left him with no reasonable possibility of intermediate examination, and with the knowledge that the absence of reasonable care in the preparation or putting up of the products will result in an injury to the consumer's life or property, owes a duty to the consumer to take that reasonable care.
>
> It is a proposition which I venture to say no one in Scotland or England who was not a lawyer would for one moment doubt. It will be an advantage to make it clear that the law in this matter, as in most others, is in accordance with sound common sense. I think this appeal should be allowed.

Lord Thankerton, agreeing with Lord Atkin, stated:

> In my opinion, the existence of a legal duty under such circumstances is in conformity with the principles of both the law of Scotland and the law of England. The English cases demonstrate how impossible it is to catalogue finally, amid the ever varying types of human relationships, those relationships in which a duty to exercise care arises apart from contract, and each of these cases relates to its own set of circumstances, out of which it was claimed that the duty had arisen. In none of these cases were the circumstances identical with the present case as regards that which I regard as the essential element in this case – namely, the manufacturer's own action in bringing himself into direct relationship with the party injured.

The other judge in the majority was Lord Macmillan. The following important extract is taken from his speech:

> The law takes no cognisance of carelessness in the abstract. It concerns itself with carelessness only where there is a duty to take care and where failure in that duty causes damage. In such circumstances carelessness assumes the legal quality of negligence and entails the consequences in the law of negligence. What, then, are the circumstances which give rise to this duty to take care? In the daily contacts of social and business life human beings are thrown into, or place themselves in, an infinite variety of relations with their fellows; and the law can refer only to the standards of the reasonable man in order to determine whether any particular relation gives rise to a duty to take care as between those who stand in that relation to each other. The grounds of action may be as various and manifold as human errancy; and the conception of legal responsibility may develop in adaptation to altering social conditions and standards. The criterion of judgment must adjust and adapt itself to the changing circumstances of life. The categories of negligence are never closed. The cardinal principle of liability is that the party complained of should owe a duty to take care, and that the party complaining should be able to prove that he has suffered damage in consequence of a breach of that duty. Where there is room for diversity of view, it is in determining what circumstances will establish such a relationship between the parties as to give rise, on the one side, to a duty to take care, and on the other side to a right to have care taken.

Lord Macmillan had earlier in his speech surveyed, as had Lord Atkin, the authorities, but both their speeches are marked out by their willingness to consider wider issues in deciding whether to impose a duty in the circumstances in question. They approached the matter as a tort action rather than a contractual action and took into account changing social and economic circumstances in reaching their decision. So by a narrow majority the House decided this landmark case in favour of consumers and against immunity from action for manufacturers.

We shall be returning to the issue of liability for products in a later chapter, where we shall see that the common law has been supplemented by strict liability under the Consumer Protection Act 1987 under European influence. However, the case of *Donoghue v Stevenson* is significant in the context of the present discussion for the attempt to discover this evasive general principle feeding through the cases. The neighbour principle based on reasonable foreseeability has to be the most cited in the common law world. It is sometimes, perhaps mistakenly, referred to as the wide ratio of the case, with the statement by Lord Atkin as to the extent of the manufacturer's duty being regarded as the narrow ratio. It is safer to suggest that the narrow ratio is the true one, whereas the neighbour test is merely a more abstract expression of principle. The narrow ratio can be seen as a more concrete illustration of the neighbour principle.

Post-*Donoghue*

It is thought that the neighbour principle enabled courts to deal much more easily with novel situations, namely problems which had not troubled the courts previously and, as a result, were not covered by an existing precedent. This may or may not have been the case in the immediate post-*Donoghue* years, but by 1970 we have Lord Reid, in the case of *Home Office v Dorset Yacht Co Ltd*,[26] making a significant statement about the principle:

> My Lords, on September 21, 1962, a party of Borstal trainees were working on Brownsea Island in Poole Harbour under the supervision and control of three Borstal officers. During that night seven of them escaped and went aboard a yacht which they found nearby. They set this yacht in motion and collided with the respondents' yacht which was moored in the vicinity. Then they boarded the respondents' yacht. Much damage was done to this yacht by the collision and some by the subsequent conduct of these trainees. The respondents sue the appellants, the Home Office, for the amount of this damage.
>
> The case comes before your Lordships on a preliminary issue whether the Home Office or these Borstal officers owed any duty of care to the respondents capable of giving rise to a liability in damages. So it must be assumed that the respondents can prove all that they could prove on the pleadings if the case goes to trial. The question then is whether on that assumption the Home Office would be liable in damages. It is admitted that the Home office would be vicariously liable if an action would lie against any of these Borstal officers.
>
> The case for the Home Office is that, under no circumstances, can Borstal officers owe any duty to any member of the public to take care to prevent trainees under their control or supervision from injuring him or his property. If that is the law, then inquiry into the facts of this case would be a waste of time and money because, whatever the facts may be, the respondents must lose. That case is based on three main arguments. Firstly it is said that there is virtually no authority for imposing a duty of this kind. Secondly it is said that no person can be liable for a wrong done by another who is of full age and capacity and who is not the servant or acting on behalf of that person. And thirdly it is said that public policy

26 [1970] AC 1004, 1025.

> (or the policy of the relevant legislation) requires that these officers should be immune from any such liability.
>
> The first would at one time have been a strong argument. About the beginning of this century most eminent lawyers thought that there were a number of separate torts involving negligence, each with its own rules, and they were most unwilling to add more. They were of course aware from a number of leading cases that in the past the courts had from time to time recognised new duties and new grounds of action. But the heroic age was over; it was time to cultivate certainty and security in the law; the categories of negligence were virtually closed. The Attorney General invited us to return to those halcyon days, but, attractive though it may be, I cannot accede to his invitation.
>
> In later years there has been a steady trend towards regarding the law of negligence as depending on principle so that, when a new point emerges, one should ask not whether it is covered by authority but whether recognised principles apply to it. *Donoghue v Stevenson* [1932] AC 562 may be regarded as a milestone, and the well-known passage in Lord Atkin's speech should I think be regarded as statement of principle. It is not to be treated as if it were a statutory definition. It will require qualification in new circumstances. But I think the time has come when we can and should say that it ought to apply unless there is some justification or valid explanation for its exclusion.

The other arguments referred to by Lord Reid will be dealt with later in this chapter. For the moment we are concerned with his statement relating to the neighbour principle. He would seem to be suggesting above that, where the principle can be applied, it creates a *prima facie* duty, ie that the court should treat the novel case as a notional duty case unless there is good reason not to. This was elaborated upon in *Anns v Merton London Borough Council*[27] by Lord Wilberforce:

> Through the trilogy of cases in this House: *Donoghue v Stevenson* [1932] AC 562; *Hedley Byrne & Co Ltd v Heller & Partners Ltd* [1964] AC 465; and *Dorset Yacht Co v Home Office* [1970] AC 1004; the position has now been reached that, in order to establish that a duty of care arises in a particular situation, it is not necessary to bring the facts of that situation within those of previous situations in which a duty of care has been held to exist. Rather, the question has to be approached in two stages. First one has to ask whether, as between the alleged wrongdoer and the person who has suffered damage, there is a sufficient relationship of proximity or neighbourhood such that, in the reasonable contemplation of the former, carelessness on his part may be likely to cause damage to the latter – in which case a *prima facie* duty of care arises. Secondly, if the first question is answered affirmatively, it is necessary to consider whether there are any considerations which ought to negative, or to reduce or limit the scope of, the duty or the class of person to whom it is owed or the damages to which a breach of it may give rise: see *Dorset Yacht* case [1970] AC 1004, *per* Lord Reid at p 1027.

Post-*Anns*

It is doubtful whether Lord Wilberforce would have appreciated at the time what was to follow. His test, known as the 'two-stage' approach, has been subjected to immense criticism throughout the middle to late 1980s. It was seen

27 [1978] AC 728 at pp 751–52.

by certain members of the judiciary as being a dangerous principle, in that it seemed to represent a considerable change of emphasis in the approach to be taken in novel cases. It was taken to be saying that a *prima facie* duty arose once it was established that there was reasonable foreseeability of harm, and it was then for the defendant to bring forward arguments of policy to suggest that he should have immunity from suit. It was feared that this would lead to litigants seeking to overturn existing decisions in favour of immunity, thus defeating established expectations. This was particularly felt to be the case in two areas, namely liability for omissions and economic loss. The floodgates would be widely ajar under such a broadly sweeping principle.

There was also a fear that the action in negligence would swallow up other areas of established law with a similar set of results. This was perceived as being especially true in relation to contract, but there were seen to be ramifications for other areas, eg public law and other torts such as defamation. A predictable reaction set in, lead principally but not exclusively by Lord Keith. His first reported attack came in the case of *Governors of the Peabody Donation Fund v Sir Lindsay Parkinson & Co Ltd*,[28] after citing both Lord Reid in the *Home Office* case and Lord Wilberforce's two-stage approach in the *Anns* case. He continued:

> There has been a tendency in some recent cases to treat these passages as being of themselves of a definitive character. This is a temptation which should be resisted. The true question in each case is whether the particular defendant owed to the particular plaintiff a duty of care having the scope which is contended for, and whether he was in breach of that duty with consequent loss to the plaintiff. A relationship of proximity in Lord Atkin's sense must exist before any duty of care can arise, but the scope of the duty must depend on all the circumstances of the case. In *Dorset Yacht Co v Home Office* [1970] AC 1004, 1038, Lord Morris of Borth-y-Gest, after observing that at the conclusion of his speech in *Donoghue v Stevenson* [1932] AC 562, Lord Atkin said that it was advantageous if the law 'is in accordance with sound common sense' and expressing the view that a special relation existed between the prison officers and the yacht company which gave rise to a duty on the former to control their charges so as to prevent them doing damage, continued, at p1039: 'Apart from this I would conclude that, in the situation stipulated in the present case, it would only be fair and reasonable that a duty of care should exist but that it would be contrary to the fitness of things were it not so. I doubt whether it is necessary to say, in cases where the court is asked whether in a particular situation a duty existed, that the court is called upon to make a decision as to policy. Policy need not be invoked where reason and good sense will at once point the way. If the test as to whether in some particular situation a duty of care arises may in some cases have to be whether it is fair and reasonable that it should so arise, the court must not shrink from being the arbiter. As Lord Radcliffe said in his speech in *Davis Contractors Ltd v Fareham Urban District Council* [1956] AC 696, 728, the court is "the spokesman of the fair and reasonable man".'
>
> So in determining whether or not a duty of care of particular scope was incumbent upon a defendant it is material to take into consideration whether it is just and reasonable that it should be so.

28 [1985] AC 210 at p 240.

At this stage a third requirement has been introduced in order to determine the duty issue in novel cases. Viewed critically, it might be argued that the criterion 'just and reasonable' is already inherent in both stages of Lord Wilberforce's approach and, therefore, adds nothing, a point which shall be returned to later.

The attack continued, but this time by another judge, Lord Brandon, in one of the influential economic loss cases, the *Aliakmon*.[29] Talking of the passage containing Lord Wilberforce's two stage approach, he said:

> The first observation which I would make is that that passage does not provide, and can not in my view have been intended by Lord Wilberforce to provide, a universally applicable test of the existence and scope of a duty of care in the law of negligence.

After citing Lord Keith in Peabody above, he continued:

> The second observation which I would make is that Lord Wilberforce was dealing from what he said, with the approach to the questions of the existence and scope of a duty of care in a novel type of factual situation which was not analogous to any factual situation in which the existence of such a duty had already been held to exist.

This last paragraph clearly expresses the fear that an unbridled principle being used in resolving duty issues will defeat settled expectations by its potential to allow the rethinking of existing precedents. The fear should have been unreal, as Lord Brandon acknowledges that Lord Wilberforce was only considering novel situations.

Lord Bridge joined the fray in *Curran v Northern Ireland Co-ownership Housing Association Ltd*.[30] In his view *Anns*:

> ... may be said to represent the high water mark of a trend in the development of the law of negligence by your lordships' House towards the elevation of the 'neighbourhood' principle derived from the speech of Lord Atkin in *Donoghue v Stevenson* [1932] AC 562 into one of general application from which a duty of care may always be derived unless there are clear countervailing considerations to exclude it.

The case was one concerning the exercise of a statutory power and cut across the boundaries of public and private law, as did the actual decision in the *Anns* case. This will be discussed in more detail later, but the point here is the court's concern that the neighbour principle might usurp the function of public law by providing a private law remedy in negligence. This and other concerns lay behind the Privy Council's decision in a case heard shortly after *Curran*. In *Yuen Kun-yeu v Attorney General of Hong Kong*[31] Lord Keith continued the assault on the two stage approach as follows:

> Their lordships venture to think that the two-stage test formulated by Lord Wilberforce for determining the existence of a duty of care in negligence has been elevated to a degree of importance greater than it merits, and greater perhaps than its author intended. Further, the expression of the first stage of the test carries with it a risk of misinterpretation. As Gibbs CJ pointed out in *Sutherland Shire Council v Heyman* (at 13) there are two possible views of what Lord

---

29 [1986] 2 All ER 145 at p 153.

30 [1987] 2 All ER 13 at p 17.

31 [1987] 2 All ER 705 at p 710.

Wilberforce meant. The first view, favoured in a number of cases mentioned by Gibbs CJ, is that he meant to test the sufficiency of proximity simply by the reasonable contemplation of likely harm. The second view, favoured by Gibbs CJ himself, is that Lord Wilberforce meant the expression 'proximity or neighbourhood' to be a composite one, importing the whole concept of necessary relationship between the plaintiff and defendant described by Lord Atkin in *Donoghue v Stevenson* [1932] AC 562 at 580, [1932] All ER Rep 1 at 11. In their lordships' opinion the second view is the correct one. As Lord Wilberforce himself observed in *McLoughlin v O'Brian* [1982] 2 All ER 298 at 303, [1983] AC 410 at 420, it is clear that foreseeability does not of itself, and automatically, lead to a duty of care. There are many other statements to the same effect. The truth is that the trilogy of cases referred to by Lord Wilberforce each demonstrate particular sets of circumstances, differing in character, which were adjudged to have the effect of bringing into being a relationship apt to give rise to a duty of care. Foreseeability of harm is a necessary ingredient of such a relationship, but it is not the only one. Otherwise there would be liability in negligence on the part of one who sees another about to walk over a cliff with his head in the air, and forbears to shout a warning.

The last sentence reflects one of the other concerns militating against the imposition of liability, in that the law has consistently taken the robust view that there is no liability for omissions. We shall have cause to discuss this category of case later, but in this context the fear was that the neighbour principle would have a dramatic and radical effect on liability in that area. The *Yuen KunYeu* case itself was concerned with that issue as well as the public law/private law dichotomy. It is also the first case in which the Australian case of *Sutherland Shire Council v Heyman*[32] rears its head in its full glory, the beginning of a process justifiably described by Howarth as an 'almost ritual incantation of an obscure Australian case ...'.[33]

In that case Brennan J thought that the law should develop 'novel categories of negligence incrementally and by analogy with established categories, rather than by a massive extension of *prima facie* duty of care restrained only by indefinable "considerations which ought to negative, or to reduce or limit the scope of the duty or the class of person to whom it is owed"'. The assault on *Anns* did not stop there and it was inevitable that the House of Lords would eventually get round to both doing away with the two-stage test completely and overturn its actual decision in *Anns*. Before we get to this point we need to consider the case of *Hill v Chief Constable of West Yorkshire*,[34] in which Lord Keith once again carried on his crusade against *Anns*, although at this stage he was apparently content to accept the decision in *Anns* and indeed called in aid Lord Wilberforce's second stage to deny liability to the plaintiff on grounds of public policy. His comments are relatively mild in relation to the two-stage test in this particular case as can be seen in the following extract:

Counsel for the appellant, however, sought to equiparate the situation to that which resulted in liability on the ground of negligence in *Anns v Merton London Borough* [1977] AC 728. There the borough were under a duty, imposed by

32 (1985) 60 ALR 1.

33 *Op cit* p 31.

34 [1988] 2 All ER 238.

> legislation, to supervise compliance with building by-laws, in particular as regards the construction of foundations. It was held that though the borough had a discretion whether or not to carry out an inspection of foundations in any particular case, in order to check compliance, once a decision had been made to carry out an inspection the borough owed to future owners and occupiers of the building in question a common law duty to exercise reasonable care in the inspection. In the present case, so it was maintained, the respondent, having decided to investigate the Sutcliffe murders, owed to his potential future victims a duty to do so with reasonable care.
>
> The foundation of the duty of care was said to be reasonable foreseeability of harm to potential future victims if Sutcliffe were not promptly apprehended. Lord Atkin's classic propositions in *McAlister (or Donoghue) v Stevenson* [1932] AC 562 at 580, [1932] All ER Rep 1 at 11 were prayed in aid, as was Lord Wilberforce's well-known two stage test of liability in negligence in *Anns v Merton* [1977] 2 All ER 492 at 498, [1978] AC at 751–52.
>
> It has been said almost too frequently to require repetition that foreseeability of likely harm is not in itself a sufficient test of liability in negligence. Some further ingredient is invariably needed to establish the requisite proximity of relationship between the plaintiff and the defendant, and all the circumstances of the case must be carefully considered and analysed in order to ascertain whether such an ingredient is present. The nature of the ingredient will be found to vary in a number of different categories of decided cases. In the *Anns* case there was held to be a sufficient proximity of relationship between the borough and future owners and occupiers of a particular building, the foundations of which it was decide to inspect, and there was also a close relationship between the borough and the builder who had constructed the foundations.
>
> In *Home Office v Dorset Yacht Co Ltd* [1970] 2 All ER 294 at 326, [1970] AC 1004 at 1060 Lord Diplock said of Lord Atkin's proposition: 'Used as a guide to characteristics which will be found to exist in conduct and relationships which give rise to a legal duty of care this aphorism marks a milestone in the modern development of the law of negligence. But misused as a universal it is manifestly false.'
>
> Earlier, he had said [1970] 2 All ER 294 at 324, [1970] AC 1004 at 1060: '... the judicial development of the law of negligence rightly proceeds by seeking first to identify the relevant characteristics that are common to the kinds of conduct and relationship between the parties which are involved in the case for decision and the kinds of conduct and relationships which have been held in the previous decisions of the courts to give rise to a duty of care.'

We shall have cause to return to the *Hill* case when discussing issues concerning the immunity of the police and matters of public policy below. The case does represent another stab in the back for the Wilberforce approach. The final blows, however, were administered in the cases of *Murphy v Brentwood*[35] and *Caparo Industries plc v Dickman*.[36] After quoting once again Lord Wilberforce's statement in *Anns*, Lord Keith went on predictably as follows:

> I observe at this point that the two-stage test has not been accepted as stating a universally applicable principle. Reservations about it were expressed by myself in *Governors of Peabody Donation Fund v Sir Lindsay Parkinson & Co* Ltd [1984] 3 All

35 [1990] 2 All ER 908.

36 [1990] 1 All ER 568.

> ER 529 at 534, [1985] AC 210 at 240, by Lord Brandon in *Leigh & Sillivan Ltd v Aliakmon Shipping Co Ltd, The Aliakmon* [1986] 2 All ER 145 at 153, [1986] AC 785 at 815, and by Lord Bridge in *Curran v Northern Ireland Co-ownership Housing Association Ltd (Stewart third party)* [1987] 2 All ER 13, [1987] AC 718. In *Sutherland Shire Council v Heyman* (1985) 60 ALR 1 at 43–44, where the High Court of Australia declined to follow Anns, Brennan J expressed his disagreement with Lord Wilberforce's approach, saying: 'It is preferable in my view, that the law should develop novel categories of negligence incrementally and by analogy with established categories, rather than by a massive extension of a *prima facie* duty of care restrained only by indefinable considerations which ought to negative, or to reduce or limit the scope of the duty or the class of person to whom it is owed.'
>
> In the Privy Council case of *Yeun KunYeu v Attorney-General of Hong Kong* [1987] 2 All ER 705 at 710, [1988] AC 175 at 191 that passage was quoted with approval and it was said ([1987] 2 All ER 705 at 712, [1988] AC 175 at 194): 'In view of the direction in which the law has since been developing, their lordships consider that for the future it should be recognised that the two-stage test ... is not to be regarded as in all the circumstances a suitable guide to the existence of a duty of care.'
>
> Finally, in the *Yuen Kun Yeu* case [1987] 2 All ER 705 at 712, [1988] AC 175 at 193 and in *Hill v Chief Constable of West Yorkshire* [1988] 2 All ER 238 at 243, [1989] AC 53 at 63 I expressed the opinion, concurred in by the other members of the House who participated in the decisions, that the second stage test only came into play where some particular consideration of public policy excluded any duty of care. As regards the ingredients necessary to establish such a duty in novel situations, I consider that an incremental approach on the lines indicated by Brennan J in the *Sutherland Shire* case is to be preferred to the two stage test.

In *Caparo Industries plc v Dickman*, Lord Bridge, after mentioning all the usual cases referred to above by Lord Keith, moved on to say:[37]

> What emerges is that, in addition to the foreseeability of damage, necessary ingredients in any situation giving rise to a duty of care are that there should exist between the party owing the duty and the party to whom it is owed a relationship characterised by the law as one of 'proximity' or 'neighbourhood' and that the situation should be one in which the court considers it is fair, just and reasonable that the law should impose a duty of a given scope on the one party for the benefit of the other. But it is implicit in the passages referred to that the concepts of proximity and fairness embodied in these additional ingredients are not susceptible of any such precise definition as would be necessary to give them utility as practical test, but amount in effect to little more than convenient labels to attach to the features of different specific situations, which, on a detailed examination of all the circumstances, the law recognises pragmatically as giving rise to a duty of care of a given scope. Whilst recognising, of course, the importance of the underlying general principles common to the whole field of negligence, I think the law has now moved in the direction of attaching greater significance to the more traditional categorisation of distinct and recognisable situations as guides to the existence, the scope and the limits of the varied duties of care which the law imposes.

37 At pp 573–74.

His Lordship then trots out Brennan J's statement about the incremental approach, mentioned by Lord Keith in the previous extract. Lord Oliver is Lord Bridge's main ally in *Caparo*:[38]

> There are, of course, cases where, in any ordinary meaning of the words, a relationship of proximity (in the literal sense of 'closeness') exists but where the law, whilst recognising the fact of the relationship, nevertheless denies a remedy to the injured party on the ground of public policy. *Rondel v Worsley* [1967] 3 All ER 993, [1969] AC 191 was such a case, as was *Hill v Chief Constable of West Yorkshire* [1988] 2 All ER 238, [1989] AC 53, so far as concerns the alternative ground of that decision. But such cases do nothing to assist in the identification of those features from which the law will deduce the essential relationship on which liability depends and, for my part, I think that it has to be recognised that to search for any single formula which will serve as a general test of liability is to pursue a will-o'-the-wisp. The fact is that once one discards, as it is now clear that one must, the concept of foreseeability of harm as the single exclusive test, of the existence of the duty of care, the attempt to state some general principle which will determine liability in an infinite variety of circumstances serves not to clarify the law but merely to bedevil its development in a way which corresponds with practicality and common sense.

Post-*Caparo*

Howarth has complained that the word 'proximity' has 'begun to float in a sea of meaninglessness'.[39] Elsewhere, he comments in vitriolic style:[40]

> What the 'proximity' concept and analogical reasoning have in common is that they both allow judges to avoid committing themselves. Since nobody can say what 'proximity' means, it can be asserted in every case to require whatever result is convenient. Similarly, analogies can be accepted as appropriate or rejected as 'unhelpful' as the need arises. This is a state of affairs no doubt agreeable to judges themselves, but one which is neither intellectually satisfying nor helpful for the practitioner with clients to advise. The unavoidable conclusion seems to be that the law lords simply do not know what to do about negligence, and have very little notion where to go next.

Jones is equally scathing:[41]

> It is not clear from the decisions of the House of Lords in *Caparo* and *Murphy* whether the return to 'traditional categories' is intended to replace, or merely supplement, the tripartite test for the duty of care developed in the 1980s. The concepts of 'proximity' or what is 'just and reasonable' or 'fair' are just as empty of content, beg as many questions as Lord Wilberforce's wide generalisations, and thus are open to many of the objections directed at the *Anns* two-stage test. It remains to be seen whether the practical application of the duty of care is any easier or more certain now that future extensions of liability can occur only on an ad hoc, incremental basis.

In some recent cases, however, there may be perceived to be a slight swing back in favour of plaintiffs in novel cases, although the judges have at least paid lip

38 At p 585.

39 *Textbook on Torts*, p 32.

40 (1991) CLJ 58 at 60.

41 *Textbook on Torts*, pp 29–30.

service to the incremental approach at times. This can be seen in some of the latest cases such as *White v Jones*[42] and *Spring v Guardian Assurance plc*.[43] We shall have cause to return to these cases in the economic loss chapter. Perhaps we have not, after all, returned quite to the dark days of legal development as epitomised by Lord Buckmaster's narrow and closed analysis of the pre-*Donoghue* case law.

Specific areas of difficulty

So far we have discussed the duty concept almost entirely in the abstract. We now need to turn attention to some of the difficult areas where the courts have struggled to articulate the reasons for the imposition of no or a limited duty on the defendant. Immunity is sometimes granted in accordance with the type of conduct of the defendant, particularly in relation to omissions. In other cases it is the status of the defendant which is selected by the court as the main criterion for refuting liability, such as public authorities, the police and certain members of the legal profession. In other instances it is the type of harm which the courts are reluctant to recognise as requiring protection against. The two principle types are psychiatric harm and economic loss, both of which have been granted the luxury of a chapter each. In the remaining part of this chapter, we shall look at materials on the problems of liability for omissions and the immunities granted according to the status of the defendant, such as the authorities and the police.

Omissions

The traditional view has been that the law does not impose liability for negligent omissions, rather it is concerned with the situation where the defendant in carrying out an activity does so badly. This is the difference between nonfeasance and misfeasance, but the line separating the two is often blurred. For example, the plaintiff may allege that the defendant, when driving his car, failed to keep a proper lookout for other road users and collided with the plaintiff's vehicle as a result. This looks like an omission, but is really part of the activity of driving and seen as part of an overall positive act. In other instances, the defendant may perform his activity so inadequately that it may be he has not performed it at all, namely, it amounts to an omission.

However, there are examples of pure omission, such as the person who watches a child drowning in a canal and does nothing to effect a rescue. The law generally refuses to impose a positive duty on such a person to act for the benefit of another. After all, it is argued, it is the law of contract which is concerned with positive duties to act for the benefit of others and in contract one has to provide some benefit in favour of the other party in order to sue for failure to perform the relevant obligation. It would be going too far to impose a general obligation of such a nature in the absence of consideration. Other more pragmatic reasons are usually put forward to support non-liability in this area. For example, upon whom would the duty be imposed if a number of people

42 [1995] 1 All ER 691.

43 [1994] 3 WLR 354.

were present watching the child drown in the canal? What would be the extent of the duty? Would it be met by merely calling the emergency services or must the potential defendant try to effect a rescue by risking, if that be the case, her own life or safety?

There are, however, situations where the law has overcome its theoretical and pragmatic objections to the imposition of liability for omissions. These have been identified as including the situation where the defendant has undertaken the task, although gratuitously, where the defendant has some relationship with the plaintiff over third parties or is in control of land or dangerous items. In these situations the law will impose a duty, but we are often still left with a difficulty as to what is comprised in any such duty. In *Smith v Littlewoods Organisation Ltd*[44] the House of Lords was asked to consider the liability of the defenders in relation to a vacant cinema which they had acquired. It seems that vandals managed to enter the premises and start a fire which damaged adjacent properties owned by the plaintiffs. The House decided against the pursuers, but only Lord Goff considered the matter in terms of duty, as follows:

> My Lords, the Lord President (Lord Elmslie) founded his judgment on the proposition that the defenders, who were both owners and occupiers of the cinema, were under a general duty to take reasonable care for the safety of premises in the neighbourhood.
>
> Now if this proposition is understood as relating to a general duty to take reasonable care *not to cause damage* to premises in the neighbourhood (as I believe that the Lord President intended it to be understood) then it is unexceptionable. But it must not be overlooked that a problem arises when the pursuer is seeking to hold the defender responsible for having failed to *prevent* a third party from causing damage to the pursuer or his property by the third party's own deliberate wrongdoing. In such a case, it is not possible to invoke a general duty of care; for it is well recognised that there is no *general* duty of care to prevent third parties from causing such damage. The point is expressed very clearly in Hart and Honore, *Causation in the Law* (2nd edn, 1985 p 196), where the authors state: 'The law might acknowledge a general principle that, whenever the harmful conduct of another is reasonably foreseeable, it is our duty to take precautions against it ... But, up to now, no legal system has gone so far as this ...'
>
> The same point is made in Fleming, *The Law of Torts* (6th edn, 1983 p 200), where it is said: '... there is certainly no *general* duty to protect others against theft or loss' (Fleming's emphasis).
>
> I wish to add that no such general duty exists even between those who are neighbours in the sense of being occupiers of adjoining premises. There is no general duty on a householder, that he should act as a watchdog or that his house should act as a bastion, to protect his neighbour's house.
>
> Why does the law not recognise a general duty of care to prevent others from suffering loss or damage caused by the deliberate wrongdoing of third parties. The fundamental reason is that the common law does not impose liability for what are called pure omissions. If authority is needed for this proposition, it is to be found in the speech of Lord Diplock in *Home Office v Dorset Yacht Co Ltd* [1970] 2 All ER 294 at 296, [1970] AC 1004 at 1006, where he said: 'The very parable of the good Samaritan (Luke 10:30) which was evoked by Lord Atkin in *Donoghue v Stevenson* [1932] AC 562, [1932] All ER Rep 1 illustrates, in the conduct of the

44 [1987] 1 All ER 710.

priest and of the Levite who passed by on the other side, an omission which was likely to have as its reasonable and probable consequence damage to the health of the victim of the thieves, but for which the priest and Levite would have incurred no civil liability in English law.'

Lord Diplock then proceeded to give examples which show that, carried to extremes, this proposition may be repugnant to modern thinking. It may therefore require, one day, to be reconsidered especially as it is said to provoke an 'invidious comparison with affirmative duties of good neighbourliness in most countries outside the common law orbit' (see Fleming, *The Law of Torts* (6th edn, 1983 p 138), but it is of interest to observe that, even if we do follow the example of those countries, in all probability we will, like them, impose strict limits on any such affirmative duty as may be recognised.

In one recent French decision, the condition was imposed that the danger to the claimant must be 'grave, imminent, constant ... *necessitant une intervention immediate*', and that such an intervention must not involve any *'risque pour le prevenu ou pour un tiers'*: see Lawson and Markesinis, *Tortious Liability for Unintentional Harm in the Common Law and the Civil Law* (1982) vol 1, pp 74–75. The latter requirement is consistent with our own law, which likewise imposes limits on steps required to be taken by a person who is under an affirmative duty to prevent harm being caused by a source of danger which has arisen without his fault (see *Goldman v Hargrave* [1966] 2 All ER 989, [1967] AC 645), a point to which I shall return later. But the former requirement indicates that any affirmative duty to prevent deliberate wrongdoing by third parties, if recognised in English law, is likely to be strictly limited. I mention this because I think it important that we should realise that problems like that in the present case are unlikely to be solved by a simple abandonment of the common law's strict approach to liability for pure omissions.

Another statement of principle, which has been much quoted, is the observation of Lord Sumner in *Weld-Blundell v Stephens*: '... even though A is in fault, he is not responsible for injury to C which B, a stranger to him, deliberately chooses to do.'

This *dictum* may be read as expressing the general idea that the voluntary act of another, independent of the defender's fault, is regarded as a *novus actus interveniens* which, to use the old metaphor, 'breaks the chain of causation'. But it also expresses a general perception that we ought not to be held responsible in law for the deliberate wrongdoing of others. Of course, if a duty of care is imposed to guard against deliberate wrongdoing by others, it can hardly be said that the harmful effects of such wrongdoing are not caused by such breach of duty. We are therefore thrown back to the duty of care. But one thing is clear, and that is that liability in negligence for harm caused by the deliberate wrongdoing of others cannot be founded simply on foreseeability that the pursuer will suffer loss or damage by reason of such wrongdoing. There is no such general principle. We have therefore to identify the circumstances in which such liability may be imposed.

That there are special circumstances in which a defender may be held responsible in law for injuries suffered by the pursuer through a third party's deliberate wrongdoing is not in doubt. For example, a duty of care may arise from a relationship between the parties which gives rise to an imposition or assumption of responsibility on or by the defender, as in *Stansbie v Troman* [1948] 1 All ER 599, [1948] 2 KB 48, where such responsibility was held to arise from contract. In that case a decorator, left alone on the premises by the householder's wife, was held liable when he went out leaving the door on the latch and a thief entered the house and stole property. Such responsibility might well be held to exist in other cases where there is no contract, as for example where a person left alone in a house has entered as a licensee of the occupier. Again, the defender may be vicariously liable for the third party's act; or he may be held liable as an occupier to a visitor on his land. Again, as appears from the *dictum* of Dixon J in *Smith v Leurs* (1945) 70 CLR 256 at 262, a duty may arise from a special relationship between the defender and the third party, by virtue of which the defender is responsible for controlling the third party: see, for example, *Home Office v Dorset Yacht Co Ltd*. More pertinently, in a case between adjoining occupiers of land, there may be liability in nuisance if one occupier causes or permits persons to gather on his land, and they impair his neighbour's enjoyment of his land. Indeed, even if such persons come onto his land as trespassers, the occupier may, if they constitute a nuisance, be under an affirmative duty to abate the nuisance. As I pointed out in *P Perl (Exporters) Ltd v Camden London BC* [1983] 3 All ER 161 at 172, [1984] QB 342 at 359, there may well be other cases.

These are all special cases. But there is a more general circumstance in which a defender may be held liable in negligence to the pursuer, although the immediate cause of the damage suffered by the pursuer is the deliberate wrongdoing of another. This may occur where the defender negligently causes or permits to be created a source of danger, and it is reasonably foreseeable that third parties may interfere with it and sparking off the danger, thereby cause damage to persons in the position of the pursuer. The classic example of such a case is, perhaps, *Haynes v Harwood* [1935] 1 KB 146, [1934] All ER Rep 103, where the defendant's carter left a horse-drawn van unattended in a crowded street and the horses bolted when a boy threw a stone at them. A police officer who suffered injury in stopping the horses before they injured a woman and children was held to be entitled to recover damages from the defendant. There, of course, the defendant's servant had created a source of danger by leaving his horses unattended in a busy street. Many different things may have caused them to bolt, a sudden noise or movement for example, or, as happened, the deliberate action of a mischievous boy. But all such events were examples of the very sort of thing which the defendant's servant ought reasonably to have foreseen and to have guarded against by taking appropriate precautions. In such a case, Lord Sumner's *dictum* in *Weld-Blundell v Stephens* [1920] AC 956 at 986, [1920] All ER Rep 32 at 47 can have no application to exclude liability.

Haynes v Harwood was a case concerned with the creation of a source of danger in a public place. We are concerned in the present case with an allegation that the defenders should be held liable for the consequences of deliberate wrongdoing by others who were trespassers on the defenders' property. In such a case it may be said that the defenders are entitled to use their property as their own and so should not be held liable if, for example, trespassers interfere with dangerous things on their land. But this is, I consider, too sweeping a proposition. It is well established that an occupier of land may be liable to a trespasser who has suffered injury on his land; though in *British Railways Board v Herrington* [1972] 1 All ER 749, [1972] AC 877, in which the nature and scope of such liability was reconsidered by your Lordships' House, the standard of care so imposed on occupiers was drawn so narrowly so as to take proper account of the rights of occupiers to enjoy the use of their land. It is, in my opinion, consistent with the existence of such liability that an occupier who negligently causes or permits a source of danger to be created on his land, and can reasonably foresee that third parties may trespass on his land and, interfering with the source of danger, may spark it off, thereby causing damage to the person or property of those in the vicinity, should be held liable to such a person for damage so caused to him. It is useful to take the example of a fire hazard, not only because that is the relevant hazard which is alleged to have existed in present case, but also because of the intrinsically dangerous nature of fire hazards as regards neighbouring property. Let me give an example of circumstances in which an occupier of land might be held liable for damage so caused. Suppose that a person is deputed to buy a substantial quantity of fireworks for a village fireworks display on Guy Fawkes night. He stores them, as usual, in an unlocked garden shed abutting onto a neighbouring house. It is well known that he does this. Mischievous boys from the village enter as trespassers and, playing with the fireworks, cause a serious fire which spreads to and burns down the neighbouring house. Liability might well be imposed in such a case, for, having regard to the dangerous and tempting nature of fireworks, interference by naughty children was the very thing which, in the circumstances, the purchaser of the fireworks ought to have guarded against.

But the liability should only be imposed under this principle in cases where the defender has negligently caused or permitted the creation of a source of danger on his land, and where it is foreseeable that third parties may trespass on his land and spark it off, thereby damaging the pursuer or his property. Moreover, it is not to be forgotten that, in ordinary households in this country, there are nowadays many things which might be described as possible sources of fire if interfered with by third parties, ranging from matches and fire-lighters to electric irons and gas cookers and even oil-fired central heating systems. These are the common places of modern life, and it would be quite wrong if householders were to be held liable in negligence for acting in a socially acceptable manner.

No doubt the question whether liability should be imposed on defenders in a case where a source of danger has been sparked off by the deliberate wrongdoing is a question to be decided on the facts of each case, and it would, I think, be wrong for your Lordships' House to anticipate the manner in which the law may develop; but I cannot help thinking that cases where liability will be so imposed are likely to be rare.

There is another basis on which a defender may be held liable for damage to neighbouring property caused by fire started on his (the defender's) property by the deliberate wrongdoing of a third party. This arises where he has knowledge or means of knowledge that a third party has created or is creating a risk of fire, or indeed has started a fire on his premises, and then fails to take such steps as are reasonably open to him (in the limited sense as explained by Lord Wilberforce in *Goldman v Hargrave* [1966] 2 All ER 989 at 995–96, [1967] 1 AC 645 at 663–64) to prevent any such fire from damaging neighbouring property. If, for example, an occupier of property has knowledge, or means of knowledge, that intruders are in the habit of trespassing on his property and starting fires there, thereby creating a risk that fire may spread to and damage neighbouring property, a duty to take reasonable steps to prevent such damage may be held to fall on him. He could, for example, take reasonable steps to keep intruders out. He could also inform the police; or he could warn his neighbours and invite their assistance. If the defender is a person of substantial means, for example a large public company, he might even be expected to employ some agency to keep a watch on the premises. What is reasonably required would, of course, depend on the particular facts of the case. I observe that in *Goldman v Hargrave* such liability was held to sound in nuisance; but it is difficult to believe that, in this respect, there can be any material distinction between liability in nuisance and liability in negligence.

I turn to the authorities. Your lordships were referred in the course of argument to two Scottish cases concerned with fire hazards. The first was *Carrick Furniture House Ltd v Paterson* 1978 SLT (Notes) 48. In that case, in allowing proof before answer, the Lord Ordinary (Allanbridge) found on the facts that the building in question, which contained considerable quantities of inflammable material, constituted a fire hazard, and that the risk of a vandal setting fire to the premises was not too remote. The case is only briefly reported; but it provides an indication that cases of this kind cannot normally be disposed of on a plea to the relevancy but have to be allowed to go to proof. In the second case, *Thomas Graham & Co Ltd v Church of Scotland General Trustees* 1982 SLT (Sh Ct) 26, Sheriff Macvicar QC held that the defenders, who were occupiers of a disused church, were liable to the pursuers whose neighbouring property suffered damage by reason of a fire started in the church by unknown vandals. He relied, *inter alia*, on the facts: that the church was situated in an area of Glasgow which was subject to vandalism on a large scale; that, to the knowledge of the defenders, on a number of previous occasions vandals had entered the church and caused damage there; that the vandals had also lit small fires in the church and that a responsible inspector had expressed the opinion that the building was a serious fire hazard; that there was no evidence that the defenders, or anyone on their behalf, had applied their minds to the question of the fire hazard, and that there was ample evidence to support the view that, if they had, and had taken advice on the matter, they would have been told that the building was a serious fire risk; and that for two months before the fire the building was not lock-fast. I incline to the opinion that this case can best be classified under the second of two heads of liability to which I have referred, on the basis that the defenders had the means of knowledge that a risk of fire had been created or was being created by third parties on their land, and yet they did nothing to prevent such risk of fire from damaging neighbouring property.

The leading Commonwealth case, in which an occupier of land was held liable for damage caused to his neighbour's property by a fire which started on his own land without his fault (when lightning struck a tall tree) and which he negligently failed to prevent from spreading onto his neighbour's land, is *Goldman v Hargrave* itself. But a case more similar to the two Scottish cases to which I have referred is perhaps the American case of *Torrack v Corpamerica Inc* (1958) 144 A 2d 703, where it was alleged that the defendant's derelict property was frequented by children and vagrants and had been condemned by the fire marshal as a fire menace, and that thereafter a fire was deliberately started by a third person on the property which spread to and damaged the plaintiff's neighbouring property; there the defendant's motion for summary judgment was denied. In so holding, Judge Christie relied on earlier cases to the same effect, *viz Prince v Chehalis Savings and Loan Association* (1936) 186 Wash 372, and *Arneil v Schnitzer* (1944) 173 ORE 179.

Turning to the facts of the present case, I cannot see that the defenders should be held liable under either of the two heads of liability. First, I do not consider that the empty cinema could properly be described as an unusual danger in the nature of a fire hazard. As the Lord President pointed out (*Squires v Perth and Kinross DC* 1986 SLT 272 at 276): 'There was nothing about the building, so far as we know from the evidence, to suggest that it could easily be set alight.'

This conclusion was, in my judgment, entirely justified on the evidence in the case; and it is, I consider, fatal to any allegation that the defenders should be held liable on the ground that they negligently caused or permitted the creation of an unusual source of danger in the nature of a fire hazard.

Nor can I see that the defenders should be held liable for having failed to take reasonable steps to abate a fire risk created by third parties on their property without their fault. If there was any such fire risk, they had no means of knowing that it existed. If anybody (eg the police) considered that there was such a risk they could, and should, have contacted the defenders (a well-known public company, whose particulars were given on a notice outside the cinema) by telephone to warn them of the situation; but they did not do so. In any event, on the evidence, the existence of such a risk was not established. As the Lord President observed (at 276–77): 'It is, in my opinion, significant that no witness who spoke about the increasing use of the cinema by intruding children, and the witnesses included the minister of St Paul's Church, the session clerk and the beadle, and also Mr Maloco, reported to the police or the defenders what they had observed. If it had crossed their minds that it was likely that the children would set fire to the building and put neighbouring properties at risk, it is inconceivable that they would not have taken immediate steps, by reporting to the police and the defenders, to bring the use of premises by children to an end. My experience of life, which I am entitled to bring to bear as a juryman would, has not taught me that empty buildings to which vandals gain access are likely to be set on fire by them ...'

In the course of his argument before your lordships, counsel for the appellants placed reliance on the decision of the Inner House of the Court of Session in *Squires v Perth and Kinross DC* 1986 SLT 30. That was a case concerned not with liability in respect of a fire hazard, but with liability in respect of a theft by a burglar who had gained access to the pursuer's jeweller's shop through a flat above, which was empty because it was being renovated by building contractors who were held to be in occupation of the flat. It was held that the contractors, as occupiers, were liable in negligence to the pursuers for the loss of the jewellery stolen from the shop, on the ground that any person in occupancy and control of the flat above would have readily foreseen the likelihood of what in fact occurred. It appears that the fact that the flat above was empty was plainly apparent from, in particular, the presence of the scaffolding at the front of the building; and complaints had been made on a number of occasions that the contractors did not keep the flat secure, for example, because windows were left open and unglazed to accommodate scaffolding. It was a remarkable feature of the case that the burglar himself, one Sneddon, gave evidence at the trial; and it transpired from his evidence that, although his attention was drawn to the possibility of breaking into the jeweller's shop through the empty flat by seeing the scaffolding and open windows of the flat facing the High Street, he in fact approached the flat from behind, climbing over a building about 12–15 feet high overall. He found the door into the yard behind the shop and flat unsecured, but nevertheless climbed over a wall into the yard and then climbed a drainpipe to a balcony, from which he entered the flat through a door which was open. Having entered the flat, he broke into the jeweller's shop through the floor of the flat and the ceiling of the shop. In these circumstances, assuming that the defenders were in breach of duty in leaving the flat insecure, I feel, with all respect, serious doubts about the decision on the issue of causation, since it is difficult to imagine that an experienced and practised housebreaker, as Sneddon was held to be, would have been deterred from entering the flat even if the door on the balcony had been secured. I am not surprised therefore to find that Lord Dunpark shared the same doubts (at 40). Furthermore, I find it difficult to understand why the question of contributory negligence on the part of the pursuers was not considered. The pursuers were just as aware of the risk as the defenders were; yet, although (as was found) an alarm system is often fitted to the roof of premises such as those of the pursuers, and is relatively inexpensive, they did not take this precaution. They seem to have assumed that, although it was their shop which was likely to attract thieves, they were entitled to rely on the contractors working above, rather than on themselves, to prevent the thieves entering through the ceiling of the shop. Indeed, if it had been thought appropriate, in the circumstances, to employ a watchman to guard the jeweller's shop, the pursuers would apparently have considered that that expense should not fall on themselves but on the contractors working above. I do not think that that can be right.

In truth the case raises a more fundamental question, which is whether an occupier is under a general duty of care to occupiers of adjacent premises to keep his premises lock-fast in order to prevent thieves entering his premises and thereby gaining access to the adjacent premises. Let us suppose that, in *Squires v Perth and Kinross DC*, the defenders had expressly warned the pursuers, by notice, that extensive work was going to be done to the flat above, and that this would mean that for a period of time scaffolding would be erected and all the windows of the flat would be removed. Would it then be objectionable that the pursuers should have to look to their own defences against thieves, in the light of these circumstances? I do not think so. Then, should it make any difference that no such notice was given, but it was obvious what the contractors were doing? Again, I do not think so. Then, suppose that the occupiers of the flat above the shop were an ordinary family and, when they went on holiday, in all the hustle and bustle of getting their children and animals and possessions into their car, they forgot to lock their front door. While they were away a passing thief, seeing that the flat was unoccupied because the curtains were drawn, went up and tried the front door and, finding it unlocked, gained access to the flat and thence entered the jeweller's shop below and robbed it. Should the occupiers of the flat be held liable to the jewellers in negligence? Again, I do not think so; and I add that I do not think that it would make any difference that it was well known that burglars were operating in the neighbourhood. It is not difficult to multiply these homely examples of cases where a thief may gain access to a house or flat which is not lock-fast: eg where an old lady goes out to spend the day with her married daughter and leaves a ground floor window open for her cat; or where a stone deaf asthmatic habitually sleeps with his bedroom window wide open at night; or where an elderly gentleman leaves his french windows open when he is weeding at the bottom of his garden, so that he can hear the telephone. For my part, I do not think that liability can be imposed on an occupier of property in negligence simply because it can be said that it is reasonably foreseeable, or even (having regard, for example, to some particular temptation to thieves in adjacent premises) that it is highly likely, that if he fails to keep his property lock-fast a thief may gain access to his property and thence to the adjacent premises. So to hold must presuppose that the occupier of property is under a general duty to prevent thieves from entering his property to gain access to neighbouring property, where there is a sufficient degree of foresight that this may occur. But there is no general duty to prevent third parties from causing harm to others, even though there is a high degree of foresight that they may do so. The practical effect is that everybody has to take such steps as he thinks fit to protect his own property, whether house or flat or shop, against thieves. He is able to take his own precautions; and, in deciding what precautions to take, he can and should take into account the fact that, in the ordinary course of life, an adjacent property is likely to be from time to time unoccupied (often obviously so, and sometimes for a considerable period of time) and is also likely from time to time not to be lock-fast. He has to form his own judgment as to the precautions which he should take, having regard to all the circumstances of the case, including (if it be the case) the fact that his premises are a jeweller's shop which offers a special temptation to thieves. I must confess that I do not find this practical result objectionable. For these reasons I consider, with all respect, that *Squires v Perth and Kinross DC* was wrongly decided.

The present case is, of course, concerned with entry not by thieves but by vandals. Here the point can be made that, whereas an occupier of property can take precautions against thieves, he cannot (apart from insuring his property and its contents) take effective precautions against physical damage caused to his property by a vandal who has gained access to adjacent property and has there created a source of danger which has resulted in damage to his property by eg fire or escaping water. Even so, the same difficulty arises. Suppose, taking the example I have given of the family going away on holiday and leaving their front door unlocked, it was not a thief but a vandal who took advantage of that fact; and that the vandal, in wrecking the flat, caused damage to the plumbing which resulted in a water leak and consequent damage to the shop below. Are the occupiers of the flat to be held liable in negligence for such damage? I do not think so, even though it may be well known that vandalism is prevalent in the neighbourhood. The reason is the same, that there is no general duty to prevent third parties from causing damage to others, even though there is a high degree of foresight that this may occur. In the example I have given, it cannot be said that the occupiers of the flat have caused or permitted the creation of a source of danger (as in *Haynes v Harwood* [1935] 1 KB 146, [1934] All ER 103 or in the example of the fireworks which I gave earlier) which they ought to have guarded against; nor of course were there any special circumstances giving rise to a duty of care. The practical effect is that the owner of the damaged premises (or, in the vast majority of case, his insurers) who is left with a worthless claim against the vandal, rather than the occupier of the property which the vandal entered (or his insurers), a conclusion which I find less objectionable than one which may throw an unreasonable burden on ordinary householders. For these reasons, I consider that both *Lamb v Camden London Borough* [1981] 2 All ER 408, [1981] QB 625 and *King v Liverpool City Council* [1986] 3 All ER 544, [1986] 1 WLR 890 were rightly decided; but I feel bound to say, with all respect, that the principle propounded by Lord Wylie in *Evans v Glasgow DC* 1978 SLT 17 at 19, *viz* that there is: 'a general duty on owners or occupiers of property ... to take reasonable care to see that it [is] proof against the kind of vandalism which was calculated to affect adjoining property', is, in my opinion, too wide.

I wish to emphasise that I do not think that the problem in these cases can be solved simply through the mechanism of foreseeability. When a duty of care is cast on a person to take precautions against the wrongdoing of third parties, the ordinary standard of foreseeability applies; and so the possibility of such wrongdoing does not have to be very great before liability is imposed. I do not subscribe to the opinion that liability for the wrongdoing of others is limited because of the unpredictability of human conduct. So, for example, in *Haynes v Harwood* [1935] 1 KB 146, [1934] All ER Rep 103, liability was imposed although it cannot have been at all likely that a small boy would throw a stone at the horses left unattended in the public road, and in *Stansbie v Troman* [1948] 1 All ER 599, [1948] 2 KB 48 liability was imposed although it cannot have been at all likely that a thief would take advantage of the fact that the defendant left the door on the latch while he was out. *Per contra*, there is at present no general duty at common law to prevent persons from harming others by their deliberate wrongdoing, however foreseeable such harm may be if the defender does not take steps to prevent it.

Of course, if persons trespass on the defender's property and the defender either knows or has the means of knowing that they are doing so and that in doing so they constitute a danger to neighbouring property, then the defender may be under an affirmative duty to take reasonable steps to exclude them, in the limited sense explained by Lord Wilberforce in *Goldman v Hargrave* [1966] 2 All ER 989 at 995–96, [1967] 1 AC 645 at 663–64, but that is another matter. I incline to the opinion that this duty arises from the fact that the defender, as occupier, is in exclusive control of the premises on which the danger has arisen.

In preparing this opinion, I have given careful consideration to the question whether *P Perl (Exporters) Ltd v Camden London BC* [1983] 3 All ER 161, [1984] QB 342, in which I myself was a member of the Court of Appeal, was correctly decided. I have come to the conclusion that it was, though on rereading it I do not think that my own judgment was very well expressed. But I remain of the opinion that, to impose a general duty on occupiers to take reasonable care to prevent others from entering their property, would impose an unreasonable burden on ordinary householders and an unreasonable curb on the ordinary enjoyment of their property; and I am also of the opinion that to do so would be contrary to principle. It is very tempting to try to solve all the problems of negligence by reference to an all-embracing criterion of foreseeability, thereby effectively reducing all decisions in this field to questions of fact. But this comfortable solution is, alas, not open to us. The law has to accommodate all the untidy complexity of life; and there are circumstances where considerations of practical justice impel us to reject a general imposition of liability for foreseeable damage. An example of this phenomenon is to be found in cases of pure economic loss, where the so-called 'floodgates' argument (an argument recognised by Lord Blackburn as long ago as 1875 in *Cattle v Stockton Waterworks Co Ltd* (1875) 10 QB 453 at 457, [1874–80] All ER Rep 220 at 223, the force of which is accepted not only in common law countries but also civil law countries such as the Federal Republic of Germany) compels us to recognise that to impose a general liability based on a simple criterion of foreseeability would impose an intolerable burden on defendants. I observe that in *Junior Bookshops Ltd v Veitchi Co Ltd* [1982] 3 All ER 201, [1983] 1 AC 520 some members of the House of Lords succumbed, perhaps too easily, to the temptation to adopt a solution based simply on 'proximity'. In truth, in cases such as these, having rejected the generalised principle, we have to search for special cases in which, on narrower but still identifiable principles, liability can properly be imposed. That is a task which I attempted to perform in *Leigh Sillivan Ltd v Aliakmon Shipping Co Ltd, The Aliakmon* [1985] 2 All ER 44, [1985] QB 350, by identifying a principle of transferred loss, a principle which has not, so far, achieved recognition by other members of the House of Lords. As the present case shows, another example of this phenomenon is to be found in cases where the plaintiff has suffered damage through the deliberate wrongdoing of a third party; and it is not surprising that, once again, we should find the courts seeking to identify specific situations in which liability can properly be imposed. Problems such as these are solved in Scotland, as in England, by means of the mechanism of the duty of care; though we have nowadays to appreciate that the broad general principle of liability for foreseeable damage is so widely applicable that the function of the duty of care is not so much to identify cases where liability is imposed as to identify those where it is not (see *Anns v Merton London Borough* [1977] 2 All ER 492 at 498–99, [1978] AC 728 at 752 *per* Lord Wilberforce.) It is perhaps not surprising that our brother lawyers in France find themselves able to dispense with any such concept, achieving practical justice by means of a simple concept of '*faute*'. But since we all live in the same social and economic environment and since the judicial function can, I believe, be epitomised as an educated reflex to facts, we find that, in civil law countries as in common law countries, not only are we beset by the same practical problems, but broadly speaking we reach the same

> practical solutions. Our legal concepts may be different, and may cause us sometimes to diverge; but we have much to learn from each other in our common efforts to achieve practical justice founded on legal principle.
>
> For these reasons I would dismiss these appeals.

The other four judges also favoured dismissing the appeal. Three of them, Lord Brandon, Griffiths and Mackay were of the view that there was a general duty on the defenders to exercise reasonable care to ensure that their premises did not become a source of danger, but that in the circumstances there was no breach of that duty. It is evident that there is judicial reluctance to impose affirmative duties of action, this case being a leading example of that trend. However, there are a number of ways to refute liability. Lord Goff talked primarily in terms of duty, the others in terms of whether there was a breach. Equally, as we shall see later, the issue can be approached from the angle of causation and remoteness. Lord Goff's approach was taken in the recent case of *Topp v London Country Bus (South West) Ltd*.[45] This can be seen from the brief extract from Dillon LJ's speech in the Court of Appeal:

> ... the plaintiff's claim is founded in negligence on the basis that the bus company, knowing that there must be a threat that a bus left ready to be driven away might be stolen and that whoever stole it, a joyrider, might drive dangerously and kill or injure someone else or damage property, was in breach of duty in failing to collect the bus or see that it was locked, without an ignition key and not capable of being driven away.
>
> Mr Hetherington submitted that there was a particular danger because the lay-by was outside or near to a public house. I do not think he suggested that its proximity to the hospital added any particular danger. He put his case in three ways: firstly, that the bus was in special category of risk as a source of danger on the highway; secondly, that even if it was not in a special category as a source of danger, there was a sufficiently high risk to attract a duty of care; thirdly, that the judge, in seeking to apply the tests laid down in *Caparo Industries plc v Dickman* [1990] 2 AC 605, drew too rigid a line, instead of dealing with the case simply on its own facts, and his reasons were flawed. But Mr Hetherington has to accept the general proposition which is to be found in the speech of Lord Goff of Chievley in *Smith v Littlewoods Organisation Ltd* [1987] AC 241, 272: 'Even though A is in fault, he is not responsible for injury to C which B, a stranger to him, deliberately chooses to do ... [that] may be read as expressing the general idea that the voluntary act of another, independent of the defender's fault, is regarded as a *novus actus interveniens* which, to use the old metaphor, "breaks the chain of causation".'
>
> In so far as the case is put on the basis that to leave the bus unlocked, and with the key in the ignition, on the highway near a public house is to create a special risk in a special category, it is pertinent to refer to a passage in the judgment of Robert Goff LJ in *P Perl (Exporters) Ltd v Camden London Borough Council* [1984] QB 342, 359: 'In particular, I have in mind certain cases where the defendant presents the wrongdoer with the means to commit the wrong, in circumstances where it is obvious or very likely that he will do so – as, for example, where he hands over a car to be driven by a person who is drunk, or plainly incompetent, who then runs over the plaintiff.'

45 [1993] 1 WLR 976.

> But the sort of cases to which Robert Goff LJ was there referring are far different from the present case. It may be added that there is no evidence that the malefactor had been frequenting the public house; we do not know who he was, nor is there any evidence or presumption that persons who do frequent that a particular public house are particularly likely to steal vehicles and engage in joy-riding.

A plaintiff, therefore has an uphill struggle to persuade a court that his case falls within one of the narrow categories of case in which a duty is imposed in relation to negligent omissions. After *Anns*, it was feared that the *prima facie* duty doctrine might remove the distinction between misfeasance and nonfeasance. Nowhere is this fear better expressed than in the strident discussion by Smith and Burns, culminating in the following extract:[46]

> The *prima facie* duty doctrine of Lord Wilberforce in the *Anns* case, ignoring as it does the distinction between misfeasance and nonfeasance, assumes the existence, the breach of which gives rise to right to compensation, so the duty never need be justified. One need then only show on terms of utilitarian calculus, economic analysis, political ideas of fairness or a religious sense of right or wrong, dressed up in the amorphous language of public policy, that the defendant ought to have done what he failed to do, so the unjustified *prima facie* duty is confirmed.
>
> Fifty years after the decision of *Donoghue v Stevenson*, the pendulum has now swung from over-particularisation to the other extreme of over-generalisation and, in spite of all warnings of even Lord Atkin himself,[47] nearly all negligence cases are being forced onto the Procrustean bed of his 'neighbour principle'. When that principle is applied not only to misfeasance, but to nonfeasance as well, in the form of the *prima facie* duty doctrine, the autonomy of the law as a separate social institution, independent of morality, which has been the hallmark of English jurisprudence, inevitably suffers. In retrospect, it is possible to conclude that the decision in *Donoghue v Stevenson* has not been entirely beneficial for the law of negligence.

This must now be read in the light of the discussion above on the general duty of care in negligence and the return to the incremental approach, as well as the fact that there does not seem to have been the anticipated avalanche of cases ignoring the distinction between acts and omissions. The line has been firmly held. This may be something to do with the fact that a number of the omissions type cases have involved defendants who for other reasons have been able to claim immunity. Many of the cases, for example, have been claims against regulatory agencies or similar public bodies and at the same time have been claims for financial loss. Others have been against the police where it is perceived that there are special considerations as we shall see below.

46 (1983) 46 MLR 147 at 161–63.

47 At pp 583–84.

IMMUNITY BASED ON THE DEFENDANT'S STATUS

It has long been the case that certain types of persons are entitled to immunity however careless they might have been. Well-established examples include judges and witnesses in the court room, as well as advocates in the way they conduct trials.[48] The immunity of the barrister extends to pre-trial work which is so intimately connected with the way the matter is to be conducted in court.[49] The most recent cases have involved actions taken against the police in respect of the way in which they have conducted investigations into crime. The leading case is one we have met already, *Hill v Chief Constable of West Yorkshire*,[50] the case concerning the so-called Yorkshire Ripper. Lord Keith gave the main judgment and, after discussing the *Dorset Yacht* case, continued:

> The *Dorset Yacht* case was concerned with the special characteristics or ingredients beyond reasonable foreseeability of likely harm which may result in civil liability for failure to control another man to prevent his doing harm to a third. The present case falls broadly into the same category. It is plain that vital characteristics which were present in the *Dorset Yacht* case and which led to the imposition of liability are here lacking. Sutcliffe was never in the custody of the police force. Miss Hill was one of a vast number of the female general public who might be at risk from his activities but was at no special distinctive risk in relation to them, unlike the owners of yachts moored off Brownsea Island in relation to the foreseeable conduct of the Borstal boys. It appears from the passage quoted from the speech of Lord Diplock in the *Dorset Yacht* case that, in his view, no liability would rest on a prison authority which carelessly allowed the escape of an habitual criminal, for damage which he subsequently caused, not in the course of attempting to make good his getaway to persons at special risk, but in further pursuance of his general criminal career to the person or property of members of the general public. The same rule must apply as regards failure to recapture the criminal before he had time to resume his career. In the case of an escaped criminal his identity and description are known. In the instant case the identity of the wanted criminal was at the material time unknown and it is not averred that any full or clear description of him was ever available. The alleged negligence of the police consists in a failure to discover his identity. But, if there is no general duty of care owed to individual members of the public by the responsible authorities to prevent the escape of a known criminal or to recapture him, there cannot reasonably be imposed on any police force a duty of care similarly owed to identify and apprehend an unknown one. Miss Hill cannot for this purpose be regarded as a person at special risk simply because she was young and female. Where the class of potential victims of a particular habitual criminal is a large one the precise size of it cannot in principle affect the issue. All the householders are potential victims of a habitual burglar, and all females of an habitual rapist. The conclusion must be that although there existed reasonable foreseeability of likely harm to such as Miss Hill if Sutcliffe were not identified and apprehended, there is absent from the case any such ingredient or characteristic as led to the liability of the Home Office in the *Dorset Yacht* case. Nor is there present any additional characteristic such as might make up the

48 *Rondel v Worsley* [1969] 1 AC 191.

49 *Saif Ali v Sydney Mitchell & Co* [1980] AC 198.

50 [1988] 2 All ER 238.

deficiency. The circumstances of the case are therefore not capable of establishing a duty of care owed towards Miss Hill by the West Yorkshire police.

That is sufficient for the disposal of the appeal. But in my opinion there is another reason why an action for damages in negligence should not lie against the police in circumstances such as those of the present case, and that is public policy. In *Yuen Kun Yeu v AG of Hong Kong* [1987] 2 All ER 705 at 712, [1988] AC 175 at 193, I expressed the view that the category of cases where the second stage of Lord Wilberforce's two-stage test in *Anns v Merton London Borough* [1977] 2 All ER 492 at 498, [1978] AC 728 at 752 might fail to be applied was a limited one, one example of that category being *Rondel v Worsley* [1967] 3 All ER 993, [1969] 1 AC 191. Application of that second stage is, however, capable of constituting a separate and independent ground for holding that the existence of liability in negligence should not be entertained. Potential existence of such liability may in many instances be in the general public interest, as tending towards the observance of a higher standard of care in the carrying on of various different types of activity. I do not, however, consider that this can be said of police activities. The general sense of public duty which motivates police forces is unlikely to be appreciably reinforced by the imposition of such liability so far as concerns their function in the investigation and suppression of crime. From time to time they make mistakes in the exercise of that function, but it is not to be doubted that they apply their best endeavours to the performance of it. In some instances the imposition of liability may lead to the exercise of a function being carried on in a detrimentally defensive frame of mind. The possibility of this happening in relation to the investigative operations of the police cannot be excluded. Further, it would be reasonable to expect that if potential liability were to be imposed it would not be uncommon for actions to be raised against police forces on the ground that they had failed to catch some criminal as soon as they might have done, with the result that he went on to commit further crimes. Whilst some such actions might involve allegations of a simple and straightforward type of failure, for example that a police officer negligently tripped and fell while pursuing a burglar, others would be likely to enter into the general nature of a police investigation, as indeed the present action would seek to do. The manner of conduct of such an investigation must necessarily involve a variety of decisions to be made on matters of policy and discretion, for example as to which particular line of inquiry is most advantageously to be pursued and what is the most advantageous way to deploy the available resources. Many such decisions would not be regarded by the courts as appropriate to be called in question, yet elaborate investigation of the facts might be necessary to ascertain whether or not this was so. A great deal of police time, trouble and expense might be expected to have to be put into the preparation of the defence to the action and the attendance of witnesses at the trial. The result would be a significant diversion of police manpower and attention from their most important function, that of suppression of crime. Closed investigations would require to be reopened and re-traversed, not with the object of bringing any criminal to justice but to ascertain whether or not they had been competently conducted. I therefore consider that Glidewell LJ, in his judgment in the Court of Appeal in the present case, was right to take the view that the police were immune from an action of this kind on grounds similar to those which in *Rondel v Worsley* were held to render a barrister immune from actions for negligence in his conduct of proceedings in court (see [1987] 1 All ER 1173 at 1183–84, [1988] QB 60 at 76).

My Lords, for these reasons I would dismiss the appeal.

Lord Templeman stated:

> The question for determination in this appeal is whether an action for damages is an appropriate vehicle for investigating the efficiency of a police force. The present action will be confined to narrow, albeit perplexing, questions, for example, whether, discounting hindsight, it should have been obvious to a senior officer that Sutcliffe was a prime suspect, whether a senior police officer should not have been deceived by an evil hoaxer, whether an officer interviewing Sutcliffe should have been better briefed and whether a report on Sutcliffe should have been given greater attention. The court would have to consider the conduct of each police officer, to decide whether the policeman failed to attain the standard of care of a hypothetical average policeman. The court would have to decide whether an inspector is to be condemned for failing to display the acumen of Sherlock Holmes and whether a constable is to be condemned for being as obtuse as Dr Watson. The appellant will presumably seek evidence, for what it is worth, from retired police inspectors, who would be asked whether they would have been misled by the hoaxer and whether they would have identified Sutcliffe at an earlier stage. At the end of the day the court might or might not find that there had been negligence by one or more members of the police force. But that finding would not help anybody or punish anybody.

Lord Templeman and the other three Law Lords agreed with Lord Keith that the appeal should be dismissed. A similar line was taken in a rash of cases brought against the police for failing to take adequate steps to discover why a burglar alarm had been activated,[51] for failure to prevent serious physical harassment of a schoolboy and his family by a schoolteacher, even where there was an argument for saying that there was close degree of proximity,[52] and for failure to warn of road hazards after an accident.[53]

PUBLIC AUTHORITIES

The courts have clearly set their face against the imposition of any general duty in negligence on the police, with some minor exceptions. To that extent the position is reasonably straightforward. The same cannot be said of the liability of public authorities in common law negligence. Here we meet the divide between public and private law head on. Public authorities are given discretionary powers of infinite variety so as to carry out their functions. If they fail to use their powers or use them carelessly, thus causing loss to the plaintiff, is the latter entitled to bring a common law action in negligence to recover that loss? There may be public law remedies available but which will not normally provide the plaintiff with the desired compensation. Does the availability of these alternatives affect the existence of a common law duty? The courts have said that an action at common law is only possible if the authority has acted *ultra vires* its powers and also that a decision is only challengeable at common law if the decision falls within the operational aspect of the exercise of the power as opposed to the policy or discretionary area. These various issues are addressed in the following extracts. One complicating factor concerns the status

51 *Alexandrou v Oxford* [1993] 4 All ER 328.

52 *Osman v Ferguson* [1993] 4 All ER 344.

53 *Ancell v McDermott* [1993] 4 All ER 355.

of some of Lord Wilberforce's statements in the *Anns* case, as it should be recalled that the decision in *Anns* was overturned in *Murphy v Brentwood*. However, it is suggested that his comments in the extract below remain unaffected by the *Murphy* decision.

Having discussed the facts of *Anns*, Lord Wilberforce continued:[54]

What is the extent of the local authority's duty towards these persons? Although, as I have suggested, a situation of 'proximity' existed between the council and owners and occupiers of the houses, I do not think that a description of the council's duty can be based upon the 'neighbourhood' principle alone or upon merely any such factual relationship as 'control' as suggested by the Court of Appeal. So to base it would be to neglect an essential factor which is that the local authority is a public body, discharging functions under statute: its powers and duties are definable in terms of public, not private, law. The problem which this type of action creates is to define the circumstances in which the law should impose, over and above, or perhaps alongside, these public law powers and duties, a duty in private law towards individuals such that they may sue for damages in a civil court. It is in this context that the distinction sought to be drawn between duties and mere powers has to be examined.

Most, indeed probably all, statutes relating to public authorities or public bodies, contain in them a large area of policy. The courts call this 'discretion', meaning that the decision is one for the authority or body to make, and not for the courts. Many statutes also prescribe or at least presuppose the practical execution of policy decisions: a convenient description of this is to say that in addition to the area of policy or discretion, there is an operational area. Although this distinction between the policy area and the operational area is convenient, and illuminating, it is probably a distinction of degree; many 'operational' powers or duties have in them some element of 'discretion'. It can safely be said that the more 'operational' a power or duty may be, the easier it is to superimpose upon it a common law duty of care.

I do not think that it is right to limit this to a duty to avoid causing extra or additional damage beyond what must be expected to arise from the exercise of the power or duty. That may be correct when the act done under the statute *inherently* must adversely *affect* the interest of individuals. But many other acts can be done without causing any harm to anyone – indeed may be directed to preventing harm from occurring. In these cases the duty is the normal one of taking care to avoid harm to those likely to be affected.

Let us examine the Public Health Act 1936 in the light of this. Undoubtedly it lays out a wide area of policy. It is for the local authority, a public and elected body, to decide upon the scale of resources which it can make available in order to carry out its functions under part two of the Act – how many inspectors, with what expert qualifications, it should recruit; how often inspections are to be made; what tests are to be carried out – must be for its decision. It is no accident that the Act is drafted in terms of functions and powers rather than in terms of positive duty. As was well said, public authorities have to strike a balance between the claims of efficiency and thrift (Du Parcq LJ in *Kent v East Suffolk Rivers Catchment Board* [1940] 1 KB 319, 338); whether they get the balance right can only be decided through the ballot box, not the courts. It is said – there are reflections of this in the judgments in *Dutton v Bognor Regis Urban District Council* [1972] 1 QB 373 – that the local authority is under no duty to inspect, and this is

54 [1978] at 753–55.

> used as the foundation for an argument, also found in some of the cases, that if it need not inspect at all, it cannot be liable for negligent inspection. If it were to be held so liable, so it is said, councils would simply decide against inspection. I think this is too crude an argument. It overlooks the fact that local authorities are public bodies operating under statute with a clear responsibility for public health in their area. They must, and in fact do, make their discretionary decisions responsibly and for reasons which accord with the statutory purpose: see *Ayr Harbour Trustees v Oswald* (1883) 8 App Cas 623, 639, *per* Lord Watson: 'the powers which [s 10] confers are discretionary ... But it is the plain import of the clause that the harbour trustees ... shall be vested with, and shall avail themselves of, these discretionary powers, whenever and as often as they may be of the opinion that the public interest will be promoted by their exercise'.
>
> If they do not exercise their discretion in this way they can be challenged in the courts. Thus, to say that councils are under no duty to inspect is not a sufficient statement of the position. They are under a duty to give proper consideration to the question whether they should inspect or not. Their immunity from attack, in the event of failure to inspect, in other words, though great is not absolute. And because it is not absolute, the necessary premise for the proposition 'if no duty to inspect, then no duty to take care in inspection' vanishes.
>
> Passing then to the duty as regards inspection, if made; on principle there must surely be a duty to exercise reasonable care. The standard of care must be related to the duty to be performed – namely to ensure compliance with the bylaws. It must be related to the fact that the person responsible for construction in accordance with the bylaws is the builder, and that the inspector's function is supervisory. It must be related to the fact that, once the inspector has passed the foundations, they will be covered up with no subsequent opportunity for inspection. But this duty, heavily operational though it may be, is still a duty arising under the statute. There may be a discretionary element in its exercise, discretionary as to the time and manner of inspection, and the techniques to be used. A plaintiff complaining of negligence must prove, the burden being on him, that action taken was not within the limits of discretion bona fide exercised, before he can begin to rely upon the common law duty of care. But if he can do this, he should, in principle, be able to sue.

In *Rowling v Takaro Properties Ltd*,[55] Lord Keith made some observations on the policy/operational distinction, in giving the judgment of the Privy Council. The finance minister of New Zealand was sued in respect of his decision to refuse consent to the issue of shares of Takaro to an overseas company, this being part of a financial package to rescue Takaro which was lost as a result of the delay. The minister's decision was declared *ultra vires* and Takaro now brought a common law action for damages. The case was ultimately decided on the basis that there was no breach, but the duty issue was discussed as follows:

> The Court of Appeal found no difficulty in holding that a duty of care rested on the minister; indeed, Cooke J went so far as to observe that the question of liability to Takaro seemed to him relatively straightforward.
>
> For reasons which will appear, their lordships do not find it necessary to reach any final conclusion on the question of the existence, or (if it exists) the scope, of the duty of care resting on a minister in a case such as the present; and they have come to the conclusion that it would not be right for them to do so, because the matter was not fully exposed before them in argument. In particular, no

55 [1988] 1 All ER 163 at 171–73.

reference was made in argument to the extensive academic literature on the subject of the liability of public authorities in negligence, study of which can be of such great assistance to the courts in considering areas of law which, as in the case of negligence, are in a continuing state of development. Even so, such is the importance of the present case, especially in New Zealand, that their Lordships feel that it would be inappropriate, and perhaps be felt to be discourteous, if they were to make no reference to the relevant considerations affecting the decision whether a duty of care should arise in a case such as the present.

Quilliam J considered the question with particular reference to the distinction between policy (or planning) decisions and operational decisions. His conclusion was expressed as follows ([1986] 1 NZLR 22 at 35): 'The distinction between the policy and the operational areas can be both fine and confusing. Various expressions have been used instead of operational, eg "administrative" or "business powers". It may not be easy to attach any of these labels to the decision of the minister in this case, but what appears to me to emerge clearly enough is that, for the reasons I have indicated, his decision was the antithesis of policy or discretion. I therefore equate it with having been operational. The result of that conclusion is that I consider the *prima facie* existence of a duty of care has been established'.

Their Lordships feel considerable sympathy with Quilliam J's difficulty in solving the problem by simple reference to this distinction. They are well aware of the references in the literature to this distinction (which appears to have originated in the United States of America) and of the critical analysis to which it has been subjected. They incline to the opinion, expressed in the literature, that this distinction does not provide a touchstone of liability, but rather is expressive of the need to exclude altogether those cases in which the decision under attack is of such a kind that a question whether it has been made negligently is unsuitable for judicial resolution, of which notable examples are discretionary decisions on the allocation of scarce resources or the distribution of risks (see especially the discussion in Craig, *Administrative Law* (1983) pp 534–38). If this is right, classification of the relevant decision as a policy or planning decision in this sense may exclude liability; but a conclusion that it does not fall within that category does not, in their lordships' opinion, mean that a duty of care will necessarily exist.

It is at this stage that it is necessary, before concluding that a duty of care should be imposed, to consider all the relevant circumstances. One of the considerations underlying certain recent decisions of the House of Lords (*Governors of the Peabody Donation Fund v Sir Lindsay Parkinson & Co Ltd* [1984] 3 All ER 529, [1985] AC 210) and of the Privy Council (*Yuen Kun Yeu v AG of Hong Kong* [1987] 2 All ER 705, [1987] 3 WLR 776) is the fear that a too literal application of the well-known observation of Lord Wilberforce in *Anns v Merton London Borough* [1977] 2 All ER 492 at 498, [1978] AC 728 at 751–52 may be productive of a failure to have regard to, and analyse and weigh, all the relevant considerations in considering whether it is appropriate that a duty of care should be imposed. Their Lordships consider that question to be of an intensely pragmatic character, well suited for gradual development but requiring most careful analysis. It is one on which all common law jurisdictions can learn much from each other because, apart from exceptional cases, no sensible distinction can be drawn in this respect between the various countries and social conditions existing in them. It is incumbent on the courts in different jurisdictions to be sensitive to each other's reactions; but what they are all searching for in others, and each of them is striving to achieve, is a careful analysis and weighing of the relevant competing considerations.

It is in this spirit that a case such as the present has, in their Lordships' opinion, to be approached. They recognise that the decision of the minister is capable of being described as having been of a policy rather than an operational character; but, if the function of the policy/operational dichotomy is as they have already described it, the allegation of negligence in the present case is not, they consider, of itself of such a character as to render the case unsuitable for judicial decision. Be that as it may, there are certain considerations which militate against the imposition of liability in a case such as the present.

Their Lordships wish to refer in particular to certain matters which they consider to be of importance. The first is that the only effect of a negligent decision, such as is here alleged to have been made, is delay. This is because the processes of judicial review are available to the aggrieved party; and, assuming that the alleged error of law is so serious that it can be properly described as negligent, the decision will assuredly be quashed by a process which, in New Zealand as in the United Kingdom, will normally be carried out with promptitude.

The second is that, in the nature of things, it is likely to be very rare indeed that an error of law of this kind by a minister or other public authority can properly be categorised as negligent. As is well known, anybody, even a judge, can be capable of misconstruing a statute; and such misconstruction, when it occurs, can be severely criticised without attracting the epithet 'negligent'. Obviously, this simple fact points rather to the extreme unlikelihood of a breach of duty being established in these case, a point to which their lordships will return; but it is nevertheless a relevant factor to be taken into account when considering whether liability in negligence should properly be imposed.

The third is the danger of overkill. It is to be hoped that, as general rule, imposition of liability in negligence will lead to a higher standard of care in the performance of the relevant type of act; but sometimes not only may this not be so, but the imposition of liability may even lead to harmful consequences. In other words, the cure may be worse than the disease. There are reasons for believing that this may be so in cases where liability is imposed on local authorities whose building inspectors have been negligent in relation to the inspection of foundations, as in the *Anns* case itself, because there is a danger that the building inspectors of some local authorities may react to that decision by simply increasing, unnecessarily, the requisite depth of foundations, thereby imposing a very substantial and unnecessary financial burden on members of the community. A comparable danger may exist in such cases as the present, because, once it became known that liability in negligence may be imposed on the ground that a minister has misconstrued a statute and so acted *ultra vires*, the cautious civil servant may go to extreme lengths in ensuring that legal advice, or even the opinion of the court, is obtained before decisions are taken, thereby leading to unnecessary delay in a considerable number of cases.

Fourth, it is very difficult to identify any particular case in which it can properly be said that a minister is under a duty to seek legal advice. It cannot, their lordships consider, reasonably be said that a minister is under a duty to seek legal advice in every case in which he is called on to exercise a discretionary power conferred on him by legislation; and their lordships find it difficult to see how cases in which a duty to seek legal advice should be imposed should be segregated from those in which it should not. In any event, the officers of the relevant department will be involved; the matter will be processed and presented to the minister for decision in the usual way, and by this means his mind will be focused on the relevant issue. Again, it is not to be forgotten that the minister, in exercising his statutory discretion, is acting essentially as a guardian of the public

> interest; in the present case, for example, he was acting under legislation enacted not for the benefit of applicants for consent to share issues but for the protection of the community as a whole. Furthermore, he is, so far as their lordships are aware, normally under no duty to exercise his discretion within any particular time; and if, through a mistaken construction of the statute, he acts *ultra vires* and delay thereby occurs before he makes an *intra vires* decision, he will have in any event to exercise his discretion anew and, if his discretion is then exercised in the plaintiff's favour, the effect of the delay will only be to postpone the receipt by the plaintiff of a benefit which he had no absolute right to receive.

The issue of common law negligence and the exercise of statutory duties and powers has recently been considered by the House of Lords in the consolidated cases, *X and others (minors) v Bedfordshire County Council, M (a minor) v Newham London Borough Council and others, E (a minor) v Dorset County Council*.[56] The cases concerned allegations relating to duties and powers concerning the physical and educational welfare of children. The House accepted the argument in all but one instance that the claims had been rightly struck out as not disclosing a cause of action. The case is important for the observations of Lord Browne-Wilkinson who gave the leading judgment. He begins his judgment with an analysis of the general problems in this area. He observed that there are four ways in which to bring a claim for private law damages, namely: actions for breach of statutory duty without more; actions based on careless performance of a statutory duty in the absence of a common law action; actions based on a common law duty arising from a statutory duty or power; and finally, misfeasance in a public office. Leaving aside the latter as not relevant in the case, His Lordship discussed each of the others. This is what he said in relation to the third type of action:[57]

> In this category, the claim alleges either that a statutory duty gives rise to a common law duty of care owed to the plaintiff by the defendant to do or refrain from doing a particular act, or (more often) that in the course of carrying out a statutory function the defendant has brought about such a relationship between himself and the plaintiff as to give rise to a duty of care at common law. A further variant is a claim by the plaintiff that, whether or not the authority is itself under a duty of care to the plaintiff, its servant in the course of performing the statutory function was under a common law duty of care for breach of which the authority is vicariously liable.
>
> Mr Munby QC, in his reply in the *Newham* case, invited your Lordships to lay down the general principles applicable in determining the circumstances in which the law would impose a common law duty of care arising from the exercise of statutory powers or duties. I have no doubt that, if possible, this would be most desirable. But I have found it quite impossible either to detect such principle in the wide range of authorities and academic writings to which we were referred or to devise any such principle *de novo*. The truth of the matter is that statutory duties now exist over such a wide range of diverse activities and take so many different forms that no one principle is capable of being formulated applicable to all cases. However, in my view it is possible in considering the problems raised by these particular appeals to identify certain points which are of significance.

56 [1995] 3 All ER 353.

57 At pp 367–71.

(1) *Co-existence of statutory duty and common law duty of care*

It is clear that a common law duty of care may arise in the performance of statutory functions. But a broad distinction has to be drawn between:

(a) cases in which it is alleged that the authority owes a duty of care in the manner in which it exercises a statutory discretion; and

(b) cases in which a duty of care is alleged to arise from the manner in which the statutory duty has been implemented in practice.

An example of (a) in the educational field would be a decision whether or not to exercise a statutory discretion to close a school, being a decision which necessarily involves the exercise of a discretion. An example of (b) would be the actual running of a school pursuant to the statutory duties. In such a latter case a common law duty to take reasonable care for the physical safety of the pupils will arise. The fact that the school is being run pursuant to a statutory duty is not necessarily incompatible with a common law duty of care arising from the proximate relationship between a school and the pupils it has agreed to accept. The distinction is between (a), taking care in exercising a statutory discretion whether or not to do an act, and (b), having decided to do that act, taking care in the manner in which you do it.

(2) *Discretion, justiciability and the policy/operational test*

(a) *Discretion*

Most statutes which impose a statutory duty on local authorities confer on the authority a discretion as to the extent to which, and the methods by which, such a statutory duty is to be performed. It is clear both in principle and from the decided cases that the local authority cannot be liable in damages for doing that which Parliament has authorised. Therefore, if the decisions complained of fall within the ambit of such statutory discretion, they cannot be actionable in common law. However, if the decision complained of is so unreasonable that it falls outside the ambit of the discretion conferred upon the local authority, there is no *a priori* reason for excluding all common law liability.

That this is the law is established by the decision in the *Dorset Yacht* case and by that part of the decision in *Anns v Merton London Borough* [1977] 2 All ER 492, [1978] AC 728 which, so far as I am aware, has largely escaped criticism in later decisions. In the *Dorset Yacht* case [1970] 2 All ER 294 at 301, [1970] AC 1004 at 1031 Lord Reid said: 'Where Parliament confers a discretion the position is not the same. Then there may, and almost certainly will, be errors of judgment in exercising such a discretion and Parliament cannot have intended that members of the public should be entitled to sue in respect of such errors. But there must come a stage when the discretion is exercised so carelessly or unreasonably that there has been no real exercise of the discretion which Parliament has conferred. The person purporting to exercise his discretion has acted in abuse or excess of his power. Parliament cannot be supposed to have granted immunity to persons who do that.' (See also [1970] 2 All ER 294 at 306, [1970] AC 1004 at 1037 *per* Lord Morris.)

Lord Diplock, as I have said, took a rather different line, making it a condition precedent to any common law duty arising that the decision impugned should be shown to be *ultra vires* in the public law sense. For myself, I do not believe that it is either helpful or necessary to introduce public law concepts as to the validity of a decision into the question of liability at common law for negligence. In public law a decision can be *ultra vires* for reasons other than *Wednesbury* unreasonableness (see *Associated*

Provincial Picture Houses Ltd v Wednesbury Corpn [1947] 2 All ER 680, [1948] KB 223) (eg breach of the rules of natural justice) which have no relevance to the question of negligence. Moreover, it leads, in my judgment mistakenly, to the contention that claims for damages for negligence in the exercise of statutory powers should for procedural purposes be classified as public law claims and therefore, under *O'Reilly v Mackman* [1982] 3 All ER 1124, [1983] 2 AC 237, should be brought in judicial review proceedings: see *Lonrho plc v Tebbit* [1992] 4 All ER 280. However, although I consider that the public law doctrine of *ultra vires* has, as such, no role to play in the subject under discussion, the remarks of Lord Diplock were plainly directed to the fact that the exercise of a statutory discretion cannot be impugned unless it is so unreasonable that it falls altogether outside the ambit of the statutory discretion. He said ([1970] 2 All ER 294 at 332, [1970] AC 1004 at 1068): 'These considerations lead me to the conclusion that neither the intentional release of a Borstal trainee under supervision, nor the unintended escape of a Borstal trainee still under detention which was the consequence of the application of a system of relaxed control intentionally adopted by the Home Office as conducive to the reformation of trainees, can have been intended by Parliament to give rise to any cause of action on the part of any private citizen unless the system adopted was so unrelated to any purpose of reformation that no reasonable person could have reached a *bona fide* conclusion that it was conducive to that purpose. Only then would the decision to adopt it be *ultra vires* in public law.'

Exactly the same approach was adopted by Lord Wilberforce in *Anns v Merton London Borough* [1977] 2 All ER 492 at 501, [1978] AC 728 at 755, when, speaking of the duty of a local authority which had, in fact, inspected a building under construction, he said: 'But this duty, heavily operational though it may be, is still a duty arising under the statute. There may be a discretionary element in its exercise, discretionary as to the time and manner of inspection, and the techniques to be used. A plaintiff complaining of negligence must prove, the burden being on him, that action taken was not within the limits of a discretion *bona fide* exercised, before he can begin to rely on a common law duty of care.'

It follows that in seeking to establish that a local authority is liable at common law for negligence in the exercise of a discretion conferred by statute, the first requirement is to show that the decision was outside the ambit of the discretion altogether; if it was not, a local authority cannot itself be in breach of any duty of care owed to the plaintiff.

In deciding whether or not this requirement is satisfied, the court has to assess the relevant factors taken into account by the authority in exercising the discretion. Since what are under consideration are discretionary powers conferred on public bodies for public purposes the relevant factors will often include policy matters, for example social policy, the allocation of finite financial resources between the different calls made upon them or (as in the *Dorset Yacht* case) the balance between pursuing desirable social aims as against the risk to the public inherent in so doing. It is established that the courts cannot enter upon the assessment of such 'policy' matters. The difficulty is to identify in any particular case whether or not the decision in question is a 'policy' decision.

(b) Justiciability and the policy/operational dichotomy

In English law the first attempt to lay down the principles applicable in deciding whether or not a decision was one of policy was made by Lord

Wilberforce in *Anns v Merton London Borough* [1977] 2 All ER 492 at 500, [1978] AC 728 at 754: 'Most, indeed probably all, statutes relating to public authorities or public bodies, contain in them a large area of policy. The courts call this "discretion", meaning that the decision is one for the authority or body to make, and not for the courts. Many statutes, also, prescribe or at least presuppose the practical execution of policy decisions; a convenient description of this is to say that in addition to the area of policy or discretion, there is an operational area. Although this distinction between the policy area and the operational area is convenient and illuminating, it is probably a distinction of degree; many "operational" powers or duties have in them some element of "discretion". It can safely be said that the more "operational" a power or duty may be, the easier it is to superimpose on it a common duty of care.'

As Lord Wilberforce appreciated, this approach did not provide a hard and fast test as to those matters which were open to the court's decision. In *Rowling v Takaro Properties Ltd* [1988] 1 All ER 163, [1988] AC 473 the Privy Council reverted to the problem. In that case the trial judge had found difficulty in applying the policy/operational test, but having classified the decision in question as being operational, took the view that as a result there was a common law duty of care. [His Lordship quoted from the speech of Lord Keith set out above.]

From these authorities I understand the applicable principle to be as follows. Where Parliament has conferred a statutory discretion on a public authority, it is for that authority, not for the courts, to exercise the discretion; nothing which the authority does within the ambit of the discretion can be actionable at common law. If the decision complained of falls outside the statutory discretion, it *can* (but not necessarily will) give rise to common law liability. However, if the factors relevant to the exercise of the discretion include matters of policy, the court cannot adjudicate on such policy matters and therefore cannot reach the conclusion that the decision was outside the ambit of the statutory discretion. Therefore a common law duty of care in relation to the taking of decisions involving policy matters cannot exist.

(3) If justiciable, the ordinary principles of negligence apply

If the plaintiff's complaint alleges carelessness, not in the taking of a discretionary decision to do some act, but in the practical manner in which that act has been performed (eg the running of a school) the question whether or not there is a common law duty of care falls to be decided by applying the usual principles, ie those laid down in *Caparo Industries plc v Dickman* [1990] 1 All ER 568 at 573–74, [1990] 2 AC 605 at 617–18. Was the damage to the plaintiff reasonably foreseeable? Was the relationship between the plaintiff and the defendant sufficiently proximate? Is it just and reasonable to impose a duty of care? See *Rowling v Takaro Properties Ltd* and *Hill v Chief Constable of West Yorkshire* [1988] 2 All ER 238, [1989] AC 53.

However, the question whether there is such a common law duty, and if so its ambit, must be profoundly influenced by the statutory framework within which the acts complained of were done. The position is directly analogous to that in which a tortious duty of care owed by A to C can arise out of the performance by A of a contract between A and B. In *Henderson v Merrett Syndicates Ltd* [1994] 3 All ER 506, [1994] 3 WLR 761 your lordships held that A (the managing agent) who had contracted with B (the members' agent) to render certain services for C (the names) came under a duty of care to C in the performance of those services. It is clear that any tortious duty of care

> owed to C in those circumstances could not be inconsistent with the duty owed in contract by A to B. Similarly, in my judgment, a common law duty of care cannot be imposed on a statutory duty if the observance of such common law duty of care would be inconsistent with, or have a tendency to discourage, the due performance by the local authority of its statutory duties.

Having decided, albeit reluctantly,[58] that some of the allegations in the abuse cases were justiciable, His Lordship proceeded to consider the direct liability of the local authorities at common law:

> I turn then to consider whether, in accordance with the ordinary principles laid down in *Caparo Industries v Dickman* [1990] 1 All ER 568, [1990] 2 AC 605, the local authority in the *Bedfordshire* case owed a direct duty of care to the plaintiffs. The local authority accepts that they could foresee damage to the plaintiffs if they carried out their statutory duties negligently and that the relationship between the authority is sufficiently proximate. The third requirement laid down in *Caparo* is that it must be just and reasonable to impose a common law duty of care in all the circumstances. It was submitted that this third requirement is only applicable in cases where the plaintiff's claim is for pure economic loss and that it does not apply where, as in the child abuse cases, the claim is for physical damage. I reject this submission; although *Caparo* and many other of the recent cases were decisions where only pure economic loss was claimed, the same basic principles apply to claims for physical damage and were applied in, for example, *Hill v Chief Constable of West Yorkshire* [1988] 2 All ER 238, [1989] AC 53.
>
> Is it, then, just and reasonable to superimpose a common law duty of care on the local authority in relation to the performance of its statutory duties to protect children? In my judgment it is not. Sir Thomas Bingham took the view, with which I agree, that the public policy consideration which has first claim on the loyalty of the law is that wrongs should be remedied and that very potent counter-considerations are required to override that policy (see [1994] 4 All ER 602 at 619, [1994] 2 WLR 554 at 572). However, in my judgment there are such considerations in this case.
>
> First, in my judgment a common law duty of care would cut across the whole statutory system set up for the protection of children at risk. As a result of the ministerial directions contained in the HMSO booklet *Working Together*, the protection of such children is not the exclusive territory of the local authority's social services. The system is inter-disciplinary, involving the participation of the police, educational bodies, doctors and others. At all stages the system involves joint discussions, joint recommendations and joint decisions. The key organisation is the child protection conference, a multi-disciplinary body which decides whether to place the child on the child protection register. This procedure by way of joint action takes place, not merely because it is good practice, but because it is required by guidance having statutory force binding on the local authority. The guidance is extremely detailed and extensive; the current edition of *Working Together* runs to 126 pages. To introduce into such a system a common law duty of care enforceable against only one of the participant bodies would be manifestly unfair. To impose such liability on all the participant bodies would lead to almost impossible problems of disentangling as between the respective bodies the liability, both primary and by way of contribution, of each for reaching a decision found to be negligent.

58 At p 380.

Second, the task of the local authority and its servants in dealing with children at risk is extraordinarily delicate. Legislation requires the local authority to have regard not only to the physical well-being of the child but also to the advantages of not disrupting the child's family environment; see eg s 17 of the 1989 Act. In one of the child abuse cases, the local authority is blamed for removing the child precipitately; in the other, for failing to remove the children from their mother. As the *Report of the Inquiry into Child Abuse in Cleveland 1987* (Cm 412) (the Cleveland Report) said (p 244): 'It is a delicate line to tread between taking action too soon and not taking it soon enough. Social services, whilst putting the needs of the child first, must respect the rights of the parents; they also must work if possible with the parents for the benefit of the children. These parents themselves are often in need of help. Inevitably a degree of conflict develops between those objectives'.

Next, if a liability in damages were to be imposed, it might well be that local authorities would adopt a more cautious and defensive approach to their duties. For example, as the Cleveland Report makes clear, on occasions the speedy decision to remove the child is sometimes vital. If the authority is to be made liable in damages for a negligent decision to remove a child (such negligence lying in the failure properly first to investigate the allegations) there would be a substantial temptation to postpone making such a decision until further inquiries have been made in the hope of getting more concrete facts. Not only would the child in fact being abused be prejudiced by such delay, the increased workload inherent in making such investigations would reduce the time available to deal with other cases and other children.

The relationship between the social worker and the child's parents is frequently one of conflict, the parent wishing to retain the care of the child, the social worker having to consider whether to remove it. This is fertile ground in which to breed ill feeling and litigation, often hopeless, the cost of which both in terms of money and human resources will be diverted from the performance of the social service for which they were provided. The spectre of vexatious and costly litigation is often urged as a reason for not imposing a legal duty. But the circumstances surrounding cases of child abuse make the risk a very high one which cannot be ignored.

If there were no other remedy for maladministration of the statutory system for the protection of children, it would provide substantial argument for imposing a duty of care. But the statutory complaints procedures contained in s 76 of the 1980 Act and the much fuller procedures now available under the 1989 Act provide a means to have grievances investigated, though not to recover compensation. Further, it was submitted (and not controverted) that the local authorities' ombudsman would have power to investigate cases such as these.

Finally, your lordships' decision in *Caparo v Dickman* lays down that, in deciding whether to develop novel categories of negligence, the court should proceed incrementally and by analogy with decided categories. We were not referred to any category of case in which a duty of care has been held to exist which is in any way analogous to the present cases. Here, for the first time, the plaintiffs are seeking to erect a common law duty of care in relation to the administration of a statutory social welfare scheme. Such a scheme is designed to protect weaker members of society (children) from harm done to them by others. The scheme involves the administrators in exercising discretions and powers which could not exist in the private sector and which, in many cases, bring them into conflict with those who, under the general law, are responsible for the child's welfare. To my mind, the nearest analogies are the cases where a common law duty of care has

> been sought to be imposed upon the police (in seeking to protect vulnerable members of society from wrongs done to them by others) or statutory regulators of financial dealings who are seeking to protect investors from dishonesty. In neither of those cases has it been thought appropriate to superimpose on the statutory regime a common law duty of care giving rise to a claim in damages for failure to protect the weak against the wrongdoer: see *Hill v Chief Constable of West Yorkshire* and *Yuen Kun Yeu v AG of Hong Kong* [1987] 2 All ER 705, [1988] AC 175. In the latter case, the Privy Council, whilst not deciding the point, said that there was much force in the argument that if the regulators had been held liable in that case the principles leading to such liability 'would surely be equally applicable to a wide range of regulatory bodies, not only in the financial field, but also, for example, to the factory inspectorate and social workers, to name only a few'. (See [1987] 2 All ER 705 at 717–16, [1988] AC 175 at 198.)
>
> In my judgment, the courts should proceed with great care before holding liable in negligence those who have been charged by Parliament with the task of protecting society from the wrongdoing of others.

His Lordship made similar noises in relation to the *Dorset* education cases and concluded by saying:

> In my judgment, as in the child abuse cases, the courts should hesitate long before imposing a common law duty of care in the exercise of discretionary powers or duties conferred by Parliament for social welfare purposes. The aim of the 1981 [Education] Act was to provide, for the benefit of society as a whole, an administrative machinery to help one disadvantaged section of society. The statute provides its own detailed machinery for securing that the statutory purpose is performed. If, despite the complex machinery for consultation and appeals contained in the Act, the scheme fails to provide the benefit intended that is a matter more appropriately remedied by way of the ombudsman looking into the administrative failure than by way of litigation.

His Lordship hesitates in this case to say explicitly whether any of the challenged decisions fell within or without the policy area, which is a pity. He prefers to assume that the issues, or at least some of them, are justiciable, but then dashes the plaintiffs' hopes by denying a duty of care at common law on the basis of the third prong of the duty test, ie that it is not just and reasonable to impose a duty. This was surely an ideal opportunity for the House to clarify the policy/operational distinction with some concrete, real life examples. The judge also plays the familiar alternative remedy card and finishes in the child abuse cases by throwing in the incremental approach as a final crushing blow to the plaintiffs' cases.

The alternative remedy approach used as one of the many reasons to decide against the imposition of a duty was adopted in the case of *Jones v Department of Employment*,[59] where the plaintiff's claim for benefit was refused by an adjudication officer but was allowed on appeal. The plaintiff sued the department for the alleged negligence of its adjudication officer. It was held that no duty was owed. Glidewell LJ observed:

> Having regard to the non-judicial nature of the adjudication officer's responsibilities, and in particular to the fact that the statutory framework provides a right of appeal which, if a point of law arises, can eventually bring the

59 [1988] 2 WLR 572.

> matter to this court, it is my view that the adjudication officer is not under any common law duty of care. In other words, I agree with Mr Laws that his decision is not susceptible of challenge at common law unless it be shown he is guilty of misfeasance.
>
> Indeed, in my view, it is a general principle that, if a government department or officer, charged with the making of decisions whether certain payments should be made, is subject to a statutory right of appeal against his decisions, he owes no duty of care in private law. Misfeasance apart, he is only susceptible in public law to judicial review or to the right of appeal provided by the statute under which he makes his decision.

Similar sentiments were expressed by Slade J.[60]

In one of the regulatory cases in the financial services sector, *Yuen Kun Yeu*, Lord Keith expressed the considerations which militated against the imposition of a duty on the Commissioner of Deposit - Taking Companies in Hong Kong for failing to revoke the registration of a company which had consequently been allowed to continue taking deposits. The allegation was that the commissioner knew or ought to have known that the company was being run fraudulently. In denying a duty, his lordship stated:

> ... the discretion given to the commissioner to register or de-register such companies, so as effectively to confer or remove the right to do business, was also an important part of the protection afforded. No doubt it was reasonably foreseeable by the commissioner that, if an uncreditworthy company were placed on or allowed to remain on the register, persons who, in the future, were to deposit money with it, would be at risk of losing that money. But mere foreseeability of harm does not create a duty, and future would-be depositors cannot be regarded as the only persons whom the commissioner should properly have in contemplation. In considering the question of removal from the register, the immediate and probably disastrous effect on existing depositors would be very relevant factor. It might be a very delicate choice whether the best course was to de-register a company forthwith or to allow it to continue in business with some hope that, after appropriate measures by management, its financial position would improve.

It would seem clear from the discussion above in the various case extracts that public authority liability at common law is minimal. At times the courts seem to be taking a similarly restrictive line to that taken in breach of statutory duty. The immunity of public authorities is great, almost absolute to use the slightly altered words of Lord Wilberforce in the much maligned *Anns* case.[61]

---

60 At pp 509–510.

61 See p 44 above.

CHAPTER 3

BREACH OF DUTY

INTRODUCTION

The second element which a plaintiff must establish in a negligence action is that the defendant was in breach of duty. It is often the most difficult element to satisfy and in the majority of cases, made up primarily of road traffic accidents and work-related injuries, it is the singular, most contentious issue. In these types of cases the duty issue is rarely a problem, as the case will normally fall within one of the established categories of duty situation. Most of the trial judge's deliberations will be taken up with this issue. Even if the plaintiff can show that the situation is one in which a notional duty is owed to him/her, and in addition that the defendant's conduct caused him/her harm, s/he will fail unless she can establish on the balance of probabilities that the defendant's conduct fell below the standard set by the law. There are two issues involved here:

(1) what is the standard of care required of the defendant in law; and

(2) has this defendant fallen below the standard demanded of him?

This latter question is often described as being one of fact, but this may disguise the fact that a judge, in deciding whether the defendant's conduct had the character of negligence, may be making inferences from what are called the primary facts. For example, in a road accident the judge is required to find the facts surrounding the incident from the witnesses. What were the weather conditions, was the road well lit if the accident took place at night, what was the speed of the defendant's vehicle? The answers are the primary facts, but in deciding from these as to whether the defendant's driving amounted to fault, the judge will often be making a value judgment. In a sense such a decision is properly regarded as one of mixed fact and law. In nearly all civil trials these days the judge sits without a jury and is therefore the arbiter of both fact and law. This makes it extremely difficult at times to ascertain whether the judge is dealing with a matter of law or fact, as the distinction becomes blurred.

This can be crucial when it comes to the issue of an appeal. Rarely will the appeal courts interfere with the trial judge's view of the facts on the basis that it is the judge's task to evaluate the strength of the evidence by seeing the witnesses in the court room being cross-examined. However, inferences from the primary facts may well be treated almost like statements about the law and be challengeable on appeal. There is also an important point about the precedent value of decisions made on the breach issue. As the actual decision may depend on the facts, the value of any particular decision is likely to be minimal. The endless citing of cases decided on the breach point is not to be encouraged, rather the cases that follow may be seen as containing guiding factors only.

A further word of warning is needed. The courts often use the word duty in the context of breach when they are concerned whether a defendant was required by the appropriate standard of care to do a specific thing; eg a judge might suggest that the defendant was under a duty to sound his car horn when approaching a dangerous junction. In this context, the word is being used to signify that this is something the reasonable person would have done in these circumstances.

STANDARD OF CARE

The standard of care is based on what the reasonable person would or would not do in the particular circumstances. The starting point for any discussion is traditionally the brief statement of Alderson B in *Blyth v Birmingham Waterworks Co*:[1]

> Negligence is the omission to do something which a reasonable man, guided upon those considerations which ordinarily regulate the conduct of human affairs, would do, or the doing of something which a prudent and reasonable man would not do.

The reasonable man is clearly an abstraction designed, some would argue, to enable a judge to hide his subjective view, which it must be, behind a cloak of objectivity and thus appear impartial towards the parties to the case. One of the leading statements on the reasonable man is that of Lord Macmillan in *Glasgow Corpn v Muir*:[2]

> My Lords, the degree of care for the safety of others which the law requires human beings to observe in the conduct of their affairs varies according to the circumstances. There is no absolute standard, but it may be said generally that the degree of care required varies directly with the risk involved. Those who engage in operations inherently dangerous must take precautions which are not required of persons engaged in the ordinary routine of daily life. It is, no doubt, true that in every act which an individual performs there is present potentiality of injury to others. All things are possible, and, indeed, it has become proverbial that the unexpected always happens, but, while the precept *alterum non laudere* requires us to abstain from intentionally injuring others, it does not impose liability for every injury which our conduct may occasion. In Scotland, at any rate, it has never been a maxim of the law that a man acts at his peril. Legal liability is limited to those consequences of our acts which a reasonable man of ordinary intelligence and experience so acting would have in contemplation. 'The duty to take care', as I essayed to formulate it in *Bourhill v Young*,[3] 'is the duty to avoid doing or omitting to do anything which may have as its reasonable and probable consequence injury to others, and the duty is owed to those to whom injury may reasonably and probably be anticipated if the duty is not observed'. This, in my opinion, expresses the law of Scotland and I apprehend that it is also the law of England.
>
> The standard of foresight of the reasonable man is, in one sense, an impersonal test. It eliminates the personal equation and is independent of the idiosyncrasies of the particular person whose conduct is in question. Some persons are by nature unduly timorous and imagine every path beset with lions. Others, of more robust temperament, fail to foresee or nonchalantly disregard even the most obvious dangers. The reasonable man is presumed to be free both from over-apprehension and from over-confidence, but there is a sense in which the

1 (1856) 11 Exch 781 at 784.

2 [1943] AC 448 at 456.

3 [1943] AC 92 at 104.

> standard of care of the reasonable man involves in its application a subjective element. It is still left to the judge to decide what, in the circumstances of the particular case, the reasonable man would have had in contemplation, and what, accordingly, the party sought to be made liable ought to have foreseen. Here there is room for diversity of view, as, indeed, is well illustrated in the present case. What to one judge may seem far-fetched may seem to another both natural and probable.

This quotation encapsulates the search for objectivity, the desire to establish a single objective standard of conduct. There is, of course, a warning in the final three sentences, reinforcing the point made earlier that a judge must make inferences from the primary facts which may well reflect his personal view of what the reasonable person would have done or not done in the particular circumstances. The theory is that there is one single standard, but practice may suggest otherwise, as we shall see.

The standard in any particular field of activity may be affected by policy considerations; eg in road traffic cases there is a tendency for the courts to treat the slightest momentary lapse of attention by a driver as negligence. The reasons for this come out in the case extracted below, *Nettleship v Weston*.[4] In this case the Court of Appeal held that a learner driver owed the same duty as the competent and experienced driver. On the issue of varying standards, Megaw LJ stated:

> As I see it, if this doctrine of varying standards were to be accepted as a part of the law on these facts, it could not logically be confined to the duty of care owed by learner drivers. There is no reason in logic why it should not operate in a much wider sphere. The disadvantages of the resulting unpredictability, uncertainty and, indeed, impossibility of arriving at fair and consistent decisions outweigh the advantages. The certainty of a general standard is preferable to the vagaries of a fluctuating standard.
>
> As a first example of what is involved, consider the converse case: the standard of care (including skill) owed, not by the driver to the passenger, but by the passenger-instructor to the learner driver. Surely the same principle of varying standards, if it is a good principle, must also be available to the passenger, if he is sued by the driver for alleged breach of the duty of care in supervising the learner driver. On this doctrine, the standard of care, or skill, owed by the instructor, *vis-à-vis* the driver, may vary according to the knowledge which the learner driver had, at some moment time, as to the skill and experience of the particular instructor. Indeed, if logic is to prevail, it would not necessarily be the knowledge of the driver which would be the criterion. It would be the expectation which the driver reasonably entertained of the instructor's skill and experience, if that reasonable expectation were greater than the actuality.
>
> Thus, if the learner driver knew that the instructor had never tried his hand previously even at amateur instructing, or if, as may be the present case, the driver knew that the instructor's experience was confined to two cases of amateur instructing some years previously, there would, under this doctrine, surely be a lower standard than if the driver knew that the instructor was professional or that he had substantial experience in the recent past. But what the standard would be, and how it would or should be assessed, I know not. For one has cut oneself adrift from the standard of the competent and experienced

4 [1971] 3 All ER 581.

instructor which, up to now, the law has required without regard to the particular personal skill, experience, physical characteristics or temperament of the individual instructor, and without regard to a third party's knowledge or assessment of those qualities or characteristics.

Again, when one considers the requisite standard of care of the learner driver, if this doctrine were to apply, would not logic irresistibly demand that there should be something more than a mere, single, conventional standard, applicable to anyone who falls into the category of learner driver, ie of anyone who has not yet qualified for (or perhaps obtained) a full licence? That standard itself would necessarily vary over a wide range, not merely with the actual progress of the learner, but also with the passenger's knowledge of that progress; or, rather, if the passenger has in fact over-estimated the driver's progress, it would vary with the passenger's reasonable assessment of the progress at the relevant time. The relevant time would not necessarily be the moment of the accident.

Lord Denning observed in the same case:

Mrs Weston is clearly liable for the damage to the lamp post. In the civil law, if a driver goes off the road on to the pavement and injures a pedestrian, or damages property, he is *prima facie* liable. Likewise if he goes on to the wrong side of the road. It is no answer for him to say: 'I was a learner driver under instruction. I was doing my best and could not help it.' The civil law permits no such excuse. It requires of him the same standard as of any other driver. 'It eliminates the personal equation and is independent of the idiosyncrasies of the particular person whose conduct is in question': see *Glasgow Corpn v Muir*[5] *per* Lord Macmillan. The learner driver may be doing his best, but his incompetent best is not good enough. He must drive in as good a manner as a driver of skill, experience and care, who is sound in wind and limb, who makes no errors of judgment, has good eyesight and hearing, and is free from any infirmity: see *Richley v Faull*[6] and *Watson v Thomas S Whitney & Co Ltd*.[7]

The high standard thus imposed by the judges is, I believe, largely the result of the policy in the Road Traffic Acts. Parliament requires every driver to be insured against third-party risks, so that a person injured by a motor car should not be left to bear the loss on her own, but should be compensated out of the insurance fund. The fund is better able to bear it than she can. But the injured person is only able to recover if the driver is liable in law. So the judges see to it that she is liable, unless she can prove care and skill of a high standard: see *The Merchant Prince*[8] and *Henderson v Henry E Jenkins & Sons Ltd*.[9] Thus we are, in this branch of the law, moving away from the concept of 'no liability without fault'. We are beginning to apply the test 'on whom should the risk fall?' Morally the learner driver is not at fault; but legally she is liable to be because she is insured and the risk should fall on her.

Not all judges would express this point quite in the overt way that Lord Denning did above, but nonetheless it does seem to be the case that in relation to accidents involving vehicles on the public roads that the courts are more willing to attribute fault to the driver. Legal liability in many instances is being

5 [1943] 2 All ER 44 at 48, [1943] AC 448 at 457.

6 [1965] 3 All ER 109, [1965] 1 WLR 1454.

7 [1966] 1 All ER 122, [1966] 1 WLR 57.

8 [1892] P 179, [1891–94] All ER Rep 396.

9 [1969] 3 All ER 756, [1970] AC 282.

divorced from any moral responsibility, as Megaw LJ confirms later in his judgment in *Nettleship*:

> It is not a valid argument against such a principle that it attributes tortious liability to one who may not be morally blameworthy. For tortious liability has in many cases ceased to be based on moral blameworthiness.

We can see similar considerations being applied in *Roberts v Ramsbottom*,[10] where a driver had suffered a stroke shortly before going out in his car and this had impaired his ability to judge speed and distance. It was held that he was nonetheless liable. Towards the end of his judgment, Neill J commented:

> I therefore consider that the defendant is liable in law for his driving when he collided with the Triumph car in Bolton Road. I also consider that the plaintiffs would be entitled to succeed, if necessary, on the alternative ground put forward, ie that the defendant continued to drive when he was unfit to do so and when he should have been aware of his unfitness. He was aware that he had been feeling queer and had hit the van. Owing to his mental state he was unable to appreciate that he should have stopped. As I have said, and I repeat, the defendant was in no way morally to blame, but this is irrelevant to the question of legal liability in this case. An impairment of judgment does not provide a defence. I consider that the defendant was in law guilty of negligence in continuing to drive because he was aware of his disabling symptoms and of his first collision, even though he was not able to appreciate their proper significance.

At first instance, the judge in *Marshall v Osmond*[11] took the view that a policeman in hot pursuit of a criminal driving a vehicle did not owe the criminal the same duty of care which he would owe to a lawful and innocent user of the highway. In the Court of Appeal, Sir John Donaldson MR said:[12]

> I think that the duty owed by a police driver to the suspect is, as Mr Spokes on behalf of the plaintiff has contended, the same duty as that owed to anyone else, namely to exercise such care and skill as is reasonable in all the circumstances. The vital words in that proposition of law are 'in all the circumstances', and of course one of the circumstances was that the plaintiff bore all the appearance of having been somebody engaged in a criminal activity for which there was a power of arrest ... As I see it, what happened was that this police officer pursued a line in steering his car which would, in the ordinary course of events, have led to his ending up sufficiently far away from the Cortina to clear its open door. He was driving on a gravelly surface, at night, in what were no doubt stressful circumstances. There is no doubt that he made an error of judgment because, in the absence of an error of judgment, there would have been no contact between the cars. But I am far from satisfied on the evidence that the police officer was negligent ... It follows that I would dismiss this appeal.

The other two judges agreed with the Master of the Rolls. The road traffic cases are to be contrasted with the attitude of the courts towards finding professional persons liable for breach of duty, particularly, but not exclusively, the medical profession.

---

10 [1980] 1 All ER 7.

11 [1982] 3 WLR 120 at 124.

12 [1983] 3 WLR 13 at 15.

Factors taken into account

We shall now consider the factors that the courts have developed in trying to decide the issue as to whether the defendant has fallen below the requisite standard. The test is reasonable care in all the circumstances, as we have already seen. The factors set out below are to be considered as guidelines to enable the courts to decide the fault issue. The difficulty is to know what weight to give to any one factor in any given case, a delicate balancing to be achieved by the judge. In assessing whether the reasonable person would have done or omitted to do something to avoid foreseeable harm to the plaintiff, the courts consider the magnitude of the harm, the seriousness of the injury should the risk materialise, the cost and practicability of the precautions needed to eliminate the risk, and the social utility of the defendant's activity. These are considered below.

Magnitude of the risk

The harm suffered by the plaintiff must be foreseeable. If it is not the defendant is not liable. Nor is the defendant liable if the risk is foreseeable but the risk of damage is small. The more likely it is that a risk will materialise, the less the defendant is entitled to ignore the risk. It has to be borne in mind that nearly every activity involves an element of risk. The magnitude of the risk was discussed by the House of Lords in *Bolton v Stone*.[13] The plaintiff was struck by a cricket ball outside her home, the ball having been hit out of the cricket ground. The House decided against her. Lord Oaksey stated:

> My Lords, I have come to the conclusion in this difficult case that the decision of Oliver J ought to be restored. Cricket has been played for about 90 years on the ground in question and no ball has been proved to have struck anyone on the highways near the ground until the respondent was struck, nor has there been any complaint to the appellants. In such circumstances was it the duty of the appellants, who are the committee of the club, to take some special precautions other than those they did take to prevent such an accident as happened? The standard of care in the law of negligence is the standard of an ordinary careful man, but, in my opinion, an ordinarily careful man does not take precautions against every foreseeable risk. He can, of course, foresee the possibility of many risks, but life would be almost impossible if he were to attempt to take precautions against every risk which he can foresee. He takes precautions against risks which are reasonably likely to happen.
>
> Many foreseeable risks are extremely unlikely to happen and cannot be guarded against except by almost complete isolation. The ordinarily prudent owner of a dog does not keep his dog always on a lead on a country highway for fear it may cause injury to a passing motor cyclist, nor does the ordinarily prudent pedestrian avoid the use of the highway for fear of skidding motor cars. It may well be that, after this accident, the ordinarily prudent committee man of a similar cricket ground would take some further precaution, but that is not to say that he would have taken a similar precaution before the accident.

Lord Reid's judgment contains a fuller discussion and a large extract is set out below:

13 [1951] 1 All ER 1078.

My Lords, it was readily foreseeable that an accident such as befell the respondent might possibly occur during one of the appellants' cricket matches. Balls had been driven into the public road from time to time, and it was obvious that if a person happened to be where a ball fell that a person would receive injuries which might or might not be serious. On the other hand, it was plain that the chance of that happening was small. The exact number of times a ball has been driven into the road is not known, but it is not proved that this has happened more than about six times in 30 years. If I assume that it has happened on average once in three seasons I shall be doing no injustice to the respondent's case. Then there has to be considered the chance of a person being hit by a ball falling in the road. The road appears to be an ordinary side road giving access to a number of private houses, and there is no evidence to suggest that the traffic on this road is other than one might expect on such a road. On the whole of that part of the road where a ball could fall, there would often be nobody and seldom any great number of people. It follows that the chance of a person ever being struck even in a long period of years was very small.

This case, therefore, raises sharply the question – what is the nature and extent of the duty of a person who promotes on his land operations which may cause damage to persons on an adjoining highway? Is it that he must not carry out or permit an operation which he knows or ought to know clearly can cause such damage, however improbable that result may be, or is it that he is only bound to take into account the possibility of such damage if such damage is a likely or probable consequence of what he does or permits, or if the risk of damage is such that a reasonable man, careful of the safety of his neighbour, would regard the risk as material?

I do not know of any case where this question has had to be decided or even where it has been fully discussed. Of course there are many cases in which somewhat similar questions have arisen, but, generally speaking, if injury to another person from the defendants' acts is reasonably foreseeable the chance that the injury will result is substantial, and it does not matter in which way the duty is stated.

In such cases I do not think that much assistance is to be got from analysing the language which a judge has used. More assistance is to be got from cases where judges have clearly chosen their language with care in setting out a principle, but even so, statements of the law must be read in the light of the facts of the particular case. Nevertheless, making all allowances for this, I do find at least a tendency to base duty rather on the likelihood of damage to others than on its foreseeability alone.

... I think that reasonable men do, in fact, take into account the degree of risk and do not act on a bare possibility as they would if the risk were more substantial. ...

Counsel for the respondent in the present case had to put his case so high as to say that, at least as soon as one ball had been driven into the road in the ordinary course of a match, the appellants could and should have realised that that might happen again, and that, if it did, someone might be injured, and that that was enough to put on the appellants a duty to take steps to prevent such an occurrence. If the true test is foreseeability alone I think that must be so. Once a ball has been driven on to a road without there being anything extraordinary to account for the fact, there is clearly a risk that another will follow, and if it does there is clearly a chance, small though it may be, that somebody may be injured.

On the theory that it is foreseeability alone that matters it would be irrelevant to consider how often a ball might be expected to land in the road and it would not matter whether the road was the busiest street or the quietest country lane. The

> only difference between these cases is the degree of risk. It would take a great deal to make me believe that the law has departed so far from the standards which guide ordinary careful people in ordinary life. In the crowded conditions of modern life even the most careful person cannot avoid creating some risks and accepting others. What a man must not do, and what a careful man tries not to do, is to create a risk which is substantial. Of course, there are numerous cases where special circumstances require that a higher standard shall be observed and where that is recognised by the law, but I do not think that this case comes within any such special category. ... In my judgment, the test to be applied here is whether the risk of damage to a person on the road was so small that a reasonable man in the position of the appellants, considering the matter from the point of view of safety, would have thought it right to refrain from taking steps to prevent the danger. In considering that matter I think that it would be right to take into account, not only how remote is the chance that person might be struck, but also how serious the consequences are likely to be if a person is struck, but I do not think it would be right to take into account the difficulty of remedial measures.
>
> If cricket cannot be played on a ground without creating a substantial risk, then it should not be played there at all. I think that this is in substance the test which Oliver J applied in this case. He considered whether the appellants' ground was large enough to be safe for all practical purposes and held that it was. This is a question, not of law, but of fact and degree. It is not an easy question, and it is one on which opinions may differ. I can only say that, having given the whole matter repeated and anxious consideration, I find myself unable to decide this question in favour of the respondent. I think, however, that this case is not far from the borderline. If this appeal is allowed, that does not, in my judgment, mean that, in every case where cricket has been played on a ground for a number of years without accident or complaint, those who organise matches there are safe to go on in reliance on past immunity. I would have reached a different conclusion if I had thought that the risk here had been other than extremely small because I do not think that a reasonable man, considering the matter from the point of view of safety, would or should disregard any risk unless it is extremely small.

The case was considered by the Privy Council in *Wagon Mound (No 2)*[14] by Lord Reid once again. After stating the principle applied in *Bolton v Stone* he continued:

> It does not follow that, no matter what the circumstances may be, it is justifiable to neglect a risk of such a small magnitude. A reasonable man would only neglect such a risk if he had some valid reason for doing so: eg that it would involve considerable expense to eliminate the risk. He would weigh the risk against the difficulty of eliminating it. If the activity which caused the injury to Miss Stone had been an unlawful activity there can be little doubt but that *Bolton v Stone* ... would have been decided differently. In their Lordships' judgment *Bolton v Stone* did not alter the general principle that a person must be regarded as negligent if he does not take steps to eliminate a risk which he knows or ought to know is a real risk and not a mere possibility which would never influence the mind of the reasonable man. What that decision did was to recognise and give effect to the qualification that it is justifiable not to take steps to eliminate a real risk if it is small and if the circumstances are such that a reasonable man, careful of the safety of his neighbour, would think it right to neglect it.

14 [1966] 2 All ER 709 at 717.

In the present case there was no justification whatever for discharging the oil into Sydney harbour. Not only was it an offence to do so, but it also involved considerable loss financially. If the ship's engineer had thought about the matter, there could have been no question of balancing the advantages and disadvantages. From every point of view it was both his duty and his interest to stop the discharge immediately.

It follows that in their Lordships' view the only question is whether a reasonable man, having the knowledge and experience to be expected of the chief engineer of the *Wagon Mound*, would have known that there was real risk of the oil on the water catching fire in some way. If it did, serious damage to ships or other property was not only foreseeable but very likely. Their Lordships do not dissent from the view of the trial judge that the possibilities of damage[15] 'must be significant enough in a practical sense to require a reasonable man to guard against them', but they think he may have misdirected himself in saying:[16] 'there does seem to be a real practical difficulty, assuming that some risk of fire damage was foreseeable, but not a high one, in making a factual judgment as to whether this risk was sufficient to attract liability if damage should occur'.

In this difficult chapter of the law decisions are not infrequently taken to apply to circumstances far removed from the facts which give rise to them, and it would seem that here too much reliance has been placed on some observations in *Bolton v Stone* and similar observations in other cases.

In their Lordships' view a properly qualified and alert engineer would have realised there was real risk here, and they do not understand Walsh J to deny that, if a real risk can properly be described as remote, it must then be held to be not reasonably foreseeable. That is a possible interpretation of some of the authorities; but this is still an open question and on principle their Lordships cannot accept this view. If a risk is one which would occur to the mind of a reasonable man in the position of the defendant's servant and which he would not brush aside as far-fetched, and if the criterion is to be what that reasonable man would have done in the circumstances, then surely he would not neglect such a risk if action to eliminate it presented no difficulty, involved no disadvantage and required no expense.

In the present case the evidence shows that the discharge of so much oil on to the water must have taken a considerable time, and a vigilant ship's engineer would have noticed the discharge at an early stage. The findings show that he ought to have known that it is possible to ignite this kind of oil on water, and that the ship's engineer ought to have known that this had in fact happened before. The most that can be said to justify inaction is that he would have known that this could only happen in very exceptional circumstances; but this does not mean that a reasonable man would dismiss such risk from his mind and do nothing when it was so easy to prevent it. If it is clear that the reasonable man would have realised or foreseen and prevented the risk, then it must follow that the appellants are liable in damages. The learned judge found this a difficult case. He said that this matter is[17] 'one on which different minds would come to different conclusions'. Taking a rather different view of the law from that of the learned judge, their Lordships must hold that the respondents are entitled to succeed on this issue.

15 [1963] 1 Lloyd's Rep at 411.

16 At 413.

17 At 424.

Other cases to be contrasted with *Bolton v Stone* are *Miller v Jackson*[18] and *Hilder v Associated Portland Cement Manufacturers Ltd.*[19] In the former, case brought in nuisance as well as negligence, the majority of the Court of Appeal held that the cricket club was negligent because that case:

> ... so far from being one incident of an unprecedented nature about which complaint is being made, this is a series of incidents, or perhaps a continuing failure to prevent incidents from happening, coupled with the certainty that they are going to happen again. The risk of injury to persons and property is so great that on each occasion when a ball comes over the fence and causes injury to the plaintiffs, the defendants are guilty of negligence.[20]

In the latter case, children were allowed to play football on a patch of ground adjoining a busy highway. On one occasion the ball went into the roadway causing a motor cyclist to fall from his bike, fracturing his skull. Ashworth J took the view that:

> In the present case, the relevant circumstances include the situation of The Green and, in particular, the existence of King Edward Road along one side, the amount of traffic using the road, the ages of the children using The Green, the nature of their amusements and the frequency with which The Green is used. A reasonable man in the position of the defendants would, in my view, consider all these circumstances and, in addition, would consider first whether there was any risk of damage to persons using the road as a result of the children's activities; and second whether that risk (if any) was so small that he could rightly refrain from taking steps to prevent the danger. If he considered the matter in this way, he would be acting in accordance with the test laid down by Lord Reid in *Bolton v Stone*. In my judgment, a reasonable man would come to the conclusion that there was a risk of damage to persons using the road and that risk was not so small that he could safely disregard it. While it is true that a football itself is unlikely to damage a person or vehicle on the road in the way that might occur with a cricket ball or a golf ball, I think that the sudden appearance of a football in front of a cyclist or motor cyclist is quite likely to cause him to fall or to swerve into the path of another vehicle, and in either event sustain serious injury.

The courts rarely use any kind of statistical material in their attempt to decide what is a real risk, or what is likely or what is probable. However, in *Haley v London Electricity Board*, a case where a blind man using a white stick fell over an obstacle near the end of a trench made by the defendant's workmen, Lord Reid commented:[21]

> In deciding what is reasonably foreseeable one must have regard to common knowledge. We are all accustomed to meeting blind people walking alone with their white sticks on city pavements. No doubt there are many places open to the public where, for one reason or another, one would be surprised to see blind persons walking alone, but a city pavement is not one of them; and a residential street cannot be different from any other. The blind people whom we meet must live somewhere, and most of them probably left their homes unaccompanied. It may seem surprising that blind people can avoid ordinary obstacles so well as

18 [1977] 3 All ER 338.

19 [1961] 3 All ER 709.

20 At 348 *per* Geoffrey Lane LJ.

21 [1964] 3 All ER 185 at 188.

they do, but we must take account of the facts. There is evidence in this case about the number of blind people in London and it appears from government publications that the proportion in the whole country is near 1 in 500. By no means all are sufficiently skilled or confident to venture out alone, but the number who habitually do so must be very large. I find it quite impossible to say that it is not reasonably foreseeable that a blind person may pass along a particular pavement on a particular day.

No question can arise in this case of any great difficulty in affording adequate protection for the blind. In considering what is adequate protection again one must have regard to common knowledge. One is entitled to expect of a blind person a high degree of skill and care, because none but the most foolhardy would venture to go out alone without having that skill and exercising that care. We know that in fact blind people do safely avoid all ordinary obstacles on pavements; there can be no question of padding lamp posts as was suggested in one case.[22] A moment's reflection, however, shows that a low obstacle in an unusual place is a grave danger. On the other hand, it is clear from the evidence in this case and also I think from common knowledge that quite a light fence some two feet high is an adequate warning. There would have been no difficulty in providing such a fence here. The evidence is that the Post Office always provides one, and that the respondents have similar fences which are often used. Indeed the evidence suggests that, the only reason why there was no fence here was that the accident occurred before the necessary fences had arrived. So, if the respondents are to succeed, it can only be on the ground that there was no duty to do more than safeguard ordinary able-bodied people.

I can see no justification for laying down any hard and fast rule limiting the classes of persons for whom those interfering with a pavement must make provision. It is said that it is impossible to tell what precautions will be adequate to protect all kinds of infirm pedestrians or that taking such precautions would be unreasonably difficult or expensive. I think that such fears are exaggerated, and it is worth recollecting that, when courts sought to lay down specific rules as to the duties of occupiers, the law became so unsatisfactory that Parliament had to step in and pass the Occupiers' Liability Act 1957. It appears to me that the ordinary principles of the common law must apply in the streets as well as elsewhere, and that fundamentally they depend on what a reasonable man, careful of his neighbour's safety, would do having the knowledge which a reasonable man, in the position of the defendant, must be deemed to have.

The other Lords of Appeal agreed with Lord Reid and the blind plaintiff's appeal was allowed.

Seriousness of the harm

The judge in the extract from his judgment in *Hilder* above, referred to the fact that a cricket or golf ball by its nature may cause serious injury if it strikes a person, unlike the football in that case. However, the judge commented about the potential danger of a ball being kicked into the road causing cyclists to swerve to avoid it. In his view the seriousness of the harm which may occur if the risk, however small, materialises, is something to be put in the balance against the magnitude of the risk. This is best exemplified by the case of *Paris v Stepney Borough Council*,[23] where a one-eyed man was employed as a fitter at the

22 See *M Kibbin v City of Glasgow Corpn* (1920) SC 590 at 598.

23 [1951] 1 All ER 42.

garage of the council. When he was working on a vehicle a chip of metal flew off a bolt he was hammering and went in his good eye with the result that he lost sight in that eye as well. By a majority the House of Lords decided in favour of the plaintiff, although all five judges were agreed on the question as to whether the seriousness of the harm is a factor. Lord Oaksey expressed the point as follows:

> The duty of an employer towards his servant is to take reasonable care for the servant's safety in all the circumstances of the case. The fact that the servant has only one eye, if that fact is known to the employer, and that, if he loses it he will be blind, is one of the circumstances which must be considered by the employer in determining what precautions, if any, shall be taken for the servant's safety. The standard of care which the law demands is the care which the ordinarily prudent employer would take in all the circumstances. As the circumstances may vary infinitely it is often impossible to adduce evidence of what care an ordinarily prudent employer would take. In some cases, of course, it is possible to prove that it is ordinary practice for employers to take or not take a certain precaution, but in such a case as the present where a one-eyed man has been injured, it is unlikely that such evidence can be adduced. The court has, therefore, to form its own opinion of what precautions the notional ordinarily prudent employer would take.
>
> In the present case the question is whether an ordinarily prudent employer would supply goggles to a one-eyed workman whose job it was to knock bolts out of a chassis with a steel hammer while the chassis was elevated on a ramp so that the workman's eye was close to and under the bolt. In my opinion, Lynskey J was entitled to hold that an ordinary prudent employer would take that precaution. The question was not whether the precaution ought to have been taken with ordinary two-eyed workmen, and it was not necessary, in my opinion, that Lynskey J should decide that question – nor did he purport to decide it, although it is true that he stated the question in one sentence too broadly. The risk of splinters of steel breaking off a bolt and injuring a workman's eye or eyes may be, and I think is, slight, and it is true that the damage to a two-eyed workman if struck by a splinter in the eye or eyes may be serious, but it is for the judge at trial to weigh up the risk of injury and the extent of the damage and to decide whether, in all the circumstances including the fact that the workman was known to be one-eyed and might become a blind man if his eye was struck, an ordinarily prudent employer would supply such a workman with goggles. It is a simple and inexpensive precaution to take to supply goggles and a one-eyed man would not be likely, as a two-eyed man might be, to refuse to wear the goggles.

Lord Simonds stated:

> I see no valid reason for excluding as irrelevant the gravity of the damage which the employee will suffer if an accident occurs, and with great respect to the judgments of the Court of Appeal I cannot accept the view, neatly summarised by Asquith LJ ([1949] 2 All ER 843), that the greater the risk of injury is, but the risk of greater injury is not, a relevant circumstance. I find no authority for such a proposition nor does it appear to me to be founded on any logical principle.

Lord Morton's view was:

> I think that the more serious the damage which will happen if an accident occurs, the more thorough are the precautions which an employer must take. If I am right as to this general principle, I think it follows logically that if A and B, who are engaged on the same work, run precisely the same risk of an accident

happening, but if the results of an accident will be more serious to A than to B, precautions which are adequate in the case of B may not be adequate in the case of A, and it is the duty of the employer to take such additional precautions for the safety of A as may be reasonable. The duty to take reasonable precautions is one which is owed by the employer to every individual workman.

Cost and practicality of precautions

This factor has already been well ventilated in the cases discussed above. The duty is to take reasonable care and it is not an absolute standard. Many accidents could be prevented but at what cost? A defendant is not expected to go beyond reasonable precautions and the court has to make an assessment of just how easy or difficult it would have been to act differently and what the impact might be on others if the defendant had taken alternative action. In *Paris* the issue was clear cut – the supply of one pair of goggles was not going to break the bank and it would only delay the workman momentarily whilst he put the goggles on. The goggles would be hardly likely to impede his progress with his work. An economist might argue that once the overall cost of the precautions, including the impact on others if the precaution were to be taken, exceed the cost of the accident, then the defendant is excused from taking those precautions.

Presumably, this thought was in the minds of the House of Lords in *Latimer v AEC Ltd*.[24] The plaintiff slipped on the oily surface in part of the factory where he was employed. The factory had been badly flooded and, when the water dispersed, it left an oily film which was only partially covered by sawdust. The House of Lords decided against the workman on the basis that the employer was not at fault in the circumstances. Lord Tucker stated:

> In the present case, the respondents were faced with an unprecedented situation following a phenomenal rainstorm. They set 40 men to work on cleaning up the factory when the flood subsided and used all the available supply of sawdust, which was approximately 3 tons. The judge has found that they took every step which could reasonably have been taken to deal with the conditions which prevailed before the night shift came on duty, and he has negatived every specific allegation of negligence pleaded, but he has held the respondents liable because they did not close the factory down, or the part of the factory where the accident occurred, before the commencement of the night shift.
>
> I do not question that such a drastic step may be required on the part of a reasonably prudent employer if the peril to his employees is sufficiently grave, and to this extent it must always be a question of degree. But, in my view, there was no evidence in the present case which could justify a finding of negligence on the part of the respondents to take this step. The question was never canvassed in evidence, nor was sufficient evidence given as to the condition of the factory as a whole to enable a satisfactory conclusion to be reached. The learned judge seems to have accepted the reasoning of counsel for the appellant to the effect that the floor was slippery; that slipperiness is a potential danger; that the respondents must be taken to have been aware of this; that, in the circumstances, nothing could have been done to remedy the slipperiness; that the respondents allowed the work to proceed; that an accident due to slipperiness occurred; and that the respondents are, therefore liable.

24 [1953] 2 All ER 449.

> This is not the correct approach. The problem is perfectly simple. The only question was: has it been proved that the floor was so slippery that, remedial steps not being possible, a reasonably prudent employer would have closed down the factory rather than allow his employees to run the risks involved in continuing work? The learned judge does not seem to me to have posed the question to himself, nor was there sufficient evidence before him to have justified an affirmative answer. The absence of any evidence that anyone in the factory during the afternoon or night shift, other that the appellant, slipped or experienced any difficulty, or that any complaint was made by or on behalf of the workers, all points to the conclusion that the danger was, in fact, not such as to impose on a reasonable employer the obligation placed on the respondents by the trial judge. I agree that the appeal be dismissed.

Closing the factory would have meant loss of production for the employer and lost wages for the appellant's fellow employees, and such a drastic step was not justified in the circumstances according to the House of Lords.

Social utility of the defendant's activity

A risk may be one which the reasonable man might run if the social utility of his activity is such that it is given more weight over other factors. In *Watt v Hertfordshire County Council*[25] the plaintiff, a fireman, was injured by a lifting jack which was not properly secured on the vehicle on which he was travelling. It was believed that the jack was needed in an emergency and consequently it was decided not to wait for the proper engine to carry it. It was held that the defendant council was not liable. Denning LJ in a brief judgment said:

> It was well settled that, in measuring due care, you must balance the risk against the measures necessary to eliminate the risk. To that proposition there ought to be added this: you must balance the risk against the end to be achieved. If this accident had occurred in a commercial enterprise without any emergency there could be no doubt that the servant would succeed. But the commercial end to make profit is very different from the human end to save life or limb. The saving of life or limb justifies taking considerable risk, and I am glad to say that there have never been wanting in this country men of courage ready to take those risks, notably in the fire service.
>
> In this case the risk involved in sending out the lorry was not so great as to prohibit the attempt to save life. I quite agree that fire engines, ambulances and doctors' cars should not shoot past the traffic lights when they show a red light. That is because the risk is too great to warrant the incurring of the danger. It is always a question of balancing the risk against the end. I agree that this appeal should be dismissed.

In *Daborn v Bath Tramways Motor Co*[26] Asquith LJ commented:

> In determining whether a party is negligent, the standard of care is that which is reasonably to be demanded in the circumstances. A relevant circumstance to take into account may be the importance of the end to be served by behaving in this way or in that. As has often been pointed out, if all trains in this country were restricted to a speed of 5mph, there would be fewer accidents, but our national

25 [1954] 1 WLR 835.

26 [1946] 2 All ER 333.

> life would be intolerably slowed down. The purpose to be served, if sufficiently important, justifies the assumption of abnormal risk.
>
> The relevance of this applied to the present case is this: during the war which was, at the material time, in progress, it was necessary for many highly important operations to be carried out by means of motor vehicles with left-hand drives, no others being available. So far as this was the case, it was impossible for the drivers of such cars to give the warning signals which could otherwise be properly demanded of them. Meanwhile, it was essential that the ambulance service should be maintained. It seems to me, in those circumstances, it would be demanding too high and an unreasonable standard of care from the drivers of such cars to say to them: 'Either you must give signals which the structure of your vehicle renders impossible or you must not drive at all.'
>
> It was urged by counsel for the defendants that these alternatives were not exhaustive, since the driver of such a car should, before executing a turn, stop his car, move to the right-hand seat and look backwards to see if another car was attempting to overtake him and then start up again. Counsel for the plaintiff has satisfied me that such a procedure, besides involving possible delay, might be wholly ineffective. I think that the plaintiff did all that in the circumstances she could reasonably be required to do if you include in those circumstances, as I think you should:
>
> (1) the necessity in time of national emergency of employing all transport resources which were available; and
>
> (2) the inherent limitations and incapacity of this particular form of transport.
>
> In considering whether reasonable care has been observed, one must balance the risk against the consequences of not assuming that risk, and in this instance this calculation seems to me to work out in favour of the plaintiff.

A collision had occurred between the left hand ambulance driven by the plaintiff. It was held that the defendant was negligent in attempting to overtake the ambulance, but the contentious issue was whether the plaintiff was negligent. The other two members of the Court of Appeal agreed with view of Asquith LJ above.

Special standards

So far we have been considering the standard of care in a general sense. We now need to consider the situations in which the standard may vary dependent on the especial skill of the defendant or his lack of experience, eg a child. The discussion will then focus on the standard of care demanded in sporting competition.

Professional persons

Where the defendant is alleged to have some special expertise and the harm to the plaintiff comes about whilst the defendant is exercising his calling, the standard of care is clearly not that of the reasonable person in the street. The test for the professional person was spelt out in the case of *Bolam v Friern Hospital Management Committee*[27] by McNair J:

27 [1957] 2 All ER 118.

In the ordinary case which does not involve any special skill, negligence in law means this: some failure to do some act which a reasonable man in the circumstances would do, or doing some act which a reasonable man in the circumstances would not do; and if that failure or doing of that act results in injury, then there is a cause of action.

How do you test whether this act or failure is negligent? In an ordinary case it is generally said that you judge that by the action of the man in the street – he is the ordinary man. In one case it has been said that you judge it by the conduct of the man on the top of a Clapham omnibus – he is the ordinary man. But where you get a situation which involves the use of some special skill or competence, then the test whether there has been negligence or not is not the test of the man on the top of a Clapham omnibus, because he has not got this special skill. The test is the standard of the ordinary skilled man exercising and professing to have that special skill. A man need not possess the highest expert skill at the risk of being found negligent. It is well established law that it is sufficient if he exercises the ordinary skill of an ordinary competent man exercising that particular art.

This test is commonly referred to as the *Bolam* test and, as we shall see shortly, it is thought to be of general application, although the case itself was concerned with alleged medical negligence. It has been approved at the highest level on more than one occasion, eg in *Whitehouse v Jordan*[28] and *Maynard v West Midlands Regional Health Authority*.[29] The test was also applied by the majority of the Court of Appeal in the case of *Wilsher v Essex Area Health Authority*.[30] In this case, it was argued by the health authority that the standard of care expected of eg a newly qualified doctor, was that of the competent doctor possessing the same formal qualifications and experience as the newly qualified doctor. One of the judges in the majority on this particular point dealt with this argument as follows:

The second proposition (advanced on behalf of the defendants) directs attention to the personal position of the individual member of the staff about whom the complaint is made. What is expected of him is as much as, but no more than, can reasonably be required of a person having his formal qualifications and practical experience. If correct, this proposition entails that the standard of care which a patient is entitled to demand will vary according to the chance of recruitment and rostering. The patient's right to complain of faulty treatment will be more limited if he has been entrusted to the care of a doctor who is a complete novice in the particular field (unless perhaps he can point to some fault of supervision further up the hierarchy) than if he has been in the hands of a doctor who has already spent months on the same ward, and his prospects of holding the health authority vicariously liable for the consequences of any mistreatment will be correspondingly reduced.

To my mind, this notion of a duty tailored to the actor, rather that to the act which he elects to perform, has no place in the law of tort. Indeed, the defendants did not contend that it could be justified by any reported authority on the general law of tort. Instead, it was suggested that the medical profession is a special case. Public hospital medicine has always been organised so that young doctors and nurses learn on the job. If the hospitals abstained from using inexperienced

28 [1981] 1 All ER 267.

29 [1985] 1 All ER 635.

30 [1986] 3 All ER 801.

> people, they could not staff their wards and theatres, and the junior staff could never learn. The longer term interests of patients as a whole are best served by maintaining the present system, even if this may diminish the legal rights of the individual patients; for, after all, medicine is about curing, not litigation.
>
> I acknowledge the appeal of this argument, and recognise that a young hospital doctor who must get onto the wards in order to qualify without necessarily being able to decide what kind of patient he is going to meet is not in the same position as another professional man who has a real choice whether or not to practice in a particular field. Nevertheless, I cannot accept that there should be a special rule for doctors in public hospitals; I emphasise public, since presumably those employed in private hospitals would be in a different category. Doctors are not the only people who gain their experience, not only from lectures or from watching others perform, but from tackling live clients or customers, and no case was cited to us which suggested that any such variable duty of care was imposed on others in a similar position. To my mind, it would be a false step to subordinate the legitimate expectation of the patient that he will receive, from each person concerned with his care, a degree of skill appropriate to the task which he undertakes to an understandable wish to minimise the psychological and financial pressures on hard-pressed young doctors.
>
> For my part, I prefer the third of the propositions which have been canvassed. This relates the duty of care, not to the individual, but to the post which he occupies. I would differentiate 'post' from 'rank' or 'status'. In a case such as the present, the standard is not just that of the averagely competent and well-informed houseman (or whatever the position of the doctor), but of such a person who fills a post in a unit offering a highly specialised service. But, even so, it must be recognised that different posts make different demands. If it is borne in mind that the structure of hospital medicine envisages that the lower ranks will be occupied by those of whom it would be wrong to expect too much, the risk of abuse by litigious patients can be mitigated, if not entirely eliminated.

Glidewell LJ, agreeing with Mustill LJ after stating that the Bolam test was the appropriate one to apply, commented:

> If I understand him correctly, Sir Nicholas Browne-Wilkinson VC would apply a less stringent test to a newly qualified practitioner who has accepted an appointment in order to gain experience. The suggested test would only hold such a doctor liable 'for acts or omissions which a careful doctor with his qualifications and experience would not have done or omitted'. With great respect, I do not believe this is the correct test. In my view, the law requires the trainee or learner to be judged by the same standard as his more experienced colleagues. If it did not, inexperience would frequently be urged as a defence to an action for professional negligence.
>
> If this test appears unduly harsh in relation to the inexperienced, I should add that, in my view, the inexperienced doctor called on to exercise a specialist skill will, as part of that skill, seek the advice and help of his superiors when he does or may need it. If he does seek such help, he will often have satisfied the test, even though he may himself have made a mistake. It is for this reason that I agree that Dr Wiles was not negligent. He made a mistake in inserting the catheter into a vein, and a second mistake in not recognising the signs that he had done so on the X-ray. But, having done what he thought right, he asked Dr Kawa, the senior registrar, to check what he had done, and Dr Kawa did so. Dr Kawa failed to recognise the indication on the X-ray that the catheter was in the vein, and some hours later himself inserted a replacement catheter, again in the

> vein, and again failed to recognise that it was in the vein. Whichever of the suggested tests of negligence should be applied to Dr Wiles, we are all agree that Dr Kawa was negligent, and that the defendants must therefore be liable for any damage to the plaintiff proved to have been caused by that negligence.

As was suggested by Glidewell LJ in the above extract, Sir Nicholas Browne-Wilkinson took a more lenient view of the standard expected of an inexperienced junior doctor. However, there are no other reported cases where such an argument has succeeded and, moreover, this point was not argued on appeal,[31] so it is reasonable to assume that the majority view in *Wilsher* on this issue represents the current state of the law.

This accords with the view expressed by Megaw LJ in *Nettleship v Weston* extracted earlier in this chapter as to the practical impossibility of the application of fluctuating standards to driving. There, however, the similarity ends. We saw earlier that the slightest inattention by a driver is likely to be branded as fault. The same is hardly true when we are considering cases of alleged medical negligence. The courts are reluctant to impose liability on the medical profession except, so it appears, in the most glaring illustrations of faulty conduct. This will be clear from the discussion below on common practice where we meet the second so-called *Bolam* test.

However, before going on to that, we shall look at the case of *Whitehouse v Jordan* as a prime example of the reluctance of the judiciary to label mistakes by doctors as being fault. Briefly, a senior registrar used the 'trial by forceps' method of delivery of a baby where the mother had been in labour for a long time. It was alleged that the registrar spent too much time on this method before proceeding to delivery by Caesarean section. The baby sustained severe brain damage. The trial judge held that this was negligent on the part of the doctor but the House of Lords confirmed the decision of the Court of Appeal overturning the trial judge's decision. The case is significant for the fact that the House, as did the Court of Appeal, interfered with matters normally solely within the province of the trial judge, namely the decision as to the primary facts. They skirted round this problem by suggesting that the issue in question was an inference from the primary facts and therefore susceptible to challenge in the appeal courts. There seems little doubt, however, that this was blatant and unwarranted interference by the higher courts to extend immunity to the medical profession, to some extent based on the notion of defensive medicine.

In the context of the immunity of the police in carrying out their investigations into crime, we saw the argument concerning defensive policing, that the imposition of liability has adverse effects on the behaviour of the police. This is a similar argument as applied to medicine, entailing doctors engaging in expensive and time wasting investigations when all that the patient has is a headache, for example. This, like the floodgates argument, is much exaggerated in this country but it does have a hold on the minds of some of the judiciary, it would seem. Lord Fraser in *Whitehouse* commented:

> Referring to medical men, Lord Denning MR said ([1980] 1 All ER 650 at 658): 'If they are to be found liable [sc for negligence] whenever they do not effect a cure,

31 [1988] 1 All ER 871, where the plaintiff's case failed on causation.

> or whenever any thing untoward happens, it would do a great disservice to the profession itself.' That is undoubtedly correct, but he went on to say this: 'We must say, and say firmly, that in a professional man an error of judgment is not negligent.' Having regard to the context, I think that Lord Denning MR must have meant to say that an error of judgment 'is not *necessarily* negligent'. But in my respectful opinion, the statement as it stands is not an accurate statement of the law. Merely to describe something as an error of judgment tells us nothing about whether it is negligent or not. The true position is that an error of judgment may, or may not, be negligent; it depends on the nature of the error. If it is one that would have not been made by a reasonably competent professional man professing to have the standard and type of skill that the defendant held himself out as having, and acting with ordinary care, then it is negligent. If on the other hand, it is an error that a man, acting with ordinary care, might have made, then it is not negligence.

Despite the rap over the knuckles for Lord Denning MR, the House nonetheless agreed that this was not an error of judgment in the legal fault sense.

It was indicated above that it was thought that the *Bolam* test applied to other professions. It has been applied to a firm of auctioneers and valuers in *Luxmoore May v Messenger May Baverstock*,[32] where Slade LJ stated:

> The defendants are a firm of provincial auctioneers and valuers who deal with many kinds of chattels. Mr Royle, an expert witness called by the plaintiffs, fairly described them as 'general practitioners'. In the court below, as in this court, the defendants, relying on an analogy with medical practitioners, cited most authoritatively the decision of the House of Lords in *Maynard v West Midlands Regional Health Authority* [1985] 1 All ER 635, [1984] 1 WLR 634. There Lord Scarman endorsed the following passage from the judgment of the Lord President (Clyde) in *Hunter v Hanley* 1955 SC 200 at 204–05: 'In the realm and diagnosis of treatment there is ample scope for genuine difference of opinion and one man is not negligent merely because his conclusion differs from that of other professional men. ... The true test for establishing negligence in diagnosis or treatment on the part of a doctor is whether he has been proved to be guilty of such failure as no doctor of ordinary skill would be guilty if acting with ordinary care. ...
>
> The defendants submitted to Simon Brown J that they were to be regarded as akin to general practitioners and that:
>
> (1) the required standard of skill and care allows for differing views, and even a wrong view, without the practitioner holding that view (necessarily) being held in breach of duty;
>
> (2) the standard is to be judged by reference only to what may be expected of the general practitioner, not the specialist, here provincial auctioneers, rather than one of the leading auction houses; and
>
> (3) compliance with the required standard is to be judged by reference to the actual circumstances confronting the practitioners at the material time, rather than with the benefit of hindsight.
>
> The judge 'unhesitatingly' accepted these propositions, and so would I. In my judgment, those propositions, read together with the passage from the judgment of the Lord President (Clyde), set out more or less all that needs to be said as to the nature of the legal duty falling on the defendants in the present case. I would

32 [1990] 1 All ER 1067.

> merely add one important rider. The valuation of pictures of which the artist is unknown, pre-eminently involves an exercise of opinion and judgment, most particularly in deciding whether an attribution to any particular artist should be made. Since it is not an exact science, the judgment in the very nature things may be fallible, and may turn out to be wrong. Accordingly, provided that the valuer has done his job honestly and with due diligence, I think that the court should be cautious before convicting him of professional negligence merely because he failed to spot a 'sleeper' [an antique of unrecognised worth] or the potentiality of a 'sleeper'.

The same point was not made in the case of *Philips v Whiteley*,[33] where the issue was the standard of care to be expected of a jeweller carrying out ear piercing. Goddard J took the following line:

> In this case, the first thing that I have to consider is the standard of care demanded from Mr Couzens – or, I should say, from Whiteleys, because Whiteleys were the people who undertook to do this piercing. It is not easy in any case to lay down a particular canon or standard by which the care can be judged, but, while it is admitted here, and admitted on all hands, that Mr Couzens did not use the same precautions of procuring an aseptic condition of his instruments as a doctor or surgeon would use, I do not think that he could be called upon to use that degree of care. Whiteleys have to see that whoever they employ for the operation uses the standard of care and skill that may be expected from a jeweller, and, of course, if the operation is negligently performed – if, for instance, a wholly unsuitable instrument were used, so that the ear was badly torn, or something of that sort happened – undoubtedly they would be liable. So, too, if they did not take that degree of care to see that the instruments were clean which one would expect a person of the training and standing of a jeweller to use.
>
> To say, however, that jeweller warrants or undertakes that he will use instruments which have the degree of surgical cleanliness that a surgeon brings about when he is going to perform a serious operation, or indeed any operation, is, I think, putting the matter too high. The doctors all seem to agree in this case that, if a lady went to a surgeon for the piercing of her ears, he would render his instruments sterile. After all, however, aseptic surgery is a thing of very modern growth. As anybody who has read the life of Lord Lister or the history of medicine in the last 50 or 60 years knows, it is not so many years ago that the best surgeon in the land knew nothing about even antiseptic surgery. Then antiseptic surgery was introduced, and that was followed by aseptic surgery. I do not think that a jeweller holds himself out as a surgeon or professes that he is going to conduct the operation of piercing a lady's ears by means of aseptic surgery, about which it is not to be supposed that he knows anything.
>
> If a person wants to ensure that the operation of piercing her ears is going to be carried out with the proportion of skill and so forth that a Fellow of the Royal College of Surgeons would use, she must go to a surgeon. If she goes to a jeweller, she must expect that he will carry it out in the way that one would expect a jeweller to carry it out. One would expect that he would wash his instruments. One would expect that he would take some means of disinfecting his instrument, just in the same way as one knows that the ordinary layman, when he is going to use a needle to prick a blister or prick a little gathering on a finger, generally takes the precaution to put the needle in a flame, as I think Mr

33 [1938] 1 All ER 566.

> Couzens did. I accept the evidence of Mr Couzens as to what he says he did on this occasion – how he put his instrument in a flame before he left his shop, and how he washed his hands, and so forth. I think that he did. I see no reason to suppose that he is not telling me the absolute truth when he says what he did, and, as Dr Pritchard, who holds the very high qualification of a Fellow of the Royal College of Physicians, said, for all practical purposes that is enough. That is to say, for the ordinary everyday matters that would be regarded as enough. It is not a degree of surgical cleanliness, which is a different thing from ordinary cleanliness. It is not the cleanliness which a doctor would insist upon, because, as I say, Mr Couzens is not a doctor. He was known not to be a doctor. One does not go to a jeweller to get one's ears attended to if one requires a doctor in attendance to do it. If one wants a doctor in attendance, one goes to his consulting room or one has him come to see one. I do not see any ground here for holding that Mr Couzens was negligent in the way in which he performed this operation. It might be better, and I think it probably would, if he boiled his instrument beforehand at his place, or if he took a spirit lamp with him and boiled his instrument at the time, but in view of the medical evidence, the evidence of Dr Pritchard, which I accept, I see no ground for holding that Mr Couzens departed from the standard of care which you would expect that a man of his position and his training, being what he held himself out to be, was required to possess. Therefore, the charge of negligence fails.

In *Wells v Cooper*[34] the Court of Appeal had to decide the requisite standard of care owed by an amateur carpenter when fixing a door handle. The plaintiff sustained injury when he had to pull hard on the handle and the three-quarter inch screws came away. Jenkins LJ, reading the judgment of the court found for the defendant and had this to say on the standard of care:

> ... we think that the standard of care and skill to be demanded of the defendant in order to discharge his duty of care to the plaintiff in the fixing of the new handle in the present case must be the degree of care and skill to be expected of a reasonably competent carpenter doing the work in question. This does not mean that the degree of care and skill required is to be measured by reference to the contractual obligations as to the quality of his work assumed by a professional carpenter working for reward, which would, in our view, set the standard too high. The question is simply what steps would a reasonably competent carpenter wishing to fix a handle such as this securely to a door such as this have taken with a view to achieving that object. ...
>
> In relation to a trifling and perfectly simple operation such as the fixing of the new handle, we think that the defendant's experience of domestic carpentry is sufficient to justify his inclusion in the category of reasonable competent carpenters. The matter then stands thus. The defendant, a reasonably competent carpenter, used three-quarter inch screws, believing them to be adequate for the purpose of fixing the handle. There is no doubt that he was doing his best to make the handle secure and believed that he had done so. Accordingly, he must be taken to have discharged his duty of reasonable care, unless the belief that three-quarter inch screws would be adequate was one which no reasonably competent carpenter could reasonably entertain, or, in other words, an obvious blunder which should at once have been apparent to him as a reasonably competent carpenter. The evidence adduced on the plaintiff's side failed, in the judge's view, to make that out.

34 [1958] 2 QB 265.

Common practice

Where the defendant acts in accordance with common practice this may be evidence that he is not at fault, but it should not be regarded as conclusive of the issue. Likewise a failure to follow such practice may be some, but not necessarily conclusive, evidence of fault. In *Brown v Rolls Royce Ltd*,[35] Lord Keith of Avonholm stated:

> A common practice in like circumstances not followed by an employer may no doubt be a weighty circumstance to be considered by judge or jury in deciding whether failure to comply with this practice, taken along with all the other material circumstances in the case, yields an inference of negligence on the part of the employers.

A word of caution was expressed by Montrose[36] in the context of a discussion of the second *Bolam* test to be considered immediately below:

> Though it is submitted that the doctrine that mere conformity with practice is legally well established, analysis is required in order that its limits and value may be ascertained. In the first place it is important to distinguish between average practices and average standards, between what the ordinary man does and what the ordinary man thinks ought to be done. His practice is not a necessary determinant of his ethics.

The average standard is not purely the aggregate of average practices is the useful point being made here. Montrose was being extremely critical of the following passage from the *Bolam* case:

> A doctor is not guilty of negligence if he has acted in accordance with a practice accepted as proper by a responsible body of medical men skilled in that particular art. I do not think there is much difference in sense. It is just a different way of expressing the same thought. Putting it the other way round, a doctor is not negligent if he is acting in accordance with such a practice, merely because there is a body of opinion that takes a contrary view. At the same time, that does not mean that a medical man can obstinately and pig-headedly carry on with some old technique if it has been proved to be contrary to what is really substantially the whole of informed medical opinion. Otherwise you might get men today saying: 'I don't believe in anaesthetics. I don't believe in antiseptics. I am going to continue to do my surgery in the way it was done in the 18th century.' That clearly would be wrong.

In *Bolam*, the plaintiff, who was suffering from depression, agreed to treatment by electro-convulsive therapy. There were two bodies of opinion as to whether the subject of such treatment should be given relaxant drugs and/or manual control should be used whilst being treated. The plaintiff was not given any drugs and sustained serious leg and hip injuries when he fell off the bed on which he was lying. The jury found for the defendant.

Similar issues were raised in the *Maynard* case before the House of Lords. Lord Scarman's judgment contains the significant facts:

> The present case may be classified as one of clinical judgment. Two distinguished consultants, a physician and a surgeon experienced in the treatment of chest diseases formed judgment as to what was, in their opinion, in the best interests of

35 [1960] 1 All ER 577.

36 [1958] 21 MLR 259 at 262.

> their patient. They recognised that tuberculosis was the most likely diagnosis. But in their opinion there was an unusual factor, *viz* swollen glands in the mediastinum unaccompanied by any evidence of lesion in the lungs. Hodgkin's disease, carcinoma, and sarcoidosis were, therefore, possibilities. The danger they thought was Hodgkin's disease; though unlikely, it was, if present, a killer (as treatment was understood in 1970) unless remedial steps were taken in its early stage. They therefore decided on mediastinoscopy, an operational procedure which would provide them with a biopsy from the swollen gland which could be subjected to immediate microscopic examination. It is said that the evidence of tuberculosis was so strong that it was unreasonable and wrong to defer diagnosis and to put their patient to the risks of the operation. The case against them is not mistake or carelessness in performing the operation, which it is admitted was properly carried out, but an error of judgment in requiring the operation to be undertaken.
>
> A case which is based on an allegation that fully considered decision of two consultants in the field of their special skill was negligent clearly presents certain difficulties of proof. It is not enough to show that there is a body of competent professional opinion which considers that theirs was the wrong decision, if there also exists a body of professional opinion, equally competent, which supports the decision as reasonable in the circumstances. It is not enough to show that subsequent events show that the operation need never have been performed, if at the time the decision to operate was taken it was reasonable in the sense that a responsible body of medical opinion would have accepted it as proper. ...
>
> I would only add that a doctor who professes to exercise a special skill must exercise the ordinary skill of his speciality. Differences of opinion and practice exist, and will always exist, in the medical as in other professions. There is seldom any one answer exclusive of all others to problems of professional judgment. A court may prefer one body of opinion to the other, but that is no basis for a conclusion of negligence. ...
>
> ... My Lords, even before considering the reasons given by the majority of the Court of Appeal for reversing the findings of negligence, I have to say that a judge's 'preference' for one body of distinguished professional opinion to another also professionally distinguished is not sufficient to establish in a practitioner whose actions have received the seal of approval of those whose opinions, truthfully expressed, honestly held, were not preferred. If this was the real reason for the judge's finding, he erred in law even though elsewhere in his judgment he stated the law correctly. For, in the realm of diagnosis and treatment, negligence is not established by preferring one respectable body of professional opinion to another. Failure to exercise the ordinary skill of a doctor (in the appropriate speciality, if he be a specialist) is necessary. ...
>
> It is certainly true that only rarely will the House itself review questions of fact. But the duty to do so does occasionally arise. Cases of professional negligence, where the primary facts are not in dispute, do sometimes require a review of the inferential findings, particularly in a case such as this where there are grounds for believing that the judge misunderstood some of the expert evidence.

Some would perhaps say that the judiciary has surrendered its role to the medical profession in cases such as this. One thing is certain is that the courts are only too willing to interfere with the decisions of the court at first instance where allegations of medical negligence are concerned. By way of contrast, the Privy Council did not shrink from holding that a customary conveyancing practice in Hong Kong was negligent. In *Edward Wong Finance Co Ltd v Johnson Stokes and Master*,[37] Lord Brightman discussed the practice:

> As already indicated, the prevalence of the Hong Kong style of completion is established beyond a peradventure. It is peculiarly well adapted to the conditions in Hong Kong. It has obvious advantages to both solicitors and their clients. Their Lordships intend to say nothing to discourage its continuance. However, in assessing whether the respondents fell short of the standard of care which they owed towards the appellants, three questions must be considered: first, does the practice, as operated by the respondents in the instant case involve a foreseeable risk; if so, could that risk have been avoided; and if so, were the respondents negligent in failing to take avoiding action?
>
> In the opinion of their Lordships, the risk of loss to the appellants by placing the money at the disposition of the vendors' solicitor unquestionably involved a foreseeable risk, the risk of an embezzlement by the recipient. Such a risk is usually remote, but is none the less foreseeable. ...
>
> Their Lordships turn to the question whether the risk could have been avoided in the instant case. The answer, in their Lordships' view, is that it could readily have been avoided without in any way undermining the basic features of the Hong Kong style of completion. For example, all that is needed in such a case is that the purchaser's or lender's solicitor should take reasonable steps to satisfy himself that the vendor's or borrower's solicitor has authority from his client to receive the purchase money or loan; and, in the case of property already subject to a mortgage which is to be discharged, so much of the purchase price or loan as is needed to discharge the prior mortgage could be paid by cheque or draft in favour of the mortgagee or his duly authorised agent, and not by a draft in favour of the vendor's solicitor. Simple precautions such as these would ensure that the purchaser or lender was placed by his solicitor in the favourable position which he ought to occupy when he parts with his money, that is to say, he would have an unanswerable claim against the other side for specific performance of that party's obligation to execute the appropriate assurances. ...
>
> The risk inherent in the Hong Kong style of completion as operated in the instant case being foreseeable, and readily avoidable, there can only be an affirmative to the third question, whether the respondents were negligent in not foreseeing and avoiding that risk.

It seems highly contradictory for the Privy Council on the one hand to declare that the practice used on this occasion was negligent, but to sanction its use generally as being suitable for the prevailing conditions in Hong Kong. It must be seriously doubted whether this decision can sit with the *Bolam* test, which, as pointed out already, has been approved of by the House of Lords in at least two cases. In one of those cases, *Sidaway v Bethlem Royal Hospital Governors*,[38] the House applied *Bolam* to a different situation, in that normally the test applies to treatment and diagnosis in the medical field, but in *Sidaway* it was extended to the doctor' duty to warn a patient of inherent risks in operational procedures.

The plaintiff was in considerable pain and agreed to an operation on her spinal column with a view to relieving that pain. The operation was carried out with the appropriate degree of skill, but the operation resulted in other damage which was a very small risk inherent in the operation. The plaintiff claimed in

37 [1984] 1 AC 296.

38 [1985] 1 All ER 643.

negligence on the basis that she was not told of the possible risk of side effects and that she was owed a duty by the surgeon to warn of any such risks. Her claim was unsuccessful but there was some difference in view between their Lordships on the precise extent, if any, of the duty to warn in such circumstances. We shall start with Lord Scarman, who took a somewhat different view from the others on the scope of such duty, whilst agreeing with the result reached by his fellow judges:

> But was the judge correct in treating the 'standard of competent professional opinion' as the criterion in determining whether a doctor is under a duty to warn his patient of the risk, or risks, inherent in the treatment which he recommends. Skinner J and the Court of Appeal in the instant case held that he was correct. Bristow J adopted the same criterion in *Chatterton v Gerson* [1981] 1 All ER 257, [1981] QB 432. The implications of this view of the law are disturbing. It leaves the determination of a legal duty to the judgment of doctors. Responsible medical judgment may, indeed, provide the law an acceptable standard in determining whether a doctor in diagnosis or treatment has complied with his duty. But is it right that medical judgment should determine whether there exists a duty to warn of risk and its scope? It would be a strange conclusion if the courts should be led to conclude that our law, which undoubtedly recognises a right in the patient to decide whether he will accept or reject the treatment proposed, should permit the doctors to determine whether and in what circumstances a duty arises requiring the doctor to warn his patient of the risks inherent in the treatment which he proposes.
>
> The right of 'self-determination', the description applied by some to what is no more and no less than the right of a patient to determine for himself whether he will or will not accept the doctor's advice, is vividly illustrated where the treatment recommended is surgery. A doctor who operates without the consent of his patient is, save in cases of emergency or mental disability, guilty of the civil wrong of trespass to the person; he is also guilty of the criminal offence of assault. The existence of the patient's right to make his own decision, which may be seen as a basic human right protected by the common law, is the reason why a doctrine embodying a right of the patient to be informed of the risks of surgical treatment has been developed in some jurisdictions in the United States of America and has found favour with the Supreme Court of Canada.
>
> Known as the 'doctrine of informed consent', it amounts to this: where there is a 'real' or a 'material' risk inherent in the proposed operation (however competently and skilfully performed), the question whether and to what extent a patient should be warned before he gives his consent is to be answered, not by reference to medical practice, but by accepting as a matter of law that, subject to all proper exceptions (of which the court, not the profession, is the judge), a patient has the right to be informed of the risks inherent in the treatment which is proposed. The profession, it is said, should not be judge in its own cause; or, less emotively but more correctly, the courts should not allow medical opinion as to what is best for the patient to override the patient's right to decide for himself whether he will submit to the treatment offered him. ...
>
> Unless statute has intervened to restrict the range of judge-made law, the common law enables the judges, when faced with a situation where a right recognised by law is not adequately protected, either to extend existing principles to cover the situation or to apply an existing remedy to redress the injustice. There is here no novelty, but merely the application of the principle *ubi jus ibi remedium*. If, therefore, the failure to warn a patent of the risks inherent in the operation which is recommended does constitute a failure to respect the

patient's right to make his own decision, I can see no reason in principle why, if the risk materialises and injury or damage is caused, the law should not recognise and enforce a right in the patient to compensation by way of damages.

For the reasons already given, the *Bolam* principle does not cover the situation. The facts of this very case expose its limitation. Mr Falconer lacked neither care for his patient's health and well-being nor professional skill in the advice and treatment which he offered. But did he overlook or disregard his patient's right to determine for herself whether or not to have the operation? Did he fail to provide her with the information necessary for her to make a prudent decision? There is, in truth, no evidence to answer these questions. Mrs Sidaway's evidence was not accepted; and Mr Falconer was dead. Assume, however, that he did overlook this aspect of his patient's situation. Since neither his advice nor his treatment could be faulted on the *Bolam* test, his patient may have been deprived of the opportunity to exercise her right of decision in the light of the information which she, had she received it, might reasonably have considered to be of importance in making up her mind.

On the *Bolam* view of the law, therefore, even if she established that she was so deprived by the lack of warning, she would have no remedy in negligence unless she could also prove that there was no competent and respected body of medical opinion which was in favour of no warning. Moreover, the tort of trespass to the person would not provide her with a remedy, for Mrs Sidaway did consent to the operation. Her complaint is that her consent resulted from ignorance of a risk, known by the doctor but not made known by him to her, inherent in the operation. Nor would the law of contract offer her a sure way forward. Medical treatment, as in her case, is frequently given today under arrangements outside the control of the law of contract.

One point is clear, however. If a failure to warn of risk is actionable in English law, it must be because it is in the circumstances a breach of the doctor's duty of care; in other words, the doctor must be shown to be negligent. English law has not accepted a 'no fault' basis for the liability of a doctor to compensate a patient for injury arising in the course of medical treatment. If, however, the *Bolam* principle is to be applied to the exclusion of any other test to advice and warning, there will be cases in which a patient who suffers injury through ignorance of a risk known to the doctor has no remedy. Is there any difficulty in holding that the doctor's duty of care is sufficiently extensive to afford a patient in that situation a remedy, if as a result she suffers injury or damage? I think not ...

It is, I suggest, a sound and reasonable proposition that the doctor should be required to exercise care in respecting the patient's right of decision. He must acknowledge that, in very many cases, factors other than the purely medical will play a significant part in his patient's decision-making process. The doctor's concern is with the health and the relief of pain – these are the medical objectives. But a patient may well have in mind circumstances, objectives and values which he may reasonably not make known to the doctor but which may lead him to a different decision from that suggested by a purely medical opinion. The doctor's duty can be seen, therefore, to be one which requires him, not only to advise as to the medical treatment, but also to provide his patient with the information needed to enable the patient to consider and balance the medical advantages and risks alongside other relevant matters, eg his family, business or social responsibilities, of which the doctor may be only partially, if at all, informed.

I conclude, therefore, that there is room in our law for a legal duty to warn a patent of the risks inherent in the treatment proposed and that, if such a duty be

> held to exist, its proper place is as an aspect of the duty of care owed by the doctor to his patient. ...
>
> In a medical negligence case where the issue is as to advice and information given to the patient as to the treatment proposed, the available options and the risk, the court is concerned primarily with a patient's right. The doctor's duty arises from his patient's right. If one considers the scope of the doctor's duty by beginning with the right of the patient to make his own decision whether he will or will not undergo the treatment proposed, the right to be informed of significant risk and the doctor's corresponding duty are easy to understand, for the proper implementation of the right requires that the doctor be under a duty to inform his patient of the material risks inherent in the treatment. And it is plainly right that a doctor may avoid liability for failure to warn of a material risk if he can show that he reasonably believed that communication to the patent of the existence of the risk would be detrimental to the health (including, of course, the mental health) of his patient. ...
>
> My conclusion as to the law is therefore this. To the extent that I have indicated, I think that English law must recognise a duty of the doctor to warn his patient of risk inherent in the treatment which he is proposing; and especially so if the treatment be surgery. The critical limitation is that the duty is confined to material risk. The test of materiality is whether, in the circumstances of the particular case, the court is satisfied that a reasonable person would be likely to attach significance to the risk. Even if the risk be material, the doctor will not be liable if, on a reasonable assessment of the patient's condition, he takes the view that a warning would be detrimental to his patient's health.

The opposition to Lord Scarman was led by Lord Bridge as follows:

> The important question which this appeal raises is whether the law imposes any, and if so what, different criterion as the measure of the medical man's duty of care to his patient when giving advice with respect to a proposed course of treatment. It is clearly right to recognise that a conscious adult patient of sound mind is entitled to decide for himself whether or not he will submit to a particular course of treatment proposed by the doctor, most significantly surgical treatment under general anaesthesia. This entitlement is the foundation of the doctrine of 'informed consent' which has led in certain American jurisdictions to decisions and, in the Supreme Court of Canada, to dicta on which the appellant relies, which would oust the *Bolam* test and substitute an 'objective' test of a doctor's duty to advise the patient of the advantages and disadvantages of undergoing the treatment proposed, and more particularly to advise the patient of the risks involved.
>
> There are, it appears to me at least theoretically, two extreme positions which could be taken. It could be argued that, if the patient's consent is to be fully informed, the doctor must specifically warn him of *all* risks involved in the treatment offered, unless he has some sound clinical reason not to do so. Logically, this would seem to be the extreme to which a truly objective criterion of the doctor's duty would lead. Yet this position finds no support from any authority to which we have been referred in any jurisdiction. It seems to be generally accepted that there is no need to warn of the risks inherent in all surgery under general anaesthesia. This is variously explained on the ground that the patient may be expected to be aware of such risks or that they are relatively remote. If the law is to impose on the medical profession, a duty to warn of risks to secure 'informed consent' independently of accepted medical opinion of what is appropriate, neither of these explanations for confining the

duty to special as opposed to general surgical risks, seems to me wholly convincing.

At the other extreme it could be argued that, once the doctor has decided what treatment is, on balance of advantages and disadvantages, in the patient's best interest, he should not alarm the patient by volunteering a warning of any risk involved, however grave and substantial, unless specifically asked by the patient. I cannot believe that contemporary medical opinion would support this view, which would effectively exclude the patient's right to decide in the very type of case where it is most important that he should be in a position to exercise that right and, perhaps even more significantly, to seek a second opinion whether he should submit himself to the significant risk which has been drawn to his attention. I should perhaps add at this point, although the issue does not strictly arise in this appeal, that, when questioned specifically by a patient of apparently sound mind about risks involved in a particular treatment proposed, the doctor's duty must, in my opinion, be to answer both truthfully and as fully as the questioner requires.

The decision mainly relied on to establish a criterion of the doctor's duty to disclose the risks inherent in a proposed treatment which is prescribed by the law and can be applied independently of any medical opinion or practice is that of the District of Columbia Circuit Court of Appeals in *Canterbury v Spence* (1972) 464 F 2d 772. The judgment of the court (Wright, Leventhal and Robinson JJ), delivered by Robinson J, expounds the view that an objective criterion of what is a sufficient disclosure of risk is necessary to ensure that the patient is enabled to make an intelligent decision and cannot be left to be determined by the doctors.

... I recognise the logical force of the *Canterbury* doctrine, proceeding from the premise that the patient's right to make his own decision must at all costs be safeguarded against the kind of medical paternalism which assumes that 'doctor knows best'. But, with all respect, I regard the doctrine as quite impractical in application for three principal reasons. First, it gives insufficient weight to the realities of the doctor/patient relationship. A very wide variety of factors must enter into a doctor's clinical judgment, not only as to what treatment is appropriate for a particular patient, but also as to how best to communicate to the patient the significant factors necessary to enable the patient to make an informed decision whether to undergo the treatment.

The doctor cannot set out to educate the patient to his own standard of medical knowledge of all the relevant factors involved. He may take the view, certainly with some patients, that the very fact of his volunteering, without being asked, information of some remote risk involved in the treatment proposed, even though he describes it as remote, may lead to that risk assuming an undue significance in the patient's calculations. Second, it would seem to me quite unrealistic in any medical negligence action to confine the expert medical evidence to an explanation of the primary medical factors involved and to deny the court the benefit of evidence of medical opinion and practice on the particular issue of disclosure which is under consideration. Third, the objective test which *Canterbury* propounds seems to me to be so imprecise as to be almost meaningless. If it is left to individual judges to decide for themselves what 'a reasonable person in the patient's position' would consider a risk of sufficient significance that he should be told about it, the outcome of litigation in this field is likely to be quite unpredictable. ...

Having rejected the *Canterbury* doctrine as a solution to the problem of safeguarding the patient's right to decide whether he will undergo a particular treatment advised by his doctor, the question remains whether that right is sufficiently safeguarded by the application of the *Bolam* test without qualification to the determination of the question – what risks inherent in a proposed treatment should be disclosed? The case against a simple application of the *Bolam* test is cogently stated by Laskin CJC, giving the judgment of the Supreme Court of Canada in *Reible v Hughes* (1980) 114 DLR (3d) 1 at 13: 'To allow expert medical evidence to determine what risks are material and, hence, should be disclosed and, correlatively, what risks are not material is to hand over to the medical profession the entire question of the scope of the duty of disclosure, including the question whether there has been a breach of that duty. Expert medical evidence is, of course, relevant to findings as to the risks that reside in or are a result of recommended surgery or other treatment. It will also have a bearing on their materiality, but this is not a question that is to be concluded on the basis of the expert medical evidence alone. The issue under consideration is a different issue from that involved, where the question is whether the doctor carried out his professional activities by applicable professional standards. What is under consideration here is the patient's right to know what risks are involved in undergoing or foregoing certain surgery or other treatment.'

I fully appreciate the force of this reasoning, but can only accept it subject to the important qualification that a decision over what disclosure of risk is best calculated to assist a particular patient to make a rational choice whether or not to undergo a particular treatment must primarily be a matter of clinical judgment. It would follow from this that the issue whether non-disclosure in a particular case should be condemned as a breach of the doctor's duty of care is an issue to be decided primarily on the basis of expert medical evidence, applying the *Bolam* test. But I do not see that this approach involves the necessity 'to hand over to the medical profession the entire question of the scope of the duty of disclosure, including the question whether there has been a breach of that duty'.

Of course, if there is a conflict of evidence whether a responsible body of medical opinion approves of non-disclosure in a particular case, the judge will have to resolve that conflict. But, even in a case where, as here, no expert witness in the relevant medical field condemns the non-disclosure as being in conflict with accepted and responsible medical practice, I am of the opinion that the judge might, in certain circumstances, come to the conclusion that disclosure of a particular risk was so obviously necessary to an informed choice on the part of a patient that no reasonably prudent medical man would fail to make it. The kind of case I have in mind would be an operation involving a substantial risk of grave adverse consequences as for example the 10% risk of a stroke from the operation which was the subject of the Canadian case of *Reibl v Hughes* (1980) 114 DLR (3d) 1. In such a case, in the absence of some cogent clinical reason why the patient should not be informed, a doctor, recognising and respecting his patient's right of decision, could hardly fail to appreciate the necessity for an appropriate warning.

In the instant case I can see no reasonable ground on which the judge could properly reject the conclusion to which the unchallenged medical evidence led in the application of the *Bolam* test. The trial judge's assessment of the risk at 1–2% covered both nerve root and spinal cord damage and covered a spectrum of possible ill-effects 'ranging from the mild to the catastrophic'. In so far as it is possible and appropriate to measure such risks in percentage terms (some of the expert medical witnesses called expressed a marked and understandable reluctance to do so), the risk to the spinal cord of such severity as the appellant in fact suffered was, it would appear, certainly less than 1%. But there is no yardstick either in the judge's findings or in the evidence to measure what

> fraction of 1% that risk represented. In these circumstances, the appellant's expert witness's agreement that the non-disclosure complained of accorded with a practice accepted as proper by a responsible body of neurosurgical opinion, afforded the respondents a complete defence to the appellant's claim.

Lord Bridge's protestations to the contrary, this nonetheless appears to be abject surrender to the medical profession. His Lordship's arguments against the 'prudent patient' test are highly unconvincing. In any event, his views seem to reflect the current state of the law on the subject. Another case which emphasises the plaintiff's difficulties in bringing medical negligence claims is *Roe v Ministry of Health.*[39] The plaintiffs underwent operations and were given spinal anaesthetic. Unfortunately, this had been kept in a phenol solution and the phenol had seeped through invisible cracks in the glass containing the anaesthetic, causing the plaintiffs to be permanently paralysed. Denning LJ in his usual style commented:

> If the anaesthetists had foreseen that the ampoules might get cracked with cracks that could not be detected on inspection they would, no doubt, have dyed the phenol a deep blue; and this would have exposed the contamination. But I do not think their failure to foresee this was negligence. It is so easy to be wise after the event and to condemn as negligence that which was only misadventure. We ought always to be on guard against it, especially in cases against hospitals and doctors. Medical science has conferred great benefits on mankind, but these benefits are attended by considerable risks. Every surgical operation is attended by risks. We cannot take the benefits without taking the risks. Every advance in technique is also attended by risks. Doctors, like the rest of us, have to learn by experience; and experience often teaches in a hard way. Something goes wrong and shows up a weakness, and then it is put right. That is just what happened here. Dr Graham sought to escape the danger of infection by disinfecting the ampoule. In escaping that known danger he, unfortunately, ran into another danger. He did not know that there could be undetectable cracks, but it was not negligent for him not to know it at that time. We must not look at the 1947 accident with 1954 spectacles.

The other two judges also agreed that the appeal by the plaintiffs should be dismissed. Of course, once the possibility that this could happen became known, the risk would be foreseeable and the precaution easy to take as was mentioned in the extract from Denning LJ's judgment.

Children

There is a dearth of authority on the liability of children as defendants, but it would seem that the standard of care is such that can reasonably be expected of a child of the same age as the defendant. Often, children will not be worth suing, which perhaps goes some way towards explaining the lack of case law. However, the High Court of Australia has had the opportunity to consider the problem in *McHale v Watson,*[40] where a 12 year old boy threw a sharp piece of metal, 'like a dart', at a post. It missed the post and struck a young girl. The majority of the court thought that the age of the boy was a relevant consideration in assessing the standard of care. Kitto J stated:

---

39 [1954] 2 All ER 131.

40 [1966] 115 CLR 199.

... a defendant does not escape liability by proving that he is abnormal in some respect which reduces his capacity for foresight or prudence.

The principle is, of course, applicable to a child. The standard of care being objective, it is no answer for him, any more than it is for an adult, to say that the harm he caused was due to his being abnormally slow-witted, quick-tempered, absent-minded or inexperienced. But it does not follow that he cannot rely in his defence upon a limitation upon the capacity for foresight or prudence, not as being personal to himself, but as being characteristic of humanity at his stage of development and in that sense normal. By doing so he appeals to a standard of ordinariness, to an objective and not a subjective standard. In regard to the things which pertain to foresight and prudence – experience, understanding of causes and effects, balance of judgment, thoughtfulness – it is absurd, indeed it is a misuse of language, to speak of normality in relation to persons of all ages taken together. In those things normality is, for children, something different from what normality is for adults; the very concept of normality is a concept of rising levels until 'years of discretion' are attained. The law does not arbitrarily fix upon any particular age for this purpose, and tribunals of fact may well give effect to different views as to the age at which normal adult foresight and prudence are reasonably to be expected in relation to particular sets of circumstances. But up to that stage the normal capacity to exercise those two qualities necessarily means the capacity which is normal for a child of the relevant age; and it seems to me that it would be contrary to the fundamental principle that a person is liable for harm that he causes by falling short of an objective criterion of 'propriety' in his conduct – propriety, that is to say, as determined by a comparison with the standard of care reasonably to be expected in the circumstances from the normal person – to hold that, where a child's liability is in question, the normal person to be considered is someone other than a child of corresponding age.

Assistance on the subject is not to be found in the shape of specific decision in England or in this country, and judicial opinion in the United States and Canada have varied both in result and reasoning. It seems to me, however, that strong support for the view I have indicated is provided by the decisions on the cognate subject of contributory negligence. It is true that contributory negligence is not a breach of legal duty; it is only a failure to take reasonable care for one's own safety. But I must respectfully disagree with those who think that the deficiencies of foresight and prudence that are normal during childhood are irrelevant in determining what care it is reasonable for a child to take for the safety of others, though relevant in determining what care it is reasonable for a child to take for himself. The standard is objective in contributory negligence no less than in negligence, in the sense that an ordinary capacity for care is postulated and is notionally applied to the circumstances of the case in order to determine what a reasonable person would have done or refrained from doing, regardless of the actual capacity for foresight or prudence possessed by the individual plaintiff or defendant. ...

On the findings which must be accepted, what the respondent did was the unpremeditated, impulsive act of a boy not yet of an age to have an adult's realisation of the danger of edged tools or an adult's wariness in the handling of them. It is, I think, a matter for judicial notice that the ordinary boy of 12 suffers from a feeling that a piece of wood and a sharp instrument have a special affinity. To expect a boy of that age to consider before throwing the spike whether the timber was hard or soft, to weigh the chances of being able to make the spike stick in the post, and to foresee that it might glance off and hit the girl,

> would be, I think, to expect a degree of sense and circumspection which nature ordinarily withholds till life has become less rosy.

Perhaps this will remain a problem which troubles the courts infrequently. It would be interesting to speculate whether old age might be a factor in the assessment of fault?

Sporting competition

We must now turn to an area which has produced a fair amount of litigation over the years and is likely to do so in the future, namely the standard of care owed in sporting competitions. There are a number of different relationships involved here, namely: that between competitor and spectator; that between competitor and fellow competitor; and that between organiser and spectator. The leading case is *Woolridge v Sumner*,[41] where a film cameraman trying to get a close-up of a horse and rider was struck by a horse and rider in the course of a competition. The Court of Appeal found that there was no negligence by the rider. Sellers LJ said:

> In my opinion, a competitor or player cannot, at least, in the normal case of competition or game, rely on the maxim *volenti non fit inuria* in answer to a spectator's claim, for there is no liability unless there is negligence, and the spectator comes to witness skill and with the expectation that it will be exercised. But, provided the competition or game is being performed within the rules and the requirement of the sport, and by a person of adequate skill and competence, the spectator does not expect his safety to be regarded by the participant. If the conduct is deliberately intended to injure someone whose presence is known, or is reckless and in disregard of all safety of others so that it is a departure from the standards which might reasonably be expected in anyone pursuing the competition or game, then the performer might well be held liable for any injury his act caused.
>
> There would, I think, be a difference, for instance, in assessing blame which is actionable between an injury caused by a tennis ball or a racket accidentally thrown in the course of play into the spectators at Wimbledon and a ball hit or a racket thrown into the stands in temper or annoyance when play was not in progress. The relationship of spectator and competitor or player is a special one, as I see it, as the standard of conduct of the participant, as accepted and expected by the spectator, is that which the sport permits or involves. The different relationship involves its own standard of care. There can be no better evidence that Mr Holladay was riding within the rules than that he won, not withstanding this unfortunate accident in the course of the event, and I do not think that it can be said that he was riding recklessly and in disregard of all safety or even, on this evidence, without skill.

Diplock LJ went on:

> A reasonable spectator attending voluntarily to witness any game or competition knows, and presumably desires, that a reasonable participant will concentrate his attention on winning, and if the game or competition is a fast-moving one will have to exercise his judgment and attempt to exert his skill in what, in the analogous context of contributory negligence, is sometimes called 'the agony of the moment'. If the participant does so concentrate his attention and

41 [1962] 2 All ER 978.

consequently does exercise his judgment and attempt to exert his skill in circumstances of this kind which are inherent in the game or competition in which he is taking part, the question whether any mistake he makes amounts to a breach of duty to take reasonable care must take account of those circumstances.

The law of negligence has always recognised that the standard of care which a reasonable man will exercise depends on the conditions under which the decision to avoid the act or omission relied on as negligence has to be taken. The case of the workman engaged on repetitive work in the noise and bustle of the factory is a familiar example. More apposite for present purposes are the collision cases where a decision has to be made on the spur of the moment. 'A's negligence makes collision so threatening that, though by the appropriate measure B could avoid it, B has not really time to think and by mistake takes the wrong measure. B is not to be held guilty of any negligence and A wholly fails.' (*Admiralty Comrs v SS Volute* [1921] All ER Rep at p 197; [1922] 1 AC at p 136).

A fails not because of his own negligence; there has never been any contributory negligence rule in Admiralty. He fails because B has exercised such care as is reasonable in the circumstances in which he has not really time to think. No doubt, if he has got into those circumstances as a result of breach of duty of care which he owes to A, A can succeed on this antecedent negligence; but a participant in a game or competition gets into the circumstances in which he has no time or very little time to think by his decision to take part in the game or competition at all. It cannot be suggested that the participant, at any rate if he has some modicum of skill, is by the mere act of participating in breach of his duty of care to a spectator who is present for the very purpose of watching him do so. If, therefore, in the course of the game or competition, at a moment when he really has not time to think, a participant by mistake takes a wrong measure, he is not, in my view, to be held guilty of any negligence.

Furthermore, the duty which he owes is a duty of care, not a duty of skill. Save where a consensual relationship exists between a plaintiff and a defendant by which the defendant warrants his skill, a man owes no duty to his neighbour to exercise any special skill beyond that which an ordinary reasonable man would acquire before indulging in the activity in which he is engaged at the relevant time. It may well be that a participant in a game or competition would be guilty of negligence to a spectator if he took part in it when he knew or ought to have known that his lack of skill was such that, even if he exerted it to the utmost, he was likely to cause injury to a spectator watching him. No question of this arises in the present case. It was common ground that Mr Holladay was an exceptionally skilful and experienced horseman.

The practical result of this analysis of the application of the common law of negligence to participant and spectator would, I think, be expressed by the common man in some such terms as these: 'A person attending a game or competition takes the risk of any damage caused to him by any act of a participant done in the course of, and for the purposes of, the game or competition, notwithstanding that such act may involve an error of judgment or a lapse of skill, unless the participant's conduct is such as to evince a reckless disregard of the spectator's safety. The spectator takes the risk because such an act involves no breach of the duty of care owed by the participant to him. He does not take the risk by virtue of doctrine expressed or obscured by the maxim *volenti non fit injuria.*'

The issue was further ventilated in the later case of *Wilks v The Cheltenham Home Guard Motor Cycle Club*,[42] where spectators were injured whilst in an enclosure when a motor cycle involved in a scrambling event veered off the course and into them. The plaintiff spectators were unsuccessful in their claims and in the course of his judgment Lord Denning MR stated:

> Let me first try to state the duty which lies on a competitor in a race. He must, of course, use reasonable care. But that means reasonable care having regard to the fact that he is a competitor in a race in which he is expected to go 'all out' to win. Take a batsman at the wicket. He is expected to hit a six, if he can, even if it lands among the spectators. So also in a race, a competitor is expected to go as fast as he can, so long as he is not foolhardy. In seeing if a man is negligent, you ask what a reasonable man in his place would or would not do. In a race a reasonable man would do everything he could to win, but he would not be foolhardy. That, I think, is the standard of care expected of him. We were referred to *Woolridge v Sumner* ([1962] 2 All ER 978, [1963] 2 QB 43). It is, I think, different. It concerned a horse show where horses were to display their paces, but not to race. The riders ought not to give their horses their heads so as to go too fast. On that account the decision was criticised by Dr Goodhart (78 LQR 490–96). His criticism may be justified. But he points out that it is different in a race when a rider is expected to go 'all out' to win. In a race the rider is, I think, liable if his conduct is such as to evince a reckless disregard of the spectators' safety; in other words if his conduct is foolhardy.
>
> The judge in this case found that the driver was reckless ... I must say that I can see no evidence to support those findings of the judge. There was no evidence whatever of greatly excessive speed. It was not even suggested by the plaintiffs. The rider was only going at 20–25mph along the straight and 10mph when he went into the spectators. There was no evidence of want of skill. He had ridden motor cycles a lot and had been 'scrambling', ie riding and racing over rough ground, for three years. No doubt he 'lost control' of his motor cycle, else he would not have gone over the wrecking rope. But loss of control is just one of those things that may happen in a motor cycle 'scramble'. It takes place over rough ground with undulations and hazards liable to cause the most skilful rider to go out of control or to have a spill. It is no more negligence than it is when a horse at a point-to-point runs out at a jump.

Edmund Davies LJ in the same case was in favour of a slightly different test:

> Lord Denning MR has already referred to the decision of this court in *Woolridge v Sumner* and I respectfully share his difficulty in accepting the view there expressed that a competitor in such events as this is to be held liable only if he acts in reckless disregard of the spectators' safety. For my part, I would with deference adopt the view of Dr Goodhart that the proper test is whether injury to a spectator has been caused 'by an error of judgment that a reasonable competitor, being the reasonable man of the sporting world, would not have made'. But the decision is, if I may say so, most valuable in pointing out those special features which are inherent in competitive events and which everyone takes for granted. I have here particularly in mind the observation of Sellers LJ that:[43] '... provided the competition or game is being performed within the rules and the requirement of the sport and by a person of adequate skill and

42 [1971] 2 All ER 369.

43 [1962] 2 All ER at 983, [1963] 1 QB at 56.

> competence, the spectator does not expect his safety to be regarded by the participant'.
>
> Nevertheless, although in the very nature of things the competitor is all out to win and that is exactly what the spectators expect of him, it is in my judgment still incumbent on him to exercise such degree of care as may reasonably be expected in all the circumstances. For my part, therefore, I would hold him liable only for damage caused by errors of judgment or lapse of skill going beyond such as, in the stress of circumstances, may reasonably be regarded as excusable.

So far the discussion in the extracts has focused on the potential liability of competitors towards spectators. One of the issues in *Harrison v Vincent* concerned the possible liability of organisers of an event towards competitors. The sidecar passenger on a motor cycle combination was badly injured when the cycle left the track during competition and struck a recovery vehicle parked in a slip road some 30–40 m from the course. The slip road was there as is required under the rules of such competitions to enable riders to escape from the track at dangerous points if they lost control of their vehicle. The recovery vehicle was projecting partially into the slip road. On the issue of foreseeability, Sir John Arnold P said:

> Riders may take a larger or smaller care for their own safety. Moreover, perhaps, riders may be more or less imaginative when contemplating the risks which a particular circumstance could set up. But management have a quite different obligation. It is their function, as it seems to me, to assess as carefully as they can precisely those contingencies which a more or less carefree competitor might ignore. All in all it seems to me, looked at from the point of view of a responsible and careful management, that the sort of thing that happened in this case was within the reasonable contemplation to the point at which it could possibly be foreseen for the purposes of assessing a breach of duty. Much must depend on the distance off the track of the place at which the limited obstruction – for it was a limited obstruction – was permitted to occur on the escape route. There must come a point at which the distance was so great as to render the foreseeability so slight as to absolve the organisers.

The Court of Appeal unanimously decided that, on the facts, the organisers were at fault. It should perhaps be remembered that the organisers' decision to park the vehicle in or near to the slip road was unlikely to be one made in the agony of the moment, unlike decisions of the competitors involved in the race. As a consequence, more can be demanded of the organisers in terms of foreseeability, both in relation to their potential liability to competitors but also in relation to possible claims by spectators brought against them.

Finally, we need to consider the position as between the competitors. In *Condon v Basi*,[44] the Court of Appeal briefly touched upon this type of case. The plaintiff was tackled by the defendant during the course of a football match and sustained a broken leg. It was held that the tackle was to be classed as serious foul play and amounted to negligence. Sir John Donaldson preferred to take the line that there was a general standard of care applicable in such circumstances, taking into account the activity being undertaken by the parties at the relevant time, which in the context of a game of football 'are quite different from those which affect you when you are going for a walk in the countryside'. The other

44 [1985] 2 All ER 453.

way of considering the matter is to argue that the plaintiff consents to certain risks inherent in the game. He continued:

> ... it was submitted by counsel on behalf of the defendant that the standard of care was subjective to the defendant and not objective, and if he was a wholly incompetent football player, he could do things without risk of liability which a competent football player could not do. For my part, I reject that submission. The standard is objective, but objective in a different set of circumstances. Thus there will of course be a higher degree of care required of a player in a First Division football match than of a player in a local league football match.

The Master of the Rolls also stated that not every breach of the rules of the game will necessarily result in a finding of negligence.

It seems that the courts are unwilling to employ the consent argument in this context, although it is usually acknowledged that the same result can be achieved whichever approach is used.

Proof of breach

The plaintiff has the legal burden of proving, on the balance of probabilities, that the defendant was in breach of his duty of care. We are here concerned with any short cuts that may be available to enable a plaintiff to satisfy this burden. Sometimes, in actions for breach of statutory duty, the relevant statute will give a party injured by the breach a civil action in damages, eg see s 41 Consumer Protection Act 1987. The Civil Evidence Act 1968 may also provide useful assistance to a plaintiff in appropriate cases:

Section 11

(1) In any civil proceedings the fact that a person has been convicted of an offence by or before any court in the United Kingdom or by a court martial there or elsewhere shall (subject to subsection (3) below) be admissible in evidence for the purpose of proving, where to do so is relevant to any issue in those proceedings, that he committed that offence, whether he was so convicted upon a plea of guilty or otherwise and whether or not he is a party to the civil proceedings; but no conviction other than a subsisting one shall be admissible in evidence by virtue of this section.

(2) In any civil proceedings in which by virtue of this section a person is proved to have been convicted of an offence by or before any court in the United Kingdom or by a court martial there or elsewhere:

- (a) he shall be taken to have committed that offence unless the contrary is proved; and
- (b) without prejudice to the reception of any other admissible evidence for the purpose of identifying the facts on which the conviction was based, the contents of any document which is admissible as evidence of the conviction. and the contents of the information, complaint, indictment or charge-sheet on which the person in question was convicted, shall be admissible in evidence for that purpose.

(3) Nothing in this section shall prejudice the operation of section 13 of this Act or any other enactment whereby a conviction or a finding of fact in any criminal proceedings is for the purposes of any other proceedings made conclusive evidence of any fact.

The common law has also developed its own principle to aid a plaintiff in difficult circumstances, namely the doctrine of *res ipsa loquitur*, the facts speak for themselves. This is thought to transfer the evidentiary burden to a defendant in appropriate circumstances. However, there is some controversy about this as will be observed in the extracts below. It is worth, perhaps, starting the discussion with a short extract forming the conclusion of an article by Atiyah on the doctrine.[45] Having discussed the cases decided up to the time of writing, he comments:

> The upshot of all this seems to be that, while English judges are reluctant openly to acknowledge the fact, the application of *res ipsa loquitur* in English courts has frequently had the effect of casting a legal burden of proof on the defendant, while a contrary view is taken in Australia. A reasonably impartial commentator may be forgiven if he pays tribute to the clarity of the views expressed by Australian judges while deploring the result in policy terms, and at the same time welcomes the results generally arrived at by English judges while deploring their inability to express their views more clearly.

Turning to the English cases, Lord Pearson stated in the case of *Henderson v Jenkins*:[46]

> My Lords, in my opinion, the decision in this appeal turns on what is sometimes called 'the evidential burden of proof', which is to be distinguished from the formal (or legal or technical) burden of proof ... For the purposes of the present case the distinction can be simply stated in this way. In an action for negligence the plaintiff must allege, and has the burden of proving, that the accident was caused by negligence on the part of the defendants. That is the issue throughout the trial, and in giving judgment at the end of the trial the judge has to decide whether he is satisfied on a balance of probabilities that the accident was caused by negligence on the part of the defendants, and if he is not so satisfied the plaintiff's action fails. The formal burden of proof does not shift. But if, in the course of the trial, there is proved a set of facts which raises a *prima facie* inference that the accident was caused by negligence on the part of the defendants, the issue will be decided in the plaintiff's favour unless the defendants, by their evidence, provide some answer which is adequate to displace the *prima facie* inference. In this situation there is said to be an evidential burden of proof resting on the defendants. I have some doubts whether it is strictly correct to use the expression 'burden of proof' with this meaning, as there is a risk of it being confused with the formal burden of proof, but it is a familiar and convenient usage.

In *Henderson* brake failure caused a lorry to career out of control on a hill, resulting in the death of the plaintiff's husband. The brake pipe had become corroded and it was a defect difficult to observe without removing other parts of the lorry. The majority of the House of Lords found for the plaintiff on the basis that the defendants, by failing to put forward evidence of the past history of the vehicle, had failed to discharge the inference of negligence raised by the facts as set out by the plaintiff. This conclusion is controversial to say the least, but the approach commented on by Atiyah noted above was similarly adopted

45 (1972) 35 MLR 337.

46 [1969] 3 All ER 756.

in the later case of *Ward v Tesco Stores Ltd*,[47] where a woman slipped on some spilt yoghurt on the supermarket floor. Below is an extract from the judgment of Lawton LJ:

> The relevant principles were enunciated in the classical judgment of Erle CJ in *Scott v London and St Katherine Docks Co* (1865) 3 H & C 596, 601: 'Where the thing is shown to be under the management of the defendant or his servants, and the accident is such as in the ordinary course of things does not happen if those who have the management use proper care, it provides reasonable evidence, in the absence of explanation by the defendants that the accident arose from want of care.'
>
> Now, in this case the floor of this supermarket was under the management of the defendants and their servants. The accident was such as in the ordinary course of things does not happen if floors are kept clean and spillages are dealt with as soon as they occur. If an accident does happen because the floors are covered with spillage, then in my judgment some explanation should be forthcoming from the defendants to show that the accident did not arise from any want of care on their part; and in the absence of any explanation the judge may give judgment for the plaintiff. Such burden of proof as there is on defendants in such circumstances is evidential, not probative. The judge thought that *prima facie* the accident would not have happened had the defendants taken reasonable care. In my judgment he was justified in taking that view because the probabilities were that the spillage had been on the floor long enough for it to have been cleaned up by a member of the staff.

Ormrod LJ, dissenting, thought that the accident could quite easily have happened without any want of care on the part of the defendants and took the view that the *res ipsa* principle was not applicable. Megaw LJ agreed with Lawton LJ. These two cases suggest that the English courts have been prepared to apply the principle very readily in some cases and that, despite statements to the contrary, the effect has been to transfer the legal burden of proof to the defendant, a policy with which Atiyah, quoted above, seems perfectly comfortable. In a more recent case, we may have witnessed something of a retreat from this position. In *Ng Chun Pui v Lee Chuen Tat*,[48] the Privy Council considered the application of the *res ipsa* principle to a case where a vehicle had suddenly gone out of control, crossed the central reservation and collided with a bus. The defendants, in response to reliance on the *res ipsa* doctrine, called evidence to the effect that an untraced vehicle had cut into the lane where the defendants' vehicle was travelling and caused it to swerve out of control. The judge found for the plaintiffs on the basis that the defendants had failed to discharge the burden of proof placed on them under the *res ipsa* principle. Commenting on this, Lord Griffiths, delivering the opinion of the Privy Council, said:

> In their Lordships' opinion this shows a misunderstanding of the so-called doctrine of *res ipsa loquitur*, which is no more than the use of a Latin maxim to describe a state of the evidence from which it is proper to draw an inference of negligence. Although it has been said in a number of cases, it is misleading to talk of the burden of proof shifting to the defendant in a *res ipsa loquitur* situation.

47 [1976] 1 All ER 219.

48 [1988] RTR 298.

> The burden of proving negligence rests throughout the case on the plaintiff. Where the plaintiff has suffered injuries as a result of an accident which ought not to have happened if the defendant had taken due care, it will often be possible for the plaintiff to discharge the burden of proof by inviting the court to draw the inference that, on the balance of probabilities, the defendant must have failed to exercise due care, even though the plaintiff does not know in what particular respects the failure occurred.
>
> ... So, in an appropriate case the plaintiff establishes a *prima facie* case by relying on the fact of the accident. If the defendant adduces no evidence there is nothing to rebut the inference of negligence and the plaintiff will have proved his case. But if the defendant does adduce evidence that evidence must be evaluated to see if it is reasonable to draw the inference from the mere fact of the accident. Loosely speaking this may be referred to as a burden on the defendant to show he was not negligent, but that only means that faced with a *prima facie* case of negligence the defendant will be found negligent unless he produces evidence that is capable of rebutting the *prima facie* case. Resort to the burden of proof is a poor way to decide a case; it is the duty of the judge to examine all the evidence at the end of the case and decide whether on the facts he finds to have been proved, and on the inferences he is prepared to draw, he is satisfied that negligence has been established. In so far as resort is had to the burden of proof, the burden remains at the end of the case as it was at the beginning upon the plaintiff to prove that his injury was caused by the negligence of the defendants.

This seems a clear enough statement of the limited effect of the application of the principle, but it still remains the case that in some instances in the past the courts have, in practice, permitted the formal burden of proof to be transferred to the defendant.

CHAPTER 4

CAUSATION AND REMOTENESS OF DAMAGE

INTRODUCTION

The third element required to be established by the plaintiff in a negligence action is that the defendant's breach of duty caused the damage sustained by the plaintiff. This in itself comprises two issues: causation and remoteness of damage. The plaintiff must first of all establish that the breach physically caused or materially contributed to the plaintiff's damage. This is sometimes referred to as causation in fact. If the answer to this question is positive in favour of the plaintiff, the second question comes into play. Is the plaintiff's loss too remote a consequence of the breach? This is often regarded as a question of law as opposed to one of fact, unlike the answer to the first question.

The remoteness issue is sometimes referred to as causation in law, but, in order to avoid confusion, this second issue will be referred to as remoteness of damage. Its function is, as a matter of legal policy, to set limits to the liability of the defendant in the interests of justice and fairness. To hold a defendant liable for all the consequences which may follow from his faulty conduct is thought to go too far. At times it is difficult to differentiate the function of remoteness from that of duty of care, and often the same result can be achieved by denying that there is a duty or by accepting the argument that the plaintiff's damage is too remote. However, the point should not be obscured that, frequently when deciding issues of physical causation, especially where the court can only speculate as to what happened after the event, the judges may be engaging in a similar exercise, in that a decision on physical cause may well not be value-free. In effect, the causation/remoteness requirements can be seen as a further significant control mechanism employed by the courts to limit the number of successful plaintiffs.

The concepts of causation and remoteness are of course important to a greater or lesser degree in all torts, but are seen to be more problematic in the context of the tort of negligence. We shall consider first of all causation in fact.

CAUSATION IN FACT

The commonly accepted test for resolving factual causation issues is the so-called 'but-for' test. Would the plaintiff have suffered the harm he did but for the defendant's fault? If the answer is in the negative, the plaintiff has at least slipped through the first net cast by the law. If the opposite conclusion is reached, then in normal circumstances the defendant's breach of duty has been eliminated as a cause of the plaintiff's harm. The remoteness question need not be put. The test can be described as a crude preliminary filter which rules out some events from being the cause of the plaintiff's damage. Just how crude and unscientific the test is can perhaps be gathered from the cases extracted below.

In *Barnett v Chelsea and Kensington Hospital Management Committee*[1] the plaintiff was the widow of a night-watchman who had died of arsenic poisoning as a result of drinking some tea whilst on duty. Feeling unwell, he had gone to the casualty department of the defendants' hospital but the duty casualty officer refused to see him, instructing the deceased to go home and see his own doctor. Nield J in his judgment, after deciding that a duty was owed to the deceased, said:

There are two main questions here: has the plaintiff established on the balance of probabilities,

(1) that the medical casualty officer was negligent, and, if so,

(2) that such negligence caused the death of the deceased?

The first of those questions can be divided into four other questions:

(1) should the doctor have seen the deceased;

(2) should he have examined the deceased;

(3) should he have admitted the deceased to the wards; and

(4) should he have treated or caused to be treated the deceased?

The first two of those four questions can be answered together.

It is not, in my judgment, the case that a casualty officer must always see the caller at his department. Casualty departments are misused from time to time. If the receptionist, for example, discovers that the visitor is already attending his own doctor and merely wants a second opinion, or if the caller has a small cut which the nurse can perfectly well dress herself, then the casualty officer need not be called. However, apart from such thing as this, I find the opinion of the witness Dr Sydney Lockett entirely acceptable ... Without doubt the casualty officer should have seen and examined the deceased. His failure to do either cannot be described as an excusable error as submitted. It was negligence. It is unfortunate that he himself at the time was a tired and unwell doctor, but there was no one else to do that which it was his duty to do. Having examined the deceased, I think the first and provisional diagnosis would have been one of food poisoning.

The third question is, should he have admitted the deceased to the wards? It is sufficient to say that I accept Dr Lockett's opinion that, having regard to all the circumstances, it was the casualty officer's duty to have admitted him.

The fourth question is, should the casualty officer have treated the deceased or caused him to be treated? And it is the case that, once admitted, the deceased's case could have gone to the medical registrar or to others if such was the desire. The immediate purpose of admission would be for observation and diagnosis. No one who has listened to the evidence can doubt that arsenical poisoning is extremely difficult to diagnose. Professor Camps accepted some figures put to him, which were that out of 6,000 deaths between 1955 and 1965 from poisoning only five were due to arsenical poisoning, and that of the 3,000,000–4,000,000 people admitted to about 5,000 hospitals in the course of a year, only 60 are cases of arsenical poisoning or potassium loss. I conclude that, after a period of observation and after taking the patient's blood pressure and subjecting him to other general tests, and upon a reconsideration of the history, in particular the fact that vomiting had occurred within 20 minutes of drinking the tea, and also finding loss of fluid, the doctor would have rejected the provisional diagnosis of

1 [1969] 1 QB 428.

food or staphylococcal poisoning and have decided that it might well have been a case of metallic poisoning. In any event, I am satisfied that the deceased's condition of dehydration and severe malaise was such that intravenous treatment should have been given. Further, I think it would have become plain that it was necessary to test a specimen of the deceased's blood and in the end to send certain other specimens away for analysis to discover what poison it was which was causing the deceased's condition.

Thus it is that I find that under all four headings the defendants were negligent and in breach of their duty in that they or their servants or agents did not see or examine and did not admit and did not treat the deceased.

It remains to consider whether it is shown that the deceased's death was caused by that negligence or whether, as the defendants have said, the deceased must have died in any event. In his concluding submission Mr Pain submitted that the casualty officer should have examined the deceased, and had he done so he would have caused tests to be made which would have indicated the treatment required, and that, since the defendants were at fault in these respects, therefore the onus of proof passed to the defendants to show that the appropriate treatment would have failed and authorities were cited to me. I find myself unable to accept that argument, and I am of the view that the onus of proof remains upon the plaintiff, and I have in mind (without quoting it) the decision cited by Mr Wilmers in *Bonnington Castings Ltd v Wardlaw* [1956] AC 613. However, were it otherwise and the onus did pass to the defendants, then I would find that they have discharged it, as I would proceed to show.

There has been put before me a timetable which I think is of much importance. The deceased attended at the casualty department at five or ten minutes past eight in the morning. If the casualty officer had got up and dressed and come to see the three men and examined them and decided to admit them, the deceased (and Dr Lockett agreed with this) could not have been in bed in a ward before 11 am. I accept Dr Goulding's evidence that an intravenous drip would not have been set up before 12 noon, and if potassium loss was suspected it could not have been discovered until 12.30 pm. Dr Lockett, dealing with this, said: 'If this man had not been treated until after 12 noon the chances of survival were not good.'

Without going in detail into the considerable volume of technical evidence which has been put before me, it seems to me to be the case that, when death results from arsenical poisoning it is brought about by two conditions: on the one hand dehydration and on the other disturbance of the enzyme processes. If the principal condition is one of enzyme disturbance – as I am of the view it was here – then the only method of treatment which is likely to succeed is the use of the specific antidote which is commonly called BAL. Dr Goulding said in the course of his evidence: 'The only way to deal with this is to use the specific BAL. I see no reasonable prospect of the deceased being given BAL before the time at which he died' – and at a later point in his evidence – 'I feel that, even if the fluid loss had been discovered, death would have been caused by the enzyme disturbance. Death might have occurred later'.

I regard that evidence as very moderate, and it might be a true assessment of the situation to say that there was no chance of BAL being administered before the death of the deceased.

For those reasons, I find that the plaintiff has failed to establish, on the balance of probabilities, that the defendants' negligence caused the death of the deceased.

The case is a graphic illustration of the point that, even if the defendant is shown to be careless, as was the case there, liability will only ensue if there is a causal link between the carelessness and the damage. The judge took the view that the deceased was going to die in any event whatever the casualty officer or others might have done. There can really be little complaint about this decision, but there has been criticism of the use of the 'but for' test in cases such as *McWilliams v Sir William Arrol & Co Ltd*.[2] Here the widow was claiming damages from her late husband's employers for failing to supply a safety belt when he was carrying out work as a steel erector. He fell to his death from a tower on which he was working at the time. The House decided against the widow on the basis that, even if a belt had been supplied, the deceased would not have worn it. Viscount Kilmuir commented:

> The evidence demonstrates to a high degree of probability that, if safety belts had been available, the deceased would, in any event, not have worn one. On this aspect the Lord Ordinary and the learned judges of the First Division found in favour of the respondents and rejected the appellant's contention. There were a number of witnesses, called for the appellant and for these respondents, with wide experience in structural steel operations including, in some instances, work on tower cranes such as that in which the deceased was engaged. The combined effect of evidence was that steel erectors never wear safety belts except in certain, very special, circumstances which do not include the erection of scaffolds for riveters on tower cranes. No witness deponed to having ever seen a safety belt worn in the course of such work, and there was ample evidence from these respondents' employees and from others that safety belts were not worn when such work was being carried out. ... There was overwhelming evidence that the deceased did not normally wear a safety belt, and in particular it was proved that he had been engaged in erecting riveters' scaffolds on the crane from which he fell, at heights greater than that from which he fell, and at times when safety belts were available, and that he had not on such occasions worn or asked for a safety belt. In my opinion, it was clearly open to a court to infer that the deceased would not have worn a safety belt even if it were available.
>
> Finally, it was submitted that if the deceased's hypothetical refusal to wear a safety belt must be recognised as the effective cause of his not wearing one and hence of his death, the failure of the respondents to provide a safety belt should not be ignored as a causative factor. The answer in my view must be that there are four steps of causation:
>
> (1) a duty to supply a safety belt;
>
> (2) a breach;
>
> (3) that, if there had been a safety belt the deceased would have used it; and
>
> (4) that, if there had been a safety belt the deceased would not have been killed.
>
> If the irresistible inference is that the deceased would not have worn a safety belt had it been available, then the first two steps in the chain of causation cease to operate.
>
> On the second submission, that the first respondents should have exhorted or instructed the deceased to use a safety belt, I considered carefully the argument based on the extent of the danger. I have, however, come to the conclusion that it fails. There was a strong feeling among steel erectors that safety belts were certainly cumbersome and might be dangerous except in very special circumstances which did not operate here.
>
> ... I would dismiss the appeal.

2 [1962] 1 WLR 295.

Viscount Simonds expressed his view as follows:

> My Lords, I do not doubt that it is part of the law of Scotland as it is part of the law of England that a causal connection must be established between a breach by an employer of his duty at common law or under a statute and the damage suffered by his employee: eg see *Bonnington Castings v Wardlaw*. If a contrary principle is thought to be established in *Roberts v Dorman Long & Co Ltd* [1953] 1 WLR 942. I cannot reconcile that case with *Wardlaw*. It may, however, be said that, where the employer is in breach of his duty, there is in that fact some *prima facie* evidence of a causal connection between the breach and the subsequent damage. So far in this case I would go with the appellant. It is the next step that I cannot take. For, it having been found as a fact by the Lord Ordinary, and their Lordships of the First Division having unanimously concurred in that finding, that it would be totally unrealistic to hold that the failure to provide a belt was the cause of the accident, the learned counsel for the appellant was driven to the argument that the evidence on which that finding was based was inadmissible or at any rate of no weight. This argument I cannot accept.
>
> The evidence showed conclusively that the deceased himself on this and similar jobs had, except on two special occasions (about which the evidence was doubted by the Lord Ordinary), persistently abstained from wearing a safety belt and that other steel erectors had adopted a similar attitude. Nor was their attitude irrational or foolhardy. They regarded belts as cumbersome and even dangerous and gave good reason for thinking so. It was, however, urged that, on this single occasion, the deceased might have changed his mind and that the respondents did not and could not prove that he had not done so.
>
> My Lords, I would agree that, just as a claim against a dead man's estate must always be jealously scrutinised, so also an inference unfavourable to him should not be drawn except upon a strong balance of probability. But there is justice to the living as well as to the dead, and it would be a denial of justice if the court thought itself bound to decide in favour of the deceased because he might, if living, have told a tale so improbable that it could convince nobody. That, my lords, is this case and in my opinion the courts below were amply justified in receiving the evidence given (not only by the respondents' witnesses) as to the attitude adopted by the deceased and other steelworkers to the wearing of belts and acting upon it. ...
>
> The appeal should, in my opinion, be dismissed.

Lord Reid, also in favour of dismissing the appeal, stated:

> It has been suggested that the decision of this House in *Bonnington Castings Ltd v Wardlaw* lays down new law and increases the burden on pursuers. I do not think so. It states what has always been the law – a pursuer must prove his case. He must prove that the fault of the defender caused, or contributed to, the danger which he has suffered. But proof need not be by direct evidence. If general practice or a regulation requires that some safety appliance shall be provided, one would assume that it is of some use, and that a reasonable man would use it. So the initial onus on the pursuer to connect the failure to provide the appliance with the accident would normally be discharged by proving the circumstances which led to the accident, and it is only where the evidence throws doubt on either of these assumptions that any difficulty would arise. Normally it would be left to the defender to adduce evidence, if he could, to displace these assumptions. So in practice it would be realistic, even if not theoretically accurate, to say that the onus is generally on the defender to show that the man would not have used the appliance even if it had been available. But in the end,

> when all the evidence has been brought out, it rarely matters where the onus originally lay, the question is which way the balance of probability has come to rest. ...
>
> I can find nothing to justify holding either that there ought to have been a general practice to exhort skilled and experienced steel erectors to use these belts, or that this man ought to have been specially urged to use a belt when doing work on this tower.

Lord Devlin, in dismissing the appeal, made the point that:

> This question of the burden of proof is frequently important when what is in issue is what a dead workman did. Without his evidence it may be difficult to prove that negligence by the employers was an effective cause of the death; once negligence is proved, the fact that the workman cannot be called to account for his actions often defeats the proof of contributory negligence. But in the present case the question is not what the deceased actually did but what he would have done in circumstances that never arose. Whether the workman is alive or dead, this cannot be proved positively as a matter of fact but can only be inferred as a matter of likelihood or probability. Even when the workman himself is perforce silent, there may be plenty of material, as there is in this case, from which an inference can be drawn one way or the other; and then the question of burden of proof is unimportant ... here the question is not what the deceased did but what he would have done. That is a matter incapable of direct proof; it must be a matter of inference. His statement about what he would have done, if he were alive to make it, is only one of the factors which the court would have to take into consideration in its task at arriving at the correct inference. A man's actions in the past may well be a safer guide than his own forecast of his action in the future.
>
> In my judgment, the courts below were right to receive and consider the evidence that the deceased had never used a safety belt in the past when it was available. That is material from which it is permissible to draw the inference that he probably would not have used one if it had been provided on the day of his death. I think also, though with more hesitation, that the courts below were right in considering for what it was worth the evidence of the general practice of steel erectors, though without some evidence of the deceased's attitude towards safety belts I do not think it would have been worth much.
>
> Undoubtedly a court should be very careful about finding what one may call hypothetical contributory negligence. A defendant, whose negligence has prevented the matter in issue from being put directly to the proof, must expect that a court will be very careful to make sure that it is acting upon legitimate inference and not upon speculation. But in the present case the evidence, even if it were confined to the deceased's own past acts, is in my opinion conclusive. If he had been injured only by the fall and could have gone into the witness-box, and if he had there sworn that he would have been wearing a safety belt if one had been available that morning, I do not see how he could have been believed.

The case has been heavily criticised for the very point that some of their Lordships recognised that they were engaging in a highly speculative guessing game, whereas there were two obvious certainties. One was that the victim was dead and the second was that the employers had definitely not provided any safety belt on this occasion.

There are a number of other difficult issues which arise in the attempt to employ the 'but for' test.

The extent of the harm

The defendant is only to be held liable to the extent that his fault caused harm or further harm to the plaintiff. A useful illustration of this is provided by the case of *Performance Cars Ltd v Abraham*.[3] The defendant negligently damaged the plaintiff's Rolls Royce causing damage to its front wing. To satisfactorily make good the damage it was necessary to re-spray the lower half of the vehicle. The vehicle, however, had been involved in an earlier accident which also necessitated a similar re-spray which had not as yet been done. The Court of Appeal found for the defendant on this issue. Lord Evershed's judgment contained the following discussion:

> The fact in the present case is that the defendant struck a motor car already damaged, the damage including the necessity in any case of re-spraying the whole of the lower part of the body. The case is, to my mind, rendered less easy because the re-spraying is something special to the character of this particular and rather luxurious motor car. But the principle, as it seems to me, is the same as that applicable to the example stated by my brother Donovan in the course of the argument. Suppose a man wrongfully damages my motor car by splintering part of the windscreen so that, as the inevitable result, I must have a new windscreen, the cost of which is damage properly flowing from the wrongful act I have suffered. Then, suppose that before my windscreen has in fact been replaced, if you will, while I am driving my motor car to the place where the new windscreen is to be fitted, another wrongdoer strikes my car and splinters another part of my windscreen. If the plaintiffs are right, it must follow that I can claim, if I have not already actually recovered from the first wrongdoer, the cost of replacing the windscreen from the second. And the same result would, as it seems to me, follow if the first damage to my windscreen had been my own fault or if, in the present case, the plaintiffs had by their own fault damaged the back of their Rolls Royce motor car.
>
> I do not multiply examples but I have in the end felt compelled to the conclusion that the necessity for re-spraying was not the result of the defendant's wrongdoing because that necessity already existed. The Rolls Royce, when the defendant struck it, was in a condition which already required that it should be re-sprayed in any event.

The other two judges agreed with the above analysis.

In *Cutler v Vauxhall Motors Ltd*[4] the Court of Appeal applied similar reasoning to a personal injury case. The plaintiff sustained a graze on his right ankle as a result of the negligence of his employers. He was found to have a pre-existing varicose vein condition which would probably have required operating on some five years in the future. However, as a result of the graze, the operation had to be performed more or less immediately. The plaintiff claimed the loss of wages whilst undergoing the operation and for the discomfort involved in the operation. The majority of the Court of Appeal rejected this part of his claim. Edmund Davies LJ commented:

> The issue, then, is whether such financial loss as has accrued can in no circumstances be affected by looking into the future. In most cases such a

3 [1962] 2 QB 33.

4 [1970] 2 All ER 56.

> question does not arise, and it has become the convenient practice, where damages for personal injuries are claimed, to divide them into (a) special and (b) general damages. The former include accrued and ascertained financial loss and these have to be expressly pleaded, while the prospect of future financial loss forms part of general damages. But the task confronting the court is the comprehensive one of assessing the *totality* of damages to be awarded, even though it performs it in stages. In doing so, the court is undoubtedly entitled to have regard to circumstances which have arisen between the accident and the trial – indeed, it must. Thus, it has to bear in mind that unemployment in the industry might have prevented the injured plaintiff from earning all the wages claimed to have already been lost (*Rouse v Port of London Authority* [1953] 2 Lloyd's Rep 179). ... In the same way, it is required to have regard to future contingencies. Accordingly, the defendant may call evidence to establish that the plaintiff's prospects of future uninterrupted employment at the same wages were precarious, owing to his poor state of health or to uncertain industrial conditions. This forward-looking is essential if the court is to perform its task of taking into account the actual consequences which have resulted from the tort. ...
>
> Why, then, should the court be prevented from adverting to future probabilities when considering whether the plaintiff is entitled to recover, under his general claim for 'damages', financial loss which at the date of trial he had undoubtedly sustained? There being no reasonable grounds for regarding as probable in the present case that the plaintiff would die before 1970 or 1971 (he has certainly survived until 1970), or that for any other reason he would not then lose, as a result of the inevitable operation, a sum at least equivalent to £173, on what legal principle should the defendants be made liable to pay that sum? ... On the known facts, were the plaintiff held entitled to recover the £173 presently lost, the result would be that the defendants would be recouping him for a loss which, had there been no accident at all, in all probability he would himself have been obliged to bear. While the point is a novel one, on principle I do not think that their liability to do this has been established.

Karminski LJ stated:

> What has to be ascertained here are the actual consequences to the plaintiff of the defendants' wrongdoing. There can be no doubt that one consequence, and an immediate one, was the graze to his right ankle. The damage so caused by the graze was valued by the judge at £10. Taken in isolation, this sum cannot be criticised as too small; but the graze set off a varicose condition in both legs which required surgical treatment. The varicose condition was in existence before the accident, and would have required surgical treatment in any event in the foreseeable future. The accident merely advanced the date of the operation.
>
> The immediate result of the operation was to cost the plaintiff £173 in lost wages, and at first impression there is much to be said in favour of his being compensated for the loss; but on consideration I have come to the conclusion that it would be wrong to ignore the strong probability on the evidence that in any event this loss was inevitable, though at a later date. To ignore this probability would be to put the plaintiff ... in a better position than he was before the wrong.

Russell LJ dissented as follows:

> I do not consider that the probability that the plaintiff would have undergone the same operation four or five years later exempts the defendants from all liability for damages for pain and suffering attributable to the operation. I do not think that it is a correct approach to say that on a balance of probabilities this would have happened some years later anyway. The pain and suffering of the operation is a certainty caused by the tort; the saving from the same operation in the future

> is only a probability, albeit a strong probability. Giving to the matter the best consideration that I can, I think that there should be a very considerable but not total offset against the damages for pain and suffering, but I do not think that this offset should leave the plaintiff with less than £100 under the head of general damages for pain and suffering in addition to the £10.

There is much force on Russell LJ's point about the certainty created by the defendant's negligence and that his approach of discounting for future contingencies rather than the all or nothing approach of the other two judges is the preferred method.

Successive causes

The inadequacy of the 'but for' test is plain for all to see in situations where the plaintiff has suffered two separate injuries, the one succeeding the other. This is perhaps best illustrated by looking at two House of Lords' decisions where this issue was fully ventilated. The first of these is *Baker v Willoughby*[5] where the plaintiff sustained an injury to his leg in an accident for which the defendant was liable, subject to some contributory negligence. Subsequent to the accident, but before the hearing of the action against the defendant, the plaintiff was shot in the same leg during an armed robbery and the leg had to be amputated more or less immediately. The issue before the House was whether the subsequent loss of the leg had to be taken into account, thus reducing the plaintiff's damages against the defendant. The leading judgment was given by Lord Reid:

> The appellant argues that the loss which he suffered from the car accident has not been diminished by his second injury. He still suffers the same kind of loss of the amenities of life and he still suffers from reduced capacity to earn, though these may have been to some extent increased. And he will still suffer these losses for as long as he would have done because it is not said that the second injury curtailed his expectation of life.
>
> The respondent on the other hand argues that the second injury removed the very limb from which the earlier disability had stemmed, and that therefore no loss suffered thereafter can be attributed to the respondent's negligence. He says that the second injury submerged or obliterated the effect of the first and that all loss thereafter must be attributed to the second injury. The trial judge rejected this argument which he said was more ingenious than attractive. But it was accepted by the Court of Appeal.
>
> The respondent's argument was succinctly put to your Lordships by his counsel. He could not run before the second injury; he cannot run now. But the cause is now quite different. The former cause was an injured leg but now he has no leg and the former cause can no longer operate. His counsel was inclined to agree that, if the first injury had caused some neurosis or other mental disability, that disability might be regarded as still flowing from the first accident. Even if it had been increased by the second accident the respondent might still have to pay for that part which he caused. I agree with that, and I think that any distinction between a neurosis and a physical injury depends on a wrong view of what is the proper subject for compensation. A man is not compensated for the physical injury; he is compensated for the loss which he suffers as a result of that injury. His loss is not in having a stiff leg; it is in his inability to lead a full life, his

5 [1970] AC 467.

inability to enjoy those amenities which depend on freedom of movement and his inability to earn as much as he used to earn or could have earned if there had been no accident. In this case the second injury did not diminish any of these. So why should it be regarded as having obliterated or superseded them?

If it were the case that in the eye of the law an effect could only have one cause, then the respondent might be right. It is always necessary to prove that any loss for which damages can be given was caused by the defendant's negligent act. But it is a commonplace that the law regards many events as having two causes; that happens whenever there is contributory negligence, for then the law says that the injury was caused both by the negligence of the defendant and by the negligence of the plaintiff. And generally it does not matter which negligence occurred first in point of time.

... In the present case the robber is not responsible or liable for the damage caused by the respondent; he would only have to pay for additional loss to the appellant by reason of his now having an artificial limb instead of a stiff leg

It is argued – if a man's death before the trial reduces the damages, why do injuries which he has received before the trial not also reduce the damages? I think it depends on the nature and result of the later injuries. Suppose that, but for the first injuries, the plaintiff could have looked forward to 20 years of working life and that the injuries inflicted by the defendant reduced his earning capacity. Then, but for the later injuries, the plaintiff would have recovered for loss of earning capacity during 20 years. And then suppose that later injuries were such that, at the date of trial, his expectation of life had been reduced to two years. Then he could not claim for 20 years of loss of earning capacity because in fact he will only suffer loss of earning capacity for two years. Thereafter he will be dead and the defendant could not be required to pay for a loss which it is now clear that the plaintiff will in fact never suffer. But that is not this case; here the appellant will continue to suffer from the disabilities caused by the car accident for as long as he would have done if his leg had never been shot and amputated.

If the later injury suffered before the date of the trial either reduces the disabilities from the injury for which the defendant is liable, or shortens the period during which they will be suffered by the plaintiff, then the defendant will have to pay less damages. But if the later injuries merely become a concurrent cause of the disabilities caused by the injury inflicted by the defendant, then in my view they cannot diminish the damages. Suppose that the plaintiff has to spend a month in bed before the trial because of some illness unconnected with the original injury, the defendant cannot say that he does not have to pay anything in respect of that month. During that month the original injuries and the new illness are concurrent causes of his inability to work and that does not reduce the damages. ...

I would allow the appeal and restore the judgment of Donaldson J.

Lord Pearson also made some valuable comments:

There is a plausible argument for the defendant on the following lines. The original accident, for which the defendant is liable, inflicted on the plaintiff a permanently injured left ankle, which caused pain from time to time, diminished his mobility and so reduced his earning capacity, and was likely to lead to arthritis. The proper figure of damages for those consequences of the accident, as assessed by the judge before making his apportionment, was £1,600. That was the proper figure for those consequences if they were likely to endure for a normal period and run a normal course. But the supervening event, when the robbers shot the plaintiff in his left leg necessitated an amputation of the left leg above the knee. The consequences of the original accident therefore have ceased.

He no longer suffers pain in his left ankle, because there no longer is a left ankle. He will never have arthritis. There is no longer any loss of mobility through stiffness or weakness of the left ankle, because it is no longer there. The injury to the left ankle, resulting from the original accident, is not still operating as one of two concurrent causes both producing discomfort and disability. It is not operating at all nor causing anything. The present state of disablement, with the stump and the artificial leg on the left side, was caused wholly by the supervening event and not at all by the original accident. Thus the consequences of the original accident have been submerged and obliterated by the greater consequences of the supervening event.

That is the argument, and it is formidable. But it must not be allowed to succeed, because it produces manifest injustice. The supervening event has not made the plaintiff less lame nor less disabled nor less deprived of amenities. It has not shortened the period over which he will be suffering. It has made him more lame, more disabled, more deprived of amenities. He should not have less damages through being worse off than might have been expected.

The nature of the injustice becomes apparent if the supervening event is treated as a tort (as indeed it was) and if one envisages the plaintiff suing the robbers who shot him. They would be entitled, as the saying is, to 'take the plaintiff as they find him' (*Performance Cars Ltd v Abraham* [1962] 1 QB 33). They have not injured and disabled a previously fit and able-bodied man. They have only made an already lame and disabled man more lame and more disabled. Take, for example, the reduction of earnings. The original accident reduced his earnings from £x per week to £y per week, and the supervening event further reduced them from £y per week to £z per week. If the defendant's argument is correct, there is, as Mr Griffiths pointed out, a gap. The plaintiff recovers from the defendant the £x–y, not for the whole period of the remainder of his working life, but only for the short period up to the date of the supervening event. The robbers are liable only for the £y–z from the date of the supervening event onwards. In the Court of Appeal an ingenious attempt was made to fill the gap by holding that the damages recoverable from the later tortfeasors (the robbers) would include a novel head of damage, *viz* the diminution of the plaintiff's damages recoverable from the original tortfeasor (the defendant). I doubt whether that would be an admissible head of damage; it looks too remote. In any case it would not help the plaintiff, if the later tortfeasors could not be found or were indigent and uninsured. These later tortfeasors cannot have been insured in respect of the robbery which they committed.

I think a solution of the theoretical problem can be found in cases such as this by taking a comprehensive and unitary view of the damage caused by the original accident. Itemisation of the damages by dividing them into heads and sub-heads is often convenient, but is not essential. In the end judgment is given for a single lump sum of damages and not for a total of items set out under heads and sub-heads. The original accident caused what may be called a 'devaluation' of the plaintiff, in the sense that it produced a general reduction of his capacity to do things, to earn money and to enjoy life. For that devaluation the original tortfeasor should be and remain responsible to the full extent, unless before the assessment of the damages something has happened which either diminishes the devaluation (eg if there is an unexpected recovery from some of the adverse effects of the accident) or by shortening the expectation of life diminishes the period over which the plaintiff will suffer from the devaluation. If the supervening event is a tort, the second tortfeasor should be responsible for the additional devaluation caused by him. ...

> I would allow the appeal and restore the judgment of Donaldson J both in respect of the total amount of the damages and in respect of the apportionment.

The other three judges agreed with Lord Reid. The above must be sharply contrasted with the approach taken in the other case. In *Jobling v Associated Dairies Ltd*[6] the plaintiff suffered an accident at work as a result of the defendant's negligence. He sustained a serious back injury and claimed, by way of general damages, loss of future earnings. Before the trial took place it was found that the plaintiff was suffering from a condition not connected to the accident which would render him totally disabled within a few months. The issue before the House of Lords was whether the fact of the disability arising from natural causes was to be taken into account in relation to that part of the claim concerned with future loss of earnings. We shall consider an extract from Lord Wilberforce's judgment first of all:

> In an attempt to solve the present case, and similar cases of successive causes of incapacity according to some legal principle, a number of arguments have been invoked.
>
> 1 Causation arguments – The unsatisfactory character of these is demonstrated by *Baker v Willoughby* [1970] AC 467. I think that it can now be seen that Lord Reid's theory of concurrent causes, even if workable on the particular facts of *Baker v Willoughby* (where successive injuries were sustained by the same limb), is as a general solution not supported by the authority he invokes ... nor workable in other cases. I shall not enlarge upon this point in view of its more than sufficient treatment in other opinions.
>
> 2 The 'vicissitudes' argument – This is that, since, according to accepted doctrine, allowance – and if necessary some discount – has to be made in assessing loss of future earnings for the normal contingencies of life, amongst which 'illness' is normally enumerated, so, if one of these contingencies becomes actual before the date of trial, this actuality must be taken into account. Reliance is here placed on the apophthegm 'the court should not speculate when it knows'. This argument has a good deal of attraction, but it has its difficulties; it raises at once the question whether a discount is to be made on account of all possible 'vicissitudes', or only on account of 'non-culpable' vicissitudes (ie such that if they occur there will be no cause of action against anyone, the theory being that the prospect of being injured by a tort is not a normally foreseeable vicissitude) or only on account of 'culpable' vicissitudes (such as *per contra*). And, if this distinction is to be made, how is the court to act when a discounted vicissitude happens before trial? Must it attempt to decide whether there was culpability or not? And how is it to do this if, as is likely, the alleged culprit is not before it?
>
> ... In spite of these difficulties, the 'vicissitude' argument is capable in some, perhaps many cases, of providing a workable and reasonably just rule, and I would certainly not discountenance its use, either in the present case or in others.
>
> The fact, however, is that, to attempt a solution of these and similar problems, where there are successive causes of incapacity in some degree, upon classical lines ('the object of damages for tort is to place the plaintiff in as good as if', etc ... 'the defendant must compensate for the loss caused by his wrongful act no more' – 'the defendant must take the plaintiff as he finds him', etc) is, in many cases, no longer possible. We do not live in a world governed by the pure common law

6 [1982] AC 794.

and its logical rules. We live in a mixed world where a man is protected against misfortune by a whole web of rules and dispositions, with a number of timid legislative interventions. To attempt to compensate him upon the basis of selected rules without regard to the whole must lead to logical inconsistencies, or to over, or under, compensation.

... In the present, and in other, industrial injury cases, there seems to me no justification for disregarding the fact that the injured man's employer is insured – indeed since 1972 compulsorily insured – against liability to his employees. The state has decided, in other words, on a spreading of risk. There seems to me no more justification for disregarding the fact that the plaintiff – presumably, we have not been told otherwise – is entitled to sickness and invalidity benefit in respect of his myelopathy, the amount of which may depend on his contribution record, which in turn may have been affected by his accident. So we have no means of knowing whether the plaintiff would be over-compensated if he were, in addition, to receive the assessed damages from his employer, or whether he would be under-compensated if left to his benefit. It is not easy to accept a solution by which a partially incapacitated man becomes worse off in terms of damages and benefit through a greater degree of incapacity. Many other ingredients, of weight in either direction, may enter into individual cases. Without any satisfaction I draw from this conclusion that no general, logical or universally fair rule can be stated which will cover, in a manner consistent with justice, cases of supervening events whether due to tortious, non-culpable or wholly accidental events.

The courts can only deal with each case as best they can in a manner so as to provide just and sufficient but not excessive compensation, taking all factors into account. I think that this is what *Baker v Willoughby* did – and indeed Lord Pearson reached his decision in this way: the rationalisation of the decision as to which I at least have doubts, need and should not be applied to other cases. In the present case the Court of Appeal reached the unanswerable conclusion that to apply *Baker v Willoughby* to the facts of the present case would produce an unjust result, and I am willing to accept the corollary that justice, so far as it can be perceived, lies the other way and that the supervening myelopathy should not be disregarded. If rationalisation is needed, I am willing to accept the 'vicissitudes' argument as the best available. I should be more firmly convinced of the merits of the conclusion if the whole pattern of benefits had been considered, in however general a way. The result of the present case may be lacking in precision and rational justification, but so long as we are content to live in a mansion of so many different architectures, this is inevitable.

I would dismiss the appeal.

Lord Edmund Davies commented:

My Lords, it is a truism that cases of cumulative causation of damage can present problems of great complexity. I can formulate no convincing juristic or logical principles supportive of this House in *Baker v Willoughby* [1970] AC 467, and none were there propounded.

Abandoning the search for logical principles and adverting solely to questions of policy, it may therefore be that *Baker v Willoughby* is acceptable on its own facts. ...

What is clear is that where, as in the present appeal, the question in issue relates to the assessment of damages when, a tort having been committed, the victim is overtaken before trial by a wholly unconnected and disabling illness, the decision in *Baker v Willoughby* [1970] AC 467, has no application. Your Lordships are therefore untrammelled by precedent. The effect of the Court of Appeal's

> decision is that no considerations of policy warrant the imposition on the respondent of liability for the loss of earnings after the emergence of myelopathy. That is in accordance with the long-established and eminently reasonable principle that the onset of illness is one of the vicissitudes of life relevant to the assessment of damages. And it is of some interest to note that this view was evidently shared at all stages by learned counsel for the plaintiff in *Baker v Willoughby* itself, and had been anticipated as long ago as 1961 by Glanville Williams ([1961] CLJ 62, 76). I believe the Court of Appeal decision was entirely correct, and I would dismiss the appeal.

Lord Russell was also in favour of dismissing the appeal, commenting on the 'vicissitudes' argument as follows:

> My Lords, it is well established that, in assessing compensation for damage caused to a plaintiff by a tortfeasor, among other considerations is the consequent loss or reduction in earning capacity in the working life of the plaintiff. It is also well established that it is appropriate, in arriving at an estimated figure under that head, that some allowance or discount should be made for the ordinary vicissitudes of life. It is also well established that, if by the time of trial, facts emerge which make known a vicissitude of life as applicable to the plaintiff, that knowledge should replace that which would have been only an estimate; where there is knowledge estimation has no part.

Lord Keith, for his part, launched an attack on *Baker v Willoughby* in the following terms:

> It is implicit in that decision that the scope of the 'vicissitudes' principle is limited to supervening events of such a nature as either to reduce the disabilities resulting from the accident or else to shorten the period during which they will be suffered. I am of opinion that failure to consider or even advert to this implication weakens the authority of the *ratio decidendi* of the case, and must lead to the conclusion that in its full breadth it is not acceptable. The assessment of damages for personal injuries involves a process of *restitutio in integrum*. The object is to place the injured plaintiff in as a good a position as he would have been in but for the accident. He is not to be placed in a better position. The process involves a comparison between the plaintiff's circumstances as regards capacity to enjoy the amenities of life and to earn a living as they would have been if the accident had not occurred, and his actual circumstances in those respects following the accident. In considering how matters might have been expected to turn out if there had been no accident, the 'vicissitudes' principle says that it is right to take into account events, such as illness, which not uncommonly occur in the ordinary course of human life. If such events are not taken into account, the damages may be greater than are required to compensate the plaintiff for the effects of the accident, and that result would be unfair to the defendant.
>
> Counsel for the appellant sought to draw a distinction between the case where the plaintiff, at the time of the tortious injury, is already suffering from a latent undetected condition which later develops into a disabling illness, and the case where the inception of the illness occurs wholly at a later date. In the former case, so it was maintained, the illness would properly fall to be taken into account in diminution of damages, upon the principle that the tortfeasor takes his victim as he finds him, but in the latter case it would not. There is no trace of the suggested distinction in any of authorities, and in my opinion it is unsound and apt to lead to great practical difficulties, providing ample scope for disputation among medical men. What would be the position, it might be asked, of an individual

having a constitutional weakness making him specially prone to illness generally, or an hereditary tendency to some specific disease.

I am therefore of opinion that the majority in *Baker v Willoughby* were mistaken in approaching the problems common to the case of a supervening tortious act and to that of supervening illness wholly from the point of view of causation. While it is logically correct to say that, in both cases, the original tort and the supervening event may be concurrent causes of incapacity, that does not necessarily, in my view, provide the correct solution. In the case of supervening illness, it is appropriate to keep in view that this is one of the ordinary vicissitudes of life, and when one is comparing the situation resulting from the accident with the situation had there been no accident, to recognise that the illness would have overtaken the plaintiff in any event, so that it cannot be disregarded in arriving at proper compensation, and no more than proper compensation.

Additional considerations come into play when dealing with the problems arising where the plaintiff has suffered injuries from two or more successive and independent tortious acts. In that situation it is necessary to secure that the plaintiff is fully compensated for the aggregate effects of all his injuries. As Lord Pearson noted in *Baker v Willoughby* it would clearly be unjust to reduce the damages awarded for the first tort because of the occurrence of the second tort, damages for which are to be assessed on the basis that the plaintiff is already partially incapacitated. I do not consider it necessary to formulate any precise juristic basis for dealing with this situation differently from the case of supervening illness. It might be said that a supervening tort is not one of the ordinary vicissitudes of life, or that it is too remote a possibility to be taken into account, or that it can properly be disregarded because it carries its own remedy.

None of these formulations, however, is entirely satisfactory. The fact remains that the principle of full compensation requires that a just and practical solution should be found. In the event that damages against two successive tortfeasors fall to be assessed at the same time, it would be highly unreasonable if the aggregate of both awards were less than the total loss suffered by the plaintiff. The computation should start from an assessment of that total loss. The award against the second tortfeasor cannot in fairness to him fail to recognise that the plaintiff whom he injured was already, to some extent, incapacitated. In order that the plaintiff may be fully compensated, it becomes necessary to deduct the award so calculated from the assessment of the plaintiff's total loss and award the balance against the first tortfeasor. If that be the correct approach, it follows that, in proceedings against the first tortfeasor alone, the occurrence of the second tort cannot be successfully relied on by the defendant as reducing the damages which he must pay. That, in substance, was the result of the decision in *Baker v Willoughby*, where the supervening event was a tortious act, and to that extent the decision was, in my view, correct.

Before leaving the case, it is right to face up to the fact that, if a non-tortious supervening event is to have the effect of reducing damages but a subsequent tortious act is not, there may in some cases be difficulty in ascertaining whether the event in question is or is not of a tortious character, particularly in the absence of the alleged tortfeasor. Possible questions of contributory negligence may cause additional complications. Such difficulties are real, but are not sufficient, in my view, to warrant the conclusion that the distinction between tortious and non-tortious supervening events should not be accepted. The court must simply do its best to arrive at a just assessment of damages in a pragmatic way in the light of the whole circumstances of the case.

My Lords, for these reasons I would dismiss the appeal.

Lord Bridge added his weight to the debate as follows:

> The vicissitudes principle itself, it seems to me, stems from the fundamental proposition of law that the object of every award of damages for monetary loss is to put the party wronged so far as possible in the same position, no better and no worse, as he would be in if he had not suffered the wrong in respect of which he claims. To assume that an injured plaintiff, if not injured, would have continued to earn his full wages for a full working life, is very probably to over-compensate him. To apply a discount, in respect of possible future loss of earnings, arising from independent causes, may under-compensate him. When confronted by future uncertainty, the court assesses the prospects and strikes a balance between these opposite dangers as best it can. But when the supervening illness or injury which is the independent cause of loss of earning capacity has manifested itself before trial, the event has demonstrated that, even if the plaintiff had never sustained the tortious injury, his earnings would now be reduced or extinguished. To hold the tortfeasor, in this situation, liable to pay damages for a notional continuing loss of earnings attributable to the tortious injury, is to put the plaintiff in a better position than he would be in if he had never suffered the tortious injury. Put more shortly, applying well-established principles for the assessment of damages at common law, when a plaintiff injured by the defendant's tort is wholly incapacitated from earning by supervening illness or accidental injury, the law will no longer treat the tort as a continuing cause of any loss of earning capacity. ...
>
> Having reached the conclusion that the *ratio decidendi* of *Baker's* case [1970] AC 467 cannot be sustained, it remains to consider whether the case should still be regarded as authority, as a decision on its own facts for the proposition that, when two successive injuries are both caused tortiously, the supervening disability caused by the second tort should, by way of exception to the general rule arising from the application of the vicissitudes principle, be disregarded when assessing the liability of the first tortfeasor for damages for loss of earnings caused by the first tort. I find it difficult to attribute such authority to the decision, when both the Court of Appeal and this House were expressly invited to adopt that proposition, and both, in different ways, declined the invitation. There is a powerful, perhaps irresistible, attraction in the argument that, in the circumstances envisaged, the aggregate of the damages recoverable by the plaintiff, should, provided both tortfeasors can be found and can meet their liability, be sufficient to cover the aggregate loss of earnings, past and future, which results from the combined effect of both injuries. But whether this end is properly achieved as between the two tortfeasors, by apportioning liability on the principle which commended itself to the Court of Appeal, or on the principle for which Mr Griffiths contended in argument, seems to me a very difficult question. ... In these circumstances, the proper conclusion seems to me to be that the question should remain open for decision on another occasion, if and when it arises.
>
> However that may be, for the reasons indicated earlier in this speech, I would dismiss the appeal.

The precise status of *Baker* is not clear from these judgments. What is clear is that the normal 'vicissitudes' argument is to hold sway where there is a tort followed by a supervening incapacity brought about by a non-tortious event. Whether the distinction between tortious and non-tortious events is a valid one is open to some doubt.

Multiple causes

A classic illustration of the lack of sophistication inherent in the 'but for' test is to be found in what Howarth describes as the 'two hunter' problem.[7] It does not appear to be a problem which has so far troubled the English courts but there have been cases in other jurisdictions. A and B are out hunting and both fire shots, one of which hits the plaintiff. It is not possible to say whose bullet hit the plaintiff. The 'but for' test does not help, nor would it help if both bullets hit the plaintiff and it is clear that both inflicted what would have been fatal injuries each in their own right. Applying the 'but for' and balance of probability tests results in the plaintiff failing in these types of situation. Often, however, the courts resolve this issue in favour of the plaintiff.[8] Where the plaintiff is only struck by one bullet, to make both defendants liable means making a mistake against one of them. However, to deny the plaintiff a claim in such circumstances involves the court in making two mistakes, one in favour of the defendant whose actual bullet struck the plaintiff and one against the plaintiff himself, because after all someone's bullet did strike him. The court is thus choosing the lesser of the two evils. Where the victim is struck fatal blows by both bullets, a finding against both defendants is not unfair because they are both at fault.

Proof of causation

Another extremely difficult area where there is much conflicting opinion is that in relation to the proof of causation. There are some complex cases on this issue. The starting point would appear to be the awkward case of *McGhee v National Coal Board*.[9] The plaintiff, an employee of the defendants, was working in their brick kilns and was exposed to brick dust. The defendants provided no washing facilities and the plaintiff used to cycle home covered in the dust. After working in the kilns for a short spell the plaintiff was found to be suffering from dermatitis and the evidence showed that the fact that after work the plaintiff was cycling home covered in the dust added materially to the risk that he might contract the disease. We shall consider Lord Reid's comments first of all:

> It has always been the law that a pursuer succeeds if he can show that fault of the defender caused or materially contributed to his injury. There may have been two separate causes but it is enough if one of the causes arose from fault of the defender. The pursuer does not have to prove that this cause would of itself have been enough to cause him injury. That is well illustrated by the decision of this House in *Bonnington Castings v Wardlaw*.[10] There the pursuer's disease was caused by an accumulation of noxious dust in his lungs. The dust which he inhaled over a period came from two sources. The defenders were not responsible for one source but they could and ought to have prevented the other. The dust from the latter source was not in itself sufficient to cause the disease but the pursuer succeeded because it made a material contribution to his injury. The respondents seek to distinguish *Wardlaw's* case by arguing that then it was

7 At pp 94–95.

8 See Howarth, p 95 and *Cook v Lewis* [1952] 1 DLR 1.

9 [1972] 3 All ER 1008.

10 [1956] 1 All ER 615, [1956] AC 613.

proved that every particle of dust inhaled played its part in causing the onset of the disease, whereas in this case it is not proved that every minor abrasion played its part.

In the present case the evidence does not show – perhaps no one knows – just how dermatitis of this type begins. It suggests to me that there are two possible ways. It may be that an accumulation of minor abrasions of the horny layer of skin is a necessary precondition for the onset of the disease. Or it may be that the disease starts at one particular abrasion and then spreads, so that multiplication of abrasions merely increases the number of places where the disease can start and in that way increases the risk of its occurrence.

I am inclined to think that the evidence points to the former view. But in a field where so little appears to be known with certainty I could not say that that is proved. If it were, then this case would be indistinguishable from *Wardlaw's* case. But I think that in cases like this we must take a broader view of causation. The medical evidence is to the effect that the fact that the man had to cycle home caked with grime and sweat added materially to the risk that this disease might develop. It does not and could not explain just why this is so. But experience shows that it is so. Plainly that must be because what happens while the man remains unwashed can have a causative effect, although just how the cause operates is uncertain. I cannot accept the view expressed in the Inner House that once the man left the brick kiln he left behind the causes which made him liable to develop dermatitis. That seems to me quite inconsistent with a proper interpretation of the medical evidence. Nor can I accept the distinction drawn by the Lord Ordinary between materially increasing the risk that the disease will occur and making a material contribution to its occurrence.

There may be some logical ground for such a distinction where our knowledge of all the material factors is complete. But it has often been said that the legal concept of causation is not based on logic or philosophy. It is based on the practical way in which the ordinary man's mind works in the everyday affairs of life. From a broad and practical viewpoint I can see no substantial difference between saying that what the respondents did materially increased the risk of injury to the appellant, and saying that what the respondents did made a material contribution to his injury.

I would therefore allow this appeal.

Lord Wilberforce had some important points to make in his judgment as follows:

The Lord Ordinary, while finding that the respondents were at fault in not providing shower baths for their men who, like the appellant, worked under hot and dusty conditions in the kilns, yet dismissed the appellant's claim because he was not satisfied that the appellant had shown, on the balance of probabilities, that this breach of duty caused or materially contributed to his injury. This reasoning was approved by the First Division. In order to evaluate it, it is necessary to amplify the findings and inferences.

In the first place, the holding that there was a breach of duty by the respondents was founded on the evidence of the appellant's medical expert that washing by shower baths is the only method of any practical use by which the risk of dermatitis, in the relevant conditions, can be reduced. Possible damaging agents, the doctor said, should be removed as soon as possible: washing is standard practice in all industrial medicine. The respondents must, from their experience with occupations involving the production of dust, have been aware of this, and as one would expect, there were showers available at the nearby Prestongrange Colliery which men on the kilns could use until the colliery was closed in 1963.

There was, therefore, a solid basis for a finding that showers ought to have been provided. It was inherent in this finding that the employers should have foreseen that, unless showers were available at the place of work, there would be an increased risk of dermatitis occurring.

But it was not enough for the appellant to establish a duty or breach of it. To succeed in his claim he had to satisfy the court that a causal connection existed between the default and the disease complained of, ie according to the formula normally used, that the breach of duty caused or materially contributed to the injury. Here two difficulties arose. In the first place, little is known as to the exact causes of dermatitis. The experts could say that it tends to be caused by a breakdown of the layer of heavy skin covering the nerve ends provoked by friction caused by dust, but had to admit that they knew little of the quantity of dust or the time of exposure necessary to cause a critical change. Secondly, there could be little doubt that the appellant's dermatitis resulted from a combination, or accumulation, of two causes: exposure to dust while working in hot conditions in the kiln; and the subsequent omission to wash thoroughly before leaving the place of work. The second of these, but not the first, was, on the findings, attributable to the fault of the respondents. The appellant's expert was unable to attribute the injury to the second of these causes for he could not say that, if the appellant had been able to wash off the dust by showers, he would not have contracted the disease. He could not do more than say that the failure to provide showers materially increased the chance, or risk, that dermatitis might set in.

My lords, I agree with the judge below to the extent that, merely to show that a breach of duty increases the risk of harm is not, *in abstracto*, enough to enable the pursuer to succeed. He might, on this basis, still be met by successful defences. Thus, it was open to the respondents, while admitting, or being unable to contest that their failure had increased the risk, to prove, if they could, as they tried to do, that the appellant's dermatitis was 'non-occupational'.

But the question remains whether a pursuer must necessarily fail if, after he has shown a breach of duty, involving an increase of risk of disease, he cannot positively prove that this increase of risk caused or materially contributed to the disease while his employers cannot positively prove to the contrary. In this intermediate case there is an appearance of logic in the view that the pursuer, on whom the onus lies, should fail – a logic which dictated the judgments below. The question is whether we should be satisfied in factual situations like the present, with this logical approach. In my opinion, there are further considerations of importance. First, it is a sound principle that, where a person has, by breach of duty of care, created a risk and injury occurs within that area of risk, the loss should be borne by him unless he shows that it had some other cause. Secondly, from the evidential point of view one may ask, why should a man who is able to show that his employer should have taken certain precautions, because without them there is a risk, or an added risk, of injury or disease, and who in fact sustains exactly that injury or disease, have to assume the burden of proving more; namely, that it was the addition to the risk, caused by the breach of duty, which caused or materially contributed to the injury?

In many cases of which the present is typical, this is impossible to prove, just because honest medical opinion cannot segregate the causes of an illness between compound causes. And if one asks which of the parties, the workman or the employers should suffer from this inherent evidential difficulty, the answer as a matter of policy or justice should be that it is the creator of the risk who, *ex hypothesi*, must be taken to have foreseen the possibility of damage, who should bear its consequences.

There are analogies in this field of industrial disease. In cases concerned with pneumoconiosis, the courts faced with a similar, although not identical, evidential gap, have bridged it by having regard to the risk situation of the pursuer. Pneumoconiosis being a disease brought on by cumulative exposure to dust particles, the courts have held that where the exposure was to a compound aggregate of 'faulty' particles and 'innocent' particles, the workman should recover, so long as the addition of the 'faulty' particles (ie those produced by some fault of the employers) was material, which I take to mean substantial, or not negligible (*Bonnington Castings Ltd v Wardlaw; Nicholson v Atlas Steel Foundry & Engineering Co Ltd.*[11] *Wardlaw's* case was decided with full acceptance of the principle that a pursuer must prove not only negligence but also that such fault caused or materially contributed to his injury (*per* Lord Reid)[12] and the pursuer succeeded because negligently-produced dust made a material contribution to the total dust which injured him. I quote from the opinion of Lord Keith of Avinholm:[13] 'It was the atmosphere inhaled by the [pursuer] that caused his illness, and it is impossible, in my opinion, to resolve the components of that atmosphere into particles caused by the fault of the [defenders] and particles not caused by the fault of the [defenders], as if they were separate and independent factors in his illness. *Prima facie* the particles inhaled are acting cumulatively, and I think the natural inference is that, had it not been for the cumulative effect, the [pursuer] would not have developed pneumoconiosis when he did, and might not have developed it at all.'

The evidential gap which undoubtedly existed there (ie the absence of proof that but for the addition of the 'guilty' dust the disease would not have been contracted) is similar to that in the present case and is expressed to be overcome by inference.

In *Nicholson's* case, the pursuer was similarly affected by an indivisible aggregate of silica dust. He succeeded because (I quote from the opinion of Viscount Simonds)[14] 'Owing to the default of the respondents, the deceased was exposed to a greater degree of risk than he should have been' – the excess not being negligible, and according to Lord Cohen,[15] because the respondents' default had materially increased the risk and so, on the balance of probabilities, caused or materially contributed to his injury.

The present factual situation has its differences; the default here consisted not in adding a material quantity to the accumulation of injurious particles, but by failure to take a step which materially increased the risk that the dust already present would cause injury. And I must say that, at least in the present case, to bridge the evidential gap by inference seems to me something of a fiction, since it was precisely this inference which the medical expert declined to make. But I find in the cases quoted an analogy which suggests the conclusion that, in the absence of proof that the culpable condition had, in the result, no effect, the employers should be liable for an injury, squarely within the risk which they created and that they, not the pursuer, should suffer the consequence of the impossibility, foreseeably inherent in the nature of his injury, of segregating the precise consequence of their default.

I would allow this appeal.

11 [1957] 1 All ER 776, [1957] 1 WLR 613.

12 [1956] 1 All ER at 618, [1956] AC at 620.

13 At 622 and 626.

14 [1957] 1 All ER at 781, [1957] 1 WLR at 620.

15 At 784 at 624.

Lords Simon of Glaisdale and Kilbrandon were in favour of allowing the appeal, as was also Lord Salmon, who added:

> In the circumstances of the present case, the possibility of a distinction existing between (a) having materially increased the risk of contracting the disease, and (b) having materially contributed to causing the disease, may no doubt be fruitful source of interesting academic discussions between students of philosophy. Such a distinction is, however, far too unreal to be recognised by the common law.

The filling of the evidentiary gap in this fashion has not been universally acclaimed. In *Wilsher v Essex Area Health Authority*[16] the House of Lords had to deal with the causation issue where the plaintiff had been born suffering from a number of illnesses. As a result of negligence he was given an excess of oxygen. It was later discovered that that he was suffering from an incurable eye condition. There were potentially five other sources of his eye condition in addition to the excess oxygen. The House decided against the plaintiff. Lord Bridge gave the only judgment, the others all agreed with him. After discussing in much depth *McGhee's* case he went on:

> The conclusion I draw from these passages is that *McGhee v National Coal Board* laid down no new principle of law whatever. On the contrary, it affirmed the principle that the onus of proving causation lies on the pursuer or plaintiff. Adopting a robust and pragmatic approach to the undisputed primary facts of the case, the majority concluded that it was a legitimate inference of fact that the defenders' negligence had materially contributed to the pursuer's injury. The decision, in my opinion, is of no greater significance than that, and the attempt to extract from it some esoteric principle which in some way modifies, as a matter of law, the nature of the burden of proof of causation which a plaintiff or pursuer must discharge once he has established a relevant breach of duty, is a fruitless one.
>
> In the Court of Appeal in the instant case, Sir Nicholas Browne-Wilkinson VC, being in a minority, expressed his view on causation with understandable caution. But I am quite unable to find any fault with the following passage in his dissenting judgment ([1986] 3 All ER 801 at 834–35, [1987] QB 730 at 779): 'To apply the principle in *McGhee v National Coal Board* [1972] 3 All ER 1008, [1973] 1 WLR 1 to the present case would constitute an extension of that principle. In *McGhee* there was no doubt that the pursuer's dermatitis was physically caused by brick dust; the only question was whether the continued presence of such brick dust on the pursuer's skin after the time when he should have been provided with a shower caused or materially contributed to the dermatitis which he contracted. There was only one possible agent which could have caused the dermatitis, *viz* brick dust, and there was no doubt that the dermatitis from which he suffered was caused by that brick dust. In the present case the question is different. There are a number of different agents which could have caused the RLF [eye condition]. Excess oxygen was one of them. The defendants failed to take reasonable precautions to prevent one of the possible causative agents (eg excess oxygen) from causing RLF. But no one can tell in this case whether excess oxygen did or did not cause or contribute to the RLF suffered by the plaintiff. The plaintiff's RLF may have been caused by some completely different agent or agents, eg hypercarbia, intraventricular haemorrhage, apnoea or patent ductus

16 [1988] 1 All ER 871.

arteriosus. In addition to oxygen, each of those conditions has been implicated as a possible cause of RLF. This baby suffered from each of those conditions at various times in the first two months of his life. There is no satisfactory evidence that excess oxygen is more likely than any of those other four candidates to have caused RLF in this baby. To my mind, the occurrence of RLF following a failure to take a necessary precaution to prevent excess oxygen causing RLF provides no evidence and raises no presumption that it was excess oxygen rather than one or more of the four other possible agents which caused or contributed to RLF in this case. The position, to my mind, is wholly different from that in *McGhee*, where there was only one candidate (brick dust) which could have caused the dermatitis, and the failure to take a precaution against brick dust causing dermatitis was followed by dermatitis caused by brick dust. In such a case, I can see the common sense, if not the logic, of holding that, in the absence of any other evidence, the failure to take the precaution caused or contributed to the dermatitis. To the extent that certain members of the House of Lords decided the question on inferences from evidence or presumptions, I do not consider the present case falls within their reasoning. A failure to take preventive measures against one out of five possible causes is no evidence as to which of those five caused the injury.'

This effectively disposed of the appeal in Lord Bridge's view, although it must be stressed at no stage did Lord Bridge overrule *McGhee*. The court was just not prepared to bridge the wider evidentiary gap. A further case which emphasises just how heavily the dice are loaded against plaintiffs in this sort of case is *Kay v Ayrshire and Arran Health Board*.[17] In this case there were only two competing alleged causes of the deafness of the plaintiff child, meningitis and an excessive overdose of penicillin negligently administered by the appellant's employee. Lord Keith was of the view that:

> Medical knowledge, as revealed in the course of the evidence, clearly demonstrates that deafness is a common sequela of meningitis. Statistics indicate that it occurs in about a third of all cases of pneumococcal meningitis. They also indicate, it is true, that prospects of a full recovery free of sequelae are somewhat better in the case of children aged between six months and two and a half years than in that of children aged below or above that bracket. Andrew was aged two years and five months at the material time, but no important significance can reasonably be attached to that. The weight of the evidence in this case, as the judges of the First Division found, is that the deafness was caused by the meningitis, and that there was no causal connection between the deafness and the overdose of penicillin.
>
> Counsel for the appellant placed some reliance on *McGhee v National Coal Board* [1972] 3 All ER 1008, [1973] 1WLR 1. That was a case where the pursuer had been employed in an environment where he was exposed to brick dust, a known cause of dermatitis. The pursuer contracted dermatitis and claimed damages from his employers on the ground of their negligence in failing to provide adequate washing facilities, including showers, a precaution normally taken by prudent employers in like circumstances. The employers admitted negligence, but maintained that their failure had not been proved to have caused the pursuer's dermatitis. In the state of medical knowledge it was not possible for medical witnesses to explain the process by which the dermatitis developed, and the pursuer's expert could do no more than say that the failure to provide showers

17 [1987] 2 All ER 417.

> materially increased the risk that the pursuer would contract the disease. He could not say that, if the pursuer had been able to wash off the dust immediately after ceasing work, he would not have contracted it. It was held in your Lordships' House that a sufficient causal connection between the failure to provide showers and the contraction of dermatitis had been established.
>
> In my opinion the decision does not assist the present appellant. Had there been acceptable medical evidence here that an overdose of penicillin administered intrathecally was known to increase the risk that the meningitis, which the penicillin was intended to treat, would cause deafness, the decision would have been in point. It would be immaterial that medical science was unable to demonstrate the precise mechanism whereby the risk was increased. But as it is, there is in the instant case no such medical evidence. It is true that there are few recorded cases of overdoses of penicillin administered for the purpose of treating actual or suspected meningitis. But the paucity of such cases, none of which supports the suggested causal connection, cannot in itself make good the lack of appropriate evidence.
>
> My Lords, for these reasons I would dismiss the appeal.

The rest of their Lordships approached the matter in a similar fashion to that adopted by Lord Keith. This approach must be contrasted with that taken in a road accident case, *Fitzgerald v Lane*,[18] where the Court of Appeal this time found for the plaintiff. The latter had walked briskly onto a pelican crossing against the lights. In the centre of the road he was struck by the car driven by the first defendant and thrown onto the other side of the road, where he was struck by a car driven by the second defendant coming in the opposite direction. All three parties were held responsible for the accident. Nourse LJ stated:

> The submissions of counsel for the second defendant were to the following effect. He said that, if the plaintiff was to recover against the second defendant, he had to prove that the collision with the latter's car occurred before he had suffered, or fully suffered, the injury or injuries which caused his tetraplegia. If he could not prove that, he could not prove that the second defendant had caused or contributed to the condition. This was a question of historic fact which the judge's finding had answered against the plaintiff. It could not be resolved by an application of the *McGhee* principle, which was confined to cases where the evidential gap was the product of the imperfect state of medical knowledge.
>
> I do not think that these submissions are correct. I think that they would emaciate the *McGhee* principle to an extent not countenanced by the decision in *Wilsher's* case, perhaps reducing it to no principle at all. Their validity rests largely on the proposition that the *McGhee* principle can apply to this case only if it is shown that the plaintiff had not suffered, or fully suffered, the injury or injuries which caused his tetraplegia before the fourth impact occurred. The correctness of that proposition must be tested by a consideration of *Wilsher's* case, in order to see whether any of the other possible causes of the plaintiff's retrolental fibroplasia had materialised before the catheter had first been negligently inserted in one of his veins. If none of them had, there might be good support for the proposition, because it could then be said that the comparable question of historic fact had never arisen in that case. However, it is admittedly difficult to discern from the judgments what the true position was. And it must

18 [1987] 2 All ER 455.

> be said that some at least of the conditions referred to by Sir Nicholas Browne-Wilkinson VC are conditions which would have been caused by the plaintiff's extreme pre-maturity and would presumably have existed from the moment of his birth (see [1986] 3 All ER 801 at 834, [1987] 2 WLR 425 at 466). This factual obscurity is unfavourable to the proposition, because it suggests that the order in which the various possible causes occurred or materialised was not regarded as being a matter of any importance. Accordingly, I think that *Wilsher's* case must be approached on the footing that there were several other possible causes the plaintiff's disability, any one or more of which could have occurred or materialised before the negligent act.
>
> In these circumstances, the proposition on which counsel's submissions were largely built is not made out. Nor do I think that there is anything in the submission that the *McGhee* principle is confined to cases where the evidential gap is the product of an imperfect state of medical knowledge in a general sense. It is true that both *McGhee's* case and *Wilsher's* case were cases of that kind, but to confine the principle to them alone would raise distinctions which could not be allowed in the application of one which is said to have been adopted in the interests of justice. The distinction sought to be made in the present case is a good example. There is no satisfactory distinction between a case where the evidential gap is the product of an imperfect state of medical knowledge in a general sense and one where it is the product of the inability of each of two medical witnesses to say which of four impacts was more likely than any of the other three to have caused the plaintiff's tetraplegia.
>
> An examination of these niceties has been brought on us by the ingenuity of the submissions of counsel for the second defendant. Having done my best to dispose of them, I gladly return to the principle.
>
> ... Does the principle apply to the state of affairs which is found to have existed in the present case? I think that it does. It is an established fact that the negligent driving of the second defendant and his collision with the plaintiff, to whom he owed a duty of care, created a risk that injury of a kind which can cause tetraplegia would be caused to the plaintiff. The plaintiff did suffer an injury or injuries which caused tetraplegia. The collision with the second defendant' s car was one of three possible causes of the condition. In *McGhee* there were two, in *Wilsher* about five. It is not suggested that any distinction is to be made solely because there are two defendants in this case. It does not matter whether the risk was created before or after the third impact had occurred, or whether the fourth impact in fact caused or contributed to the plaintiff's condition. A benevolent principle smiles on these factual uncertainties and melts them all away.

After a lengthy discussion and much soul-searching, it would appear, Slade LJ had the following to say:

> In the end, however, on the particular facts of the present case, I have come to the conclusion that the *McGhee* principle was rightly applied for these short reasons. Counsel's submissions focused attention on the moment of impact between the plaintiff and the second defendant's car. In my judgment, however, attention should be focused on the moment when the second defendant's negligent course of conduct began, that is to say (if my assessment of the facts is right) when he first saw the plaintiff on the pavement hurrying towards the crossing and failed to brake immediately. At that moment of time the plaintiff was a fit and able man.. If this is the right way to look at the matter, applying the *McGhee* principle ... I have no difficulty in holding that the second defendant, by failing to brake when he should have done, created a risk that physical injury involving

tetraplegia would be caused to the plaintiff or increased the existing risk that such injury would ensue.

It does not seem that the case is affected by the House of Lords' decision in *Wilsher*. The status of the principle in *McGhee* must still be in some doubt, however and the debate may continue for a long time yet.

Lost chance

The final causal riddle, at least for the time being, is that relating to the lost chance. This is best epitomised in the case of *Hotson v East Berkshire Area Health Authority*[19] where the plaintiff fell out of a tree and sustained a serious hip injury. The injury was not correctly diagnosed for five days by which time the chance of a good recovery, estimated at 25%, had been lost. The judge awarded the plaintiff 25% of the damages he would have received on a full liability basis to reflect the lost chance. The Court of Appeal affirmed the judge's decision. In allowing the authority's appeal, Lord Bridge had this to say:

> [The judge] reached the conclusion that the question was one of quantification and thus arrived at his award to the plaintiff of one quarter of the damages appropriate to compensate him for the consequences of the avascular necrosis.
>
> It is here, with respect, that I part company with the judge. The plaintiff's claim was for damages for physical injury and consequential loss alleged to have been caused by the authority's breach of their duty of care. In some cases, perhaps particularly medical negligence cases, causation may be so shrouded in mystery that the court can only measure statistical chances. But that was not so here. On the evidence there was a clear conflict as to what had caused the avascular necrosis. The authority's evidence was that the sole cause was the original traumatic injury to the hip. The plaintiff's evidence, as its highest, was that the delay in treatment was a material contributory cause. This was a conflict, like any other, about some relevant past event which the judge could not avoid resolving on a balance of probabilities. Unless the plaintiff proved on a balance of probabilities that the delayed treatment was at least a material contributory cause of the avascular necrosis, he failed on the issue of causation and no question of quantification could arise. But the judge's findings of fact ... are unmistakably to the effect that on the balance of probabilities the injury caused by the plaintiff's fall left insufficient blood vessels intact to keep the epiphysis alive. This amounts to a finding of fact that the fall was the sole cause of the avascular necrosis.

Lord Mackay spoke in a similar vein:

> As I have said, the fundamental question of fact to be answered in this case related to a point in time before the negligent failure to treat began. It must, therefore, be a matter of past fact. It did not raise any question of what might have been the situation in a hypothetical state of facts. To this problem the words of Lord Diplock in *Mallett v McGonagle* [1969] 2 All ER 178 at 191, [1970] AC 166 at 176 apply: 'In determining what did happen in the past a court decides on the balance of probabilities. Anything that is more probable than not it treats as certain.'
>
> In this respect this case is the same, in principle, as any other in which the state of facts existing before alleged negligence came into play has to be determined. For

19 [1987] 2 All ER 909.

> example, if a claimant alleges that he sustained a certain fracture in a fall at work and there is evidence that indeed he had fallen at work, but shortly before he had fallen at home and sustained the fracture, the court would have to determine where the truth lay. If the claimant denied the previous fall, there would be evidence, both for and against the allegation, that he had so fallen. The issue would be resolved on the balance of probabilities. If the court held on that balance that the fracture was sustained at home, there could be no question of saying that since all that had been established was that it was more probable than not that the injury was not work-related, there was a possibility that it was work-related and that this possibility or chance was a proper subject of compensation.
>
> I should add in this context that where on disputed evidence a judge reaches a conclusion on the balance of probabilities it will not usually be easy to assess a specific measure of probability for the conclusion at which he has arrived. As my noble and learned friend Lord Bridge observed in the course of the hearing, a judge deciding disputed questions of fact will not ordinarily do it by use of a calculator.
>
> On the other hand, I consider that it would be unwise in the present case to lay it down as a rule that a plaintiff could never succeed by proving loss of chance in a medical negligence case ... In these circumstances I think it unwise to do more than say that, unless and until this House departs from the decision in *McGhee*, your Lordships cannot affirm the proposition that in no circumstances can evidence of a loss of chance resulting from the breach of a duty of care found a successful claim for damages, although there was no suggestion that the House regarded such a chance as an asset in any sense.

In the light of this last part of the extract, one wonders if the plaintiff in that case could not succeed for a lost chance, then just who else could ever be in a better position? What is the basis of the plaintiff's claim in this type of case. It may be argued that the damage is the loss of the chance in which case, on the balance of probabilities, the defendant's negligence has caused the plaintiff to lose that chance.[20] In addition, the courts have recognised the loss of a chance in contract claims.[21]

REMOTENESS OF DAMAGE

Supposing that the plaintiff successfully negotiates the causation hurdle, s/he must then establish that his/her damage is not too remote a consequence of the defendant's breach of duty. This will depend on her satisfying the test of remoteness established in the important case known as the *Wagon Mound (No 1)*,[22] perhaps unkindly described by Howarth as 'the greatest mistake of 20th century British tort jurisprudence'.[23]

The facts in this case have already been discussed in the previous chapter on breach of duty. The plaintiffs in this instance were the owners of the wharf upon which the welding operations were being carried out by their employees. The claim was for the destruction of the wharf by fire. The previous test of

20 See Stapleton, [1988] 104 LQR p 391 *et seq*.

21 See *Chaplin v Hicks* [1911] 2 KB 786.

22 [1961] AC 388.

23 *Textbook on Tort*, p 30.

remoteness of damage was established in the case *Re Polemis and Furness Withy & Co*[24] favouring a direct consequence test. The Privy Council rejected this test, as will be evident from the extracts from Lord Simonds' judgment:

> Enough has been said to show that the authority of *Polemis* has been severely shaken, though lip-service has from time to time been paid to it. In their Lordships' opinion it should no longer be regarded as good law. It is not probable that many cases will, for that reason, have a different result, though it is hoped that the law will therefore be simplified and that in some cases, at least, palpable injustice will be avoided. For it does not seem consonant with current ideas of justice or morality that, for an act of negligence, however slight or venial, which results in some trivial foreseeable damage, the actor should be liable for all consequences, however unforeseeable and however grave, so long as they can be said to be 'direct'. It is a principle of civil liability, subject only to qualifications which have no present relevance, that a man must be considered to be responsible for the probable consequences of his act. To demand more of him is too harsh a rule, to demand less is to ignore that civilised order requires the observance of a minimum standard of behaviour.
>
> This concept applied to the slowly developing law of negligence has led to a great variety of expressions which can, as it appears to their Lordships, be harmonised with little difficulty, with the single exception of the so-called rule in *Polemis.* For, if it is asked why a man should be responsible for the natural or necessary or probable consequences of his act (or any other similar description of them), the answer is that it is not because they are natural or necessary or probable, but because, since they have this quality, it is judged by the standard of the reasonable man that he ought to have foreseen them. Thus it is that, over and over again it has happened that in different judgments in the same case, and sometimes in a single judgment, liability for a consequence has been imposed on the ground that it was reasonably foreseeable or, alternatively, on the ground that it was natural or necessary or probable. The two grounds have been treated as coterminous, and so they largely are. But, where they are not, the question arises to which the wrong answer was given in *Polemis.* For, if some limitation must be imposed upon the consequences for which the negligent actor is to be held responsible – and all are agreed that some limitation there must be – why should that test (reasonable foreseeability) be rejected which, since he is judged by what the reasonable man ought to foresee, corresponds with the common conscience of mankind, and a test (the 'direct' consequence) be substituted which leads to nowhere but the never-ending and insoluble problems of causation. ...
>
> It is, no doubt proper when considering tortious liability for negligence to analyse its elements and to say that the plaintiff must prove a duty owed to him by the defendant, a breach of that duty by the defendant, and consequent damage. But there can be no liability until the damage has been done. It is not the act but the consequences on which tortious liability is founded. Just as (as it has been said) there is no such thing as negligence in the air, so there is no such thing as liability in the air. Suppose an action brought by A for damages caused by the carelessness (a neutral word) of B, for example, a fire caused by the careless spillage of oil. It may, of course, become relevant to know what duty B owed to A, but the only liability that is in question is the liability for damage by fire. It is vain to isolate the liability from its context and to say that B is or is not liable, and then to ask for what damage he is liable. For his liability is in respect of that damage and no other. If, as admittedly it is, B's liability (culpability) depends on

24 [1921] 3 KB 560.

> the reasonable foreseeability of the consequent damage, how is that to be determined except by the foreseeability of the damage which in fact happened – the damage in suit? And, if that damage is unforeseeable so as to displace liability at large, how can the liability be resorted so as to make compensation payable?
>
> But it is said, a different position arises if B's careless act has been shown to be negligent and has caused some foreseeable damage to A. Their Lordships have already observed that to hold B liable for consequences, however unforeseeable, of a careless act, if, but only if, he is at the same time liable for some other damage however trivial, appears to be neither logical nor just. This becomes more clear if it is supposed that similar unforeseeable damage is suffered by A and C but other foreseeable damage, for which B is liable, by A only. A system of law which would hold B liable to A but not to C for the similar damage suffered by each of them could not easily be defended. Fortunately, the attempt is not necessary. For the same fallacy is at the root of the proposition. It is irrelevant to the question whether B is liable for unforeseeable damage that he is liable for foreseeable damage, as irrelevant as would the fact that he had trespassed on Whiteacre be to the question whether he has trespassed on Blackacre. Again, suppose a claim by A for damage by fire by the careless act of B. Of what relevance is it to that claim that he has another claim arising out of the same careless act? It would surely not prejudice his claim if that other claim failed; it cannot assist if it succeeds. Each of them rests on its own bottom, and will fail if it can be established that the damage could not reasonably be foreseen. We have come back to the plain common sense stated by Lord Russell of Killowen in *Bourhill v Young*.[25] As Denning LJ said in *King v Phillips*[26]: 'there can be no doubt since *Bourhill v Young* that the test of liability for shock is foreseeability of injury by shock.' Their Lordships substitute the word 'fire' for 'shock' and endorse this statement of the law.

The Privy Council allowed the appeal on the basis that damage by fire, on the evidence, was not reasonably foreseeable. What was foreseeable was that there would be some damage caused by the fouling of the slipways belonging to the respondents, but that is all. The rationale for the change of principle to reasonable foreseeability of the type of harm from directness appears to be that the latter is arbitrary in its application and could result in manifest injustice. The reasonable foreseeability test brings the test for remoteness into line with the test for establishing duty and allows the court to take policy factors into account in deciding whether certain types of damage are to be excluded. As to whether the principle has made any difference in result is difficult to establish, although some take the view that most cases would be decided no differently had the directness test been applied to the facts. It seems that the English courts have tended to apply the reasonable foreseeability test. There have been some considerable difficulties following *Wagon Mound (No 1)* and these are considered in the cases below.

Type of harm

There is considerable ambiguity inherent in the phrase 'type of harm'. It can be broadly or narrowly construed, and it could be argued that courts draw its

25 [1943] AC 92 at 101.

26 [1953] 1 QB 429 at 441.

scope widely or narrowly depending on the result to be achieved. This is perhaps best illustrated by looking at the extracts from the following cases. In *Bradford v Robinson Rentals*[27] the plaintiff's employers sent him on a long journey without adequate heating and in extremely cold weather. He suffered from frostbite as a result of the cold. Rees J stated:

> So far as the principles of law applicable to this case are concerned, they may be shortly stated. The defendants, as the plaintiff's employers, were under a duty at common law to take reasonable steps to avoid exposing the plaintiff to a reasonably foreseeable risk of injury. It was strongly argued on behalf of the defendants that injury to his health suffered by the plaintiff in this case by frostbite or cold injury was not reasonably foreseeable. There was no evidence that, before the plaintiff started the journey, either the plaintiff himself or the defendants' servants ... actually contemplated that the plaintiff might suffer from frostbite if he were required to carry out the journey. However, I am satisfied that any reasonable employer in possession of all the facts known to [his servants] would have realised ... that, if the plaintiff was required to carry out the journey, he would certainly be subjected to a real risk of some injury to his health arising from prolonged exposure to an exceptional degree of cold. No doubt the kinds of injury to health due to prolonged exposure to an exceptional degree of cold are commonly thought to include, for example, that the victim might suffer from a common cold or in a severe case from pneumonia, or that he might suffer from chilblains on his hands and feet. The question which I have to consider is whether the plaintiff has established that the injury to his health by 'frostbite' (and I use the lay term for convenience), which is admittedly unusual in this country, is nevertheless of the type and kind of injury which was reasonably foreseeable. The law does not require that the precise nature of the injury must be reasonably foreseeable before liability for its consequences is attributed. ...
>
> In these circumstances I hold that the defendants did, by sending the plaintiff out on this journey, expose him to a reasonably foreseeable risk of injury arising from exposure to severe cold and fatigue. This breach of duty caused the plaintiff to suffer from frostbite or cold injury with serious consequences.

The result in this case is in vivid contrast to that reached in *Tremain v Pike*,[28] where the plaintiff contracted Weil's disease during the course of his employment as a herdsman after coming into contact with rats which had infested the defendants' farm. In refusing the claim, Payne J commented:

> The kind of damage suffered here was a disease contracted by contact with rats' urine. This, in my view, was entirely different in kind from the effect of a rat bite, or food poisoning by the consumption of food or drink contaminated by rats. I do not accept that all illness or infection arising from an infestation of rats should be regarded as of the same kind. ...
>
> It may be that it is less satisfactory in this case to ask the question whether the infection is different in kind from other sequelae of rat infestation which might be foreseeable, as that leads to disputation about what is meant by difference in kind, than to ask the direct question whether, on the facts of this case, the leptospirosis was reasonably foreseeable by the defendants. In my opinion. one has only to ask that question and the answer is inescapably 'no'.

27 [1967] 1 All ER 267.

28 [1969] 3 All ER 1303.

The differing outcomes in these two cases are a product of the wide or narrow way in which the type or kind of harm is categorised. In *Bradford* the court considered whether harm by cold was reasonably foreseeable, not harm by frostbite. In *Tremain*, the question asked was whether Weil's disease was reasonably foreseeable. Clearly it was not, certainly at that time, but the narrowness of the question produced the inevitable response.

Manner of occurrence

It is said in the cases that the precise way in which the harm has come about does not have to be reasonably foreseeable before the plaintiff can succeed. Again there are contrasting and confusing cases on this point. In *Hughes v Lord Advocate*[29] a manhole was left open overnight by workmen. The hole was surrounded by paraffin lamps. A young boy knocked or lowered one of the lamps into the hole and an explosion followed, the boy falling into the hole and being badly burned. In allowing the appeal in favour of the young boy, Lord Guest observed:

> Concentration has been placed in the courts below on the explosion which, it was said, could not have been foreseen because it was caused in a unique fashion by the paraffin forming into vapour and being ignited by the naked flame of the wick. But this, in my opinion, is to concentrate on what is really a non-essential element in the dangerous situation created by the allurement. The test might be better put thus: was the igniting of paraffin outside the lamp by the flame a foreseeable consequence of the breach of duty? In the circumstances, there was a combination of potentially dangerous circumstances against which the Post Office had to protect the appellant. If these formed an allurement to children it might have been foreseen that they would play with the lamp, that it might tip over, that it might be broken, and that when broken the paraffin might spill and be ignited by the flame. All these steps in the chain of causation seem to have been accepted by all the judges in the courts below as foreseeable. But because the explosion was the agent which caused the burning and was unforeseeable, therefore, the accident, according to them, was not reasonably foreseeable. In my opinion, this reasoning is fallacious. An explosion is only one way in which burning can be caused. Burning can also be caused by the contact between the liquid paraffin and a naked flame. In the one case paraffin vapour and in the other case liquid paraffin is ignited by fire. I cannot see that these are two different types of accident. They are both burning accidents and in both cases the injuries would be burning injuries. Upon this view the explosion was an immaterial event in the chain of causation. It was simply one way in which burning might be caused by the potentially dangerous paraffin lamp.

Lord Pearce, also in favour of allowing the appeal, stated:

> In the case of an allurement to children it is particularly hard to foresee with precision the exact shape of the disaster that will arise. The allurement in this case was the combination of a red paraffin lamp, a ladder, a partially closed tent, and a cavernous hole within it, a setting well fitted to inspire some juvenile adventure that might end in calamity. The obvious risks were burning and conflagration and a fall. All these in fact occurred, but unexpectedly the mishandled lamp, instead of causing an ordinary conflagration, produced a violent explosion. Did the explosion create an accident and damage of a different

29 [1963] AC 837.

> type from the misadventure and damage that could be foreseen? In my judgment it did not. The accident was but a variant of the foreseeable. It was, to quote the words of Denning LJ in *Roe v Minister of Health*,[30] 'within the risk created by the negligence'. No unforeseeable, extraneous, initial occurrence fired the train. The children's entry into the tent with the ladder, the descent into the hole, the mishandling of the lamp, were all foreseeable. The greater part of the path to injury had thus been trodden, and the mishandled lamp was quite likely to spill at that stage and cause a conflagration. Instead, by some curious chance of combustion, it exploded and no conflagration occurred, it would seem, until after the explosion. There was thus an unexpected manifestation of the apprehended physical dangers. But it would be, I think, too narrow a view to hold that those who created the risk of fire are excused from the liability for the damage by fire because it came by way of explosive combustion. The resulting damage, though severe, was not greater than, or different in kind from, that which might have been produced had the lamp spilled and produced a more normal conflagration in the hole.
>
> I would therefore allow the appeal.

The other judges were also in favour of allowing the appeal.

The contrasting case is *Doughty v Turner Manufacturing Co Ltd*,[31] where the Court of Appeal took a different line altogether. An asbestos cover slipped into a cauldron of hot molten liquid. The liquid erupted and the plaintiff sustained personal injuries when it came over the side of the cauldron. Lord Pearce gave the first judgment and commented:

> In the present case the evidence showed that nobody supposed that an asbestos cement cover could not safely be immersed in the bath. The judge took the view, which Mr James concedes was correct, that if the defendants had deliberately immersed this cover in the bath as part of the normal process, they could not have been held liable for the resulting explosion. The fact that they inadvertently knocked it into the bath cannot of itself convert into negligence that which they were entitled to do deliberately. In the then state of their knowledge, for which the judge, rightly on the evidence, held them in no way to blame, the accident was not foreseeable.
>
> ... In the present case the potential eruptive qualities of the covers when immersed in great heat were not suspected and they were not a known source of danger, but Mr James argues that the cause of injury was the escape of the hot liquid from the bath and that injury through the escape of liquid from the bath by splashing was foreseeable. The evidence shows that splashes caused by sudden immersion, whether of the metal objects for which it was intended or any other extraneous object, were a foreseeable danger which should carefully be avoided. The falling cover might have ejected the liquid by a splash and in the result it did eject the liquid, though in a more dramatic fashion. Therefore, he argues, the actual accident was merely a variant of foreseeable accidents by splashing. It is clear, however, both by inference and by one explicit observation, that the judge regarded splashes as being in quite a different category. Moreover, according to the evidence, it seems that the cover never did create a splash; it appears to have slid into the liquid at an angle of some 45° and dived obliquely downwards. Further, it seems somewhat doubtful whether the cover falling only

30 [1954] 2 QB 66 at 85.

31 [1964] 1 QB 518.

> from a height of 4–6 inches, which was the difference in level between the liquid and the sides, could have splashed any liquid outside the bath. And when (if ever) the plaintiff was in the area in which he could be hit by a mere splash (apparently the liquid being heavy, if splashed, would not travel further than a foot from the bath) the cover had already slid into the liquid without splashing. Indeed, it seems from the plaintiff's evidence that, when he first came onto the scene, the cover was already half in and half out of the liquid. On broader grounds, however, it would be quite unrealistic to describe this accident as a variant of the perils from splashing ... There was an eruption due to chemical changes underneath the surface of the liquid as opposed to a splash caused by displacement from bodies falling on to its surface. In my judgment, the reasoning in *Hughes v Lord Advocate*[32] cannot be extended far enough to cover this case.

His Lordship seems to have decided this case on the basis that there had been no breach of duty, despite mentioning the leading cases on remoteness, perhaps a timely reminder that foreseeability is crucial at every stage in a negligence action. Harman LJ seemed to approach the issue from the remoteness angle in the following brief extract:

> In my opinion, the damage here was of an entirely different kind from the foreseeable splash. Indeed, the evidence showed that any disturbance of the material resulting from the immersion of the hardboard was past an appreciable time before the explosion happened. This latter was caused by the disintegration of the hardboard under the great heat to which it was subjected and the consequent release of the moisture enclosed within it. This had nothing to do with the agitation caused by the dropping of the board into the cyanide. I am of the opinion that it would be wrong on these facts to make another in-road on the doctrine of foreseeability, which seems to me a satisfactory solvent of this type of difficulty.

Diplock LJ ploughed a similar furrow:

> ... in the present case the defendant's duty owed to the plaintiff in relation to the only foreseeable risk, that is of splashing, was to take reasonable care to avoid knocking the cover into the liquid or allowing it to slip in in such a way as to cause a splash which would injure the plaintiff. Failure to avoid knocking it into the liquid, or allowing it to slip in, was of itself no breach of duty to the plaintiff. It is not clear on the evidence whether the dropping of the cover on to the liquid caused any splash at all. The judge made no finding on this. The reasoning in his judgment is not sufficiently explicit to make it clear whether the point argued by Mr James, with which I am now dealing, formed part of his *ratio decidendi*, though some of his observations in the course of the hearing suggest that it was not. However that may be, it is incontrovertible that, even if there was some slight splash when the cover fell on to the liquid, the plaintiff was untouched by it and it caused him no injury. There was thus, in the circumstances of this case, no breach of duty to the plaintiff involved in inadvertently knocking the cover into the liquid or inadvertently allowing it to slip in.

The case is difficult to reconcile with *Hughes*, but perhaps the solution is to treat the case as one in which the court in reality took the view that the defendants were not at fault. It is noticeable that Diplock LJ also finished on the point that there was no breach of duty. It could be argued that the harm caused to the plaintiff was outside the risk created by the negligence (if any), whereas in *Hughes* the harm was still within the risk created by the breach of duty.

32 *Ibid* 837.

Extent of the harm

Provided the type or kind of harm is reasonably foreseeable, it does not matter that the extent of the harm goes beyond what was reasonably foreseeable. In *Vacwell Engineering v BDH Chemicals*,[33] as a result, amongst other things, of negligence, an explosion occurred which caused considerable damage to the plaintiffs' premises. One of the issues concerned the foreseeability of the extent of the harm. Rees J dealt with this point succinctly:

> Here it was a foreseeable consequence of the supply of boron tribromide without a warning – and *a fortiori* with an irrelevant warning about harmful vapour – that in the ordinary course of industrial use it could come into contact with water and cause a violent reaction and possibly an explosion. It would also be foreseeable that some damage to property would or might result. In my judgment the explosion and the type of damage being foreseeable, it matters not in law that the magnitude of the former and the extent of the latter were not.

Egg-shell skull rule

Following the *Wagon Mound (No 1)* there was some concern about the precise status of the so-called egg-shell skull rule, namely, the defendant must take his/her victim as s/he finds him. Whether it had survived was soon resolved in the case of *Smith v Leech Brain & Co Ltd*.[34] The deceased was burnt on his lower lip by a piece of molten metal. The burn was instrumental in causing cancer in some pre-malignant tissues and the victim died from cancer some three years later. It was held that the defendants were liable for breach of duty. On the question of the egg-shell skull rule, Lord Parker CJ stated:

> For my part, I am quite satisfied that the judicial committee in the *Wagon Mound* case did not have what I may call, loosely, the thin skull cases in mind. It has always been the law of this country that a tortfeasor takes his victim as he finds him ... it seems to me that this is plainly a case which comes within the old principle. The test is not whether these employers could reasonably have foreseen that a burn would cause cancer and that he would die. The question is whether these employers could reasonably foresee the type of injury he suffered, namely, the burn. What, in the particular case, is the amount of damage which he suffers as a result of that burn, depends upon the characteristics and constitution of the victim.

The matter came before the Court of Appeal in *Robinson v The Post Office*,[35] where the plaintiff workman as result of the negligence of the first defendants sustained a graze to his shin. He was given an injection of anti-tetanus serum which brought about an allergic reaction resulting in serious illness. The Post Office was held liable for the full extent of the plaintiff's illness. Orr LJ, giving the judgment of the court, said, after reviewing the various authorities:

> In the present case the judge held that it was plainly foreseeable:
>
> (1) that if oil was negligently allowed to escape onto a ladder a workman was liable to slip and sustain the type of wound in question; and
>
> (2) that such injury might well require medical treatment;

---

33 [1971] 1 QB 88.

34 [1962] 2 QB 405.

35 [1974] 2 All ER 737.

> and on this basis alone he was prepared to hold the defendants liable for encephalitis, but he held in addition that, having regard to the nature of the plaintiff's work and the area in which he was working, it was also foreseeable that some form of anti-tetanus prophylactic would be deemed necessary. In the result he concluded that every relevant matter was foreseeable except the terrible extent of the injury which was due to the plaintiff's allergy to a second dose of ATS, in respect of which the Post Office must take their victim as they found him.
>
> On this appeal, counsel for the Post Office did not challenge the correctness of Lord Parker CJ's reasoning and conclusion in the *Leech Brain* case and accepted that some at least of the subsequent decisions fell within the same principle, but he claimed that an essential link which was missing in the present case was that it was not foreseeable that administration of a form of anti-tetanus prophylaxis would itself give rise to a rare serious illness. In our judgment, however, there was no missing link and the case is governed by the principle that the Post Office had to take their victim as they found him, in this case with an allergy to a second dose of ATS. ... In our judgment the principle that a defendant must take the plaintiff as he finds him involves that, if a wrongdoer ought reasonably to foresee that as result of his wrongful act the victim may require medical treatment, he is, subject to the principle of *novus actus interveniens*, liable for the consequences of the treatment applied, although he could not reasonably foresee those consequences or that they could be serious.

We shall have cause to come back to this case in considering the alleged negligence of the hospital in its treatment of the plaintiff and the issue of *novus actus interveniens* (new intervening cause) mentioned in that last extract.

Plaintiff's economic state

One significant issue which has never really been resolved following *Wagon Mound (No 1)* is that concerning the plaintiff's impoverished state at the time of the breach of duty and whether the plaintiff can successfully claim from the tortfeasor for extra expense incurred as a result of his lack of means. The issue was explored in the House of Lords case known as the *Liesbosch Dredger*,[36] where the dredger was negligently sunk by the defendants' ship. The plaintiffs, because of financial embarrassment, were forced to hire another vessel at a high rate of hire. Lord Wright commented:

> The respondents' tortious act involved the physical loss of the dredger; that loss must somehow be reduced to terms of money. But the appellants' actual loss in so far as it was due to their impecuniosity arose from that impecuniosity as a separate and concurrent cause, extraneous to and distinct in character from the tort; the impecuniosity was not traceable to the respondents' acts, and in my opinion was outside the legal purview of the consequences of these acts. The law cannot take account of everything that follows a wrongful act; it regards some subsequent matters as outside the scope of its selection, because 'it was for the law to judge the cause of causes', or consequences of consequences. Thus the loss of a ship by collision due to the other vessel's sole fault may force the ship owner into bankruptcy and that again may involve his family in suffering, loss of education or opportunities in life, but no such loss could be recovered from the wrongdoer. In the varied web of affairs, the law must abstract some

36 [1933] AC 449.

> consequences as relevant, not perhaps on grounds of pure logic but simply for practical reasons. In the present case, if the appellants' financial embarrassment is to be regarded as a consequence of the respondents' tort, I think it is too remote, but I prefer to regard it as an independent cause, though its operative effect was conditioned by the loss of the dredger. ... Nor is the appellants' financial disability to be compared with that physical delicacy or weakness which may aggravate the damage in the case of personal injuries, or with the possibility that the injured man in such a case may be either a poor labourer or a highly paid professional man. The former class of circumstances goes to the extent of actual physical damage and the latter consideration goes to interference with profit-earning capacity; whereas the appellants' want of means was, as already stated, extrinsic.

All the other Law Lords agreed with the above, but it seems difficult to see the difference between this situation and the rule that a defendant must take his victim as he finds him. There have been subsequent cases in which the case has been distinguished,[37] and Howarth, with good cause, doubts whether the case would survive if the House had to reconsider the issue.[38]

Intervening events

Sometimes the defendant's negligence is accompanied by another event or events which may be said to contribute to the plaintiff's injury. Where this event comes after the breach of duty but before the harm to the plaintiff the court has to decide whether the original defendant is liable for the plaintiff's harm. It is traditional to use the language of causation, *novus actus interveniens* or the causative potency of the negligence, in order to describe the decision as to whether the defendant is to be held liable. On the other hand, the matter may be expressed in terms of remoteness of damage, ie the damage was of a type that was/was not reasonably foreseeable. Howarth is sceptical[39] about the usefulness of the foreseeability test in many of the following cases and suggests that courts have returned to a directness test to resolve difficult issues. We need to consider the different types of intervening event, namely the intervening natural event, the situation where there is intervening negligence by a third party, the controversial area of deliberate third party interventions, and finally intervening acts of the plaintiff herself.

Intervening natural events

It seems that an intervening natural event will normally break the chain of causation, unless it can be argued that the defendant's breach has either increased the likelihood of further damage from a natural event, or it has made the plaintiff more susceptible to damage. In the case of *Carslogie SS Co Ltd v Royal Norwegian Government*[40] a ship was damaged in a collision through the fault of the other ship. The ship was temporarily repaired but needed

37 See, eg, *Dodd Properties (Kent) Ltd v Canterbury City Council* [1980] 1 WLR 433.

38 *Op cit* p 126.

39 *Op cit* pp 136–56.

40 [1952] AC 292.

permanent repair, and set off for port to have these done. On the way the ship was further damaged by heavy weather and required 30 days in port for repair, but otherwise would have only needed 10 days for the repair of the initial damage. It was held that the defendants were not liable for this supervening damage as it was not in any sense a consequence of the collision. In addition, the House held that the plaintiff was not entitled to loss of profit for the 10 day period. Viscount Jowitt stated:

> ... the fact remains that when she entered the dock at New York she was not a profit-earning machine by reason of the heavy-weather damage which had rendered her unseaworthy. If there had been no collision she would have been detained in dock for 30 days to repair this damage.

The other judges took a similar line. The intervening natural event overwhelmed the defendant's breach of duty and reduced its causative potency to next to nothing.

Intervening negligent acts by third parties

The issues become more complex here. It is clear that a negligent intervention by a third party may be considered too remote as not being reasonably foreseeable, or be regarded as constituting a new intervening cause, but there is no universal rule to that effect. *The Oropesa*[41] is a good illustration. Two vessels collided and both were to blame for the collision. The master of one of the ships sent a lifeboat with some of the crew in it to the other to consider salvage. The sea was rough and the boat capsized and several crew members were drowned. Actions were brought against the owners of the ships by the families of the deceased crew. The issue was whether the action of the master of the ship in sending his men across in the boat was a *novus actus interveniens*. Lord Wright gave the only judgment of the Court of Appeal, stating as follows:

> The defendants deny liability on the ground that there was no legal connection between the breach of duty and death of the deceased. Certain well-known formulae are invoked, such as the chain of causation was broken and that there was a *novus actus interveniens*. These phrases, sanctified as they are by standing authority, only mean that there was not such a direct relationship between the act of negligence and the injury that the one can be treated as flowing directly from the other. Cases have been cited which show great difference of opinion on the true answer in the various circumstances to the question whether the damage was direct or too remote. I find it very difficult to formulate any precise and all-embracing rule. I do not think that the authorities which have been cited succeed in settling that difficulty. It may be said that in dealing with the law of negligence it is possible to state general propositions, but when you come to apply those principles to determine whether there has been actionable negligence in any particular case, you must deal with the case on its facts.
>
> What were the facts here? The master of the *Manchester Regiment* was faced with a very difficult proposition. His ship was helpless, without any means of propulsion or of working any of her important auxiliary apparatus, a dead lump in the water, and he had only the saving thought that she might go on floating so long as her bulkheads did not give way. He had great faith in his ship, but he realised that there was a heavy sea, with a heavy gale blowing and that he was in

41 [1943] P 32.

> a very perilous plight. ... In those circumstances the master decided to go to *The Oropesa* where, no doubt, he thought he would find valuable help and advice. Nobody suggests that he was acting unreasonably or improperly in doing so, or indeed that he was doing anything but his duty. ... If, therefore, the test is whether what was done was reasonable, there can be no doubt that the actions ... of the master ... were reasonable. Whether the master took exactly the right course is another matter. He may have been guilty of an error of judgment, but, as I read the authorities, that would not affect the question whether the action he took and its consequences flowed directly from the negligence of *The Oropesa*. ... There was an unbroken sequence of cause and effect between the negligence which caused *The Oropesa* to collide with the *Manchester Regiment*, and the action [of the master], which was dictated by the exigencies of the position. It cannot be severed from the circumstances affecting both ships. ...
>
> There are some propositions which are beyond question in connection with this class of case. One is that human action does not *per se* sever the connected sequence of acts. The mere fact that human action intervenes does not prevent the sufferer from saying that the injury which is due to that human action as one of the elements in the sequence is recoverable from the original wrongdoer.

It is not altogether clear from the above whether there was an express finding of negligence in respect of the master's decision to cross to *The Oropesa*. It is not, therefore, possible to argue that it is an authority for saying that a negligent intervention may not break the causation chain. However, that it may do so can be gathered from the case of *Knightly v Johns*,[42] where the first defendant caused a serious accident at or near the exit to a road tunnel. A police inspector, having forgotten to seal off the far end of the tunnel, sent a police motor cyclist, the plaintiff, back along the tunnel against the oncoming traffic. The plaintiff was struck by a vehicle coming the other way. Both the first defendant and the police inspector were found to be negligent. On the question of whether the latter's intervening breach of duty severed the chain of causation, Stephenson LJ, with whom the other two judges in the Court of Appeal agreed, said:

> It is plain that [the judge] was asking himself the right question and applying the right law. He was, I think, rightly taking the law to be that, in considering the effects of carelessness, as in considering the duty to take care, the test is reasonable foreseeability, which I understand to mean foreseeability of something of the same sort being likely to happen, as against its being a mere possibility which would never occur to the mind of a reasonable man or, if it did, would be neglected as too remote to require precautions or to impose responsibility. ... The question to be asked is accordingly whether the whole sequence of events is a natural and probable consequence of Mr John's negligence and a reasonably foreseeable result of it. In answering the question it is helpful but not decisive to consider which of these events were deliberate choices to do positive acts and which were mere omissions or failures to act; which acts and omissions were innocent mistakes or miscalculations and which were negligent having regard to the pressures and the gravity of the emergency and the need to act quickly. Negligent conduct is more likely to break the chain of causation than conduct which is not. Positive acts will more easily constitute new causes than inaction. Mistakes and mischances are to be expected when human beings, however well trained, have to cope with a crisis; what exactly they will be cannot be predicted, but if those which occur are natural the

42 [1982] 1 All ER 851.

> wrongdoer cannot, I think, escape responsibility for them and their consequences simply by calling them improbable or unforeseeable. He must accept the risk of some unexpected mischances ... but what mischances?
>
> The answer to this difficult question must be dictated by common sense, rather than logic on the facts and circumstances of each case. In this case it must be answered in the light of the true view to be taken of the events leading up to Inspector Sommerville's acts, or rather his act and omission, and the plaintiff's and PC Easthope's, acts. I have expressed my view of all these links in the chain leading from Mr Johns' negligence to the plaintiff's collision with Mr Cotton. I have decided, respectfully disagreeing with the judge, that the inspector was negligent in failing to close the tunnel and, respectfully agreeing with the judge, that the plaintiff was not negligent in riding the wrong way after being ordered to do so by the inspector or in deciding on the spur of the moment to ride his motor cycle close to the wall in lane one.
>
> I am also of the opinion that the inspector's negligence was not a concurrent cause running with Mr Johns' negligence, but a new cause disturbing the sequence of events leading from Mr Johns' overturning of his car to the plaintiff's accident and interrupting the effect of it. This would, I think, have been so had the inspector's negligence stood alone. Coming as it did on top of the muddle and misunderstanding of Mr Williams' telephone call and followed by the inspector's order to remedy his own negligence by a dangerous manoeuvre, it was the real cause of the plaintiff's injury and made that injury too remote from Mr Johns' wrongdoing to be a consequence of it. ... In my judgment, too much happened here – too much went wrong, the chapter of accidents and mistakes was too long and varied – to impose on Mr Johns' liability for what happened to the plaintiff in discharging his duty as a police officer, although it would not have happened had not Mr Johns negligently overturned his car. The ordinary course of things took an extraordinary course. The length and the irregularities of the line leading from the first accident to the second have no parallel in the reported rescue cases, in all of which the plaintiff succeeded in establishing the original wrongdoer's liability. It was natural, it was probable, it was foreseeable, it was indeed certain, that the police would come to the overturned car and control the tunnel traffic. It was also natural and probable and foreseeable that some steps would be taken in controlling the traffic and clearing the tunnel and some things be done that might be more courageous than sensible. The reasonable hypothetical observer would anticipate some human errors, some forms of what might be called folly, perhaps even from trained police officers, and some unusual and unexpected accidents in the course of their rescue duties. But would he anticipate such a result as this from so many errors as these, so many departures from the common sense procedure prescribed by the standing orders for just such an emergency as this?

The Court of Appeal in *Robinson v Post Office* also touched upon the issue of intervening cause. Orr LJ commented:

> The judge, having found that Dr MacEwan was not negligent in deciding to administer ATS, and that, although he was negligent in failing to administer a proper test dose, such negligence had no causative effect, it is, in our judgment, impossible for the Post Office to rely on any negligence of the doctor as a *novus actus interveniens*.

The judge also indicated that anything short of negligence could not amount to a *novus actus*, which point counsel for the Post Office sought to argue.

Deliberate intervention by third parties

We need now to consider the issue of whether a deliberate act by a third party will be regarded as breaking the chain of causation. Sometimes the courts consider this as a duty issue,[43] in other cases as a causation/remoteness question. We shall be considering it from the latter perspective in this section, having already considered it from a duty viewpoint in Chapter 3. However, it will be apparent that, whether the matter is approached as one of duty or causation, the courts are extremely reluctant to impose liability on the original tortfeasor for further damage caused by a deliberate, often criminal act by a third party.

It has been said that, in order to satisfy the remoteness test, the plaintiff must show that the third party's deliberate act was very likely to happen following the defendant's breach of duty, or is the very thing to be guarded against.[44] This approach has not been followed all that consistently in the cases, and there is judicial divergence as to how the matter is to be dealt with. This is best exemplified in the case of *Lamb v Camden London Borough Council*,[45] where the plaintiffs alleged that as a result of the council's negligence squatters had invaded their empty property and caused significant damage to it. The differing approaches of the judges to the issue should be noted, although they agree on the result. After criticising Lord Reid's test in *Home Office v Dorset Yacht Co* ('very likely to happen'), Lord Denning MR went on:

> If Lord Reid's test is wrong, what is the alternative test? Logically, I suppose that liability and compensation should go hand in hand. If reasonable foresight is the criterion in negligence, so also it should be in remoteness of damage. ... To my mind that alternative test is also not acceptable. It would extend the range of compensation far too widely. ...
>
> The truth is that all these three – duty, remoteness and causation – are all devices by which the courts limit the range of liability for negligence or nuisance. As I said recently, in *Compania Financiera 'Soleado' SA v Hamoor Tanker Corpn Inc* [1981] 1 WLR 274, 281 EF '... it is not every consequence of a wrongful act which is the subject of compensation. The law has to draw the line somewhere'. Sometimes it is done by limiting the range of persons to whom the duty is owed. Sometimes it is done by saying that there is a break in the chain of causation. At other times it is done by saying that the consequence is too remote to be ahead of damage. All these devices are useful in their way. But ultimately it is a question of policy for the judges to decide. ...
>
> Looking at the question as one of policy, I ask myself: whose job was it to do something to keep out the squatters? And, if they got in to evict them? To my mind the answer is clear. It was the job of the owner of the house, Mrs Lamb, through her agents. That is how everyone in the case regarded it. It has never been suggested in the pleadings or elsewhere that it was the job of the council. No one ever wrote to the council asking them to do it. The council were not in occupation of the house. They had no right to enter it. All they had done was to break the water main outside and cause the subsidence. After they had left the site, it was Mrs Lamb *herself* who paved the way for the squatters by moving out

43 See, eg, *Perl v Camden London Borough Council* [1984] QB 342.

44 See, eg, *Stansbie v Troman* [1948] 2 KB 48.

45 [1981] QB 625.

all her furniture and leaving the house unoccupied and unfurnished. There was, then, if not before, on the judge's findings, a reasonably foreseeable risk that squatters might enter. She ought to have taken steps to guard against it. She says that she locked the doors and pulled the shutters. That turned out to be insufficient, but it was her responsibility to do more. At any rate, when the squatters did get in on the first occasion in 1974, it was then her agents who acted on her behalf. They got the squatters out. Then, at any rate, Mrs Lamb or her agents ought to have done something effective. But they only put up a few boards at a cost of £10. Then there was the second invasion in 1975. Then her agents did recognise her responsibility. They did what they could to get the squatters out. They eventually succeeded. But no one ever suggested throughout that it was the responsibility of the council.

In her evidence Mrs Lamb suggested that she had not the money to do more. I do not think that the judge accepted the suggestion. Her agents could well have made the house secure for a modest sum which was well within her capabilities.

On broader grounds of policy I would add this: the criminal acts here – malicious damage and theft – are usually covered by insurance. By this means the risk of loss is spread throughout the community. It does not fall heavily on one pair of shoulders alone. The insurers take the premium to cover just this sort of risk and should not be allowed, by subrogation, to pass it on to others. ... It is commonplace nowadays for the courts, when considering policy, to take insurance into account. ...

So here, it seems to me that if Mrs Lamb was insured against damage to the house and theft, the insurers should pay the loss. If she was not insured, that is her misfortune. Taking all these policy matters into account, I think the council are not liable for the acts of these squatters. I would dismiss this appeal.

Oliver LJ expressed himself somewhat differently:

The views which Lord Reid there expressed are not reflected in the speeches of the others of their Lordships in the case and were, I think, *obiter*, since there was no scope for argument on the assumed facts that the damage which occurred was not the very thing that was likely to happen. But, *obiter* or no, Lord Reid's opinion must be at least of the very highest persuasive authority. For my part, however, I very much doubt whether he was, in what he said regarding the likelihood of the act of a third party, intending to bring back into the test of remoteness some further philosophical consideration of nexus or direct or indirect causation. As it seems to me, all that Lord Reid was saying was this: that, where as a matter of fact the consequence which the court is considering is one which results from or would not have occurred but for the intervention of some independent human agency over which the tortfeasor has no control, it has to approach the problem of what could be reasonably foreseen by the tortfeasor, and thus of the damage for which he is responsible, with particular care.

The immediate cause is known. It is the independent human agency, and one has therefore to ask, on what basis can the act of that person be attributed back to the tortfeasor? It may be because the tortfeasor is responsible for his actions or because the third party act which has precipitated the damage is the very thing that the tortfeasor is employed to prevent. But what is the position in the absence of some such consideration? Few things are less predictable than human behaviour and if one is asked whether in any given situation a human being may behave idiotically, irrationally, or even criminally, the answer must always be that that is a possibility, for every society has its proportion of idiots and criminals. It cannot be said that you cannot foresee the possibility that people will do stupid or criminal acts, because people are constantly doing stupid or

Loan Receipt
Liverpool John Moores University
Library Services

Borrower Name: Yarwood, Jade
LAWJYARW
Borrower ID: ********

Sourcebook on tort /
31111008027359
Due Date: 02/04/2019 23:59:00 BST

Total items: 1
26/03/2019 23:18

Please keep your receipt in case of dispute.

> criminal acts. But the question is not what is foreseeable merely as a possibility but what would the reasonable man actually foresee if he thought about it, and all that Lord Reid seems to me to be saying is that the hypothetical reasonable man in the position of the tortfeasor cannot be said to foresee the behaviour of another person unless that behaviour is such as would, if viewed objectively, be very likely to occur.
>
> Thus, for instance, if by my negligent driving I damage another motorist's car, I suppose that theoretically I *could* foresee that, whilst he leaves it by the roadside to go and telephone his garage, some ill-intentioned passer-by may jack it up and remove the wheels. But I cannot think that it could be said that, merely because I have created the circumstances in which a theft might become possible, I ought reasonably to foresee that it would happen. ...
>
> To apply a straight test of foreseeability or likelihood to hypothetical circumstances which could arise in relation to the acts of independent third parties in the case of, for instance, carelessness on the part of servants of the Home Office does ... produce some astonishing results. Suppose that, as a result of the carelessness of a prison officer, a prisoner escapes and commits a crime of the same type as that for which he is in custody a fortnight later and 400 miles away from the place at which he escaped? Is it any less foreseeable that he will do so than that he will steal his rail fare from a house adjoining the prison? And is the Home Office to be liable without limit until the prisoner is apprehended? Does it make any difference if he is, at the date of his escape, on remand or due for parole?
>
> Happily such hypothetical questions do not, on the view that I take, have to be answered in the instant case, but whether or not it is right to regard questions of remoteness according to some flexible test of the policy of the law from time to time (upon which I prefer at the moment to express no view). I concur with Lord Denning MR in regarding the straight test of foreseeability, at least in cases where the acts of independent third parties are concerned, as one which can, unless subjected to some further limitation, produce results which extend the ambit of liability beyond all reason.
>
> Speaking for myself, I would respectfully regard Lord Reid's test as a workable and sensible one, subject only to this – that I think that he may perhaps have understated the *degree* of likelihood required before the law can or should attribute the free act of a responsible third person to the tortfeasor. Such attribution cannot, as I think, rationally be made simply on the basis of some geographical or temporal proximity and even 'likelihood' is a somewhat uncertain touchstone. It may be that some more stringent standard is required. There may, for instance, be circumstances in which the court would require a degree of likelihood amounting almost to inevitability before it fixes a defendant with responsibility for the act of a third party over whom he has and can have no control. On the official referee's finding, however, that does not arise here and the problem can be left for a case in which it directly arises.

Watkins LJ introduced a twist to the assessment of remoteness as follows:

> It seems to me that, if the sole and exclusive test of remoteness is whether the fresh damage which has arisen from an event or act which is reasonably foreseeable or reasonably foreseeable as a possibility, or likely or quite likely to occur, absurd even bizarre results might ensue in actions for damages for negligence. Why, if this test were to be rigidly applied to the facts in the *Dorset Yacht* case [1970] AC 1004, one can envisage the Home Office being found liable for the damage caused by an escaped Borstal boy committing a burglary in John O'Groats. This would plainly be a ludicrous conclusion.

> I do not think that words such as 'among others', 'possibility', 'likely' or 'quite likely' assist in the application of the test of reasonable foreseeability. If the crisply stated test which emanates from the *Wagon Mound (No 1)* [1961] AC 388 is to be festooned with additional words supposedly there for the purpose of amplification or qualification, an understandable application of it will become impossible. In my view *The Wagon Mound* test should always be applied without any of the gloss which is from time to time applied to it.
>
> But when so applied it cannot in all circumstances in which it arises conclude consideration of the question of remoteness, although in the vast majority of cases it will be adequate for this purpose. In other cases, the present one being an example of these in my opinion, further consideration is necessary, always providing, of course, that a plaintiff survives the test of reasonable foreseeability.
>
> This is because the very features of an event or act for which damages are claimed themselves suggest that the event or act is not upon any practical view of it remotely in any way connected with the original act of negligence. These features will include such matters as the nature of the event or act, the time it occurred, the place where it occurred, the identity of the perpetrator and his intentions and responsibility, if any, for taking measures to avoid the occurrence and matters of public policy.
>
> A robust and sensible approach to this very important area of study of remoteness will more often than not produce, I think, an instinctive feeling that the event or act being weighed in the balance is too remote to sound in damages for the plaintiff. I do not pretend that in all cases the answer will come easily to the inquirer. But that the question must be asked and answered in all these cases I have no doubt.
>
> To return to the present case, I have the instinctive feeling that squatters' damage is too remote. I could not possibly come to any other conclusion, although on the primary facts I, too, would regard that damages or something like it as reasonably foreseeable in these times.
>
> We are here dealing with unreasonable conduct of an outrageous kind. It is notorious that squatters will take the opportunity of entering and occupying any house, whether it be damaged or not, which is found to be unoccupied for more than a very temporary duration. In my opinion this kind of anti-social and criminal behaviour provides a glaring example of an act which inevitably, or almost so, is too remote to cause a defendant to pay damages for the consequences of it.

The three judgments in this case illustrate all too well the point that the remoteness test based on reasonable foreseeability is unhelpful when dealing with third party interventions of the type in that case. There is clear unease amongst the judiciary with the test and that is perhaps why Lord Denning MR prefers to base his decision on what he calls policy grounds, Oliver LJ uses a more orthodox approach of causation and *novus actus*, whereas poor Watkins LJ has to be content with a mere instinctive feeling.

This case must be contrasted with that of *Ward v Cannock Chase District Council*,[46] where, on broadly similar facts, Scott J came to a different conclusion, distinguishing *Lamb* on this point. The judge stated:

46 [1985] 3 All ER 537.

It was, in my judgment, a reasonably foreseeable consequence of the breaches of duty committed by the council that 3 and 4 Mossley would spend some time unoccupied.

The actual manner in which the property became unoccupied was not, by any stretch of the imagination, foreseeable. No one could have foreseen that Mr Boulton, the council and the county council would have taken the steps they did in order to force the Ward family out of occupation. But it was, none the less, in my view, a highly likely possibility that 3 and 4 The Mossley, if caused serious damage by the collapse of no 5 and if the damage was not promptly repaired, would have to be vacated. It was also, in my judgment, reasonably foreseeable that, if nos 3 and 4 were unoccupied, vandals and thieves might cause them damage. Given the record of vandalism and thievery at The Mossley it was, to my mind, virtually certain that, if nos 3 and 4 remained unoccupied for any length of time, they would receive the attention of vandals and thieves.

This case is, in my view, different on its facts from *Lamb v Camden Borough* in two important respects. First, the likelihood of unoccupied property receiving the attention of vandals was very much higher at The Mossley in Rugely than in Hampstead. In Hampstead it might have been foreseen as a possibility. At The Mossley it ought to have been foreseen as highly likely. Second, in *Lamb v Camden London Borough* the standpoint from which the foreseeability of the vandal damage was judged, at least by Oliver LJ, was the negligent act. What damage would a reasonable man actually foresee as likely to be caused to Mrs Lamb's house by the burst water main? That was the question which Oliver LJ thought should be asked. The answer did not include vandal damage. But the corresponding question in present case has to be asked not simply from the standpoint of the council's negligent omission to keep nos 5 and 6 in a safe condition, but from the stand point of the council's continued failure to repair the damage to 3 and 4 The Mossley caused by the collapse of nos 5 and 6. If the reasonable man were asked what damage to 3 and 4 The Mossley he would foresee if there were an indefinite failure to repair the serious damage which had been caused on 9 October 1982, his answer would, in my view, be that the property would have to be vacated and that further damage would be caused by vandals. ...

In the present case, if the breaches of duty committed by the council had not happened, 3 and 4 The Mossley would not have become unoccupied and would not have been damaged by the vandals. There is, in my view, a chain of causation leading from the breaches of duty to the damage sought to be recovered. Whether the chain of causation must be held to be broken by the intervention of independent third parties, namely the vandals, depends, in my view, on whether or not that intervention was itself a reasonably foreseeable consequence of one or other of the breaches of duty relied on. In my judgment, in the present case, the intervention was reasonably foreseeable. It was, applying Lord Reid's test, 'the very thing that was likely to happen' if the serious damage to nos 3 and 4 were left indefinitely unrepaired. The approach recommended by Watkins LJ leads, in my view, to the same conclusion. There seems to me to be a clear connection between the damage done by the vandals and thieves to 3 and 4 The Mossley and the failure by the council to repair the damage done when nos 5 and 6 collapsed. Common sense seems to me to justify imposing on the council liability for the consequences of its own failure.

The above judgment is a curious mixture of tests of causation and remoteness of damage which exemplifies what was said earlier to the effect that the judiciary is uncomfortable with present test of remoteness of damage as expressed in the

Wagon Mound (No 1). Another case which caused some difficulty for the judge is *Meah v McCreamer (No 2)*.[47] The plaintiff suffered severe head injuries in an accident caused by the driver of a car in which he was a passenger, the injuries resulting in a personality change leaving him with a tendency to attack women. Two of his rape victims sued him successfully for damages and he sought to obtain an indemnity in respect of these awards from the defendant. He was unsuccessful, the judge commenting:

> Both my intellectual and instinctive response to the matter ... is that the loss is not recoverable either from the driver of the car or that driver's insurers. I consider that this approach is supported by the following considerations. First of all, if a victim of these attacks had had a child, would the defendant, that is the driver, and his insurers be responsible for maintaining that child? The person who raped the mother certainly should be so responsible, but, in my view, it would be contrary to common sense to suggest that a careless driver should have to saddle himself with that sort of long-term expense.
>
> Again, one of the victims who sought damages yesterday before me alleged that the consequence of the attack on her was the break-up of her marriage. I did not accept that that was indeed the consequence. But, if I had come to a different conclusion, are the driver and his insurers to be taken to have foreseen that this would be the result of his negligent driving? I answer the question 'no'.
>
> Furthermore, I bear in mind that where a person sustains the sort of personal injuries that this plaintiff sustained, many years later he could attack a further victim. He is detained at the present time and is regarded as a category A prisoner for this very reason. Is the court required to give a declaration to the plaintiff that he is entitled to be, in effect, indemnified in respect of any claim brought against him in respect of any further attack of this nature?

The judge decided against the plaintiff on what might in this context be the unusually safer ground of public policy that the plaintiff should not be indemnified for the consequences of his crime.

These cases emphasise just how difficult it is to rationalise decisions in terms of causation and remoteness of damage in many of the cases that come before the courts.

Act of the plaintiff

We must finally consider the position where the act of the plaintiff intervenes between the breach of duty by the defendant and at least some of the plaintiff's damage. We shall look at two contrasting cases. The first is *McKew v Holland & Hannen & Cubitts (Scotland) Ltd*.[48] The plaintiff was injured at work as a result of the negligence of his employer. As a consequence, his leg would unexpectedly give way. On leaving some premises, as he was going down some stairs, his leg gave way and he jumped in an attempt to remain upright but he fell awkwardly and fractured his ankle. He claimed for this additional damage against his employers. In rejecting his claim, Lord Reid said:

> In my view the law is clear. If a man is injured in such a way that his leg may give way at any moment he must act reasonably and carefully. It is quite possible

47 [1986] 1 All ER 943.

48 [1969] 3 All ER 1621.

> that, in spite of all reasonable care, it may give way in circumstances such that as a result he sustains further injury. Then that second injury was caused by his disability which in turn was caused by the defender's fault. But if the injured man acts unreasonably he cannot hold the defender liable for injury caused by his own unreasonable conduct. His unreasonable conduct is *novus actus interveniens*. The chain of causation has been broken and what follows must be regarded as caused by his own conduct and not by the defender's fault or the disability caused by it. Or one may say that unreasonable conduct of the pursuer and what follows from it is not the natural and probable result of the original fault of the defender or of the ensuing disability.
>
> I do not think that foreseeability comes into this. A defender is not liable for a consequence of a kind which is not foreseeable. But it does not follow that he is liable for every consequence which a reasonable man could foresee. What can be foreseen depends almost entirely on the facts of the case, and it is often easy to foresee unreasonable conduct or some other *novus actus interveniens* as being quite likely. But that does not mean that the defender must pay for damage caused by the *novus actus*. It only leads to trouble that, if one tries to graft on to the concept of foreseeability, some rule of law to the effect that a wrongdoer is not bound to foresee something which in fact he could readily foresee as quite likely to happen. For it is not at all unlikely or unforeseeable that an active man who has suffered such a disability will take some quite unreasonable risk. But if he does he cannot hold the defender liable for the consequences.
>
> So, in my view the question here is whether the second accident was caused by the appellant doing something unreasonable. It was argued that the wrongdoer must take his victim as he finds him and that that applies not only to a thin skull but also to his intelligence. But I shall not deal with that argument because there is nothing in the evidence to suggest that the appellant is abnormally stupid. This case can be dealt with equally well by asking whether the appellant did something which a moment's reflection would have shown him was an unreasonable thing to do.
>
> He knew that his left leg was liable to give way suddenly and without warning. He knew that this stair was steep and that there was no hand rail. He would have realised, if he had given the matter a moment's thought, that he could only safely descend the stair if he either went extremely slowly and carefully so that he could sit down if his leg gave way, or waited for the assistance of his wife and brother-in-law. But he chose to descend in such a way that when his leg gave way he could not stop himself.

The other Law Lords were all in favour of dismissing the appeal also.

The other case is *Wieland v Cyril Lord Carpets Ltd*.[49] As a result of the defendants' negligence, the plaintiff had to wear a collar which prevented her from using her bifocal glasses as well as she might. She fell down some stairs and sustained further injuries. The High Court judge took the view that:

> In my view the injury and damage suffered because of the second fall are attributable to the original negligence of the defendants so as to attract compensation. ... It can be said that it is foreseeable that one injury may affect a person's ability to cope with the vicissitudes of life and thereby be a cause of another injury and if foreseeability is required, that is to say, if foreseeability in this context, foreseeability of this general nature will, in my view, suffice.

49 [1969] 3 All ER 1006.

The difficulty facing the judge in *Pigney v Pointer's Transport Services Ltd*[50] was whether the defendants could be held liable for the suicide of the plaintiff's husband following head injuries received by the husband as a result of the defendant's negligence. The judge took the view:

> I have no doubt on the evidence that the deceased would not have committed suicide if he had not been in a condition of acute neurotic depression induced by the accident. In this sense the injury which he sustained in the accident was a *causa sine qua non* of the accident. It is equally clear that the immediate cause of his death was that he hanged himself in a fit of acute depression. That he might do this was clearly a matter which could not reasonably have been foreseen by the defendants. ...
>
> Whilst the death of the deceased was not the kind of damage one would expect to result from the injury he received, I am satisfied that his death was, to use Scrutton LJ's words 'directly traceable' to the physical injury which he sustained, due to the lack of care of the defendants for his safety.

The last three decisions are also firm evidence of the shortcomings of the test established in the *Wagon Mound (No 1)* and the return to the old-fashioned concepts of causation.

50 [1957] 1 WLR 1121.

CHAPTER 5

LIABILITY FOR PSYCHIATRIC INJURY

INTRODUCTION

Twenty years ago or even less, this chapter would have been titled *Nervous shock*. Nowadays the new title is preferred as the former expression has been labelled as inaccurate and misleading by commentators and the judiciary. However, the term nervous shock will still be used on occasions. The topic has a chapter to itself, although other writers might include it in the general chapter on the duty of care in negligence. This does not signify that it has become a tort in its own right, but rather that it is a species of negligence with its own special rule of liability. Whether or not it is a tort in its own right can be debated elsewhere since, whether it is or not, does not really affect in substance the way in which the material is assembled or considered. By way of comparison with claims for economic loss, considered in the next chapter, there have been fewer cases on claims for psychiatric harm. However, the prevalence of this type of claim is on the increase if the incidence of the reported cases is anything to go by. To date there have been four House of Lords' decisions on claims for psychiatric harm.

The picture is one of gradual development of the principles in cases since the beginning of the century, with a slow broadening of the grounds for imposing liability. Liability for what was until recently called nervous shock was initially kept within extremely narrow confines for a number of reasons. The floodgates fear, the spectre of fraudulent claims and the initial lack of development in psychiatry, allied to the promotion of self reliance; all these factors persuaded the courts, at least in the early years of this type of liability, that tight control should be maintained over claims.

Initially, the courts would only recognise claims where the plaintiff had also suffered some physical injury as a consequence of the defendant's negligence, the rationale presumably being that psychiatric harm was much more likely as a consequence where there was also some physical damage to the plaintiff. Nowadays such a plaintiff would be called a primary victim, as opposed to the secondary victim, who normally would have witnessed the defendant putting, as a result off his negligence, the primary victim in danger. This distinction is now of some importance as a result of a recent House of Lords case discussed below. It is fair to say that the most problematic areas of the law in this context arise in relation to these so-called secondary victims, with the courts erecting barriers to recovery for just the reasons mentioned briefly above. These barriers take the form of familial, spatial and temporal proximity which must normally be established by the secondary victim in order to satisfy the duty of care requirement. We shall consider first of all the cases involving primary victims.

PRIMARY VICTIMS

Primary victims are those persons who are either physically injured by the breach of duty by the defendant or are in fear of their own safety, although in the event they do not actually sustain bodily injuries, In both types of case the victim suffers from a psychiatric illness. As was mentioned above, at first the law was not prepared to consider claims for nervous shock without the accompanying bodily injury. The position changed somewhat in the case of *Dulieu v White & Sons*[1] where the Court of Appeal considered a claim by a woman for nervous shock when a horse-drawn van was negligently driven into the public house in which she was working. She was not actually struck by it but was in fear of being so struck. Kennedy LJ asked:

> If impact be not necessary, and if, as must be assumed here, the fear is proved to have naturally and directly produced physical effects, so that the ill results of the negligence which caused the fear are as measurable in damages as the same results would be if they arose from an actual impact, why should not an action for those damages lie just as well as it lies where there has been an actual impact? It is not, however, to be taken that, in my view, every nervous shock occasioned by negligence and producing physical injury to the sufferer gives a cause of action. There is, I am inclined to think, at least one limitation. The shock, where it operates through the mind, must be a shock which arises from a reasonable fear of immediate personal injury to oneself. A has, I conceive, no legal duty not to shock B's nerves by the exhibition of negligence towards C, or towards the property of B or C.

The judge was in favour of allowing the plaintiff's claim. The statement in the last sentence of the brief extract from his judgment must now be read in the light of the cases below. His fellow judge, Phillimore J, said:

> I think there may be cases in which A owes a duty to B not to inflict a mental shock on him or her, and that in such a case, if A does inflict such a shock upon B – as by terrifying B – and physical damage thereby ensues, B may have an action for the physical damage, though the medium through which it has been inflicted is the mind.

It should be noted at this stage that both of the judges make it clear that the shock must manifest itself in some physical condition, eg the serious illness of the plaintiff and premature birth of the baby she was carrying at the time in that particular case. The history of nervous shock liability took another turn in subsequent cases because, despite Kennedy LJ's statement above that psychiatric damage to a witness of injury to another party through the negligence of the defendant was not actionable, that is precisely the way in which the law progressed, and little thought was given to there being any distinction between primary and secondary victims. That is, until recently. In the case of *Page v Smith*,[2] in only the fourth case to come before the House on this topic, it was necessary to decide whether the plaintiff could succeed in a claim for nervous shock where foreseeability of physical harm alone was present on the facts and the plaintiff was already suffering from the illness known as ME. It had been decided, as we shall see below, that to recover for psychiatric injury the plaintiff had to establish that harm by shock was reasonably foreseeable. The majority of the House decided that, as long as personal injury harm, whether physical or mental, was reasonably foreseeable, then a primary

1 [1901] 2 KB 669.

2 [1995] 2 All ER 736.

victim could succeed in a shock claim. Lord Browne-Wilkinson, agreeing in the main with Lord Lloyd of Berwick's analysis, in view of the fact that it was a majority decision added some words of his own as follows:

> In my view this case is bedevilled by use of the description 'nervous shock' to describe any injury suffered otherwise than by a chain of demonstrably physical causes. The law has long recognised tangible physical damage to the plaintiff as a head of damage. Medical science has now advanced so far that the process whereby an impact causing direct physical injury to one limb or organ of the body can be demonstrated to have caused physical damage to another limb or organ. Lawyers can readily accept that such consequential, physical damage is the consequence of the original impact. Hence there is a willingness to accept that all such tangible physical damage is foreseeable.
>
> Medical science has also demonstrated that there are other injuries the body can suffer as a consequence of an accident, such injuries not being demonstrably attributable to physical injury to the plaintiff. Injuries of this type may take two forms. First, physical illness or injury not brought about by a chain of demonstrable physical events but by mental or emotional stresses, ie by a psychiatric route. Examples are a heart attack or a miscarriage produced by shock. In this case, the end-product is a physical condition, although it has been brought about by a process which is not demonstrably a physical one but lies in the mental or nervous system. The second form is psychiatric illness itself which is brought about by mental or emotional stresses, ie by a psychiatric route. Because medical science has so far been less successful in demonstrating the nature of psychiatric illness and the processes whereby it is brought about by the psychiatric route, the courts have been more reluctant to accept the risk of such illness as being foreseeable. But since the decision of this House in *McLoughlin v O'Brian* [1982] 2 All ER, [1983] 1 AC 410 it has been established that, in certain circumstances, a defendant can be liable for illness or injury, whether psychiatric or physical, produced in a plaintiff by purely psychiatric processes, without any direct physical impact on, or injury to, the limbs or organs of the plaintiff. That case also establishes that such a process is, in certain circumstances, to be treated as foreseeable by a defendant.
>
> It follows that, in the present case, the fact that the plaintiff suffered no tangible physical injury is irrelevant to the question whether or not he is entitled to recover damages for the recrudescence of his illness. On the judge's findings, the plaintiff suffered injury (the recrudescence of his illness) by the psychiatric route, ie by reason of shock exacerbating his condition. The question, therefore, is whether the driver of a car should reasonably foresee that a person involved in an accident may suffer psychiatric injury of some kind (whether or not accompanied by physical injury). I have no doubt that he should. It is not physical injury alone which causes illness or injury; physical or psychiatric illness occurs quite apart from physical injury.
>
> ... I am, therefore, of the opinion that any driver of a car should reasonably foresee that, if he drives carelessly, he will be liable to cause injury, either physical or psychiatric or both, to other users of the highway who become involved in an accident. Therefore he owes to such persons a duty of care to avoid such injury. In the present case the defendant could not foresee the exact type of psychiatric damage suffered by the plaintiff who, due to his ME, was an 'eggshell personality'. But that is of no significance since the defendant did owe a duty of care to prevent foreseeable damage, including psychiatric damage. Once such a duty of care is established, the defendant must take his victim as he finds him. ... In my judgment, the law will be more effective if it accepts that the result

> of being involved in a collision may include both physical and psychiatric damage.

Lord Lloyd of Berwick, in giving the leading judgment for the majority view, after discussing the proximity requirements in relation to secondary victims, commented:

> None of these mechanisms are required in the case of a primary victim. Since liability depends on foreseeability of physical injury, there could be no question of the defendant finding himself liable to all the world. Proximity of relationship cannot arise, and proximity in time and space goes without saying.
>
> Nor in the case of a primary victim is it appropriate to ask whether he is a person of 'ordinary phlegm'. In the case of physical injury there is no such requirement. The negligent defendant, or more usually his insurer, takes his victim as he finds him. The same should apply in the case of psychiatric injury. There is no difference in principle ... between an eggshell skull and an eggshell personality. Since the number of potential claimants is limited by the nature of the case, there is no need to impose any further limit by reference to a person of ordinary phlegm. Nor can I see any justification for doing so.
>
> As for bogus claims, it is sometimes said that if the law were such as I believe it to be, the plaintiff would be able to recover damages for a fright. This is not so. Shock by itself is not the subject of compensation, any more than fear or grief or any other human emotion occasioned by the defendant's negligent conduct. It is only when shock is followed by recognisable psychiatric illness that the defendant may be held liable.
>
> There is another limiting factor. Before a defendant can be held liable for psychiatric injury suffered by a primary victim, he must at least have foreseen the risk of physical injury. So that if ... the defendant bumped his neighbour's car while parking in the street, in circumstances in which he could not reasonably foresee that the occupant would suffer any physical injury at all, or suffer injury so trivial as not to found an action in tort, there could be no question of his being held liable for the onset of hysteria. Since he could not reasonably foresee any injury, physical or psychiatric, he would owe the plaintiff no duty of care. That example is, however, far removed from the present.
>
> So I do not foresee any great increase in unmeritorious claims. The court will, as ever, have to be vigilant to discern genuine shock resulting in recognised psychiatric illness. But there is nothing new in that. The floodgates argument has made regular appearances in this field ... I do not regard it as a serious obstacle here ... The test in every case ought to be whether the defendant can reasonably foresee that his conduct will expose the plaintiff to risk of personal injury ... If so, then he comes under a duty of care to that plaintiff ... In the case of a secondary victim, the question will usually turn on whether the foreseeable injury is psychiatric, for the reasons already explained. In the case of a primary victim the question will almost always turn on whether the foreseeable injury is physical. But it is the same test in both cases, with different applications. There is no justification for regarding physical and psychiatric injury as different kinds of injury. Once it is established that the defendant is under a duty of care to avoid causing personal injury to the plaintiff, it matters not whether the injury in fact sustained is physical, psychiatric or both.
>
> ... Applying that test in the present case, it was enough to ask whether the defendant should have reasonably foreseen that the plaintiff might suffer physical injury as a result of the defendant's negligence, so as to bring him within the range of the defendant's duty of care. It was unnecessary to ask, as a

> separate question, whether the defendant should reasonably have foreseen injury by shock; and it is irrelevant that the plaintiff did not, in fact, suffer any external physical injury.
>
> ... In conclusion, the following propositions can be supported.
>
> (1) In cases involving nervous shock, it is essential to distinguish between the primary victim and secondary victims.
>
> (2) In claims by secondary victims the law insists on certain control mechanisms, in order as a matter of policy to limit the number of potential claimants. Thus, the defendant will not be liable unless psychiatric injury is foreseeable in a person of normal fortitude. These control mechanisms have no place where the plaintiff is the primary victim.
>
> (3) In claims by secondary victims, it may be legitimate to use hindsight in order to be able to apply the test of reasonable foreseeability at all. Hindsight, however, has no part to play where the plaintiff is a primary victim.
>
> (4) Subject to the above qualifications, the approach in all cases should be the same, namely, whether the defendant can reasonably foresee that his conduct will expose the plaintiff to the risk of personal injury, whether physical or psychiatric. If the answer is yes, then the duty of care is established, even though physical injury does not in fact occur. There is no justification for regarding physical and psychiatric injury as different 'kinds of damage'.
>
> (5) A defendant who is under a duty of care to the plaintiff, whether as primary or secondary victim, is not liable for damages for nervous shock unless the shock results in some recognised psychiatric illness. It is no answer that the plaintiff was predisposed to psychiatric illness. Nor is it relevant that the illness takes a rare form or is of unusual severity. The defendant must take his victim as he finds him.

SECONDARY VICTIMS

Whilst the distinction between secondary and primary victims has only recently received significant emphasis, most of the reported litigation has been concerned with plaintiffs who would be regarded as secondary victims. The first of these cases was *Hambrook v Stokes*.[3] In this case a majority of the Court of Appeal held that a woman put in fear of the safety of her children by the defendant's negligence had a viable claim for nervous shock. One of the judges in that majority, Bankes LJ stated:

> Upon the authorities as they stand, the defendant ought to have anticipated that if his lorry ran away down this narrow street, it might terrify some woman to such an extent, through fear of some immediate bodily injury to herself, that she would receive such a mental shock as would injure her health. Can any real distinction be drawn from the point of view of what the defendant ought to have anticipated and what, therefore, his duty was, between that case and the case of a woman whose fear is for her child, and not for herself?
>
> Take a case in point as a test. Assume two mothers crossing this street at the same time when this lorry comes thundering down, each holding a small child by the hand. One mother is courageous and devoted to her child. She is terrified, but thinks only of the damage to the child, and not at all about herself. The other

3 [1925] 1 KB 141.

> woman is timid and lacking in the motherly instinct. She is also terrified, but thinks only of damage to herself and not at all about her child. The health of both mothers is seriously affected by the mental shock occasioned by the fright. Can any real distinction be drawn between the two cases? Will the law recognise a cause of action in the case of the less deserving mother, and none in the case of the more deserving one? Does the law say that the defendant ought reasonably to have anticipated the non-natural feeling of the timid mother, and not the natural feeling of the courageous mother? I think not. ...
>
> I wish to confine my decision to cases where the facts are indistinguishable in principle from the facts of the present case, and in the present case I am merely deciding that, in my opinion, the plaintiff would establish a cause of action if he proved to the satisfaction of the jury all the material facts on which he relies – namely, that the death of his wife resulted from the shock occasioned by the running away of the lorry, that the shock resulted from what the plaintiff's wife either saw or realised by her own unaided sense, and not from something which someone told her, and that the shock was due to a reasonable fear of immediate personal injury either to herself or to her children.

Atkin LJ, who agreed with Bankes LJ, said:

> The legal effects of injury by shock have undoubtedly developed in the last 30–40 years. At one time the theory was held that damage at law could not be proved in respect of personal injuries, unless there was some injury which was variously called 'bodily' or 'physical', but which necessarily excluded an injury which was only 'mental'. There can be no doubt at the present day that this theory is wrong. It is perhaps irrelevant to discuss at length how it arose. It may be due partly to a false analogy between the action of negligence and the action of trespass to the person involving some sort of impact with the person; and in part to the law following a belated psychology which falsely removed mental phenomena from the world of physical phenomena. ...
>
> In my opinion it is not necessary to treat this cause of action as based upon a duty to take reasonable care to avoid administering a shock to wayfarers. The cause of action ... appears to be created by breach of the ordinary duty to take reasonable care to avoid inflicting personal injuries, followed by damage, even though the type of damage may be unexpected – namely, shock. The question appears to be as to the extent of the duty, and not as to remoteness of damage. If it were necessary, however, I should accept the view that the duty extended to the duty to take care to avoid threatening personal injury to a child in such circumstances as to cause damage by shock to a parent or guardian then present, and that the duty was owed to the parent or guardian; but I confess that upon this view of the case I should find it difficult to explain why the duty was confined to the case of parent or guardian and child, and did not extend to other relations of life also involving intimate associations; and why it did not eventually extend to bystanders.

The issue of bystanders came up in the next important case on nervous shock, namely, *Bourhill v Young*,[4] a case in which the pursuer unsuccessfully claimed damages for shock against the driver of a motor bike which negligently collided with a car a short distance form her. The deceased motor cyclist and the pursuer were in no way related. Lord Russell of Killowen, in rejecting the appeal by the pursuer, argued:

4 [1943] AC 92.

> Can it be said that John Young could reasonably have anticipated that a person, situated as was the appellant, would be affected by his proceeding towards Colinton at the speed at which he was travelling? I think not. His road was clear of pedestrians. The appellant was not within his vision, but was standing behind the solid barrier of the tramcar. His speed in no way endangered her. In these circumstances I am unable to see how he could reasonably anticipate that, if he came into collision with a vehicle coming across the tramcar into Glenlockhart Road, the resultant noise would cause physical injury by shock to a person standing behind the tramcar. In my opinion, he owed no duty to the appellant, and was, therefore, not guilty of any negligence in relation to her.

Lord Macmillan, also in favour of dismissal, stated:

> It is no longer necessary to consider whether the infliction of what is called mental shock may constitute an actionable wrong. The crude view that the law should take cognisance only of physical injury resulting from actual impact has been discarded, and it is now well recognised that an action will lie for injury by shock sustained through the medium of the eye or the ear without direct contact. The distinction between mental shock and bodily injury was never a scientific one, for mental shock is presumably in all cases the result of, or at least accompanied by, some physical disturbance in the sufferer's system. And a mental shock may have consequences more serious than those resulting from physical impact. But in the case of mental shock there are elements of greater subtlety than in the case of an ordinary physical injury and these elements may give rise to debate as to the precise scope of legal liability....In the present instance the late John Young was clearly negligent in a question with the occupants of the motor car with which his cycle collided. He was driving at an excessive speed in a public thoroughfare and he ought to have foreseen that he might consequently collide with any vehicle which he might meet in his course, for such an occurrence may reasonably and probably be expected to ensue from driving at a high speed in a street. But can it be said that he ought further to have foreseen that his excessive speed, involving the possibility of collision with another vehicle, might cause injury by shock to the appellant? The appellant was not in his line of vision, for she was on the other side of a tramcar which was standing between him and her when he passed, and it was not until he had proceeded some distance beyond her that he collided with the motor car. The appellant did not see the accident and she expressly admits that her 'terror did not involve any element of reasonable fear of immediate bodily injury to herself'. She was not so placed that there was any reasonable likelihood of her being affected by the cyclist's careless driving. In these circumstance I am of the opinion with the majority of the learned judges of the Second Division that the late John Young was under no duty to the appellant to foresee that his negligence in driving at an excessive speed and consequently colliding with a motor car might result in injury to her, for such a result could not reasonably and probably be anticipated. He was, therefore, not guilty of negligence in a question with the appellant.

Lord Wright, dismissing the appeal also, commented:

> The present case, like many others of this type, may, however, raise the different question whether the appellant's illness was not due to her peculiar susceptibility. She was eight months gone in pregnancy. Can it be said, apart from everything else, that it was likely that a person of normal nervous strength would have been affected in the circumstances by illness as the appellant was? Does the criterion of reasonable foresight extend beyond people of ordinary health or susceptibility, or does it take into account the peculiar susceptibilities or

> infirmities of those affected which the defendant neither knew of nor could reasonably be taken to have foreseen? Must the manner of conduct adapt itself to such special individual peculiarities? If extreme cases are taken, the answer appears to be fairly clear, unless, indeed, there is knowledge of extraordinary risk. One who suffers from the terrible tendency to bleed on slight contact, which is denoted by the term 'bleeder', cannot complain if he mixes with the crowd and suffers severely, perhaps fatally, from being merely brushed against. There is no wrong done there. ...
>
> What is now being considered is the question of liability, and this, I think, in a question whether there is a duty owing to members of the public who come within the ambit of the act, must generally depend on a normal standard of susceptibility. This, it may be said, is somewhat vague. That is true, but definition involves limitation which it is desirable to avoid further than is necessary in a principle of law like negligence which is widely ranging and is still in the stage of development. It is here, as elsewhere, a question of what the hypothetical reasonable man, viewing the position, I suppose *ex post facto*, would say it was proper to foresee. What danger of particular infirmity that would include must depend on all the circumstances, but generally, I think, a reasonably normal condition, if medical evidence is capable of defining it, would be the standard.
>
> The test of the plaintiff's extraordinary susceptibility, if unknown to the defendant, would in effect make him an insurer. The lawyer likes to draw fixed and definite lines and is apt to ask where the thing is to stop. I should reply it should stop where in the particular case the good sense of the jury or of the judge decides ... Upon these, can it be said that a duty is made out, and breach of that duty, so that the damage which is found is recoverable? I think not. The appellant was completely outside the range of the collision. She merely heard a noise, which upset her, without her having any definite idea at all ... She saw nothing of the actual accident, or, indeed, any marks of blood until later. I cannot accept that John Young could reasonably have foreseen, or, more correctly, the reasonable hypothetical observer could reasonably have foreseen, the likelihood that anyone placed as the appellant was, could be affected in the manner in which she was. In my opinion, John Young was guilty of no breach of duty to the appellant, and was not in law responsible for the hurt which she sustained. I may add that the issue of duty or no duty is, indeed, a question for the court, but it depends on the view taken of the facts. In the present case both courts below have taken the view that the appellant has, on the facts of the case, no redress, and I agree with their view.

As similar line was taken by Lord Porter saying:

> In the present case the appellant was never herself in any bodily danger nor reasonably in fear of danger either for herself or others. She was merely a person who, as a result of the action, was emotionally disturbed and rendered physically ill by that emotional disturbance. The question whether emotional disturbance or shock, which a defender ought reasonably to have anticipated as likely to follow from his reckless driving, can ever form the basis of a claim is not in issue. It is not every emotional disturbance or every shock which should have been foreseen. The driver of a car or vehicle, even though careless, is entitled to assume that the ordinary frequenter of the streets has sufficient fortitude to endure such incidents as may from time to time be expected to occur in them, including the noise of a collision and the sight of injury to others, and is not to be considered negligent towards one who does not possess the customary phlegm.

Lord Thankerton went along with his colleagues in rejecting the appeal. As is evident from the extracts above, some of their Lordships seemed to be saying that the appellant was outside the area of reasonable foreseeability of harm by shock on the basis of purely geographical considerations. If the woman had been round the other side of the tramcar with the accident in full view, would the result have been any different? On the basis of Lord Porter's reasoning above, presumably, and justifiably, not. This is perhaps the preferred view of the decision, namely, that normally mere bystanders cannot recover. We shall return to this issue later.

The next important case on liability for psychiatric harm is *McLoughlin v O'Brian*[5] in which the House of Lords took the opportunity to air their Lordships' views on this apparently developing area of the law of negligence. The plaintiff was told of an accident involving her husband and children. She went to the hospital some two hours after the accident and saw them in a very sorry state indeed, and was informed that one young daughter had died as a result of the accident. Her appeal was allowed by the House but the method of achieving this result varies somewhat as between the judges. Lord Wilberforce's judgment is usually regarded as the leading one and we shall start with this as follows:

> Although we continue to use the hallowed expression 'nervous shock', English law, and common understanding, have moved some distance since recognition was given to this symptom as a basis for liability. Whatever is known about the mind-body relationship (and the area of ignorance seems to expand with that knowledge), it is now accepted by medical science that recognisable and severe physical damage to the human body and system may be caused by the impact, through the senses, of external events on the mind. There may thus be produced what is identifiable an illness as any that may be caused by direct physical impact. It is safe to say this, in general terms, is understood by the ordinary man or woman who is hypothesised by the courts in situations where claims for negligence are made. Although in the only one case which has reached this House (*Bourhill v Young* [1943] AC 92) a claim for damages in respect of 'nervous shock' was rejected on its facts, the House gave clear recognition to the legitimacy, in principle, of claims of that character. As the result of that and other cases, assuming they are accepted as correct, the following position has been reached:
>
> 1 While damages cannot, at common law, be awarded for grief and sorrow, a claim for damages for 'nervous shock' caused by negligence can be made without the necessity of showing direct impact or fear of immediate personal injuries for oneself. The reservation made by Kennedy J in *Dulieu v White & Sons* [1901] 2 KB 669, though taken up by Sargant LJ in *Hambrook v Stokes Brothers* [1925] 1 KB 141, has not gained acceptance, and although the respondents, in the courts below, reserved their right to revive it, they did not do so in argument. I think that it is now too late to do so. The arguments on this issue were fully and admirably stated by the Supreme Court of California in *Dillon v Legg* (1968) 29 ALR 3d 1316.
>
> 2 A plaintiff may recover damages for 'nervous shock' brought on by injury caused not to him or herself but to a near relative, or by the fear of such injury. So far (subject to 5 below), the cases do not extend beyond the spouse

5 [1982] 2 WLR 982.

or children of the plaintiff (*Hambrook v Stokes Brothers* [1925] 1 KB 141, *Boardman v Sanderson* [1964] 1 WLR 1317, *Hinz v Berry* [1970] 2 QB 40 – including foster children – (where liability was assumed), and see *King v Phillips* [1953] 1 QB 429).

3 Subject to the next paragraph, there is no English case in which a plaintiff has been able to recover nervous shock damages where the injury to the near relative occurred out of sight and earshot of the plaintiff. In *Hambrook v Stokes Brothers* an express distinction was made between shock caused by what the mother saw with her own eyes and what she might have been told by bystanders, liability being excluded in the latter case.

4 An exception from, or I would prefer to call it an extension of, the latter case has been made where the plaintiff does not see or hear the incident but comes upon its immediate aftermath. In *Boardman v Sanderson* the father was in earshot of the accident to his child and likely to come upon the scene; he did so and suffered damage from what he then saw. In *Marshall v Lionel Enterprises Inc* [1972] 2 OR 177 the wife came immediately upon the badly injured body of her husband. And in *Benson v Lee* [1972] VR 879, a situation existed with some similarity to the present case. The mother was in her home 100 yards away, and, on communication by a third party, ran out to the scene of the accident and there suffered shock. Your Lordships have to decide whether or not to validate these extensions.

5 A remedy on account of nervous shock has been given to a man who came upon a serious accident involving numerous people immediately thereafter and acted as a rescuer of those involved (*Chadwick v British Railways Board* [1967] 1 WLR 912). 'Shock' was caused neither by fear for himself nor by fear or horror on account of a near relative. The principle of 'rescuer' cases was not challenged by the respondents and ought, in my opinion, to be accepted. But we have to consider whether, and how far, it can be applied to cases such as the present.

Throughout these developments, as can be seen, the courts have proceeded in the traditional manner of the common law from case to case, upon a basis of logical necessity. If a mother, with or without accompanying children, could recover on account of fear for herself, how can she be denied recovery on account of fear for her accompanying children? If a father could recover had he seen his child run over by a backing car, how can he be denied recovery if he is in the immediate vicinity and runs to the child's assistance? If a wife and mother could recover if she had witnessed a serious accident to her husband and children, does she fail because she was a short distance away and immediately rushes to the scene (Cf *Benson v Lee*)? I think that, unless the law is to draw an arbitrary line at the point of direct sight and sound, these arguments require acceptance of the extension mentioned above under 4 in the interest of justice.

If one continues to follow the process of logical progression, it is hard to see why the present plaintiff also should not succeed. She was not present at the accident, but she came very soon upon its aftermath. If, from a distance of some 100 yards (Cf *Benson v Lee*), she had found her family by the roadside, she would have come within principle 4 above. Can it make any difference that she comes upon them in an ambulance, or, as here, in a nearby hospital, when, as the evidence shows, they were in the same condition, covered with oil and mud and distraught with pain? If Mr Chadwick can recover, when acting in accordance with normal and irresistible human instinct, and indeed moral compulsion, he goes to the scene of an accident, may not a mother recover if, acting under the same motives, she goes to where her family can be found?

I could agree that a line can be drawn above her case with less hardship than would have been apparent in *Boardman v Sanderson* [1964] 1 WLR 1317 and *Hinz v Berry* [1970] 2 QB 40, but so to draw it would not appeal to most people's sense of justice. To allow her claim may be, I think it is, upon the margin of what the process of logical progression would allow. But where the facts are strong and exceptional, and, as I think, fairly analogous, her case ought, *prima facie* to be assimilated to those which have passed the test.

To argue from one factual situation to another and to decide by analogy is a natural tendency of the human and legal mind. But the lawyer still has to inquire whether, in so doing, he has crossed some critical line behind which he ought to stop. That is said to be the present case. The reasoning by which the Lords Justices decided not to grant relief to the plaintiff is instructive. Both Stephenson LJ and Griffiths LJ accepted that the 'shock' to the plaintiff was foreseeable; but from this, at least in presentation they diverge. Stephenson LJ considered that the defendants owed a duty of care to the plaintiff, but that for reasons of policy the law should stop short of giving her damages; it should limit relief to those on or near the highway at or near the time of the accident caused by the defendants' negligence. He was influenced by the fact that the courts of this country, and of other common law jurisdictions, had stopped at this point; it was indicated by the barrier of commercial sense and practical convenience. Griffiths LJ took the view that, although the injury to the plaintiff was foreseeable, there was no duty of care. The duty of care of drivers of motor vehicles was, according to decided cases, limited to persons and owners of property on the road or near to it who might be directly affected. The line should be drawn at this point. It was not even in the interest of those suffering shock as a class to extend the scope of the defendants' liability; to do so would quite likely delay their recovery by immersing them in the anxiety of litigation.

I am impressed by both of these arguments, which I have only briefly summarised. Though differing in expression, in the end, in my opinion, the two presentations rest upon a common principle, namely that, at the margin, the boundaries of a man' s responsibility for acts of negligence have to be fixed as a matter of policy. Whatever is the correct jurisprudential analysis, it does not make any essential difference whether one says, with Stephenson LJ, that there is a duty but, as a matter of policy, the consequences of breach of it ought to be limited at a certain point, or whether, with Griffiths LJ, one says that the fact that the consequences may be foreseeable does not automatically impose a duty of care, does not do so in fact where policy indicates the contrary. This is an approach which one can see very clearly from the way in which Lord Atkin stated the neighbour principle in *Donoghue v Stevenson* [1932] AC 56, 580: 'persons who are so closely and directly affected by my act that I ought reasonably to have them in contemplation as being so affected ...' This is saying that foreseeability must be accompanied and limited by the law's judgment as to persons who ought, according to its standards of value or justice, to have been in contemplation. Foreseeability, which involves a hypothetical person, looking with hindsight at an event which has occurred, is a formula adopted by English law, not merely for defining, but also for limiting, the persons to whom duty may be owed, and the consequences for which an actor may be held responsible. It is not merely an issue of fact to be left to be found as such. When it is said to result in a duty of care being owed to a person or class, the statement that there is a 'duty of care'denotes a conclusion into the forming of which considerations of policy have entered. That foreseeability does not of itself, and automatically, lead to a duty of care is, I think, clear. ...

We must then consider the policy arguments. In doing so we must bear in mind that cases of 'nervous shock', and the possibility of claiming damages for it, are not necessarily confined to those arising out of accidents on public roads. To state, therefore, a rule that recoverable damages must be confined to persons on or near the highway is to state not a principle in itself, but only an example of a more general rule that recoverable damages must be confined to those within sight and sound of an event caused by negligence or, at least, to those in close, or very close, proximity to such a situation. The policy arguments against a wider extension can be stated under four heads.

First, it may be said that such extension may lead to a proliferation of claims, possibly fraudulent, to the establishment of an industry of lawyers and psychiatrists who will formulate a claim for nervous shock damages, including what in America is called the customary miscarriage, for all, or many, road accidents and industrial accidents.

Second, it may be claimed that an extension of liability would be unfair to defendants, as imposing damages out of proportion to the negligent conduct complained of. In so far as such defendants are insured, a large additional burden will be placed on insurers, and ultimately upon the class of persons insured – road users or employers.

Third, to extend liability beyond the most direct and plain cases would greatly increase evidentiary difficulties and tend to lengthen litigation.

Fourth, it may be said – and the Court of Appeal agreed with this – that an extension of the scope of liability ought only to be made by the legislature after careful research. This is the course which has been taken in New South Wales and the Australian Capital territory.

The whole argument has been well summed up by Dean Prosser (Prosser, *Torts*, 4th edn (1971), p 256): 'The reluctance of the courts to enter this field, even where the mental injury is clearly foreseeable, and the frequent mention of the difficulties of proof, the facility of fraud and the problem of finding a place to stop and draw the line suggest that here it is the nature of the interest invaded and the type of damage which is the real obstacle.'

Since he wrote, the type of damage has, in this country at least, become more familiar and less deterrent to recovery. And some of the arguments are susceptible of answer. Fraudulent claims can be contained by the courts, who, also, can cope with evidentiary difficulties. The scarcity of cases which have occurred in the past, and the modest sums recovered, give some indication that fears of a flood of litigation may be exaggerated – experience in other fields suggests that such fears usually are. If some increase does occur, that may only reveal the existence of a genuine social need; that legislation has been found necessary in Australia may indicate the same thing.

But, these discounts accepted, there remains in my opinion, just because 'shock' in its nature is capable of affecting so wide a range of people, a real need for the law to place some limitation upon the extent of admissible claims. It is necessary to consider three elements inherent in any claim: the class of persons whose claims should be recognised; the proximity of such persons to the accident; and the means by which the shock is caused. As regards the class of persons, the possible range is between the closest range of family ties – of parent and child, or husband and wife – and the ordinary bystander. Existing law recognises the claims of the first; it denies that of the second, either on the basis that such persons must be assumed to be possessed of fortitude sufficient to enable them to endure the calamities of modern life, or that the defendants cannot be expected to compensate the world at large. In my opinion, these positions are justifiable,

> and since the present case falls within the first class, it is strictly unnecessary to say more. I think, however, that it should follow that other cases involving less close relationships must be very carefully scrutinised. I cannot say that they should never be admitted. The closer the tie (not merely in relationship, but in care) the greater the claim for consideration. The claim in any case, has to be judged in the light of other factors, such as proximity to the scene in time and place, and the nature of the accident.
>
> As regards proximity to the accident, it is obvious that this must be close in both time and space. It is, after all, the fact and consequence of the defendant's negligence that must be proved to have caused the 'nervous shock'. Experience has shown that to insist on direct and immediate sight or hearing would be impractical and unjust and that, under what may be called the 'aftermath' doctrine, one who, from close proximity, comes very soon upon the scene should not be excluded.
>
> ... Finally, and by way of reinforcement of 'aftermath' cases, I would accept, by analogy with 'rescue' situations, that a person of whom it could be said that one could expect nothing else than that he or she would come immediately to the scene – normally a parent or spouse – could be regarded as being within the scope of foresight and duty. Where there is not immediate presence, account must be taken of the possibility of alterations in the circumstances, for which the defendant should not be responsible.
>
> Subject only to these qualifications, I think that a strict test of proximity by sight or hearing should be applied by the courts.
>
> Lastly, as regards communication, there is no case in which the law has compensated shock brought about by communication by a third party ... The shock must come through sight or hearing of the event or of its immediate aftermath. Whether some equivalent of sight or hearing, eg through simultaneous television, would suffice may have to be considered.
>
> My Lords, I believe that these indications, imperfectly sketched, and certainly to be applied with common sense to individual situations in their entirety, represent either the existing law, or the existing law with only such circumstantial extension as the common law process may legitimately make. They do not introduce a new principle. Nor do I see any reason why the law should retreat behind the lines already drawn. I find on this appeal that the appellant's case falls within the boundaries of the law so drawn. I would allow her appeal.

Without doubt this was at the time the fullest account of the law so far undertaken in any case. Not all His Lordship's colleagues, whilst agreeing in the result, were of the same mind as to how that result was to be achieved. Lord Scarman commented as follows:

> The appeal raises directly a question as to the balance in our law between the functions of judge and legislature. The common law, which in a constitutional context includes judicially developed equity, covers everything which is not covered by statute. It knows no gaps; there can be no '*casus omissus*'. The function of the court is to decide the case before it, even though the decision may require the extension or adaptation of a principle, or in some cases the creation of new law to meet the justice of the case. But, whatever the court decides to do, it starts from a baseline of existing principle and seeks a solution consistent with or analogous to a principle or principles already recognised.
>
> The distinguishing feature of the common law is this judicial development and formation of principle. Policy considerations will have to be weighed; but the

> objective of the judges is the formulation of principle. And, if principle inexorably requires a decision which entails a degree of policy risk, the court's function is to adjudicate according to principle, leaving policy curtailment to the judgment of Parliament. Here lies the true role of the two law-making institutions in our constitution. By concentrating on principle the judges can keep the common law alive, flexible and consistent, and can keep the legal system clear of policy problems which neither they, nor the forensic process which it is their duty to operate, are equipped to resolve. If principle leads to results which are thought to be socially unacceptable, Parliament can legislate to draw a line or map out a new path.
>
> The real risk to the common law is not its movement to cover new situations and new knowledge but lest it should stand still, halted by a conservative judicial approach. If that should happen ... there would be a danger of the law becoming irrelevant to the consideration, and inept in its treatment, of modern social problems. Justice would be defeated. The common law has, however, avoided this catastrophe by the flexibility given it by generations of judges. Flexibility carries with it, of course, certain risks, notably a degree of uncertainty in the law and the 'floodgates' risk which so impressed the Court of Appeal in the present case.
>
> The importance to be attached to certainty and the size of the 'floodgates' risk vary from one branch of the law to the other. What is required of the law in its approach to a commercial transaction will be very different from the approach appropriate to problems of tortious liability for personal injuries. In some branches of the law, notably that now under consideration, the search for certainty can obstruct the law, in its pursuit of justice, and can become the enemy of the good ... The 'floodgates' argument may be exaggerated. Time alone will tell; but I foresee social and financial problems if damages for 'nervous shock' should be made available to persons other than parents and children who, without seeing or hearing the accident, or being present in the immediate aftermath, suffer nervous shock in consequence of it. There is, I think, a powerful case for legislation such as has been enacted in New South Wales and the Australian Capital Territories.
>
> Why then should not the courts draw the line, as the Court of Appeal manfully tried to do in this case? Simply, because the policy issue as to where to draw the line is not justiciable. The problem is one of social, economic and financial policy. The considerations relevant to a decision are not such as to be capable of being handled within the limits of the forensic process.
>
> My Lords, I would allow the appeal for the reasons developed by my noble and learned friend, Lord Bridge of Harwich, while putting on record my view that there is here a case for legislation.

Turning, therefore, to the speech of Lord Bridge, he observed:

> The basic difficulty of the subject arises from the fact that the crucial answers to the questions which it raises lie in the difficult field of psychiatric medicine. The common law gives no damages for the emotional distress which any normal person experiences when someone he loves is killed or injured. Anxiety and depression are normal human emotions. Yet an anxiety neurosis or a reactive depression may be recognisable psychiatric illnesses, with or without psychosomatic symptoms. So, the first hurdle which a plaintiff claiming damages of the kind in question must surmount is to establish that he is suffering, not merely grief, distress or any other normal emotion, but a positive psychiatric illness. That is here not in issue. A plaintiff must then establish the necessary chain of causation in fact between his psychiatric illness and the death or injury

of one or more third parties negligently caused by the defendant. Here again this is not in dispute in the instant case. But when causation in fact is in issue, it must no doubt be determined by the judge on the basis of the evidence of psychiatrists.

Thus, here comes the all-important question. Given the fact of the plaintiff's psychiatric illness caused by the defendant's negligence in killing or physically injuring another, was the chain of causation from the one event to the other, considered *ex post facto* in the light of all that has happened, 'reasonably foreseeable' by the 'reasonable man'? A moment's thought will show that the answer to that question depends on what knowledge is to be attributed to the hypothetical reasonable man of the operation of cause and effect in psychiatric medicine. There are at least two theoretically possible approaches. The first is that the judge should receive the evidence of psychiatrists as to the degree of probability that the particular cause would produce the particular effect, and apply to that the appropriate legal test of reasonable foreseeability as the criterion of the defendant's duty of care. The second is that the judge, relying on his own opinion of the operation of cause and effect in psychiatric medicine, as fairly representative of that of the educated layman, should treat himself as the reasonable man and form his own view of the primary facts as to whether the proven chain of cause and effect was reasonably foreseeable.

In principle, I think that there is much to be said for the first approach. Foreseeability, in any given set of circumstances, is ultimately a question of fact. If a claim in negligence depends on whether some defect in a complicated piece of machinery was foreseeably a cause of injury, I apprehend that the judge will decide that question on the basis of the expert evidence of engineers. But the authorities give no support to this approach in relation to the foreseeability of psychiatric illness. The judges, in all the decisions we have been referred to, have assumed that it lay within their own competence to determine whether the plaintiff's 'nervous shock' (as lawyers quaintly persist in calling it) was in any given circumstances a sufficiently foreseeable consequence of the defendant's act or omission relied on as negligent to bring the plaintiff within the scope of those to whom the defendant owed a duty of care.

To depart from this practice and treat the question of foreseeable causation in this field, and hence the scope of the defendant's duty, as a question of fact to be determined in the light of the expert evidence adduced in each case would, no doubt, be too large an innovation in the law to be regarded as properly within the competence ... of your Lordships' House. Moreover, psychiatric medicine is far from being an exact science. The opinion of its practitioners may differ widely. Clearly it is desirable in this, as in any other, field that the law should achieve such a measure of certainty as is consistent with the demands of justice. It would seem that the consensus of informed judicial opinion is probably the best yardstick available to determine whether, in any given circumstances, the emotional trauma resulting from the death or injury of third parties, or indeed the threat of such death or injury, *ex hypothesi* attributable to the defendant's negligence, was a foreseeable cause in law, as well as the actual cause in fact, of the plaintiff's psychiatric or psychosomatic illness. But the word I would emphasise in the foregoing sentence is 'informed'.

For too long earlier generations of judges have regarded psychiatry and psychiatrists with suspicion, if not hostility. Now, I venture to hope, that attitude has quite disappeared. No judge who has spent any length of time trying personal injury claims in recent years would doubt that physical injuries can give rise not only to organic but also to psychiatric disorders. The sufferings of the patient from the latter are no less real and frequently no less painful and disabling than from the former. Likewise, I would suppose that the legal profession well understands that an acute emotional trauma, like a physical trauma, can well cause a psychiatric illness in a wide range of individuals whom it would be wrong to regard as having any abnormal psychological make-up. It is in comparatively recent times that these insights have come to be generally accepted by the judiciary. It is only by giving effect to these insights in the developing law of negligence that we can do justice to an important, though no doubt small, class of plaintiffs whose genuine psychiatric illnesses are caused by negligent defendants.

My Lords, in the instant case I cannot help thinking that the learned trial judge's conclusion that the appellant's illness was not the foreseeable consequence of the respondents' negligence was one to which, understandably, he felt himself driven by the authorities. Free of authority, and applying the ordinary criterion of reasonable foreseeability to the facts, with an eye 'enlightened by progressive awareness of mental illness' (the language of Stephenson LJ [1981] QB 599, 612), any judge must, I would think, share the view of all three members of the Court of Appeal, with which I understand all your Lordships agree, that, in the words of Griffiths LJ, at p 617, it was 'readily foreseeable that a significant number of mothers exposed to such an experience might break down under the shock of the event and suffer illness'.

The question, then, for your Lordships' decision, is whether the law as a matter of policy draws a line which exempts from liability a defendant whose negligent act or omission was actually and foreseeably the cause of the plaintiff's psychiatric illness and, if so, where the line is to be drawn. In thus formulating the question, I do not, of course, use the word 'negligent' as prejudging the question whether the defendant owes the plaintiff a duty, but I do use the word 'foreseeably' as connoting the normally accepted criterion of such a duty. ...

In approaching the question whether the law should, as a matter of policy, define the criterion of liability in negligence for causing psychiatric illness by reference to some test other than that of reasonable foreseeability, it is well to remember that we are concerned only with the question of liability of a defendant who is, *ex hypothesi*, guilty of fault in causing the death, injury or danger which has in turn triggered the psychiatric illness. A policy which is to be relied on to narrow the scope of the negligent tortfeasor's duty must be justified by cogent and readily intelligible considerations, and must be capable of defining the appropriate limits of liability by reference to factors which are not purely arbitrary. A number of policy considerations which have been suggested as satisfying these requirements appear to me, with respect, to be wholly insufficient. I can see no grounds whatever for suggesting that to make the defendant liable for reasonably foreseeable psychiatric illness caused by his negligence would be to impose a crushing burden on him out of proportion to his moral responsibility. However liberally the criterion of reasonable foreseeability is interpreted, both the number of successful claims in this field and the quantum of damages they will attract are likely to be moderate. I cannot accept as relevant the well known phenomenon that litigation may delay recovery from a psychiatric illness. If this were a valid policy consideration, it would lead to the conclusion that psychiatric illness should be excluded altogether from the heads of damage which the law will recognise. It cannot justify limiting the cases in which damages will be awarded for psychiatric illness by reference to the circumstances of its causation. To attempt to draw a line at the furthest point which any of the decided cases happen to have reached, and to say that it is for the legislature, not the courts, to extend the limits of liability any further, would be, to my mind, an unwarranted abdication of the court's function of developing and adapting principles of the common law to changing conditions, in a particular corner of the common law which exemplifies, *par excellence*, the important and indeed necessary part which that function has to play.

In the end I believe that the policy question depends on weighing against each other two conflicting considerations. On the one hand, if the criterion of liability is to be reasonable foreseeability *simpliciter*, this must, precisely because questions of causation in psychiatric medicine give rise to difficulty and uncertainty, introduce an element of uncertainty into the law and open the way to a number of arguable claims which a more precisely fixed criterion of liability would exclude. I accept that the element of uncertainty is an important factor. I believe that the 'floodgates' argument, however, is, as it always has been, greatly exaggerated. On the other hand, it seems to me inescapable that any attempt to define the limit of liability by requiring, in addition to reasonable foreseeability, that the plaintiff claiming damages for psychiatric illness should have witnessed the relevant accident, should have been present at or near the place where it happened, should have come upon its aftermath and thus have had some direct perception of it, as opposed to merely learning of it after the event, should be related in some particular degree to the accident victim – to draw a line by reference to any of these criteria must impose a largely arbitrary limit of liability.

I accept the importance of the factors indicated in the guidelines suggested by Tobriner J in *Dillon v Legg* 29 ALR 3d 1316 as bearing upon the *degree* of foreseeability of the plaintiff's psychiatric illness. But let me give two examples to illustrate what injustice would be wrought by any such hard and fast lines of policy as have been suggested. First, consider the plaintiff who learned after the event of the relevant accident. Take the case of a mother who knows that her husband and children are staying in a certain hotel. She reads in her morning newspaper that it has been the scene of a disastrous fire. She sees in the paper a photograph of unidentifiable victims trapped on the top floor waving for help from the windows. She learns shortly afterwards that all her family have perished. She suffers an acute psychiatric illness. That her illness in these circumstances was a reasonably foreseeable consequence of the events resulting from the fire is undeniable. Yet, is the law to deny her damages as against a defendant whose negligence was responsible for the fire simply on the ground that an important link in the chain of causation of her psychiatric illness was supplied by her imagination of the agonies of mind and body in which her family died, rather than by direct perception of the event?

Second, consider the plaintiff who is unrelated to the victims of the relevant accident. If rigidly applied, an exclusion of liability to him would have defeated the plaintiff's claim in *Chadwick v British Railways Board* [1967] 1 WLR 912. The Court of Appeal treated that case as a special category because Mr Chadwick was a rescuer. Now, the special duty owed to a rescuer who voluntarily places himself in physical danger to save others is well understood, and is illustrated by *Haynes v Harwood* [1935] 1 KB 146, the case of the constable injured in stopping a runaway horse in a crowded street. But in relation to the psychiatric consequences of witnessing such terrible carnage as must have resulted from the Lewisham train disaster, I would find it difficult to distinguish in principle the position of the rescuer, like Mr Chadwick, from a mere spectator as, for example, an uninjured or only slightly injured passenger in the train, who took no part in the rescue operations but was present at the scene after the accident for some time, perforce observing the rescue operations while he waited for transport to take him home.

> My Lords, I have no doubt that this is an area of the law of negligence where we should resist the temptation to try yet once more to freeze the law in a rigid posture which would deny justice to some who, in the application of the classic principles of negligence derived from *Donoghue v Stevenson* [1932] AC 562, ought to succeed, in the interests of certainty, where the very subject matter is uncertain and continuously developing, or in the interests of saving defendants and their insurers from the burden of having sometimes to resist doubtful claims. I find myself in complete agreement with Tobriner J in *Dillon v Legg*, 29 ALR 3d 1316, 1326 that the defendant's duty must depend on reasonable foreseeability and '... must necessarily be adjudicated only upon a case-by-case basis. We cannot now predetermine a defendant's obligation in every situation by a fixed category; no immutable rule can establish the extent of that obligation for every circumstance of the future'.
>
> To put the matter in another way, if asked where the thing is to stop, I should answer, in an adaptation of the language of Lord Wright (in *Bourhill v Young* [1943] AC 92, 110) and Stephenson LJ [1981] QB 599, 612, 'Where in the particular case the good sense of the judge, enlightened by progressive awareness of mental illness, decides'.
>
> I regret that my noble and learned friend, Lord Edmund-Davies, who criticises my conclusion that in this area of the law there are no policy considerations sufficient to justify limiting the liability of negligent tortfeasors by reference to some narrower criterion than that of reasonable foreseeability, stops short of indicating his view as to where the limit of liability should be drawn or as to the nature of the policy considerations (other than the 'floodgates' argument, which I understand he rejects) which he would invoke to justify such a limit.
>
> My Lords, I would accordingly allow the appeal.

Lord Edmund-Davies commented:

> In my judgment, the proposition that 'the policy issue ... is not justiciable' is as novel as it is startling. So novel is it in relation to this appeal that it was never mentioned during the hearing before your Lordships. And it is startling because, in my respectful judgment, it runs counter to well-established and wholly acceptable law. ...
>
> My Lords ... I hold that policy issues *are* 'justiciable'. Their invocation calls for close scrutiny, and the conclusion may be that its nature and existence have not been established with the clarity and cogency required before recognition can be granted to any legal doctrine, and before any litigant can properly be deprived of what would otherwise be his manifest legal rights.

Notwithstanding the clear disagreement amongst the judges as to whether policy is a matter for the courts, they all agree on the result in the case under appeal. Is it any more worrying that the judges should all reach the same conclusion by varying routes, than if they all purported to use the same approach but came to different results? There is no doubt that, in result, this case pushed the gate a little further ajar, by resorting to the vague and imprecise nature of the so-called aftermath test. This will become apparent on a reading of the extracts in the case discussed below, *Alcock v Chief Constable of the South Yorkshire Police.*[6] It will perhaps become evident that the approach of Lords Wilberforce and Edmund-Davies were preferred by the House in this case. No one who saw the television pictures of the scenes at Hillsborough in 1989 could

6 [1991] 4 All ER 907.

forget the enormity of the disaster as nearly 100 people were crushed to death at the Leppings Lane end of the ground. A number of relatives brought actions against the police for psychiatric harm as a result of what they saw. Some of the issues had not been litigated before; for example, some claimants had seen the disaster unfold on the television. The House of Lords had the unique opportunity to consider a number of claims at the same time and settle the boundaries of liability in this troublesome area of the law. Lord Keith gave the first judgment. He stated:

> It was argued for the appellants in the present case that reasonable foreseeability of the risk of injury to them in the particular form of psychiatric illness was all that was required to bring home liability to the respondent. In the ordinary case of direct physical injury suffered in an accident at work or elsewhere, reasonable foreseeability of the risk is indeed the only test that need be applied to determine liability. But injury by psychiatric illness is more subtle, as Lord Macmillan observed in *Bourhill v Young* [1942] All ER 396 at 402, [1943] AC 92 at 103. In the present type of case it is a secondary sort of injury brought about by the infliction of physical injury, upon another person. That can affect those closely connected with that person in various ways. One way is by subjecting a close relative to the stress and strain of caring for the injured person over a prolonged period, but psychiatric illness due to such stress and strain has not so far been treated as founding a claim in damages. So I am of the opinion that, in addition to reasonable foreseeability, liability for injury in the particular form of psychiatric illness must depend in addition upon a requisite relationship of proximity between the claimant and the party said to owe the duty. ...
>
> The concept of a person being closely and directly affected has been conveniently labelled 'proximity', and this concept has been applied in certain categories of cases, particularly those concerned with pure economic loss, to limit and control the consequences as regards liability which would follow if reasonable foreseeability were the sole criterion.
>
> As regards the class of persons to whom the duty may be owed to take reasonable care to avoid inflicting psychiatric illness through nervous shock sustained by reason of physical injury or peril to another, I think it is sufficient that reasonable foreseeability should be the guide. I would not seek to limit the class by reference to particular relationships such as husband and wife or parent and child. The kinds of relationship which may involve close ties of love and affection are numerous, and it is the existence of such ties which leads to mental disturbance when the loved one suffers a catastrophe. They may be present in family relationships or those of close friendship, and may be stronger in the case of engaged couples than in that of persons who have been married to each other for many years. It is common knowledge that such ties exist, and reasonably foreseeable that those bound by them may in certain circumstances be at real risk of psychiatric illness if the loved one is injured or put in peril. The closeness of the tie would, however, require to be proved by the plaintiff, though no doubt being capable of being presumed in appropriate cases. The case of a bystander unconnected with the victims of an accident is difficult. Psychiatric injury to him would not ordinarily, in my view, be within the range of reasonable foreseeability, but could not perhaps be entirely excluded from it if the circumstances of a catastrophe occurring very close to him were particularly horrific.
>
> In the case of those within the sphere of reasonable foreseeability the proximity factors mentioned by Lord Wilberforce in *McLoughlin v O'Brian* [1982] 2 All ER 298 at 304, [1983] 1 AC 410 at 422, must, however, be taken into account in

judging whether a duty of care exists. The first of these is proximity of the plaintiff to the accident in time and space. For this purpose the accident is to be taken to include its immediate aftermath, which in *McLoughlin's* case was held to cover the scene at the hospital which was experienced by the plaintiff some two hours after the accident. In *Jaensch v Coffey* (1984) 54 ALR 417 the plaintiff saw her injured husband at the hospital to which he had been taken in severe pain before and between his undergoing a series of emergency operations, and the next day stayed with him in the intensive care unit and thought he was going to die. She was held entitled to recover damages for the psychiatric illness she suffered as a result. Deane J said (at 462–63): '... the aftermath of the accident extended to the hospital to which the injured person was taken and persisted for so long as he remained in the state produced by the accident up to and including immediate post-accident treatment ... Her psychiatric injuries were the result of the impact upon her of the facts of the accident itself and its aftermath while she was present at the aftermath of the accident at the hospital.'

As regards the means by which the shock is suffered, Lord Wilberforce said in *McLoughlin's* case [1982] 2 All ER 298 at 305, [1983] 1 AC 410 at 423 that it must come through sight or hearing of the event or its immediate aftermath. He also said that it was surely right that the law should not compensate shock brought about by communication by a third party. On that basis it is open to serious doubt whether *Hevican v Ruane* [1991] 3 All ER 65 and *Ravenscroft v Rederiaktiebolaget Transatlantic* [1991] 3 All ER 73 were correctly decided, since in both of these cases the effective cause of the psychiatric illness would appear to have been the fact of a son's death and the news of it.

Of the present appellants, two – Brian Harrison and Robert Alcock – were present at the Hillsborough ground, both of them in the west stand, from which they witnessed the scenes in pens 3 and 4. Brian Harrison lost two brothers, while Robert Alcock lost a brother-in-law and identified the body at the mortuary at midnight. In neither of these cases was there any evidence of particularly close ties of love and affection with the brothers or brother-in-law. In my opinion the mere fact of the particular relationship was insufficient to place the plaintiff within the class of persons to whom a duty of care could be owed by the defendant as being foreseeably at risk of psychiatric illness by reason of injury or peril to the individuals concerned. The same is true of the other plaintiffs who were not present at the ground and who lost brothers, or in one case a grandson.

I would, however, place in the category of members to which risk of psychiatric illness was reasonably foreseeable Mr and Mrs Copoc, whose son was killed, and Alexandra Penk, who lost her fiancé. In each of these cases the closest ties of love and affection fall to be presumed from the fact of the particular relationship, and there is no suggestion of anything which might tend to rebut that presumption. These three all watched scenes from Hillsborough on television, but none of these depicted suffering of recognisable individuals, such being excluded by the broadcasting code of ethics, a position known to the defendant. In my opinion the viewing of these scenes cannot be equiparated with the viewer being within 'sight or hearing of the event or its immediate aftermath', to use the words of Lord Wilberforce in *McLoughlin v O'Brian* [1982] 2 All ER 298 at 305, [1983] 1 AC 410 at 423, nor can the scenes reasonably be regarded as giving rise to shock, in the sense of a sudden assault on the nervous system. They were capable of giving rise to anxiety for the safety of relatives known or believed to be present in the area affected by the crush, and undoubtedly did so, but this is very different from seeing the fate of the relative or his condition after the event. The viewing of the television scenes did not create the necessary degree of proximity.

My Lords, for these reasons I would dismiss each of these appeals.

The following is an extract from Lord Ackner's speech:

> It is now generally accepted that an analysis of the reported cases of nervous shock establishes that it is a type of claim in a category of its own. Shock is no longer a variant of physical injury but a separate kind of damage. Whatever may be the pattern of the future development of the law in relation to this cause of action, the following propositions illustrate that the application simpliciter of the reasonable foreseeability test is, today, far from being operative.
>
> (1) Even though the risk of psychiatric illness is reasonably foreseeable, the law gives no damages if the psychiatric injury was not induced by shock. Psychiatric illnesses caused in other ways, such as from experience of having to cope with the deprivation consequent upon the death of a loved one, attracts no damages. Brennan J in *Jaensch's* case (1984) 54 ALR 417 at 429 gave as examples: the spouse who has been worn down by caring for a tortiously injured husband or wife and who suffers psychiatric illness as a result, but who, nevertheless, goes without compensation; a parent made distraught by the wayward conduct of a brain-damaged child and who suffers psychiatric illness as a result also has no claim against the tortfeasor liable to the child.
>
> (2) Even where the nervous shock and the subsequent psychiatric illness caused by it could both have been reasonably foreseen, it has been generally accepted that damages for merely being informed of, or reading, or hearing about the accident are not recoverable. In *Bourhill v Young* [1942] 2 All ER 396 at 402, [1943] AC 92 at 103, Lord Macmillan only recognised the action lying where the injury by shock was sustained 'through the medium of the eye or the ear without direct contact'. Certainly Brennan J in his judgment in *Jaensch's* case 54 ALR 417 at 430 recognised that 'A psychiatric illness induced by mere knowledge of a distressing fact is not compensatable; perception by the plaintiff of the distressing phenomenon is essential'. That seems also to have been the view of Bankes LJ in *Hambrook v Stokes Bros* [1925] 1 KB 141 at 152, [1924] All ER Rep 110 at 117. I agree with my noble and learned friend Lord Keith of Kinkel that the validity of each of the recent decisions at first instance of *Hevican v Ruane* [1991] 3 All ER 65 and *Ravenscroft v Rederiaktiebolaget Transatlantic* [1991] 3 All ER 73 is open to serious doubt.
>
> (3) Mere mental suffering, although reasonably foreseeable, if unaccompanied by physical injury, is not a basis for a claim for damages. To fill this gap in the law a very limited category of relatives are given a statutory right by the Administration of Justice Act 1982, s 3, inserting a new s 1A into the Fatal Accidents Act 1976 to bring an action claiming damages for bereavement.
>
> (4) As yet there is no authority establishing that there is liability on the part of the injured person, his or her estate, for mere psychiatric injury which was sustained by another by reason of shock, as a result of a self-inflicted death, injury or peril of the negligent person, in circumstances where the risk of such psychiatric injury was reasonably foreseeable. On the basis that there must be a limit at some reasonable point to the extent of the duty of care owed to third parties which rests upon everyone in all his actions, Lord Robertson, the Lord Ordinary, in his judgment in *Bourhill*'s case [1941] SC 395 at 399, did not view with favour the suggestion that a negligent window cleaner who loses his grip and falls from a height, impaling himself on spiked railings, would be liable for the shock-induced psychiatric illness occasioned to a pregnant woman looking out of the window of a house situated on the opposite side of the street.

(5) 'Shock', in the context of this cause of action, involves the sudden appreciation by sight or sound of a horrifying event which violently agitates the mind. It has yet to include psychiatric illness caused by the accumulation over a period of time of more gradual assaults on the nervous system. ...

The three elements

Because 'shock' in its nature is capable of affecting such a wide range of persons, Lord Wilberforce in *McLoughlin v O'Brian* [1982] 2 All ER 298 at 304, [1983] 1 AC 410 at 422 concluded that there was a real need for the law to place some limitation upon the extent of admissible claims and, in this context, he considered that there were three elements inherent in any claim. It is common ground that such elements do exist and are required to be considered in connection with all these claims. The fundamental difference in approach is that on behalf of the ... plaintiffs it is contended that the consideration of these three elements is merely part of the process of deciding whether, as a matter of fact, the reasonable foreseeability test is satisfied. On behalf of the chief constable it is contended that these elements operate as a control or limitation on the mere application of the reasonable foreseeability test. They introduce the requirement of 'proximity' as conditioning the duty of care.

The three elements are:

(1) the class of persons whose claims should be recognised;

(2) the proximity of such persons to the accident-in time and space; and

(3) the means by which the shock has been caused.

The class of persons whose claim should be recognised

When dealing with the possible range of the class of persons who might sue, Lord Wilberforce contrasted the closest of ties – parent and child and husband and wife – with that of the ordinary bystander. He said that, while existing law recognises the claims of the first, it denied that of the second, either on the basis that such persons must be assumed to be possessed with fortitude sufficient to enable them to endure the calamities of modern life, or that defendants cannot be expected to compensate the world at large. He considered that these positions were justified, that other cases involving less close relationships must be very carefully considered. ...

I respectfully share the difficulty expressed by Atkin LJ in *Hambrook v Stokes Bros* [1925] 1 KB 141 at 158-59, [1924] All ER Rep 110 at 117 – how do you explain why the duty is confined to the case of parent or guardian and child and does not extend to other relations of life also involving intimate associations; and why does it not eventually extend to bystanders? As regards the latter category, while it may be very difficult to envisage a case of a stranger, who is not actively and foreseeably involved in a disaster or its aftermath, other than in the role of rescuer, suffering shock-induced psychiatric injury by mere observation of apprehended or actual injury of a third person in circumstances that could be considered reasonably foreseeable, I see no reason in principle why he should not if, in the circumstances, a reasonably strong-nerved person would have been so shocked. In the course of argument your Lordships were given, by way of an example, that of a petrol tanker careering out of control into a school in session and bursting into flames. I would not be prepared to rule out a potential claim by a passer-by so shocked by the scene as to suffer psychiatric illness.

As regards claims to those in the close family relationships referred to by Lord Wilberforce, the justification for admitting such claims is the presumption, which I would accept as being rebuttable, that the love and affection normally associated with persons in those relationships is such that a defendant ought reasonably to contemplate that they may be so closely and directly affected by his conduct as to suffer shock resulting in psychiatric illness. While as a generalisation more remote relatives and, a *fortiori*, friends, can reasonably be expected not to suffer illness from the shock, there can well be relatives and friends whose relationship is so close and intimate that their love and affection for the victim is comparable to that of the normal parent, spouse or child of the victim and should for the purpose of this cause of action be so treated. ...

Whether the degree of love and affection in any given relationship, be it that of relative or friend, is such that the defendant, in the light of the plaintiffs' proximity to the scene of the accident in time and space and its nature, should reasonably have foreseen the shock-induced psychiatric illness, has to be decided on a case-by-case basis. ...

The proximity of the plaintiff to the accident

It is accepted that the proximity to the accident must be close both in time and space. Direct and immediate sight or hearing of the accident is not required. It is reasonably foreseeable that injury by shock can be caused to a plaintiff, not only through the sight or hearing of the event, but of its immediate aftermath.

Only two of the plaintiffs before us were at the ground. However, it is clear from *McLoughlin's* case that there may be liability where subsequent identification can be regarded as part of the 'immediate aftermath' of the accident. Mr Alcock identified his brother-in-law in a bad condition in the mortuary at about midnight, that is some eight hours after the accident. This was the earliest of the identification cases. Even if this identification could be described as apart of the 'aftermath', it could not in my judgment be described as part of the *immediate* aftermath. *McLoughlin's* case was described by Lord Wilberforce as being upon the margin of what the process of logical progression from case to case would allow. Mrs McLoughlin had arrived at the hospital within an hour or so after the accident. Accordingly, in the post-accident identification cases before their Lordships, there was not sufficient proximity in time and space to the accident.

The means by which the shock is caused

Lord Wilberforce concluded that the shock must come through sight or hearing of the event or its immediate aftermath, but specifically left for later consideration whether some equivalent of sight or hearing, eg through simultaneous television, would suffice (see [1982] 2 All ER 298 at 305, [1983] 1 AC 410 at 423). Of course it is common ground that it was clearly foreseeable by the chief constable that the scenes at Hillsborough would be broadcast live and that amongst those who would be watching would be parents and spouses and other relatives and friends of those in the pens behind the goal at the Leppings Lane end. However he would also know of the code of ethics which the television authorities televising this event could be expected to follow, namely that they would not show pictures of suffering by recognisable individuals. Had they done so, Mr Hytner accepted that this would have been a *novus actus* breaking the chain of causation between the chief constable's alleged breach of duty and the psychiatric illness. As the chief constable was reasonably entitled to expect to be the case, there were no such pictures.

Although the television pictures certainly gave rise to feelings of the deepest anxiety and distress, in the circumstances of this case the simultaneous television broadcasts of what occurred cannot be equated with the 'sight or hearing of the event or its immediate aftermath'. Accordingly shocks sustained by reason of these broadcasts cannot found a claim. I agree, however, with Nolan LJ that simultaneous broadcasts of a disaster cannot in all cases be ruled out as providing the equivalent of the actual sight or hearing of the event or its immediate aftermath. Nolan LJ gave an example of a situation where it was reasonable to anticipate that the television cameras, whilst filming and transmitting pictures of a special event of children travelling in a balloon, in which there was media interest, particularly amongst the parents, showed the balloon suddenly bursting into flames (see [1991] 3 All ER 88 at 122). Many other such situations could be imagined where the impact of the simultaneous television pictures would be as great, if not greater, than the actual sight of the accident.

Conclusion

Only one of the plaintiffs who succeeded before Hidden J, namely Brian Harrison, was at the ground. His relatives who died were his two brothers. The quality of brotherly love is well known to differ widely – from Cain and Abel to David and Jonathan. I assume that Mr Harrison's relationship with his brothers was not an abnormal one. His claim was not presented upon the basis that there was such a close and intimate relationship between them as gave rise to that very special bond of affection which would make his shock-induced psychiatric illness reasonably foreseeable by the Chief Constable. Accordingly, the learned judge did not carry out the requisite close scrutiny of their relationship. Thus there was no evidence to establish the necessary proximity which would make his claim reasonably foreseeable and, subject to the other factors, to which I have referred, a valid one. The other plaintiff who was present at the ground, Robert Alcock, lost a brother-in-law. He was not, in my judgment, reasonably foreseeable as a potential sufferer from shock-induced psychiatric illness, in default of very special facts, and none was established. Accordingly their claims must fail, as must those of the other plaintiffs who only learnt of the disaster by watching simultaneous television. I, too, would therefore dismiss these appeals.

Lord Oliver also gave a substantial speech, some of which is contained in the following extract:

The failure of the law in general to compensate for injuries sustained by persons unconnected with the event precipitated by a defendant's negligence must necessarily import the lack of any legal duty owed by the defendant to such persons. That cannot, I think, be attributable to some arbitrary but uneducated rule of 'policy' which draws a line as the outer boundary of the area of duty. Nor can it rationally be made to rest upon such injury being without the area of reasonable foreseeability. It must, as it seems to me, be attributable simply to the fact that such persons are not, in contemplation of law, in a relationship of sufficient proximity to, or directness with, the tortfeasor as to give rise to a duty of care, though no doubt 'policy', if that is the right word, or perhaps more properly, the impracticability or unreasonableness of entertaining claims to the ultimate limits of the consequences of human activity, necessarily plays a part in the court's perception of what is sufficiently proximate.

What is more difficult to account for is why, when the law in general declines to extend the area of compensation to those whose injury arises only from the circumstances of their relationship to the primary victim, an exception has arisen in those cases in which the event of injury to the primary victim has been actually witnessed by the plaintiff and the injury claimed is established as stemming from that fact. That such an exception exists is now too well established to be called in question. What is less clear, however, is the ambit of the duty in such cases or, to put it another way, what is the essential characteristic of such cases that marks them off from those cases of injury to uninvolved persons in which the law denies any remedy for injury of precisely the same sort.

Although it is convenient to describe the plaintiff in such a case as a 'secondary' victim, that description must not be permitted to obscure the absolute essentiality of establishing a duty owed by the defendant directly to him – a duty which depends not only upon the reasonable foreseeability of damage of the type which has in fact occurred to the particular plaintiff, but also upon the proximity or directness of the relationship between the plaintiff and the defendant. The difficulty lies in identifying the features which, as between two persons who may suffer effectively identical psychiatric symptoms as a result of the impression left upon them by an accident, establish in the case of one who was present at or near the scene of the accident a duty in the defendant which does not exist in the case of one who was not.

The answer cannot, I think, lie in the greater foreseeability of the sort of damage which the plaintiff has suffered. The traumatic effect on, for instance, a mother on the death of her child is as readily foreseeable in a case where the circumstances are described to her by an eye witness at the inquest as it is in a case where she learns of it at a hospital immediately after the event. Nor can it be the mere suddenness or unexpectedness of the event, for the news brought by a policeman hours after the event may be as sudden and unexpected to the recipient as the occurrence of the event is to the spectator present at the scene. The answer has, as it seems to me, to be found in the existence of a combination of circumstances from which the necessary degree of 'proximity' between the plaintiff and the defendant can be deduced. And, in the end, it has to be accepted that the concept of 'proximity' is an artificial one which depends more upon the court's perception of what is the reasonable area for the imposition of liability than upon any logical process of analogical deduction.

The common features of all the reported cases of this type decided in this country ... and in which the plaintiff succeeded in establishing liability are, first, that in each case there was a marital or parental relationship between the plaintiff and the primary victim; second, that the injury for which damages were claimed arose from the sudden and unexpected shock to the plaintiff's nervous system; third, that the plaintiff in each case was either personally present at the scene of the accident or was in the more or less immediate vicinity and witnessed the aftermath shortly afterwards, and fourth, that the injury suffered arose from witnessing the death of, extreme danger to, or injury and discomfort suffered by the primary victim. Lastly, in each case there was not only an element of physical proximity to the event but a close temporal connection between the plaintiff's perception of it combined with a close relationship of affection between the plaintiff and the primary victim.

It must, I think, be from these elements that the essential requirement of proximity is to be deduced, to which can be added the reasonable foreseeability on the part of the defendant that, in that combination of circumstances, there was a real risk of injury of the type sustained by the particular plaintiff as a result of his or her concern for the primary victim. There may indeed be no primary 'victim' in fact. It is, for instance, readily conceivable that a parent may suffer injury, whether physical or psychiatric, as a result of witnessing a negligent act which places his or her child in extreme jeopardy but from which, in the event, the child escapes unharmed. ...

The principal argument in the appeal has centred round the question whether, as the appellants contend, the decision of this House in *McLoughlin v O'Brian* [1982] 2 All ER 298, [1983] 1 AC 410 establishes, as the criterion of a duty owed by the defendants to the plaintiff, a simple test of the foreseeability of injury of the type in fact sustained or whether, as the respondent maintains, that case imports also a necessary requirement, either as a matter of public policy or as a measure of proximity, of the existence of some close blood or marital relationship between the appellants and the victims of the negligent conduct ... In this House, although the members of the Appellate Committee were unanimous in allowing the appeal, the speeches displayed distinct differences of approach. All were agreed that actually witnessing or being present at or near the scene of an accident was not essential to ground liability in an appropriate case, but that the duty might equally be owed to one who comes upon the immediate aftermath of the event. Thus, such a person, given always the reasonable foreseeability of the injury in fact sustained and of such persons witnessing it, may be within the area of proximity in which a duty of care may be found to exist.

The diversity of view arose at the next stage, that is to say that of ascertaining whether the relationship between the plaintiff and the primary victim was such as to support the existence of such a duty. That can be expressed in various ways. It may be asked whether, as a matter of policy of the law, a relationship outside the categories of those in which liability has been established by past decisions can be considered sufficiently proximate to give rise to the duty, quite regardless of the question of foreseeability. Or it may be asked whether injury of the type with which these appeals are concerned can ever be considered to be reasonably foreseeable where the relationship between the plaintiff and the primary victim is more remote than that of an established category. Or, again, it may be asked whether, even given proximity and foreseeability, nevertheless the law must draw an arbitrary line at the boundary of the established category or some other wider or narrower category of relationships beyond which no duty will be deemed to exist.

Lord Wilberforce appears to have favoured the last of these three approaches, but found it, in the event, unnecessary to determine the boundary since the case then before the House concerned a claim within a category which had already been clearly established. He did not altogether close the door to an enlargement of the area of possible duty but observed ([1982] 2 All ER 298 at 304, [1983] 1 AC 410 at 422): '... other cases involving less close relationships must be very carefully scrutinised. I cannot say that they should never be admitted. The closer the tie (not merely in relationship but in care) the greater the claim for consideration. The claim, in any case, has to be judged in the light of the other factors, such as proximity to the scene in time and place, and the nature of the accident.'

In so far as this constituted an invitation to courts, seised of similar problems in the future, to draw lines determined by their perception of what public policy requires, it was an invitation accepted by Parker LJ in the Court of Appeal in the instant case. It was his view that liability should, as a matter of policy, determine at the relationship of parent or spouse and should be restricted to persons present at or at the immediate aftermath of the incident from which the injury arose. The approach of Lord Edmund-Davies and Lord Russell of Killowen, as I read their speeches, was similar to that of Lord Wilberforce. On the other hand, Lord Bridge of Harwich, with whom Lord Scarman agreed, rejected an appeal to policy considerations as a justification for fixing arbitrary lines of demarcation of the duty in negligence. Lord Bridge propounded simply a criterion of the reasonable foreseeability by the defendant of the damage to the plaintiff which had occurred, without necessarily invoking physical presence at or propinquity to the accident or its aftermath or any particular relationship to the primary victim as limiting factors, although, of course, clearly these elements would be important in the determination of what, on the facts of any given case, would be reasonably foreseeable. ...

Counsel for the appellants and for the respondent respectively have invited your Lordships to accept or reject one or other of these two approaches on the footing that they represent mutually exclusive alternatives, and to say, on the one hand, that the only criterion for the establishment of liability is the reasonable foreseeability of damage in accordance with the views expressed by Lord Bridge (which, it is urged, existed in the case of each of the appellants), or, on the other hand, that liability must, as a matter of public policy, be decreed to stop at the case of a spouse or parent and in any event must be restricted to injury to a person who was physically present at the event or at its aftermath and witnessed one or the other.

My Lords, for my part I have not felt able to accept either of these two extreme positions nor do I believe that the views in *McLoughlin v O'Brian* [1982] 2 All ER 298, [1983] 1 AC 410 are as irreconcilable as has been suggested. If I may say so with respect, the views expressed by Lord Bridge are open to the criticism that, on their face, they entirely ignore the critical element of proximity to which reference has been made, taking us back to the 'demonstrably too wide' proposition of Brett MR in *Heaven v Pender* (18830 11 QBD 503, [1881] All ER Rep 35). But the critical part played by this element is very clearly expressed by Lord Bridge himself in his speech in *Caparo Industries plc v Dickman* [1990] 1 All ER 568 at 574, 576–78, [1990] 2 AC 605 at 618, 621, 623, and I do not believe for one moment that, in expressing his view with regard to foreseeability in *McLoughlin v O'Brian*, he was overlooking that element which is, after all, implicit in any discussion of tortious negligence based upon Lord Atkin's classic statement of principle, ... or was doing more than meeting the argument which had been advanced that, even given foreseeability, an immutable line either had been, or ought to be, drawn by the law at the furthest point reached by previously decided cases. Equally, I do not read Lord Wilberforce (whose remarks in this context were, in any event, *obiter* since the question of fixing lines of demarcation by reference to public policy did not in fact arise) as excluding altogether a pragmatic approach to claims of this nature.

In any event, there is in many cases, as for instance cases of direct physical injury in a highway accident, an almost necessary coalescence of the twin elements of foreseeability and proximity, the one flowing from the other. But where such divergence is not self-evident, the question of proximity requires separate consideration. In deciding it the court has reference to no defined criteria, and the decision necessarily reflects to some extent the court's concept of what policy – or perhaps common sense – requires.

My Lords, speaking for myself, I see no logic and no virtue in seeking to lay down as a matter of 'policy' categories of relationship within which claims may succeed and without which they are doomed to failure *in limine*. So rigid an approach would, I think, work great injustice and cannot be rationally justified. Obviously a claim for damages for psychiatric injury by a remote relative of the primary victim will factually require most cautious scrutiny and faces considerable evidentiary difficulties. Equally obviously, the foreseeability of such injury to such a person will be more difficult to establish than similar injury to a spouse or parent of the primary victim. But these are factual difficulties and I can see no logic and no policy reason for excluding claims by more remote relatives.

Suppose, for instance, that the primary victim has lived with the plaintiff for 40 years, both being under the belief that they are lawfully married. Does she suffer less shock or grief because it is subsequently discovered that their marriage was invalid? The source of the shock and distress in all these cases is the affectionate relationship which existed between the plaintiff and the victim, and the traumatic effect of the negligence is equally foreseeable given that relationship, however the relationship arises. Equally, I would not exclude the possibility envisaged by my noble and learned friend Lord Ackner of a successful claim, given circumstances of such horror as would be likely to traumatise even the most phlegmatic spectator, by a mere bystander.

That is not, of course, to say that the closeness of the relationship between plaintiff and the primary victim is irrelevant, for the likelihood or unlikelihood of a person in that relationship suffering shock of the degree claimed from the event, must be a most material factor to be taken into account in determining whether that consequence was reasonably foreseeable. In general, for instance, it might be supposed that the likelihood of trauma of such degree as to cause psychiatric illness would be less in the case of a friend or a brother-in-law than in that of a parent or fiancé.

But in every case the underlying and essential postulate is a relationship of proximity between the plaintiff and defendant and it is this, as it seems to me, which must be the determining factor in the instant appeals. No case prior to the hearing before Hidden J ([1991] 1 All ER 353, [1991] 2 WLR 814) from which these appeals arise has countenanced an award of damages for injuries suffered where there was not at the time of the event a degree of physical propinquity between the plaintiff and the event caused by the defendant's breach of duty to the primary victim, nor where the shock sustained by the plaintiff was not either contemporaneous with the event or separated from it by a relatively short interval of time. The necessary element of proximity between plaintiff and defendant is furnished, at least in part, by both physical and temporal propinquity and also by the sudden and direct visual impression on the plaintiff's mind of actually witnessing the event or its immediate aftermath. ...

Grief, sorrow, deprivation and the necessity for caring for loved ones who have suffered injury or misfortune must, I think, be considered as ordinary and inevitable incidents of life which, regardless of individual susceptibilities, must be sustained without compensation. It would be inaccurate and hurtful to suggest that grief is made any the less real or deprivation more tolerable by a more gradual realisation, but to extend liability to cover injury in such cases would be to extend the law in a direction for which there is no pressing policy need and in which there is no logical stopping point. In my opinion, the necessary proximity cannot be said to exist where the elements of immediacy, closeness of time and space, and direct visual or aural perception are absent.

I would agree with the view expressed by Nolan LJ that there may well be circumstances where the element of visual perception may be provided by witnessing the actual injury to the primary victim on simultaneous television, but that is not the case in any of the instant appeals, and I agree with my noble and learned friend Lord Keith of Kinkel that, for the reasons he gives, the televised images seen by the various appellants cannot be equiparated with 'sight or hearing of the event'. Nor did they provide the degree of immediacy required to sustain a claim for damages for nervous shock.

That they were sufficient to give rise to worry and concern cannot be in doubt, but in each case other than those of Brian Harrison and Robert Alcock, who were present at the ground, the appellant learnt of the death of the victim at second hand and many hours later. As I read the evidence, the shock in each case arose not from the original impact of the transmitted image which did not, as has been pointed out, depict the suffering of recognised individuals. These images provided no doubt the matrix for imagined consequences giving rise to grave concern and worry, followed by a dawning consciousness over an extended period that the imagined consequence had occurred, finally confirmed by news of the death and, in some cases, subsequent visual identification of the victim. The trauma is created in part by such confirmation and, in part by, the linking in the mind of the plaintiff of that confirmation to the previously absorbed image. To extend the notion of proximity in cases of immediately created nervous shock to this more elongated and, to some extent, retrospective process may seem a logical analogical development. But, as I shall endeavour to show, the law in this area is not wholly logical and, whilst having every sympathy with the appellants whose suffering is not in doubt and is not to be underrated, I cannot for my part see any pressing reason of policy for taking this further step along a road which must ultimately lead to virtually limitless liability.

Whilst, therefore, I cannot, for the reasons which I have sought to explain, accept Mr Woodward QC's submission that it is for your Lordships to lay down, on grounds of public policy, an arbitrary requirement of the existence of a particular blood or marital as a precondition of liability, I equally believe that further pragmatic extensions of the accepted concepts of what constitutes proximity must be approached with the greatest caution. *McLoughlin v O'Brian* was a case which itself represented an extension not, as I think, wholly free from difficulty, and any further widening of the area of potential liability to cater for the expanded and expanding range of media of communication ought, in my view, to be undertaken rather by Parliament, with full opportunity for public debate and representation, than by a process of judicial extrapolation.

In the case of both Brian Harrison and Robert Alcock, although both were present at the ground and saw scenes which were obviously distressing and such as to cause grave worry and concern, their perception of the actual consequences of the disaster to those whom they were related was again gradual. In my judgment, the necessary proximity was lacking in their cases too, but I also agree with my noble and learned friend Lord Keith of Kinkel that there is also lacking the necessary element of reasonable foreseeability, Accordingly, I too would dismiss the appeals, and it follows from what I have said that I agree that the correctness of the decisions in *Hevican v Ruane* [1991] 3 All ER 65 and *Ravenscroft v Rederiaktiebolaget Transatlantic* [1991] 3 All ER 73 must be seriously doubted.

I would only add that I cannot, for my part, regard the present state of the law as either entirely satisfactory or as logically defensible. If there exists a sufficient degree of proximity to sustain a claim for damages for nervous shock, why it may justifiably be asked, does not that proximity also support that perhaps more easily foreseeable loss which the plaintiff may suffer as a direct result of the death or injury from which the shock arises. That it does not is, I think, clear from *Hinz v Berry* [1970] 1 All ER 1074 esp at 1076–77, [1970] 2 QB 40 esp at 44 *per* Lord Pearson. But the reason why it does not has, I think, to be found, not in logic, but in policy. Whilst not dissenting from the case-by-case approach advocated by Lord Bridge in *McLoughlin's* case, the ultimate boundaries within which claims for damages in such cases can be entertained must, I think, depend in the end upon considerations of policy.

For example, in his illuminating judgment in *Jaensch v Coffey* (1984) 54 ALR 417 Deane J expressed the view that no claim could be entertained as a matter of law in a case where the primary victim is the negligent defendant himself and the shock to the plaintiff arises from witnessing the victim's self-inflicted injury. The question does not, fortunately, fall to be determined in the instant case, but I suspect that an English court would be likely to take a similar view. But if that be so, the limitation must be based upon policy rather than upon logic, for the suffering and shock of a wife or mother at witnessing the death of her husband

> or son is just as immediate, just as great and just as foreseeable, whether the accident be due to the victim's own or to another's negligence, and if the claim is based, as it must be, on the combination of proximity and foreseeability, there is certainly no logical reason why a remedy should be denied in such a case.
>
> Indeed, Mr Hytner QC, for the appellants, has boldly claimed that it should not be. Take, for instance, the case of a mother who suffers shock and psychiatric injury through witnessing the death of her son when he negligently walks in front of an on-coming motor car. If liability is to be denied in such a case, such a denial can only be because the policy of the law forbids such a claim, for it is difficult to visualise a greater proximity or a greater degree of foreseeability. Moreover, I can visualise great difficulty arising, if this be the law, where the accident, though not solely caused by the primary victim, has been materially contributed to by his negligence. If, for instance, the primary victim is himself 75% responsible for the accident, it would be a curious and wholly unfair situation if the plaintiff were enabled to recover damages for his or her traumatic injury from the person responsible only in a minor degree, whilst he in turn remained unable to recover any contribution from the person primarily responsible since the latter's negligence *vis-à-vis* the plaintiff would not even have been tortious.
>
> Policy considerations such as this could, I cannot help feeling, be much better accommodated if the rights of persons injured in this way were to be enshrined in and limited by legislation as they have been in the Australian statute law to which my noble and learned friend, Lord Ackner, has referred.

In a short speech, Lord Jauncey of Tullichettle made similar comments to his fellow judges and agreed that the appeals should be dismissed. Lord Lowry merely agreed with the other Law Lords. This case was obviously a serious attempt by the House, short of legislation, to settle the boundaries of liability for damage by shock. Before commenting on some of the issues, some points need elaborating upon in the light of subsequent events. Reference was made in some of the judgments to two cases, the correctness of which was doubted. One of these, *Ravenscroft's*[7] case, was reversed by the Court of Appeal[8] in the light of the decision and comments in *Alcock*. In this case the news of the death of the plaintiff's son was communicated to her by her husband. In the other, *Hevican v Ruane*,[9] the judge's decision must be seriously doubted, as the father was told of his son's death by a third party and then went to the mortuary to see the body.

In the case of *Brice v Brown*[10] the plaintiff suffered severe psychiatric illness as a result of an accident in which she sustained trivial injuries, but her daughter was more seriously injured. The defendant argued that the precise nature and extent of the illness had to be shown to be reasonably foreseeable. In dismissing this argument, Stuart Smith LJ said:

> The fact that the tortfeasor could not foresee the precise name the psychiatrists were to put on the condition or the precise mental or psychological process that led to the result is immaterial. So is the fact that a completely normal person would not have suffered the consequences that the plaintiff in fact suffered. In my judgment the plaintiff is entitled to recover in law.

---

7 [1991] 3 All ER 73.

8 [1992] 2 All ER 470.

9 [1991] 3 All ER 65.

10 [1984] 1 All ER 997.

Presumably, in this case the court was satisfied that a person of normal fortitude would have suffered from some psychiatric harm, or possibly it could be argued that the plaintiff was a primary victim in any event, in which case the 'take your victim as you find him' rule would apply.

Another issue not dealt with in *Alcock* is the question of whether a plaintiff can recover for psychiatric illness resulting from witnessing one's property negligently damaged by the defendant. This point was considered, somewhat briefly, by the Court of Appeal on a preliminary issue in *Attia v British Gas*,[11] All three judges agreed that there was no theoretical objection to there being a claim in such circumstances. The extract below is taken from the judgment of Bingham LJ:

> Whether the psychiatric damage suffered by this plaintiff as a result of the carelessness of the defendants was reasonably foreseeable is not something which can be decided as a question of law. In considering the present question of principle reasonable foreseeability must for the present be assumed in the plaintiff's favour. So the question is whether, assuming everything else in the plaintiff's favour, this court should hold his claim to be bad in law because the mental or emotional trauma which precipitated the plaintiff's psychiatric damage was caused by her witnessing the destruction of her home and property, rather than apprehending or witnessing personal injury or the consequences of personal injury.
>
> It is submitted, I think rightly, that this claim breaks new ground. No analogous claim has ever, to my knowledge, been upheld or even advanced. If, therefore, it were proper to erect a doctrinal boundary stone at the point which the onward march of recorded decisions has so far reached, we should answer the question of principle in the negative and dismiss the plaintiff's action, as the deputy judge did. But I should for my part erect the boundary stone with a strong presentiment, that it would not be long before a case would arise so compelling on its facts as to cause the stone to be moved to a new and more distant resting place. The suggested boundary line is not, moreover, one that commends itself to me as either fair or convenient.
>
> Examples which arose in argument illustrate the point. Suppose, that a scholar's life's work of research or composition were destroyed before his eyes as a result of a defendant's careless conduct, causing the scholar to suffer reasonably foreseeable psychiatric damage. Or suppose that a householder returned home to find that his most cherished possessions had been destroyed through the carelessness of an intruder in starting a fire or leaving a tap running, causing reasonably foreseeable psychiatric damage to the owner. I do not think a legal principle which forbade recovery in these circumstances could be supported. The only policy argument relied on as justifying or requiring such a restriction was the need to prevent a proliferation of claims, the familiar floodgates argument. This is not an argument to be automatically discounted. But nor is it, I think, an argument which can claim a very impressive record of success. All depends on one's judgment of the likely result of a particular extension of the law. I do not myself think that refusal by this court to lay down the legal principle for which the defendants contend, or (put positively) our acceptance that a claim such as the plaintiff's may in principle succeed, will lead to a flood of claims or actions, let alone a flood of successful claims or actions. Insistence that psychiatric damage must be reasonably foreseeable, coupled with a clear recognition that a

11 [1987] 3 All ER 455.

> plaintiff must prove psychiatric damage as I have defined it, and not merely grief, sorrow or emotional distress, will in my view enable the good sense of the judge to ensure ... that the thing stops at the appropriate point. His good sense provides a better, more flexible mechanism of control than a necessarily arbitrary rule of law. ...
>
> I am accordingly of opinion that this appeal should be allowed. The case should be remitted to a judge for trial of all live issues related to reasonable foreseeability, causation and damage on the footing that, if the plaintiff succeeds on all these issues, her claim may in principle be upheld.

It might strike some as odd that the Court of Appeal was prepared to countenance such a claim as a possibility when claims were rejected in the *Alcock* case, where the harm caused by the defendant's negligence was physical harm to the primary victim. Is the loss of property in the way it occurred in *Attia* more worthy of consideration as a factor in bringing about psychiatric illness?

The remaining issue to be discussed was mentioned in *Alcock*; this concerns the thorny problem of the bystander witnessing a particularly horrific accident. It will be recalled that some of their Lordships were not prepared to rule out a claim in such circumstances. It has not taken long for the Court of Appeal to have to rule on this one. As if on cue, in 1993 litigation on the *Piper Alpha* disaster spilled into the Court of Appeal, though the facts of the incident preceded the Hillsborough disaster. In *McFarlane v EE Caledonia Ltd*[12] the plaintiff was a worker on the oil rig in question, but on the relevant night he was off duty on a support vessel nearby. He witnessed the brunt of the disaster from that vessel which never got nearer than 100 m to the devastated platform. Stuart Smith LJ gave the judgment of the court:

> In *Alcock v Chief Constable of South Yorkshire Police* [1991] 4 All ER 907 at 923, [1992] 1 AC 310 at 407 Lord Oliver of Aylmerton identified two categories of those who suffered nervous shock through fear of injury. Firstly, those involved mediately or immediately as a participant in the event who feared injury to themselves, and secondly, those who are no more than passive and unwilling witnesses of injury caused to others. In the present case the judge held that the plaintiff was a participant.
>
> There are I think basically three situations in which a plaintiff may be a participant when he sustains psychiatric injury through fear of physical injury to himself. First, where he is in the actual area of danger created by the event, but escapes physical injury by chance or good fortune. Such a person would be one who, while actually on the *Piper Alpha* rig at the time of the fire, escaped physical injury but might well be in fear for his life or safety. Second, where the plaintiff is not actually in danger, but because of the sudden and unexpected nature of the event he reasonably thinks that he is ... Third, the situation may arise where the plaintiff, who is not originally within the area of danger, comes into it later. In the ordinary way, such a person, who is a volunteer, cannot recover if he has freely and voluntarily entered the area of danger. That is not something that the tortfeasor can reasonably foresee, and the plaintiff may also be met with a defence of *volenti non fit injuria*. However, if he comes as a rescuer, he can recover. This is because a tortfeasor who has put A in peril by his negligence

12 [1994] 2 All ER 1.

must reasonably foresee that B may come to rescue him, even if it involves risking his own safety. ...

It is submitted by Mr Wilkinson that the plaintiff was a rescuer and that, even if his injury did not result from fear for his own safety, he was entitled to recover because it was due to his experiences in rescuing the survivors ... But the judge held that the plaintiff was not a rescuer even though he was on board the *Tharos* which went to assist in rescue operations. I agree with the judges' conclusions. The plaintiff was never actively involved in the operation beyond helping to move blankets with a view to preparing the heli-hangar to receive casualties, and encountering and perhaps assisting two walking injured as they arrived on the *Tharos*.

This is no criticism of him; he had no role to play and there is no reason to doubt that he would have given more help if he could. But since the defendant's liability to a rescuer depends on his reasonable foreseeability, I do not think that a defendant could reasonably foresee that this very limited degree of involvement could possibly give rise to psychiatric injury.

Secondly, it is submitted that the plaintiff was obliged to witness the catastrophe at close range, and that it was of such a horrendous nature that, even as a bystander, the defendants owed him a duty of care. Mr Wilkinson relies on *dicta* of three of their Lordships in *Alcock v Chief Constable of the South Yorkshire Police*. ...

Mr Wilkinson submits that it is hardly possible to imagine anything more horrific than the holocaust on the *Piper Alpha*, especially to the plaintiff who knew that some of his mates were on board. I share Lord Keith's difficulty. The whole basis of the decision in *Alcock v Chief Constable of South Yorkshire Police* is that, where the shock is caused by fear of injury to others as opposed to fear of injury to the participant, the test of proximity is not simply reasonable foreseeability. There must be a sufficiently close tie of love and affection between the plaintiff and the victim. To extend the duty to those who have no such connection is to base the test purely on foreseeability.

It seems to me that there are great practical problems as well. Reactions to horrific events are entirely subjective; who is to say that it is more horrific to see a petrol tanker advancing out of control on a school, when perhaps unknown to the plaintiff none of the children are in the building but are somewhere safe, than to see a child or group of children run over on a pedestrian crossing? There must be few scenes more harrowing than seeing women and children trapped at the window of a blazing building, yet many people gather to witness these calamities.

In my judgment, both as a matter of principle and policy the court should not extend the duty to those who are mere bystanders or witnesses of horrific events unless there is a sufficient degree of proximity, which requires both nearness in time and place and a close relationship of love and affection between plaintiff and victim.

Even if I am wrong in this view, I think the plaintiff faces insuperable difficulty in this case. Not only is there no finding that it was reasonably foreseeable that a man of ordinary fortitude and phlegm would be so affected by what he saw, a finding which I would certainly decline to make on the evidence, but there is the finding that the plaintiff was probably not such a person. I think this is fatal to this submission.

I would therefore allow the appeal.

If the plaintiff, this last point apart, could not succeed on these facts, then liability to a pure bystander cannot be said to exist despite the *dicta* in *Alcock*. It is not without significance that the Appeal Committee refused leave to appeal in the *Piper Alpha* case. Further, the claim in the case of *Robertson v Forth Road Bridge Joint Board (No 2)*[13] was given short shrift by the Outer House. The judge, after commenting that neither pursuer as fellow workers of the deceased, who had been swept by the wind off the back of a vehicle and over the side of the bridge, could satisfy the close tie of love and affection requirement and, concluding that neither were participants, stated:

> There remains finally the possibility that an accident can be so horrific as to involve the ordinary bystander. Although this was canvassed in the case of *Alcock*, and was the basis of the remedy sought in *McFarlane*, it is clear that in circumstances very considerably more appalling than the present case such a remedy was not found, and indeed it would appear that no case on this basis has been successfully pled. Again, while I have no doubt that the pursuers suffered genuine and deep distress as a result of this incident, I do not think they can justify their present claim on the ground that the accident witnessed was so horrific that even an ordinary bystander would foreseeably suffer serious nervous shock leading to psychiatric injury.

In the light of the above, it is hardly surprising that there are calls for reform of the law in this controversial area. The main focus of criticism has been on the severe barriers to recovery placed by the heavy-handed proximity requirements facing secondary victims. The courts seem to approach this from the aspect of the notional duty of care which causes considerable confusion. The point is forcefully made, as usual, by Howarth in relation to the requirements of close ties of love and affection, temporal and spatial proximity as follows:

> The point is that proof of the relationship has nothing at all to do with foreseeability, but concerns instead factual causation (did the relationship make any difference?) and in turn, fault (would a reasonable person have taken such a risk into account?) and remoteness (was the overwhelmingly more important cause the relationship, which was the plaintiff's doing, rather that the accident?). Similarly, the sight, sound and aftermath restrictions are matters of causation and fault.

The proximity requirements have also come under attack elsewhere.[14] The Law Commission in its recent consultation paper[15] has recommended provisionally that the sight, sound and aftermath requirements should be relaxed in respect of certain very close relationships. These extra restrictions are considered to be unnecessary as claims can be kept in check by insisting on reasonable foreseeability, a genuine psychiatric illness and some form of close tie of love and affection. Frequent reference was made in the cases to legislation in parts of Australia on this topic. Below is the text of a statutory provision for New South Wales which might turn out to be a model, or at least a starting point, for any English legislation.

---

13 1994 SLT 568

14 See Teff, *Negligently Inflicted Nervous Shock*, (1983) 99 LQR 100.

15 *Liability for Psychiatric Illness*, 1995, Consultation Paper no 137.

New South Wales Law Reform (Miscellaneous Provisions) Act 1944

Section 4

(1) – The liability of any person in respect of injury caused by an act, neglect or default by which another person is killed, injured or put in peril, shall extend to include liability for injury arising wholly or in part from mental or nervous shock sustained by:

(a) a parent or the husband or wife of the person so killed, injured or put in peril; or

(b) any other member of the family of the person so killed, injured or put in peril where such person was killed, injured or put in peril within the sight or hearing of such member of the family.

...

(5) – 'Member of the family' means the husband, wife, parent, child, brother, sister, half-brother or half-sister in relation to whom the expression is used.

'Parent' includes-father, mother, grandfather, grandmother, step-father, step-mother and any other person in *loco parentis* to another.

'Child' includes son, daughter, grandson, granddaughter, step-son, step-daughter and any other person to whom another stands in *loco parentis*.

Some interesting points arise from this. One is that there is no mention of any requirement of reasonable foreseeability as is required at common-law. Another is that, in relation to two groups of people, the spatial and temporal aspects of the proximity requirement have been dispensed with in s 4(1)(a). They are, however, still very much a requirement where the relationship is regarded by the statute at least, as less close as in s 4(1)(b). The extremely wide meaning given to family should be noted. Where is the 'quality of the relationship' criterion so favoured by the common law? What about rescuers, other participants in the events leading up to the injury to the primary victim, and bystanders? Are they precluded from bringing claims or is it possible for them to resort once again to the common law? It may well be the case that the statute does not replace the common law rules on liability for psychiatric injury in the particular jurisdiction, in which case, presumably, a plaintiff could pursue a case outside the scope of the legislation. There are many questions to be considered and answered before legislation, if ever, is to be put into place on this topic.

CHAPTER 6

LIABILITY FOR ECONOMIC LOSS

We must now consider the awkward topic of liability for negligently inflicted economic loss, an extremely complex and controversial area of tort law. Howarth states:[1]

> Economic loss is notoriously difficult, especially for beginning students. Unlike most of negligence law, which concerns everyday matters such as road accidents and accidents at work, economic loss is largely about areas of life, especially shipping and international trade, which are not widely known about. It is truly said that, when learning tort law, students find the facts of the cases easy to understand but the law incomprehensible, whereas in contract law it is the other way round. Economic loss cases, unfortunately, seem to combine the incomprehensible aspects of both subjects.
>
> The reason for the difficulty of economic loss is, however, important for understanding it. Economic loss cases are usually about plaintiffs who might have expected to have contractual claims against the defendants, but who turn out not to have such claims and who in consequence try to sue in negligence instead.

The uneasy relationship between these two areas of law will be considered at stages in this chapter, as it has clearly bedevilled the cases and the principles under discussion. Contract and tort meet head on here and the question of which, if any, is the dominant one comes up time and again.

Generally, the law has set its face against claims for pure economic loss outside contract. Furthermore, tort law is meagre with its remedies for deliberately inflicted economic loss, so it is hardly surprising that it does not welcome with open arms claims for such loss when it is negligently inflicted.

Economic loss may be, and often is, recoverable in negligence actions provided the plaintiff can show that she has suffered some personal injury or property damage with which the financial loss claim can be linked. Such economic loss is often called consequential economic loss, in the sense that it is a consequence of some personal injury or property damage.

We shall explore this point fully in the discussion below, as it is fundamental to the question of recoverability in many of the cases. We shall also be giving much consideration to the major and notable exception to non-recoverability, namely, the principle in the *Hedley Byrne* case. As we shall discover there have been other cases in which claims for free-standing financial loss have been upheld. It is these sorts of cases which are perplexing as there does not seem to be any coherent principle underlying them.

PURE ECONOMIC LOSS

The first enquiry is into what is meant by the phrase 'pure economic loss'. The use of the word 'pure' tends to suggest that the loss in question must be untainted and stand apart from other types of loss suffered by a plaintiff in any

---

1 *Textbook on Tort*, p 267.

particular case. It is loss unconnected with, eg, personal injury damage. In a claim for personal injuries following negligence by a defendant, the plaintiff may well be unable to resume work. In such circumstances, the plaintiff's claim will include, as a head of damage, an item representing future loss of earnings. This is a normal head of damage which is clearly economic loss, but it is dependent or linked with the personal injuries sustained by the plaintiff. The loss is not pure economic loss, but is consequential on the damage to the plaintiff's body or mind. The distinction between property damage and pure economic loss is, perhaps, much more difficult to detect at times. We shall look at some of the cases to illustrate the distinction. The first one of these is the case of *Weller v The Foot and Mouth Disease Research Institute*,[2] in which the institute negligently released the foot and mouth virus which infected local cattle. As a consequence, movement of cattle was forbidden for some time. The plaintiff was a cattle auctioneer who claimed his loss of profits on the auctions which had to be cancelled. After quoting extensively from Lord Atkin's neighbour principle, Widgery J continued:

> Applying this principle, counsel for the plaintiff says that, since the defendants should have foreseen the damage to his clients but nevertheless failed to take proper precaution against the escape of the virus, their liability is established. It may be observed that, if this argument is sound, the defendants' liability is likely to extend far beyond the loss suffered by the auctioneers, for in an agricultural community the escape of foot and mouth disease virus is a tragedy which can foreseeably affect almost all business in that area. The affected beasts must be slaughtered, as must others to whom the disease may conceivably have spread. Other farmers are prohibited from moving their cattle and may be unable to bring them to market at the most profitable time; transport contractors who make their living by the transport of animals are out of work; dairymen may go short of milk, and sellers of cattle feed suffer loss of business. The magnitude of these consequences must not be allowed to deprive the plaintiffs of their rights, but it emphasises the importance of this case.
>
> The difficulty facing counsel for the plaintiffs is that there is a great volume of authority ... to the effect that a plaintiff suing in negligence for damages as a result of an act or omission of a defendant cannot recover if the act or omission did not directly injure, or at least threaten directly to injure, the plaintiff's person or property but merely caused consequential loss as, for example, by upsetting the plaintiff's business relations with a third party who was the direct victim of the act or omission. The categories of negligence never close, but when the court is asked to recognise a new category, it must proceed with some caution.
>
> I think it important to remember at the outset that, in the cases to which I have referred, the act or omission relied on as constituting a breach of the duty to take care was an act or omission which might foreseeably have caused direct injury to the person or property of another. The world of commerce would come to a halt and ordinary life would become intolerable if the law imposed a duty on all persons at all times to restrain from conduct which might foreseeably cause detriment to another, but where an absence of reasonable care may foreseeably cause direct injury to the person or property of another, a duty to take such care exists. ...

2 [1965] 3 All ER 560.

> In the present case, the defendants' duty to take care to avoid the escape of the virus was due to the foreseeable fact that the virus might infect cattle in the neighbourhood and cause them to die The duty of care is accordingly owed to the owners of cattle in the neighbourhood, but the plaintiffs are not owners of cattle and have no proprietary interest in anything which might conceivably be damaged by the virus if it escaped. Even if the plaintiffs have a proprietary interest in the premises known as Farnham Market, these premises are not in jeopardy. In my judgment, therefore, the plaintiffs' claim in negligence fails even if the assumptions of fact most favourable to them are made.

Although the judge does not say so expressly, the auctioneer's losses were regarded as purely economic. They were not in any way related to any personal injury or property damage. Local farmers would clearly have fallen within the latter category and have recovered their consequential economic losses.

Another useful case is *Spartan Steel & Alloys Ltd v Martin & Co (Contractors) Ltd*,[3] where the facts were simple but the consequences complex. In this case the defendants' employee negligently severed the electricity cable which supplied the plaintiffs' factory with electricity. The latter claimed for the damage to a melt in their furnace at the time, the loss of profit on that melt, the material being virtually worthless as a result, and in addition they claimed for loss of profits on further melts whilst the supply was still discontinued. Lord Denning MR, one of the judges in the majority in the Court of Appeal, stated:

> At bottom I think the question of recovering economic loss is one of policy. Whenever the courts draw a line to mark out the bounds of *duty*, they do it as a matter of policy so as to limit the responsibility of the defendant. Whenever the courts set bounds to the *damages* recoverable – saying that they are, or are not, too remote – they do it as a matter of policy so as to limit the liability of the defendant.
>
> In many of the cases where economic loss has been held not to be recoverable, it has been put on the ground that the defendant was under no *duty* to the plaintiff. Thus, where a person is injured in a road accident by the negligence of another, the negligent driver owes a duty to the injured man himself, but he owes no duty to the servant of the injured man ... nor to the master of the injured man, ... nor to anyone else who suffers loss because he had a contract with the injured man, ... nor indeed to anyone who only suffers economic loss on account of the accident. ... Likewise, when property is damaged by the negligence of another, the negligent tortfeasor owes a duty to the owner or possessor of the chattel, but not to one who suffers loss only because he had a contract entitling him to use the chattel or giving him the right to receive it at some later date.
>
> In other cases, however, the defendant seems clearly to have been under a duty to the plaintiff, but the economic loss has not been recovered because it is too remote.
>
> ... The more I think about these cases, the more difficult I find it to put each into its proper pigeon-hole. Sometimes I say: 'There was no duty.' In others I say: 'the damage was too remote', so much so that I think the time has come to discard those tests which have proved so elusive. It seems to me better to consider the particular relationship in hand, and see whether or not, as a matter of policy, economic loss should be recoverable. Thus in *Weller v Foot and Mouth Disease*

3 [1972] 3 All ER 557.

Research Institute [1965] 3 All ER 560 it was plain that the loss suffered by the auctioneers was not recoverable no matter whether it is put on the ground that there was no duty or that the damage was too remote. ...

So I turn to the relationship in the present case. It is of common occurrence. The parties concerned are the electricity board who are under a statutory duty to maintain supplies of electricity in their district; the inhabitants of the district, including the factory, who are entitled by statute to a continuous supply of electricity for their use; and the contractors who dig up the road. Similar relationships occur with other statutory bodies, such as gas and water undertakings. The cable may be damaged by the negligence of the statutory undertaker, or by negligence of the contractor, or by accident without any negligence by anyone; and the power may have to be cut off whilst the cable is repaired. Or the power may be cut off owing to a short circuit in the power house; and so forth. If the cutting off of the supply causes economic loss to the consumers, should it as a matter of policy be recoverable? And against whom?

The first consideration is the position of the statutory undertakers. If the board do not keep up the voltage or pressure of electricity, gas or water – or, likewise, if they shut it off for repairs – and thereby cause economic loss to their consumers, they are not liable in damages, not even if the cause of it is due to their own negligence ... one thing is clear, the board have never been held liable for economic loss only. If such be the policy of the legislature in regard to electricity boards, it would seem right for the common law to adopt a similar policy in regard to contractors. If the electricity boards are not liable for economic loss due to negligence which results in the cutting off of the supply, nor should a contractor be liable.

The second consideration is the nature of the hazard, namely, the cutting of the supply of electricity. This is a hazard which we all run. It may be due to a short circuit, to a flash of lightning, to a tree falling on the wires, to an accidental cutting of the cable, or even to the negligence of someone or other. And when it does happen, it affects a multitude of persons; not as a rule by way of physical damage to them or their property, but by putting them to inconvenience, and sometimes to economic loss. The supply is usually restored in a few hours, so the economic loss is not large.

Such a hazard is regarded by most people as a thing they must put up with – without seeking compensation from anyone. Some there are who install a stand-by system. Others seek refuge by taking out an insurance policy against breakdown in the supply. But most people are content to take the risk on themselves. When the supply is cut off, they do not go running round to their solicitors. They do not try to find out whether it was anyone's fault. They just put up with it. They try to make up the economic loss by doing more work the next day. This is a healthy attitude which the law should encourage.

The third consideration is this. If claims for economic loss were permitted for this particular hazard, there would be no end of claims. Some might be genuine, but many might be inflated, or even false. A machine might not have been in use anyway, but it would be easy to put it down to the cut in the supply. It would be well-nigh impossible to check the claims. If there was economic loss on one day, did the applicant do his best to mitigate it by working harder next day? And so forth. Rather than expose claimants to such temptation and defendants to such hard labour – on comparatively small claims – it is better to disallow economic loss altogether, at any rate when it stands alone, independent of any physical damage.

> The fourth consideration is that, in such a hazard as this, the risk of economic loss should be suffered by the whole community who suffer the losses – usually, but comparatively small losses – rather than on one pair of shoulders, that is on the contractor on whom the total of them, all added together, might be very heavy.
>
> The fifth consideration is that the law provides for deserving cases. If the defendant is guilty of negligence which cuts off the electricity supply and causes actual physical damage to person or property, that physical damage can be recovered. ... Such cases will be comparatively few. They will be readily capable of proof and will easily be checked. They should be and are admitted.
>
> These considerations lead me to the conclusion that the plaintiffs should recover for the physical damage to the one melt (£368), and the loss of profit on that melt consequent thereon; but not for the loss of profit on the four melts (£1,767), because that was economic loss independent of the physical damage. I would therefore allow the appeal and reduce the damages to £768.

Agreeing with the above, Lawton LJ commented:

> This is not the first time a negligent workman has cut an electricity supply cable nor the first claim for damages arising out of such an incident. When in practice at the Bar I myself advised in a number of such cases. Most practitioners acting for insurers under the so-called 'public liability" types of policy will have had similar professional experiences; if not with electrical supply, with gas and water mains. Negligent interference with such services is one the facts of life and can cause a lot of damage, both physical and financial. Water conduits have been with us for centuries; gas mains for nearly a century and a half; electricity supply cables for about three-quarters of a century; but there is not a single case in the English law reports which is an authority for the proposition that mere financial loss resulting from negligent interruption of such services is recoverable.

Dissenting, Edmund-Davies LJ said:

> Having considered the intrinsic nature of the problem presented in this appeal, and having consulted the relevant authorities, my conclusion, as already indicated, is that an action lies in negligence for damages in respect of purely economic loss, provided that it was reasonably foreseeable and direct consequence of failure in a duty of care. The application of such rule can undoubtedly give rise to difficulties in certain sets of circumstances, but so can the suggested rule that economic loss may be recovered, *provided* it is directly consequential on physical damage. Many alarming situations were conjured up in the course of counsel's arguments before us. In their way, they were reminiscent of those formerly advanced against awarding damages for nervous shock; for example, the risk of fictitious claims and expensive litigation, the difficulty of disproving the alleged cause and effect, and the impossibility of expressing such a claim in financial terms. But I suspect that they ... would for the most part be resolved either on the ground that no duty of care was owed to the injured party or that the damages sued for were irrecoverable, *not* because they were simply financial but because they were too remote.
>
> ... Such good sense as I possess guides me to the conclusion that it would be wrong to draw in the present case any distinction between the first, spoilt 'melt' and the four 'melts' which, but for the defendants' negligence, would admittedly have followed it. That is simply another way of saying that I consider the plaintiffs are entitled to recover the entirety of the financial loss they sustained.

The line drawn by the majority in this case has the merit of being a clear one, although, as Edmund-Davies LJ observed above, it seems somewhat arbitrary.

The distinction between economic loss which is recoverable and that which is not has not always been so easy to formulate. Difficulty has arisen in a number of the shipping cases where the result of the case seems to depend on the precise form of the contract made between the buyer of goods, the seller and the ship owner. This is perhaps best illustrated by looking at one such case, *Leigh & Sillavan Ltd v Aliakmon Shipping Co Ltd, The Aliakmon*.[4] The purchasers contracted to buy from the sellers a quantity of steel coils which were to be shipped c&f from Korea to the UK. As a result of negligence of the ship owners the steel was damaged during the voyage. Before the damage was discovered the sellers tendered the bill of lading but the purchasers could not meet the payment. The contract was varied by agreement so as to enable the purchasers to take delivery of the steel, but they would hold the bill of lading as agents of the sellers and the steel would be held to the sole order of the sellers. The effect of this arrangement was that the purchasers did not have title to the steel. They sued the ship owners in contract and negligence. The House dismissed the purchasers' appeal. Lord Brandon delivered the only judgment, the others all agreeing with him, as follows:

> My Lords, under the usual kind of CIF or c&f contract of sale, the risk in the goods passes from the seller to the buyer on shipment, as is exemplified by the obligation of the buyer to take up and pay for the shipping documents even though the goods may already have suffered damage or loss during their carriage by sea. The property in the goods, however, does not pass until the buyer takes up and pays for the shipping documents. Those include a bill of lading relating to the goods which has been indorsed by the seller in favour of the buyer. By acquiring the bill of lading so indorsed the buyer becomes a person to whom the property in the goods has passed on or by reason of such indorsement, and so, by virtue of s 1 of the Bills of Lading Act 1855, has vested in him all the rights of suit, and is subject to the same liabilities in respect of the goods as if the contract contained in the bill of lading had been made with him.
>
> In terms of the present case this means that, if the buyers had completed the c&f contract in the manner intended, they would have been entitled to sue the ship owners for the damage to the goods in contract under the bill of lading, and no question of any separate duty of care in tort would have arisen. In the events which occurred, however, what had originally been a usual kind of c&f contract of sale had been varied so as to become, in effect, a contract of sale ex-warehouse at Immingham.
>
> The contract as so varied was, however, unusual in an important respect. Under an ordinary contract of sale ex-warehouse both the risk and property in the goods would pass from the seller to the buyer at the same time, that time being ascertained by the intention of the parties. Under this varied contract, however, the risk had already passed to the buyers on shipment because of the original c&f terms, and there was nothing in the new terms which caused it to revert to the sellers.
>
> The buyers, however, did not acquire any rights of suit under the bill of lading by virtue of s 1 of the Bills of Lading Act 1855. This was because, owing to the sellers' reservation of the right of disposal of the goods, the property in the goods did not pass to the buyers on or by reason of the indorsement of the bill of lading, but only on payment of the purchase price by the buyers to the sellers

4 [1986] 2 All ER 145.

after the goods had been discharged and warehoused at Immingham. Hence the attempt of the buyers to establish a separate claim against the ship owners founded in the tort of negligence.

My Lords, there is a long line of authority for a principle of law that, in order to enable a person to claim in negligence for loss caused to him by reason of loss of or damage to property, he must have had either the legal ownership of or a possessory title to the property concerned at the time when the loss or damage occurred, and it is not enough for him to have only had contractual rights in relation to such property which have been adversely affected by the loss or damage to it. ...

None of these cases concerns a claim by CIF or c&f buyers of goods to recover, from the owners of the ship in which the goods are carried, loss suffered by reason of want of care in the carriage of the goods resulting in their being lost or damaged at a time when the risk in the goods, but not yet the legal property in them, has passed to such buyers.

The question whether such a claim would lie however, came up for decision in *Margarine Union GmbH v Cambay Prince SS Co Ltd, The Wear Breeze* [1967] 3 All ER 775, [1969] 1 QB 219. In that case CIF buyers had accepted four delivery orders in respect of as yet undivided portions of a cargo of copra in bulk shipped under two bills of lading. It was common ground that, by doing so, they did not acquire either the legal property in, or a possessory title to, the portions of copra concerned; they only acquired the legal property later when four portions each of 500 tons were separated from the bulk on or shortly after discharge in Hamburg. The copra having been damaged by want of care by the ship owners' servants or agents in not properly fumigating the holds of the carrying ship before loading, the question arose whether the buyers were entitled to recover from the ship owners in tort for negligence the loss which they had suffered by reason of the copra having been so damaged. Roskill J held that they were not, founding his decision largely on the principle of law established by the line of authority to which I have referred. ...

My Lords, counsel for the buyers did not question any of the cases in the long line of authority to which I have referred except *The Wear Breeze*. He felt obliged to accept the continuing correctness of the rest of the cases (the other non-recovery cases) because of the recent decision of the Privy Council in *Candlewood Navigation Corpn Ltd v Mitsui OSK Lines Ltd, The Mineral Transporter, The Ibaraki Maru* [1985] 2 All ER 935, [1986] AC I, in which those cases were again approved and applied, and to which it will be necessary for me to refer more fully later. He contended, however, that *The Wear Breeze* was either wrongly decided at the time, or at any rate should be regarded as wrongly decided today, and should accordingly be overruled.

In support of this contention, counsel for the buyers relied on five main grounds. The first ground was that the characteristics of a CIF or c&f contract for sale differed materially from the characteristics of the contracts concerned in the other non-recovery cases. The second ground was that, under a CIF or c&f contract, the buyer acquired immediately on shipment of the goods the equitable ownership of them. The third ground was that the law of negligence had developed significantly since 1969 when *The Wear Breeze* was decided, in particular as a result of the decisions of your Lordships' House in *Anns v Merton London Borough* [1977] 2 All ER 492, [1978] AC 728 and *Junior Books Ltd v Veitchi Co Ltd* [1982] 3 All ER 201, [1983] 1 AC 520. In this connection reliance was placed on two decisions, at first instance in which *The Wear Breeze* had either not been followed or treated as no longer being good law. The fourth ground was that any rational system of law would provide a remedy for persons who suffered the kind of loss which the buyers suffered in the present case. The fifth ground was the judgment of Robert Goff LJ in the present case, so far as related to the buyers' right to sue the ship owners in tort for negligence. I shall examine each of these grounds in turn.

Ground 1: difference in characteristics of a CIF or c&f contract

My Lords, under this head counsel for the buyers said that, in the other non-recovery cases, the plaintiffs who failed were not persons who had contracted to buy the property to which the defendants' want of care had caused loss or damage; they were rather persons whose contractual rights entitled them either to have the use or services of the property concerned and thereby made profits (eg the time charter cases), or to render services to the property concerned and thereby earn remuneration (eg the towage cases). By contracts, buyers under a CIF or c&f contract of sale were persons to whom it was intended that the legal ownership of the goods should later pass, and who were therefore prospectively, though not presently, the legal owners of them.

I recognise that this difference in the characteristics of a CIF or c&f contract of sale exists, but I cannot see why it should of itself make any difference to the principle of law to be applied. In all these cases what the plaintiffs are complaining of is that, by reason of their contracts with others, loss of or damage to property, to which, when it occurred, they had neither a proprietary nor a possessory title, has caused them to suffer loss; and the circumstance that, in the case of CIF or c&f buyers, they are, if the contract of sale is duly completed, destined later to acquire legal ownership of the goods after the loss or damage has occurred, does not seem to me to constitute a material distinction in law.

Ground 2: equitable ownership

My Lords, under this head counsel for the buyers puts forward two propositions of law. The first proposition was that a person who has the equitable ownership of goods is entitled to sue in tort for negligence anyone, who by want of care, causes them to be lost or damaged without joining the legal owner as a party to the action. The second proposition was that a buyer who agrees to buy goods in circumstances where, although ascertained goods have been appropriated to the contract, their legal ownership remains in the seller, acquires on such appropriation the equitable ownership of the goods. Applying those two propositions to the facts of the present case, counsel for the buyers submitted that the goods, the subject matter of the c&f contract, had been appropriated to the contract on or before shipment at Inchon, and that from then on, while the legal ownership of the goods remained in the sellers, the buyers became equitable owners of them, and could therefore sue the ship owners in tort for negligence for the damage done to them without joining the sellers.

In my view, the first proposition cannot be supported. There may be cases where a person who is the equitable owner of certain goods has also a possessory title to them. In such a case he is entitled, by virtue of his possessory title rather than his equitable ownership, to sue in tort for negligence anyone whose want of care has caused loss of or damage to the goods without joining the legal owner as a party to the action ... If, however, the person is the equitable owner of the goods and no more, then he must join the legal owner as a party to the action, either as co-plaintiff if he is willing or co-defendant if he is not. This has always been the law in the field of equitable ownership of land and I see no reason why it should not also be so in the field of equitable ownership of goods.

With regard to the second proposition, I do not doubt that it is possible, in accordance with established equitable principles, for equitable interests in goods to be created and to exist. It seems to me, however, extremely doubtful whether equitable interests in goods can be created or exist within the confines of an ordinary contract of sale. ...

Ground 3: development of the law of negligence since 1969

... Counsel for the buyers said, rightly in my view, that the policy reason for excluding a duty of care in cases like *The Mineral Transporter* and what I earlier called the other non-recovery cases was to avoid the opening of the floodgates so as to expose a person guilty of want of care to unlimited liability to an indefinite number of other persons whose contractual rights have been adversely affected by such want of care. Counsel for the buyers went on to argue that, recognition by the law of a duty of care owed by ship owners to a CIF or c&f buyer, to whom the risk, but not yet the property in the goods carried in such ship owners' ship, has passed, would not of itself open any floodgates of the kind described. It would, he said, only create a strictly limited exception to the general rule, based on the circumstance that the considerations of policy on which that general rule was founded did not apply to that particular case. I do not accept that argument. If an exception to the general rule were to be made in the field of carriage by sea, it would no doubt have to be extended to the field of carriage by land, and I do not think that it is possible to say that no undue increase in the scope of a person's liability for want of care would follow.

In any event, where a general rule, which is simple to understand and easy to apply, has been established by a long line of authority over many years, I do not think that the law should allow special pleading in a particular case within the general rule to detract from its application. If such detraction were to be permitted in one particular case, it would lead to attempts to have it permitted in a variety of other particular cases, and the result would be that the certainty, which the application of the general rule presently provides, would be seriously undermined. Yet certainty of the law is of the utmost importance, especially but by no means only, in commercial matters. I therefore think that the general rule, reaffirmed as it has been so recently by the Privy Council in *The Mineral Transporter*, ought to apply to a case like the present one, and that there is nothing in what Lord Wilberforce said in the *Anns* case which would compel a different conclusion. ...

Ground 4: the requirements of a rational system of law

My Lords, under this head counsel for the buyers submitted that any rational system of law ought to provide a remedy for persons who suffered the kind of loss which the buyers suffered in the present case, with the clear implication that, if your Lordships' House were to hold that the remedy for which he contended was not available, it would be lending its authority to an irrational feature of English law. I do not agree with this submission for, as I shall endeavour to show, English law does, in all normal cases, provide a fair and adequate remedy for loss of or damage to goods the subject matter of a CIF or c&f contract, and the buyers in this case could easily, if properly advised at the time when they agreed to the variation of the original c&f contract, have secured to themselves the benefit of such a remedy.

As I indicated earlier, under the usual CIF or c&f contract the bill of lading issued in respect of the goods is indorsed and delivered by the seller to the buyer against payment by the buyer of the price. When that happens, the property in the goods passes from the sellers to the buyers on or by reason of such indorsement, and the buyer is entitled, by virtue of s 1 of the Bills of Lading Act 1855, to sue the ship owner for loss of or damage to the goods on the contract contained in the bill of lading. The remedy so available to the buyer is adequate and fair to both parties, and there is no need for any parallel or alternative remedy in tort for negligence.

In the present case, as I also indicated earlier, the variation of the original c&f contract agreed between the sellers and the buyers produced a hybrid contract of an extremely unusual character. It was extremely unusual in that, what had originally been an ordinary c&f contract became, in effect, a sale ex-warehouse at Immingham, but the risk in the goods during their carriage by sea remained with the buyers as if the sale had still been on a c&f basis. In this situation the persons who had the right to sue the ship owners for loss of or damage to the goods on the contract contained in the bill of lading were the sellers, and the buyers, if properly advised, should have made it a further term of the variation that the sellers should either exercise this right for their account ... or assign such right to them to exercise for themselves. If either of these two precautions had been taken, the law would have provided the buyers with a fair and adequate remedy for their loss.

These considerations show, in my opinion, not that there is some lacuna in English law relating to these matters, but only that the buyers, when they agreed to the variation of the original contract of sale, did not take steps to protect themselves which, if properly advised, they should have done. To put the matter quite simply, the buyers, by the variation to which they agreed, were depriving themselves of the right of suit under s1 of the Bills of Lading Act 1855 which they would otherwise have had, and commercial good sense required that they should obtain the benefit of an equivalent right in one or other of the two different ways which I have suggested.

Ground 5: the judgment of Robert Goff LJ

My Lords, after a full examination of numerous authorities relating to the law of negligence Goff LJ said ([1985] 2 All ER 44 at 77, [1985] QB 350 at 399): 'In my judgment, there is no good reason in principle or in policy, why the c&f buyer should not have ... a direct cause of action. The factors which I have already listed point strongly towards liability. I am particularly influenced by the fact that the loss in question is of a character which will ordinarily fall on the goods' owner, who will have a good claim against the ship owner, but in a case such as the present the loss may, in practical terms, fall on the buyer. It seems to me that the policy reasons pointing towards a direct right of action by the buyer against the ship owner in a case of this kind outweigh the policy reasons which generally preclude recovery for purely economic loss. There is here no question of any wide or indeterminate liability being imposed on wrongdoers; on the contrary, the ship owner is simply held liable to the buyer in damages for loss which he would ordinarily be liable to the goods' owner. There is a recognised principle underlying the imposition of liability, which can be called "the principle of transferred loss". Furthermore, that principle can be formulated. For the purpose of the present case, I would formulate it in the following deliberately narrow terms, while recognising that it may require modification in the light of experience. Where A owes a duty of care in tort not to cause physical damage to B's property, and commits a breach of that duty in circumstances in which the loss of, or the physical damage to, the property will ordinarily fall on B, but (as is reasonably foreseeable) such loss or damage, by reason of a contractual relationship between B and C, falls on C, then C will be entitled, subject to the terms of any contract restricting A's liability to B, to bring an action in tort against A in respect of such loss or damage to the extent that it falls on him, C. To that proposition there must be exceptions. In particular, there must, for the reasons I have given, be an exception in the case of contracts of insurance. I have

> also attempted to draw the principle as to exclude the case of the time charterer who remains liable for hire for the chartered ship while under repair following collision damage, though this could if necessary be treated as another exception having regard to the present state of the authorities.'
>
> With the greatest possible respect to Robert Goff LJ, the principle of transferred loss which he here enunciated, however useful in dealing with future factual situations it may be in theory, is not only not supported by authority, but is on the contrary inconsistent with it. Even if it were necessary to introduce such a principle in order to fill a genuine *lacuna* in the law, I should myself, perhaps because I am more faint hearted than Robert Goff LJ, be reluctant to do so. As I have tried to show earlier, however, there is in truth no such *lacuna* in the law which requires to be filled. Neither Sir John Donaldson MR nor Oliver LJ was prepared to accept the introduction of such a principle and I find myself entirely in agreement with their unwillingness to do so.

The extracts from the judgment illustrate only too well the judiciary's growing reluctance at that time to contemplate the overturning of existing precedents. We have seen in the chapter on duty earlier that the reaction to the two-stage test in *Anns* had already begun to set in by this time and the battleground was generally the area of liability for economic loss. Why should the defendant ship owner's liability depend so arbitrarily on a quirk as it did in this case? The defendants were not likely to know what had passed between the sellers and buyers and must have been anticipating the imposition of liability had the normal state of affairs occurred. How can this be seen as creating indeterminate liability? The mythical certainty argument once again raises its head in this case and is once again overplayed. Be that as it may, unless the plaintiff can show that he has a sufficient proprietary or possessory interest in the damaged property, then he will be unable to recover, even though to all intents and purposes, because of the transfer of the risk, he is the owner of the goods.

There is another area of difficulty surrounding the thorny issue of what amounts to pure economic loss. This arose in the now, in England and Wales at least, discredited *Anns* case. In discussing the type of damage in that case, Lord Wilberforce commented:

> To allow recovery for such damage to the house follows, in my opinion, from normal principle. If classification is required, the relevant damage is, in my opinion, material, physical damage, and what is recoverable is the amount of expenditure necessary to restore the dwelling to a condition in which it is no longer a danger to health or safety of persons occupying and possibly (depending on the circumstances) expenses arising from necessary displacement.

Although it did not seem from the above that it was necessary to classify the damage in such a way, it did at least counter arguments that the damage was purely economic in nature. However, there has of course been a subsequent reclassification by the House of the type of damage. This process started in the case of *D & F Estates v Church Commissioners for England*.[5] The plaintiffs were lessees and occupiers of a flat in a block built several years before by the third defendants. The latter had employed a sub-contractor to do some of the original plastering work in the flat and the plaintiff was claiming in tort for the cost of repairing and renewing defective plaster work carried out by the sub-

5 [1988] 2 All ER 992.

contractors. After a lengthy survey of the law, including a study of the Defective Premises Act 1972, Lord Bridge stated:

> These principles are easy enough to comprehend and probably not difficult to apply when the defect complained of is in a chattel supplied complete by a single manufacturer. If the hidden defect in the chattel is the cause of personal injury or of damage to property other than the chattel itself, the manufacturer is liable. But if the hidden defect is discovered before any such damage is caused, there is no longer any room for the application of the *Donoghue v Stevenson* principle. The chattel is now defective in quality, but it is no longer dangerous. It may be valueless or it may be capable of economic repair. In either case the economic loss is recoverable in contract by a buyer or hirer of the chattel entitled to the relevant warranty of quality, but is not recoverable in tort by a remote buyer or hirer of the chattel.
>
> If the same principle applies in the field of real property to the liability of the builder of a permanent structure which is dangerously defective, that liability can only arise if the defect remains hidden until the defective structure causes personal injury or damage to property other than the structure itself. If the defect is discovered before any damage is done, the loss sustained by the owner of the structure, who has to repair or demolish it to avoid a potential source of danger to third parties, would seem to be purely economic. Thus, if I acquire a property with a dangerously defective garden wall which is attributable to the bad workmanship of the original builder, it is difficult to see any basis in principle on which I can sustain an action in tort against the builder for the cost of either repairing or demolishing the wall. No physical damage has been caused. All that has happened is that the defect in the wall has been discovered in time to prevent damage occurring. I do not find it necessary for the purpose of deciding the present appeal to express any concluded view as to how far, if at all, the *ratio decidendi* of *Anns v Merton London Borough* [1977] 2 All ER 492, [1978] AC 728 involves a departure from this principle, establishing a new cause of action in negligence against a builder when the only damage alleged to have been suffered by the plaintiff is the discovery of the defect in the very structure which the builder erected.
>
> My example of the garden wall, however, is that of a very simple structure. I can see that more difficult questions may arise in relation to a more complex structure like a dwelling house. One view would be that such a structure should be treated in law as a single indivisible unit. On this basis, if the unit becomes a potential source of danger when a hitherto hidden defect in construction manifests itself, the builder, as in the case of the garden wall, should not in principle be liable for the cost of remedying the defect. ...
>
> However, I can see that it may well be arguable that in the case of complex structures, as indeed possibly in the case of complex chattels, one element of the structure should be regarded for the purpose of the application of the principles under discussion as distinct from another element, so that damage to one part of the structure caused by a hidden defect in another part may qualify to be treated as damage to 'other property', and whether the argument should prevail may depend on the circumstances of the case. It would be unwise and it is unnecessary for the purpose of deciding the present appeal to attempt to offer authoritative solutions to these difficult problems in the abstract. ...
>
> In the instant case the only hidden defect was in the plaster. The only item pleaded as damage to other property was 'cost of cleaning carpets and other possessions damaged or dirtied by falling plaster – £50'. Once it appeared that the plaster was loose, any danger of personal injury or of further injury to other

property could have been simply avoided by the timely removal of the defective plaster. The only function of plaster on walls and ceilings, unless it is elaborately decorative, is to serve as a smooth surface on which to place decorative paper or paint. Whatever case there may be for treating a defect in some part of the structure of a building as causing damage to 'other property' when some other part of the building is injuriously affected, as for example cracking in walls caused by defective foundations, it would seem to me entirely artificial to treat the plaster as distinct from the decorative surface placed on it. Even if it were so treated, the only damage to 'other property' caused by the defective plaster would be the loss of value of existing decorations occasioned by the necessity to remove loose plaster which was in danger of falling. When the loose plaster in flat 37 was first discovered in 1980, the flat was in any event being redecorated.

It seems to me clear that the cost of replacing the defective plaster itself, either as carried out in 1980 or as intended to be carried out in the future, was not an item of damage for which the builder ... could possibly be made liable in negligence under the principle of *Donoghue v Stevenson* or any legitimate development of that principle. To make him so liable would be to impose on him, for the benefit of those with whom he had no contractual relationship, the obligation of one who warranted the quality of the plaster as regards materials, workmanship and fitness for purpose. I am glad to reach the conclusion that this is not the law, if only for the reason that a conclusion to the opposite effect would mean that the courts, in developing the common law, had gone much further than the legislature were prepared to go in 1972, after comprehensive examination of the subject by the Law Commission, in making builders liable for defects in the quality of their work to all who subsequently acquire interests in buildings they have erected. The statutory duty imposed by the 1972 Act was confined to dwelling houses and limited to defects appearing within six years. The common law duty, if it existed, could not be so confined or so limited. I cannot help feeling that consumer protection is an area of law where legislation is much better left to the legislators.

Lord Oliver, after reviewing some of the case law, commented:

These propositions [ie those in *Anns*] involve a number of entirely novel concepts. In the first place, in no other context has it previously been suggested that a cause of action in tort arises in English law for the defective manufacture of an article which causes no injury other than injury to the defective article itself. If I buy a second-hand car to which there has been fitted a pneumatic tyre which, as a result of carelessness in manufacture, is dangerously defective and which bursts, causing injury to me or to the car, no doubt the negligent manufacturer is liable in tort on the ordinary application of *Donoghue v Stevenson*. But if the tyre bursts without causing any injury other than to itself or if I discover the defect before a burst occurs, I know of no principle on which I can claim to recover from the manufacturer in tort the cost of making good the defect which, in practice, could only be the cost of supplying and fitting a new tyre. That would be, in effect, to attach to goods a non-contractual warranty of fitness which would follow the goods into whosoever hands they came. Such a concept was suggested, *obiter*, by Lord Denning MR in *Dutton's* case [1972] 1 All ER 462 at 474, [1972] 1 QB 373 at 396, but it was entirely unsupported by any authority and is, in my opinion, contrary to principle.

The proposition that damages are recoverable in tort for negligent manufacture, when the only damage sustained is either an initial defect in or subsequent injury to the very thing that is manufactured, is one which is peculiar to the construction of a building and is, I think, logically explicable only on the hypothesis suggested by my noble and learned friend Lord Bridge, that in the case of such a complicated structure the other constituent parts can be treated as separate items of property distinct from that portion of the whole which has given rise to the damage, for instance in *Anns'* case, treating the defective foundations as something distinct from the remainder of the building. So regarded, this would be no more than the ordinary application of the *Donoghue v Stevenson* principle. It is true that in such a case the damages would, and in some cases might be restricted to, the costs of replacing or making good the defective part, but that would be because such remedial work would be essential to the repair of the property which had been damaged by it. ...

My Lords, I have to confess that the underlying logical basis for, and the boundaries of, the doctrine emerging from *Anns v Merton London Borough* are not entirely clear to me, and it is in any event unnecessary for the purposes of the instant appeal to attempt a definitive exposition. This much at least seems clear – that in so far as the case is authority for the proposition that a builder responsible for the construction of the building is liable in tort at common law for damage occurring through his negligence to the very thing which he has constructed, such liability is limited directly to cases where the defect is one which threatens the health or safety of occupants or of third parties and (possibly) other property.

... The case cannot, in my opinion, properly be adapted to support the recovery of damages for pure economic loss going beyond that, and for the reasons given by my noble and learned friend Lord Bridge, with whose analysis I respectfully agree, such loss is not in principle recoverable in tort unless the case can be brought within the principle of reliance established by *Hedley Byrne*. In the instant case the defective plaster caused no damage to the remainder of the building, and in so far as it presented a risk of damage to other property or to the person of any occupant that was remediable simply by the process of removal. I agree, accordingly, for the reasons which my noble and learned friend Lord Bridge has given, that the cost of replacing the defective plaster is not an item for which the builder can be held liable in negligence. I too would dismiss the appeal.

The other three Law Lords agreed with the above.

The final nail in the coffin of the argument – that the damage in the defective building cases was physical damage – came, of course, in *Murphy v Brentwood District Council*.[6] On very similar facts to those in *Anns*, the House of Lords departed from the decision in that case. On the crucial question of the nature of the damage, Lord Keith observed:

In *Anns*, the House of Lords approved, subject to explanation, the decision of the Court of Appeal in *Dutton v Bognor Regis UDC* [1972] 1 All ER 462, [1972] 1 QB 373 at 396), in that case Lord Denning MR observed: 'Counsel for the council submitted that the liability of the council would, in any case, be limited to those who suffered bodily harm; and did not extend to those who only suffered economic loss. He suggested, therefore, that although the council might be liable if the ceiling fell down and injured a visitor, they would not be liable simply because the house was diminished in value. ... I cannot accept this submission. The damage done here was not solely economic loss; it was physical damage to the house. If counsel's submission were right, it would mean that, if the inspector negligently passes the house as properly built and it collapses and injures a person, the council are liable; but, if the owner discovers the defect in time to

6 [1990] 2 All ER 908.

repair it – and he does repair it – the council are not liable. That is an impossible distinction. They are liable in either case. I would say the same about the manufacturer of an article. If he makes it negligently, with a latent defect (so that it breaks to pieces and injures someone), he is undoubtedly liable. Suppose that the defect is discovered in time to prevent the injury. Surely he is liable for the cost of repair.'

The jump which is here made, from liability under the *Donoghue v Stevenson* principle for damage to person or property caused by a latent defect in a carelessly manufactured article, to liability for the cost of rectifying a defect in such an article which is *ex hypothesi* no longer latent, is difficult to accept. As Stamp LJ recognised in the same case, there is no liability in tort on a manufacturer towards the purchaser from a retailer of an article which turns out to be useless or valueless through defects due to careless manufacture (see [1972] 1 All ER 426 at 489–90, [1972] 1 QB 373 at 414–15). The loss is economic. It is difficult to draw a distinction in principle between an article which is useless or valueless and one which suffers from a defect which would render it dangerous in use, but which is discovered by the purchaser in time to avert any possibility of injury. The purchaser may incur expense in putting right the defect, or, more probably, discard the article. In either case the loss is purely economic. Stamp LJ appears to have taken the view that, in the case of a house, the builder would not be liable to a purchaser where the defect was discovered in time to prevent injury, but that a local authority which had failed to discover the defect by careful inspection during the course of construction was so liable. ...

In *D & F Estates Ltd v Church Commissioners for England* [1988] 2 All ER 992, [1989] AC 177 both Lord Bridge and Lord Oliver expressed themselves as having difficulty in reconciling the decision in *Anns* with pre-existing principle, and as being uncertain as to the nature and scope of such new principle as it introduced. Lord Bridge suggested that, in the case of a complex structure such as a building, one element of the structure might be regarded for *Donoghue v Stevenson* purposes as distinct from another element, so that damage to one part of the structure caused by a hidden defect in another part might qualify to be treated as damage to 'other property' (see [1988] 2 All ER 992 at 1006, [1989] AC 177 at 206).

I think it would be unrealistic to take this view as regards a building, the whole of which had been erected and equipped by the same contractor. In that situation the whole package provided by the contractor would, in my opinion, fall to be regarded as one unit rendered unsound as such by a defect in the particular part. On the other hand, where, for example, the electric wiring had been installed by a sub-contractor and, due to a defect caused by a lack of care, a fire occurred which destroyed the building, it might not be stretching ordinary principles too far to hold the electrical sub-contractor liable for the damage ...

Lord Bridge also gave a view in this case. The following is a brief extract from his judgment:

If a manufacturer negligently puts into circulation a chattel containing a latent defect which renders it dangerous to persons or property, the manufacturer ... will be liable in tort for injury to persons or damage to property which the chattel causes. But if a manufacturer produces and sells a chattel which is merely defective in quality, even to the extent that it is valueless for the purpose for which it is intended, the manufacturer's liability at common law arises only under, and by reference to, the terms of any contract to which he is a party in relation to the chattel; the common law does not impose on him any liability in tort to persons to whom he owes no duty in contract but who, having acquired the chattel, suffer economic loss because the chattel is defective in quality. If a dangerous defect in a chattel is found before it causes any personal injury or damage to property, because the danger is now known and the chattel cannot be safely used unless the defect is repaired, the defect becomes merely a defect in quality.

The chattel is either capable of repair at economic cost or it is worthless and must be scrapped. In either case the loss sustained by the owner or hirer of the chattel is purely economic. It is recoverable against any party who owes the loser a relevant contractual duty, but it is not recoverable in tort in the absence of a special relationship of proximity imposing on the tortfeasor a duty of care to safeguard the plaintiff from economic loss. There is no such special relationship between the manufacturer of a chattel and a remote owner or hirer.

I believe that these principles are equally applicable to buildings. If a builder erects a structure containing a latent defect which renders it dangerous to persons or property, he will be liable in tort for injury to persons or damage to property resulting from that dangerous defect. But, if the defect becomes apparent before any injury or damage has been caused, the loss sustained by the building owner is purely economic. If the defect can be repaired at economic cost, that is the measure of the loss. If the building cannot be repaired, it may have to be abandoned as unfit for occupation and therefore valueless. These economic losses are recoverable if they flow from breach of a relevant contractual duty, but, here again, in the absence of a special relationship of proximity they are not recoverable in tort.

The only qualification I would make to this is that, if a building stands so close to the boundary of the building owner's land that, after discovery of the dangerous defect, it remains a potential source of injury to persons or property on neighbouring land or on the highway, the building owner ought, in principle, to be entitled to recover in tort from the negligent builder the cost of obviating the danger, whether by repair or demolition, so far as that cost is necessarily incurred in order to protect himself from potential liability to third parties. ...

In my speech in the *D & F Estates* case [1988] 2 All ER 992 at 1006–07, [1989] AC 177 at 206–07 I mooted the possibility that, in complex structures or complex chattels, one part of a structure or chattel might, when it caused damage to another part of the same structure or chattel, be regarded in the law of tort as having caused damage to 'other property' for the purpose of the application of *Donoghue v Stevenson* principles. I expressed no opinion as to the validity of this theory, but put it forward for consideration as a possible ground on which the facts considered in *Anns* might be distinguishable from the facts which had to be considered in *D & F Estates* itself. I shall call this for convenience 'the complex structure theory' and it is, so far as I can see, only if, and to the extent that this theory can be affirmed and applied, that there can be any escape from the conclusions I have indicated above. ...

The complex structure theory has, so far as I know, never been subjected to express and detailed examination in any English authority. ...

A critical distinction must be drawn here between some part of a complex structure which is said to be a 'danger' only because it does not perform its proper function in sustaining the other parts, and some distinct item incorporated in the structure which positively malfunctions so as to inflict positive damage on the structure in which it is incorporated. Thus, if a defective central heating boiler explodes and damages a house or a defective electrical installation malfunctions and sets the house on fire, I see no reason to doubt that the owner of the house, if he can prove that the damage was due to the negligence of the boiler manufacturer in the one case or the electrical contractor in the other, can recover damages in tort on *Donoghue v Stevenson* principles.

But the position in law is entirely different where, by reason of the inadequacy of the foundations of the building to support the weight of the superstructure, differential settlement and consequent cracking occurs. Here, once the first cracks appear, the structure as a whole is seen to be defective and the nature of the defect is known. Even if, contrary to my view, the initial damage could be regarded as damage to other property caused by a latent defect, once the defect is known the situation of the building owner is analogous to that of the car owner who discovers that the car has faulty brakes. He may have a house which, until repairs are effected, is unfit for habitation, but, subject to the reservation I have expressed with respect to ruinous buildings at or near the boundary of the owner's property, the building no longer represents a source of danger and, as it deteriorates, will only damage itself.

For these reasons the complex structure theory offers no escape from the conclusion that damage to a house itself which is attributable to a defect in the structure of the house is not recoverable in tort on *Donoghue v Stevenson* principles, but represents purely economic loss which is recoverable in contract or tort by reason of some special relationship of proximity which imposes on the tortfeasor a duty of care to protect against economic loss.

Lord Oliver was also in this case and commented in similar vein:

... despite the categorisation of the damage as 'material, physical damage' (see *Anns* [1977] 2 All ER 492 at 505, [1978] AC 728 at 759 per Lord Wilberforce), it is, I think, incontestable on analysis that what the plaintiffs suffered was pure pecuniary loss and nothing more. If one asks 'what were the damages to be awarded for?', clearly they were not to be awarded for injury to health or person of the plaintiffs, for they had suffered none. But equally clearly, although the 'damage' was described, both in the Court of Appeal in *Dutton* and in this House in *Anns*, as physical or material damage, this simply does not withstand analysis. To begin with, it makes no sort of sense to accord a remedy where the defective nature of the structure has manifested itself by some physical symptom, such as a crack or a fractured pipe, but to deny it where the defect has been brought to light by, for instance, a structural survey in connection with a proposed sale.

... In the speech of Lord Bridge and in my own speech in *D & F Estates v Church Commissioners for England* [1988] 2 All ER 992. [1989] AC 177 there was canvassed what has been called 'the complex structure theory'. This has rightly been criticised by academic writers, although I confess that I thought that both Lord Bridge and I had made it clear that it was a theory which was not embraced with any enthusiasm but was advanced as the only logically possible explanation of the categorisation of the damage in *Anns* as 'material, physical damage'. Lord Bridge has, in the course of his speech in the present case, amply demonstrated the artificiality of the theory and, for the reasons which he has given, it must be rejected as a viable explanation of the underlying basis for the decision in *Anns*.

However that decision is analysed, therefore, it is in the end inescapable that the only damage for which compensation was to be awarded and which formed the essential foundation of the action was pecuniary loss and nothing more. The injury which the plaintiff suffers in such a case is that his consciousness of the possible injury to his own health or safety or that of others puts him in a position in which, in order to enable him either to go on living in the property or to exploit its financial potentiality without that risk, whether substantial or insubstantial, he has to expend money in making good the defects which have now become patent. ...

The fact is that the categorisation of the damage in *Anns* as 'material, physical

> damage', whilst at first sight lending to the decision some colour of consistency with the principle of *Donoghue v Stevenson*, has served to obscure not only the true nature of the claim but, as a result, the nature and scope of the duty on the breach of which the plaintiffs in that case were compelled to rely. ...
>
> I frankly doubt whether ... the categorisation of the damage as 'material', 'physical', 'pecuniary' or 'economic' provides a particularly useful contribution. Where it does, I think, serve a useful purpose is in identifying those cases in which it is necessary to search for and find something more than the mere reasonable foreseeability of damage which has occurred as providing the degree of 'proximity' necessary to support the action. ... The infliction of physical injury to the person or property of another universally requires to be justified. The causing of economic loss does not. If it is to be categorised as wrongful it is necessary to find some factor beyond the mere occurrence of the loss and the fact that its occurrence could be foreseen. Thus the categorisation of damage as economic serves at least the useful purpose of indicating that something more is required, and is one of the unfortunate features of *Anns* that it resulted initially in this essential distinction being lost sight of.

Lord Jauncey made similar, although briefer comments on the nature of the damage and the complex structure theory. Lord Mackay, in a very short speech, agreed with the comments of the others. The case settles the issue of the nature of the damage in such circumstances, although it is an analysis which is not universally accepted in the common law world.[7]

GENERAL RULE AGAINST RECOVERY

The importance of the distinction between property damage on the one hand and pure economic loss on the other should be evident from the preceding discussion. There is, and has been for well over 100 years, a rule against recovery for pure financial loss. Its very antiquity is one of the compelling reasons, so it is said, for its continuance. The case of *Cattle v Stockton Waterworks Co*[8] is traditionally cited in this context as the authority for this proposition. Blackburn J stated:

> In the present case there is no pretence for saying that the defendants were malicious or had any intention to injure anyone. They were, at most, guilty of a neglect of duty, which occasioned injury to the property of Knight, but which did not injure any property of the plaintiff. The plaintiff's claim is to recover the damage which he has sustained by his contract with Knight becoming less profitable, or, it may be, a losing contract, in consequence of this injury to Knight's property. We think this does not give him any right of action.

This statement was reinforced by the following comments of Lord Penzance in *Simpson and Co v Thomson, Burrell*,[9] a case where two ships belonging to the same person collided. The underwriters paid the insurance on the lost ship and then in their own right sought to claim from the fund lodged in court by the owner of the ships as proprietor of the negligent ship. Lord Penzance, in rejecting the claim, stated:

---

7 See, for example, *Invercargill City Council v Hamlin* [1996] 1 All ER 756.

8 (1875) LR 10 QB 453.

9 (1877) 3 App Case 279.

> ... in the argument ... the learned counsel for the respondents took their stand upon a much broader ground. They contended that the underwriters, by virtue of the policy which they entered into in respect of this ship, had an interest of their own in her welfare and protection, inasmuch as any injury or loss sustained by her would indirectly fall upon them as a consequence of their contract; and that this interest was such as would support an action by them in their own names and behalf against a wrongdoer. This proposition virtually affirms a principle which I think your Lordships will do well to consider with some care, as it will be found to have a much wider application and signification than any which may be involved in the incidents of a contract of insurance. The principle involved seems to me to be this – that where damage is done by a wrongdoer to a chattel not only the owner of that chattel, but all those who by contract with the owner have bound themselves to obligations which are rendered more onerous, or have secured to themselves advantages which are rendered less beneficial by the damage done to the chattel, have a right of action against the wrongdoer although they have no immediate or reversionary property in the chattel, and no possessory right by reason of any contract attaching to the chattel itself, such as by lien or hypothecation.
>
> This, I say, is the principle involved in the respondents' contention. If it be a sound one, it would seem to follow that if, by the negligence of a wrongdoer, goods are destroyed which the owner of them had bound himself by contract to supply to a third person, this person as well as the owner has a right of action for any loss inflicted on him by their destruction.
>
> But if this be true as to injuries done to chattels, it would seem to be equally so as to injuries to the person. An individual injured by a negligently driven carriage has an action against the owner of it. Would a doctor, it may be asked, who had contracted to attend him and provide medicines for a fixed sum by the year, also have a right of action in respect of the additional cost of attendance and medicine cast upon him by that accident? And yet it cannot be denied that the doctor had an interest in his patient's safety. In like manner an actor or singer bound for a term to a manager is disabled by the wrongful act of a third person to the serious loss of the manager. Can the manager recover damages for that loss from the wrongdoer? Such instances might be indefinitely multiplied, giving rise to rights of action which in modern communities, where every complexity of mutual relation is daily created by contract, might be both numerous and novel.
>
> My Lords, I have given these illustrations because I fail to see any distinction in principle between them and the right asserted by the underwriters in the present case; and if I am right in so regarding them, they show at least how much would be involved in a decision by your Lordships whereby that right should be affirmed.
>
> But the ground upon which I will ask your Lordships to reject this contention of the respondents' counsel is this – that upon the cases cited no precedent or authority has been found or produced to the House for an action against the wrongdoer except in the name, and therefore, in point of law, on the part of one who had either some property in, or possession of, the chattel injured. On the other hand, the existence of authorities in which the suit has been brought in the name of the owner, though for the benefit of persons having a collateral interest, is somewhat strong to show that such persons had no right of action in themselves. For it is to be presumed that a person having such a right would pursue it directly, and not indirectly through the name of another.

The very antiquity of the rule against recovery of pure economic loss is, in a sense, a measure of its vitality. The reason for the support given to the rule in recent years has been based on the overplayed floodgates argument, the fear of undermining other areas of law such as contract and defamation and the promotion of an individualistic, self-reliant ethos amongst members of the community. Economic loss is seen as a fact of life and must be borne stoically, without resort to litigation at every little reversal in fortune. But to every general rule there are, of course, exceptions, and it these that the courts spend most of their time debating, as we shall see.

The notable exception

So far the discussion has centred on negligent acts where the general rule holds sway. We must now consider developments in the law relating to negligent statements giving rise to pure economic loss. Prior to 1963, it had always been thought that there was no liability at common law for damages for such loss caused by a negligent mis-statement. This was inferred from the case of *Derry v Peek*,[10] a case concerning unsuccessful allegations of fraudulent misrepresentation made against directors of a company who issued a company prospectus containing false statements. The House of Lords decided against the plaintiff on the basis that there was no fraud proved against the defendants. But as a result of some of the statements by their Lordships it was assumed that nothing short of fraud would suffice to enable a plaintiff to claim damages for a misrepresentation. The law relating to actionable misrepresentation, it appeared, was divided into only two categories, namely fraudulent and non-fraudulent (innocent), and unless there was actual fraud, a claim for damages was barred even if there was evidence of carelessness by the maker of the statement.

The first chink of light appeared in the case of *Candler v Crane Christmas & Co*[11] in the dissenting judgment of Denning LJ. The majority of the Court of Appeal decided that, in the absence of a contractual or fiduciary relationship, the defendant accountants did not owe a duty of care to the plaintiff, a potential investor in the company, in preparing the accounts and balance sheet of the company in question. The accounts had been negligently prepared and the person preparing them knew that they were wanted for the purpose of inducing the plaintiff to invest in the company, which he did to his detriment. Denning LJ commented:

> I come now to the great question in the case: did the defendants owe a duty of care to the plaintiff? If the matter were free from authority, I should have said that they clearly did owe a duty of care to him. They were professional accountants who prepared and put before him these accounts, knowing that he was going to be guided by them in making an investment in the company. On the faith of those accounts he did make the investment, whereas, if the accounts had been carefully prepared, he would not have made the investment at all. The result is he has lost money. In the circumstances, had he not every right to rely on the accounts being prepared with proper care, and is he not entitled to redress from the defendants on whom he relied? I say he is. ...

10 (1889) 14 App Case 337.

11 [1951] 2 KB 164.

Let me now be constructive and suggest the circumstances in which I say that a duty to use care in making a statement does exist apart from a contract in that behalf. First, what persons are under such a duty? My answer is those persons, such as accountants, surveyors, valuers and analysts, whose profession and occupation it is to examine books, accounts and other things, and to make reports on which other people – other than their clients – rely in the ordinary course of business. Their duty is not merely a duty to use care in their reports. They have also a duty to use care in their work which results in their reports. Herein lies the difference between these professional men and other persons who have been held to be under no duty to use care in their statements, such as promoters who issue a prospectus, ... and trustees who answer inquiries about the trust funds. ... Those persons do not bring, and are not expected to bring, any professional knowledge or skill into the preparation of their statements. They can only be made responsible by the law affecting persons generally, such as contract, estoppel, innocent misrepresentation or fraud.

It is, however, very different with persons who engage in a calling which requires special knowledge and skill. From very early times it has been held that they owe a duty of care to those who are closely and directly affected by their work, apart altogether from any contract or undertaking in that behalf. It is, I think, also applicable to professional accountants. They are not liable, of course, for casual remarks made in the course of conversation, nor for other statements made outside their work, or not made in their capacity as accountants, ... but they are, in my opinion, in proper cases, apart from any contract in the matter, under a duty to use reasonable care in the preparation of their accounts and in the making of their reports.

Second, to whom do these professional people owe this duty? I will take accountants, but the same reasoning applies to the others. They owe the duty, of course, to their employer or client, and also, I think, to any third person to whom they themselves show the accounts, or to whom they know their employer is going to show the accounts so as to induce him to invest money or take some other action on them. I do not think, however, the duty can be extended still further so as to include strangers of whom they have heard nothing and to whom their employer without their knowledge may choose to show their accounts. Once the accountants have handed their accounts to their employer, they are not, as a rule, responsible for what he does with them without their knowledge or consent ... there are some cases – of which the present is one – where the accountants know all the time, even before they present their accounts, that their employer requires the accounts to show to a third person so as to induce him to act on them, and then they themselves or their employers, present the accounts to him for the purpose. In such cases I am of the opinion that the accountants owe a duty of care to the third person. ...

Third, to what transactions does the duty of care extend? It extends, I think, only to those transactions for which the accountants knew their accounts were required. For instance, in the present case it extends to the original investment of £2,000 which the plaintiff made in reliance on the accounts, because the defendants knew that the accounts were required for his guidance in making that investment, but it does not extend to the subsequent £200 which he invested after he had been two months with the company. This distinction, that the duty only extends to the very transaction in mind at the time, is implicit in the decided cases.

Thus a doctor, who negligently certifies a man to be a lunatic when he is not, is liable to him, although there is no contract in the matter, because the doctor knows that his certificate is required for the very purpose of deciding whether the man should be detained or not, but an insurance company's doctor owes no duty to the insured person, because he makes his examination only for the purposes of the insurance company. ... So, also, a Lloyd's surveyor who, on surveying for classification purposes, negligently passes a mast as sound when it is not, is not liable to the owner for damage caused by it breaking, because the surveyor makes his survey only for the purpose of classifying the ship for the Yacht Register and not otherwise. ... Again, a scientist or expert (including a marine hydrographer) is not liable to his readers for careless statements in his published works. He publishes his work simply to give information, and not with any particular transaction in mind. When, however, a scientist or an expert makes an investigation and report for the very purpose of a particular transaction, then, in my opinion, he is under a duty of care in respect of that transaction.

It will be noticed that I have confined the duty to cases where the accountant prepares his accounts and makes his report for the guidance of the very person in the very transaction in question. That is sufficient for the decision of this case. I can well understand it would be going too far to make an accountant liable to any person in the land who chooses to rely on the accounts in matters of business, for that would expose him, in the words of Cardozo CJ in *Ultramares Corp v Touche* (28) (174 NE 444), to '... liability in an indeterminate amount for an indeterminate time to an indeterminate class'.

Whether he would be liable if he prepared his accounts for the guidance of a specific class of transactions, I do not say. I should have thought he might be. ...

My conclusion is that a duty to use care in statement is recognised by English law, and that its recognition does not create any dangerous precedent when it is remembered that it is limited in respect of the persons by whom and to whom it is owed and the transactions to which it applies.

One final word. I think the law would fail to serve the best interests of the community if it should hold that accountants and auditors owe a duty to no one but their client. Its influence would be most marked in cases where the client is a company or firm controlled by one man. It would encourage accountants to accept the information which the one man gives them without verifying it, and to prepare and present the accounts rather as a lawyer prepares and presents a case, putting the best appearance on the accounts they can without expressing their personal opinion on them.

This is, to my way of thinking, an entirely wrong approach. There is a great difference between the lawyer and the accountant. The lawyer is never called on to express his personal belief in the truth of his client's case, whereas the accountant, who certifies the accounts of his client, is always called on to express his personal opinion whether the accounts exhibit a true and correct view of his client's affairs, and he is required to do this, not so much for the satisfaction of his own client, but more for the guidance of shareholders, investors, revenue authorities, and others who may have to rely on the accounts in serious matters of business.

If we should decide this case in favour of the defendants, there will be no reason why accountants should ever verify the word of one man in a one-man company, because there will be no one to complain about it. The one man who gives them wrong information will not complain if they do not verify it. He wants their backing for the misleading information he gives them, and he can only get it if they accept his word without verification. It is just what he wants so as to gain his own ends. And the persons who are misled cannot complain because the accountants owe no duty to them. If such be the law, I think it is to be regretted,

> for it means that the accountants' certificate, which should be a safeguard, becomes a snare for those who rely on it. I do not myself think that it is the law. In my opinion, accountants owe a duty of care not only to their own clients, but also to all those whom they know will rely on their accounts in the transactions for which those accounts are prepared.

Although a dissenting judgment, this statement has exerted a powerful influence in the development of the principle of liability for negligent misstatement at common law. This will be amply illustrated in the leading case on the topic, *Hedley Byrne & Co Ltd v Heller & Partners Ltd*,[12] where a bank, it was alleged, gave a false statement to the plaintiff as a result of negligence. Although the bank was found not liable on the basis of an effective disclaimer of liability, the House of Lords significantly held that there could be a duty of care outside contract for a negligent misrepresentation giving rise to pure economic loss. The duty was expressed variously. We shall consider first extracts from Lord Reid's speech as follows:

> Apart altogether from authority, I would think that the law must treat negligent words differently from negligent acts. The law ought so far as possible to reflect the standards of the reasonable man. ... The most obvious difference between negligent words and negligent acts is this. Quite careful people often express definite opinions on social or informal occasions, even when they see that others are likely to be influenced by them; and often they do that without taking that care which they would take if asked for their opinion professionally, or in a business connection. The appellants agree that there can be no duty of care on such occasions ... but it is at least unusual casually to put into circulation negligently-made articles which are dangerous. A man might give a friend a negligently-prepared bottle of home-made wine and his friend's guests might drink it with dire results; but it is by no means clear that those guests would have no action against the negligent manufacturer.
>
> Another obvious difference is that a negligently-made article will only cause one accident, and so it is not very difficult to find the necessary degree of proximity or neighbourhood between the negligent manufacturer and the person injured. But words can be broadcast with or without the consent or foresight of the speaker or writer. It would be one thing to say that the speaker owes a duty to a limited class, but it would be going very far to say that he owes a duty to every ultimate 'consumer' who acts on those words to his detriment. It would be no use to say that a speaker or writer owes a duty, but can disclaim responsibility if he wants to. He, like the manufacturer, could make it part of a contract that he is not liable for his negligence; but that contract would not protect him in a question with a third party if the third party was unaware of it.
>
> So it seems to me that there is good sense behind our present law that, in general, an innocent but negligent misrepresentation gives no cause of action. There must be something more than the mere mis-statement ... the most natural requirement would be that expressly or by implication from the circumstances the speaker or writer has undertaken some responsibility, and that appears to me not to conflict with any authority which is binding on this House. Where there is a contract there is no difficulty as regards the contracting parties; the question is whether there is a warranty. The refusal of English law to recognise any *jus quaesitum tertio* causes some difficulties, but they are not relevant here. There are cases where a person does not merely make a statement, but performs a gratuitous

12 [1963] 2 All ER 575.

service. I do not intend to examine the case about that, but at least they show that, in some cases, that a person owes a duty of care apart from any contract, and to that extent they pave the way to holding that there can be a duty of care in making a statement of fact or opinion which is independent of contract.

... It must now be taken that *Derry v Peek* did not establish any universal rule that in the absence of contract an innocent misrepresentation cannot give rise to an action ...

A reasonable man, knowing that he was being trusted or that his skill and judgment were being relied on, would, I think, have three courses open to him. He could keep silent or decline to give the information or advice sought; he could give an answer with a clear qualification that he accepted no responsibility for it or that it was given without that reflection or inquiry which a careful answer would require; or he could simply answer without any such qualification. If he chooses to adopt the last course he must, I think, be held to have accepted some responsibility for his answer being given carefully, or to have accepted a relationship with the inquirer which requires him to exercise such care as the circumstances require.

If that is right then it must follow that *Candler v Crane, Christmas & Co* was wrongly decided ... it was obvious to the defendants that the plaintiff was relying on their skill or judgment on their having exercised that care which, by contract, they owed to the company, and I think that any reasonable man in the plaintiff's shoes would have relied on that. This seems to me a typical case of agreeing to assume a responsibility; they knew why the plaintiff wanted to see the accounts and why their employers, the company, wanted them to be shown to him, and agreed to show them to him without even a suggestion that he should not rely on them ...

Lord Reid decided that there was no duty in the end because of the disclaimer.

Lord Morris was the next to consider the question of whether a notional duty could exist in such circumstances:

My Lords, it seems to me that if A assumes a responsibility to B to tender him deliberate advice, there could be liability if the advice is negligently given. I say 'could be' because the ordinary courtesies and exchanges of life would become impossible if it were sought to attach legal obligation to every kindly and friendly act. But the principle of the matter would not appear to be in doubt. If A employs B (who might, for example, be a professional man such as an accountant or a solicitor or a doctor) for reward to give advice, and if the advice is negligently given, there could be a liability on B to pay damages. The fact that the advice is given in words would not, in my view, prevent liability from arising. ... It is said, however, that where careless (but not fraudulent) mis-statements are in question there can be no liability in the maker of them unless there is either some contractual or fiduciary relationship with a person adversely affected by the making of them or unless, through the making of them, something is created or circulated or some situation is created which is dangerous to life, limb or property. In logic I can see no essential reason for distinguishing injury which is caused by a reliance on the safety of the staging to a ship, or by reliance on the safety for use of the contents of a bottle of hair wash or a bottle of some consumable liquid. It seems to me, therefore, that if A claims that he has suffered injury or loss as a result of acting upon some mis-statement made by B, who is not in any contractual or fiduciary relationship with him, the inquiry that is first raised is whether B owed any duty to A. If he did the further inquiry is raised as the nature of the duty. There may be circumstances under which the only duty owed by B to A is the duty of being honest; there may be

> circumstances under which B owes to A the duty, not only of being honest, but also a duty of taking reasonable care. The issue in the present case is whether the bank owed any duty to Hedleys and, if so, what the duty was. ...
>
> My Lords, I consider that ... it should now be regarded as settled that if someone possessed of special skill undertakes, quite irrespective of contract, to apply that skill for the assistance of another person who relies on such skill, a duty of care will arise. The fact that the service is to be given by means of, or by the instrumentality of, words can make no difference. Furthermore if, in a sphere in which a person is so placed that others could reasonably rely on his judgment or his skill or on his ability to make careful inquiry, a person takes it on himself to give information or advice to, or allows his information or advice to be passed on to, another person who, as he knows or should know, will place reliance on it, then a duty of care will arise.
>
> I do not propose to examine the facts of particular situations or the facts of recent decided cases in the light of this analysis, but I proceed to apply it to the facts of the case now under review. As I have stated, I approach the case on the footing that the bank knew that what they said would in fact be passed on to some unnamed person who was a customer of National Provincial Bank. ... In these circumstances I think that some duty towards the unnamed person, whoever it was, was owed by the bank. There was a duty of honesty. The great question, however, is whether there was a duty of care; the bank need not have answered their inquiry from National Provincial Bank Ltd. It appears, however, that it is a matter of banking convenience or courtesy and presumably of mutual business advantage that inquiries between banks will be answered. The fact that it is most unlikely that the bank would have answered a direct inquiry from Hedleys does not affect the question as to what the bank must have known as to the use that would be made of any answer that they gave, but it cannot be left out of account in considering what it was the bank undertook to do. ...
>
> There was, in the present case, no contemplation of receiving anything like a formal report such as might be given by some concern charged with the duty (probably for reward) of making all proper and relevant inquiries concerning the nature, scope and extent of a company's activities, and of obtaining and marshalling all available evidence as to its credit, efficiency, standing and business reputation. There is much to be said, therefore, for the view that, if a banker gives a reference in the form of a brief expression of opinion in regard to creditworthiness, he does not accept, and there is not expected from him any higher duty than that of giving an honest answer. I need not, however, seek to deal further with this aspect of the matter, which perhaps cannot be covered by any statement of general application, because in my judgment the bank in the present case, by the words which they employed, effectively disclaimed any assumption of a duty of care. They stated that they only responded to the inquiry on the basis that their reply was without responsibility. If the inquirers chose to receive and act upon the reply they cannot disregard the definite terms upon which it was given. They cannot accept a reply given with a stipulation and then reject the stipulation.

We now turn to Lord Hodson who, having stated that he preferred Denning LJ's view in *Candler*, proceeded:

> Was there any special relationship here? I cannot exclude from consideration the actual terms in which the reference was given and I cannot see how the appellants can get over the difficulty which those words put in their way. They cannot say that the respondents are seeking to, as it were, contract out of their duty by use of language which is insufficient for the purpose, if the truth of the

> matter is that the respondents never assumed a duty of care nor was such a duty imposed on them.

Lord Devlin's speech contains probably the most important discussion of the duty issue. He commented as follows:

> So before I examine the authorities, I shall explain why I think that the law, if settled how counsel for the respondents says that it is, would be defective. As well as being defective in the sense that it would leave a man without a remedy where he ought to have one and where it is well within the scope of the law to give him one, it would also be profoundly illogical. The common law is tolerant of much illogicality especially on the surface; but no system of law can be workable if it has not got logic at the root of it.
>
> Originally it was thought that the tort of negligence must be confined entirely to deeds and could not extend to words. That was supposed to be decided by *Derry v Peek*. I cannot imagine that anyone would now dispute that, if this were the law, the law would be gravely defective. The practical proof of this is that the supposed deficiency was, in relation to the facts in *Derry v Peek*, immediately made good by Parliament. Today it is unthinkable that the law would permit directors to be as careless as they liked in the statements that they made in a prospectus.
>
> A simple distinction between negligence in word and negligence in deed might leave the law defective, but at least it would be intelligible. This is not, however, the distinction which is drawn in counsel for the respondents' argument and it is one which would be unworkable. A defendant who is given a car to overhaul and repair if necessary is liable to the injured driver:
>
> (a) if he overhauls it and repairs it negligently and tells the driver that it is safe when it is not;
>
> (b) if he overhauls it and negligently finds it not to be in need of repair, and tells the driver that it is safe when it is not; and
>
> (c) if he negligently omits to overhaul it at all and tells the driver that it is safe when it is not.
>
> It would be absurd in any of these cases to argue that the proximate cause of the driver's injury was not what the defendant did or failed to do, but his negligent statement on the faith of which the driver drove the car and for which he could not recover. In this type of case where, if there were a contract, there would undoubtedly be a duty of service, it is not practicable to distinguish between the inspection or examination, the acts done or omitted to be done, and the advice or information given. Neither in this case nor in *Candler v Crane, Christmas & Co* … has counsel for the respondents argued that the distinction lies there.
>
> This is why the distinction is now said to depend on whether financial loss is caused through physical injury or whether it is caused directly. The interposition of the physical injury is said to make a difference of principle. I can find neither logic nor common sense in this. If, irrespective of contract, a doctor negligently advises a patient that he can safely pursue his occupation and he cannot, and the patient's health suffers and he loses his livelihood, the patient has a remedy. But if the doctor negligently advises him that he cannot safely pursue his occupation when in fact he can and he loses his livelihood, there is said to be no remedy. Unless, of course, the patient was a private patient and the doctor accepted half a guinea for his trouble: then the patient can recover all.
>
> I am bound to say, my lords, that I think this to be nonsense. It is not the sort of nonsense that can arise even in the best system of law out of the need to draw nice distinctions between borderline cases. It arises, if it is the law, simply out of

a refusal to make sense. The line is not drawn on any intelligible principle. It just happens to be the line which those, who have been driven from the extreme assertion that negligent statements in the absence of contractual or fiduciary duty give no cause of action, have in the course of their retreat so far reached. ...

In my opinion the appellants in their argument tried to press *Donoghue v Stevenson* too hard. They asked whether the principle of proximity should not apply as well to words as to deeds. I think that it should, but as it is only a general conception it does not get them very far. Then they take the specific proposition laid down in *Donoghue v Stevenson* and try to apply it literally to a certificate or banker's reference. That will not do, for a general conception cannot be applied to pieces of paper in the same way as to articles of commerce, or to writers in the same way as to manufacturers. An inquiry into the possibilities of intermediate examination of a certificate will not be fruitful. The real value of *Donoghue v Stevenson* to the argument in this case is that it shows how the law can be developed to solve particular problems. Is the relationship between the parties in this case such that it can be brought within a category giving rise to special duty. As always in English law the first step in such an inquiry is to see how far the authorities have gone, for new categories in the law do not spring into existence overnight.

It would be surprising if the sort of problem that is created by the facts of this case had never until recently arisen in English law. As a problem it is a by-product of the doctrine of consideration. If the respondents had made a nominal charge for the reference, the problem would not exist. If it were possible in English law to construct a contract without consideration, the problem would move at once out of the first and general phase into the particular; and the question would be, not whether on the facts of the case there was a special relationship, but whether on the facts of the case there was a contract.

The respondents in this case cannot deny that they were performing a service. Their sheet anchor is that they were performing it gratuitously and therefore no liability for its performance can arise. My Lords, in my opinion this is not the law. A promise given without consideration to perform a service cannot be enforced as a contract by the promisee; but if the service is in fact performed and done negligently, the promisee can recover in an action in tort. ...

My Lords, it is true that this principle of law has not yet been clearly applied to a case where a service, which the defendant undertakes to perform, is or includes the obtaining and imparting of information. But I cannot see why it should not be; and if it had not been thought erroneously that *Derry v Peek* negatived any liability for negligent statements, I think that by now it probably would have been. It cannot matter whether the information consists of fact or opinion or a mixture of both, nor whether it was obtained as a result of special inquiries or comes direct from facts already in the defendant's possession or from his general store of professional knowledge. One cannot, as I have already endeavoured to show, distinguish in this respect between a duty to inquire and a duty to state.

I think, therefore, that there is ample authority to justify your Lordships in saying now that the categories of special relationships, which may give rise to a duty to take care in word as well as in deed, are not limited to contractual relationships or to relationships of fiduciary duty, but include also relationships which, in the words of Lord Shaw in *Nocton v Lord Ashburton*,[13] are 'equivalent to

13 [1914] AC at p 972.

contract', that is, where there is an assumption of responsibility in circumstances in which, but for the absence of consideration, there would be a contract.

Where there is an express undertaking, an express warranty as distinct from mere representation, there can be little difficulty. The difficulty arises in discerning those cases in which the undertaking is to be implied. In this respect the absence of consideration is not irrelevant. Payment for advice or information is very good evidence that it is being relied on and that the informer or adviser knows that it is. Where there is no consideration, it will be necessary to exercise greater care in distinguishing between social and professional relationships, and between those which are of a contractual nature and those which are not. It may often be material to consider whether the adviser is acting purely out of good nature or whether he is getting his reward in some indirect form. The service that a bank performs in giving a reference is not done simply out of a desire to assist commerce. It would discourage the customers of the bank if their deals fell through because the bank had refused to testify to their credit when it was good.

I have had the advantage of reading all the opinions prepared by your Lordships, and of studying the terms which your Lordships have framed by way of definition of the sort of relationship which gives rise to responsibility towards those who act on information or advice and so creates a duty of care towards them. I do not understand any of your Lordships to hold that it is a responsibility imposed by law on certain types of persons or in certain sorts of situations. It is a responsibility that is voluntarily accepted or undertaken, either generally where a general relationship, such as that of solicitor and client or banker and customer, is created, or specifically in relation to a particular transaction.

In the present case the appellants were not the customers or potential customers of the bank. Responsibility can attach only to the single act, ie the giving of the reference, and only if the doing of that act implied a voluntary undertaking to assume responsibility. This is a point of great importance because it is, as I understand it, the foundation for the ground on which in the end the House dismisses the appeal. I do not think it possible to formulate with exactitude all the conditions under which the law will, in a specific case, imply a voluntary undertaking, any more than it is possible to formulate those in which it will imply a contract. But in so far as your Lordships describe the circumstances in which an implication will ordinarily be drawn, I am prepared to adopt any one of your Lordships' statements as showing the general rule; and I pay the same respect to the statement by Denning LJ, in his dissenting judgment in *Candler v Crane, Christmas & Co*, about the circumstances in which he says a duty to use care in the making of statements exists. ...

I shall content myself with the proposition that, wherever there is a relationship equivalent to contract, there is a duty of care. Such a relationship may be either general or particular. Examples of a general relationship are those of solicitor and client and banker and customer ... there may well be others yet to be established. Where there is a general relationship of this sort it is unnecessary to do more than prove its existence and the duty follows. Where, as in the present case, what is relied on is a particular relationship created *ad hoc*, it will be necessary to examine the particular facts to see whether there is an express or implied undertaking of responsibility.

I regard this proposition as an application of the general conception of proximity. Cases may arise in the future in which a new and wider proposition, quite independent of any notion of contract, will be needed. There may, for example, be cases in which a statement is not supplied for the use of any particular person, any more than in *Donoghue v Stevenson* the ginger beer was supplied for

> consumption by any particular person; and it will then be necessary to return to the general conception of proximity and to see whether there can be evolved from it, as was done in *Donoghue v Stevenson*, a specific proposition to fit the case. When that has to be done, the speeches of your Lordships today as well as the judgment of Denning LJ to which I have referred ... will afford good guidance as to what ought to be said. I prefer to see what shape such cases take before committing myself to any formulation, for I bear in mind Lord Atkin's warning ... against placing unnecessary restrictions on the adaptability of English law. I have, I hope, made it clear that I take quite literally the *dictum* of Lord Macmillan that 'the categories of negligence are never closed'. English law is wide enough to embrace any new category or proposition that exemplifies the principle of proximity.
>
> I have another reason for caution. Since the essence of the matter in the present case and in others of the same type is assumption of responsibility, I should like to guard against the imposition of restrictive terms, notwithstanding that the essential condition is fulfilled. If a defendant says to a plaintiff, 'Let me do this for you, do not waste your money in employing a professional, I will do it for nothing and you can rely on me', I do not think that he could escape liability simply because he belonged to no profession or calling, had no qualifications or special skill and did not hold himself out as having any. The relevance of these factors is to show the unlikelihood of a defendant in such circumstances assuming a legal responsibility, and as such they may often be decisive. But they are not theoretically conclusive, and so cannot be the subject of definition. It would be unfortunate if they were. For it would mean that plaintiffs would seek to avoid the rigidity of the definition by bringing the action in contract ... and setting up something that would do for consideration. That to my mind would be an undesirable development in the law; and the best way of avoiding it is to settle the law so that the presence or absence of consideration makes no difference.

Lord Devlin went on to say that the disclaimer was effective to prevent their being an assumption of responsibility, deciding the case in favour of the respondent bank. Lord Pearce also added his views as follows:

> The reason for some divergence between the law of negligence in word and that of negligence in act is clear. Negligence in word creates problems different from those of negligence in act. Words are more volatile than deeds. They travel fast and far afield. They are used without being expended and take effect in combination with innumerable facts and other words. Yet they are dangerous and can cause vast financial damage. How far they are relied on unchecked ... must in many cases be a matter of doubt and difficulty. If the mere hearing or reading of words were held to create proximity, there might be no limit to the persons to whom the speaker or writer could be liable. Damage by negligent acts to persons or property on the other hand is more visible and obvious; its limits are more easily defined and it is with this damage that the earlier cases were more concerned. ...
>
> How wide the sphere of the duty of care in negligence is to be laid depends ultimately on the courts' assessment of the demands of society for protection from the carelessness of others. Economic protection has lagged behind protection in physical matters where there is injury to person or property. It may be that the size and width of the range of possible claims has acted as a deterrent to extension of economic protection. ...
>
> The true rule is that innocent misrepresentation *per se* gives no right to damages. If the misrepresentation was intended by the parties to form a warranty between

the two contracting parties, it gives on that ground a right to damages ... if an innocent misrepresentation is made between the parties in a fiduciary relationship it may, on that ground, give a right to claim damages for negligence. There is also, in my opinion, a duty of care created by special relationships which, though not fiduciary, give rise to an assumption that care as well as honesty is demanded.

Was there such a special relationship in the present case as to impose on the respondents a duty of care to the appellants as the undisclosed principals for whom National Provincial Bank was making the inquiry? The answer to that question depends on the circumstances of the transaction. If, for instance, they disclosed a casual social approach to the inquiry, no such special relationship or duty of care would be assumed. ... To import such a duty the representation must normally, I think, concern a business or professional transaction whose nature makes clear the gravity of the inquiry and the importance and influence attached to the answer ... a most important circumstance is the form of the inquiry and answer. Both were here plainly stated to be without liability. Counsel for the appellants argues that those words are not sufficiently precise to exclude liability for negligence. Nothing, however, except negligence could, in the facts of this case, create a liability. ... I do not, therefore, accept that, even if the parties were already in contractual or other special relationship, the words would give no immunity to a negligent answer. But in any event they clearly prevent a special relationship from arising. They are part of the material from which one deduces whether a duty of care and a liability for negligence is assumed. If both parties say expressly (in a case where neither is deliberately taking advantage of the other) that there shall be no liability, I do not find it possible to say that a liability was assumed. ...

This is clearly the most important case in tort law next to *Donoghue v Stevenson* itself. It is clear, however, that the principle is restricted in its scope for the reasons referred to in the judgments above, particularly that of Lord Pearce, namely the 'volatile' nature of words. The special relationship must be established if there is to be duty of care. It seems that the principle, sometimes called the detrimental reliance principle, states that a duty will arise where advice or information is given in a business context by a person with special skill or knowledge to the plaintiff and the latter in fact relies on that advice or information to his detriment, and that reliance is reasonable. This, however, is not the only formulation to describe the required relationship, but for the present it will be used as the basis for the further discussion.

One issue which arose fairly early on, following the birth of the principle, was what was meant by the business context or connection. In the case of *Mutual Life & Citizens' Assurance Co Ltd v Evatt*,[14] the majority opinion given by Lord Diplock suggested that the principle was restricted to those 'carrying on a business or profession of giving advice or undertaking enquiries of that kind'. However, the preferred view seems to be that contained in the dissenting opinion subscribed to by Lords Reid and Morris, both of whom significantly were in the *Hedley Byrne* case:

In our judgment it is not possible to lay down hard and fast rules as to when a duty of care arises in this or in any other class of case where negligence is alleged. When, in the past, judges have attempted to lay down rigid rules or

14 [1971] 1 All ER 150.

> classifications or categories, they have later had to be abandoned. But it is possible and necessary to determine the principles which have to be applied in determining whether, in given circumstances, any duty to take care arises. In this class of case no duty beyond the duty to give an honest answer can arise when advice is given casually or in a social context, and the reason is that it would be quite unreasonable for the enquirer to expect more in such circumstances and quite unreasonable to impose any greater duty on the adviser. The law must keep in step with the habits of the reasonable man and consider whether ordinary people would think they had some obligation beyond merely giving an honest answer.
>
> It may be going too far to say that a duty to take care can only arise where advice is sought and given in a business or professional context, for there might be unusual cases requiring a wider application of this principle. But for the present purposes we think that the appropriate question is whether this advice was given on a business occasion or in the course of the appellant company's business activities. ...
>
> Much of the argument was directed to establishing that a person giving advice cannot be under any duty to take care unless he has some special skill, competence, qualification or information with regard to the matter on which his advice is sought. But then how much skill or competence must he have? Even a man with a professional qualification is seldom an expert on all matters dealt with by members of his profession. Must the adviser be an expert or specialist in the matter on which his advice is sought? And when it comes to matters of business or finance where those whose business it is to deal with such matters generally have no recognised formal qualification, how is the sufficiency of the adviser's special skill or competence to be measured?
>
> If the adviser is invited in a business context to advise on a certain matter, and he chooses to accept that invitation and to give without warning or qualification what appears to be considered advice, is he allowed to turn round later and say that he was under no duty to take care because, in fact, he had no sufficient skill or competence to give the advice? ... In our judgment, when an enquirer consults a businessman in the course of his business and makes it plain to him that he is seeking considered advice, and intends to act on it in a particular way, any reasonable businessman would realise that, if he chooses to give advice without any warning or qualification, he is putting himself under a moral obligation to take some care. It appears to us to be well within the principles established by the *Hedley Byrne* case to regard his action in giving such advice as creating a special relationship between him and the enquirer, and to translate his moral obligation into a legal obligation to take such care as is reasonable in the whole circumstances.

It was stated above that the preferred view was that of the minority, and this was the line taken in the Court of Appeal in the case of *Esso Petroleum Co Ltd v Mardon*,[15] where the defendant was induced to contract with the plaintiffs on the strength of a statement made by one of their negotiators, in relation to the throughput of a petrol station the defendant was considering taking off the hands of the plaintiff. The statement was inaccurate in the circumstances. In his counterclaim the defendant alleged breach of warranty and breach of duty in tort based on the statement. It was held that there was a breach of warranty. In

15 [1976] 2 All ER 5.

addition, it was held that there was a concurrent breach of duty in the tort of negligence. Lord Denning MR dealt with the issues thus:

> A professional man may give advice under a contract for reward; or without a contract, in pursuance of a voluntary assumption of responsibility, gratuitously without reward. In either case he is under one and the same duty to use reasonable care. ... In the one case it is by reason of a term implied by law. In the other, it is by reason of a duty imposed by law. For a breach of that duty, he is liable in damages; and those damages should be, and are, the same, whether he is sued in contract or tort.
>
> It follows that I cannot accept counsel for Esso's proposition. It seems to me that *Hedley Byrne*, properly understood, covers this particular proposition; if a man, who has or professes to have special knowledge or skill, makes a representation by virtue thereof to another – be it advice, information or opinion – with the intention of inducing him to enter into a contract with him, he is under a duty to use reasonable care to see that the representation is correct, and that the advice, information or opinion is reliable. If he negligently gives unsound advice or misleading information or expresses an erroneous opinion, and thereby induces the other side into a contract with him, he is liable in damages. ...
>
> Applying this principle, it is plain that Esso professed to have – and did in fact have – special knowledge or skill in estimating the throughput of a filling station. They made the representation – they forecast a throughput of 200,000 gallons – intending to induce Mr Mardon to enter into a tenancy on the faith of it. They made it negligently – it was a 'fatal error' – and thereby induced Mr Mardon to enter into a contract of tenancy that was disastrous to him. For this misrepresentation they are liable in damages.

It is implicit in the above that Lord Denning MR was accepting the point that, so long as the statement was made in a business context, the principle could apply. It would be difficult to say that the negotiator for Esso was in the business of giving advice or information; his job was to persuade prospective tenants or purchasers to take on the petrol station. Ormrod LJ was much more explicit:

> Like Lawson J, I much prefer the reasoning of the minority in this [*Evatt's*] case and think that it should be followed. If the majority view were to be accepted, the effect of *Hedley Byrne* would be so radically curtailed as to be virtually eliminated.

He also agreed with Lord Denning MR that the principle could apply in a two party as well as a three party situation, although the *Hedley Byrne* case itself was concerned with the situation where A makes a statement to B which induces B to contract with C. In *Esso* the principle was held to be applicable to a situation where A makes a pre-contractual statement to B which induces B to contract with A. Of course, there is some overlap with the statutory remedy contained in s 2 Misrepresentation Act 1967, although there are significant differences between the common law action and that under the statute, in particular the difference in the burden of proof which, under the Act, is placed on the defendant.

The principle has spawned a massive amount of litigation and has been applied in numerous cases since 1963. Some attempt was made in 1990, in the case of *Caparo Industries plc v Dickman*,[16] to restrict the scope of the principle in

16 [1990] 1 All ER 568.

the wake of the attack on the two-stage approach to the duty of care question in general. The respondents were shareholders in a company whose accounts had been prepared by auditors. On the basis of these accounts they purchased more shares and eventually they took over the company. They brought an action for negligence against the auditors in the auditing of the accounts, as they were misleading and inaccurate. After surveying a number of the cases in which it had been held that there was a duty under the principle, Lord Bridge continued:

> The salient feature of all these cases is that the defendant giving advice or information was fully aware of the nature of the transaction which the plaintiff had in contemplation; knew that the advice or information would be communicated to him directly or indirectly; and knew that it was very likely that the plaintiff would rely on that advice or information in deciding whether or not to engage in the transaction in contemplation. In these circumstances the defendant could clearly be expected, subject always to the effect of any disclaimer of responsibility, specifically to anticipate that the plaintiff would rely on the advice or information given by the defendant for the very purpose for which he did in the event rely on it. So also the plaintiff, subject again to the effect of any disclaimer, would in that situation reasonably suppose that he was entitled to rely on the advice or information communicated to him for the very purpose for which he required it.
>
> The situation is entirely different where a statement is put into more or less general circulation and may foreseeably be relied on by strangers to the maker of the statement for any one of a variety of different purposes which the maker of the statement has no specific reason to anticipate. To hold the maker of the statement to be under a duty of care in respect of the accuracy of the statement to all and sundry, for any purpose for which they may choose to rely on it, is not only to subject him, in the classic words of Cardozo CJ, to 'liability in an indeterminate amount for an indeterminate time to an indeterminate class' (see *Ultramares Corp v Touche* (1931) 255 NY 170 at 179), it is also to confer on the world at large a quite unwarranted entitlement to appropriate for their own purposes the benefit of the expert knowledge or professional expertise attributed to the maker of the statement. ...
>
> These considerations amply justify the conclusion that auditors of a public company's accounts owe no duty of care to members of the public who rely on the accounts in deciding to buy shares in the company. If the duty of care were owed so widely, it is difficult to see any reason why it should not equally extend to all who rely on the accounts in relation to other dealings with a company, as lenders or merchants extending credit to the company. A claim that such a duty was owed by auditors to a bank lending to a company was emphatically and convincingly rejected by Millett J in *Al Saudi Banque v Clark Pixley (a firm)* [1989] 3 All ER 361, [1990] 2 WLR 344. The only support for an unlimited duty of care owed by auditors for the accuracy of their accounts to all who may foreseeably rely on them is to be found in some jurisdictions in the United States of America, where there are striking differences in the law in different states. In this jurisdiction I have no doubt that the creation of such an unlimited duty would be a legislative step which it would be for Parliament, not the courts, to take.
>
> The main submissions for *Caparo* are that the necessary nexus of proximity between it and the auditors giving rise to a duty of care stems from:
>
> (1) the pleaded circumstances indicating the vulnerability of Fidelity to a take-over bid, and from the consequent probability that another company, such as *Caparo*, would rely on the audited accounts in deciding to launch a take-over bid; or

(2) the circumstance that *Caparo* was already a shareholder in Fidelity when it decided to launch its take-over bid in reliance on the accounts.

In relation to the first of these two submissions, *Caparo* applied, in the course of the hearing, for leave to amend para 16(2) of the statement of claim by adding the words 'or alternatively that it was highly probable that such persons would rely on the accounts for that purpose'.

The case which gives most assistance to Caparo in support of this submission is *Scott Group Ltd v McFarlane* [1978] 1 NZLR 553. The audited, consolidated accounts of a New Zealand public company and its subsidiaries overstated the assets of the group because of an admitted accounting error. Under the relevant New Zealand legislation its accounts were, as in England, accessible to the public. The circumstances of the group's affairs were such as to make it highly probable that it would attract a take-over bid. The plaintiffs made such a bid successfully and, when the accounting error was discovered, claimed from the auditors in respect of the shortfall in the assets. Quilliam J held that the auditors owed the plaintiffs no duty of care (see [1975] 1 NZLR 582). The majority of the New Zealand Court of Appeal (Woodhouse and Cooke JJ) held that the duty of care arose from the probability that the company would attract a take-over bid and the bidder would rely on the audited accounts, although Cooke J held that the shortfall in the assets below that erroneously shown in the accounts did not amount to a loss recoverable in tort. Richmond P held that no duty of care was owed. He said ([1978] 1 NZLR 553 at 566): 'All the speeches in *Hedley Byrne* seem to me to recognise the need for a "special" relationship – a relationship which can properly be treated as giving rise to a special duty to use care in statement. The question in any given case is whether the nature of the relationship is such that one party can fairly be held to have assumed a responsibility to the other as regards the reliability of the advice or information. I do not think that such a relationship should be found to exist unless, at least, the maker of the statement was, or ought to have been, aware that his advice or information would in fact be made available to, and relied on, by a particular person or class of persons for the purposes of a particular transaction or type of transaction. I would especially emphasise that, to my mind, it does not seem reasonable to attribute an assumption of responsibility unless the maker of the statement ought, in all the circumstances, both in preparing himself for what he said and in saying it, to have directed his mind, and to have been able to direct his mind, to some particular and specific purpose for which he was aware that his advice or information would be relied on. In many situations that purpose will be obvious. But the annual accounts of a company can be relied on in all sorts of ways and for many purposes.'

I agree with this reasoning, which seems to me to be entirely in line with the principles to be derived from the authorities to which I have earlier referred, and not to require modification in any respect which is relevant for present purposes by reference to anything said in this House in *Smith v Eric S Bush*. I should in any event be extremely reluctant to hold that the question, whether or not an auditor owes a duty of care to an investor buying shares in a public company, depends on the degree of probability that the shares will prove attractive either *en bloc* to a take-over bidder or piecemeal to individual investors. It would be equally wrong, in my opinion, to hold an auditor under a duty of care to anyone who might lend money to a company, by reason only that it was foreseeable as highly probable that the company would borrow money at some time in the year following publication of its audited accounts, and that lenders might rely on those accounts in deciding to lend. I am content to assume that the high probability of a take-over bid in reliance on the accounts which the proposed amendment of the statement of claim would assert, but I do not think that it assists *Caparo's* case. ...

The position of auditors in relation to the shareholders of a public limited liability company arising from the relevant provisions of the Companies Act 1985 is accurately summarised in the judgment of Bingham LJ in the Court of Appeal ([1989] 1 All ER 798 at 804, [1989] QB 653 at 680–81): 'The members, or shareholders, of the company are its owners. But they are too numerous, and in most cases too unskilled, to undertake the day-to-day management of that which they own. So responsibility for day-to-day management of the company is delegated to directors. The shareholders, despite their overall powers of control, are, in most companies for most of the time, investors and little more. But it would, of course, be unsatisfactory and open to abuse if the shareholders received no report on the financial stewardship of their investment, save from those to whom the stewardship has been entrusted. So provision is made for the company in general meeting to appoint an auditor (Companies Act 1985, s 384) whose duty is to investigate and form an opinion on the adequacy of the company's accounting records and returns and the correspondence between the company's accounting records and returns and its accounts (s 237). The auditor has then to report to the company's members (among other things) whether in his opinion the company's accounts give a true and fair view of the company's financial position (s 236). In carrying out his investigation and in forming his opinion, the auditor necessarily works very closely with the directors and officers of the company. He receives his remuneration from the company. He naturally, and rightly, regards the company as his client. But he is employed by the company to exercise his professional skill and judgment for the purpose of giving the shareholders an independent report on the reliability of the company's accounts and thus on their investment. ... The auditor's report must be read before the company in general meeting and must be open to inspection by any member of the company (s 241). It is attached to and forms part of the company's accounts (ss 238(3) and 239). A copy of the company's accounts (including the auditor's report) must be sent to every member (s 240). Any member of the company, even if not entitled to have a copy of the accounts sent to him, is entitled to be furnished with a copy of the company's last accounts on demand and without charge (s 246).'

No doubt these provisions establish a relationship between the auditors and the shareholders of a company, on which the shareholder is entitled to rely for the protection of his interest. But the crucial question concerns the extent of the shareholder's interest which the auditor has a duty to protect. The shareholders of a company have a collective interest in the company's proper management and, in so far as a negligent failure of the auditor to report accurately on the state of the company's finances deprives the shareholders of the opportunity to exercise their powers in general meeting to call the directors to book and to ensure that errors in management are corrected, the shareholders ought to be entitled to a remedy. But in practice no problem arises in this regard since the interest of the shareholders in the proper management of the company's affairs is indistinguishable from their interest in the company itself, and any loss suffered by the shareholders, eg by the negligent failure of the auditor to discover and expose a misappropriation of funds by a director of the company, will be recouped by a claim against the auditor in the name of the company, not by individual shareholders.

I find it difficult to visualise a situation arising in the real world in which the individual shareholder could claim to have sustained a loss in respect of his existing shareholding, referable to the negligence of the auditor, which could not be recouped by the company. But on this part of the case your Lordships were much pressed with the argument that such a loss might occur by a negligent undervaluation of the company's assets in the auditor's report relied on by the individual shareholder in deciding to sell his shares at an undervalue.

The argument then runs thus. The shareholder is entitled to rely on the auditor's report as the basis of his investment decision to sell his existing shareholding. If he sells at an undervalue he is entitled to the loss from the auditor. There can be no distinction in law between the shareholder's investment decision to sell the shares he has or to buy additional shares. It follows, therefore, that the scope of the duty of care owed to him by the auditor extends to cover any loss sustained consequent on the purchase of additional shares in reliance on the auditor's negligent report.

I believe this argument to be fallacious. Assuming, without deciding that a claim by a shareholder to recover a loss suffered by selling his shares at an undervalue attributable to an undervaluation of the company's assets in the auditor's report could be sustained at all, it would not be by reason of any reliance by the shareholder on the auditor's report in deciding to sell; the loss would be referable to the depreciatory effect of the report on the market value of the shares before even the decision of the shareholder to sell was taken. A claim to recoup a loss alleged to flow from the purchase of overvalued share, on the other hand, can only be sustained on the basis of the purchaser's reliance on the report. The specious equation of 'investment decisions' to sell or to buy, as giving rise to parallel claims, thus appears to me to be untenable. Moreover, the loss in the case of the sale would be a loss of part of the shareholder's existing holding, which, assuming a duty of care owed to individual shareholders, it might sensibly lie within the scope of the auditor's duty to protect. A loss, on the other hand, resulting from the purchase of the additional shares, would result from a wholly independent transaction having no connection with the existing shareholding. ...

Assuming for the purpose of the argument that the relationship between the auditor of a company and individual shareholders is of sufficient proximity to give rise to a duty of care, I do not understand how the scope of the duty can possibly extend beyond the protection of any individual shareholder from losses in the value of the shares which he holds. As a purchaser of additional shares in reliance on the auditor's report, he stands in no different position from any other investing member of the public to whom the auditor owes no duty.

I would allow the appeal and dismiss the cross-appeal.

Lord Roskill agreed with the others but added:

My Lords, I confess that, like Lord Griffiths in *Smith v Eric S Bush* [1989] 2 All ER 514 at 534, [1989] 2 WLR 790 at 813, I find considerable difficulty in phrases such as 'voluntary assumption of responsibility' unless they are to be explained as meaning no more than the existence of circumstances in which the law will impose a liability on a person making the allegedly negligent statement to the person to whom that statement is made, in which case the phrase does not help to determine in what circumstances the law will impose that liability or, indeed, its scope. The submission that there is a virtually unlimited and unrestricted duty of care in relation to the performance of an auditor's statutory duty to certify a company's accounts, a duty extending to anyone who may use those accounts for any purpose such as investing in the company or lending their company money, seems to me untenable. No doubt it can be said to be foreseeable that those accounts may find their way into the hands of persons who may use them for such purposes or, indeed, other purposes and lose money as a result. But to impose a liability in those circumstances is to hold, contrary to all recent authorities, that foreseeability alone is sufficient, and to ignore the statutory duty which enjoins the preparation of, and certification of, those accounts.

I think that, before the existence and scope of any liability can be determined, it is necessary first to determine for what purposes and in what circumstances the information in question is to be given. If a would-be investor or predator commissions a report which he will use, and which the maker of the report knows he will use, as a basis for his decision whether or not to invest or whether or not to make a bid, it may not be difficult to conclude that, if the report is negligently prepared and as a result a decision is taken in reliance on it and financial losses then follow, a liability will be imposed on the maker of that report. But I venture to echo the caution expressed by my noble and learned friend Lord Oliver that, because different cases may display common features, they are necessarily all cases in which the same consequences regarding liability or the scope of liability will follow. Moreover, there may be cases in which the circumstances in which the report was commissioned justify the inclusion of, and reliance on, a disclaimer such as succeeded in the *Hedley Byrne* case, but by reason of subsequent statutory provisions failed in *Smith v Eric S Bush*.

Lord Oliver, after making comments about the general duty of care and the two stage approach, extracted in the duty chapter above, continued:

The damage which may be occasioned by the spoken or written word is not inherent. It lies always in the reliance by somebody on the accuracy of that which the word communicates, and the loss or damage consequential on that person having adopted a course of action on the faith of it. In general, it may be said that, when any serious statement, whether it takes the form of a statement of fact or advice, is published or communicated, it is foreseeable that the person who reads or receives it is likely to accept it as accurate and to act accordingly. It is equally foreseeable that, if it is inaccurate in a material particular, the recipient who acts on it may suffer a detriment which, if the statement had been accurate, he would not have undergone. But it is now clear that mere foreseeability is not of itself sufficient to ground liability, unless by reason of the circumstances it itself constitutes also the element of proximity (as in the case of direct physical damage) or unless it is accompanied by other circumstances from which that element may be deduced.

One must, however, be careful about seeking to find any general principle which will serve as a touchstone for all cases, for even within the limited category of what, for the sake of convenience, I may refer to as 'the negligent statement cases', circumstances may differ infinitely, and, in a swiftly developing field of law, there can be no necessary assumption that those features which have served in one case to create the relationship between the plaintiff and the defendant on which liability depends, will necessarily be determinative of liability in the different circumstances of another case. There are, for instance, at least four and possibly more situations in which damage or loss may arise from reliance on the spoken or written word and it must not be assumed that because they display common features of reliance and foreseeability they are necessarily in all respects analogous.

To begin with, reliance on a careless statement may give rise to direct physical injury which may be caused either to the person who acts on the faith of the statement or to a third person. One has only to consider, for instance, the chemist's assistant who mislabels a dangerous medicine, a medical man who gives negligent telephonic advice to a parent with regard the treatment of a sick child, or an architect who negligently instructs a bricklayer to remove the keystone of an archway. ... In such cases it is not easy to divorce foreseeability *simpliciter* and the proximity which follows from the virtual inevitability of damage if the advice is followed. Again, economic loss may be inflicted on a third party as a result of the act of the recipient of the advice or information carried out in reliance on it. ... For present purposes, however, it is necessary to consider only those cases of economic damage suffered directly by a recipient of the statement or advice as a result of his personally having acted in reliance on it.

... it is not easy to cull from the speeches in the *Hedley Byrne* case any clear attempt to define or classify the circumstances which give rise to the relationship of proximity on which the action depends and, indeed, Lord Hodson expressly stated (and I respectfully agree) that he did not think it possible to catalogue the special features which must be found to exist before the duty of care will arise in the given case (see [1963] 2 All ER 575 at 601, [1964] AC 465 at 514). Lord Devlin is to the same effect (see [1963] 2 All ER 575 at 611, [1964] AC 465 at 530). The nearest that one gets to the establishment of a criterion for the creation of a duty in the case of a negligent statement is the emphasis to be found in all the speeches on 'the voluntary assumption of responsibility' by the defendant. This is a convenient phrase but it is clear that it was not intended to be a test for the existence of the duty for, on analysis, it means no more than that the act of the defendant in making the statement or tendering the advice was voluntary, and that the law attributes to it an assumption of responsibility if the statement or advice is inaccurate and is acted on. It tells us nothing about the circumstances from which such attribution arises.

The point that is, as it seems to me, significant in the present context, is the unanimous approval in this House of the judgment of Denning LJ in *Candler's* case [1951] 1 All ER 426 at 434, [1951] 2 KB 164 at 181, in which he expressed the test of proximity in these words: 'Did the accountants know that the accounts were required for submission to the plaintiff and use by him?' In so far as this might be said to imply that the plaintiff must be specifically identified as the ultimate recipient, and that the precise purpose for which the accounts were required must be known to the defendant before the necessary relationship can be created, Denning LJ 's formulation was expanded in the *Hedley Byrne* case, where it is clear that, but for an effective disclaimer, liability would have attached. The respondents were not aware of the actual identity of the advertising firm for which the credit reference was required nor of its precise purpose, save that it was required in anticipation of the placing of advertising contracts. Furthermore, it is clear that 'knowledge' on the part of the respondents embraced not only actual knowledge, but such knowledge as would be attributed to a reasonable person placed as the respondents were placed.

What can be deduced from the *Hedley Byrne* case, therefore, is that the necessary relationship between the maker of a statement or giver of advice (the adviser) and the recipient who acts in reliance on it (the advisee) may typically be held to exist where:

(1) the advice is required for a purpose, whether particularly specified or generally described, which is made known, either actually or inferentially, to the adviser at the time when the advice is given;

(2) the adviser knows, either actually or inferentially, that his advice will be communicated to the advisee, either specifically or as a member of an ascertainable class, in order that it should be used by the advisee for that purpose;

(3) it is known, either actually or inferentially, that the advice so communicated is likely to be acted on by the advisee for that purpose without independent inquiry; and

(4) it is so acted on by the advisee to his detriment.

That is not, of course, to suggest that these conditions are either conclusive or exclusive, but merely the actual decision in the case does not warrant any broader propositions. ...

In seeking to ascertain whether there should be imposed on the adviser a duty to avoid the occurrence of the kind of damage which the advisee claims to have suffered, it is not, I think, sufficient to ask simply whether there existed a 'closeness' between them in the sense that the advisee had a legal entitlement to receive the information on the basis of which he has acted, or in the sense that the information was intended to serve his interest or to protect him. One must, I think, go further and ask – in what capacity was his interest to be served and from what was he intended to be protected? A company's annual accounts are capable of being utilised for a number of purposes and, if one thinks about it, it is entirely foreseeable that they may be so employed.

But many of such purposes have absolutely no connection with the recipient's status or capacity, whether as a shareholder, voting or non-voting, or as a debenture-holder. Before it can be concluded that the duty is imposed to protect the recipient against harm which he suffers by reason of the particular use that he chooses to make of the information which he receives, one must, I think, first ascertain the purpose for which the information is required to be given ... if the conclusion is reached that the very purpose of providing the information is to serve as the basis for making investment decisions or giving investment advice, it is not difficult then to conclude also that the duty imposed on the adviser extends to protecting the recipient against loss occasioned by an unfortunate investment decision which is based on carelessly inaccurate information ... I do not believe and I see no grounds for believing that, in enacting the statutory provisions, Parliament had in mind the provision of information for the assistance of purchasers of shares or debentures in the market, whether they be already the holders of shares or other securities, or persons having no previous proprietary interest in the company.

It is unnecessary to decide the point on this appeal, but I can see more force in the contention that one purpose of providing the statutory information might be to enable the recipient to exercise whatever rights he has in relation to his proprietary interest by virtue of which he receives it, by way, for instance, of disposing of that interest. I can, however, see no ground for supposing that the legislature was intending to foster a market for the existing holders of shares or debentures, by providing information for the purpose of enabling them to acquire such securities from other holders who might be minded to sell. ...

In my judgment, accordingly, the purpose for which the auditors' certificate is made and published is that of providing those entitled to receive the report with information to enable them to exercise, in conjunction, those powers which their respective proprietary interests confer on them, and not for the purposes of individual speculation with a view to profit. ...

To widen the scope of the duty to include loss caused to an individual by reliance on the accounts for a purpose for which they were not supplied and were not intended, would be to extend it beyond the limits which are so far deducible from the decisions of this House. It is not, as I think, an extension which either logic requires or policy dictates and I, for my part, am not prepared to follow the majority of the Court of Appeal in making it. In relation to the

> purchase of shares of other shareholders in a company, whether in the open market or as a result of an offer made to all or a majority of the existing shareholders, I can see no sensible distinction, so far as a duty of care is concerned, between a potential purchaser who is, *vis-à-vis* the company, a total outsider and one who is already the holder of one or more shares. ...

Lord Jauncey of Tullichettle, in a much shorter speech, agreed with the above, and Lord Ackner concurred with the comments of his fellow judges.

In two cases immediately following this decision, the Court of Appeal had to decide on closely similar facts. In *James McNaughton Papers Group Ltd v Hicks Anderson & Co (a firm)*,[17] draft accounts were prepared by the defendants to assist the chairman of a company about to be taken over in the negotiations. These accounts were shown to the plaintiffs who were the potential bidders for the company, who alleged that they had relied on them to their detriment. The Court of Appeal allowed the defendants' appeal on the basis that the accounts were only in draft form and were only prepared for the company which was the subject of the take-over. Neill LJ observed as follows:

> ... in England a restrictive approach is now adopted to any extension of the scope of the duty of care beyond the person directly intended by the maker of the statement to act on it, and ... that in deciding whether a duty of care exists in any particular case it is necessary to take all the circumstances into account, but ... that ... it is possible to identify certain matters which are likely to be of importance in most cases in reaching a decision as to whether a duty or not exists. ...
>
> (1) *The purpose for which the statement is made*
>
> In some cases the statement will have been prepared or made by the 'adviser' for the express purpose of being communicated to the 'advisee' (to adopt the labels used by Lord Oliver). In such a case it may often be right to conclude that the advisee was within the scope of the duty of care. In many cases, however, the statement will have been prepared or made, or primarily prepared or made, for a different purpose, and for the benefit of someone other than the advisee. In such cases it will be necessary to look carefully at the precise purpose for which the statement was communicated to the advisee.
>
> (2) *The purpose for which the statement was communicated*
>
> Under this heading it will be necessary to consider the purpose of, and the circumstances surrounding, the communication. Was the communication made for information only? Was it made for some action to be taken and, if so, what action and by whom? These are some of the questions which may have to be addressed.
>
> (3) *The relationship between the adviser, the advisee and any relevant third party*
>
> Where the statement was made or prepared in the first instance to or for the benefit of someone other than the advisee, it will be necessary to consider the relationship between the parties. Thus it may be that the advisee is likely to look to the third party and through him to the adviser for advice or guidance. Or the advisee may be wholly independent and in a position to make any necessary judgments himself.

17 [1991] 1 All ER 134.

> *(4) The size of any class to which the advisee belongs*
>
> Where there is a single advisee or he is a member of only a small class, it may sometimes be simple to infer that a duty of care was owed to him. Membership of a large class, however, may make such an inference more difficult, particularly where the statement was made in the first instance for someone outside the class.
>
> *(5) The state of knowledge of the adviser*
>
> The precise state of knowledge of the adviser is one of the most important matters to examine. Thus it will be necessary to consider his knowledge of the purpose for which the statement was made or required in the first place, and also his knowledge of the purpose for which the statement was communicated to the advisee. In this context knowledge includes not only actual knowledge, but also such knowledge as would be attributed to a reasonable person in the circumstances in which the adviser was placed. On the other hand any duty of care will be limited to transactions or types of transactions of which the adviser had knowledge, and will only arise where 'the adviser knows or ought to know that [the statement or advice] will be relied on by a particular person or class of persons in connection with that transaction'; see *per* Lord Oliver in the *Caparo Industries* case [1990] 1 All ER 568 at 592, [1990] 2 AC 605 at 641. It is also necessary to consider whether the adviser knew that the advisee would rely on the statement without obtaining independent advice.
>
> *(6) Reliance by the advisee*
>
> In cases where the existence of a duty of care is in issue it is always useful to examine the matter from the point of view of the plaintiff. As I have ventured to say elsewhere the question 'who is my neighbour?' prompts the response 'consider first those who would consider you to be their neighbour'. One should therefore consider whether, and to what extent, the advisee was entitled to rely on the statement to take the action that he did take. It is also necessary to consider whether he did in fact rely on the statement, whether he did or should have used his own judgment, and whether he did or should have sought independent advice. In business transactions conducted at arm's length it may sometimes be difficult for an advisee to prove that he was entitled to act on a statement without taking any independent advice, or to prove that the adviser knew, actually or inferentially, that he would act without taking such advice.

In the other case it seems that a different conclusion was reached. In *Morgan Crucible Co plc v Hill Samuel Bank Ltd*[18] the difference was that further representations were made once an identified bidder had emerged. In delivering the only judgment, Slade LJ said:

> In these circumstances, we are of the opinion that it is at least arguable that the present case can be distinguished from *Caparo* on its assumed facts. On such facts, each of the directors, in making the relevant representations, was aware that Morgan Crucible would rely on them for the purpose of deciding whether or not to make an increased bid, *and intended that they should*; this was one of the purposes of the defence documents and the representations contained therein. Morgan Crucible did rely on them for this purpose. In these circumstances, subject to questions of justice and reasonableness, we think it plainly arguable that there was a relationship of proximity between the directors and Morgan Crucible sufficient to give rise to a duty of care, particularly bearing in mind that much of the information on which the accounts and profit forecast was based was presumably available to the defendants alone.

18 [1991] 1 All ER 148.

The crucial point here is that made in italics in the above extract, as the plaintiffs were comfortably able to satisfy points (1) and (2) in the list in the judgment of Neill LJ in the previous case. Whether this heralds a more restrictive approach, as is claimed by that judge, is open to question. Perhaps it is safer to suggest that the parameters of the *Hedley Byrne* principle have been more sharply defined than hitherto.

RELIANCE

The issue of reliance is fundamental to the principle at two levels in a sense. The advisee must establish actual reliance, ie causation, in that she must show that, acting on the advice or information, she did so to her detriment and sustained a loss. The other point is that the plaintiff must show that her reliance was reasonable in the circumstances. This is likely to be the crucial issue in many cases and, in a sense, is tied up with the other elements. It is only where the advice is given in a business context that the reliance will be reasonable. Similarly, only if the reliance of the plaintiff is within the purpose for which the advice or information is given will that reliance be seen as being reasonable. The most useful cases for discussing this issue in some depth are those concerning the liability of surveyors in respect of house valuations. We shall consider these next.

The first of these was the High Court case of *Yianni v Evans*[19] which, despite its lowly status in the court hierarchy, was an extremely significant case. The Yiannis were purchasing a house at the lower end of the market with the aid of a building society mortgage. The society, as is required by law, instructed the defendants to carry out a basic valuation of the property in question to see whether it was worth at least the amount that the society was preparing to lend. The Yiannis did not have their own survey carried out but relied on the fact that the valuer had reported favourably on the property. The house needed considerable work doing on it, far exceeding the purchase price. The Yiannis sued the valuer in negligence. After surveying the case law the judge, Park J, said:

> Accordingly, guided by the passages in the judgment of Denning LJ in *Candler's* case and the speeches in the House of Lords cases, I conclude that, in this case, the duty of care would arise if, on the evidence, I am satisfied that the defendants knew that their valuation of 1 Seymour Road, in so far as it stated that the property provided adequate security for an advance of £12,000, would be passed on to the plaintiffs who, notwithstanding the building society's literature and the service of the notice under s 30 of the 1962 Act, in the defendants' reasonable contemplation would place reliance on its correctness in making their decision to buy the house and mortgage it to the building society. What therefore does the evidence establish?
>
> These defendants are surveyors and valuers. It is their profession and occupation to survey and make valuations of houses and other property. They make reports about the condition of property they have surveyed. Their duty is not merely to use care in their reports, they also have a duty to use care in their work which results in their reports. On the instructions of the building society, the defendants

19 [1981] 3 All ER 592.

sent a representative to 1 Seymour Road to make a survey and valuation of that property. He knew that the object of the survey was to enable the defendants, his employers, to submit a report to the building society for the use of the directors in discharging their duty under s 25 of the Act. The report, therefore, had to be directed to the value of the property and to any matter likely to affect its value. The defendants knew, therefore, that the director or other officer in the building society who considered their report would use it for the purpose of assessing the adequacy of 1 Seymour Road as security for an advance.

There is no evidence that the building society had access to any other reports or information for this purpose, or that the defendants believed or assumed that the building society would have any information beyond that contained in their report. Accordingly, the defendants knew that the director or other officer of the building society who dealt with the plaintiffs' application would rely on the correctness of this report in making, on behalf of the society, the offer of a loan on the security of 1 Seymour Road. The defendants, therefore, knew that the plaintiffs would receive from the building society an offer to lend £12,000, which sum, as the defendants also knew, the plaintiffs desired to borrow. It was argued that, as the information contained in the defendants' report was confidential to the directors, the defendants could not have foreseen that the contents of their report would be passed on to the plaintiffs.

But the contents of the report were never passed on. This case is not about the contents of the entire report, it is about that part of the report which said that 1 Seymour Road was suitable as security for a loan of £12,000. The defendants knew that that part would have to be passed on to the plaintiffs, since the reason for the plaintiffs' application was to obtain a loan of £12,000. Accordingly, the building society's offer of £12,000, when passed on to the plaintiffs, confirmed to them that 1 Seymour Road was sufficiently valuable to cause the building society to advance on its security 80% of the purchase price. Since that was also the building society's view, the plaintiffs' belief was not unreasonable.

It was argued that there was no reasonable likelihood that the plaintiffs would rely on the fact that the defendants had made a valuation report to the building society or, alternatively, that the defendants could not reasonably have foreseen or contemplated, first, that the plaintiffs would rely on the valuation in the report or, second, that they would act unreasonably in failing to obtain an independent surveyor's report for their own guidance. These submissions were founded on the fact that the defendants would know that the plaintiffs would have been provided with the building society's literature and that the building society, for its own protection, would have served with their offer the statutory notice pursuant to s 30 of the 1962 Act.

Now these defendants, plainly, are in a substantial way of business as surveyors and valuers. ... They must have on their staff some members of the Royal Institute of Chartered Surveyors. The terms of the building society's request to them to value 1 Seymour Road indicated that they had regularly carried out valuations for the Halifax, and no doubt for other building societies. Mr Hunter's evidence is that, for some six years, over 90% of applicants for a building society mortgage have relied on the building society's valuation, as represented by the building society's offer of an advance, as a statement that the house in question is worth at least that sum.

These applicants, and in particular applicants at the lower end of the property market, do not read building society literature, or, if they do, they ignore the advice to have an independent survey and also the terms of the statutory notice. Mr Hunter's evidence was unchallenged. No witness was called to suggest that

> he had in any way misrepresented the beliefs, conduct and practice of the typical applicant. I think that Mr Hunter is telling me what was common knowledge in the professional world of building societies and of surveyors and valuers employed or instructed by them. I am satisfied that the defendants were fully aware of all these matters.
>
> The defendants' representative who surveyed and valued 1 Seymour Road noted the type of dwelling house it was, its age, its price and the locality in which it was situated. It was plainly a house at the lower end of the property market. The applicant for a loan would therefore almost certainly be a person of modest means who, for one reason or another, would not be expected to obtain an independent valuation, and who would be certain to rely, as the plaintiffs in fact did, on the defendants' valuation as communicated to him in the building society's offer. I am sure that the defendants knew that their valuation would be passed on to the plaintiffs and that the defendants knew that the plaintiffs would rely on it when they decided to accept the building society's offer.

The approach taken by the judge in this case received strong approval in the House of Lords in the joined cases of *Smith v Eric S Bush* and *Harris v Wyre Forest District Council*[20] where, on very similar facts, Lord Templeman stated:

> In general I am of the opinion that, in the absence of a disclaimer of liability, the valuer who values a house for the purpose of a mortgage, knowing that the mortgagee will rely and the mortgagor will probably rely on the valuation, knowing that the purchaser mortgagor has in effect paid for the valuation, is under a duty to exercise reasonable skill and care and that duty is owed to both parties to the mortgage for which the valuation is made.

Lord Griffiths also stated:

> I have come to the conclusion that *Yianni's* case was correctly decided. I have already given my view that the voluntary assumption of responsibility is unlikely to be a helpful or realistic test in most cases. I therefore return to the question: in what circumstances should the law deem those who give advice to have assumed responsibility to the person who acts on the advice or, in other words, in what circumstances should a duty of care be owed by the adviser to those who act on his advice? I would answer: only if it is foreseeable that, if the advice is negligent, the recipient is likely to suffer damage, that there is a sufficiently proximate relationship between the parties and that it is just and reasonable to impose the liability.
>
> In the case of a surveyor valuing a small house for a building society or local authority, the application of these three criteria leads to the conclusion that he owes a duty of care to the purchaser. If the valuation is negligent and is relied on, damage in the form of economic loss to the purchaser is obviously foreseeable. The necessary proximity arises from the surveyor's knowledge that the overwhelming probability is that the purchaser will rely on his valuation. The evidence was that surveyors knew that approximately 90% of purchasers did so, and the fact that the surveyor only obtains the work because the purchaser is willing to pay his fee. It is just and reasonable that the duty should be imposed, for the advice is given in a professional as opposed to a social context and liability for breach of the duty will be limited both as to its extent and amount. The extent of the liability is limited to the purchaser of the house; I would not extend it to subsequent purchasers. The amount of the liability cannot be very great because it relates to a modest house.

20 [1989] 2 All ER 514.

> There is no question here of creating a liability of indeterminate amount to an indeterminate class. I would certainly wish to stress that, in cases where the advice has not been given for the specific purpose of the recipient acting on it, it should only be in cases when the adviser knows that there is a high degree of probability that some other identifiable person will act on the advice, that a duty of care should be imposed. It would impose an intolerable burden on those who give advice in a professional or commercial context if they were to owe a duty, not only to those to whom they give advice, but to any other person who might choose to act on it.

The other three Law Lords agreed with their two fellow judges. The other issue in this case related to the disclaimer contained in the mortgage documents and whether this was covered by the Unfair Contract Terms Act 1977. The House decided that the Act did apply, and held that the disclaimers were unreasonable. They also rejected the argument that the relevant disclaimer was a denial of an assumption of responsibility and prevented the duty arising in the first place. This would have side-stepped the Act and the House was not prepared to sanction such an approach. The court must consider whether the duty has arisen, disregarding the disclaimer. It must then go on to consider the effect of the disclaimer as regulated by the 1977 Act and decide on its reasonableness under s 2(2). The assumption of responsibility test as a basis for establishing a duty has had a chequered history. As we shall see below, somewhat extraordinarily, it has been revived in recent cases, despite apparently having been laid to rest in *Caparo* and *Smith v Eric S Bush*.

Before leaving the *Hedley Byrne* principle, it is worth looking at an amazing case called *Chaudry v Prabhakar*,[21] where it was held that a friend of the plaintiff, who agreed to purchase a car on the latter's behalf, owed a duty under the principle to exercise care in the selection of a suitable vehicle. The defendant, and presumably former friend, of the plaintiff was not even a mechanic but did have some knowledge of cars. Stuart-Smith LJ in the Court of Appeal said:

> It seems to me that all the necessary ingredients are here present. The plaintiff clearly relied on the first defendant's skill and judgment and, although it may not have been great, it was greater than hers and was quite sufficient for the purpose of asking the appropriate questions of the second defendant. The first defendant also knew that the plaintiff was relying on him. Indeed he told her that she did not need to have it inspected by a mechanic and she did not do so on the strength of his recommendation. It was clearly in a business connection, because he knew that she was there and then going to commit herself to buying the car for £4,500 through his agency.

The case seems to be an extreme one, and interestingly May LJ comments that he was not altogether sure that the duty point was correctly conceded by counsel for the first defendant. Nonetheless a salutary warning for those who do favours for a friend.

21 [1988] 3 All ER 718.

OTHER EXCEPTIONAL CASES

There are other instances of courts accepting that there is, exceptionally, a duty situation which do not seem to fall squarely within the principle discussed immediately above, although there have been recent attempts to drag at least some of them, belatedly in some cases, into the *Hedley Byrne* fold. Unfortunately, there does not seem to be any explicit principle informing these cases and they appear to be rather *ad hoc*, even random, exceptions to the general rule against recovery. Their existence, however untidy from a doctrinal point of view, must be acknowledged and accepted. We shall now look at some of these.

One such case is *Ministry of Housing and Local Government v Sharp*,[22] where the ministry lost the valuable benefit of a charge over a property, as a result of the negligence of a clerk employed in the local land charges registry for the area in which the property was situated. The local search made by the purchaser's solicitor was returned without mention of the charge, thus the purchaser took the property free of the charge, leaving the ministry with a personal unsecured claim against the vendor. The ministry sued the defendant on the basis of negligence. Lord Denning MR, in discussing the liability of the clerk, said:

> I have no doubt that the clerk is liable. He was under a duty at common law to use due care. That was a duty he owed to any person-incumbrancer or purchaser who, he knew or ought to have known, might be injured if he made a mistake. ...
>
> In my opinion the duty to use due care in a statement arises, not from any voluntary assumption of responsibility, but from the fact that the person making it knows, or ought to know, that others, being his neighbours in this regard, would act on the faith of the statement being accurate. That is enough to bring the duty into being. It is owed, of course, to the person to whom the certificate is issued and who he knows is going to act on it. ... But it is also owed to any person who he knows, or ought to know, will be injuriously affected by a mistake, such as the incumbrancer here.

Salmon LJ commented:

> The present case does not precisely fit into any category of negligence yet considered by the courts. The ministry has not been misled by any careless statement made to it by the defendants or made by the defendants to someone else who the defendants knew would be likely to pass it on to a third party, such as the ministry, in circumstances in which the third party might reasonably be expected to rely on it. ... I am not, however, troubled by the fact that the present case is, in many respects, unique.
>
> ... it has been argued in the present case that, since the council did not voluntarily make the search or prepare the certificate for their clerk's signature, they did not voluntarily assume responsibility for the accuracy of the certificate and, accordingly, owed no duty of care to the minister. I do not accept that, in all cases, the obligation to take reasonable care necessarily depends on a voluntary assumption of responsibility. Even if it did, I am far from satisfied that the council did not voluntarily assume responsibility in the present case. On the contrary, it seems to me that they certainly chose to undertake the duty of searching the register and preparing the certificate. There was nothing to compel

22 [1970] 1 All ER 1009.

> them to discharge this duty through their servant. It obviously suited them better that this somewhat pedestrian task should be performed by one of their comparatively minor servants than by their clerk, so that he might be left free to carry out other far more difficult and important functions on their behalf.
>
> I do not think that it matters that the search was made at the request of the purchaser and that the certificate was issued to him. It would be absurd if a duty of care were owed to a purchaser but not to an incumbrancer. The rules made under many of the statutes creating local land charges do not apply s 17(3); they do, however, apply s 17(1) and (2) of the Land Charges Act 1925. If, in such cases, a clear certificate is carelessly given, it will be the purchaser and not the incumbrancer who will suffer. Clearly land may be worth much more unencumbered than if it is subject to a charge. The purchaser who buys on the faith of a clear certificate might suffer very heavy financial loss if the certificate turns out to be incorrect. Such a loss is reasonably to be foreseen as a result of any carelessness in the search of the register or the preparation of the certificate.
>
> The proximity between the council and the purchaser is even closer than that between the plaintiff and the defendants in *Candler v Crane, Christmas & Co*. The council even received a fee, although a small one, for the certificate. Clearly a duty to take care must exist in such a case. Our law would be grievously defective if the council did owe a duty of care to the purchaser in the one case but no duty to the incumbrancer in the other. The damage in each case is equally foreseeable. It is, in my view, irrelevant that in the one case the certificate is issued to the person it injures and in the other case it is not. The purchaser is deceived by the certificate about his legal rights when s 17(3) of the Land Charges Act 1925 does not apply, whilst the incumbrancer's legal rights are taken away by the certificate when s 17(3) does apply. In my view the proximity is as close in one case as in the other, and certainly sufficient to impose on the council through their servant a duty to take reasonable care.

It would be hard to describe this case as a detrimental reliance case as the injured party did not rely on the statement in the certificate. They could hardly be said to do so when, in all probability, they were not aware that a search was being done and a certificate issued. On the other hand there is little danger of indeterminate liability in view of the fact that there could only ever be one potential plaintiff whose identity was known to the defendants.

Another exceptional case, coming in the aftermath of the *Anns* case, was that of *Junior Books Ltd v Veitchi Co Ltd*,[23] in which the pursuers contracted with a builder for the construction of a factory. The pursuers nominated the defenders as sub-contractors for the flooring work in the factory. The floor was defective, causing severe financial loss to the pursuers which included loss of profits, which was considered to be pure economic loss. By a majority, the House found for the pursuers. Lord Brandon dissented, and not surprisingly, Lord Keith was less than enthusiastic, although agreeing with the other three of their Lordships in the result. He was particularly concerned with the impact that allowing an action in these circumstances would have on commercial practice in relation to warranties and guarantees, a point laboured by Lord Brandon. The leading judgment was that of Lord Roskill, and after discussing the cases he went on:

23 [1982] 3 All ER 201.

> Turning back to the present appeal I therefore ask, first, whether there was the requisite degree of proximity so as to give rise to the relevant duty of care relied on by the respondents [pursuers]. I regard the following facts as of crucial importance in requiring an affirmative answer to that question:
>
> (1) the appellants were nominated sub-contractors;
>
> (2) the appellants were specialists in flooring;
>
> (3) the appellants knew what products were required by the appellants and their main contractors and specialised in the production of those products;
>
> (4) the appellants alone were responsible for the composition and construction of the flooring;
>
> (5) the respondents relied on the appellants' skill and experience;
>
> (6) the appellants, as nominated sub-contractors, must have known that the respondents relied on their skill and experience;
>
> (7) the relationship between the parties was as close as it could be short of actual privity of contract;
>
> (8) the appellants must be taken to have known that, if they did the work negligently (as it must be assumed that they did), the resulting defects would at some time require remedying by the respondents expending money on the remedial measures, as a consequence of which the respondents would suffer financial or economic loss.

This case caused considerable controversy and was considered by some to be the final straw, in that it paved the way for the obliteration of contract law by the all-powerful, overwhelming tort of negligence. This somewhat hysterical reaction, of course, found its way into the cases and started the beginning of the end for the two-stage approach. The desire to preserve the integrity of other areas of law, in particular contract law, came to the fore in a number of cases and, whilst being openly polite about *Junior Books*, the judges found reasons not to apply it to the case before them.[24] The fear was that consumers would be able to sue manufacturers for the value or cost of repair of shoddy goods, involving difficulties of what would amount to breach, namely, was the standard equivalent to that expected in the contract between retailer and purchaser (ie merchantable or satisfactory quality). Perhaps the irony is that it may soon be the case that, under European Treaty obligations, such a position may have to be achieved.[25]

Another significant dent in the rule against recovery for pure economic loss was made by the decision in *Ross v Caunters (a firm)*,[26] the basic facts of which are included in the judgment of Sir Robert Megarry VC below:

> In this case the facts are simple and undisputed, and the point of law that it raises is short; yet it has taken five days to argue, and over 30 authorities from both sides of the Atlantic have very properly been cited, some at considerable length. In broad terms, the question is whether solicitors who prepare a will are liable to a beneficiary under it if, through their negligence, the gift to the

24 See eg *Muirhead v Industrial Tank Specialities Ltd* [1985] 3 All ER 703; *Greater Nottingham Co-operative Society Ltd v Cementation Piling and Foundations Ltd* [1988] 2 All ER 971.

25 See the Green Paper, COM (93) 509 final.

26 [1979] 3 All ER 580.

> beneficiary is void. The solicitors are liable, of course, to the testator or his estate for a breach of the duty that they owed to him, though as he has suffered no financial loss it seems that his estate could recover no more than nominal damages. Yet it is said that, however careless the solicitors were, they owed no duty to the beneficiary, and so they cannot be liable to her.
>
> If this is right, the result is striking. The only person who has a valid claim has suffered no loss, and the only person who has suffered a loss has no valid claim. However grave the negligence, and however great the loss, the solicitors would be under no liability to pay substantial damages to anyone. No doubt they would be liable to the testator if the mistake was discovered in his lifetime, though in that case the damages would, I think, be merely the cost of making a new and valid will, or otherwise putting matters right. But the real question is whether the solicitors are under any liability to the disappointed beneficiary.

After an able and admirable analysis of the case law and principles, the judge expressed the view that the case did not sit easily within the *Hedley Byrne* mould, and that it was probably more akin to *Donoghue v Stevenson*. He also dismissed the arguments, based on policy by counsel for the defendant firm, as tenuous, and in summary put forward his conclusions thus:

> (1) ... there is no longer any rule that a solicitor, who is negligent in his professional work, can be liable only to his client in contract; he may be liable both to his client and to others in the tort of negligence.
>
> (2) The basis of the solicitor's liability to others is either an extension of the *Hedley Byrne* principle or, more probably, a direct application of the principle in *Donoghue v Stevenson*.
>
> (3) A solicitor, who is instructed by his client to carry out a transaction that will confer a benefit on an identified third party, owes a duty of care towards that third party in carrying out that transaction, in that the third party is a person within his direct contemplation as someone who is so closely and directly affected by his acts or omissions that he can reasonably foresee that the third party is likely to be injured by those acts or omissions.
>
> (4) The mere fact that the loss to such a third party, caused by the negligence, is purely financial and is in no way a physical injury to person or property, is no bar to the claim against the solicitor.
>
> (5) In such circumstances there are no considerations which suffice to negative or limit the scope of the solicitor's duty to the beneficiary.

There was some doubt about the correctness of this decision but, after some 15 years, the House of Lords has finally resolved, by a majority (3–2), that a solicitor does owe a duty in such circumstances. In *White v Jones*[27] the solicitor negligently failed to carry out the testator's instructions to prepare a new will including his two daughters, the plaintiffs, as beneficiaries. It is hardly a surprise to find Lord Keith dissenting, using the incremental case-by-case analogical approach, saying:

> The intention to benefit the plaintiffs existed only in the mind of the testator, and if it had received legal effect would have given them only a *spes successionis* of an ambulatory character. ...
>
> Upon the whole matter I have found the conceptual difficulties involved in the plaintiffs' claim, which are fully recognised by all your Lordships, to be too

27 [1995] 1 All ER 691.

> formidable to be resolved by any process of reasoning compatible with existing principles of law.

The leading judgment was given by Lord Goff, who summarised the conceptual difficulties as follows:

> (1) First, the general rule is well established that a solicitor acting on behalf of a client owes a duty of care only to his client. The relationship between a solicitor and his client is nearly always contractual, and the scope of the solicitor's duties will be set by the terms of his retainer; but a duty of care owed by a solicitor to his client will arise concurrently in contract and in tort. ... But, when a solicitor is performing his duties to his client, he will generally owe no duty of care to third parties.
>
> ... As I have said, the scope of the solicitor's duties to his client are set by the terms of his retainer; and as a result it has been said that the content of his duties is entirely within the control of his client. The solicitor can, in theory at least, protect himself by the introduction of terms into his contract with his client; but, it is objected, he could not similarly protect himself against any third party to whom he might be held responsible, where there is no contract between him and the third party.
>
> In these circumstances, it is said, there can be no liability of the solicitor to a beneficiary under a will who has been disappointed by reason of negligent failure by the solicitor to give effect to the testator's intention. There can be no liability in contract, because there is no contract between the solicitor and the disappointed beneficiary; if any contractual claim was to be recognised, it could only be by way of an *ius quaesitum tertio*, and no such claim is recognised in English law. Nor could there be any liability in tort because, in the performance of his duties to his client, a solicitor owes no duty of care in tort to a third party such as a disappointed beneficiary under his client's will.
>
> (2) A further reason is given which is said to reinforce the conclusion that no duty of care is owed by the solicitor to the beneficiary in tort. Here, it is suggested, is one of the situations in which a plaintiff is entitled to damages if, and only if, he can establish a breach of contract by the defendant. First, the plaintiff's claim is one for purely financial loss; and as a general rule, apart from cases of assumption of responsibility arising under the principle in *Hedley Byrne v Heller*, no action will lie in respect of such loss in the tort of negligence. Furthermore, in particular, no claim will lie in tort for damages in respect of a mere loss of an expectation, as opposed to damages in respect of damage to an existing right or interest of the plaintiff. Such a claim falls within the exclusive zone of contractual liability; and it is contrary to principle that the law of tort should be allowed to invade that zone.
>
> ... The present case, it is suggested, falls within that exclusive zone. Here, it is impossible to frame the suggested duty except by reference to the contract between the solicitor and the testator – a contract to which the disappointed beneficiary is not a party, and from which, therefore, he can derive no rights. Second, the loss suffered by the disappointed beneficiary is not in reality a loss at all; it is, more accurately, a failure to obtain a benefit. All that has happened is that what is sometimes called a *spes succesionis* has failed to come to fruition. As a result, he has not become better off, but he is not made worse off. A claim in respect of such loss of expectation falls, it is said, clearly within the exclusive zone of contractual liability.
>
> (3) A third, and distinct, objection is that, if liability in tort was recognised in cases such as *Ross v Caunters*, it would be impossible to place any sensible bounds to cases in which such recovery was allowed. In particular, the same

liability should logically be imposed in cases where an *inter vivos* transaction was ineffective, and the defect was not discovered until the donor was no longer able to repair it. Furthermore, liability could not logically be restricted to cases where a specific, named beneficiary was disappointed, but would inevitably have to be extended to cases in which wide, even indeterminate, classes of persons could be said to have been adversely affected.

(4) Other miscellaneous objections were taken though, in my opinion, they were without substance, in particular:

(a) since the testator himself owes no duty to the beneficiary, it would be illogical to impose any such duty on his solicitor – I myself cannot however see any force in this objection;

(b) to enable the disappointed beneficiary to recover from the solicitor would have undesirable, and indeed fortuitous, effect of substantially increasing the size of the testator's estate – even of doubling it in size – because it would not be possible to recover any part of the estate which had lawfully devolved upon others by an unrevoked will or on an intestacy, even though that was not in fact the testator's intention. I cannot however see what impact this has on the disappointed beneficiary's remedy. It simply reflects the fact that those who received the testator's estate, either under an unrevoked will or on an intestacy, were lucky enough to receive a windfall; and in consequence the estate is, so far as the testator and the disappointed beneficiary are concerned, irretrievably lost.

(5) There is, however, another objection of a conceptual nature. ... In the present case ... there was no act of the defendant solicitor which could be characterised as negligent. All that happened was that the solicitor did nothing at all for a period of time, with the result that the testator died before his new testamentary intentions could be implemented in place of the old. As a general rule, however, there is no liability in tortious negligence for an omission, unless the defendant is under some pre-existing duty. Once again, therefore, the question arises how liability can arise in the present case in the absence of a contract.

Against these conceptual problems are set the arguments in favour of what Lord Goff calls 'the impulse to do practical justice'. He continues:

(1) In the forefront stands the extraordinary fact that, if such a duty is not recognised, the only persons who might have a valid claim (ie the testator and his estate) have suffered no loss, and the only person who has suffered a loss (ie the disappointed beneficiary) has no claim ... it can therefore be said that, if the solicitor owes no duty to the intended beneficiaries, there is a lacuna in the law which needs to be filled. This I regard as being a point of cardinal importance in the present case.

(2) The injustice of denying such a remedy is reinforced if one considers the importance of legacies in a society which recognises (subject only to the incidence of inheritance tax, and statutory requirements for provision for near relatives) the right of citizens to leave their assets to whom they please, and in which, as a result, legacies can be of great importance to individual citizens, providing very often the only opportunity for a citizen to acquire a significant capital sum; or to inherit a house, so providing a secure roof over the heads of himself and his family; or to make special provision for his or her old age. In the course of the hearing before the appellate committee, Mr Matheson (who was instructed by the Law Society to represent the appellant

solicitors) placed before the committee a schedule of the claims of the character of that in the present case notified to the Solicitors' Indemnity Fund following the judgment of the Court of Appeal below. It is striking that, where the amount of the claim was known, it was, by today's standards, of a comparatively modest size. This perhaps indicates that it is where a testator instructs a small firm of solicitors that mistakes of this kind are most likely to occur, with the result that it tends to be people of modest means, who need the money so badly, who suffer.

(3) There is a sense in which the solicitors' profession cannot complain if such a liability be imposed on their members. If one of them has been negligent in such a way as to defeat his client's testamentary intentions, he must regard himself as very lucky indeed if the effect of the law is that he is not liable to pay damages in the ordinary way. It can involve no injustice to render him subject to such a liability, even if the damages are payable, not to his client's estate for distribution to the disappointed beneficiary (which might have been the preferred solution), but direct to the disappointed beneficiary.

(4) That such a conclusion is required as a matter of justice is reinforced by consideration of the role played by solicitors in society. The point was well made by Cooke J in *Gartside v Sheffield Young & Ellis* [1983] NZLR 37 at 43, when he observed: 'To deny an effective remedy in a plain case would seem to imply a refusal to acknowledge the solicitor's professional role in the community. In practice the public relies on solicitors (or statutory officers with similar functions) to prepare effective wills'.

The question therefore arises whether it is possible to give effect in law to the strong impulse for practical justice which is the fruit of the foregoing considerations. For this to be achieved, I respectfully agree with Nicholls VC when he said that the court will have to fashion 'an effective remedy for the solicitor's breach of his professional duty to his client' in such a way as to repair the injustice to the disappointed beneficiary (see [1993] 3 All ER 481 at 489, [1993] 3 WLR 730 at 739).

After discussing the conceptual problems, and presumably deciding that the impulse to do practical justice was overwhelming, Lord Goff considered how best to achieve the desired result. Ultimately, he was compelled to turn to tort law for his solution as follows:

I therefore return to the law of tort for a solution to the problem. For the reasons I have already given, an ordinary action in tortious negligence on the lines proposed by Megarry VC in *Ross v Caunters* must, with the greatest respect, be regarded as inappropriate, because it does not meet any of the conceptual problems which have been raised. Furthermore, for the reasons I have previously given, the *Hedley Byrne* principle cannot, in the absence of special circumstances, give rise on ordinary principles to an assumption of responsibility by the testator's solicitor towards an intended beneficiary. ... In my opinion ... your Lordships' House should, in cases such as these, extend to the intended beneficiary a remedy under the *Hedley Byrne* principle by holding that the assumption of responsibility by the solicitor towards his client should be held in law to extend to the intended beneficiary, who (as the solicitor can reasonably foresee) may, as a result of the solicitor's negligence, be deprived of his intended legacy in circumstances in which neither the testator nor his estate will have a remedy against the solicitor.

Such liability will not, of course, arise in cases in which the defect in the will comes to light before the death of the testator, and the testator either leaves the will as it is or otherwise continues to exclude the previously intended beneficiary from the relevant benefit. I only wish to add that, with the benefit of experience during the 15 years in which *Ross v Caunters* has been regularly applied, we can say with some confidence that a direct remedy by the intended beneficiary against the solicitor appears to create no problems in practice. That is therefore the solution which I would recommend to your Lordships.

As I see it, not only does this conclusion produce practical justice as far as all parties are concerned, but it also has the following beneficial consequences.

(1) There is no unacceptable circumvention of established principles of the law of contract.

(2) No problem arises by reason of the loss being of a purely economic character.

(3) Such assumption of responsibility will of course be subject to any term of the contract between the solicitor and the testator, which may exclude or restrict the solicitor's liability to the testator under the principle in *Hedley Byrne*; it is true that such a term would be most unlikely to exist in practice, but as a matter of principle it is right that this largely theoretical question should be addressed.

(4) Since the *Hedley Byrne* principle is founded upon an assumption of responsibility, the solicitor may be liable for negligent omissions as well as negligent acts of commission. ... This conclusion provides justification for the decision of the Court of Appeal to reverse the decision of Turner J in the present case, although this point was not in fact raised below or before your Lordships.

(5) I do not consider that damages for loss of an expectation are excluded in cases of negligence arising under the principle in *Hedley Byrne*, simply because the cause of action is classified as tortious. Such damages may, in principle, be recoverable in cases of contractual negligence; and I cannot see that, for present purposes, any relevant distinction can be drawn between the two forms of action. In particular, an expectation loss may well occur in cases where a professional man, such as a solicitor, has assumed responsibility for the affairs of another; and I for my part can see no reason in principle why the professional man should not, in an appropriate case, be liable for such loss under the *Hedley Byrne* principle.

In the result, all the conceptual problems ... can be seen to fade innocuously away. Let me emphasise that I can see no injustice in imposing liability upon a negligent solicitor in a case such as the present where, in the absence of a remedy in this form, neither the testator's estate nor the disappointed beneficiary will have a claim for the loss caused by his negligence. This is the injustice which, in my opinion, the judges of this country should address, by recognising that cases such as these call for an appropriate remedy, and that the common law is not so sterile as to be incapable of supplying that remedy when it is required.

Both Lord Browne-Wilkinson and Lord Nolan agreed with the above analysis, both incidentally purporting to be using the incremental approach to a novel case. Lord Mustill was extremely sceptical about the practical justice arguments put forward by Lord Goff. However, the main criticism of the approach is the failure to consider the issue of reliance, which after all has been hitherto seen as the lynch-pin of liability under the *Hedley Byrne* principle. It seems that, after all, this can now be discarded in cases where an 'impulse' to do practical justice is overwhelmingly strong. Whilst not quibbling with the end result in the case, might it not have been better left in the terms expounded by the judge in *Ross v Caunters*, rather than to attempt to drag the case within the 'assumption of responsibility' test which has not, in the past at least, received universal acclaim as the true, or even a useful, basis for the *Hedley Byrne* principle?

Lord Goff also ploughed this particular furrow in *Spring v Guardian Assurance plc*,[28] although on this occasion it was a rather lonely one. In this case the plaintiff had been given a reference by his former employer which, it was alleged, was negligent in that it suggested that he was not honest and had little integrity. This more or less ensured that he was unemployable in the insurance business. He brought an action in negligence and contract against the former employer. With only Lord Keith, sticking to his guns steadfastly, dissenting, the remainder of the House found for the plaintiff. Lord Goff stated:

> The central issue in this appeal is whether a person who provides a reference in respect of another who was formerly engaged by him as a member of his staff ... may be liable in damages to that other in respect of economic loss suffered by him by reason of negligence in the preparation of the reference. That issue can, for the sake of convenience, be subdivided into two questions.
>
> (1) Whether the person who provided the reference *prima facie* owes a duty of care, in contract or tort, to the other in relation to the preparation of the reference.
>
> (2) If so, whether the existence of such a duty of care will nevertheless be negatived because it would, if recognised, *pro tanto* undermine the policy underlying the defence of qualified privilege in the law of defamation.
>
> ... *Prima facie*, ... it is my opinion that an employer who provides a reference in respect of one of his employees to a prospective future employer will ordinarily owe a duty of care to his employee in respect of the preparation of the reference. The employer is possessed of special knowledge, derived from his experience of the employee's character, skill and diligence in the performance of his duties while working for the employer. Moreover, when the employer provides a reference to a third party in respect of his employee, he does so not only for the assistance of the third party, but also, for what it is worth, for the assistance of the employee. Indeed, nowadays it must often be very difficult for an employee to obtain fresh employment without the benefit of a reference from his present or previous employer. It is for this reason that, in ordinary life, it may be the employee, rather that a prospective future employer, who asks the employer to provide the reference; and even where the approach comes from the prospective future employer, it will (apart from special circumstances) be made with either the express or tacit authority of the employee.
>
> The provision of such references is a service regularly provided by employers to their employees; indeed, references are part of the currency of the modern employment market. Furthermore, when such a reference is provided by an employer, it is plain that the employee relies upon him to exercise due skill and care in the preparation of the reference before making it available to the third party. In these circumstances, it seems to me that all the elements requisite for the application of the *Hedley Byrne* principle are present. I need only add that, in the context under consideration, there is no question of the circumstances in which the reference is being provided being, for example, so informal as to negative an assumption of responsibility by the employer.

Here, Lord Goff does at least acknowledge, but barely in passing, the reliance issue. By the time he comes across the appeal in *White v Jones* this requirement

28 [1994] 2 All ER 129.

has slipped into oblivion. On the other aspect, ie the integrity of the rules on defamation as a reason for not imposing liability, Lord Goff stated:

> ... it is, I consider, necessary to approach the question as a matter of principle. Since, for the reasons I have given, it is my opinion that, in cases such as the present, the duty of care arises by reason of an assumption of responsibility by the employer to the employee in respect of the relevant reference, I can see no good reason why the duty to exercise due skill and care which rests upon the employer should be negatived because, if the plaintiff were instead to bring an action for damage to his reputation, he would be met by the defence of qualified privilege which could only be defeated by proof of malice. It is not to be forgotten that the *Hedley Byrne* duty arises where there is a relationship which is, broadly speaking, either contractual or equivalent to contract. In these circumstances, I cannot see that principles of the law of defamation are of any relevance ... In all the circumstances, I do not think that we may fear too many ill effects from the recognition of the duty. The vast majority of employers will continue, as before, to provide careful references. But those who, as in the present case, fail to achieve that standard, will have to compensate their employees who suffer damage in consequence. Justice, in my opinion, requires that this should be done; and I, for my part, cannot see any reason in policy why that justice should be denied.

The extracts above are strangely reminiscent of the discredited two-stage approach. It is also very interesting how easily His Lordship shrugs off the defamation argument as being of no relevance. The other Law Lords, with of course the exception of Lord Keith, dealt with this argument in similar fashion. As to the negligence issue proper, both Lords Slynn and Woolf were of the view that there was a sufficiently close relationship between the plaintiff and the defendants so as to establish a duty, without mentioning the phrase 'assumption of responsibility'.

Again, few would have difficulty with the final result in this case, but there must be some concern about the way in which it was achieved. Lord Goff seems to be firmly in favour of resurrecting the 'assumption of responsibility' test as in *Henderson v Merrett Syndicates Ltd*,[29] the case involving the Lloyd's names. There was clearly reliance in that case and that reliance was eminently reasonable, so the application of the *Hedley Byrne* principle in such circumstances is not problematic. The problems are really concentrated on the two previous cases, in which His Lordship places great emphasis on the 'assumption of responsibility'. His approach may be storing up new difficulties and may have the effect of distorting the *Hedley Byrne* principle beyond recognition.

The *Henderson* case also involved detailed arguments concerning the relationship between contract and tort. It was argued that, because of the contractual framework surrounding the relationships between the names and the various types of agent, there was no scope for imposing a tortious duty. This argument was dismissed by the House. However, in the most recent case on economic loss, the contractual framework was used as one reason for denial of a duty in favour of the plaintiff. In *Marc Rich & Co v Bishop Rock Marine*[30] the claim arose from the destruction of a cargo belonging to the plaintiffs which

29 [1994] 3 All ER 506.

30 [1995] 3 All ER 307.

occurred when a ship pronounced seaworthy by an employee of the defendant classification society sank. The House of Lords found for the defendants, Lord Lloyd dissenting. Lord Steyn read the leading judgment and the following is extracted from it:

> Counsel for the cargo owners submitted that, in cases of physical damage to property in which the plaintiff has a proprietary or possessory interest, the only requirement is proof of reasonable foreseeability. For this proposition he relied on observations of Lord Oliver of Aylmerton in *Caparo Industries plc v Dickman* [1990] 1 All ER 568 at 585, [1990] 2 AC 605 at 632–33. Those observations, seen in context, do not support his argument. They merely underline the qualitative difference between cases of direct physical damage and indirect economic loss. The materiality of the distinction is plain. But since the decision in *Home Office v Dorset Yacht Co Ltd* [1970] 2 ALL ER 294, [1970] AC 1004 it has been settled law that the elements of foreseeability and proximity as well as considerations of fairness, justice and reasonableness are relevant to all cases, whatever the nature of the harm sustained by the plaintiff. Saville LJ explained ([1994] 3 All ER 686 at 692–93, [1994] 1 WLR 1071 at 1077): '... whatever the nature of the harm sustained by the plaintiff, it is necessary to consider the matter, not only by inquiring about foreseeability, but also by considering the nature of the relationship between the parties; and to be satisfied that in all the circumstances it is fair, just and reasonable to impose a duty of care. Of course ... these three matters overlap with each other and are really facets of the same thing. For example, the relationship between the parties may be such that it is obvious that a lack of care will create a risk of harm and that, as a matter of common sense and justice, a duty should be imposed. Again, in most cases the direct infliction of physical loss or injury through carelessness, it is self-evident that a civilised system of law should hold that a duty of care has been broken, whereas the infliction of financial harm may well pose a more difficult problem. Thus the three so-called requirements for a duty of care are not to be treated as wholly separate and distinct requirements, but rather as convenient and helpful approaches to the pragmatic question whether a duty should be imposed in any given case. In the end, whether the law does impose a duty in any particular circumstances depends on those circumstances ...'
>
> That seems to me a correct summary of the law as it now stands. It follows that I would reject the first argument of counsel for the cargo owners. ...
>
> It is now necessary to examine a number of other factors in order to put the case in its right perspective, and to consider whether some of those factors militate against the recognition of a duty of care. For convenience these factors can be considered under six headings, namely:
>
> (a) did the surveyor's negligence cause direct physical loss;
>
> (b) did the cargo owners rely on the surveyor's recommendations;
>
> (c) the impact of the contract between the ship owners and the owners of the cargo;
>
> (d) the impact of the contract between the classification society and the ship owners;
>
> (e) the position and role of NKK; and
>
> (f) policy factors arguably tending to militate against the recognition of a duty of care.
>
> Only after an examination of these features will it be possible to address directly the element of proximity and the question whether it is fair, just and reasonable to impose a duty of care.

(a) Direct physical loss

Counsel for the cargo owners argued that the present case involved the infliction of *direct* physical loss. At first glance the issue of directness may seem a matter of terminology rather than substance. In truth it is a material factor. The law more readily attaches the consequences of actionable negligence to directly inflicted physical loss than to indirectly inflicted physical loss. For example, if the NKK surveyor had carelessly dropped a lighted cigarette into a cargo hold known to contain a combustible cargo, thereby causing an explosion and the loss of the vessel and cargo, the assertion that the classification society was in breach of a duty of care might have been a strong one. That would be a paradigm case of directly inflicted physical loss. ... In the present case the ship owner was primarily responsible for the vessel sailing in a seaworthy condition. The role of the NKK was a subsidiary one. In my view the carelessness of the NKK surveyor did not involve the direct infliction of physical damages in the relevant sense. That by no means concludes the answer to the general question. But it does introduce the right perspective on one aspect of this case.

(b) Reliance

It is possible to visualise direct exchanges between cargo owners and a classification society, in the context of a survey on behalf of owners of a vessel laden with cargo, which might give rise to an assumption of responsibility in the sense explained by Lord Goff in *Henderson v Merrett Syndicates Ltd* [1994] 3 All ER 506 at 517–18, 533–34, [1994] 3 WLR 761 at 773, 789–91. ... In the present case there was no contact whatever between the cargo owners and the classification society. Moreover, ... in this case it is not even suggested that the cargo owners were aware that NKK had been brought in to survey the vessel ... the cargo owners simply relied on the owners of the vessel to keep the vessel seaworthy and to look after the cargo. ... In my view this feature is not necessarily decisive but also contributes to placing the claim in the correct perspective.

(c) The bill of lading contracts

The first and principal ground of the decision of Saville LJ was the impact of the terms of the bill of lading contracts. He said [1994] 3 All ER 686 at 695–95, [1994] 1 WLR 1071 at 1080: 'The Hague Rules and their successor, the Hague-Visby Rules (which are scheduled to the Carriage of Goods by Sea Act 1971), form an internationally recognised code adjusting the rights and duties existing between ship owners and those shipping goods under bills of lading ... the rules create an intricate blend of responsibilities and liabilities, rights and immunities, limitations on the amount of damages recoverable, time bars, evidential provisions, indemnities and liberties, all in relation to the carriage of goods under bills of lading. The proposition advanced by Mr Gross would add an identical or virtually identical duty owed by the classification society to that owed by the ship owners, but without any of these balancing factors, which are internationally recognised and accepted. I do not regard that as a just, fair or reasonable proposition.'

Saville LJ ended this part of his judgment by explicitly stating ([1994] 3 All ER 686 at 697, [1994] 1 WLR 1071 at 1081): 'The question is not whether the classification society is covered by the rules, but whether, in all the circumstances, it is just, fair and reasonable to require them to shoulder a responsibility which, by the rules, primarily lies on the ship owners, without the benefits of those rules or other international conventions.'

That question Saville LJ (and, by adoption, Balcombe LJ) answered in the negative. And Mann LJ was in substantial agreement on this point.

It was the principal task of counsel for the cargo owners to try to dismantle the reasoning of Saville LJ. He pointed out that Saville LJ apparently assumed that the limitation of the claim of the cargo owners against the ship owners arose under the Hague Rules. In truth, the limitation arose by reason of tonnage limitation. ... This is not a point of substance. Tonnage limitation is a part of the international code which governs the claims under consideration. It is as relevant as any limitation under the Hague Rules.

Moving on to more substantial matters, counsel for the cargo owners submitted that the allocation of risks in the Hague Rules between ship owners and the owners of cargo is irrelevant to the question whether NKK owed a duty of care to the owners of the cargo. He said the bill of lading contract on Hague Rules terms, and the international character of those rules, is only a piece of history which explains the positions in which NKK and the owners of the cargo found themselves. In the course of these submissions Mr Gross referred your Lordships to a valuable article by PF Cane, 'The Liability of Classification Societies' [1994] LMCLQ 363. Mr Cane observed trenchantly at 373: 'But why should an allocation of risks between ship owners and cargo owners be enforced as between cargo owners and classification societies? Whatever good reasons there may be to do so, the mere existence of the Hague Rules is surely not one of them.'

That is a cogent argument against the reasoning of the Court of Appeal. There is, however, a further dimension of the problem that must be considered.

The dealings between ship owners and cargo owners are based on a contractual structure, the Hague Rules and tonnage limitation, on which the insurance of international trade depends: see Dr Malcolm Clarke, 'Mis-delivery and Time Bars', [1990] LMCLQ 314. Underlying it is the system of double or overlapping insurance of cargo. Cargo owners take out direct insurance in respect of the cargo. Ship owners take out liability insurance in respect of breaches of their duties of care in respect of the cargo. The insurance system is structured on the basis that the potential liability of ship owners to cargo owners is limited under the Hague Rules and by virtue of tonnage limitation provisions. And insurance premiums payable by owners obviously reflect such limitations on the ship owners' exposure.

If a duty of care by classification societies to cargo owners is recognised in this case, it must have a substantial impact on international trade. In his article Mr Cane described the likely effect of imposing such a duty of care as follows ([1994] LMCLQ 363 at 375): 'Societies would be forced to buy appropriate liability insurance unless they could bargain with ship owners for an indemnity. To the extent that societies were successful in securing indemnities from ship owners in respect of loss suffered by cargo owners, the limitation of the liability of ship owners to cargo owners under the Hague–Visby Rules would effectively be destroyed. Ship owners would need to increase their insurance cover in respect of losses suffered by cargo owners, but at the same time, cargo owners would still need to insure against losses above the Hague-Visby recovery limit which did not result from actionable negligence on the part of a classification society. At least if classification societies are immune from non-contractual liability, they can confidently go without insurance in respect of third-party losses, leaving third parties to insure themselves in respect of losses for which they could not recover from ship owners.'

Counsel for the cargo owners challenged this analysis. On instructions he said that classification societies already carry liability risks insurance. This is no doubt right, since classification societies do not have a blanket immunity from all tortious liability. On the other hand, if a duty of care is held to exist in this case, the potential exposure of classification societies to claims by cargo owners will be large. That greater exposure is likely to lead to an increase in the cost to classification societies of obtaining appropriate liability risks insurance. Given their role in maritime trade, classification societies are likely to seek to pass on the higher cost to owners. Moreover, it is readily predictable that classification societies will require ship owners to give appropriate indemnities. Ultimately, ship owners will pay.

The result of a recognition of a duty of care in this case will be to enable cargo owners, or rather their insurers, to disturb the balance created by the Hague Rules and the Hague (Visby) Rules as well as by tonnage limitation provisions, by enabling cargo owners to recover in tort against a peripheral party to the prejudice of the protection of ship owners under the existing system. For these reasons I would hold that the international trade system tends to militate against the recognition of the claim in tort put forward by the cargo owners against the classification society.

(d) The contract between the classification society and ship owners

Mr Aikens QC, who appears for NKK, argued that the contract between the ship owners and the classification society must be a factor against the recognition of the suggested duty of care. He referred to *Pacific Associates Inc v Baxter* [1989] 2 All ER 159, [1990] 1 QB 993. That was a case where the Court of Appeal held that the network of contracts between a building owner, the head contractor, subcontractors and even suppliers militated against imposing duties in tort on peripheral parties. In the present case the classification society was not involved in such a web of contracts.

(e) The position and role of NKK

The fact that a defendant acts for the collective welfare is a matter to be taken into consideration when considering whether it is fair, just and reasonable to impose a duty of care. ... Even if such a body has no general immunity from liability in tort, the question may arise whether it owes a duty of care to aggrieved persons and, if so, in what classes of case, eg only in cases involving the direct infliction of physical harm or on a wider basis ... one would not describe classification societies as carrying on quasi-judicial functions. But it is still the case that (apart from their statutory duties) they act in the public interest. The reality is simply, that NKK ... is an independent and non-profit-making entity, created and operating for the sole purpose of promoting collective welfare, namely the safety of lives and ships at sea. In common with other classification societies, NKK fulfils a role which, in its absence, would have to be fulfilled by states. And the question is whether NKK, and other classification societies, would be able to carry out their functions as efficiently if they become the ready alternative target of cargo owners, who already have contractual claims against ship owners. In my judgment there must be some apprehension that the classification societies would adopt, to the detriment of their traditional role, a more defensive position.

(f) Policy factors

Counsel for the cargo owners argued that a decision that a duty of care existed in this case would not involve wide ranging exposure for NKK and other classification societies to claims in tort. That is an unrealistic position. If a duty is recognised in this case there is no reason why it should not extend to annual surveys, docking surveys, intermediate surveys, special surveys, boiler surveys, and so forth. And the scale of NKK's potential liability is shown by the fact that NKK conducted an average of 14,500 surveys per year over the last five years.

> At present the system of settling cargo claims against ship owners is a relatively simple one. The claims are settled between the two sets of insurers. If the claims are not settled, they are resolved in arbitration or court proceedings. If a duty is held to exist in this case as between the classification society and cargo owners, classification societies would become potential defendants in many cases. An extra layer of insurance would become involved. The settlement process would inevitably become more complicated and expensive. Arbitration proceedings and court proceedings would often involve an additional party. And often similar issues would have to be canvassed in separate proceedings since classification societies would not be bound by arbitration clauses in the contracts of carriage. If such a duty is recognised, there is a risk that classification societies might be unwilling from time to time to survey the very vessels which most urgently require independent examination. It will also divert men and resources from the prime function of classification societies, namely to save life and ships at sea. These factors are, by themselves, far from decisive. But in an overall assessment of the case they merit consideration.
>
> *Is the imposition of a duty of care fair, just and reasonable?*
>
> ... I am willing to assume (without deciding) that there was a sufficient degree of proximity in this case to fulfil that requirement for the existence of a duty of care. The critical question is whether it would be fair, just and reasonable to impose such a duty. For my part I am satisfied that the factors and arguments advanced on behalf of cargo owners are decisively outweighed by the cumulative effect, if a duty is recognised, of the matters discussed in paras (c), (e) and (f), ie the outflanking of the bargain between ship owners and cargo owners, the negative effect on the public role of NKK and the other considerations of policy. By way of summary, I look at the matter from the point of view of the three parties concerned. I conclude that the recognition of a duty would be unfair, unjust and unreasonable as against the ship owners who would ultimately have to bear the cost of holding classification societies liable, such consequence being at variance with the bargain between ship owners and cargo owners based on an internationally agreed contractual structure. It would also be unfair, unjust and unreasonable towards classification societies, notably because they act for the collective welfare and, unlike ship owners, they would not have the benefit of any limitation provisions. Looking at the matter from the point of view of the cargo owners, the existing system provides them with the protection of the Hague Rules or Hague (Visby) Rules. But that protection is limited under such rules and by tonnage limitation provisions. Under the existing system any shortfall is readily insurable. In my judgment the lesser injustice is done by not recognising a duty of care. It follows that I would reject the primary way in which counsel for the cargo owners put his case.
>
> *Assumption of responsibility*
>
> Given that the cargo owners were not even aware of NKK's examination of the ship, and that the cargo owners simply relied on the undertakings of the ship owners, it is in my view impossible to force the present set of facts into even the most expansive view of the doctrine of assumption of responsibility.

It is worth quoting some extracts from the dissenting speech of Lord Lloyd of Berwick in which he pours scorn on some of the arguments advanced above. On the relevance of the Hague Rules he states:

> I have to say that, in my opinion, the Hague Rules have little if anything to do with the case. It is true that the cargo happened to be carried under bills of lading which incorporated the Hague Rules, and that much of the world's sea borne traffic, especially in the liner trades (which this was not), is carried on similar

> terms. But the cargo might just as well have been carried under a charter-party, in common with much of the world's bulk trade. If it had been, then 'the intricate blend of liabilities and responsibilities, rights and immunities' contained in the Hague Rules would have had nothing to say on the matter, for the simple reason that the Hague Rules do not apply to charter-parties (see Article V).
>
> It would make nonsense of the law if a surveyor in the position of Mr Ducat owed a duty of care towards cargo if the contract of carriage were contained in a charter-party, which does not incorporate the Hague Rules, but not if it were contained in a bill of lading, which does. ...
>
> Then it is said that, if claims such as the present became at all frequent, the classification societies might seek to pass on the cost of insurance to ship owners ... there was no evidence one way or the other as to the cost of the insurance, or whether it would be passed on. It is mere guesswork. But having regard to the prevailing competition among classification societies, it by means follows that the cost of insurance would be passed on to ship owners; and even if it was, I doubt if it would be a significant factor in upsetting the balance of rights and liabilities under the Hague Rules. ...
>
> I am unable to see why the existence of the contract of carriage should 'militate against' a duty of care being owed by a third party in tort. The function of the law of tort is not limited to filling in gaps left by the law of contract, as this House has recently reaffirmed in *Henderson v Merrett Syndicates Ltd* [1994] 3 All ER 506 at 531, [1994] 3 WLR 761 at 787 *per* Lord Goff of Chievley. The House rejected an approach which treated the law of tort as supplementary to the law of contract, ie as providing for a tortious remedy only where there is no contract. On the contrary, the law of tort is the general law out of which parties may, if they can, contract.

On the issue of proximity, after discussing that between the surveyor and the crew and deciding that there was a sufficient relationship of proximity between them, he continued:

> What about the cargo? In some ways the relationship between Mr Ducat and the cargo was even closer. For it is a universal rule of maritime law – certainly it is the law of England – that ship and cargo are regarded as taking part in a joint venture. This is the basis on which the whole law of general average rests. ... To my mind the necessary element of proximity was not only present, but established beyond any peradventure. I would only add at this point that, if concern is felt that a decision in favour of the cargo owners would open a wide field of liability, I would reply 'not so'. There is an obvious, sensible and readily defensible line between the surveyor in the present case, where the cargo was on board and the joint venture was in peril, and a surveyor called in to carry out a periodic survey.

His Lordship was no more impressed with the argument concerning the status and role of the classification society. He went on:

> ... it was pointed out that classification societies are charitable non-profit making organisations, promoting the collective welfare and fulfilling a public role. But why should this make a difference? Remedies in the law of tort are not discretionary. Hospitals are also charitable non-profit making organisations. But they are subject to the same common duty of care under the Occupiers' Liability Acts 1957 and 1984 as betting shops and brothels.

On the insurance front again, he said:

> I agree with Bingham LJ and Taylor LJ, that the court should be wary of expressing any view on the insurance position without any evidence on the point, and should not speculate as to the effect, if any, of an extra layer of insurance on the cost of settling claims. For what it may be worth, I would for my part doubt whether it would make much difference.

In his conclusion, he continued:

> The concept of proximity, and the requirement that it should be fair, just and reasonable to impose a duty of care on the defendant in the particular circumstances of the case, have been developed as a means of containing liability for pure economic loss under the principles stated in *Donoghue v Stevenson*. At the same time, and by a parallel movement in the opposite direction, the House has, in two recent decisions, reaffirmed liability for economic loss based on the principle of assumption of responsibility as expounded by the House in *Hedley Byrne & Co Ltd v Heller & Partners Ltd*. None of these difficulties arise in the present case. We are not asked to extend the law of negligence into a new field. We are not even asked to make an incremental advance. All that is required is a straightforward application of *Donoghue v Stevenson*. ... Where the facts cry out for the imposition of a duty of care between the parties as they do here, it would require an exceptional case to refuse to impose a duty on the ground that it would not be fair, just and reasonable. Otherwise there is a risk that the law of negligence will disintegrate into a series of isolated decisions without any coherent principles at all, and the retreat from *Anns* will turn into a rout.

CONCLUSION

It is extremely hard to summarise such an extensive and complex chapter as this. The task is even harder in the light of the more recent case on economic loss into which we have briefly dipped. There is much merit in Lord Lloyd's concluding comments above. The law on liability for economic loss would seem to be a conceptual morass. The post-*Anns* attack was led principally through the medium of the economic loss cases by Lord Keith in the main, but ably supported by Lords Brandon and Bridge, both of whom no longer sit. Lord Keith is in the minority for the most part nowadays. Nonetheless, the picture, as clouded by the this most recent decision, is one of to-ing and fro-ing, presenting an extremely bewildering scene to all concerned. The doctrinal tidiness of *Hedley Byrne* has been disturbed by Lord Goff's recent attempts to revive the almost moribund test of 'assumption of responsibility'. The *Rich* case seems to take us two steps back. The discussion and the litigation is sure to continue.

CHAPTER 7

OCCUPIER'S LIABILITY

INTRODUCTION

The subject to be explored in this chapter is the liability of occupiers to visitors, whether lawful or not. The liability is based on fault and is considered to be a species of negligence, although it is now on a statutory footing both in relation to lawful visitors and to trespassers. Before the Occupiers' Liability Act 1957, this area was regulated by the common law. It was considered that the common law had created a number of difficulties which could only be resolved by statute, hence the 1957 Act. The main difficulty concerned the apparent fluctuation in the standard of care expected by the occupier depending on the precise status of the entrant onto the premises.

Briefly, the law differentiated between contractual entrants, invitees, licensees and trespassers. The latter were considered to be beyond the pale, being owed a minimal duty. The other three categories were regarded as lawful entrants, but it seems that they were treated somewhat differently when it came to the standard of care owed. The major difficulties arose at the divide between invitees and licensee on the one hand, and licensees and trespassers on the other. An invitee was owed a duty of reasonable care whereas the licensee was owed a duty to warn of danger and concealed traps of which the occupier was aware. Trespassers were owed very little at all.

Case law at the margins of these divides resulted in artificial distinctions such as the implied licence in favour of children 'allured' onto premises by machinery or other attractive objects, thus allowing the courts to treat them as lawful entrants as opposed to trespassers. Other cases involved convoluted discussions about whether the entrant was an invitee or licensee, and again courts often strained the meaning of these categories to obtain a higher standard of care for the plaintiff. Broadly, an invitee was thought to be a person who came onto the relevant premises with a purpose in common with the occupier. A licensee, on the other hand, was a person who merely had permission, express or implied, to be on the premises.

There was also a further problem concerning the difference between what is called the 'occupancy' duty and the 'activity' duty. The former is concerned with the static condition of the premises whereas the latter relates to the activities carried on there. Whether this difference was one of substance rather than one purely of description is not too clear.

These problems were perceived as necessitating reform which resulted in the introduction of the Occupiers' Liability Act 1957, although we had to wait almost a further 30 years for reform in relation to the trespasser, in the shape of the Occupiers' Liability Act 1984. As the names of the Acts suggest, the liability in issue is that of the occupier of premises, although as we shall see the word 'occupier' is widely interpreted. We shall consider first of all liability to lawful visitors followed by the position in relation to trespassers.

LIABILITY TO LAWFUL VISITORS

Section 1 of the 1957 Act provides as follows:

(1) The rules enacted by the two next following sections shall have effect, in place of the rules of the common law, to regulate the duty which an occupier of premises owes to his visitors in respect of dangers due to the state of the premises or to things done or omitted to be done on them.

(2) The rules so enacted shall regulate the nature of the duty imposed by law in consequence of a person's occupation or control of premises and of any invitation or permission he gives (or is to be treated as giving) to another to enter or use the premises, but they shall not alter the rules of the common law as to the persons on whom a duty is so imposed or to whom it is owed; and accordingly for the purpose of the rules so enacted the persons who are to be treated as an occupier and as his visitors are the same (subject to subsection (4) of this section) as the persons who would at common law be treated as an occupier and as his invitees or licensees.

(3) The rules so enacted in relation to an occupier of premises and his visitors shall also apply, in like manner and to the like extent as the principles applicable at common law to an occupier of premises and his invitees or licensees would apply, to regulate:

(a) the obligations of a person occupying or having control over any fixed or moveable structure, including any vessel, vehicle or aircraft; and

(b) the obligations of a person occupying or having control over any premises or structure in respect of damage to property, including the property of persons who are not themselves his visitors.

(4) A person entering any premises in exercise of rights conferred by virtue of an access agreement or under the National Parks and Access to the Countryside Act 1949, is not, for the purposes of this Act, a visitor of the occupier of those premises.

The important point to note is that the Act was not intended to affect the meaning given to 'occupier' at common law, and it is therefore necessary to consider the cases as to the interpretation of this word in the absence of a statutory definition.

Who is an occupier?

The leading case on this issue is *Wheat v E Lacon & Co Ltd*,[1] where the husband of the plaintiff fell down the back staircase of an inn where he was a lodger. The hand rail was short and also there was no light bulb in the fitting at the top of the stairs. The respondents owned the inn and employed a manager who lived on the premises and who had permission to take in lodgers. It was held that there was no breach of duty by anyone, but one of the central issues was: who was the occupier of the premises, the respondents or the manager? Lord Denning once again was at the forefront:

> In the Occupiers' Liability Act, 1957, the word 'occupier' is used in the same sense as it was used in the common law cases on occupiers' liability for dangerous premises. It was simply a convenient word to denote a person who

1 [1966] 1 All ER 582.

had a sufficient degree of control over premises to put him under a duty of care towards those who come lawfully on to the premises. Those persons were divided into two categories, invitees and licensees, and a higher duty was owed to invitees than to licensees; but by the year 1956 the distinction between invitees and licensees had been reduced to vanishing point. The duty of the occupier had become simply a duty to take reasonable care to see that the premises were reasonably safe for people coming lawfully on to them, and it made no difference whether they were invitees or licensees. ... The Act of 1957 confirmed the process. It did away, once and for all, with invitees and licensees and classed them all as 'visitors', and it put on the occupier the same duty to all of them, namely the common duty of care. This duty is simply a particular instance of the general duty of care, which each man owes to his 'neighbour'. ...

Translating this general principle into its particular application to dangerous premises, it becomes simply this: wherever a person has a sufficient degree of control over premises that he ought to realise that any failure on his part to use care may result in injury to a person coming lawfully there, then he is an 'occupier' and the person coming lawfully there is his 'visitor'; and the 'occupier' is under a duty to his 'visitor' to use reasonable care. In order to be an 'occupier' it is not necessary for a person to have entire control over the premises. He need not have exclusive occupation. Suffice it that he has some degree of control. He may share control with others – two or more may be 'occupiers' – and whenever this happens, each is under a duty to use care towards persons coming lawfully on to the premises, dependent on his degree of control. If each fails in his duty, each is liable to a visitor who is injured in consequence of his failure, but each may claim to contribution from the other.

In *Salmond on Torts* (14th edn, 1965) p 372, it is said that an 'occupier' is 'he who has the immediate supervision and control and the power of permitting or prohibiting the entry of other persons'. This definition was adopted ... by Diplock J in the present case ([1965] 2 All ER at p 711). There is no doubt that a person who fulfils that test is an 'occupier'. He is the person who says 'come in'; but I think that that test is too narrow by far; there are other people who are 'occupiers', even though they do not say 'come in'. If a person has any degree of control over the state of the premises it is enough. The position is best shown by examining the cases in four groups.

Firstly, where a landlord let premises by demise to a tenant, he was regarded as parting with all control over them. He did not retain any degree of control, even though he had undertaken to repair the structure. Accordingly, he was held to be under no duty to any person lawfully coming on to the premises, save only to the tenant under the agreement to repair. In *Cavalier v Pope* ([1906] AC 428) it was argued that the premises were under the control of the landlord because of his agreement to repair; but the House of Lords rejected that argument. That case has now been overruled by s 4 of the Act of 1957[2] to the extent therein mentioned.

Secondly, where an owner let floors or flats in a building to tenants, but did not demise the common staircase or the roof or some other parts, he was regarded as having retained control of all parts not demised by him. Accordingly, he was held to be under a duty in respect of those retained parts to all persons coming lawfully on to the premises ... the old cases still apply so as to show that the landlord is responsible for all parts not demised by him, on the ground that he is

2 See now s 4 Defective Premises Act 1972, *post*.

regarded as being sufficiently in control of them to impose on him a duty of care to all persons lawfully coming on to the premises.

Thirdly, where an owner did not let premises to a tenant but only licensed a person to occupy them on terms which did not amount to a demise, the owner still having the right to do repairs, he was regarded as being sufficiently in control of the structure to impose on him a duty towards all persons coming lawfully on to the premises. ...

Fourthly, where an owner employed an independent contractor to do work on premises or a structure, the owner was usually still regarded as sufficiently in control of the place as to be under a duty towards all those who might lawfully come there. ... But in addition to the owner, the courts regarded the independent contractor as himself being sufficiently in control of the place where he worked as to owe a duty of care towards all persons coming lawfully there. He was said to be an 'occupier' also. ...

In the light of these cases, I ask myself whether the respondents had a sufficient degree of control over the premises to put them under a duty to a visitor. Obviously they had complete control over the ground floor and were 'occupiers' of it. But I think that they had also sufficient control over the private portion. They had not let it out to Mr Richardson [the manager] by a demise. They had only granted him a licence to occupy it, having a right themselves to do repairs. That left them with a residuary degree of control. ... They were, in my opinion, 'an occupier' within the Act of 1957. Mr Richardson, who had a licence to occupy, had also a considerable degree of control. So had Mrs Richardson, who catered for summer guests. All three of them were, in my opinion, 'occupiers' of the private portion of the *Golfer's Arms*. There is no difficulty in having more than one occupier at one and the same time, each of whom is under a duty of care to visitors. ...

Lord Morris in the same case observed:

Section 1(1) of the Act of 1957 speaks of 'an occupier of premises'. Section 1(2) refers to a 'person's occupation or control of premises'; it goes on to refer to 'any invitation or permission he gives (or is to be treated as giving) to another to enter or use the premises'. This, I think, shows that exclusive occupation is not necessary to constitute a person an occupier. ...

This brings me to the question whether the respondents to this appeal were in occupation or control. The Richardsons were not made parties to the appeal and are not before your Lordships. No question as to their liability calls for investigation. It is impossible, however, to avoid considering how they, as well as the respondents, stood in regard to occupation or control. Much turns on the facts and also on the effect of the agreement of 3 April 1951. That was a service agreement. The respondents were called 'employers'. Mr Richardson was being employed as 'the manager' of the public house called the *Golfer's Arms*. He was being employed on the terms and conditions of the agreement. He was to devote all his time (except for holiday periods) to managing the business. ... The general result of the agreement and of the arrangements to which I have referred was that the respondents through their servant were in occupation of the whole premises. Their servant was required to be there. The contemplation, it would appear, was that the respondents would see to the condition of the premises and would effect any necessary repairs. As the residential part would constitute the home of the manager and his family it was a reasonable inference, and it would be mutually assumed that his privacy in regard to it would be respected. It would be mutually assumed that the respondents could not, as of right, enter that part save for the defined purpose of viewing its condition and state or repair. There was freedom for the manager or his wife to make contracts with and to receive and entertain visitors for reward.

The conclusion which I reach is that as regards the premises as a whole both the respondents and the manager were occupiers, but that by mutual arrangement the respondents would not (subject to certain overriding consideration) exercise control over some parts. They gave freedom to their manager to live in his home in privacy. They gave him freedom to furnish it as and how he chose. They gave him freedom to receive personal guests and also to receive guests for reward. I think it follows that both the respondents and the Richardsons were 'occupiers' *vis-à-vis* Mr Wheat and his party. Both the respondents and the Richardsons owed Mr Wheat and his party a duty. The duty was the common duty of care.

Lord Pearce commented:

It seems clear to me that Mr and Mrs Richardson had at least some occupational control of the upper part of the premises to which the appeal relates. They lived there; they provided the furniture. They, for their own benefit, took in paying guests and received them and looked after them. The paying guests would have been invitees at common law, and were visitors under the Act of 1957. Moreover, Mr and Mrs Richardson were present and able to see the state of the premises and what was being done or omitted therein. If anything was wrong, they could take steps to rectify it or have it rectified. If there was any danger, they could protect the paying guests by erecting a barrier or giving a warning or otherwise. Mr and Mrs Richardson were appropriate persons for bearing and fulfilling the common duty of care. ...

I think that the respondents, however, also had some occupational control of the upper part of the premises. The lower part, the licensed part, was occupied by the respondents through their servant, Mr Richardson, and their agent, Mrs Richardson, for the purpose of the liquor-selling business of the respondents. The agreement applied to the whole of the premises without distinguishing between the two parts. Mr Richardson, as manager for the respondents, was required as well as entitled to occupy the whole of the premises on their behalf. He was required to live in the upper part for the better performance of his duties as manager of the business of the respondents. His right to live there, and the permission to take in paying guests, were perquisites of the employment. The paying guests, though invited by the Richardsons, had the respondents' permission to come and were therefore visitors of the respondents as well as of the Richardsons. The fact that the respondents gave permission for the Richardsons to take in paying guests is important as showing that the respondents had some control over the admission of persons to the upper part of the premises. The respondents did not themselves say 'come in', but they authorised the Richardsons to say 'come in'. The respondents had, under clause 5 of the agreement, an express right to enter the premises for viewing the state of repair, and, as was conceded (correctly in my opinion), an implied right to do the repairs found to be necessary. It is fair to attribute to the respondents some responsibility for the safety of the premises for those who would, in pursuance of the authority given by the respondents, be invited to enter as paying guests the upper part of the premises. In matters relating to the design and condition of the structure they would be in a position to perform the common duty of care.

For these reasons I agree that there was, for the purpose of occupiers' liability, dual occupation of the upper part of the premises.

There are a number of observations following from the above discussion. Firstly, the case of *Fairman v Perpetual Investment Building Society*[3] shows that a landlord, by retaining control over the entrance and common stairway in a block of flats or offices, is regarded as the occupier of those parts. Secondly, using the sufficient degree of control test, it is clear that an independent contractor may be regarded as an occupier whilst working on the premises or parts of premises belonging to his employer. Indeed, there may be circumstances where the contractor is to be regarded as the sole occupier of the premises in a situation where even the owner of the premises is prevented from entering them whilst the occupier is in possession. Thirdly, it is evident that premises may be regarded as being in dual occupation for the purposes of the 1957 Act. Each occupier may have his own areas of control on the one set of premises, as in *Wheat*'s case itself. Fourthly, a landlord may have sole responsibility with regard to premises retained or for defects arising from his failure to repair. Section 4 Defective Premises Act 1972 states as follows:

(1) Where premises are let under a tenancy which puts on the landlord an obligation to the tenant for the maintenance or repair of the premises, the landlord owes to all persons who might reasonably be expected to be affected by defects in the state of the premises a duty to take such care as is reasonable in all the circumstances to see that they are reasonably safe from personal injury or from damage to their property caused by a relevant defect.

(2) The said duty is owed if the landlord knows (whether as the result of being notified by the tenant or otherwise), or if he ought in all the circumstances to have known, of the relevant defect.

(3) In this section 'relevant defect' means a defect in the state of the premises existing at or after the material time and arising from, or continuing because of, an act or omission by the landlord which constitutes or would if he had had notice of the defect, have constituted a failure by him to carry out his obligations to the tenant for the maintenance or repair of the premises; and for the purposes of the foregoing provision 'the material time' means:

(a) where the tenancy commenced before this Act, the commencement of this Act; and

(b) in all other cases, the earliest of the following times, that is to say:

(i) the time when the tenancy commences;

(ii) the time when the tenancy agreement is entered into; and

(iii) the time when possession is taken of the premises in contemplation of the letting.

(4) Where premises are let under a tenancy which expressly or impliedly gives the landlord the right to enter the premises to carry out any description of maintenance or repair of the premises, then, as from the time when he first is, or by notice or otherwise can put himself, in a position to exercise the right and so long as he is or can put himself in that position, he shall be treated for the purposes of subsections (1) to (3) above (but for no other purpose) as if he were under an obligation to the tenant for that description of maintenance or repair of the premises; but the landlord shall not owe the tenant any duty by virtue of this subsection in respect of any defect in the state of the premises

---

3 [1923] AC 74.

arising from, or continuing because of, a failure to carry out an obligation expressly imposed on the tenant by the tenancy.

(5) For the purposes of this section obligations imposed or rights given by any enactment in virtue of a tenancy shall be treated as imposed or given by the tenancy.

(6) This section applies to a right of occupation given by contract or any enactment and not amounting to a tenancy as if the right were a tenancy, and 'tenancy' and cognate expressions shall be construed accordingly.

The above section repeals s 4 of the 1957 Act referred to in the speech of Lord Denning in *Wheat*'s case above.

Who is a lawful visitor?

As we have seen, the Act has nothing to offer by way of definition of 'lawful visitor', and s 1(2) merely indicates that those who were invitees and licensees at common law were to be regarded as lawful visitors, as well as those entitled by contract to enter the premises. Since the 1957 Act the focus of attention has moved from the distinction between invitees and licensees on to that between lawful visitors and trespassers. We have seen that the implied license technique was often used to circumvent the problem in certain types of case, most notably those involving children 'allured' onto premises. There should be less need to resort to such artificiality following the enactment of the 1984 Act. More of that later.

It should be noted that there is still a tendency, just occasionally, for judges to talk in terms of invitees and licensees, but once the plaintiff is found to fall into the one or other category, nothing is supposed to turn on the distinction. They are to be regarded as lawful visitors just the same and are owed the common duty of care. Trespassers apart, there seems to be one other situation where the plaintiff is not owed a duty under the 1957 Act. The point was raised in *McGeown v Northern Ireland Housing Executive*[4] where the appellant, a tenant on a housing estate owned by the respondent, tripped in a hole in one of the footpaths crossing the estate and which was a public right of way. Lord Keith, in rejecting her appeal, said:

> The concept of licensee or visitor involves that the person in question has at least the permission of the relevant occupier to be in a particular place. Once a public right of way has been established, there is no question of permission being granted by the owner of the *solum* to those who choose to use it. They do so as of right and not by virtue of any licence or invitation. In the present case the pathway upon which the plaintiff fell had not been adopted by the highway authority, and it was therefore not responsible for the maintenance of it. Adjoining areas had been so adopted, in particular the strip of ground immediately adjoining the terrace where the plaintiff and her husband lived, and which she had to cross in order to get to or from his house. If the plaintiff was the licensee of the defendants upon the pathway where she fell she was equally their licensee upon that strip of ground. The circumstance that the highway authority was responsible under public law for its maintenance cannot logically make any difference to the position. The defendants would still owe a personal duty to the

4 [1994] 3 All ER 53.

> plaintiff to maintain the pathway in a reasonably safe condition, and be liable to her if she suffered injury owing to the area not being in such condition. That unreasonable result can be avoided if it is held that dedication as a public highway puts an end to any duty which might otherwise be owed by the housing executive.

Lord Browne-Wilkinson was the only member of the House who expressed any reservations about the consequences of the decision thus:

> To my mind it would be unfortunate if, as a result of the decision in this case, the owner of a railway bridge could, by expressly dedicating the land as a public highway or submitting to long public user, free himself from all liability to users whose presence he had encouraged. Who, other than the occupier, is to maintain these artificial structures and protect from injury those encouraged to use them by the occupier for the occupier's own business reasons?
>
> For these reasons, I am very reluctant to reach a conclusion which will leave unprotected those who, for purposes linked to the business of the owners of the soil, are encouraged, expressly or impliedly, to use facilities which the owner has provided.
>
> In the present case, I can see no escape from the logic of Lord Keith's conclusion that, after presumed dedication of the pathway as a public right of way, the housing executive ceased to owe any duty of care to the plaintiff. ...
>
> But it does not necessarily follow that the existence of a public right of way is incompatible with the owner of the soil owing a duty of care to an invitee, as opposed to a licensee. In the case of an invitee there is no logical inconsistency between the plaintiff's right to be on the premises in exercise of the right of way and his actual presence there in response to the express or implied invitation of the occupier. It is the invitation which gives rise to the occupier's duty of care to an invitee. I do not understand your Lordships to be deciding that it is impossible to be an invitee (and therefore a visitor) on land over which there is a public right of way. I wish expressly to reserve my view on that point.

Whilst it is possible to agree with the view expressed above, His Lordship's attempt to resurrect the distinction between invitees and licensees is not welcome. This approach may give rise to nice points of distinction once again. If the plaintiff is merely taking a short cut through a shopping mall or just sheltering there from the weather, is she to be treated differently from the shopper who sustains injury whilst on the premises?

It has also been held that a person using a private right of way is not owed a duty under the 1957 Act,[5] as such a person is not to be treated as a visitor. However, as we shall see, such a person, unlike the user of a public right of way, may be able to take advantage of the provisions in the 1984 Act. One further point is that, by s 2(6) of the 1957 Act, it is provided that:

> For the purposes of this section, persons who enter premises for any purpose in the exercise of a right conferred by law are to be treated as permitted by the occupier to be there for that purpose, whether they in fact have his permission or not.

This will cover the police, emergency services such as fire or ambulance crews and other statutory regulators.

5 *Holden v White* [1982] 2 All ER 328.

THE COMMON DUTY OF CARE

Section 2 of the 1957 Act reads as follows:

(1) An occupier of premises owes the same duty, the 'common duty of care', to all his visitors, except in so far as he is free to and does extend, restrict, modify or exclude his duty to any visitor or visitors by agreement or otherwise.

(2) The common duty of care is a duty to take such care as in all the circumstances of the case is reasonable to see that the visitor will be reasonably safe in using the premises for the purposes for which he is invited or permitted by the occupier to be there.

(3) The circumstances relevant for the present purpose include the degree of care, and of want of care, which would ordinarily be looked for in such a visitor, so that (for example) in proper cases:

(a) an occupier must be prepared for children to be less careful than adults; and

(b) an occupier may expect that a person, in the exercise of his calling, will appreciate and guard against any special risks ordinarily incident to it, so far as the occupier leaves him free to do so.

(4) In determining whether the occupier of premises has discharged the common duty of care to a visitor, regard is to be had to all the circumstances, so that (for example):

(a) where damage is caused to a visitor by a danger of which he had been warned by the occupier, the warning is not to be treated without more as absolving the occupier from liability, unless in all the circumstances it was enough to enable the visitor to be reasonably safe; and

(b) where damage is caused to a visitor by a danger due to faulty execution of any work of construction, maintenance or repair by an independent contractor employed by the occupier, the occupier is not to be treated without more as answerable for the danger if, in all the circumstances he had acted reasonably in entrusting the work to an independent contractor and had taken such steps (if any) as he reasonably ought in order to satisfy himself that the contractor was competent and that the work had been properly done.

(5) The common duty of care does not impose on an occupier any obligation to a visitor in respect of risks willingly accepted as his by the visitor (the question whether a risk was so accepted to be decided on the same principles as in other cases in which one person owes a duty of care to another).

Where there is more than one occupier, the specific duties will be related to those matters over which the respective occupiers are deemed to have a sufficient degree of control. For example, in *Wheat v Lacon* Lord Denning expressed this as follows:

> What did the common duty of care demand of each of these occupiers towards their visitors? Each was under a duty to take such care as 'in all the circumstances of the case' was reasonable to see that the visitor would be reasonably safe. So far as the respondents were concerned, the circumstances demanded that on the ground floor they should, by their servants, take care not only of the structure of the building, but also the furniture, the state of the floors and lighting, and so forth, at all hours of day or night when the premises were open. With regard to the private portion, however, the circumstances did not

demand so much of the respondents. They ought to have seen that the structure was reasonably safe, including the handrail, and that the system of lighting was efficient; but I doubt whether they were bound to see that the lights were properly switched on or the rugs laid safely on the floor The respondents were entitled to leave those day-to-day matters to Mr and Mrs Richardson. They, too, were occupiers. The circumstances of the case demanded that Mr and Mrs Richardson should take care of those matters in the private portion of the house. And of other matters, too. If they had realised that the handrail was dangerous, they should have reported it to the respondents. ... So far as the handrail was concerned, the evidence was overwhelming that no-one had any reason before this accident to suppose that it was in the least dangerous. So far as the light was concerned, the proper inference was that it was removed by some stranger shortly before Mr Wheat went down the staircase. Neither the respondents nor Mr and Mrs Richardson could be blamed for the act of a stranger.

On the issue of breach, Lord Morris commented:

The 'circumstances of the case' would, however, vary as between the respondents and the Richardsons. Thus, if after Mr Wheat and his party had arrived they had been ascending the main staircase, and, if it had collapsed and caused them injury, a question would have arisen whether either the respondents or the Richardsons or any or all of them had been lacking in their duty. 'The circumstances of the case' in such a situation would have, or might have, been quite different so far as the respondents were concerned from what they would have been so far as the Richardsons were concerned. If, to take another possibility, the Wheats had entered a living room of the Richardsons which had been fitted and equipped by the Richardsons and had suffered some mishap, which arose from the state or condition of the equipment or furnishings, 'the circumstances of the case' would have been, or might have been, quite different so far as the Richardsons were concerned from the circumstances as far as the respondents were concerned.

In the illustrations to which I have referred, it might or could be that there would be some failure on the part of the respondents to take care in regard to the staircase and no failure on the part of the Richardsons; so it might be or could be that there would be some failure on the part of the Richardsons in regard to some equipment or furnishing in a living room and no failure on the part of the respondents.

It may, therefore, often be that the extent of the particular control which is exercised within the sphere of joint occupation will become a pointer as to the nature and extent of the duty which reasonably devolves on a particular occupier. Did they (the respondents) negligently provide a staircase which it would be unsafe to use? I cannot think that they did. In daylight the staircase was quite safe to use. In the period of 20 years before the day Mr Wheat fell there had been no accident on the stairs. In darkness the means of illumination was provided. I cannot think that there was a failure to take reasonable care on the part of the respondents. I do not consider that they were negligent in failing to contemplate and to eliminate the possibility that someone unfamiliar with the stairs might use them in the dark or when a light was not available and might, on the assumption that the end of the handrail marked the reaching of the lowest stair, take a step onwards without feeling or testing whether such an assumption was correct.

Lord Pearce commented:

The safety of premises may depend on the acts or omissions of more than one person, each of whom may have a different right to cause or continue the state of

> affairs which creates the danger, and on each a duty of care may lie; but where separate persons are each under a duty of care the acts or omissions which would constitute a breach of that duty may vary very greatly. That which would be negligent in one may well be free from blame in the other. If the Richardsons had a dangerous hole in the carpet which they chose to put down in their sitting room, that would be negligent in them towards a visitor who was injured by it; but the respondents could fairly say that they took no interest in the Richardsons' private furnishings and that no reasonable person in their position would have noticed, or known of, or taken any steps with regard to the dangerous defect. If the construction of the staircase was unsafe, that would be negligence on the respondents' part. Whether the Richardsons would also be negligent in not warning their visitors or taking steps to reveal the danger would depend on whether a reasonable person in their position would have done so. ... In the present case the respondents are not shown to have failed in their duty of care.

Reasonable care is not an absolute guarantee of safety and there is no need for the occupier to guard against highly improbable risks. Factors to be considered will be the nature of the danger, how long it has been there and its extent, the cost and practicability of steps required to avoid the danger and the probability of injury, seriousness of the harm and so on. It must be remembered that this is still a negligence action and many of the general features involved in the assessment of the breach of duty are relevant here.

In *Sawyer v Simonds*[6] the plaintiff was injured when he fell off a bar stool in a bar belonging to the defendants. He cut his hand on some broken glass lying on the floor. The High Court judge said:

> This [the common duty of care] did not extend to the duty of *insuring* the safety of the visitor. Of course it was dangerous to allow broken glass to lie about anywhere where the public came and went. Of course broken glass should be cleared up as soon as possible. But one could not clear up broken glass unless one knew that broken glass was there to be cleared.
>
> The occupier was therefore under a duty to keep a reasonable look-out for this type of danger. The accident had occurred at a busy time in the lunch hour on a Saturday. It was the duty of the hall porter to come in every 20 minutes to clear empty glasses, and if he had seen the broken glass on the floor he would have removed it. 'Reasonable care' involved consideration of the nature of the danger, the length of time that the danger was in existence, the steps necessary to remove the danger and the likelihood or otherwise of an injury being caused. The mere fact that this unfortunate accident happened did not connote negligence. There was an adequate system in the hotel for looking out for this kind of danger. The danger of falling from a stool in this way was remote. The barman had no knowledge that glass was on the floor.

Variations in the standard of care

By virtue of s 2(3) above, the Act does allow for variation in the standard of care. As far as children are concerned the occupier must take into account that they are likely to be less careful than adults, and consequently what might enable an adult to be reasonably safe may be insufficient in relation to a child.

6 (1966) 197 Est Gaz 877.

This is illustrated by the case of *Moloney v Lambeth London Borough Council*,[7] where a child of under five years of age tripped or slipped on a staircase occupied by the defendants in a block of flats. It appears that he fell through a gap in the balustrade which would not have allowed an adult to pass through in that way. The High Court judge stated:

> There is no doubt on the evidence that the defendant local authority would know, and indeed would expect, that children of four years of age would use this staircase unaccompanied by adults. If this child had been sent down to the flat below on a message, no one would have suggested that he was too small to take something down to or go down on his own to people, to his friends. He did on occasions go down and come up unaccompanied, but the evidence is that he was a rather timid child and tended to cling to his mother; so, very often, when he went up and down, he would be with his mother. His mother said she had told him to use the handrail as he went down and, at his age, he would be using the centre bar for that purpose. When I say 'his age', I mean a person of his size.
>
> There has been produced a photograph of a little girl, on the evidence I think younger than the plaintiff, going down the staircase with great dignity, running her hand down the centre bar and using it as a handrail, demonstrating that one can come down the stairs without falling. Of course one can. But, if a person of the size of this plaintiff did lose his balance in any way going down this staircase, he was liable, in my view, to go through that gap.
>
> Evidence has been adduced to show that, in other places, the designs are such that these gaps exist, and I am quite sure they do. It is not the fact that there is a gap; it is the position of the gap and the size of the gap that is important. Using my own common sense, having heard the evidence and looking at the plan and the photographs, I consider that this staircase did not comply with the occupier's ordinary duty of care owed to a child of the age of the plaintiff.

In *Glasgow Corpn v Taylor*[8] a seven year old boy died after eating some poisonous berries growing in some public gardens under the control of the corporation. In finding for the pursuer, Lord Atkinson observed:

> They did nothing to protect the child, and contend they were not bound to do anything. There is, in my view, no resemblance between this case and those cases where mischievous boys sustain injury by interfering with or misusing natural objects, such as trees in public parks up which they may be tempted to climb, or water, ornamental or other, into which they may accidentally fall or be tempted deliberately to enter. The appearance of such objects as these is well known and unmistakable. There is nothing deceptive or misleading about them. They cannot well be mistaken for things other than, or different from, what they really are. Whereas ... there was in this belladonna plant, with the deadly berries it bore, something in the nature of a trap. The berries looked alluring and as harmless as grapes or cherries. It is averred that the defenders and their agents knew this, and also knew – which the deceased child did not – that the berries were, if eaten, highly poisonous. The defenders were, therefore, aware of the existence of a concealed or disguised danger to which the child might be exposed when he frequented their park, a danger of which he was entirely ignorant, and could not by himself reasonably discover, yet they did nothing to protect him from that danger or even inform him of its existence. ...

7 (1966) 64 LGR 440.

8 [1922] AC 44.

> The liability of defendants in cases of this kind rests, I think, in the last resort upon their knowledge that, by their action, they may bring children of tender years, unable to take care of themselves yet inquisitive and easily tempted, into contact, in a place in which they, the children, have a right to be, with things alluring or tempting to them, and possibly in appearance harmless, but which, unknown to them and well known to the defendants, are hurtful or dangerous if meddled with. I am quite unable to see any difference in principle between placing amongst children a dangerous but tempting machine, of whose parts and action they are ignorant, and growing in the vicinity of their playground a shrub whose fruit is harmless in appearance and alluring, but, in fact, most poisonous. I think, in the latter case, as in the former, the defendant would be bound, by notice or warning or some other adequate means, to protect the children from injury. In this case the averments are that the appellants did nothing of the kind. If that be true, they were, in my view, guilty of negligence, giving the pursuer a right of action.

Lord Shaw of Dunfermline commented:

> The child, having a right to be in these gardens, was, in my opinion, entitled, as were also his parents, to rely upon the gardens being left in a reasonably safe condition. Or, in the language of the Lord Justice-Clerk: 'the playground for the children must be taken as being provided as a place reasonably suitable and safe for children, and I think the parents were entitled so to regard it'. ...
>
> When the danger is familiar and obvious, no special responsibility attaches to the municipality or owner in respect of an accident having occurred to children of tender years. The reason for that appears to me to be this, that the municipality or owner was entitled to take into account that reasonable parents will not permit their children to be sent into the midst of familiar and obvious dangers except under protection or guardianship. The parent or guardian of the child must act reasonably; the municipality or owner of the park must act reasonably. This duty rests upon both and each; but each is entitled to assume it of the other.
>
> Where the dangers are not familiar and obvious, and where in particular they are or ought to be known to the municipality or owner, special considerations arise. In the case of objects, whether artificial, and so to speak, dangerous in themselves, such as loaded guns or explosives, or natural objects, such as trees bearing poisonous fruits which are attractive in appearance, it cannot be considered a reasonably safe procedure for a municipality or owner to permit the exhibition of these things with their dangerous possibilities in a place of recreation and without any special and particular watch and warning. There can be no fault on the part of a parent in relying that such obligations of safety would be duly performed by the municipality or owner; and in allowing his child accordingly to pass into the grounds unattended the parent commits no negligent act. As for the child itself, while it may do things and incur dangers by inquisitively meddling with things it should not touch, it is plain that when the incurred danger – against which no protection or sufficient warning was directed to anybody – produces its unfortunate evil effect, the municipality or owner is answerable for this, and there is no defence of contributory negligence.
>
> I do not find myself able to draw a distinction in law between natural objects such as shrubs, whose attractive fruitage may be injuriously or fatally poisonous, and artificial objects such as machines left in a public place unattended and liable to produce danger if tampered with. The act of tampering might be contributory negligence on the part of a grown-up person, but would not be so reckoned on the part of a child. ... I think that there was fault in having such a shrub where it was without definite warning of its danger and definite protection against the

> danger being incurred. To give such protection was part of the reasonable duty of the corporation, and citizens were entitled to rely upon it having been given.

Whilst the House found in favour of the pursuer in that case, there is clear reference in the last extract to the countervailing principle which may operate in this type of case, namely, the responsibility of parents for the safety of their child. In *Phipps v Rochester Corpn*,[9] a boy aged five years fell into a ditch which had been dug for the purpose of laying a sewer on a new housing estate. Some of the houses were already occupied and it was known by the corporation that children were tending to play in the area where the ditch was. Devlin J, having decided that the boy plaintiff was a licensee, continued:

> On the facts of the present case the plaintiff has, in my judgment, only to reach this stage to succeed, for there is no evidence that the defendants in this case took any steps at all. I have already expressed the view that the instructions which they gave were intended and understood to be confined to the building plots. There is no evidence that any child was ever chased off the open space, and it would seem such a hard measure that I think, if it had been done, it would have been remembered. The fact is that the defendants have already lost this point by staking their case on the contention that there were never any children to chase off. It follows that they never took any steps to show that they resented the invasion. ...
>
> I have not been able to find, in the cases that have been cited to me, any clearly authoritative formulation of the licensor's duty towards little children. I think the cases do show that judges have not allowed themselves to be driven to the conclusion that licensors must make their premises safe for little children; but they have chosen different ways of escape from that conclusion. One way, which can be supported by many *dicta*, is to say bluntly that children, no matter what their age, should get no different treatment from adults. Children must themselves bear the risks attendant of childhood; that is the way the world is made. Another way is to put on the parents the burden of contributory negligence which the child cannot himself bear. A third way is to treat the licence as being conditional on the little child being accompanied by a responsible adult.
>
> ... A fourth way is to frame the duty so as to compromise between the robustness that would make children take the world as they found it, and the tenderness which would give them nurseries wherever they go. On this view the licensor is not entitled to assume that all children will, unless they are allured, behave like adults; but he is entitled to assume that, normally, little children will, in fact, be accompanied by a responsible person and to discharge his duty of warning accordingly. The third and fourth solutions will in most cases produce the same result. They are, however, radically different in law, for in the former the unaccompanied child is a trespasser and in the latter a licensee.

After considering the various authorities, the judge rejected the first two of the possible ways of resolving the issue in the case. He then continued:

> The third principle is that of the conditional licence, and the cases show that there is excellent authority for this. Nevertheless, I think it involves difficulties. It is easy to put a condition into an express licence; the licensor can then word it as he likes. It is not easy to settle the terms of an implied condition. They must, however, be settled with some precision, because on them will turn the question whether a person using the premises is a trespasser or not. He cannot become a

9 [1955] 1 QB 450.

trespasser according to whether he falls into a pit. The law cannot wait to see whether in fact he is circumspect; he must be identifiable as a trespasser so that a legalistic licensor could turn him back at the gate. ...

I respectfully doubt whether the notion of the conditional licence would, if further developed, be found in the end to work satisfactorily. Furthermore, I think that the general principle which governs the relationship between licensors and licensees can be made to work in the case of little children without the employment of any special device. ... A licensor who tacitly permits the public to use his land without discriminating between its members must assume that the public may include little children. But as a general rule he will have discharged his duty towards them if the dangers which they may encounter are only those which are obvious to a guardian or of which he has given a warning comprehensible by a guardian.

To every general rule there are, of course, exceptions. A licensor cannot divest himself of the obligation of finding out something about the sort of people who are availing themselves of his permission and the sort of use they are making of it. He may have to take into account the social habits of the neighbourhood. No doubt, there are places where little children go to play unaccompanied. If the licensor knows or ought to anticipate that, he may have to take steps accordingly. But the responsibility for the safety of little children must rest primarily on the parents; it is their duty to see that such children are not allowed to wander about by themselves, or, at the least, to satisfy themselves that the places to which they do allow their children to go unaccompanied are safe for them to go. It would not be socially desirable if parents were, as a matter of course, able to shift the burden of looking after their children from their own shoulders to those of persons who happen to have accessible bits of land. Different considerations may well apply to public parks or to recognised playing grounds where parents allow their children to go unaccompanied in the reasonable belief that they are safe. ...

If this be the true principle to apply, then I have to consider whether the defendants ought, in this case, to have anticipated the presence of the infant plaintiff unaccompanied. I say 'unaccompanied' because the sister, while doubtless able to take care of herself as is shown by her own avoidance of the trench, was not old enough to take care of her little brother as well. There is no evidence in this case to show that little children frequently went unaccompanied on the open space in a way which ought to have brought home to the defendants that that was the use being made of their licence. Apart from evidence of that sort, I do not think that the defendants ought to have anticipated that it was a place in which children aged five years would be sent out to play by themselves. It is not an overcrowded neighbourhood; it is not as if it were the only green place in the centre of a city. The houses had gardens in which small children could play; if it be material, I believe that at the relevant time the plaintiff's garden was in fact fenced. The parents of children who might be expected to play there all live near and could have made themselves familiar with the space. They must have known that building operations were going on nearby and ought to have realised that that might involve the digging of trenches and holes. Even if it be prudent, which I do not think it is, for a parent to allow two small children out in this way on an October evening, the parents might at least have satisfied themselves that the place to which they allowed these little children to go held no dangers for them. Any parent who looked could have seen the trench and taken steps to prevent his child going there while it was still open. In my judgment, the defendants are entitled to assume that parents would behave in this naturally prudent way, and are not obliged to take it on themselves, in effect, to discharge parental duties. I conclude, therefore, that the infant plaintiff was on the land as a licensee, but that there was no breach of the defendants' duty towards him.

It should be remembered that the case preceded the enactment of the 1957 Act, and references to the duty of the defendants as licensors and the standard of care demanded must be read in the light of that fact. However, the point made by the judge on the duty of parents, although a harsh judgment in that particular case, is nonetheless valid in relation to post-Act cases. There has to be a balance struck between the respective responsibilities of occupiers and parents, not always so easy to achieve.

Another example is provided by the case of *Simkiss v Rhondda Borough Council*,[10] where the infant plaintiff was having a picnic with a friend. It appears that the plaintiff was sliding down a slope on a blanket and lost control going down the steep slope and fell into the road. After discussing the relevant case law, and in allowing the appeal of the defendants, Dunn LJ commented:

> It appears from his judgment that the judge was influenced by the fact that the borough council called no evidence of any consideration having been given to the fencing of the bluff, and the judge appears to have formed the view it was unreasonable for the borough council not to do anything about this bluff – not even to consider whether it constituted a danger. Whether that is right or not seems to me to depend on whether it was foreseeable that the bluff constituted a danger to children.
>
> The plaintiff's own father was quite clear that it did not; it never entered his head, so far as I can see from his evidence, that this little girl would try to slide down this slope on a blanket, and it seems to me from the photographs that the slope was only dangerous if somebody tried to effect to toboggan down it. I see no reason why the borough council should be required to exercise a higher standard of care than that of a reasonably prudent parent. If the exercise of reasonable care required the borough council to fence off this bluff, it seems to me it would also require them to fence every natural hazard in the Rhondda Valley which was adjacent to housing estates. The borough council are in no special position compared with other occupiers. There are many parts of the country with open spaces adjacent to houses where children play unattended, and this is to be encouraged.
>
> It is not unreasonable, in my judgment, for such occupiers to assume that the parents of children have warned them of the dangers of natural hazards, and would not allow them to play round such places unless the children appreciated the dangers.

The other two judges in the Court of Appeal agreed that the appeal should be allowed on similar grounds.

Section 2(3)(b) also contains a special rule relating to skilled visitors with regard to risks ordinarily incidental to their special callings. This is best illustrated by the case of *Roles v Nathan*,[11] in which two chimney sweeps, despite warnings and advice from an expert with regard to dangerous fumes, carried on with their work and both died from carbon monoxide fumes. The majority of the Court of Appeal found against the estates, although the

10 (1983) 81 LGR 460.

11 [1963] 2 All ER 908.

dissenting judge, Pearson LJ, claimed that he was only taking a different view on the facts rather than on the applicable law. Lord Denning MR stated:

> The householder can reasonably expect the sweep to take care of himself so far as any dangers from the flues are concerned. These chimney sweeps ought to have known that there might be dangerous fumes about and ought to have taken steps to guard against them. They ought to have known that they should not attempt to seal up the seep-hole whilst the fire was still alight. They ought to have had the fire withdrawn before they attempted to seal it up, or at any rate they ought not to have stayed in the alcove too long when there might be dangerous fumes about. All this was known to these two sweeps; they were repeatedly warned about it, and it was for them to guard against the danger. It was not for the occupier to do it, even though he was present and heard the warnings. When a householder calls in a specialist to deal with a defective installation on his premises, he can reasonably expect the specialist to appreciate and guard against the dangers arising from the defect. The householder is not bound to watch over him to see that he comes to no harm. I would hold, therefore, that the occupier here was under no duty of care to these sweeps, at any rate in regard to the dangers which caused their deaths. If it had been a different danger, as for instance if the stairs leading to the cellar gave way, the occupier might no doubt be responsible, but not for these dangers which were special risks ordinarily incidental to their calling.

Harman LJ went along similar lines:

> Here the 'person' is a chimney sweep, and the first question is: would such a person appreciate and guard against the risk of carbon monoxide gas? I should have thought that this was a special risk ordinarily incident to the trade of a sweep. There was no evidence on this point except the words of the sweeps themselves, who said that they knew all about this kind of risk. Clearly, however, they did not appreciate the degree of risk for they did not guard against it; but I should have thought that the occupier was entitled to take their word and was entitled to expect that they would take sufficient precautions having regard to the emphatic warnings of the occupier's agent ... given the previous day. He said he told them of the risks of these gases more than once.

Warning notices

We have seen that the Act covers the issue of warning notices and whether they are sufficient to satisfy the standard set by the common duty of care. It must be emphasised that the effect of a warning notice must be sharply differentiated from the effect of a notice which purports to restrict or exclude liability. A warning, if sufficient, is treated as satisfying the standard of care under the Act, and thus prevents there being a breach of duty. An exclusion clause operates on the assumption that there has been a breach of the common duty of care, but the defendant is putting the risk of any such breach either wholly or at least partially on the plaintiff. We shall deal with the latter shortly.

As to warning notices, the Act in s 2(4)(a) above states that the notice must enable the visitor to be reasonably safe. To achieve this it must be specific. It is not enough if the notice merely says, eg, 'Danger', without anything more. If there is a large hole on the premises, to be sufficient, the notice would probably have to mention this fact and more than likely give an indication of the location of the danger. This much would surely be needed to enable the visitor to avoid the hole. Returning to *Roles v Nathan*, it will be recalled that the two sweeps were given warnings by the agent for the occupier and by an expert in addition. Lord Denning on this point stated:

> I am quite clear that the warnings which were given to the sweeps were enough to enable them to be reasonably safe. The sweeps would have been quite safe if they had heeded these warnings. They should not have come back that evening and attempted to seal up the sweep-hole while the fire was still alight. They ought to have waited till next morning, and then they should have seen that the fire was out before they attempted to seal up the sweep-hole. In any case they should not have stayed too long in the sweep-hole. In short, it was entirely their own fault. The judge held that it was contributory negligence. I would go further and say that, under the Act, the occupier has, by the warnings, discharged his duty.

Harman LJ likewise said:

> There seems to me no doubt that the sweeps had been warned by the occupier through his agent ... of the danger which killed them. That, however, as the section says, does not *without more* absolve the occupier from liability. The crucial question is whether, in all the circumstances, the warning was 'enough to enable the visitor[s]' (ie the sweeps) 'to be reasonably safe'. In my judgment, it was. The occupier did not request or even authorise the sweeps to close the sweep-hole while the fire was alight. Mr Corney did not expect the return of the sweeps on Friday night; they told him that they were coming back in the morning. He had arranged that they should do the work on Saturday morning. He said also that he anticipated that the fire burning on Friday night would be out by Saturday morning, thus making the work safe. It is true that the caretaker apparently did not let the fire out, and it is said that Mr Corney failed in his duty because he did not expressly order the caretaker to do so, nor did he expressly forbid the sweeps to attempt the work with the fire on. Nevertheless, these sweeps knew as much about the danger as he did. There was no obligation on them to proceed without drawing the fire, they were free to do so, and they deliberately chose to assume the risk notwithstanding the advice given.

Pearson LJ also dissented on this point and took the view that the warnings did not enable the sweeps to be reasonably safe. It might be argued that the sweeps were at the worst, guilty of contributory negligence.

Liability for independent contractors

We have seen earlier that an independent contractor might be regarded in some situations as either a joint occupier with the owner of premises or even the sole occupier in exceptional circumstances. We are here concerned with the possibility of the owner or other occupier's liability for things done on premises where the contractor is not to be regarded as an occupier himself. The general rule in tort is that an employer of an independent contractor is not liable for the torts of the latter, even if carried out during the course of the activities covered by the contract between them, unless the duty of the occupier is regarded as non-delegable, ie a personal duty. Section 2(4)(b) above covers the issue of an occupier's potential liability for the acts of an independent contractor. Presumably, the rules in this section only apply where the duty falls in to the personal category because the occupier is not otherwise liable and the paragraph would be superfluous. There are three requirements in the provision. The occupier must:

(a) use reasonable care in entrusting the work to an independent contractor;

(b) take reasonable steps to ensure that the contractor is reasonably competent; and

(c) exercise reasonable care in order to satisfy himself that the work is properly done.

Just how far the occupier must go in order to check the work of the contractor seems to depend on the technical ability required in the task in question. In *Haseldine v Daw*[12] the occupier brought a firm of hydraulic engineers to repair the lift in a block of flats. The lift failed injuring the plaintiff. The Court of Appeal found that the occupier/landlord was not negligent in what he had done. Scott LJ argued as follows:

> The invitor is bound to take that kind of care which a reasonably prudent man in his place would take – neither more nor less. The landlord of a block of flats, as occupier of the lifts, does not profess as such to be either an electrical or, as in this case, a hydraulic engineer. Having no technical skill he cannot rely on his own judgment, and the duty of care towards his invitees requires him to obtain and follow good technical advice. If he did not do so, he would, indeed, be guilty of negligence. To hold him responsible for the misdeeds of his independent contractor would be to make him insure the safety of his lift. That duty can only arise out of contract, as in the case of an employer's duty towards his employed which, in certain circumstances, may make him responsible for the structural fitness of the premises where they are to work.
>
> In the present case the landlord was ignorant of the mechanics of his hydraulic lifts and it was his duty to choose a good expert, to trust him and then to be guided by his advice. I think that he realised his duty and wholly discharged it, so far as the safety of others was concerned, for he chose a first-class firm of lift engineers and trusted them, and over a long period of years and in connection with many lifts he found them trustworthy. The engineers evidently had a very high reputation and wide practice as lift engineers, and I can see no ground whatever for doubting that the landlord took every reasonable precaution in trusting to their examining the lift with care and reporting to him if there was any indication of danger. The landlord thus duly performed his whole duty of care to the plaintiff and others using the lift, even if they were his invitees, by contracting with the engineers and then leaving the expert problems, of which he was ignorant, entirely to his experts who possessed the requisite knowledge.

Goddard LJ also expressed a similar view:

> It seems to me that, by employing a first class firm of lift engineers to make periodical inspections of the lift, to adjust it and furnish reports upon it, the landlord did all that a reasonable man could do towards seeing that it was safe, especially when it is remembered that he also had the advantage of quarterly inspections by the insurance company's engineer. But it is argued that, if the engineers were negligent, it cannot be said that the occupier has discharged his duty. With this I cannot agree. An occupier or any other person may have, either by contract or by law, such a degree of duty imposed on him that he cannot discharge it by employing a contractor to do work for him, but where the duty is to take care that premises are safe, I cannot see how it can be discharged better than by the employment of competent contractors. Indeed, one may well ask how otherwise could the duty be discharged?

12 [1941] 2 KB 343.

Clauson LJ agreed with the other two on this point. However, by a majority the Court of Appeal allowed the plaintiff's claim against the engineers, holding that the duty under *Donoghue v Stevenson* applied to repairers of goods and was not limited solely to manufacturers.

A case to contrast with the above is *Woodward v Mayor of Hastings*,[13] in which a school pupil slipped on a step and was injured. He brought an action against the defendants for the negligence of the cleaner of the steps, to whose services they were entitled, although she was not their servant. The Court of Appeal found for the plaintiff in this case. In reading the judgment of the court, Du Parcq LJ stated:

> Two questions of fact arise. Did they use the reasonable care required? Ought they to have known of the danger which in fact existed? These questions of fact must be answered in the light of certain legal principles and of all the circumstances of the case. The defendants were governors of the school and it was inevitable that they should act through agents. They were bound to entrust to others the cleaning of the school premises, their upkeep from day to day, and the immediate supervision (so far as that was deemed necessary) of the work done in connection with that cleaning and upkeep. The careful performance of these delegated duties was necessary in order that the obligation to take reasonable care to prevent damage to invitees might be fulfilled. Cleaning must be done, and in some circumstances it has to be done carefully if danger is to be avoided. When a step, truly described by the judge as 'potentially dangerous', is covered with snow, the person entrusted with the duty of cleaning it must be careful not to leave it in a dangerous condition. If anyone has been appointed to supervise the work of the cleaner it is his duty to see that the work is carefully done. If no one has been appointed to supervise that work, then the invitors must be taken to have left the performance of the duty, for good or ill, to the cleaner.
>
> On the facts of this case we have no doubt that Mrs Clark, who was admittedly negligent, had been entrusted by the defendants with the necessary work of cleaning the premises which they occupied. They had secured, by contract, the benefit of her services for that purpose. It may be, though we think it improbable, that the defendants expected the headmaster to supervise her work. If they did, he does not appear to have done what was expected of him. If they did not, then they left the care of the premises to Mrs Clark. It is idle to suggest that Mrs Clark was not authorised to brush snow from the step. It was clearly part of her duty to do so, and no one in her position would have been likely to omit that task. Negligence having been established against her, it follows that the defendants are responsible for their agent's failure to take reasonable care for the safety of their invitee. It does not avail them to say that they did not know of the danger. Of course, the defendants, who were many miles away, did not, and could not, know of it. Their agent, however, knew, or ought to have known of it, whether we regard the headmaster as their agent to supervise the operation of cleaning or Mrs Clark as their sole agent in the matter.
>
> It is said by counsel for the defendants that Mrs Clark was the servant, not of the defendants, but of the diaconate of the Congregational Church whose premises were occupied by the defendants. We do not accept this as the true view of her position. On the contrary, we think that it is a fair inference from the evidence that, at the material time, she was subject to the control of the defendants. We will, however, assume that the defendants are right on this point, for the purpose

13 [1945] 1 KB 174.

> of examining their argument. If, said Mr Dare, an occupier's servant negligently cleans his floor so that an invitee slips on it, the occupier is liable, but if (he said) the occupier has borrowed, or obtained by contract the services of, another man's servant, and that servant is guilty of similar negligence with similar consequences, then the occupier is not liable, though the servant's master may be. In our opinion, this is not the law. Even if Mrs Clark was not temporarily under the control of the defendants and thus for the time being their servant, they are liable on the ground that they delegated to her the performance of the duty which was incumbent on them. If she is to be treated (as counsel submitted) as if she were an independent contractor; they are liable for her negligence.

The judge distinguished this case from the previous one by saying:

> The craft of the charwoman may have its mysteries, but there is no esoteric quality in the nature of the work which the cleaning of a snow-covered step demands.

The case of *Ferguson v Welsh*[14] contains some interesting observations on this aspect of the legislation. The appellant was injured whilst helping to demolish a building owned by the respondents. The contract for the work had been awarded to a Mr Spence, the third defendant, who subcontracted the work to the first and second defendants who were responsible for engaging the appellant. The latter was injured as a result of the unsafe system of work adopted by the first and second defendants. The House decided against the appellant in favour of the respondents. After setting out s 2(4)(b) of the 1957 Act, Lord Keith commented as follows:

> The enactment is designed to afford some protection from liability to an occupier who has engaged an independent contractor who has executed the work in a faulty manner. It is to be observed that it does not specifically refer to demolition, but a broad and purposive interpretation may properly lead to the conclusion that demolition is embraced by the word 'construction'. Further, the pluperfect tense employed in the last words of the paragraph 'the work *had* been properly done', might suggest that there is in contemplation only the situation where the work has been completed, but has been done in such a way that there exists a danger related to the state of the premises. That would, however, in my opinion be an unduly strict construction, and there is no good reason for narrowing the protection afforded so as not to cover liability from dangers created by a negligent act or omission by the contractor in the course of his work on the premises. It cannot have been intended not to cover, for example, dangers to visitors from falling masonry or the objects brought about by the negligence of the contractor. It may, therefore, be inferred that an occupier might, in certain circumstances, be liable for something done or omitted to be done on his premises by an independent contractor if he did not take reasonable steps to satisfy himself that the contractor was competent and that the work was being properly done.
>
> It would not ordinarily be reasonable to expect an occupier of premises, having engaged a contractor whom he has reasonable grounds for regarding as competent, to supervise the contractor's activities in order to ensure that he was discharging his duty to his employees to observe a safe system of work. In special circumstances, on the other hand, where the occupier knows or has reason to suspect that the contractor is using an unsafe system of work, it might

14 [1987] 3 All ER 777

well be reasonable for the occupier to take steps to see that the system was made safe.

The crux of the present case, therefore, is whether the council knew or had reason to suspect that Mr Spence, in contravention of the terms of his contract, was bringing in cowboy operators who would proceed to demolish the building in a thoroughly unsafe way. The thrust of the affidavit evidence admitted by the Court of Appeal was that Mr Spence had long been in the habit of subcontracting his demolition work to persons who proceeded to execute it by the unsafe method of working from the bottom up. If the evidence went to the length of indicating that the council knew or ought to have known that this was Mr Spence's usual practice, there would be much to be said for the view that they should be liable to Mr Ferguson. ... I conclude that the evidence in question would not be likely to have an important effect on the result of the action so far directed against the council.

Lord Goff observed:

I, for myself, can see no difficulty in law in reaching a conclusion that Mr Ferguson may have been a lawful visitor in relation to Mr Spence, but a trespasser in relation to the council. Once it is accepted that two persons may be in occupation of the same land, it seems to me inevitable that, on certain facts, such a conclusion may have to be reached. If it is the case that one only of such occupiers authorises a third person to come onto the land, then plainly the third person is, *vis-à-vis* that occupier, a lawful visitor. But he may not be a lawful visitor *vis-à-vis* the other occupier. Whether he is so or not must, in my opinion, depend on the question whether the occupier who authorised him to enter had authority, actual (express or implied) or ostensible, from the other occupier to allow the third party onto the land. If he had, then the third party will be, *vis-à-vis* that other occupier, a lawful visitor; if he had not, then the third party will be, *vis-à-vis* that other occupier a trespasser. No doubt, in the ordinary circumstances of life, the occupier who allows the third party to come onto the land will frequently have implied or ostensible authority so to do on behalf of the other occupier as will, I think, usually be the case when the first occupier is a builder, in occupation of a building site with the authority of the building owner, who authorises a servant or independent contractor to come onto the site. But this may not always be so, as for example where the third party is aware that the building owner has expressly forbidden the builder to allow him on the site. These problems have, as I see it, to be solved by the application of the ordinary principles of agency law.

I am content to assume, for the purposes of the present appeal, that there is evidence capable of establishing that Mr Spence did have the ostensible authority of the council to allow the Welsh brothers (and through them, Mr Ferguson) onto the land. Even so, in my judgment Mr Ferguson's action against the council must fail because I cannot see how the council could be held liable to him, in particular under the 1957 Act.

On the assumption that Mr Ferguson was the lawful visitor of the council on the land, the council owed to him the common duty of care, ie a duty 'to take such care as in all the circumstances of the case is reasonable to see that the visitor will be reasonably safe *in using the premises* for the purposes for which he is invited or permitted by the occupier to be there': see section 2(2) of the 1957 Act. I have emphasised the words 'in using the premises' because it seems to me that the key to the problem in the present case lies in those words. I can see no basis, even on the evidence now available, for holding that Mr Ferguson's injury arose from any breach by the council of that duty. There can, no doubt, be cases in which an independent contractor does work on premises which result in such premises becoming unsafe for a lawful visitor coming on them, as when a brick falls from a building under repair onto the head of a postman delivering the mail. In such circumstances the occupier may be held liable to the postman, though in considering whether he is in breach of the common duty of care there would have to be considered, *inter alia*, the circumstances specified in section 2(4)(b) of the 1957 Act. But if I ask myself, in relation to the facts of the present case, whether it can be said that Mr Ferguson's injury arose from a failure by the council to take reasonable care to see that persons in his position would be reasonably safe *in using the premises* for the relevant purposes, the answer must, I think, be 'no'. There is no question, as I see it, of Mr Ferguson's injury arising from any such failure; for it arose not from his use of the premises but from the manner in which he carried out his work on the premises. For this simple reason, I do not consider that the 1957 Act has anything to do with the present case.

I wish to add that I do not, with all respect, subscribe to the opinion that, the mere fact that an occupier may know or have reason to suspect that the contractor carrying out work on his building may be using an unsafe system of work, can of itself be enough to impose on him a liability under the 1957 Act, or, indeed, in negligence at common law, to an employee of the contractor who is thereby injured, even if the effect of using that unsafe system is to render the premises unsafe and thereby to cause the injury to the employee. I have only to think of the ordinary householder who calls in an electrician, and the electrician sends in a man who, using an unsafe system established by his employer, creates a danger in the premises which results in his suffering injury from burns. I cannot see that, in ordinary circumstances, the householder should be held liable under the 1957 Act, or even in negligence, for failing to tell the man how he should be doing his work. I recognise that there may be special circumstances which may render another person liable to the injured man together with his employer, as when they are, for some reason, joint tortfeasors, but such a situation appears to me to be quite different.

Limitations on the extent of the duty

The occupier is free, according to s 2(1) of the 1957 Act, to extend, restrict, modify or exclude his duty. Restriction or exclusion of the duty may be subject to controls in the Unfair Contract Terms Act 1977 and will be discussed below. It is accepted that an occupier may limit the extent of the duty in ways which fall short of restriction or exclusion. Section 2(2) mentions the 'purpose' for which the visitor is invited on the premises. If the visitor goes beyond that purpose, then s/he may well be considered no longer to be a lawful visitor and fall into the trespasser category. The same may be true where the visitor is permitted to be on premises for a stated time, or it is made clear that only certain parts of the premises are covered by the original permission. The point came up for consideration in *Pearson v Coleman Brothers*[15] where the seven year old plaintiff, visiting a circus, wandered off during the performance to find a toilet and was injured by a caged lion putting its paw through the bars of the cage. Lord Greene MR stated:

She was invited to a place where there was no lavatory, seeking for one and moving within the part controlled by the defendants, and not finding any place,

15 [1948] 2 KB 359.

she arrived near the runway. It seems to me impossible then to say that she was trespasser the moment she got out of the circus tent. What was she to do? ... She could not remain where she was, and, therefore, it seems to me the only proper inference was ... that, at any rate up to the crucial point when she decided to crawl under the runway, she was there pursuant to the original invitation.

Now there comes what, to my mind, is the really important point and, from the legal point of view, the most interesting part of this case. The defendants have got two adjoining pieces of land, the circus and the zoo, and there was an invitation to these children to go to the circus. A person who has two pieces of land and invited the public to come to one of them can, of course, if he chooses, limit the invitation to that one; but if the other piece is contiguous to that one and he does not indicate to his invitees that his invitation is confined to the one piece of land, he cannot be surprised if they treat his invitation as extending to both pieces.

In my opinion, if a landowner is minded to make part of his land a prohibited area he must indicate this to his invitees by appropriate means. It is no good his coming afterwards and saying 'You were not allowed to go on that piece' if, in point of fact, he has done nothing, or nothing adequate, to show that the second piece of land is a prohibited area. Whether or not proper or sufficient steps have been taken to delimit the prohibited area must, I apprehend, depend on the facts in each case.

Looking at the zoo, which in this case is said to be a prohibited area, I find what I have described as a rough and ready manner of marking it off, and indicating that nobody ought to go in there unless he goes through the proper entrance. It is a rough and ready method of doing it, and to an adult it might be very well regarded as sufficient indication that the area of the zoo is a prohibited area and is not to be accessible to anyone who does not go through the proper entrance. But we are not dealing here with an adult, but with a child who is not moving about out of mere curiosity or without any reason. We are dealing with a child in a condition which the proprietors must have contemplated as reasonably possible, namely the condition of being under an urgent necessity to find a quiet place in which to relieve herself. I ask myself, having regard to the fact that, among the invitees of the defendants, there were likely to be children needing to relieve themselves, whether in relation to that class of person the steps taken at the point in question to delimit the prohibited area of the zoo were adequate. In my opinion, the facts speak for themselves.

So, far from indicating sufficiently to a child bent on such an errand that she must not go in, there is displayed before her what, and from the photograph, is clearly not a prohibition, but a temptation. It is quite obvious that, to a little girl seeking for a quiet place, here is the ideal quiet place. It seems to me quite impossible to say that the prohibited area had, as regards a child in those circumstances, been adequately marked off by the defendants from the area into which the child was entitled to go. However the matter might have stood with regard to somebody who came on to the field as a trespasser and chose to go into that place, the fact that the little girl started as an invitee can only lead to the conclusion that the invitation extends, impliedly at least, to a place to which she would reasonably go to meet her need.

It will be observed that I have been careful to consider all the relevant facts of the case as they appear to me – the child's need, her age, the absence of any lavatory, the fact that she made a circuit round the tent and found nothing, and the fact that she did find a very attractive place in the end. The combination of all those facts is what leads me inevitably to the conclusion that the defendants in this case

> cannot succeed. I say nothing of what the position would have been in the case of an adult who had found himself in a similar need. If he had followed the same route as this girl and had crawled through the fence or under the runway, any claim by him might very well have been met with the answer: 'to you, an adult, it was quite sufficiently indicated that this was a prohibited area.' It can scarcely be necessary to stop up every hole through which an adult could crawl; adults are not expected to crawl. That might have been the answer in that case, but I only refer to it as showing the importance of paying due regard to all the facts of this case. Again I say nothing about what would have been the conclusion if this little girl, being bored with the circus performance, had chosen to go from curiosity and wandered into the zoo. The plaintiff was under a compelling need, for the satisfaction of which a convenient and inviting aperture was left in what was intended to be an enclosure of the zoo; and she is, in my opinion, justified in saying that the invitation in her case extended to this point.

The other two judges agreed wholeheartedly with this and found for the plaintiff.

Of course, if the court since 1984 comes to the conclusion that the plaintiff has gone beyond the point of remaining a visitor, all is not necessarily lost as we shall see below. It seems clear from the above case that, in order to satisfy the court that an area was prohibited, clear signs such as 'private' or 'staff only' should be displayed prominently at appropriate places. Also, the defendant may need to consider fencing or some other form of effective barrier to show that the visitor must not go beyond a certain point. This will always be a question of fact as to whether what the occupier has done will be sufficient.

Restriction or exclusion of liability

The controversial and difficult topic of attempted restriction or exclusion of liability must now be considered. It is worth repeating that there is a difference between this and the previously discussed issue of warning notices, although it may often be the case that both types of issue are covered in one particular notice relied upon by the occupier. A satisfactory warning notice discharges the duty, an exclusion clause is an attempt to relieve the consequences of a breach. We have seen already that s 2(1) of the 1957 Act permits the occupier to restrict or exclude the duty. This was so provided the notice purporting to have such effect satisfied the common law rules on sufficiency of notice, namely – have reasonable steps been taken to bring the notice to the attention of visitors, and was it drafted sufficiently wide enough to cover the events which had taken place?[16] Such a restriction could and did include cases of death or personal injury, but s 2(1) must be read in the light of s 3 of the 1957 Act and subject to the relevant controls introduced by s 2 Unfair Contract Terms Act 1977. Section 3 of the 1957 Act reads as follows:

> (1) Where an occupier of premises is bound by contract to permit persons who are strangers to the contract to enter or use the premises, the duty of care which he owes to them as his visitors cannot be restricted or excluded by that contract, but (subject to any provision of the contract to the contrary) shall include the duty to perform his obligations under the contract, whether

16 See *Ashdown v Samuel Williams* [1957] 1 QB 409; *White v Blackmore* [1972] 2 QB 651.

undertaken for their protection or not, in so far as those obligations go beyond the obligations otherwise involved in that duty.

(2) A contract shall not, by virtue of this section, have the effect, unless it expressly so provides, of making an occupier who has taken all reasonable care, answerable to strangers to the contract for dangers due to the faulty execution of any work of construction, maintenance or repair or other like operation, by persons other than himself, his servants and persons acting under his direction and control.

(3) In this section 'stranger to the contract' means a person not, for the time being, entitled to the benefit of the contract as a party to it or as the successor by assignment or otherwise of a party to it, and accordingly includes a party to the contract who has ceased to be so entitled.

(4) Where by the terms or conditions governing any tenancy (including a statutory tenancy which does not in law amount to a tenancy) either the landlord or tenant is bound, though not by contract, to permit persons to enter or use premises of which he is the occupier, this section shall apply as if the tenancy were a contract between the landlord and the tenant.

The more important restriction on the right to exclude liability is contained in s 2(1) Unfair Contract Terms Act 1977. It should be noted that the subsection prevents attempts by business occupiers from seeking to exclude their liability under the common duty of care for personal injury or death on the one hand, and under s 2(2) subjects attempts to exclude liability for property damage to a reasonableness test. There are several points to note on this.

Firstly, private occupiers are free (subject to s 3(1) above) to restrict or exclude liability under the 1957 Act, as the Unfair Contract Terms Act, in the main, only applies to business liability. The lawful visitor need not be on the business premises of the occupier necessarily in order to take advantage of the provisions of the 1977 Act. Secondly, s 14 of the 1977 Act defines business as including the activities of a profession and of a local authority. Thirdly, note the amendment to s 1(3) of the 1977 Act by the Occupiers' Liability Act 1984. This provides that liability to persons visiting business premises for educational or recreational purposes is not a business liability unless education or recreation is a business purpose of the occupier. This allows eg a farmer to grant access to part of his farm premises to a group of schoolchildren for educational or recreational purposes, and be able to restrict or exclude liability to them. Fourthly, s 2(5) of the 1957 Act preserves the *volenti* defence, but as to whether it is applicable depends on ordinary principles which will be discussed in the defences chapter in due course. It should be noted, however, that by s 2(3) of the 1977 Act, the inclusion of a notice attempting to restrict or exclude liability to which a person has agreed, or of which he is aware, is not to be taken of itself as amounting to a voluntary assumption of risk.

Liability to trespassers

This section is concerned with liability to trespassers, but certain other persons are deemed to be trespassers. They are persons who enter premises in the exercise of rights conferred by an access order or agreement under the National Parks and Access to the Countryside Act 1949 and persons lawfully using a private right of way. This means they can take advantage of the dubious benefits given by the 1984 Act. Those exercising public rights of way are not entitled to the benefit of the 1984 Act. Presumably, however, they may be entitled to the minimum common law standard owed to a trespasser under the principle in *Addie v Dumbreck*,[17] where it was stated by Lord Hailsham LC that the only duty owed to a trespasser was in circumstances where there was:

> ... some act done with the deliberate intention of doing harm to the trespasser, or at least some act done with reckless disregard of the presence of the trespasser.

This seemingly harsh rule came in for considerable criticism over the years and was, in the first place, somewhat softened in impact by the House of Lords in *British Railways Board v Herrington*,[18] in which the House developed a rather vague and unsatisfactory notion of common humanity as a basis for liability towards trespassers in some circumstances. This approach avoided, at least for a short period, the need for the courts to reach out for the implied licence cases to bring the child trespasser within the fold of the lawful visitor. The approach was not considered satisfactory and the matter was referred to the Law Commission,[19] whose report provided the basis for the 1984 Act.

Occupiers' Liability Act 1984

Section 1

(1) The rules enacted by this section shall have effect, in place of the rules of the common law, to determine–

(a) whether any duty is owed by a person as occupier of premises to persons other than his visitors in respect of any risk of their suffering injury on the premises by reason of any danger due to the state of the premises or to things done or omitted to be dine on them; and

(b) if so, what that duty is.

(2) For the purpose of this section, the persons who are to be treated respectively as an occupier of any premises (which for these purposes, include any fixed or movable structure) and as his visitors are–

(a) any person who owes in relation to the premises the duty referred to in section 2 of the Occupiers' Liability 1957 (the common duty of care); and

(b) those who are his visitors for the purposes of that duty.

(3) An occupier of premises owes a duty to another (not being his visitor) in respect of any such risk as is referred to in subsection (1) above if–

(a) he is aware of the danger or has reasonable grounds to believe it exists;

(b) he knows or has reasonable grounds to believe that the other is in the vicinity of the danger concerned or that he may come into the vicinity of the danger (in either case, whether the other has lawful authority for being in that vicinity or not); and

(c) the risk is one against which, in all the circumstances of the case, he may reasonably be expected to offer the other some protection.

---

17 [1929] AC 358.

18 [1972] AC 877.

19 *Liability for Damage or Injury to Trespassers and Related Questions of Occupiers' Liability*, Law Com no 75, Cmnd 6428, 1976.

(4) where, by virtue of this section, an occupier of premises owes a duty to another in respect of such a risk, the duty is to take such care as is reasonable in all the circumstances of the case to see that he does not suffer injury on the premises by reason of the danger concerned.

(5) Any duty owed by virtue of this section in respect of a risk may, in an appropriate case, be discharged by taking such steps as are reasonable in all the circumstances of the case to give warning of the danger concerned or to discourage persons from incurring the risk.

(6) No duty is owed by virtue of this section to any person in respect of risks willingly accepted as his by that person (the question whether a risk was so accepted to be decided on the same principles as in other cases in which one person owes a duty of care to another).

(7) No duty is owed by virtue of this section to persons using the highway, and this section does not affect any duty owed to such persons.

(8) Where a person owes a duty by virtue of this section, he does not, by reason of any breach of the duty, incur any liability in respect of any loss of or damage to property.

(9) In this section:

'highway' means any part of a highway other than a ferry or waterway;

'injury' means anything resulting in death or personal injury, including any disease and any impairment of physical or mental condition; and

'movable structure' includes any vessel, vehicle or aircraft.

This is, as the section says, intended to replace the common law on liability to trespassers but still relies on the common law for the interpretation of 'occupier' and 'lawful visitor'. It should be remembered that a person may be regarded as a lawful visitor on the basis of an implied licence, which may depend on factors such as the regularity of the alleged trespass, the knowledge of the occupier and attempts made to discourage the use of the land in question. It should also be recalled that a visitor may subsequently become a trespasser where she exceeds her permission, eg by staying beyond the time allotted, or by straying beyond the limits set by the occupier in terms of space and purpose of the visit.

The requirements in s 1(3) are cumulative. There has been little reported litigation on the Act so far. In one case, *White v St Albans City and District Council*[20] where the plaintiff fell into a deep trench on fenced-off council property, he argued that s 1(3)(b) was satisfied once it had been established that the council had thought it necessary to adopt precautions to prevent the trespass. All three judges rejected this interpretation, even thought the fence was described as inadequate to keep out all but the elderly or infirm. There was insufficient evidence that the public was using their land as a short cut.

There are some further observations on the provisions. Firstly, the Act, unlike the 1957 Act, does not cover loss of or damage to property. Secondly, when assessing the issue of breach of duty, then, presumably, the normal considerations at common law will come into play, in particular the cost and practicality of precautions. Was the danger latent or obvious; how long had it been there, and so on? Thirdly, the issue of warning notices is specifically

20 (1990) Times, 12 March.

referred to once again. In relation to trespassers, there may well be practical difficulties in bringing dangers on the land to the attention of a trespasser. The occupier has to try and anticipate, perhaps, the exact point of entry of a potential trespasser, or will it be sufficient to have a prominent notice close to the hazard in question?

The assumption of risk defence is also raised in the Act, and the detail of this will be discussed in the chapter on defences. However, it might be argued that such a defence might be appropriate to deal with the vexed issue of the injured burglar who brings a claim. A possible further defence in such an event might be the maxim, *ex turpi causa non oritur actio*, that the burglar should not be allowed to profit from his own wrongdoing. This defence will be discussed in the chapter on trespass to the person later. One final comment concerns the possibility of exclusion of the duty under the 1984 Act. A private occupier can still exclude the duty under the 1957 Act notwithstanding the 1977 Act; should this not also be the case in relation to trespassers under the 1984 Act? The latter Act is silent upon this point, but it would be rather odd if the duty to a lawful visitor could be excluded, but not that owed to the apparently less deserving trespasser.

CHAPTER 8

PRODUCT LIABILITY

INTRODUCTION

This chapter is concerned with liability for defective goods in tort, outside contract. In a sense, product liability law in this country is a strange mixture of strict contractual liability, tortious liability based on fault, and strict liability in tort under Part I Consumer Protection Act 1987. The problem with contractual liability, of course, is the tight adherence in English law to the doctrine of privity of contract, which denies the benefit of the strict contractual liability under the Sale of Goods Act 1979 (as amended) to all but the purchasing consumer, even to those in the same household who are injured by the product which was clearly intended for household use by all living under the same roof. Usually, the person who has lost the least has the benefit of such an action, the person who has lost the most does not.

In both *Preist v Last*[1] and *Daniels v White*[2] the purchasing consumer was the husband. In the first of these cases it was the wife who was scalded when the hot water bottle burst; in the second both husband and wife drank some of the contaminated lemonade. In each case the husband had a claim under the Sale of Goods Act 1893 (as it was then), but his related solely to his own losses and could not include a claim for the damage to the respective wife. In the first of the cases there was no mention of any independent claim by the wife; in the second of the cases the wife sued in tort, but nonetheless lost as we shall see soon, although her case would probably be treated differently now under the 1987 Act.

Liability prior to the Act was based on the narrow rule in *Donoghue v Stevenson*,[3] which settled the duty issue but still demanded proof of fault. This was not always so easy because, often, the consumer would know little about the manufacturing process involved in producing the product and was frequently faced with large resources of the manufacturer in attempting to pursue a claim. *Daniels v White* is a good illustration of the difficulties which might confront a consumer. There was significant criticism of the fault-based system of the law in this area.[4] The impetus for change finally came in the form of the agreed directive[5] in 1985 after protracted discussion on earlier drafts. A significant point is that Part I Consumer Protection Act 1987, the UK's response to the directive, does not replace the common law of negligence which still has a vital role to play in certain areas where the Act is not applicable. This will be particularly true in relation to claims for damage to commercial property, a major area of liability excluded from the scope of the strict liability provisions. Claims for economic loss not consequential on other types of loss falling within

1 [1903] 2 KB 148.

2 [1938] 4 All ER 258.

3 [1932] AC 562.

4 Pearson Commission, vol 1 ch 22, Law Com no 82, Cmnd 6831, 1977.

5 85/374/EEC.

the statute, if they are going to be recoverable at all, must be pursued at common law. The common law is, in addition, not restricted by the definition given to 'product' within the Act, for as we shall see, unprocessed agricultural produce and game are excluded from the remit of the legislation. The common law had, and, of course, still has its deficiencies, hence the legislation, but it is also evident that the Act itself has its detractors as we shall see. We shall consider the common law in the first instance, followed by the strict liability provisions.

COMMON LAW

The starting point for any discussion of product liability law must naturally be the case of *Donoghue v Stevenson*. It will be recalled from Chapter 2 the way in which the law had developed up to that case, in that there was only said to be a duty in negligence for a defective item if it was considered dangerous *per se*, or in the unlikely event that it could be established that the manufacturer was fraudulent. This anomalous situation was recognised for what it was by the majority in *Donoghue* and put to right. What is called the narrow rule in this case is to be found, not surprisingly, in Lord Atkin's speech. He stated:

> A manufacturer of products which he sells in such a form as to show that he intends them to reach the ultimate consumer in the form in which they left him, with no reasonable possibility of intermediate examination, and with the knowledge that the absence of reasonable care in the preparation or putting up of the products will result in injury to the consumer's life or property, owes a duty to the consumer to take that reasonable care.

The other two judges in the majority made broadly similar comments, but Lord Atkin's statement above has been taken as the foundation for product liability at common law.

Who owes the duty?

Whilst the issue in *Donoghue* concerned the liability of a manufacturer of a product, it has been held to extend to any person in the distribution chain, provided the plaintiff can establish that any such person has been at fault in relation to the product. One of the deficiencies of the common law concerned the position of the importer of goods, particularly from remote, far away places in circumstances where the manufacturer was an unlikely target for litigation. Unless the importer was found in some way to be negligent, which would be extremely unlikely, the injured plaintiff would have no claim at common law against him.

That problem apart, the common law had shown itself flexible in relation to the issue of by whom the duty was owed. For example, in *Fisher v Harrods*[6] the plaintiff sued the retailer in negligence when she sustained personal injuries following her attempt to use a cleaning fluid sold by them to another person who had given it to the plaintiff. It seems that, when she removed the screw top, the plug flew out and the liquid went into her eyes. McNair J found for the

6 [1966] 1 Lloyd's Rep 500.

plaintiff, assuming that it was a duty situation. On the scope of the duty, he had this to say:

> I have reached the conclusion, on the facts of this case, that the defendants did not measure up to the standard of care which they should have exercised. ... If they had made any inquiries they would have found out that Mr Meyer was a man of no qualifications for, or experience in, the manufacture of a cleaning product and no qualifications for making a proper choice of its constituents. Mr Meyer's only knowledge of chemistry was derived from 18 months' study in chemistry, without taking a degree, at a German university some 30 years ago. He had come to this country 30 years ago and had had no manufacturing experience at all until 1961, when he manufactured and attempted unsuccessfully to market a toilet cleaner and a shaving lotion. In that year he invented the formula which he used for the production of Couronne. He worked on its production in an old garage where the different commodities were mixed by him by hand in somewhat primitive conditions. If the defendants had taken the elementary precaution of having the Couronne examined by their own chemist, they would have found that the information given by Mr Meyer to Mr Nash was inaccurate, as it referred only to ammonia and soft soap and made no mention of the isopropyl alcohol. Even Mr Nash, who did not profess to have any professional qualifications in this field, realised that as a cleaning material it might contain properties which were dangerous.
>
> Mr Moir, an experienced industrial chemist called on behalf of the plaintiff, expressed the view that he would not expect a substance of this kind to be put on the market without some warning, this view being based on his experience of substances which are accompanied by a warning when put on the market. Dr Barent, called on behalf of the defendants, part of whose function is to advise public bodies of the hazards involved in the transport of dangerous goods, though he instanced a number of articles sold on the market without warning such as some of the bleaches, surgical spirit and Lysol, which would equally scar the eyes if it came into contact with them, was impressed by the hazard in this case arising from the inflammability of the alcohol. He accepted Mr Moir's view, which I have set out above, as being a reasonable view, though he did not agree with it on the basis of his knowledge of substances sold in bulk. ... As it seems to me, the danger of this article is that, even with a pierced plug, the contents have to be squeezed out by pressure. ...
>
> In my judgment this Couronne should not have been put on the market, even with a pierced plug, without instructions as to the manner in which the liquid was to be got out of the container and without a warning as to the danger if it came into contact with the eyes; *a fortiori* it should not have been put on the market with a blind plug without a similar or more stringent warning – such as was used later – namely 'Keep away from the eyes'. ...
>
> In my judgment the defendants' initial fault in putting this commodity on the market without making proper inquiries, and without seeing that an adequate warning of danger was affixed to the bottles, was and remained the effective cause of the plaintiff's injuries.

The issue in the case was clearly not that of duty, but one of breach, but it does show that the duty could be owed by a retailer in appropriate circumstances. Further, in the case of *Watson v Buckley, Osborne, Garrett & Co Ltd*,[7] a wholesaler was held liable for failing to test a hair dye which caused dermatitis when

7 [1940] 1 All ER 174.

applied to the plaintiff's head. The latter successfully sued the first defendant, the hairdresser in contract, and also brought an action in negligence against the distributor. The latter advertised the product as absolutely safe and harmless, and as not needing any testing before use. On the duty issue, Stable J said:

> If Ogee Ltd [the distributors] had been the manufacturers, I should have held without difficulty here that, by this advertisement which Watson saw, ... and upon which he relied, Ogee Ltd, if they had been manufacturers, of their own accord would have brought themselves into direct relationship with the consumer. It is said that here, although the manufacturers would owe such a duty, the distributors, being distributors and not manufacturers, are absolved. It seems to me that that statement must be qualified. The number of cases in which a distributor would owe a duty must, I think, be comparatively few. As it has been said, duty is not a duty in the abstract. One does not have to search for the duty *in vacuo*, but one has to look at the facts and decide whether or not the law attaches a duty out of those facts, or to those facts.
>
> The initial tortious act or careless act – carelessness would be better – was the putting of the 10% solution into the lotion, and for that the distributors were not responsible. The manufacturers were not their agents. They had no direct control over the manufacturers, and I have to ask myself whether, in law, as between this consumer and this distributor, having regard to all the circumstances of the case, there is a duty. It is extremely difficult to arrive at a legal decision without some guidance as to the sort of test one applies as to whether or not there is a duty. ...I do not think that it matters whether the man is a manufacturer or whether he is a distributor. It seems to me to be the same in the case of a person through whose hands there has passed a commodity which ultimately reaches a consumer to his detriment. Where that person has intentionally so excluded interference with, or examination of, the article by the consumer, then he has, of his own accord, brought himself into direct relationship with that consumer so as to be responsible to the consumer for any injury the consumer may sustain as a result of the distributor's negligence. The duty is there.

It has also been held that the duty is owed by repairers of goods.[8]

To whom is the duty owed?

The duty is owed to anyone to whom injury is reasonably foreseeable, whether it is injury to the person of the consumer or damage to her property. In *Lambert v Lewis*[9] the plaintiff's family was involved in a serious crash brought about by a defective coupling attaching a trailer to the towing vehicle. There was no problem in holding that the plaintiff's family was owed a duty in this instance even though they were not using the item in question. It was reasonably foreseeable that, if the coupling was defective, serious injury or death might be caused to other road users. This would no doubt also include damage to property owned by other road users and those having property adjacent to the road.

Another case of a repairer being held liable to third parties in this way is *Stennet v Hancock and Peters*.[10] A flange came off the wheel of a lorry and the

8 See *Haseldine v Daw* [1941] 2 KB 343.

9 [1982] AC 225.

10 [1939] 2 All ER 578.

owner took it for repair to the second defendant, who arranged for this to be done. A few hours later the flange came off the vehicle again while being driven along the road. It struck the plaintiff who sustained personal injuries. On the question whether the plaintiff was owed a duty by the second defendant, the judge commented:

> In this case ... there was an operation performed by a man who must have known, had he considered the matter for a moment, that it was an operation which, if he did not perform it properly, would probably result in injury to somebody upon the road. He knew that the lorry was being prepared for the purposes of being used on the road. He knew that, if it was not repaired with due care, with this wheel so assembled as to make it keep together and not fly apart upon the road, in all probability somebody would be injured as the result of his not having done that which he should have done He knew that the [first] defendant was not going to take the wheel off or submit it to any scrutiny to see whether the work had been properly done. ... It is not suggested that, by reason of the negligent performance of a contract, Peters is liable to the female plaintiff. What is said is that he is liable by reason of his negligently repairing a vehicle which he knew was going to be used upon the road, and which he knew would, if so used, be liable to inflict injury upon a passer-by. That is a different matter altogether.

STANDARD OF CARE

The standard must be that of reasonable care in all the circumstances as it is elsewhere in the tort of negligence, so the various factors discussed in Chapter 3 on breach of duty may have to be considered. It needs repeating that the standard is relative and not absolute. Proof of breach, as has already been mentioned in the introduction to this chapter, may be difficult and will depend on the nature of the defect. A plaintiff may be at a serious disadvantage if the item is a sophisticated piece of consumer equipment. However, where the alleged defect is one which can be categorised as a manufacturing defect, the courts have been more plaintiff-oriented in some of the cases. Where there is a manufacturing defect, the plaintiff is usually alleging that the there has been some error in the process or there has been a lack of quality control resulting in the article not being as designed, as in *Donoghue* itself.

The case of *Grant v Australian Knitting Mills Ltd*[11] illustrates just how favourably the courts may treat the plaintiff in some cases. The plaintiff contracted dermatitis on his legs as a result of wearing a new pair of underpants manufactured by the respondents to the appeal. It appears that excess sulphites were left in this particular pair, causing the illness. Lord Wright delivered the opinion of the Privy Council in this case and stated on the fault issue as follows:

> The facts set out in the foregoing show, in their Lordships' judgment, negligence in manufacture. According to the evidence, the method of manufacture was correct; the danger of excess sulphites being left was recognised and was guarded against; the process was intended to be foolproof. If excess sulphites were left in the garment, that could only be because someone was at fault. The

11 [1936] AC 85.

> appellant is not required to lay his finger on the exact person in all the chain who was responsible, or to specify what he did wrong. Negligence is found as a matter of inference from the existence of the defects taken in connection with all the known circumstances; even if the manufacturers could by apt evidence have rebutted that inference, they have not done so.

In *Evans v Triplex Safety Glass Co Ltd*[12] the judge was reluctant to find that there had been a failure in manufacture of a car windscreen which inexplicably shattered. The action was brought against the manufacturer of the windscreen, not that of the vehicle itself. His decision also seems to turn on issues of causation, and at times it seems that the two aspects of breach and causation merge into one. He said:

> The plaintiff must prove negligence and there must not be an opportunity for examination by an intermediate party or an ultimate purchaser. The article must reach the purchaser in the form in which it left the manufacturer. ...The plaintiff says that the proper inference for me to draw is that a flaw in this kind of glass is more susceptible to cause damage than a flaw in other glass, and the fact that it may disintegrate is, in itself, dangerous, and especially as it does so without any warning, and therefore the plaintiff should be able to recover. ...
>
> The evidence in support of the act of negligence is as follows. The plaintiff, who does not know anything about the technical aspect of the case, said he was driving along the road when the windscreen exploded without any apparent cause. I am not sure that the actual cause of the damage was a light blow on the windscreen which was not noticed by the plaintiff, but a light blow according to the defendants ought not to break the windscreen, and I am inclined to agree with this.
>
> Now the evidence given by another witness for the plaintiff was that 'toughened glass' was not suitable for use in motor cars at all because he said that, even if the glass was properly made and manufactured, changes of temperature would cause it to disintegrate. He also said that there were other causes which might make the glass disintegrate, namely improperly manufactured glass, or a stone jumping up and striking the windscreen, or a scratch on the surface. According to the evidence given by the defendants it would need a good deal more than a scratch to cause the glass to disintegrate. They say it will stand up to ordinary heat and a light blow will not cause disintegration. They point out that the glass is carefully manufactured and properly examined. It is heated up to 600°, and they say that this glass would stand up to an ordinary blow from a non-cutting instrument better than ordinary glass, and that the usual cause of disintegration was a breakage of the outside surface. In those circumstances am I to infer that properly made glass would never disintegrate without fault?
>
> In this case I do not think that I ought to infer negligence on the part of the defendants. If I take Professor Low's evidence, I ought not to draw the induction that there has been negligence because this glass disintegrated without negligence on the part of anyone. One has to remember that one has three choices as to the glass one can use. There is laminated glass, the 'toughened glass' and the ordinary plate glass, and whichever glass one takes one has to take risks. If you use a 'toughened glass windscreen' and your car is overthrown, you can get out. There seems to be more risks in using the other forms of glass. I do not accept Professor Low's evidence in full. No doubt this glass does suffer from disadvantages. If the outside surface is broken by cutting or if it is strained when

12 [1936] 1 All ER 283.

> it is being screwed into to its frame, we have disintegration. In this case I cannot draw the inference that the cause of the disintegration was the faulty manufacture. It is true that the human element may fail and then the manufacturers would be liable for negligence of their employee, but then that was not proved in this case. The disintegration may have been caused by any accident. There was every opportunity for failure on the part of the human element in fastening the windscreen, and I think that the disintegration was due rather to the fitting of the windscreen than to faulty manufacture having regard to its use on the road and the damage done to a windscreen in the course of use.

Leaving aside the causation issues for the time being in the above, it does provide a stark contrast to the approach taken in the previous case by Lord Wright in the Privy Council, where there was almost a strict liability finding. The vagaries of the evidential process, emphasising the difficulty facing consumers in these type of cases, is reinforced by the much criticised decision in *Daniels v White*. It will be recalled that Mrs Daniels brought an action in negligence against the manufacturer of the lemonade. The judge observed:

> I have to remember that the duty owed to the consumer, or the ultimate purchaser, by the manufacturer is not to ensure that his goods are perfect. All he has to do is to take reasonable care to see that no injury is done to the consumer or ultimate purchaser. In other words, his duty is to take reasonable care to see that there exists no defect that is likely to cause such injury.
>
> I listened yesterday to a description of the machinery and the method used in these works in dealing with these bottles. ... That method has been described as fool-proof, and it seems to me a little difficult to say that, if people supply a fool-proof method of cleaning, washing and filling bottles, they have not taken all reasonable care to prevent defects in their commodity. The only way in which it might be said that the fool-proof machine was not sufficient was if it could be shown that the people working it were so incompetent that they did not give the fool-proof machine a chance.
>
> It is pointed out quite rightly by Mr Busse that the question of supervision comes in. If you have 16 girls doing this process with no supervision of their work, of course all kinds of accidents may happen. A bottle may get to the filler without ever having been washed at all. A girl may upset a bottle just after it has been filled. She finds, let us say, that two teaspoonfuls of liquid have been poured out. She has to fill it up from somewhere, so she walks along to the trolley where the dirty bottles have been put, picks up the first bottle she sees there and pours the contents into the lemonade. Of course, that would be a rather curious thing for anyone to do, but it is a possible thing to happen if there is no supervision in this process.
>
> I am satisfied in this case that there is supervision. I have had called before me the works manager who has charge of all three factories. That means, of course, that he is not at one factory the whole time, but he has described to me what takes place in this particular factory, and I am satisfied that there is quite adequate supervision.

The case, it has been suggested, was wrongly decided,[13] cold comfort to Mrs Daniels. However, it does illustrate the difficulties of proof facing the consumer. This does provide a striking contrast with the *Grant* case above. Also, in *Fisher v Harrods*, it will be recalled, the court commented on the fact that the defendants

13 See *Hill v Crowe* [1978] 1 All ER 812, Jones, *op cit* p 310.

had not made any inquiries about the manufacturer and this was evidence of negligence on their part. In the *Watson* case, moreover, the judge considered whether there had been negligence on the part of the distributor of the hair dye, observing:

> Ogee Ltd were not dealing with an old-established manufacturer who had been supplying them for years. They were, in essence, dealing with a gentleman who had emerged quite unexpectedly from Spain. Although at an interview they stipulated 4% of the chromic acid – a matter of vital importance in connection with the hair dye, as I have said – that stipulation was never reduced to writing. It was never made a term of the agreement between them and the manufacturers. The percentage was never confirmed in a letter. They never saw where it was manufactured. They took no steps to ascertain under what sort of supervision the manufacture was carried on. When deliveries were made, no test of any sort, kind or description was ever made. I am not suggesting that they ought to have tested every consignment. Perhaps it would have been enough ... if they had made a sample test here and there. I was told that the test could have been made, and that it took 30 seconds. In fact, however, there was no test at all of the deliveries. Last, but by no means least, this commodity, of which they knew singularly little, and in connection with which they had taken no steps whatever to ensure that the deliveries of the commodity were in accordance with the stipulated article, was put out to the trade and to the world as being the hair dye which, in contradistinction to every other hair dye, was absolutely safe and harmless, could not harm the most sensitive skin, and positively needed no preliminary tests. I need not labour the matter. That, in my judgment, was carelessness. Before committing their name to such an assertion to all and sundry, they should have taken far greater care to ensure that that assertion was based on solid ground.

In relation to design defects, the law has been less than willing to admit these as amounting to negligence. There appear to have been remarkably few cases in the UK in which a court has found for a plaintiff in circumstances where the product has been manufactured as designed, but the plaintiff's complaint relates to the faulty design in itself, or the product has harmful side effects such as a drug. It may be that this is a result of a much more thorough analysis of the costs and benefits of the product which is seen to favour the producer of the product. In *Walton and Walton v British Leyland*[14] the court was reluctant to find the manufacturer liable for the initial, allegedly faulty design in a vehicle produced by them, which resulted in one of the wheels coming adrift whilst the vehicle was being driven.

However, there was a suggestion that the manufacturer, once aware of the problem, was under a duty at least to warn of the danger, or possibly even to arrange for the recall of vehicles potentially subject to the defect. The social utility argument is often decisive in this situation, and the fear of the excessive cost of precautions is sometimes raised to sway the argument in favour of the defendant. Many products can potentially be rendered safer, but at what cost?

Another factor favouring the defendant may be the existence of a statutory or other type of standard in accordance with which the product has been

14 (1978), unreported.

designed and produced. For example, in *Albery-Speyer and Budden v BP Oil Ltd*[15] actions were brought against the defendant oil company on the basis that their petrol contained too much lead which adversely affected children. Megaw LJ summarised the argument for the oil company thus:

> The companies had contended that they had an unanswerable case to the claims because they had, at all times, adhered to the maximum permitted limits of lead in petrol prescribed by the secretary of state under the Motor Fuel (Lead Content of Petrol) Regulations 1976 (SI No 1866), made pursuant to s 75(1) of the Control of Pollution Act 1974. But it was arguable that the suggested interpretation of the statute was incorrect and the actions could be dismissed on that ground. But the 1976 Regulations had not been attacked as *ultra vires* and the conclusion of the secretary of state was one reached by an independent person after taking proper advice, and approved by Parliament. He must have applied the criterion of the public interest in setting the permitted maximum, taking the country as a whole, and giving weight to all relevant considerations. The oil companies could not be held to be negligent and failing in their duty to the children in complying with the requirements prescribed by the secretary of state and approved by Parliament.

CAUSATION/REMOTENESS

The issues of causation and remoteness of damage may be just as live in product liability cases as in other areas of negligence. The one major point in this context is the 'intermediate examination' point which is often considered as one of causation. A producer may be able to advance the argument that his negligence is obliterated by the negligent failure of a third party to make an inspection of the product and, had this been done, the defect would have come to light. The point was a serious one in *Grant's* case. Returning to Lord Wright's opinion, he had this to say:

> The presence of the deleterious chemical in the pants, due to negligence in manufacture, was a hidden and latent defect, just as much as were the remains of the snail in the opaque bottle; it could not be detected by any examination that could reasonably be made. Nothing happened between the making of the garments and their being worn to change their condition. The garments were made by the manufacturers for the purpose of being worn exactly as they were worn, in fact, by the appellant; it was not contemplated that they should be first washed.

In *Stennet v Hancock v Peters* the judge commented:

> I think it right to say that, if upon the facts of the case, it had appeared that Hancock (the owner of the vehicle and the first defendant) should reasonably have examined the wheel before putting it into use, and had failed to do so, then there would be a *novus actus interveniens* which would break the continuity necessary to make Peters (the repairer and second defendant) liable to the female plaintiff. I cannot think, however, that it would be right to say... that a person who employs a skilled and competent repairer to repair his vehicle is omitting any duty which he owes to himself or to anybody else if he trusts to that man having done his work properly, and, in reliance upon that, takes the vehicle upon the road.

15 (1980) 124 Sol J 376.

Finally, we return to the case of *Evans v Triplex* where the issue was a live one and resulted in a decision in favour of the defendant. The judge stated:

> He [counsel for the plaintiff] has not displaced sufficiently the balance of probabilities in this case. I think that this glass is reasonably safe and possibly more safe than other glasses. One cannot help seeing that, in all these cases, one has to look with reasonable care. One has to consider the question of time. The plaintiff had had the windscreen for about a year. Then there is the possibility of examination. The suppliers of the car had every opportunity to examine the windscreen. I do not propose to lay down any rule of law; it is a question of degree and these elements must be taken into consideration. This article put into a frame and screwed – one must consider that. As I have said there is the element of time, the opportunity of examination and the opportunity of damage from other causes. ... There are a number of causes which might have caused disintegration.

Issues of causation are still relevant under the 1987 Act, and the case law above on such issues may still prove useful, for as we shall see the plaintiff still has to show that his injury was caused by the defect in the product.

We have considered some of the difficulties facing the consumer in bringing an action at common law. The various problems really came to a head or fever pitch at the time of the thalidomide litigation, an action which laid open to the public gaze the glaring inadequacies of the common law on product liability, although the many problems were not the exclusive domain of this field of liability. The Act is the attempt, with European sanction, to alleviate some of these problems.

STRICT LIABILITY

The text of Part I Consumer Protection Act 1987 reads as follows:

> 1 *Purpose and construction of Part I*
>
> (1) This part shall have effect for the purpose of making such provision as is necessary in order to comply with the product liability Directive and shall be construed accordingly.
>
> (2) In this Part, except in so far as the context otherwise requires–
>
> 'agricultural produce' means any produce of the soil, of stock farming or of fisheries;
>
> 'dependant' and 'relative' have the same meaning as they have in, respectively, the Fatal Accidents Act 1976 and the Damage (Scotland) Act 1976;
>
> 'producer' in relation to a product, means–
>
> (a) the person who manufactured it;
>
> (b) in the case of a substance which has not been manufactured but has been won or abstracted, the person who won or abstracted it; and
>
> (c) in the case of a product which has not been manufactured, won or abstracted but essential characteristics of which are attributable to an industrial or other process having been carried out (for example, in relation to agricultural produce), the person who carried out that process;

'product' means any goods or electricity and (subject to subsection (3) below) includes a product which is comprised in another product, whether by virtue of being a component part or raw material or otherwise; and

'the product liability Directive' means the Directive of the Council of the European Communities, dated 25 July 1985 (No 85/374/EEC) on the approximation of the laws, regulations and administrative provisions of the Member States concerning liability for defective products.

(3) For the purposes of this Part a person who supplies any product in which products are comprised, whether by virtue of being component parts or raw materials or otherwise, shall not be treated by reason only of his supply of that product as supplying any of the products so comprised.

2 *Liability for defective products*

(1) Subject to the following provisions of this Part, where any damage is caused wholly or partly by a defect in a product, every person to whom subsection (2) below applies shall be liable for the damage.

(2) This subsection applies to–

(a) the producer of the product;

(b) any person who, by putting his name on the product or using a trade mark or other distinguishing mark in relation to the product, has held himself out to be the producer of the product; and

(c) any person who has imported the product into a Member State from a place outside the Member States in order, in the course of any business of his, to supply it to another.

(3) Subject as aforesaid, where any damage is caused wholly or partly by a defect in a product, any person who supplied the product (whether to the person who suffered the damage, to the producer of any product in which the product in question is comprised or to any other person) shall be liable for the damage if–

(a) the person who suffered the damage requests the supplier to identify one or more of the persons (whether still in existence or not) to whom subsection (2) above applies in relation to the product;

(b) that request is made within a reasonable period after the damage occurs and at a time when it is not reasonably practicable for the person making the request to identify all those persons; and

(c) the supplier fails, within a reasonable period after receiving the request, either to comply with the request or to identify the person who supplied the product to him.

(4) Neither subsection (2) nor subsection (3) above shall apply to a person in respect of any defect in any game or agricultural produce if the only supply of the game or produce by that person to another was at a time when it had not undergone an industrial process.

(5) Where two or more persons are liable by virtue of this Part for the same damage, their liability shall be joint and several.

(6) This section shall be without prejudice to any liability arising otherwise than by virtue of this Part.

3 *Meaning of 'defect'*

(1) Subject to the following provisions of this section, there is a defect in a product for the purposes of this Part if the safety of the product is not such as persons are generally entitled to expect; and for those purposes 'safety' in

relation to a product, shall include safety with respect to products comprised in that product and safety in the context of risk of damage to property, as well as in the context of risks of death or personal injury.

(2) In determining for the purposes of subsection (1) above what persons generally are entitled to expect in relation to a product all the circumstances shall be taken into account, including–

(a) the manner in which, and purposes for which, the product has been marketed, its get-up, the use of any mark in relation to the product and any instructions for, or warnings with respect to, doing or refraining from doing anything with or in relation to the product;

(b) what might reasonably be expected to be done with or in relation to the product; and

(c) the time when the product was supplied by its producer to another;

and nothing in this section shall require a defect to be inferred from the fact alone that the safety of a product which is supplied after that time is greater than the safety of the product in question.

4 *Defences*

(1) In any civil proceedings by virtue of this Part against any person ('the person proceeded against') in respect of a defect in a product it shall be a defence for him to show–

(a) that the defect is attributable to compliance with any requirement imposed or under any enactment or with any Community obligation; or

(b) that the person proceeded against did not at any time supply the product to another; or

(c) that the following conditions are satisfied, that is to say–

(i) that the only supply of the product to another person by the person proceeded against was otherwise than in the course of a business of that person's; and

(ii) that section 2(2) above does not apply to that person or applies to him by virtue only of things done or otherwise than with a view to profit; or

(d) that the defect did not exist in the product at the relevant time; or

(e) that the state of scientific or technical knowledge at the relevant time was not such that a producer of products of the same description as the product in question might be expected to have discovered the defect if it had existed in his products whilst they were under his control; or

(f) that the defect–

(i) constituted a defect in a product ('the subsequent product') in which the product in question had been comprised; and

(ii) was wholly attributable to the design of the subsequent product or to compliance by the producer of the product in question with instructions given by the producer of the subsequent product.

(2) In this section 'the relevant time', in relation to electricity, means the time at which it was generated, being a time before it was transmitted or distributed, and in relation to any other product, means–

(a) if the person proceeded against is a person to whom subsection (2) of section 2 above applies in relation to the product, the time when he supplied the product to another;

(b) if that subsection does not apply to that person in relation to the product, the time when the product was last supplied by a person to whom that subsection does apply in relation to the product.

5 *Damage giving rise to liability*

(1) Subject to the following provisions of this section, in this Part 'damage' means death or personal injury or any loss of or damage to any property (including land).

(2) A person shall not be liable under section 2 above in respect of any defect in a product for the loss of or any damage to the product itself or for the loss of or any damage to the whole or any part of any product which has been supplied with the product in question comprised in it.

(3) A person shall not be liable under section 2 above for any loss of or damage to any property which, at the time it is lost or damaged, is not–

(a) of a description of property ordinarily intended for private use, occupation or consumption; and

(b) intended by the person suffering the loss or damage mainly for his own private use, occupation or consumption.

(4) No damages shall be awarded to any person by virtue of this Part in respect of any loss of or damage to property if the amount which would fall to be so awarded to that person, apart from this subsection and any liability for interest, does not exceed £275.

(5) In determining for the purposes of this Part who has suffered any loss of or damage to property and when any such loss or damage occurred, the loss or damage shall be regarded as having occurred at the earliest time at which a person with an interest in the property had knowledge of the material facts about the loss or damage.

(6) For the purposes of subsection (5) above the material facts about any loss of or damage to any property are such facts about the loss or damage as would lead a reasonable person with an interest in the property to consider the loss or damage sufficiently serious to justify his instituting proceedings for damages against a defendant who did not dispute liability and was able to satisfy a judgment.

(7) For the purposes of subsection (5) above a person's knowledge includes knowledge which he might reasonably have been expected to acquire–

(a) from facts observable or ascertainable by him; or

(b) from facts ascertainable by him with the help of appropriate expert advice which it is reasonable for him to seek;

but a person shall not be taken by virtue of this subsection to have knowledge of a fact ascertainable by him only with the help of expert advice unless he has failed to take all reasonable steps to obtain (and, where appropriate, to act on) that advice.

(8) Subsections (5) to (7) above shall not extend to Scotland.

6 *Application of certain enactments*

(1) Any damage for which a person is liable under section 2 above shall be deemed to have been caused–

(a) for the purposes of the Fatal Accidents Act 1976, by that person's wrongful act, neglect or default;

(2) Where–

(a) a person's death is caused wholly or partly by a defect in a product, or a person dies after suffering damage which has been so caused;

(b) a request such as mentioned in paragraph (a) of subsection (3) of section 2 above is made to a supplier of the product by that person's personal representatives or, in the case of a person whose death is caused wholly or partly by the defect, by any dependant or relative of that person; and

(c) the conditions specified in paragraphs (b) and (c) of that subsection are satisfied in relation to that request;

this Part shall have effect for the purposes of the Law Reform (Miscellaneous Provisions) Act 1934, the Fatal Accidents Act 1976 and the Damages (Scotland) Act 1976 as if liability of the supplier to that person under that subsection did not depend on that person having requested the supplier to identify certain persons or on the said conditions having been satisfied in relation to a request made by that person.

(3) Section 1 of the Congenital Disabilities (Civil Liability) Act 1976 shall have effect for the purposes of this Part as if–

(a) a person were answerable to a child in respect of an occurrence caused wholly or partly by a defect in a product if he is or has been liable under section 2 above in respect of any effect of the occurrence on a parent of the child, or would be so liable if the occurrence caused a parent of the child to suffer damage;

(b) the provisions of this Part relating to liability under section 2 above applied in relation to liability by virtue of paragraph (a) above under the said section 1; and

(c) subsection (6) of the said section 1 (exclusion of liability) were omitted.

(4) Where any damage is caused partly by a defect in a product and partly by the fault of the person suffering the damage, the Law Reform (Contributory Negligence) Act 1945 and section 5 of the Fatal Accidents Act 1976 (contributory negligence) shall have effect as if the defect were the fault of every person liable by virtue of this Part for the damage caused by the defect.

(5) In subsection (4) above 'fault' has the same meaning as in the said Act of 1945.

(6) Schedule 1 to this Act shall have effect for the purpose of amending the Limitation Act 1980 and the Prescription and Limitation (Scotland) Act 1973 in their application in relation to the bringing of actions by virtue of this Part.

(7) It is hereby declared that liability by virtue of this Part is to be treated as liability in tort for the purposes of any enactment conferring jurisdiction on any court with respect to any matter.

(8) Nothing in this Part shall prejudice the operation of section 12 of the Nuclear Installations Act 1965 (rights to compensation for certain breaches of duties confined to rights under that Act).

7 *Prohibition on exclusions from liability*

The liability of a person by virtue of this Part to a person who has suffered damage caused wholly or partly by a defect in a product, or to a dependant or relative of such a person, shall not be limited or excluded by any contract term, by any notice or any other provision.

45 *Interpretation*

(1) In this Act, except in so far as the context otherwise requires–

'aircraft' includes gliders, balloons and hovercraft;

'business' includes a trade or profession or trade association or of a local authority or other public authority;

'goods' includes substances, growing crops and things compromised in land by virtue of being attached to it and any ship, aircraft or vehicle;

'personal injury' includes any disease and any other impairment of a person's physical or mental condition;

'ship' includes any boat and any other description of vessel used in navigation; and

'substance' means any natural or artificial substance, whether in solid, liquid or gaseous form or in the form of a vapour, and includes substances that are comprised in or mixed with other goods.

46 *Meaning of 'supply'*

(1) Subject to the following provisions of this section, references in this Act to supplying goods shall be construed as references to doing of any of the following, whether as principal or agent, that is to say–

(a) selling, hiring out or lending the goods;

(b) entering into a hire-purchase agreement to furnish the goods;

(c) the performance of any contract for work and materials to furnish the goods;

(d) providing the goods in exchange for any consideration (including trading stamps) other than money;

(e) providing the goods in or in connection with the performance of any statutory function; or

(f) giving the goods as a prize or otherwise making a gift of the goods;

and, in relation to gas or water, those references shall be construed as including references to providing the service by which the gas or water is made available for use.

(2) For the purposes of any reference in this Act to supplying goods, where a person ('the ostensible supplier') supplies goods to another person ('the customer') under a hire-purchase agreement, conditional sale agreement or credit-sale agreement or under an agreement for the hiring of goods (other than a hire-purchase agreement) and the ostensible supplier–

(a) carries on business of financing the provision of goods for others by means of such agreements; and

(b) in the course of that business acquired his interest in the goods supplied to the customer as a means of financing the provision of them for the customer by a further person ('the effective supplier');

the effective supplier and not the ostensible supplier shall be treated as supplying the goods to the customer.

(3) Subject to subsection (4) below, the performance of any contract by the erection of any building or structure on any land or by the carrying out of any other building works shall be treated for the purposes of this Act as a supply of goods in so far as, but only in so far as, it involves the provision of any goods to any person by means of their incorporation into the building, structure or works.

(4) Except for the purposes of, and in relation to, notices to warn or any provision made by or under Part III of this Act, references in this Act to supplying goods shall not include references to supplying goods comprised in land where the supply is effected by the creation or disposal of an interest in the land.

THE DIRECTIVE

The Act detailed above is based upon the Directive set out below.

The Council of the European Communities

Having regard to the Treaty establishing the European Economic Community, and in particular Article 100 thereof,

Having regard to the proposal from the Commission,

Having regard to the opinion of the European Parliament,

Having regard to the opinion of the Economic and Social Committee,

Whereas approximation of laws of the Member States concerning the liability of the producer for damage caused by the defectiveness of his products is necessary because the existing divergencies may distort competition and affect the movement of goods within the common market and entail a differing degree of protection of the consumer against damage caused by a defective product to his health or property;

Whereas liability without fault on the part of the producer is the sole means of adequately resolving the problem, peculiar to our age of increasing technicality, of a fair apportionment of the risks inherent in modern technological production;

Whereas liability without fault should apply only to movables which have been industrially produced; whereas, as a result, it is appropriate to exclude liability for agricultural products and game, except where they have undergone a processing of an industrial nature which could cause a defect in these products; whereas the liability provided for in this Directive should also apply to movables which are used in the construction of immovables or are installed in immovables;

Whereas protection of the consumer requires that all producers involved in the production process should be made liable, in so far as the finished product, component part or any raw material supplied by them was defective; whereas, for the same reason, liability should extend to importers of products into the Community and to persons who present themselves as producers by affixing their name, trade mark or other distinguishing feature or who supply a product the producer of which cannot be identified;

Whereas, in situations where several persons are liable for the same damage, the protection of the consumer requires that the injured person should be able to claim full compensation for the damage from any one of them;

Whereas, to protect the physical well-being and property of the consumer, the defectiveness of the product should be determined by reference not to its fitness for use but to the lack of safety which the public at large is entitled to expect; whereas the safety is assessed by excluding any misuse of the product not reasonable under the circumstances;

Whereas a fair apportionment of risk between the injured person and the producer implies that the producer should be able to free himself from liability if he furnishes proof of certain exonerating circumstances;

Whereas the protection of the consumer requires that the liability of the producer remains unaffected by acts or omissions of other persons having contributed to causing the damage; whereas, however, the contributory negligence of the injured person may be taken into account to reduce or disallow such liability;

Whereas the protection of the consumer requires compensation for death and personal injury as well as compensation for damage to property; whereas the latter should nevertheless be limited to goods for private use or consumption and be subject to a deduction of a lower threshold of a fixed amount in order to avoid litigation in an excessive number of cases; whereas this Directive should not prejudice compensation for pain and suffering and other non-material damages payable, where appropriate, under the law applicable to the case;

Whereas a uniform period of limitation for the bringing of action for compensation is in the interests both of the injured person and of the producer;

Whereas products age in the course of time, higher safety standards are developing and the state of science and technology progresses; whereas, therefore, it would not be reasonable to make the producer liable for an unlimited period of the defectiveness of his product; whereas, therefore, liability should expire after a reasonable length of time, without prejudice to claims pending at law;

Whereas, to achieve effective protection of consumers, no contractual derogation should be permitted as regards the liability of the producer in relation to the injured person;

Whereas under the legal systems of the Member States an injured party may have a claim for damages based on grounds of contractual liability or on grounds of non-contractual liability other than that provided for in this Directive; in so far as these provisions also serve to attain the objective of effective protection of consumers, they should remain unaffected by this Directive; whereas, in so far as effective protection of consumers in the sector of pharmaceutical products is already also attained in a Member State under a special liability system, claims based on this system should similarly remain possible;

Whereas, to the extent that liability for nuclear injury or damage is already covered in all Member States by adequate special rules, it has been possible to exclude damage of this type from the scope of this Directive;

Whereas, since the exclusion of primary agricultural products and game from the scope of this Directive may be felt, in certain Member States, in view of what is expected for the protection of consumers, to restrict unduly such protection, it should be possible for a Member State to extend liability to such products;

Whereas, for similar reasons, the possibility offered to a producer to free himself from liability if he proves that the state of scientific and technical knowledge at the time when he put the product into circulation was not such as to enable the existence of the defect to be discovered may be felt in certain Member States to restrict unduly the protection of the consumer; whereas it should therefore be possible for a Member State to maintain in its legislation or to provide for new legislation that this exonerating circumstance is not admitted; whereas, in the case of new legislation, making use of this derogation should, however, be subject to a Community stand-still procedure, in order to raise, if possible, the level of protection in a uniform manner throughout the Community;

Whereas, taking into account the legal traditions in most of the Member States, it is inappropriate to set any financial ceiling on the producer's liability without fault; whereas, in so far as there are, however, differing traditions, it seems possible to admit that a Member State may derogate from the principle of unlimited liability by providing a limit for the total liability of the producer for damage resulting from a death or personal injury and caused by identical items with the same defect, provided that this limit is established at a level sufficiently high to guarantee adequate protection of the consumer and the correct functioning of the common market;

Whereas the harmonisation resulting from this cannot be total at the present stage, but opens the way towards greater harmonisation; whereas it is therefore necessary that the Council receive at regular intervals, reports from the Commission on the application of this Directive, accompanied, as the case may be, by appropriate proposals;

Whereas it is particularly important in this respect that a re-examination be carried out of those parts of the Directive relating to the derogations open to the Member States, at the expiry of a period of sufficient length to gather practical experience on the effects of these derogations on the protection of consumers and on the functioning of the common market,

Has adopted this Directive:

Article 1

The producer shall be liable for damage caused by a defect in his product.

Article 2

For the purpose of this Directive 'product' means all movables, with the exception of primary agricultural products and game, even though incorporated into another movable or into an immovable. 'Primary agricultural products' means the products of the soil, of stock-farming and of fisheries, excluding products which have undergone initial processing. 'Product' includes electricity.

Article 3

1 'Producer' means the manufacturer of a finished product, the producer of any raw material or the manufacturer of a component part and any person who, by putting his name, trade mark or other distinguishing feature on the product presents himself as its producer.

2 Without prejudice to the liability of the producer, any person who imports into the Community a product for sale, hire, leasing or any form of distribution in the course of his business shall be deemed to be a producer within the meaning of this Directive and shall be responsible as a producer.

3 Where the producer of the product cannot be identified, each supplier of the product shall be treated as its producer unless he informs the injured person, within a treasonable time, of the identity of the producer or of the person who supplied him with the product. The same shall apply, in the case of an imported product, if this product does not indicate the identity of the importer referred to in paragraph 2, even if the name of the producer is indicated.

Article 4

The injured person shall be required to prove the damage, the defect and the causal relationship between defect and damage.

Article 5

Where, as a result of the provisions of this Directive, two or more persons are liable for the same damage, they shall be liable jointly and severally, without prejudice to the provisions of national law concerning the rights of contribution or recourse.

Article 6

1 A product is defective when it does not provide the safety which a person is entitled to expect, taking all circumstances into account, including–

(a) the presentation of the product;

(b) the use to which it could reasonably be expected that the product be put;

(c) the time when the product was put into circulation.

2 A product shall not be considered defective for the sole reason that a better product is subsequently put into circulation.

Article 7

The producer shall not be liable as a result of this Directive if he proves–

(a) that he did not put the product into circulation; or

(b) that, having regard to the circumstances, it is probable that the defect which caused the damage did not exist at the time when the product was put into circulation by him or that this defect came into being afterwards; or

(c) that the product was neither manufactured by him for sale or any form of distribution for economic purpose nor manufactured or distributed by him in the course of his business; or

(d) that the defect is due to compliance of the product with mandatory regulations issued by the public authorities; or

(e) that the state of scientific and technical knowledge at the time when he put the product into circulation was not such as to enable the existence of the defect to be discovered; or

(f) in the case of a manufacturer of a component, that the defect is attributable to the design of the product in which the component has been fitted or to the instructions given by the manufacturer of the product.

Article 8

1 Without prejudice to the provisions of national law concerning the right of contribution or recourse, the liability of the producer shall not be reduced when the damage is caused both by a defect in the product and by the act or omission of a third party.

2 The liability of the producer may be reduced or disallowed when, having regard to all the circumstances, the damage is caused both by a defect in the product and by the fault of the injured person or any person for whom the injured person is responsible.

Article 9

For the purpose of Article 1, 'damage' means–

(a) damage caused by death or personal injuries;

(b) damage to, or destruction of, any item of property other than the defective product itself, with a lower threshold of 500 ECU, provided that the item of property:

   (i) is of a type ordinarily intended for private use and consumption, and

   (ii) was used by the injured person mainly for his own private use or consumption.

This Article shall be without prejudice to national provisions relating to non-material damage.

Article 10

1 Member States shall provide in their legislation that a limitation period of three years shall apply to proceedings for recovery of damages as provided for in this Directive. The limitation period shall begin to run from the day on which the plaintiff became aware, or should reasonably have become aware, of the damage, the defect and the identity of the producer.

2 The laws of Member States regulating suspension or interruption of the limitation period shall not be affected by this Directive.

Article 11

Member States shall provide in their legislation that the rights conferred upon the injured person pursuant to this Directive shall be extinguished upon the expiry of a period of 10 years from the date on which the producer put into circulation the actual product which caused the damage, unless the injured person has in the meantime instituted proceedings against the producer.

Article 12

The liability of the producer arising from this Directive may not, in relation to the injured person, be limited or excluded by a provision limiting his liability or exempting him from liability.

Article 13

This Directive shall not affect any rights which an injured person may have according to the rules of the law of contractual or non-contractual liability or a special liability system existing at the moment when this Directive is notified.

Article 14

This Directive shall not apply to injury or damage arising from nuclear accidents and covered by international conventions ratified by Member States.

Article 15

1 Each Member State may–

(a) by way of derogation from Article 2, provide in its legislation that within the meaning of Article 1 of this Directive 'product' also means primary agricultural products and game; and

(b) by way of derogation from Article 7(e), maintain or, subject to the procedure set out in paragraph 2 of this Article, provide in this legislation that the producer shall be liable even if he proves that the state of scientific and technical knowledge at the time when he put the product into circulation was not such as to enable the existence of a defect to be discovered.

2 A Member State wishing to introduce the measures specified in paragraph 1(b) shall communicate the text of the proposed measure to the Commission. The Commission shall inform the other Member States thereof.

The Member State concerned shall hold the proposed measure in abeyance for nine months after the Commission is informed and provided that in the meantime the Commission has not submitted to the Council a proposal amending this Directive on the relevant matter. However, if within three months of receiving the said information, the Commission does not advise the Member State concerned that it intends submitting such a proposal to the Council, the Member State may take the proposed measure immediately

If the Commission does submit to the Council such a proposal amending this Directive within the aforementioned nine months, the Member State concerned shall hold the proposed measure in abeyance for a further period of 18 months from the date on which the proposal is submitted.

3 Ten years after the date of notification of this Directive, the Commission shall submit to the Council a report on the effect that rulings by the courts as to the application of Article 7(e) and of paragraph 1(b) of this Article have on consumer protection and the functioning of the common market. In the light of this report the Council, acting on a proposal from the Commission and pursuant to the terms of Article 100 of the Treaty, shall decide whether to repeal Article 7(e).

Article 16

1 Any Member State may provide that a producer's total liability for damage resulting from a death or personal injury and caused by identical items with the same defect shall be limited to an amount which may not be less than 70 million ECU.

2 Ten years after the date of notification of this Directive, the Commission shall submit to the Council a report on the effect on consumer protection and the functioning of the common market of the implementation of the financial limit on liability by those Member States which have used the option provided for in paragraph 1. In the light of this report the Council, acting on a proposal from the Commission and pursuant to the terms of Article 100 of the Treaty, shall decide whether to repeal paragraph 1.

Article 17

This Directive shall not apply to products put into circulation before the date on which the provisions referred to in Article 19 enter into force.

Article 18

1 For the purposes of this Directive, the ECU shall be that defined by Regulation (EEC) No 2626/84. The equivalent in national currency shall initially be calculated at the rate obtaining on the date of adoption of this Directive.

2 Every five years the Council, acting on a proposal from the Commission, shall examine and, if need be, revise the amounts in this Directive, in the light of economic and monetary trends in the Community.

Article 19

1 Member States shall bring into force, not later than three years from the date of notification of this Directive, the laws, regulations and administrative provisions necessary to comply with this Directive. They shall forthwith inform the Community thereof.

2 The procedure set out in Article 15(2) shall apply from the date of notification of this Directive.

Article 20

Member States shall communicate the texts of the main provisions of national law which they subsequently adopt in the field governed by this Directive.

Article 21

Every five years the Commission shall present a report to the Council on the application of this Directive and, if necessary, shall submit appropriate proposals to it.

Article 22

This Directive is addressed to the Member States.

COMMENTARY

Products covered

It will have been noticed that the UK legislation has opted to leave unprocessed agricultural products and game outside the scope of the meaning of product, as is permitted by the Directive. This means that any claim for damage following the supply of unwholesome meat or poultry or similarly unfit vegetables or fruit can only be brought under the common law discussed above. It has long been held that a breach of the food legislation does not give rise to a civil remedy, merely criminal sanctions.[16] One problem may arise in relation to the wording of the 1987 Act when it talks of an 'industrial process'. This will clearly cover fish fingers, beefburgers and the like, but the Directive uses the expression 'initial processing'. Does this involve something short of a process such as the fish are subjected to before becoming fish fingers. It is possible that this wording would cover the treatment of eg fruit with chemicals to prevent decay or attack by insects or birds. It might also cover the cleaning and plucking of poultry before being put on sale. It would seem that such activity is not an 'industrial process' within the 1987 Act. There is possibly here some scope for arguing that there is a discrepancy between the UK statute and the Directive which might need at some stage a decision from the European Court.

Producer

This is given a very wide meaning so as to avoid some of the pitfalls of the common law, particularly the difficult practical problem of suing remote manufacturers. This has been to some extent resolved by imposing liability onto the first importer into the Union. A person may become a producer by subjecting game or agricultural products to an industrial process which establishes its essential characteristics. Retailers who put their own brand on goods, even though they do not make the products themselves, are regarded as producers, as are retailers or, for that matter, anybody else in the distribution chain who cannot or will not name the producer or the person who supplied the goods to them. This means great emphasis must be placed on organisations, large and small, to keep accurate records of their suppliers.

Actionable damage

Unlike the common law, the damage to be actionable under the strict liability provisions must be personal injury or death, and consumer property damage over the threshold figure of £275. As much consumer property is likely to be insured, the major benefit for the consumer is the strict liability for personal injury. The extension to consumer property is, in most cases, only of benefit to the insurance companies of consumers using the subrogation rule. Commercial property damage can only be pursued at common law, but again, in many

16 See *Square v Model Farm Dairies* [1939] 2 KB 365 on the earlier legislation, but it is thought that the position would be no different under the present legislation, the Food Safety Act 1990.

cases, this will cause a headache for the insurance companies of the owners of commercial property. Damage to the product itself, the fact that it is merely shoddy and of inferior quality, is not actionable under the Act. Likewise, damage caused to a parent product by a component part is not recoverable under the Act.

Defect

There is a complex definition of what amounts to a defective product. The standard, much like the common law, is a relative one. Just because the product causes injury does not mean to say it is defective, otherwise most products would fall into this category. The product must be judged according to standards applicable at the time of putting into circulation. It seems patently clear that the courts must become involved in a degree of cost/benefit analysis in assessing whether an item is defective. With considerable justification, Stapleton argues[17] that problems of risk assessment and policy evaluation are not eliminated in a shift from a fault-based liability to one based on defects in products which is dependent on cost/benefit assessment. She continues:

> Liability will still rest on complex and costly questions and the outcome in many cases may be just as uncertain and unpredictable as it is under negligence.

It must not be overlooked that this comment was made in an article before the UK legislation was put into place. The whole article is an extremely sceptical view of the prospects of satisfactory reform of the area of product liability. It is well and cogently argued, but so far there is little evidence to bear out the writer's worse fears. In fact, there is just no evidence of reported cases to judge one way or the other. Experience may suggest that insurance companies are significantly mush less likely to go to court where the plaintiff has the major advantage of not having to prove fault.

Defences

The Act provides a number of defences but the most controversial is that known as the 'state of the art' defence. Criticism has been directed in the first place at the very existence of this defence in a statute imposing strict liability as it seems incongruous. The burden of proof in relation to the defence is on the defendant, but nonetheless the provision of such a defence, which is more at home in fault-based systems of liability, in a scheme such as that established by the 1987 Act seems entirely inappropriate. The other criticism of the defence highlights the apparent disparity between the wording of the defence as it appears in the 1987 Act and the wording set out in the Directive. It is suggested that the defence at it stands in the UK is far too defendant-oriented in the way in which it seems to look at the state of the art from the point of view of the 'hypothetical' producer. It appears that the Commission was none too happy with the wording of the UK statute and referred the matter to the European Court of Justice. It is argued that, with the provision of the defence, another Thalidomide disaster could slip through the litigation net.

17 (1986) 6 OJLS 392.

CHAPTER 9

STRICT LIABILITY

INTRODUCTION

In the last chapter we saw that the law on product liability was a mixture of common law negligence and strict statutory liability. In this chapter we shall be looking at three areas of liability which are, or were considered to be, areas where liability was imposed without proof of fault. We shall discover that the picture is far less straightforward than that, and that there is once again this rather unsatisfactory mix of fault-based and strict liability. The three areas are liability for the escape of things (the rule in *Rylands v Fletcher*), liability for fire and, finally, liability for animals. In a sense all three areas are closely linked, but there is a tendency to treat them as distinct fields of liability. If cases of liability under the rules discussed in the previous chapter are fairly rare, then cases under these three topics must be even rarer. We shall start by considering the rule in *Rylands v Fletcher* which, as we shall see, has some similarities with the law of nuisance, the subject of the next chapter.

LIABILITY FOR ESCAPES OF THINGS

The origin for this type of liability would seem to be the case of *Rylands v Fletcher*,[1] although support for the principle expressed in that case was found in the earlier cases on nuisance and cattle trespass. Liability for such activities was considered to be strict and the trend was, on the face of it, continued in this case, although the overall trend was towards a fault-based liability elsewhere, as we shall see in the chapter on trespass to the person. In a sense, like nuisance, the rule in this case is an early form of environmental tort, although the frequency of its use would suggest that it is hardly a major player in controlling environmental hazards. However, there are indications that it was an attempt to impose control on hazardous activities affecting others, as well as a form of enterprise liability.

The defendants in the case had arranged for the construction of a reservoir on their land. Unknown to them and their contractors, there were old mine workings under the land which connected with the plaintiff's mines under his land. When the reservoir was filled the water burst through into the plaintiff's mine workings. In the Court of Exchequer Chamber, Blackburn J made his famous statement about the liability of a defendant in such a case, which came to be known as the rule in *Rylands v Fletcher*:

> The plaintiff, though free from all blame on his part, must bear the loss, unless he can establish that it was the consequence of some default for which the defendants are responsible. The question of law therefore arises, what is the obligation which the law casts on a person who, like the defendants, lawfully brings on his land something which, though harmless whilst it remains there, will naturally do mischief if it escape out of his land. It is agreed on all hands that

1 (1866) LR 1 Ex 265.

> he must take care to keep in that which he has brought on the land and keeps there, in order that it may not escape and damage his neighbours, but the question arises whether the duty which the law casts upon him, under such circumstances, is an absolute duty to keep it in at his peril, or is, as the majority of the Court of Exchequer thought, merely a duty to take all reasonable and prudent precautions in order to keep it in, but no more. If the first be the law, the person who has brought on his land and kept there something dangerous, and failed to keep it in, is responsible for all the natural consequences of its escape. If the second be the limit of his duty, he would not be answerable except on proof of negligence, and consequently would not be answerable for escape arising from any latent defect which ordinary prudence and skill could not detect.
>
> Supposing the second to be the correct view of the law, a further question arises subsidiary to the first, *viz* whether the defendants are not so far identified with the contractors whom they employed as to be responsible for the consequences of their want of care and skill in making the reservoir in fact insufficient with reference to the old shafts, the existence of which they were aware, though they had not ascertained where the shafts went to.
>
> We think that the true rule of law is, that the person who for his own purposes brings on his land and collects and keeps there anything likely to do mischief if it escapes, must keep it in at his peril, and, if he does not do so, is *prima facie* answerable for all the damage which is the natural consequence of its escape. He can excuse himself by showing that the escape was owing to the plaintiff's default; or, perhaps that the escape was the consequence of *vis major*, or the act of God; but as nothing of the sort exists here, it is unnecessary to inquire what excuse would be sufficient. The general rule, as above stated, seems on principle just. The person whose grass or corn is eaten down by the escaping cattle of his neighbour, or whose mine is flooded by the water from his neighbour's reservoir, or whose cellar is invaded by the filth of his neighbour's privy, or whose habitation is made unhealthy by the fumes and noisome vapours of his neighbour's alkali works, is damnified without any fault of his own: and it seems but reasonable and just that the neighbour, who has brought something on his own property which was not naturally there, harmless to others as long as it is confined to his own property, but which he knows to be mischievous if it gets on his neighbour's, should be obliged to make good the damage which ensues if he does not succeed in confining it to his own property. But for his act in bringing it there no mischief could have accrued, and it seems but just that he should at his peril keep it there so that no mischief may arise, or answer for the natural and anticipated consequences. And upon authority, this we think is established to be the law whether the things so brought be beasts, or water, or filth, or stenches.

This statement is treated as the true principle, although it has to be acknowledged that in the subsequently appeal from the decision of the Exchequer Chamber, Lord Cairns had something useful to say on the applicability of the principle which the courts will look for in the facts before them. This is the 'non-natural user' criterion mentioned in the extract from Lord Cairns' speech[2] below:

> My Lords, the principles on which this case must be determined appear to me to be extremely simple. The defendants, treating them as the owners or occupiers of the close on which the reservoir was constructed, might have lawfully used that close for any purpose for which it might in the ordinary course of the enjoyment

2 (1868) LR 3 HL 330.

> of land be used; and if, in what I may term the natural user of that land, there had been an accumulation of water, either on the surface or underground, and if, by the operation of the laws of nature, that accumulation of water had passed off into the close occupied by the plaintiff, the plaintiff could not have complained that that result had taken place. If he had desired to guard himself against it, it would have lain upon him to have done so, by leaving, or by interposing, some barrier between his close and the close of the defendants in order to have prevented that operation of the laws of nature. ...
>
> On the other hand if the defendants, not stopping at the natural use of their close, had desired to use it for any purpose which I may term non-natural use, for the purpose of introducing into the close that which in its natural condition was not in or upon it, for the purpose of introducing water either above or below ground in quantities and in a manner not the result of any work or operation on or under the land, and if in consequence of their doing so, or in consequence of any imperfection in the mode of their doing so, the water came to escape and to pass off into the close of the plaintiff, then it appears to me that that which the defendants were doing they were doing at their own peril; and, if in the course of their doing it, the evil arose to which I have referred, the evil, namely, of the escape of the water and its passing away to the close of the plaintiff and injuring the plaintiff, then for the consequence of that, in my opinion, the defendants would be liable.

Lord Cranworth agreed with the Lord Chancellor, dismissing the appeal. It was thought that the case only applied to dangerous things, but, as the facts of the case themselves suggest, the rule is wider in that it can apply to something which might normally be safe in smaller quantities. At times, it will be the artificial accumulation of the item on the land which gives rise to the operation of the principle.

Non-natural use

Lord Cairns, in his speech, laid emphasis on the unusual nature of the use of the land by the occupier or owner. This was discussed in *Rickards v Lothian*,[3] in which a third party had, it appears, deliberately blocked a toilet basin, causing water to overflow from the upstairs of a building to a lower floor damaging the plaintiff's property. In finding the defendant not responsible, the Privy Council commented on the non-natural user point. Lord Moulton observed:

> It is not every use to which land is put that brings into play that principle. It must be some special use bringing with it increased danger to others, and must not merely be the ordinary use of land or such use as is proper for the general benefit of the community.

Later, in justifying his view that this was a natural user of the land, His Lordship continued:

> The provision of a proper supply of water to the various parts of a house is not only reasonable, but has become, in accordance with modern sanitary views, an almost necessary feature of town life. It is recognised as being so desirable in the interests of the community that, in some form or other, it is usually made obligatory in civilised countries. Such a supply cannot be installed without causing some concurrent danger of leakage or overflow. It would be

3 [1913] AC 263.

> unreasonable for the law to regard those who install or maintain such a system of supply as doing so at their own peril, with an absolute liability for any damage resulting from its presence even when there has been no negligence.

The issue has cropped up, as might be expected, in other cases since the above. In *Read v Lyons*[4] the appellant was injured following an explosion at a munitions factory which she was inspecting at the time. On the non-natural user point, Viscount Simon commented somewhat curtly:

> I think it not improper to put on record, with all due regard to the admission and dicta in that case,[5] that if the question had hereafter to be decided whether the making of munitions in a factory at the government's request in time of war for the purpose of helping to defeat the enemy is a 'non-natural' use of land, adopted by the occupier for his 'own purposes', it would not seem to me that the house would be bound by this authority to say that it was.

Lord Macmillan in the course of his speech, aspects of which we shall return to shortly, said:

> I should hesitate to hold that, in these days and in an industrial community, it was a non-natural use of land to build a factory on it and conduct there the manufacture of explosives.

Lord Porter delicately and skillfully avoided answering this question throughout his judgment. An interesting case which also touched upon this point is *British Celanese Ltd v A H Hunt (Capacitors) Ltd*,[6] in which one of the issues was whether the escape of metal foil strips stored on the premises of the defendants fell within the rule. Lawton J stated:

> The manufacturing of electrical and electronic components in 1964, which is the material date, cannot be adjudged to be a special use, nor can bringing and storing on the premises of metal foil be a special use in itself. The way the metal foil was stored may have been a negligent one; but the use of the premises for storing such foil did not, by itself, create special risks. The metal foil was there for use in the manufacture of goods of a common type which, at all material times, were needed for the general benefit of the community.

The most full discussion of this issue occurred in the very recent case in the House of Lords, *Cambridge Water Co Ltd v Eastern Counties Leather plc*,[7] in which the House put paid to any attempt to revive the rule and retrieve it from its apparent death throes. In this case, there had been a gradual and imperceptible seepage of chemicals used by the defendants in their tanning process through the soil and layers of rock. Eventually, the chemicals hit impermeable material underground and drained into the borehole belonging to the plaintiffs. On the issue of user, Lord Goff, with whom everybody else in the House agreed, said:

> It is obvious that the expression 'ordinary use of the land' in Lord Moulton's statement of the law is one which is lacking in precision. There are some writers who welcome the flexibility which has thus been introduced into this branch of the law, on the ground that it enables judges to mould and adapt the principle of strict liability to the changing needs of society; whereas others regret the

4 [1947] AC 156.

5 *Rainham Chemical Works Ltd v Belvedere Fish Guano Co Ltd* [1921] AC 465.

6 [1969] 1 WLR 959.

7 [1994] 1 All ER 53.

> perceived absence of principle in so vague a concept, and fear that the whole idea of strict liability may as a result be undermined. A particular doubt is introduced by Lord Moulton's alternative criterion 'or such a use as is proper for the general benefit of the community'. If these words are understood to refer to a local community, they can be given some content as intended to refer to such matters as, for example, the provision of services; indeed the same idea can, without too much difficulty, be extended to, for example, the provision of services to industrial premises, as in a business park or an industrial estate.
>
> But if the words are extended to embrace the wider interests of the local community or the general benefit of the community at large, it is difficult to see how the exception can be kept within reasonable bounds ... [We] can see the introduction of another extension in the present case, when the judge invoked the creation of employment as clearly for the benefit of the local community, *viz* 'the industrial village' at Sawston. I myself, however, do not feel able to accept that the creation of employment as such, even in a small industrial complex, is sufficient of itself to establish a particular use as constituting a natural or ordinary use of land.
>
> Fortunately, I do not think that it is necessary for the purposes of the present case to attempt any redefinition of the concept of natural or ordinary use. This is because I am satisfied that the storage of chemicals in substantial quantities, and their use in the manner employed at ECL's premises, cannot fall within the exception. For the purpose of testing the point, let it be assumed that ECL was well aware of the possibility that PCE, if it escaped, could indeed cause damage, for example by contaminating any water with which it became mixed so as to render that water undrinkable by human beings. I cannot think that it would be right in such circumstances to exempt ECL from liability under the rule in *Rylands v Fletcher* on the ground that the use was natural or ordinary. The mere fact that the use is common in the tanning industry cannot, in my opinion, be enough to bring the use within the exception, nor the fact that Sawston contains a small industrial community which is worthy of encouragement or support. Indeed I feel bound to say that the storage of substantial quantities of chemicals on industrial premises should be regarded as an almost classic case of non-natural use; and I find it very difficult to think that it should be thought objectionable to impose strict liability for damage caused in the event of their escape. It may well be that, now that it is recognised that foreseeability of harm of the relevant type is a prerequisite of liability in damages under the rule, the courts may feel less pressure to extend the concept of natural use to circumstances such as those in the present case; and in due course it may become easier to control this exception, and to ensure that it has a more recognisable basis of principle.

Contained in the above extract is the clue to the loss of the case by the plaintiff, the issue of foreseeability of harm to which we shall return shortly. Therefore, the above comments were not part of the decision on the case which is unfortunate. What Lord Goff has given with the one hand, he has taken away with the other, which is doubly unfortunate. We shall return to this below.

Escape

There must be an escape. The case of *Read v Lyons* illustrates this point neatly. The plaintiff was still on the premises when she sustained her injuries. Viscount Simon observed:

'Escape', for the purpose of applying the proposition in *Rylands v Fletcher*, means escape from a place where the defendant has occupation of or control over land, to a place which is outside his occupation or control. Blackburn J several times refers to the defendant's duty as being the duty of 'keeping a thing in' at the defendant's peril, and by 'keeping in' he does not mean preventing an explosive substance from exploding but preventing a thing which may inflict mischief from escaping from the area which the defendant occupies or controls.

The plaintiff therefore lost on this point, but she can take consolation that she would have lost on the user point if the court had been pressed, or on another point discussed below relating to personal injury claims.

Status of the plaintiff

There has been some controversy over whether the plaintiff need show an interest in land in order to sustain an action. Hitherto, or at least until very recently as we shall see in the next chapter, this has been the rule in actions for private nuisance. Some have argued that the plaintiff must at least be an occupier of adjacent land since the rule is akin to nuisance. The better view, as supported by the majority of cases, is that it is not an essential requirement.[8] In the *Cambridge* case the House left open the point as to whether the rule was a free-standing tort in its own right or merely an adjunct of nuisance. Another issue that has been the focus of some attention is whether a plaintiff can sue for personal injuries. This is an issue which has afflicted the sister tort of private nuisance also. In *Read v Lyons* Lord Macmillan made some forthright statements on this topic as follows:

In my opinion the appellant's statement of claim discloses no ground of action against the respondents. The action is one of damages for personal injuries. Whatever may have been the law of England in early times, I am of the opinion that, as the law now stands, an allegation of negligence is in general essential to the relevancy of an action of reparation for personal injuries ... the process of evolution has been from the principle that every man acts at his peril and is liable for all the consequences of his acts to the principle that a man's freedom of action is subject only to the obligation not to infringe any duty of care which he owes to others. The emphasis formerly was on the injury sustained, and the question was whether the case fell within one of the accepted classes of common law actions; the emphasis now is on the conduct of the person whose act has occasioned the injury, and the question is whether it can be characterised as negligent. I do not overlook the fact there is at least one instance in the present law in which the primitive rule survives, namely in the case of animals *ferae naturae* or animals *mansuetae naturae* which have shown dangerous proclivities. The owner or keeper of such an animal has an absolute duty to confine or control it so that it shall not do injury to others, and no proof of care on his part will absolve him from responsibility. But this is probably not so much a vestigial relic of otherwise discarded doctrine as a special of practical good sense, At any rate, it is too well established to be challenged. But such an exceptional case as this affords no justification for its extension by analogy.

The appellant in her printed case in this House thus poses the question to be determined: 'Whether the manufacturer of high-explosive shells is under strict

8 See eg *Perry v Kendricks Transport Ltd* [1956] 1 WLR 85.

> liability to prevent such shells from exploding and causing harm to persons on the premises where such manufacture is carried on as well as to persons outside such premises.' Two points arise on this statement of the question. In the first place the expression 'strict liability', though borrowed from authority, is ambiguous. If it means the absolute liability of an insurer irrespective of negligence, then the answer in my opinion must be in the negative. If it means that an exacting standard of care is incumbent on manufacturers of explosive shells to prevent the occurrence of accidents causing personal injuries, I should answer the question in the affirmative, but this will not avail the appellant. In the next place, the question as stated would seem to assume that liability would exist in the present case to persons injured outside the defendants' premises without any proof of negligence on the part of the defendants. ... In my opinion persons injured by the explosion inside or outside the defendants' premises would alike require to aver and prove negligence in order to render the defendants liable. ... I am unable to accept the proposition that, in law, the manufacture of high-explosive shells is a dangerous operation which imposes on the manufacturer an absolute liability for any personal injuries which may be sustained in consequence of his operations. Strict liability, if you will, is imposed upon him in the sense that he must exercise a high degree of care, but that is all.
>
> The sound view, in my opinion, is that the law in all cases exacts a degree of care commensurate with the risk created. It was suggested that some operations are so intrinsically dangerous that no degree of care, however scrupulous, can prevent the occurrence of accidents, and that those who choose for their own ends to carry on such operations ought to be held to do so at their peril. If this were so, many industries would have a serious liability imposed on them. Should it be thought that this is a reasonable liability to impose in the public interest, it is for Parliament so to enact. In my opinion it is not the present law of England. ...
>
> The doctrine of *Rylands v Fletcher*, as I understand it, derives from a conception of mutual duties of adjoining or neighbouring landowners and its congeners are trespass and nuisance. If its foundation is to be found in the injunction *sic utere tuo ut alienum non laedas*, then it is manifest that it has nothing to do with personal injuries. The duty is to refrain from injuring not *alium* but *alienum*. The two prerequisites of the doctrine are that there must be the escape of something from one man's close to another man's close, and that that which escapes must have been brought upon the land from which it escapes in consequence of some non-natural use of that land, whatever precisely that may mean.

Lord Simonds left this point open in his speech. The other judges did not comment on the point. It was clearly not part of the decision. Subsequently, it has been said that the principle does extend to personal injuries.[9] Parker LJ in *Perry v Kendricks Transport Ltd*, stated that:

> ... nor do I think that it is open to this court to hold that the rule only applies to damage to adjoining land, or to a proprietary interest in land and not to personal injury.

The better view must be that the rule does apply to such injuries, despite the strong statement to the contrary from an eminent a judge as Lord Macmillan.

9 See *Benning v Wong* [1969] 122 CLR 249.

Defences

There are a number of defences available to a defendant including consent by the plaintiff, statutory authority, Act of God and act of a third party. We shall briefly look at the latter two. An Act of God, it would appear, nowadays will only be a defence if the event in question was something which no human foresight could have guarded against. Lord Finlay LC in *Greenock Corpn v Caledonian Rly Co*[10] said that the event in question in that case was a 'flood of extraordinary violence, but floods of extraordinary violence must be anticipated as likely to take place from time to time'. In view of improved methods of predicting the weather, an Act of God is less likely to be accepted as a defence if the event is something of the nature as occurred in that case.

The other defence to be discussed is the act of a stranger. In the *Rickards* case, it will be recalled that the damage was caused when a third party mischievously blocked the basin, causing water to cascade to the floors below. Lord Moulton continued where he left off earlier on the natural user point as follows:

> It would be still more unreasonable if, as the respondent contends, such liability were to be held to extend to the consequences of malicious acts on the part of third persons. In such matters as the domestic supply of water or gas it is essential that the mode of supply should be such as to permit ready access for the purpose of use, and hence it is impossible to guard against wilful mischief.

Returning to *Perry's* case where a boy was injured when some other children put a match into the petrol tank of a disused vehicle on the defendant's land; in rejecting the boy's claim, the members of the Court of Appeal seized upon the fact that the act was by a stranger for whom the defendant was not responsible in law under the principle. On this issue Singleton LJ commented:

> I am prepared to accept this position. If the person who interferes with something of the defendants is a person whom they might expect to be upon their ground, and if the character of the interference is something which they ought to anticipate, then they would owe some duty. The measure of that duty depends upon the circumstances, the nature of the object and the age of the children. I do not think that it can extend to that which happened in this case. Someone removed the cap. Someone threw the lighted match into the tank. There is no evidence to show that either of those things ought to be anticipated. ... The match was thrown into the tank mischievously and deliberately. It cannot be said that it was something which the defendants ought to have anticipated, and it was the act of one who was not under their control in any sense. He was a stranger.

Parker LJ also took a similar line:

> It has for a long time been an exception to the rule if the defendants can show that the act which brought about the escape was the act of a stranger, meaning thereby, someone over whom they had no control. The acts in question here, firstly, of removing the petrol cap, and secondly, of inserting a lighted match, are, as it seems to me, *prima facie* undoubtedly the acts of strangers in that sense. ... In a *Rylands v Fletcher* case the plaintiff need only prove the escape. The onus is then on the defendants to bring themselves within one of the exceptions. Once they prove that the escape was caused by the act of a stranger, whether an adult or a child, they escape liability, unless the plaintiff can go on to show that the act

10 [1917] AC 556.

> which caused the escape was an act of the kind which the occupier could reasonably have anticipated and guarded against. In that connection it seems to me that it is not sufficient for the plaintiff to show that the defendants knew that children played in the vehicle park, on the roof of a motor car or inside a coach. They must show that the defendants reasonably should have anticipated an act of a kind which would cause the escape.

Clearly, the plaintiff has an uphill struggle should the defendant be in a position to plead act of a stranger.

Remoteness of damage

The final topic to consider under the rule is that of remoteness of damage, a matter which was recently the major point in the *Cambridge Water* case, as mentioned earlier. Following the decision in *Wagon Mound (No 2)*, a case primarily brought in public nuisance it will be recalled, it had been mooted that a similar remoteness test, namely reasonable foreseeability of the type of harm, might apply in cases brought under *Rylands*, although there were those who argued that this would be incongruous in the context of a strict liability action. After discussing foreseeability of damage in nuisance, Lord Goff continued:

> It is against this background that I turn to the submission advanced by ECL before your Lordships, that there is a similar prerequisite of recovery of damages under the rule in *Rylands v Fletcher*.

His Lordship then sets out the famous statement by Blackburn J and continues:

> In that passage Blackburn J spoke of 'anything *likely* to do mischief if it escapes'; and later he spoke of something 'which he *knows* to be mischievous if it gets on to his neighbour's property', and the liability to 'answer for the natural and *anticipated* consequences'. Furthermore, time and again he spoke of the strict liability imposed upon the defendant as being that he must keep the thing in at his peril; and, when referring to liability in actions for damage occasioned by animals, he referred (at 282) to the established principle 'that it is quite immaterial whether the escape is by negligence or not'. The general tenor of his statement of principle is therefore that knowledge, or at least foreseeability of the risk, is a prerequisite of the recovery of damages under the principle; but the principle is one of strict liability in the sense that the defendant may be held liable notwithstanding that he has exercised all due care to prevent the escape from occurring.

His Lordship then considered a number of cases which suggested that foreseeability of damage was not an essential of liability under the rule, but concluded that the cases provided 'a very fragile base for any firm conclusion that foreseeability of damage has been rejected as a prerequisite of the recovery of damages' under the rule. He went on:

> The point is one on which academic opinion appears to be divided: *cf Salmond and Heuston on Torts* (20th edn, 1992) pp 324–25, which favours the prerequisite of foreseeability, and *Clerk and Lindsell on Torts* (16th edn, 1989) para 25.09, which takes a different view. However, quite apart from the indications to be derived from the judgment of Blackburn J, ... to which I have already referred, the historical connection with the law of nuisance must now be regarded as pointing towards the conclusion that foreseeability of damage is a prerequisite of the recovery of damages under the rule. I have already referred to the fact that Blackburn J himself did not regard his statement of principle as having broken

new ground; furthermore, Professor Newark has convincingly shown that the rule ... was essentially concerned with an extension of the law of nuisance to cases of isolated escape. Accordingly, since, following the observations of Lord Reid when delivering the advice of the Privy Council in *The Wagon Mound (No 2)* [1966] 2 All ER 709 at 717, [1967] 1 AC 617 at 640, the recovery of damages in private nuisance depends on foreseeability by the defendant of the relevant type of damage, it would appear logical to extend the same requirement to liability under the rule. ...

Even so, the question cannot be considered solely as a matter of history. It can be argued that the rule ... should not be regarded simply as an extension of the law of nuisance, but should rather be treated as a developing principle of strict liability from which can be derived a general rule of strict liability for damage caused by ultra-hazardous operations, on the basis of which persons conducting such operations may properly be held strictly liable for the extraordinary risk to others involved in such operations. As is pointed out in *Fleming on Torts* (8th edn, 1992) pp 327–28, this would lead to the practical result that the cost of damage resulting from such operations would have to be absorbed as part of the overheads of the relevant business, rather than be borne (where there is no negligence) by the injured person or his insurers, or even by the community at large. Such a development appears to have been taking place in the United States, as can be seen from para 519 of the *Restatement of Torts* (2nd edn, vol 3, 1977). The extent to which it has done so is not altogether clear; and I infer from para 519, and the comment in that paragraph, that the abnormally dangerous activities there referred to are such that their ability to cause harm would be obvious to any reasonable person who carried them on.

I have to say, however, that there are serious obstacles in the way of the development of the rule ... in this way. First of all, if it was so to develop, it should logically apply to all persons suffering injury by reason of the ultra-hazardous operations; but the decision of this House in *Read v Lyons* [1946] 2 All ER 471, [1947] AC 156, which establishes that there can be no liability under the rule except where the injury has been caused by an escape from land under the control of the defendant, has effectively precluded any such development. Professor Fleming has observed that 'the most damaging effect of the decision in *Read v Lyons* is that it prematurely stunted the development of a general theory of strict liability for ultra-hazardous activities' (see *Fleming on Torts*, 8th edn, 1992, p 341). Even so, there is much to be said for the view that the courts should not be proceeding down the path of developing such a general theory. In this connection, I refer in particular to the report of the Law Commission on *Civil Liability for Dangerous Things and Activities* (Law Com no 32) 1970. In paras 14–16 of the report, the Law Commission expressed serious misgivings about the adoption of any test for the application of strict liability involving a general concept of 'especially dangerous' or 'ultra-hazardous' activity, having regard to the uncertainties and practical difficulties of its application. If the Law Commission is unwilling to consider statutory reform on this basis, it must follow that judges should if anything be even more reluctant to proceed down that path.

Like the judge in the present case, I incline to the opinion that, as a general rule, it is more appropriate for strict liability in respect of operations of high risk to be imposed by Parliament, than by the courts. If such liability is imposed by statute, the relevant activities can be identified, and those concerned can know where they stand. Furthermore, statute can where appropriate lay down precise criteria establishing the incidence and scope of such liability.

> It is of particular relevance that the present case is concerned with environmental pollution. The protection and preservation of the environment is now perceived as being of crucial importance to the future of mankind; and public bodies, both national and international, are taking significant steps towards the establishment of legislation that will promote the protection of the environment, and make the polluter pay for the damage to the environment for which he is responsible – as can be seen from the WHO, EEC and national regulations to which I have previously referred. But it does not follow from these developments that a common law principle, such as the rule in *Rylands v Fletcher*, should be developed or rendered more strict to provide for liability in respect of such pollution. On the contrary, given that so much well-informed and carefully structured legislation is now being put in place for this purpose, there is less need for the courts to develop a common law principle to achieve the same end, and indeed it may well be undesirable that they should do so.
>
> Having regard to these considerations, and in particular to the step which this House has already taken in *Read v Lyons* to contain the scope of liability under the rule, ... it appears to me to be appropriate now to take the view that foreseeability of damage of the relevant type should be regarded as a prerequisite of liability in damages under the rule. Such a conclusion can, as I have already stated, be derived from Blackburn J's original statement of the law; and I can see no good reason why this prerequisite should not be recognised under the rule, as it has been in the case of private nuisance. ... It would moreover lead to a more coherent body of common law principles if the rule were to be regarded essentially as an extension of the law of nuisance to cases of isolated escapes from land, even though the rule as established is not limited to escapes which are, in fact, isolated. I wish to point out, however, that in truth the escape of the PCE from ECL's land, in the form of trace elements carried in percolating water, has not been an isolated escape, but a continuing escape resulting from a state of affairs which has come into existence at the base of the chalk aquifer underneath ECL's premises. Classically, this would have been regarded as a case of nuisance; and it would seem strange if, by characterising the case as one falling under the rule, ... the liability should thereby be rendered more strict in the circumstances of the present case. ...
>
> Turning to the facts of the present case, it is plain that, at the time when the PCE was brought onto ECL's land, and indeed when it was used in the tanning process there, nobody at ECL could reasonably have foreseen the resultant damage which occurred at CWC's borehole at Sawston.

The effect of this case in practice at least, if not theoretically, is to equate the rule with an action negligence. Aided and abetted by the other restrictions on the scope of the rule, namely, the non-natural user rule, the insistence on escape and the act of a stranger defence, this case has almost obliterated the value of this tort (if that is what it still is). The emasculation has been seen as complete and acknowledged as such by the High Court of Australia[11] when stating that the rule has now been absorbed by the principles of ordinary negligence. How this can be squared with the original statement of the rule by Blackburn J is somewhat mystifying. We must now turn our attention to liability for fire which, as we shall see, has a close connection with the above.

11 See *Burnie Port Authority v General Jones Pty Ltd* [1994] 64 AJLR 331.

LIABILITY FOR FIRE

It is not altogether clear whether liability for fire was strict at common law, although the preferred view was that it was. The position was affected by the passing of s 86 Fires Prevention (Metropolis) Act 1774 as follows:

> ... no action, suit or process whatever shall be had, maintained or prosecuted against any person in whose house, chamber, stable, barn or other building, or on whose estate any fire shall ... accidentally begin, nor shall any recompense be made by such person for any damage suffered thereby, any law, usage or custom to the contrary notwithstanding: ... provided that no contract or agreement made between landlord and tenant shall be hereby or made void.

This provision seems to make it clear that there was to be no liability in the absence of fault. It seems, therefore that there must be some blameworthy conduct by the defendant or by somebody considered to be under his control which, as we shall see, includes independent contractors. It has also been held that a defendant may be liable in nuisance and under the rule in *Rylands v Fletcher* for damage caused by fire. In fact, the latter rule seems to have assumed the major burden of responsibility for action for fire damage. It should, of course, be remembered that fire damage will normally be covered by first party insurance, and this may have a significant impact on the number of claims brought.

Fire under *Rylands v Fletcher*

One of the earliest cases which relied upon the rule was that of *Musgrove v Pandelis*[12] although, as we shall see, it could have been argued in negligence just as easily. the defendant kept a car in a garage underneath the plaintiff's premises. The premises were badly damaged by a fire which started accidentally in the garage when petrol in the car's carburettor accidentally caught fire. The fire could have easily been extinguished by the defendant's employee but he negligently failed to carry out the appropriate procedure. Finding for the plaintiff, Bankes LJ in the Court of Appeal stated:

> The defendant's main defence, apart from disputing the negligence, was founded on s 86 of the Fires Prevention (Metropolis) Act 1774, and the argument has been chiefly directed to the construction of that enactment. Lush J took the view that the statute did not apply at all; and I agree. He also held that, if that view was not correct, the fire which caused the damage did not accidentally begin within the meaning of the Act. And there also I agree. Section 86 of this Act was passed to take place of a section in almost the same words of the Act of 6 Ann, c 31, s 6. In order to see what alteration these statutes effected it is material to consider the state of the law before the earlier statute was passed. A man was liable at common law for damage done by fire originating on his own property:
>
> (1) for the mere escape of the fire;
>
> (2) if the fire was caused by the negligence of himself or his servants, or by his own wilful act;
>
> (3) upon the principle of *Rylands v Fletcher*.

12 [1919] 2 KB 43.

> This principle was not then known by that name, because *Rylands v Fletcher* was not then decided; but it was an existing principle of the common law as I shall show presently. The alteration which those statutes effected was to give protection in cases falling under the first heading of liability mentioned above. It is thus stated by Lord Denman CJ in *Filliter v Phippard* ((1847) 11 QB 347, 354.): 'The ancient law, or rather custom of England, appears to have been that a person in whose house a fire originated, which afterwards spread to his neighbour's property and destroyed it, must make good the loss.' That was the principle of the common law to which the statutes were directed. They altered the law so as to exclude the liability of a 'person in whose house, chamber, stable, barn or other building, or on whose estate any fire shall ... accidentally begin'.
>
> It is plain that the statutes did not touch the other heads of liability at common law. The second head is not within the protection; that was decided by *Filliter v Phippard* where it was held that the Act of Geo 3 did not apply to a fire which was caused either deliberately or negligently. Why, if that is the law as to the second head of liability, should it be otherwise as to the third head, the liability on the principle of *Rylands v Fletcher*? If that liability existed, there is no reason why the statute should alter it and yet leave untouched the liability for fire caused by negligence or design. That the principle of *Rylands v Fletcher* existed long before that case was decided is plain. In *Vaughan v Menlove* ((1837) 3 Bing NC 468) Tindal CJ says: 'There is a rule of law which says you must so enjoy your own property as not to injure that of another.'
>
> Park J says: 'Although the facts in this case are new in specie, they fall within a principle long established, that a man must so use his own property as not to injure others.' *Rylands v Fletcher* is merely an illustration of that old principle, and in my opinion Lush J was right in saying that this case, if it falls within that principle, is not within the protection of the statute.
>
> The question, then, is whether this motor car, with its petrol tank full or partially filled with petrol, was a dangerous thing to bring into the garage within the principle of *Rylands v Fletcher*. Mr Hawke says a motor car is not a dangerous thing unless it is in such a condition that an accident is to be apprehended. But the expectation of danger is not the basis of the principle. ... A thing may be dangerous although the danger is expected. I agree with Lush J that this motor car was dangerous within that principle. The defendant brought it, or caused it to be brought upon his premises, and he is responsible for the fire which resulted, and is not within the protection of the statute.

The other two judges agreed that the case came within the principle. Would it do so nowadays when nearly every house is built with a garage? Is parking a car there 'some special use'? Arguably, there was no need to rely on the principle anyway as there was a clear finding of negligence against the employee for which the defendant would be vicariously liable. The case did not fall within the statute because it was a case brought under the principle, but rather because the fire which caused the damage came about as a result of the negligence of the employee, even though it started innocently.

Nonetheless, the principle was applied to the facts in the more recent case of *Mason v Levy Auto Parts of England Ltd*, following the *Musgrove* case, by McKenna J, perhaps with more justification. In this case the defendant stored large quantities of combustible material in a yard very close to the plaintiff's house. A severe fire started in the yard but the cause was unknown. The defendant's fire-fighting equipment was inadequate and the fire spread to the plaintiff's property. The judge stated:

> The plaintiff takes three main points against the defendants. He says, first, that the statute does not excuse a defendant in any case where the fire begins by his negligence or that of any other person for whom he is responsible – a point established in 1847 by *Filliter v Phippard*, that the burden of disproving negligence is on the defendant who claims the protection of the statute, and that the defendant in this case has not discharged the burden. Secondly, and alternatively, he says that he (the plaintiff) has discharged the burden of proving negligence if it rests on him. If he fails on both these points, he says thirdly that the statute does not apply to a fire which arises through the storage of large quantities of combustible materials in the conditions which I have described, and that the defendant is liable if a fire of this kind damages a neighbour's property upon some principle analogous to that of *Rylands v Fletcher*.

The judge decided that the plaintiff failed on the first two points but dealt with the third in this way:

> There is, it seems to me, a choice of alternatives. The first would require the plaintiff to prove:
>
> (1) that the defendant had brought something onto his land likely to do mischief if it escaped;
>
> (2) that he had done so in the course of a non-natural user of the land; and
>
> (3) that the thing had ignited and that the fire had spread.
>
> The second would be to hold the defendant liable if:
>
> (1) he brought onto his land things likely to catch fire, and kept them there in such conditions that, if they did ignite, the fire would be likely to spread to the plaintiff's land;
>
> (2) he did so in the course of some non-natural use; and
>
> (3) the things ignited and the fire spread.
>
> The second test is, I think, the more reasonable one. To make the likelihood of damage if the thing escapes a criterion of liability, when the thing has not in fact escaped but has caught fire, would not be very sensible.
>
> So I propose to apply the second test, asking myself the two questions:
>
> (i) did the defendants in this case bring to their land things likely to catch fire, and keep them there in such conditions that, if they did ignite, the fire would be likely to spread to the plaintiff's land? If so;
>
> (ii) did the defendants do these things in the course of some non-natural user of the land?
>
> I have no difficulty in answering 'yes' to the first of those questions, but the second is more troublesome. ... I would say that the defendants' use of their land in the way described ... was non-natural. In saying that I have regard:
>
> (i) to the quantities of combustible material which the defendants brought on their land;
>
> (ii) to the way in which they stored them; and
>
> (iii) to the character of the neighbourhood.
>
> It may be that those considerations would also justify a finding of negligence. If that is so, the end would be the same as I have reached by a more laborious, and perhaps more questionable, route.

In both these cases, there is some element of blameworthiness in the conduct of the defendants which justifies the non-application of the 1774 Act, although the principle of liability is said to be strict. Perhaps it has always been the case that there is some blameworthy conduct involved in the principle beyond the mere escape of something which causes harm, and that this has only just been truly acknowledged, as was mentioned above in the main discussion on *Rylands v Fletcher*.

Negligence

There is obviously nothing remarkable in saying that a person who negligently allows a fire to cause damage to the property of another is liable for that damage. What is more perplexing is whether that person can be held liable in negligence for the fault of any other person, including an independent contractor. The subject came up for consideration by the Court of Appeal in *Balfour v Barty-King*.[13] The defendants employed an independent contractor to thaw out the frozen pipe in their premises. He applied a blow lamp to the pipe but the lagging caught fire and spread to the plaintiff's adjacent premises. Lord Goddard CJ gave the judgment of the court and, after admitting that there was no direct authority on the point, commented:

> The precise meaning to be attached to 'accidentally' has not been determined, but it is clear ... that, where the fire is caused by negligence, it is not to be regarded as accidental. Although there is a difference of opinion among eminent text writers whether, at common law, the liability was absolute or depended on negligence, at the present day it can safely be said that a person in whose house a fire is caused by negligence is liable if it spreads to that of his neighbour, and this is true whether the negligence is his own or that of his servant or guest, but he is not liable if the fire is caused by a stranger.
>
> Who, then, is a stranger? Clearly a trespasser would be in that category, but if a man is liable for the negligent act of his guest, it is, indeed, difficult to see why he is not liable for the act of a contractor whom he has invited to his house to do work on it, and who does the work in a negligent manner. ...
>
> Mr Stevenson's argument was that, in the present case, it was not the defendants' fire as the contractor was not employed to light a fire or to use a blow lamp or any other form of fire. But that is answered by the fact that the use of a blow lamp is an ordinary way of freeing frozen pipes. The negligence was in using the lamp in proximity to inflammable material. ...
>
> The defendants here had control over the contractor in that they chose him, they invited him to their premises to do work, and he could have been ordered to leave at any moment. It was left to the men who were sent how to do the work, and in our opinion the defendants are liable to the plaintiff for this lamentable occurrence, the more lamentable in that the persons ultimately responsible are insolvent.

The above was applied in the later case of *H & N Emanuel Ltd v Greater London Council*,[14] in which the council owned a site on which were some pre-fabricated bungalows due for demolition. An independent contractor was engaged by the Ministry of Works to do the work, on the understanding that no fires were to be lit. The workmen ignored this and often lit a fire, to the knowledge of the ministry, to get rid of unwanted timber. Sparks from a fire caused a further fire,

13 [1957] 1 QB 496.

14 [1971] 2 All ER 835.

damaging the plaintiff's premises. Employing the 'sufficient degree of control' test from the occupiers' liability cases, Lord Denning MR held that the GLC were the occupiers of the site:

> Adapting what I said in *Wheat v Lacon,* I would say that, for the purposes of fire, whenever a person has a sufficient degree of control over premises that he can say, with authority, to anyone who comes there, 'do' or 'do not light a fire', or 'do' or 'do not put that fire out', he as 'occupier' must answer for any fire which escapes by negligence from the premises. Applying this test, I am clear that the LCC were occupiers of this site. They were the owners of it. Their foreman had the keys of the prefabs. Anyone who wanted to do anything with them had to get permission from him.

On the issue of whether such an occupier could be liable for what the contractor had done, he said:

> After considering the cases, it is my opinion that the occupier of a house or land is liable for the escape of fire which is due to the negligence, not only of his servants, but also of his independent contractors and of his guests, and of anyone who is there with his leave or licence. The only circumstance when the occupier is not liable for the negligence is when it is the negligence of a stranger. ...
>
> Who then is a stranger? I think a 'stranger' is anyone who in lighting a fire or allowing it to escape, acts contrary to anything which the occupier could anticipate that he would do. ... Even if it is a man whom you have allowed or invited into your house, nevertheless, if his conduct in lighting a fire is so alien to your invitation that he should be regarded as a trespasser, he is a 'stranger'. ...
>
> There has been much discussion about the exact legal basis of liability for fire. The liability of the occupier can be said to be a strict liability in this sense that he is liable for the negligence not only of his servant but also of independent contractors and, indeed, of anyone except a 'stranger'. By the same token it can be said to be a 'vicarious liability', because he is liable for the defaults of others as well as his own. It can also be said to be a liability under the principle of *Rylands v Fletcher,* because fire is undoubtedly a dangerous thing which is likely to do damage if it escapes. But I do not think it necessary to put it into any one of these three categories. It goes back to the time when no such categories were thought of. Suffice it to say that the extent of the liability is now well defined as I have stated it. The occupier is liable for the escape of fire which is due to the negligence of anyone other than a stranger.

The other two judges agreed with the Master of the Rolls.

A slightly different situation arose in the case of *Honeywill and Stein Ltd v Larkin Bros,*[15] in which the plaintiffs employed the defendants as independent contractors to take photographs in the premises of a third party. As a result of the negligence of the defendants the premises were damaged by fire. Slesser LJ read the judgment of the court, stating:

> To take the photograph in the cinema with a flashlight was, on the evidence stated above, a dangerous operation in its intrinsic nature, involving the creation of fire and explosion on another's premises, that is in the cinema, the property of the cinema company. The appellants, in procuring this work to be performed by their contractors, the respondents, assumed an obligation to the cinema company which was, as we think, absolute, but which was at least an obligation to use

15 [1934] 1 KB 191.

> reasonable precautions to see that no damage resulted to the cinema company from these dangerous operations; that obligation they could not delegate by employing the respondents as independent contractors, but they were liable in this regard for the respondents' acts. For the damage actually caused the appellants were accordingly liable in law to the cinema company, and are entitled to claim and recover from the respondents damages for their breach of contract, or negligence in performing their contract to take the photographs.

There was no escape in this case, but nonetheless the court imposed liability on the appellants *vis-à-vis* the third party, on the basis of the difficult principle of non-delegable duty.

Nuisance

Liability for fire can also arise in nuisance. Although the general principles involved in that tort will be considered in the next chapter, the mention of two cases on fire at this stage is thought appropriate. In *Spicer v Smee*[16] the plaintiff's bungalow was destroyed by fire emanating from the defendant's premises. The electrical wiring on the defendant's premises had been left in a defective state by a contractor engaged by the defendant, and this had caused the fire. The defendant was not in occupation at the time as she had let the premises. The High Court judge, discussing the relevant law, observed:

> I have no doubt that there was a nuisance on this property, a nuisance which caused the damage, and it is one for which, as a matter of law, the defendant is answerable. Liability for a nuisance may exist quite independently of negligence. In negligence a plaintiff must prove a duty to take care, but not so in nuisance. In *Rapier v London Tramways Co*, Lindley LJ said ([1893] 2 Ch 588 at 600): '... if I am sued for a nuisance, and the nuisance is proved, it is no defence on my part to say, and to prove, that I have taken all reasonable care to prevent it.'
>
> Nuisance and negligence are different in their nature, and a private nuisance arises out of a state of things on one man's property whereby his neighbour's property is exposed to danger. ... I am satisfied that the state of the defendant's bungalow around that plug, with a bare wire in contact with wet wood, did constitute a nuisance on the defendant's property, and that it exposed the neighbouring property to danger and, in the end, caused the escape of a dangerous thing, to wit, fire.
>
> Mrs Smee was not the occupier. In general, the responsibility for nuisance is based on possession, but it is clear in law that, if an owner lets his premises with a nuisance thereon created by himself or by his servants or agents, he assumes liability for the continuance of that nuisance.
>
> ... the Fires Prevention (Metropolis) Act 1774, s 86, ... has no application. It has no application where the fire is due to negligence, or to nuisance created by the landlord or those for whom he is responsible.

Liability for fire was also found in nuisance in the case of *Goldman v Hargrave*,[17] where the fire started accidentally when a tree was struck by lightening, but allowed, negligently so the court held, to burn itself out and spread as a

16 [1946] 1 All ER 489.

17 [1967] AC 645.

consequence to other property from the occupier's land. Lord Wilberforce read the opinion of the Privy Council and referred to the 1774 Act as follows:

> The words 'shall accidentally begin' are simple enough, but the simplicity is deceptive. Read literally they suggest that account need be taken of nothing except the origin of the fire and that, given an accidental beginning, no supervening negligence, even deliberate act, can deprive a defendant of the benefit of the statute. But further reflection suggests a doubt both because such a result seems capable of producing absurdity and injustice, and because of the inherent difficulty of saying what the expression 'any fire' is intended to mean. A fire is an elusive entity; it is not a substance, but a changing state. The words 'any fire' may refer to the whole continuous process of combustion from birth to death, in an Olympic sense, or reference may be to a particular stage in that process – when it passes from controlled combustion to uncontrolled conflagration. Fortunately, the Act has been considered judicially and, as one would expect, the process of interpretation has taken account of these considerations.

His Lordship considered the interpretation imposed in the cases *Filliter v Phippard* and *Musgrove v Pandelis* discussed above, and continued:

> Their Lordships accept this interpretation; it makes sense of the statute, it accords with its antecedents, and it makes possible a reasonable application of it to the facts of the present case, that is to say, that the fire which damaged the respondents' property was that which arose on 1 March as the result of the negligence of the appellant. The statutory defence therefore fails.

We shall come back to this case in the context of the fuller discussion on nuisance in the next chapter.

LIABILITY FOR ANIMALS

Rather like the preceding section on fire, liability for animals is currently an untidy mix of common law fault-based liability, particularly negligence, and strict statutory liability. It has been, and remains, a topically controversial area, particularly in relation to domestic dogs. At common law originally there developed a form of strict liability based on what was called the *scienter* rule. Certain animals were regarded as a species dangerous in itself and liability for what they did was strict. In respect of animals outside such classification, the owner could be strictly liable if he knew the animal in question had dangerous tendencies. Beyond this, the owner might be liable in another tort, eg trespass, where s/he set a dog on the plaintiff, or perhaps more commonly in negligence. The *scienter* rule was abolished by the Animals Act 1971 which, however, still relies upon the principle underlying the scienter rule. Liability outside the Act still depends on the case falling within one of the other torts as before. Before going on to the Act we shall briefly consider the possibilities of an action at common law.

Common law

The main action at common law is negligence. The point came up in the case of *Draper v Hodder*[18] where a boy was badly bitten by a pack of Jack Russell terrier

18 [1972] 2 QB 560.

puppies which had not previously displayed any dangerous tendencies. The puppies were about to be fed when they attacked the plaintiff as a pack. The propensity to do this should have been known to a dog breeder such as the defendant. The dogs should have been kept in a compound to avoid this type of incident. In the Court of Appeal, Davies LJ said:

> There can, I think, be no doubt that certain modern authorities show clearly that an owner or keeper of an animal may, quite apart from the *scienter* rule, be liable for damage done by that animal if the owner or keeper puts it or allows it to be in such a position that it is reasonably foreseeable that damage may result.

The other two judges agreed with him on this. As to whether there was a breach of such duty, the judge continued:

> The logical conclusion from the evidence ... would seem to be that, whenever two or more dogs are allowed out alone, the owner ought to foresee that they will or may do damage, including even an attack on mankind.
>
> ... there was the evidence, open to criticism though it was, that there was in the circumstances a serious risk of a happening such as did occur in the present case and that the defendant, as an experienced breeder, should have anticipated and foreseen it.

On this issue Edmund Davies LJ commented:

> The defendant knew that his dogs were young and sprightly, he knew that no less than seven of them were free to go where they willed, and he knew that, in a place only some yards down the road to which at least some of his dogs regularly went, there was likely to be a very small child. Placing all reasonable reins on his foreseeability, he ought ... to have realised that risk of real harm to the child was involved. For example, he could well be bowled over by an onward rush of dogs to the dustbins, or by their subsequent antics (however innocent), sustain no insubstantial injury to face or body, for which the defendant ought clearly to be made liable.

Roskill LJ agreed with this, but went on to say:

> In reaching this conclusion I must emphasise that it does not, in my view, follow that every owner or keeper of a dog or dogs is to be held liable for negligence merely because a dog or dogs escape on to neighbouring land and cause injury on that land.

In *Tutin v Mary Chipperfield Promotions Ltd*,[19] the actress plaintiff successfully brought an action in negligence and under the Act against the defendant in relation to injuries she sustained during the course of a camel race, for which she was inadequately prepared by the defendants. In *Smith v Prendergast*[20] an owner of a scrapyard was held liable in negligence to the plaintiff child for allowing a stray dog to wander around his premises for about three weeks before it attacked the child as she went past the open yard gates. The basis for the finding of negligence lay in the failure of the defendant to attempt any systematic supervision and control, much less training of the dog, according to the Court of Appeal. It is also possible for liability for animals to be based in nuisance or under the rule in *Rylands v Fletcher* in appropriate situations. We shall now consider the Act.

---

19 (1980) 130 NLJ 807.

20 (1984) Times, 18 October.

Animals Act 1971

The Act was based on one of the earliest reports of the Law Commission.[21] The Act has replaced the pre-existing strict liability rules developed by the common law with rules of a broadly similar nature, but it also contains some amendments to the common law, particularly with regard to liability for animals straying onto the road.

1 *New Provisions as to strict liability for damage done by animals*

(1) The provisions of sections 2 to 5 of this Act replace–

(a) the rules of the common law imposing a strict liability in tort for damage done by an animal on the ground that the animal is regarded as *ferae naturae* or that its vicious or mischievous propensities are known or presumed to be known;

(b) subsections (1) and (2) of section 1 of the Dogs Act 1906 as amended by the Dogs (Amendment) Act 1928 (injury to cattle or poultry); and

(c) the rules of the common law imposing a liability for cattle trespass.

(2) Expressions used in those sections shall be interpreted in accordance with the provisions of section 6 (as well as those of section 11) of this Act.

2 *Liability for damage done by dangerous animals.*

(1) Where any damage is caused by an animal which belongs to a dangerous species, any person who is a keeper of the animal is liable for the damage, except as otherwise provided by this Act.

(2) Where damage is caused by an animal which does not belong to a dangerous species, a keeper of the animal is liable for the damage, except as otherwise provided by this Act, if–

(a) the damage is of a kind which the animal, unless restrained, was likely to cause or which, if caused by the animal, was likely to be severe; and

(b) the likelihood of the damage or of its being severe was due to characteristics of the animal which are not normally found in animals of the same species or are not normally so found except at particular times or in particular circumstances; and

(c) those characteristics were known to the keeper or were at any time known to a person who at that time had charge of the animal as that keeper's servant or, where the keeper is the head of a household, were known to another keeper of the animal who is a member of that household and under the age of 16.

3 *Liability for injury done by dogs to livestock*

Where a dog causes damage by killing or injuring livestock, any person who is a keeper of the dog is liable for the damage, except as otherwise provided by this Act.

4 *Liability for damage and expenses due to trespassing livestock*

(1) Where livestock belonging to any person strays on to land in the ownership or occupation of another and–

(a) damage is done by the livestock to the land or to any property on it which is in the ownership or possession of the other person; or

---

21 *Civil Liability for Animals*, Law Com no 13, 1967.

(b) any expenses are reasonably incurred by that other person in keeping the livestock while it cannot be restored to the person to whom it belongs or while it is detained in pursuance of section 7 of this Act, or in ascertaining to whom it belongs;

the person to whom the livestock belongs is liable for the damage or expenses, except as otherwise provided by this Act.

(2) For the purposes of this section livestock belongs to the person in whose possession it is.

5 *Exceptions to liability under sections 2 to 4*

(1) A person is not liable under sections 2 to 4 of this Act for any damage which is due wholly to the fault of the person suffering it.

(2) A person is not liable under section 2 of this Act for any damage suffered by a person who has voluntarily accepted the risk thereof.

(3) A person is not liable under section 2 of this Act for any damage caused by an animal kept on any premises or structure to a person trespassing there, if it is proved either–

(a) that the animal was not kept there for the protection of persons or property; or

(b) (if the animal was kept there for the protection of persons or property) that keeping it there for that purpose was not unreasonable.

(4) A person is not liable under section 3 of this Act if the livestock was killed or injured on land on to which it had strayed and either the dog belonged to the occupier or its presence on the land was authorised by the occupier.

(5) A person is not liable under section 4 of this Act where the livestock strayed from a highway and its presence there was a lawful use of the highway.

(6) In determining whether any liability for damage under section 4 of this Act is excluded by subsection (1) of this section the damage shall not be treated as due to the fault of the person suffering it by reason only that he could have prevented it by fencing; but a person is not liable under that section where it is proved that the straying of the livestock on to the land would not have occurred but for a breach by any other person, being a person having an interest in the land, of a duty to fence.

6 *Interpretation of certain expressions used in sections 2 to 5*

(1) The following provisions apply to the interpretation of sections 2 to 5 of this Act.

(2) A dangerous species is a species–

(a) which is not commonly domesticated in the British Islands; and

(b) whose fully grown animals normally have such characteristics that they are likely, unless restrained, to cause severe damage or that any damage they may cause is likely to be severe.

(3) Subject to subsection (4) of this section, a person is a keeper of an animal if–

(a) he owns the animal or has it in his possession; or

(b) he is the head of a household of which a member under the age of 16 owns the animal or has it in his possession;

and if at any time an animal ceases to be owned by or to be in the possession of a person, any person who immediately before that time was a keeper thereof by virtue of the preceding provisions of this subsection continues to be a keeper of the animal until another person becomes a keeper thereof by virtue of those provisions.

(4) Where an animal is taken into and kept in possession for the purpose of preventing it from causing damage or of restoring it to its owner, a person is not a keeper of it by virtue only of that possession.

(5) Where a person employed as a servant by a keeper of an animal incurs a risk incidental to his employment he shall not be treated as accepting it voluntarily.

7 *Detention and sale of trespassing livestock*

(1) The right to seize and detain any animal by way of distress damage feasant is hereby abolished.

(2) Where any livestock strays on to any land and is not then under the control of any person, the occupier of the land may detain it, subject to subsection (3) of this section, unless ordered to return it by a court.

(3) Where any livestock is detained in pursuance of this section the right to detain it ceases–

(a) at the end of the period of 48 hours, unless within that period notice of the detention has been given to the officer in charge of a police station and also, if the person detaining the livestock knows to whom it belongs, to that person; or

(b) when such amount is tendered to the person detaining the livestock as is sufficient to satisfy any claim he may have under section 4 of this Act in respect of the livestock; or

(c) if he has no such claim, when the livestock is claimed by a person entitled to its possession.

(4) Where livestock has been detained in pursuance of this section for a period of not less than 14 days, the person detaining it may sell it at a market or by public auction, unless proceedings are then pending for the return of the livestock or for any claim under section 4 of this Act in respect of it.

(5) Where any livestock is sold in the exercise of the right conferred by this section and the proceeds of the sale, less the costs thereof and any costs incurred in connection with it, exceed the amount of any claim under section 4 of this Act which the vendor had in respect of the livestock, the excess shall be recoverable from him by the person who would be entitled to the possession of the livestock but for the sale.

(6) A person detaining livestock in pursuance of this section is liable for any damage caused to it by a failure to treat it with reasonable care and supply it with adequate food and water while it is so detained.

(7) References in this section to a claim under section 4 of this Act in respect of any livestock do not include any claim under that section for damage done by or expenses incurred in respect of the livestock before the straying in connection with which it is detained under this section.

8 *Duty to take care to prevent damage from animals straying on to the highway*

(1) So much of the rules of the common law relating to liability for negligence as excludes or restricts the duty which a person might owe to others to take such care as is reasonable to see that damage is not caused by animals straying on to a highway is hereby abolished.

(2) Where damage is caused by animals straying from unfenced land to a highway, a person who placed them on the land shall not be regarded as

having committed a breach of the duty to take care by reason only of placing them there if–

(a) the land is common land, or is land situated in an area where fencing is not customary, or is a town or village green; and

(b) he had a right to place the animals on that land.

9 *Killing of or injury to dogs worrying livestock*

(1) In any civil proceedings against a person (in this section referred to as the defendant) for killing or causing injury to a dog it shall be a defence to prove–

(a) that the defendant acted for the protection of any livestock and was a person entitled to act for the protection of that livestock; and

(b) that within 48 hours of the killing or injury notice thereof was given by the defendant to the officer in charge of a police station.

(2) For the purposes of this section a person is entitled to act for the protection of any livestock if, and only if–

(a) the livestock or the land on which it is belongs to him or to any person under whose express or implied authority he is acting; and

(b) the circumstances are not such that liability for killing or causing injury to the livestock would be excluded by section 5(4) of this Act.

(3) Subject to subsection (4) of this section, a person killing or causing injury to a dog shall be deemed for the purposes of this section to act for the protection of any livestock if, and only if, either–

(a) the dog is worrying or is about to worry the livestock and there are no other reasonable means of ending or preventing the worrying; or

(b) the dog has been worrying livestock, has not left the vicinity and is not under the control of any person and there are no practicable means of ascertaining to whom it belongs.

(4) For the purposes of this section the condition stated in either of the paragraphs of the preceding subsection shall be deemed to have been satisfied if the defendant believed that it was satisfied and had reasonable ground for that belief.

(5) For the purposes of this section–

(a) an animal belongs to any person if he owns it or has it in his possession; and

(b) land belongs to any person if he is the occupier thereof.

10 *Application of certain enactments to liability under sections 2 to 4*

For the purposes of the Fatal Accident Act 1976, the Law Reform (Contributory Negligence) Act 1945 and the Limitation Act 1980 any damage for which a person is liable under sections 2 to 4 of this Act shall be treated as due to his fault.

11 *General interpretation*

In this Act–

'common land', and 'town or village green' have the same meanings as in the Commons Registration Act 1965;

'damage' includes the death of, or injury to, any person (including any disease and any impairment of physical or mental condition);

'fault' has the same meaning as in the Law Reform (Contributory Negligence) Act 1945;

'fencing' includes the construction of any obstacle designed to prevent animals from straying;

'livestock' means cattle, horses, asses, hinnies, sheep, pigs, goats and poultry, and also deer not in the wild state and, in sections 3 to 9, also, while in captivity, pheasants, partridges and grouse;

'poultry' means the domestic varieties of the following, that is to say, fowls, turkeys, geese, ducks, guinea-fowls, pigeons, peacocks and quails; and

'species' includes sub-species and variety.

Commentary

Most of the above is straight forward and unremarkable. Section 2, however, which contains the main provision in the Act, is unsurprisingly the most complex, particularly sub-s (2). If an animal belongs to a dangerous species, which is regarded as a question of law not fact, it does not matter whether that particular animal is tame nor is it relevant that it is a domesticated animal in another country, as long as it is not such in the British Islands.[22] It has also been held that the damage caused need not necessarily be related to the particular characteristic which makes the animal dangerous. In *Behrens v Bertram Mills Circus Ltd*, a case under the previous common law but nonetheless valid, Devlin J observed:

> If a tiger is let loose in a fun fair, it seems to me to be irrelevant whether a person is injured as the result of a direct attack or because on seeing it he runs away and falls over.

Where the species to which the animal in question belongs is not dangerous, the plaintiff must try and rely on the provision in s 2(2). This has been discussed in several cases at Court of Appeal level and perhaps it is best left to the judges to do the explaining. The leading case is *Cummings v Granger*.[23] The plaintiff was a trespasser in the scrapyard of the defendant when she was attacked by an Alsatian dog kept there by the defendant as a guard dog. The Court of Appeal had to consider whether the plaintiff's case fell within s 2. In so holding, Lord Denning MR said:

> The statutory liability for a tame animal like a dog is defined in s 2(2) of the 1971 Act, subject to exceptions contained in s 5. Now it seems to me that this is a case where the keeper of the dog is strictly liable unless he can bring himself within one of the exceptions. I say this because the three requirements for strict liability are satisfied. The section is very cumbrously worded and will give rise to several difficulties in the future. But in this case the judge held that the three requirements were satisfied and I agree with him for these reasons. Section 2(2)(a): this animal was a dog of the Alsatian breed. If it did bite anyone, the damage was 'likely to be severe'. Section 2(2)(b): this animal was a guard-dog kept so as to scare intruders and frighten them off. On the owner's own evidence, it used to bark and run round in circles, especially when coloured people

22 See *Tutin v Mary Chipperfield Promotions Ltd* (above); *Behrens v Bertram Mills Circus Ltd* [1957] 1 All ER 583.

23 [1977] QB 397.

> approached. Those characteristics-barking and running around to guard its territory-are not normally found in Alsatian dogs except in the circumstances where used as guard dogs. Those circumstances are 'particular circumstances' within s 2(2)(b). It was 'due' to those circumstances that the damage was likely to be severe if an intruder did enter on its territory. Section 2(2)(c): those characteristics were known to the keeper.

The other two judges took a similar line to the Master of the Rolls on this issue. The court also considered the applicability of the defences in section 5 to which we shall return shortly. In *Curtis v Betts*,[24] in which a small boy was attacked by a bull mastiff, which he knew, just as it was being loaded into the back of the defendant's Land Rover. In deciding in favour of the plaintiff, Slade LJ dealt with each of the requirements in s 2(2) in turn as follows:

> *Requirement (a)*
>
> The kind of damage in the present case was personal injury. The judge, rightly, did not find that this damage was 'of a kind which [Max], unless restrained, was likely to cause'. Indeed, he made it plain that in general Max was a docile and lazy dog. However, he found that Max's action 'in jumping up and biting a child on the side of the face was likely to cause severe damage'. By this route he found that the personal injury caused to Lee was of a kind 'which, if caused by the animal, was likely to be severe', so that the second head of requirement (a) was satisfied.
>
> Counsel for the defendants submitted that the judge's approach to requirement (a) was erroneous. In this context he referred us to and relied on a passage in North, *The Modern Law of Animals* (1972) p 56, where it is said: 'This second type of damage envisaged by s 2(2)(a) is one that must prove to be rare in practice. For there to be liability on this basis, an animal must have caused damage in circumstances where it was unlikely that an animal of that species would cause the kind of damage in question, but the animal had such abnormal characteristics that it was likely that, if it did cause damage, the damage would be severe.'
>
> He pointed out that there was no evidence or finding that Max had *abnormal* characteristics (that is to say abnormal in the case of bull mastiffs as a breed) such as rendered it likely that, if he did damage, the damage would be severe.
>
> I agree with the latter point, but, with respect to Professor North, am unable to agree with the approach to the construction of requirement (a) suggested by him, for two reasons. First, while I accept that requirements (b) and (c) have to read in conjunction with the preceding requirement (a), I see no necessity or justification for reading words into requirement (a) itself through a process of implication effected by reference to the succeeding requirements. The broad purpose of requirement (a), as I read it, is to subject the keeper of a non-dangerous animal to liability for the damage caused by it in any circumstances where the damage is of a kind which the particular animal in question, unless restrained, was likely to cause or, which if caused by that animal, was likely to be severe, provided that the plaintiff can also satisfy the additional requirements (b) and (c). While conceivably the reference to the likelihood of severity of damage may give rise to questions of degree on particular facts, I would not, for my part, ordinarily anticipate difficulty in applying requirement (a) in practice.
>
> Second, Professor North's work (including p 56) was drawn to the attention of this court in argument in *Cummings v Granger*. Nevertheless, Lord Denning MR,

24 [1990] 1 All ER 769.

with whose judgment Bridge LJ expressly agreed, himself adopted the simple approach to the construction of the second limb of requirement (a) which, with respect, seems to me the right one. In the context of requirement (a), he did not find it necessary to consider whether the dog in question has characteristics not abnormal to Alsatians.

So too in the present case. Max was a dog of bull mastiff breed. If he did bite anyone, the damage was likely to be severe. For this simple reason the judge was, in my judgment, right to hold that requirement (a) was satisfied.

Requirement (b)

The construction and application of requirement (b) give rise to rather greater difficulties. In particular, on a first reading I was puzzled by the legislature's use of the phrase 'the likelihood of the damage or if its being severe', instead of the simple phrase 'the damage', especially since the subsequent phrase 'due to' at first sight appeared to me to bear the simple meaning 'caused by'. However, another, broader, meaning is also given to the word 'due' by the *Shorter Oxford Dictionary* (3rd edn), namely 'To be ascribed or attributed'. If one reads the phrase 'due to' as bearing the broader sense of 'attributable to', I think that this particular difficulty disappears.

Just as, in my view, requirement (a) in any given case falls to be considered having regard to the particular facts of that case, so too in my view, in the consideration of requirement (b), the existence or non-existence of the relevant likelihood has to be determined having regard to the particular facts. If, therefore, the plaintiff is relying on the second limb of requirement (b), he will have to show that *on the particular facts* the likelihood of the damage or of its being severe was attributable to characteristics of the animal not normally found except at particular times or in particular circumstances corresponding with the particular facts of the case.

The broad purpose of requirement (b), as I read it, is to ensure that, even in a case falling within requirement (a), the defendant, subject to one exception, will still escape liability if, on the particular facts, the likelihood of the damage was attributable to potentially dangerous characteristics of the animal which are normally found in animals of the same species. The one exception is this. The mere fact that a particular animal shared its potentially dangerous characteristics with other animals of the same species will not preclude the satisfaction of requirement (b) if, on the particular facts, the likelihood of damage was attributable to characteristics normally found in animals of the same species at times or in circumstances corresponding with those in which the damage actually occurred. In *Cummings v Granger* [1977] 1 All ER 104 at 110, Ormrod LJ gave examples of 'a bitch with pups or an Alsatian dog running loose in a yard which it regards as its territory when a stranger enters into it'. If, in his example, the damage is caused by a bitch accompanying her pups or an Alsatian dog defending its territory, requirement (b) will be satisfied. ...

On the basis of [the] evidence, the judge was, in my opinion, entitled to find that Max had characteristics which are not normally found in bull mastiffs, except at particular times or in particular circumstances, namely the tendency to react fiercely when defending what they regarded as their own territory.

However, to establish requirement (b) the plaintiff still had to establish that the likelihood of damage was, on the particular facts, due to these characteristics. ...

In my judgment, in the light of all the evidence and of his own common knowledge and experience, it was open to the judge, albeit without expert

> evidence to support his conclusion, to infer that Max regarded his territory as including the rear of the Land Rover ... requirement (b) is thus satisfied.

The judge also concluded that the third requirement was satisfied. Stuart-Smith LJ made similar comments about requirement (a) and then went on to consider (b):

> Paragraph (b) presents more difficulty. Here again there are two limbs to the subsection. The first deals with what may, for convenience, be called permanent characteristics; the second, temporary characteristics. Dogs are not normally fierce or prone to attack humans; a dog which has a propensity to do this at all times and in all places and without discrimination to persons would clearly fall within the first limb. One that is only aggressive in particular circumstances, for example, when guarding its territory or, if a bitch, when it has a litter of pups, will come within the second limb. In the present case the judge concluded that Max fell within the second limb. ...
>
> To my mind the difficulty in the subsection arises from the first three words, 'the likelihood of'. Without these words it would be plain that para (b) was concerned with causation of damage. The plaintiff would have to prove that the damage of one of the types in para (a) was caused by either a permanent or temporary characteristic specified in para (b). This makes good sense. But the first three words seem to connote a concept of foreseeability and not causation. This would have remarkable consequences. If all that is necessary is that it be likely that a bitch with a litter of pups may have a propensity to be fierce and provided she is large enough to cause severe damage, the owner of such a bitch would be liable (if para (c) is satisfied) if the bitch causes severe damage at any time whether or not she has pups or is with them. I cannot think that this was the intention of Parliament. Although I find difficulty in giving content to the words 'the likelihood of', I am satisfied that there must be a causal link between the characteristic in question and the damage suffered. In particular where the case falls under the second limb, the temporary characteristic, the time or circumstances in which the damage is caused, must be those during which the particular characteristics are or were prone to be exhibited.

The third judge, Nourse LJ agreed with the other two and the appeal of the defendant was dismissed.

In *Wallace v Newton*[25] the plaintiff was a groom looking after horses for the defendant. One of the horses was known to be temperamental and unpredictable. During the loading of the animal into the horse box it became uncontrollable and crushed the plaintiff's arm against a bar. Park J said:

> Under s 2(2)(a) of the Animals Act 1971 the plaintiff has to establish first that the damage which she has suffered was of a kind which [the horse] was likely to cause, and on this part of the case there is no dispute. Under s 2(2)(b) the plaintiff has to establish that the likelihood of the damage was due to characteristics of [the horse] which were not normally found in horses. The question is whether the words 'characteristics which are not normally found in horses' have to be interpreted as meaning that [the horse] must be shown to have had a vicious tendency to injure people by attacking them or whether the words have to be given their ordinary natural meaning, that is that [the horse] had characteristics of a kind not usually found in horses. If the plaintiff has to establish that her injuries were due to [the horse's] vicious tendency to injure people, then her

25 [1982] All ER 106.

> claim would fail. He was not, as the plaintiff herself agreed, a vicious horse or a dangerous horse in any way in which the defendant understood that word. On the other hand, she has to establish that her injuries were due to a characteristic of [the horse] which is unusual in a horse, then she would establish this limb of her case. I think this is the meaning to be given to the words in s 2(2)(b).
>
> On the evidence I am satisfied that, certainly during the period that the plaintiff had [the horse] in her charge, the horse was unpredictable and unreliable in his behaviour and in that way was, as the plaintiff said, dangerous. The injury to her arm was due to this characteristic, which is not normally found in a horse. So, in my judgment, the plaintiff has established the second limb of her case.

The judge also found the third limb in para (c) satisfied and gave judgment for the plaintiff. Returning to dogs and liability under the Act, it was said in the brief report in the case of *Hunt v Wallis*,[26] where the defendant's border collie collided with and injured the plaintiff, that the comparison under s 2(2)(b) was with dogs of a similar breed as the one in question, rather than with all dogs in general. In *Smith v Ainger*[27] the Court of Appeal held that the keeper of a dog which had a tendency to attack other dogs was liable to the plaintiff who was knocked over by the dog when it lunged to attack the dog belonging to the plaintiff. Dealing with s 2 of the 1971 Act, Neill LJ commented:

> It was clear that paragraph (a) could be established in two quite separate ways.
>
> The words 'was likely' gave rise to difficulty. In many contexts 'likely' meant 'probable' or 'more probable than not'. But in other contexts it might have a wider meaning so that a likely event included an event 'such as might well happen' or 'where there is a material risk that it will happen' as well as events which are 'more probable than not'.
>
> In the present context the wider meaning was to be preferred. Parliament could not have intended that a keeper of a dog with a known propensity to bite strangers could escape liability by establishing that only 40% of such persons had been bitten in the past. Moreover, such a construction would represent a radical departure from the old law. ...
>
> The kind of damage concerned was personal injury to a human being caused by the direct application of force, and if the personal injury was the result of an attack by a dog it was unrealistic to distinguish between a bite and the consequences of a buffet. ...
>
> The judge was clearly satisfied that Sam was likely to attack another dog if the other dog offended him in some way. The attack in the instant case took place in a high street. In such a place another dog was very likely to be with its owner and on a lead.
>
> Furthermore, if Sam attacked the other dog there was a material risk that the owner of the other dog would intervene to defend his animal and would be bitten or buffeted as a result of his intervention.

These provisions in s 2 are hardly easy reading and have already caused a considerable amount of litigation which the Act was meant to avoid, being a substitute for the anomaly-ridden common law.

26 (1991) Times, 10 May.

27 (1990) Times, 5 June.

Defences

An example of what is covered by s 5(1) above is contained in the old case of *Marlor v Ball*,[28] in which the plaintiff had stroked a zebra which had bitten him. AL Smith LJ observed:

> Where the plaintiff did something which he had no business to do – eg by meddling, as the plaintiff in this case had done – then the defendant was not liable.

The *volenti* defence is preserved by s 5(2) of the Act, but it was unsuccessful in *Tutin* because the judge took the view that it could not be inferred that the plaintiff actress accepted or ever contemplated the negligence which was the real cause of her fall. The defence also failed in *Behrens* where the defendant tried to argue that, because the plaintiffs had seen the elephants walking past their stall every day, they had assumed the risk. Devlin J commented:

> It cannot here be contended that the passing of the elephants created an obvious danger; indeed, the case as pleaded for the defence is that the risk was very small. This plea fails.

However, the plea was accepted as valid by all three judges in *Cummings* where Lord Denning MR stated:

> The lady certainly knew the animal was there. She worked next door. She knew all about it. She must have seen this huge notice on the door 'Beware of the dog'. Nevertheless she went in, following her man friend. In the circumstances she must be taken voluntarily to have incurred this risk; so with any burglar or thief who goes on to premises knowing that there is a guard dog there. If he is bitten or injured he cannot recover. He voluntarily takes the risk of it. Even if he does not know a guard dog is there, he might be defeated by the plea '*ex turpi causa non oritur actio*'.

Bridge LJ agreed as follows:

> Clearly the two matters which must be proved in order to show that somebody has voluntarily accepted the risk are:
>
> (1) that they fully appreciated the risk; and
>
> (2) that they exposed themselves to it.
>
> The evidence of the plaintiff here was all one way as regards her appreciation of the risk. She emphasised what a fierce dog this was and how frightened she was of it. Of course her evidence was that she had not exposed herself to it, but the judge did not accept that and found that she had exposed herself to the risk. In those circumstances, I do not think that it was open to him, with respect, to draw the inference which he did that, when she exposed herself to the risk, she thought that the dog was unlikely to attack her because Mr Hobson was there, because that is contrary to her evidence.

The defence in s 5(3) was also successfully raised in this case. On this, Lord Denning MR added:

> Section 5(3) may, however, avail the keeper. It shows that if someone trespasses on property and is bitten or injured by a guard dog, the keeper of the guard dog is exempt from liability if it is proved 'that keeping it there for that purpose was not unreasonable'.

28 (1900) 16 TLR 239.

> The judge held that the owner of this dog was unreasonable in keeping it in this yard. ...
>
> I take a different view. This was yard in the East End of London where persons of the roughest type come and go. It was a scrapyard, true, but scrapyards like building sites often contain much valuable property. It was deserted at night and at weekends. If there was no protection allowed there, thieves would drive up in a lorry and remove the scrap, with no one to see them or stop them. The only reasonable way of protecting the place was to have a guard dog. True, it was a fierce dog. But why not? A gentle dog would be no good. The thieves would soon make friends with him. It seems to me that it was very reasonable or, at any rate, not unreasonable for the owner to keep this dog there.

Both Bridge LJ and Ormrod LJ made similar comments about the reasonableness of keeping a guard dog. However, The Master of the Rolls did add a significant rider to his statement above. Later in his judgment he commented:

> This accident took place in November 1971 very shortly after the Animals Act 1971 was passed. In 1975 the Guard Dogs Act 1975 was passed. It does not apply to this case. But it makes it quite clear that, in future, a person is not allowed to have a guard dog to roam about on his premises unless the dog is under the control of a handler. If he has no handler, the dog must be chained up so that it is not at liberty to roam around. If a person contravenes the 1975 Act, he can be brought before a magistrate and fined, ... but it is only criminal liability. It does not confer a right of action in any civil proceedings. It may, however, have this effect in civil proceedings; it may make it unreasonable for the defendant to let a dog free in the yard at night (as this defendant did) and it may thus deprive the defendant of a defence under s 5(3)(b). But he still might be able to rely on the defence under s 5(2) of *volenti non fit injuria*.

Such an argument may be even stronger in the light of the passing of the Dangerous Dogs Act 1991.

The Court of Appeal in *Matthews v Wicks*[29] had to consider the defence in s 5(5) of the Act in relation to livestock straying from the highway. For the defence to apply the livestock must be lawfully on the highway in the first place, and not have strayed onto the highway from a place where the owner is entitled to graze them. This is what happened in this case and the court held that the animals were not lawfully on the highway. Ralph Gibson LJ observed:

> Since the plaintiff had left his sheep to wander at will, their presence on the highway was not a 'lawful use of the highway' and the defendants succeeded under s 4 of the 1971 Act.

That concludes the discussion of the three topics in this chapter. We shall in the next chapter consider the major tort covering the use of land, namely, nuisance, which we have already considered to a small extent in this chapter.

29 (1987) Times, 25 August.

CHAPTER 10

NUISANCE

INTRODUCTION

The tort of nuisance was discussed briefly in the previous chapter, both in relation to its possible links with the rule in *Rylands v Fletcher* and as an alternative action in connection with liability for damage by fire. As an action on the case, it certainly has a long history, and yet it still has a significant role to play as a tort protecting the environment. However, its existence as a separate and viable cause of action has been challenged by two developments.

One is the all-embracing nature of the negligence action, one by-product of which we have already seen in relation to the rule in *Rylands v Fletcher*, where it has been argued that liability is nowadays to be considered as fault-based. The uneasy relationship between nuisance and negligence is a continuing and controversial point of discussion which follows below in the cases extracted. It appears that, in some cases, a failure to take care is considered as an essential requirement of the plaintiff's case; in others it seems to be still the case that the nature of the liability in nuisance is strict.

The other development has been the burgeoning of the public law controls over pollution placed in the hands, for the most part, of local authorities.[1] These mechanisms for protecting the environment are a valuable addition to the common law, although it would seem that the reverse is true, in that the common law controls in most cases will surely be taking a back seat in the fight against environmental damage. The common law may be seen as the backdrop against which the other controls now operate. We shall be considering the scope of the common law actions only in this chapter, although often the solution may lie in the public law domain.

The second point of an introductory nature is that the tort comprises two separate and, possible historically distinct, causes of action, ie public and private nuisance. Whilst it is true that they are independent actions, they often overlap, and the same set of facts may well give rise to an action in both, in addition to an action under the rule in *Rylands v Fletcher*, assuming for the moment that that is a distinct cause of action.

DISTINCTION BETWEEN PUBLIC AND PRIVATE NUISANCE

A public nuisance is normally considered to be an interference or misuse which either:

(a) affects the exercise of some public right; or

(b) substantially affects the health, safety, or convenience of a substantial number of people within the area of effect.

1 See, eg, the Environmental Protection Act 1990.

Private nuisance is commonly regarded as an unreasonable interference with the use or enjoyment of the plaintiff's land or recognised interest in land.

Public nuisance, it must be emphasised, is a crime as well as a tort, whereas private nuisance is a tort only. A civil action for a public nuisance would normally be brought by the Attorney General in what is known as a relator action, although the frequency of resort to this procedure has been considerably reduced by the introduction of the public law controls mentioned above. A private individual may bring an action in public nuisance provided s/he can show that s/he has suffered special damage over and above that suffered by the community at large. A private individual must take the initiative at all times in a private nuisance action.

Public nuisance protects a wider range of interests in that the plaintiff need not have an interest in land, as is generally thought to be the case, in a private nuisance action. Personal injury damages are definitely recoverable in a public nuisance action, provided the plaintiff can show special damage as mentioned earlier. In private nuisance, as with the rule in *Rylands v Fletcher*, the issue of recovery of such damages is not free from doubt as we shall see later. As public nuisance is a crime the prescription rule cannot apply to it. The tort of nuisance as a whole has a role to play in the prevention of damage, rather than just providing compensation for past events, by providing for the issue of an injunction in appropriate cases. We shall look at a few cases where some of these issues have been explored, before going on to look at private nuisance.

A case which shows the potential source of overlap between the causes of action is the case of *Halsey v Esso Petroleum Co Ltd*,[2] in which the defendants had an oil distribution depot close to a residential street. The residents complained of a number of things, including the escape of acid smuts which caused damage to washing on the line and to paint work on cars in the street. There were complaints about a pungent and nauseating smell emanating from the premises, as well as noise at night from two sources, boilers on the premises and large oil tankers driving along the street to obtain access to the depot. The plaintiff brought a variety of actions in private and public nuisance as well as under the rule in *Rylands v Fletcher*. Veale J made some observations on nuisance in the first place:

> So far as the present case is concerned, liability for nuisance by harmful deposits could be established by proving damage by the deposits to the property in question, provided, of course, that the injury was not merely trivial. Negligence is not an ingredient of the cause of action, and the character of the neighbourhood is not a matter to be taken into consideration. On the other hand, nuisance by smell or noise is something to which no absolute standard can be applied. It is always a question of degree whether the interference with comfort or convenience is sufficiently serious to constitute a nuisance. The character of the neighbourhood is very relevant, and all the relevant circumstances have to be taken into account. What might be nuisance in one area is by no means necessarily so in another. In an urban area, everyone must put up with a certain amount of discomfort and annoyance from the activities of neighbours, and the law must strike a fair balance between the right of the plaintiff on the one hand to the undisturbed

2 [1961] 2 All ER 145.

enjoyment of his property, and the right of the defendant on the other hand to use his property for his own lawful enjoyment. That it is how I approach this case.

It may be possible in some cases to prove that noise or smell have in fact diminished the value of the plaintiff's property in the market. That consideration does not arise in this case, and no evidence has been called in regard to it. The standard in respect of discomfort and inconvenience from noise and smell that I have to apply is that of the ordinary reasonable and responsible person who lives in this particular area of Fulham. This is not necessarily the same as the standard which the plaintiff chooses to set up for himself. It is the standard of the ordinary man, and the ordinary man, who may well like peace and quiet, will not complain for instance of the noise of traffic if he chooses to live on a main street in an urban centre, nor of the reasonable noises of industry, if he chooses to live alongside a factory. ...

I have no doubt at all that the defendants had been the cause of the emission into the atmosphere of noxious smuts which had caused damage to the plaintiff's washing and to his motor car. The smuts are noxious acid smuts, and it does not matter whether they contain sulphate or sulphuric acid. For this damage the defendants in my judgment are liable, both as for a nuisance and under *Rylands v Fletcher*. It is not necessary for the plaintiff to prove, or for me to decide, precisely why this has happened. It is necessary for the plaintiff to prove the fact of it happening, and this I am satisfied he has done. ...

I find as a fact that, over and above the occasional smell of oil which has been present from time to time for many years, during recent years and growing over the years in frequency and intensity, there has been emitted from the defendants' depot a particularly pungent smell which goes far beyond any triviality, far beyond any background smell of oil, and it is a serious nuisance to local residents including the plaintiff. ... There is something which is a nauseating smell, and this is so frequent as to be an actionable nuisance. ...

Whether or not this smell amounts to a nuisance depends of course on the whole of the circumstances, including the character of the neighbourhood and the nature, intensity and frequency of the smell. I hold that this smell, of which the witnesses have given evidence, and which may or may not be due to heated oil, does amount to a nuisance and, further, that any defence of prescription in respect of it fails because the frequency and intensity of it which constitutes the nuisance have not been continued for anything approaching 20 years.

I approach this question with caution, as counsel for the defendants asked me to do, since there has been no injury to health, but injury to health is not a necessary ingredient in the cause of action for nuisance by smell. ...

I accept the evidence of the plaintiff as to noise and I hold it is a serious nuisance, going far beyond a triviality, and one in respect of which the plaintiff is entitled to complain. Because of the noise made by the boilers, I think that the plaintiff is not so much, certainly since the throbbing of the steam pumps ceased, troubled by the noise of the electric pumps. But that is because the noise of the pumps is largely drowned by the noise of the boilers, and even if the noise of the boilers stopped, it might be that the plaintiff could justifiably complain of the noise of the pumps. ...

Bearing in mind all the relevant considerations, in my judgment the defendants are liable in nuisance for the noise of their plant, though only at night. ... This inconvenience is, as I find to be the fact, more than fanciful, more than one of mere delicacy or fastidiousness. It is an inconvenience materially interfering with the ordinary comfort physically of human existence, not merely according to the elegant or dainty modes of living, but according to plain and sober and simple notions among ordinary people living in this part of Fulham.

The question of noise does not stop there. At intervals through the night tankers leave and come to the defendants' depot. It has been urged on me that the public highway is for the use of all, and that is true. But it must be borne in mind that the tankers are not ordinary motor cars; they are not ordinary lorries which make more noise than a motor car; they are enormous vehicles, some when laden weighing 24 tons, which, apart from the loud noise of the engine, may rattle as they go, particularly when empty and especially if they hit something in the road like a grating. They all enter the depot almost opposite the plaintiff's house, which involves a sharp turn in order to do so, often changing down in to low gear at the same time. They leave by the exit gate which is also close to the plaintiff's house. ...

It is said by the defendants that, since the public highway is for the use of everyone, the plaintiff cannot complain if all that the defendants do is to make use of their right to use the public highway. I agree, if that is all the defendants have done. If a person makes an unreasonable use of the public highway, for instance by parking stationary vehicles on it, a member of the public who suffers special damage has a cause of action against him for public nuisance. Similarly, in my view, if a person makes an unreasonable use of the public highway by concentrating in one small area of the highway vehicles in motion, and a member of the public suffers special damage, he is equally entitled to complain, although in most cases concentration of moving, as opposed to stationary vehicles, will be more likely to be reasonable. ...

The noise outside and inside the plaintiff's house is, in my judgment, attributable to the defendants' mode of operation of their depot, and the principles of law to be applied seem to me to be the same as those in respect of alleged nuisance by noise of the plant itself. Applying those principles which involve consideration of the whole of the relevant circumstances, I hold that the defendants are also guilty of nuisance in this respect, but only during the night shift. ...

If these cases are more properly to be regarded as instances of public nuisance, I do not think ... that the result is any different. If I treat this part of the case as public nuisance, as counsel for the plaintiff argued in the alternative, I ask myself: is it reasonable to concentrate outside the plaintiff's house during the night, not on odd occasions, but every night, and not once a night, but at irregular intervals during the night and early hours of the morning, particularly noisy vehicles, sometimes in convoy, the noise of one of which is 83 decibels? I bear in mind the importance of the defendants' business. I also, I hope, bear in mind all the circumstances, including the circumstance that a man is entitled to sleep during the night in his own house. I have no hesitation in saying that the plaintiff has satisfied me that the defendants' use of their tankers in all the circumstances is unreasonable. On this view they are liable as for a public nuisance, since it is conceded that noise can be special damage if it affects the plaintiff more than the ordinary member of the public. On this alternative view also the defendants are liable, since I find that the plaintiff has indeed suffered special damage which is substantial and not transient or fleeting. ...

The plaintiff is therefore entitled to damages. For his damaged linen he claims £5. This is a modest claim and he is entitled to it. He is also entitled, in my view, to damages in respect of his motor car, but I do not think that the alleged loss of value due to the damaged paintwork is proved. I think a new coat of paint would have maintained the value of the motor car. ...

> Since the end of 1956 the plaintiff has suffered very considerable discomfort. It is something which cannot easily be assessed in terms of money ... I must do the best I can to ward him a sum in respect of the nuisances by noise and smell which have been inflicted on him over the last few years. On this head, which is limited to noise and smell over the past few years, I award £200. ...
>
> So far as the future is concerned, I have considered the authorities to which I have been referred by both parties. ... An injunction is a discretionary remedy, but the discretion should be exercised in accordance with accepted principles. One, but only one, of those principles is that the court is not a tribunal for legalising wrongful acts by an award of damages. I am fully conscious of the importance of the defendant's business. The question of remedy by injunction must be considered separately in respect of noise, smell, and smuts.
>
> As to the noise, I bear in mind the effect on the defendants of closing the night shift. Indeed, the evidence quantified the possible and probable loss of profit. I am asked to bear in mind the effect on the customers of the defendants, but the figures of estimated loss of profit are on the basis of the defendants making alternative arrangements to keep their customers supplied. I bear in mind that the defendants have in some respects done what they can to minimise the noise. Nevertheless, the plaintiff is entitled, in my judgment, to an injunction to limit it to the hours of the night shift, namely, ten o'clock at night to six o'clock in the morning. There will be an injunction restraining the defendants by themselves, their servants or agents from so operating their plant at the depot, and from so driving their vehicles as, by reason of noise, to cause a nuisance to the plaintiff between the hours of 10 pm and 6 am. I am prepared to suspend the operation of this order for a reasonable time so that the defendants may make appropriate arrangements.
>
> As to smell, again I think that the plaintiff is entitled to an injunction. I have felt some difficulty on this aspect of the case because I do not think that the occasional slight smell of oil *per se* is a matter which can be complained about as opposed to what is described as the pungent, rather nauseating smell. It is difficult to find the precise words which will cover my findings on the facts, but I propose to grant an injunction in general terms restraining the defendants by themselves, their servant or agents from so conducting their operations at the depot as, by reason of smell, to cause a nuisance to the plaintiff. In this case there is no limitation as to the time of day or night, but again, I am prepared to suspend the operation of my order for a reasonable time if the defendants desire to make alterations or adjustments.
>
> As to smuts, ... I do not propose either to grant an injunction or to award damages for the future. If future damage is caused by the defendants, he will be able to bring a fresh action. I take this action primarily because the whole boiler house and the offending chimneys are to be pulled down.

The case is an extremely useful illustration of many of the problems which arise in nuisance cases, all coming neatly for once within the four corners of one case. We shall be exploring further many of the points raised in this case in the discussion below.

Another case, which we shall only briefly dip into this time, is the rather odd case of *Malone v Laskey*,[3] in which the plaintiff, living with her husband on the premises and not regarded as an occupier, claimed damages for personal injury

3 [1907] 2 KB 141.

as a result a bracket falling on her. It was alleged that it had been disturbed by vibrations coming from the neighbouring premises. One brief issue in the case is whether, in a private nuisance action, the plaintiff had to show that she had a recognised interest in land in order to maintain such an action. Sir Gorrell Barnes P stated:

> The main question, however, on this part of the case is whether the plaintiff can maintain this action on the ground of vibration causing the damage complained of, and in my opinion the plaintiff has no cause of action upon that ground. Many cases were cited in the course of argument in which it had been held that actions for nuisance could be maintained where a person's rights of property had been affected by the nuisance, but no authority was cited, nor in my opinion can any principle of law be formulated, to the effect that a person who has no interest in property, no right of occupation in the proper sense of the term, can maintain an action for a nuisance arising from the vibration causes by the working of an engine in an adjoining house. On that point, therefore, I think that the plaintiff fails, and that she has no cause of action in respect of the alleged nuisance.

Fletcher Moulton LJ agreed and Kennedy LJ added:

> I am of the same opinion. On the question of vibration there is no more to be said. No question was asked of the jury whether what was done by the defendants amounted to a public nuisance, and I agree that the mere existence of vibration amounting only to a private nuisance to the occupiers of the premises gave no cause of action to the plaintiff in respect of the alleged consequences of the vibration.

The unfortunate woman did not succeed also on her negligence pleading, and it does not seem that the case was pleaded in public nuisance, in which case she might have had more luck. The contentious issue in that case was thought to have been long settled, but recently the Court of Appeal has upset the apple-cart by its decision in *Khorasandjian v Bush*.[4] In that case the plaintiff was seeking an injunction to prevent, amongst other things, the continued harassment of herself by the defendant by means of telephone calls to her parent's home in which she was then living. The action was pleaded on the basis of private nuisance. Dillon LJ, with whom Rose LJ agreed, said:

> To my mind, it is ridiculous if, in this present age, the law is that the making of deliberately harassing and pestering telephone calls to a person is only actionable in the civil courts if the recipient of the calls happens to have the freehold or a leasehold proprietary interest in the premises in which he or she has received the calls.
>
> Miss Harry Thomas submits, however, that English law does not recognise any tort of harassment or invasion of privacy or, save in the different context of such a case as *Rookes v Barnard* [1964] 1 All ER 367, [1964] AC 1129, intimidation. Therefore, she says, that, save as expressly conceded as set out above, the defendant's conduct to the plaintiff is, even on the plaintiff's version of it, under the English civil law legitimate conduct of which the plaintiff has no power or right to complain. I apprehend that it is correct, historically, that the tort of private nuisance, which originated as an action on the case, was developed in the beginning to protect private property rights, in relation to the use or enjoyment of land. It is stated in *Clerk & Lindsell on Torts* (16th edn, 1989, para 24-01) that

4 [1993] 3 All ER 669.

> 'the essence of nuisance is a condition or activity which unduly interferes with the use and enjoyment of land'.
>
> That a legal owner can obtain an injunction, on the grounds of private nuisance, to restrain persistent harassment by unwanted telephone calls to his home was decided by the Appellate Division of the Alberta Supreme Court in *Motherwell v Motherwell* (1976) 73 DLR (3d) 62. The court there rejected, by reference to English authority, a submission (at 67): 'That the common law does not have within itself the resources to recognise invasion of privacy as either included in an existing category or as a new category of nuisance, and that it has lost its original power, by which indeed it created itself, to note new ills arising in a growing and changing society, and pragmatically to establish a principle to meet the need for control and remedy; and then by categories to develop the principle as the interests of justice make themselves sufficiently apparent.'
>
> Consequently, notwithstanding *Malone v Laskey*, the court held that the wife of the owner had also the right to restrain harassing telephone calls to the matrimonial home. Clement JA who delivered the judgment of the court said (at 78): 'Here we have a wife harassed in the matrimonial home. She has a status, a right to live there with her husband and children. I find it absurd to say that her occupancy of the matrimonial home is insufficient to found an action in nuisance. In my opinion, she is entitled to the same relief as her husband, the brother.'
>
> I respectfully agree, and in my judgment this court is entitled to adopt the same approach. The court has at times to reconsider earlier decisions in the light of changed social conditions. ... If the wife of the owner is entitled to sue in respect of harassing telephone calls, then I do not see why that should not also apply to a child living at home with her parents.

Some see this as heralding a new tort of harassment. Others, more cautiously and with good cause, regard this as merely a development bringing the tort of nuisance into this century.

Before going on to discuss further the various aspects of a private nuisance action, it is worthwhile contrasting the views in two other cases at this stage. The case of *Wagon Mound (No 2)* we have already met in the chapter on breach of duty, and we shall return to it later in this chapter. At this stage it is worth commenting that that case represents a major step in the gradual take over of the tort of nuisance by its sister action on the case, negligence. This should be compared with the strict nature of the liability in *Wringe v Cohen*,[5] where the issue was whether the repairing occupier or owner of premises in bad repair which collapse and injure passers-by or adjoining owners are liable in nuisance, even if not aware of the danger. Atkinson LJ read the judgment of the court and said:

> In our judgment if, owing to want of repair, premises on a highway become dangerous and, therefore, a nuisance, and a passer-by or an adjoining owner suffers damage by their collapse, the occupier, or the owner if he has undertaken the duty of repair, is answerable whether he knew or ought to have known of the danger or not. The undertaking to repair gives the owner control of the premises, and a right of access thereto for the purpose of maintaining them in a safe condition. On the other hand, if the nuisance is created, not by want of repair, but, for example, by the act of a trespasser, or by a secret and unobservable operation of nature, such as subsidence under or near the foundations of the

5 [1940] 1 KB 229.

> premises, neither an occupier nor an owner responsible for repair is answerable, unless with knowledge or means of knowledge he allows the danger to continue. In such a case he has in no sense caused the nuisance by any act or breach of duty.

The defendant's appeal was dismissed. It provides a harsh contrast with some of the cases to be discussed later, but may be justified on public safety grounds.

We have explored in this introduction some of the similarities and differences between the two types of nuisance. We shall now consider private nuisance in more detail.

Private nuisance

The usual starting point in a discussion of private nuisance is the principle that no man is allowed to use his property to injure another which, of itself, is very little use. It does not tell us to what point the use of the property by the defendant may go before the law will intervene. There is a balance to be sought and, if possible, achieved between competing private rights as between adjoining landowners and the spurious public interest.

Interests protected

Subject to the development discussed earlier in *Khorasandjian v Bush*, the plaintiff, in order to maintain an action, must have a legally recognised interest in the land affected by the alleged nuisance. This would obviously cover the freeholder, the leaseholder and the reversioner in situations where the nuisance has caused or might cause permanent damage to the property. In fact, any interest which is capable of being protected by a grant falls within this category, and therefore, a mere licence would not seem to be sufficient. Again, the *Bush* case may have wrought a serious change in this rule.

Conduct covered

We shall see that nuisance is concerned with interferences of a physical nature which are indirect, whereas direct physical interferences would be within the scope of a trespass to land action. Nuisance, as we have already seen, however, encompasses more than just physical damage or inconvenience to property. It covers intangible interferences, which can and often are, serious interferences with the use and enjoyment of the plaintiff's own property. Into this category fall eg smells, noise and vibrations. Establishing a sex shop or a brothel in a particular area might also be examples of intangible interference. There is a tendency, as we shall see, for the law to take the physical interferences more seriously in most situations.

Activity or conduct must be unreasonable

This is the crucial issue in any private nuisance action. Was the defendant's conduct or activity reasonable in relation to the plaintiff's use and enjoyment of his own land? There has to be give and take in regard to the use of land, but has the defendant gone beyond this?

The courts consider a number of factors when assessing this question, such as whether negligence by the defendant is relevant, whether the escape was a continuing or isolated one, the nature of the locality, the social utility of the activity, the duration, frequency and intensity of the activity. We shall consider these below.

Negligence a factor?

It seems, as already indicated in the introduction to this chapter, that in some cases foreseeability as to consequences is thought to be a factor. As a general rule, it seems that this is more likely to be the case where damages are claimed by the plaintiff as opposed to the preventative remedy of the injunction. Also, where the defendant or somebody for whom he is responsible has created the alleged nuisance, negligence is not normally considered essential. However, where the nuisance resulted from a natural event or as a result of the act of a third party outside the control of the defendant, the courts will only hold that there is a nuisance as far as the defendant is concerned if some negligence, even an omission, can be laid at the defendant's door. This is well illustrated by the case of *Goldman v Hargrave*.[6] It will be recalled from previous discussions of this case that it concerned the escape of fire from the defendant's land as a result of a failure by him to extinguish a tree on his land which had been struck by lightning. Lord Wilberforce delivered the opinion of the Privy Council and stated:

> It is important at once to deal with an argument as to the facts which was advanced by the respondents at the trial. It was sought to contend that, although the fire commenced accidentally, the appellant, whether by heaping combustible material onto it after the tree had been felled, or even by permitting the tree to burn in the way in which it did on the ground, had adopted the fire as his own – *as suus ignis* – and had made use of it for his own purpose or advantage.
>
> Their Lordships (in agreement with the High Court) do not accept this view of the facts. The result of the evidence, in their Lordships' opinion, is that the appellant both up to 26 February and thereafter was endeavouring to extinguish the fire; that initially he acted with prudence, but that there came a point, about the evening of 26 February or the morning of 27 February, when, the prudent and reasonable course being to put the fire out by water, he chose to adopt the method of burning it out. That method was, according to the finding of the trial judge, unreasonable, or negligent in the circumstances; it brought a fresh risk into operation, namely the risk of a revival of the fire, under the influence of changing wind and weather, if not carefully watched, and it was from this negligence that the damage arose. That a risk of this character was foreseeable by someone in the appellant's position was not really disputed; in fact danger arising from weather conditions is given official recognition in the Bush Fires Act 1954–1958, which provides for their classification according to the degree of danger arising from them.
>
> This conclusion has an important bearing upon the nature of the legal issue which has to be decided. It makes clear that the case is not one where a person has brought a source of danger onto his land, nor one where the occupier has so used his property as to cause a danger to his neighbour. It is one where an occupier, faced with a hazard accidentally arising on his land, fails to act with reasonable prudence so as to remove the hazard. The issue is, therefore, whether

6 [1967] 1 AC 645.

in such a case the occupier is guilty of legal negligence, which involves the issue whether he is under a duty of care, and, if so, what is the scope of that duty.

Their Lordships propose to deal with these issues as stated, without attempting to answer the disputable question whether, if responsibility is established, it should be brought under the heading of nuisance or placed in a separate category. As this board has recently explained in *The Wagon Mound (No 2)* the tort of nuisance, uncertain in its boundary, may comprise a wide variety of situations, in some of which negligence plays no part, in others of which it is decisive. The present case is one where liability, if it exists, rests upon negligence and nothing else; whether it falls within or overlaps the boundaries of nuisance is a question of classification which need not here be resolved.

What then is the scope of an occupier's duty, with regard to his neighbours, as to hazards arising on his land? With the possible exception of hazard of fire ... it is only in comparatively recent times that the law has recognised an occupier's duty as one of a more positive character than merely to abstain from creating, or adding to, a source of danger or annoyance. It was for long satisfied with the conception of separate or autonomous proprietors, each of which was entitled to exploit his territory in a 'natural' manner, and none of whom was obliged to restrain or direct the operations of nature in the interest of avoiding harm to his neighbours. ...

[The case of *Sedleigh-Denfield v O'Callaghan*] establishes the occupier's liability with regard to a hazard created on his land by a trespasser, of which he has knowledge, when he fails to take reasonable steps to remove it. It was clear in that case that the hazard could have been removed by what Viscount Maugham described as the 'very simple step' of placing a grid in the proper place. ...

The appellant, inevitably, accepts the development, or statement of the law which the *Sedleigh-Denfield*[7] case contains – as it was accepted by the High Court of Australia. But he seeks to establish a distinction between the type of hazard which was there involved, namely, one brought about by human agency, such as the act of a trespasser, and one arising from natural causes or Act of God. In relation to hazards of this kind it was submitted that an occupier is under no duty to remove or to diminish it, and that his liability only commences if and when by interference with it, he negligently increases the risk or danger to his neighbour's property.

Their Lordships would first observe, with regard to the suggested distinction, that it is well designed to introduce confusion into the law. As regards many hazardous conditions arising on land, it is impossible to determine how they arose – particularly is this the case as regards fires. If they are caused by human agency, the agent, unless detected in *flagrante delicto*, is hardly likely to confess his fault. And is the occupier, when faced with the initial stages of a fire, to ask himself whether the fire is accidental or man-made before he can decide on his duty? Is the neighbour whose property is damaged bound to prove the human origin of the fire? The proposition involves that if he cannot do so, however irresponsibly the occupier has acted, he must fail. But the distinction is not only inconvenient; it lacks, in their Lordships' view, any logical foundation.

Within the class of situations in which the occupier is himself without responsibility for the origin of the fire, one may ask in vain what relevant difference there is between a fire caused by a human agency, such as a trespasser, and one caused by Act of God or nature. A difference in degree as to the potency

7 [1940] AC 880, see below.

> of the agency – one can see but none that is in principle relevant to the occupier's duty to act. It was suggested as a logical basis for the distinction that, in the case of a hazard originating in an act of man, an occupier who fails to deal with it can be said to be using his land in a manner detrimental to his neighbour, and so to be within the classical field of responsibility in nuisance, whereas this cannot be said when the hazard originates without human action so long at least as the occupier merely abstains. The fallacy of this argument is that ... the basis of the occupier's liability lies not in the use of his land; in the absence of 'adoption' there is no such use; but in the neglect of action in the face of something which may damage his neighbour, to this, the suggested distinction is irrelevant. ...
>
> So far it has been possible to consider the existence of a duty, in general terms. But the matter cannot be left there without some definition of the scope of his duty. How far does it go? What is the standard of the effort required? What is the position as regards expenditure? It is not enough to say merely that these must be 'reasonable', since what is reasonable to one man may be very unreasonable, and indeed ruinous, to another; the law must take account of the fact that the occupier on whom the duty is cast has, *ex hypothesi*, had this hazard thrust upon him through no seeking or fault of his own. His interest, and his resources, whether physical or material, may be of a very modest character either in relation to the magnitude of the hazard, or as compared with those of his threatened neighbour. A rule which required of him in such unsought circumstances in his neighbour's interest, a physical effort of which he is not capable, or an excessive expenditure of money, would be unenforceable or unjust.
>
> One may say in general terms that the existence of a duty must be based upon knowledge of the hazard, ability to foresee the consequences of not checking or removing it, and the ability to abate it. And in many cases ... where the hazard could have been removed with little effort and no expenditure, no problem arises. But other cases may not be so simple. In such situations the standard ought to be to require of the occupier what it is reasonable to expect of him in his individual circumstances. Thus, less must be expected of the infirm than of the able-bodied; the owner of a small property where a hazard arises which threatens a neighbour with substantial interests should not have to do so much as one with larger interests of his own at stake and greater resources to protect them; if the small owner does what he can and promptly calls on his neighbour to provide additional resources, he may be held to have done his duty; he should not be liable unless it is clearly proved that he could, and reasonably in his individual circumstance should, have done more.

The standard of care expected in these situations is highly subjective as is evident from the above. The approach was adopted by the Court of Appeal in the later case *Leakey v National Trust*,[8] in which the defendants' land was liable to landslip following especially dry weather and then heavy rain. The danger was pointed out to the defendants but they did nothing about it, and the plaintiffs' house was damaged when there was a major collapse onto it. On the question of whether the claim was correctly expressed in terms of nuisance, Megaw LJ, with whom Cumming Bruce J agreed, said:

> It is convenient at this stage to deal with the second proposition put forward by the defendants in the present appeal. The plaintiffs' claim is expressed in the pleadings to be founded in nuisance. There is no express reference to negligence in the statement of claim. But there is an allegation of a breach of duty, and the

8 [1980] 1 All ER 17.

> duty asserted is, in effect, a duty to take reasonable care to prevent part of the defendants' land from falling onto the plaintiffs' property. I should, for myself, regard that as being properly described as a claim in nuisance. But even if that were, technically, wrong, I do not think that the point could or should avail the defendants in this case. If it were to do so, it would be a regrettable modern instance of the forms of action successfully clanking their spectral chains; for there would be no conceivable prejudice to the defendants in this case that the word 'negligence' had not been expressly set out in the statement of claim.

Having dealt with that preliminary issue, the judge went on to discuss the duty issue as follows:

> If, as a result of the working of the forces of nature, there is, poised above my land, above my house, a boulder or a rotten tree, which is liable to fall at any moment of the day or night, perhaps destroying my house and perhaps killing or injuring me or members of my family, am I without remedy? (Of course the standard of care required may be much higher where there is risk to life or limb as contrasted with mere risk to property, but can it be said that the duty exists in the one case and not in the other?) Must I, in such a case, if my protests to my neighbour go unheeded, sit and wait and hope that the worst will not befall? If it is said that I have in such circumstances a remedy of going on my neighbour's land to abate the nuisance, that would, or might, be an unsatisfactory remedy. But in any event, if there were such a right of abatement, it would, as counsel for the plaintiff rightly contended, be because my neighbour owed me a duty. There is, I think, ample authority that, if I have the right to abatement, I have a remedy in damages if the nuisance remains unabated and causes me damage or personal injury. ...
>
> In the example which I have given above, I believe that few people would regard it as anything other than a grievous blot on the law if the law recognises the existence of no duty on the part of the owner or occupier. But take another example, at the other end of the scale, where it might be thought that there is, potentially, an equally serious injustice the other way. If a stream flows through A's land, A being a small farmer, and there is a known danger that in times of heavy rainfall, because of the configuration of A's land and the nature of the stream's course and flow, there may be an overflow, which will pass beyond A's land and damage the property of A's neighbours – perhaps much wealthier neighbours. It may require expensive works, far beyond A's means, to prevent or even diminish the risk of flooding. Is A to be liable for all the loss that occurs when the flood comes, if he has not done the impossible and carried out these works at his own expense?
>
> In my judgment there is, in the scope of the duty as explained in *Goldman v Hargrave*, a removal, or at least a powerful amelioration, of the injustice which might otherwise be caused in such a case by the recognition of the duty of care. Because of that limitation on the scope of the duty, I would say that, as a matter of policy, the law ought to recognise such a duty of care.
>
> This leads on to the question of the scope of the duty. This is discussed, and the nature and extent of the duty is explained, in the judgment in *Goldman v Hargrave*. The duty is a duty to do that which is reasonable in all the circumstances, and no more than what, if anything, is reasonable, to prevent or minimise the known risk of damage or injury to one's neighbour or his property. The considerations with which the law is familiar are all to be taken into account in deciding whether there has been a breach of duty, and, if so, what that breach is, and whether it is causative of the damage in respect of which the claim is made.

> Thus, there will fall to be considered the extent of the risk. What, so far as reasonably can be foreseen, are the chances that anything untoward will happen or that any damage will be caused? What is to be foreseen as to the possible extent of the damage if the risk becomes a reality? Is it practicable to prevent, or to minimise, the happening of any damage? If it is practicable, how simple or how difficult are the measures which could be taken, how much and how lengthy work do they involve, and what is the probable cost of such works? Was there sufficient time for preventive action to have been taken, by persons acting reasonably in relation to the known risk, between the time when it became known to, or should have been realised by, the defendant, and the time when the damage occurred? Factors such as these, so far as they apply in a particular case, fall to be weighed in deciding whether the defendant's duty of care requires, or required, him to do anything, and if so, what. ...
>
> The defendant's duty is to do that which it is reasonable for him to do. The criteria of reasonableness include, in respect of a duty of this nature, the factor of what the particular man, not the average man, can be expected to do, having regard, amongst other things, where a serious expenditure of money is required to eliminate or reduce the danger, to his means. Just as, where physical effort is required to avert an immediate danger, the defendant's age and physical condition may be relevant in deciding what is reasonable, so also logic and good sense require that, where the expenditure of money is required, the defendant's capacity to find the money is relevant. But this can only be in the way of a broad, and not a detailed, assessment; and, in arriving at a judgment on reasonableness, a similar broad assessment may be relevant in some cases as to the neighbour's capacity to protect himself from damage, whether by way of some form of barrier on his own land or by way of providing funds for expenditure on agreed works on the land of the defendant.
>
> Take, by way of example, the hypothetical instance which I gave earlier: the landowner through whose land a stream flows. In rainy weather, it is known, the stream may flood and the flood may spread to the land of neighbours. If the risk is one which can readily be overcome or lessened, for example by reasonable steps on the part of the landowner to keep the stream free from blockage by flotsam or silt carried down, he will be in breach of duty if he does nothing or he does too little. But if the only remedy is substantial and expensive works, then it might be well that the landowner would have discharged his duty by saying to his neighbours, who also know of the risk and have asked him to do something about it, 'You have my permission to come onto my land and to do agreed works at your expense', or it may be, 'on the basis of a fair sharing of expense'.

The judge decided in favour of the plaintiff by dismissing the appeal and, implicitly, therefore, must have thought that the defendants in the case before him were under a duty to do something to prevent the landslip and that expense was not a factor to be considered. It is interesting to note the reluctance of Shaw LJ to dismiss the appeal, although in the end he did so. He was somewhat sceptical as the following brief extract illustrates:

> Why should a nuisance which has its origin in some natural phenomenon, and which manifests itself without any human intervention, cast a liability on a person who has no other connection with that nuisance than the title to the land on which it chances to originate? This view is fortified inasmuch as a title to land cannot be discarded or abandoned. Why should the owner of land in such a case be bound to protect his neighbour's property and person rather than that the neighbour should protect his interests against the potential danger?

We now need to turn to the case mentioned in *Goldman v Hargrave* earlier, namely *Sedleigh-Denfield v O'Callaghan*, in which the House of Lords was called upon to consider the liability of an occupier for the acts of a trespasser on his land. In this case the alleged nuisance concerned the act of a trespasser who inserted a pipe in a ditch on the defendant's land. The pipe became blocked by debris and overflowed, flooding the plaintiff's garden. The evidence showed that the pipe had been inserted over three years before the incident complained of, and that a person authorised by the defendants cleaned the ditch out at least twice a year. Viscount Maugham said:

> The statement that an occupier of land is liable for the continuance of a nuisance created by others, eg by trespassers, if he continues or adopts it – which seem to be agreed – throws little light on the matter, unless the words 'continues or adopts' are defined. In my opinion, an occupier of land 'continues' a nuisance if, with knowledge or presumed knowledge of its existence, he fails to take any reasonable means to bring it to an end, though with ample time to do so. He 'adopts' if he makes any use of the erection, building, bank or artificial contrivance which constitutes the nuisance. ...
>
> My lords, in the present case I am of opinion that the respondents both continued and adopted the nuisance. After the lapse of nearly three years, they must be taken to have suffered the nuisance to continue, for they neglected to take the very simple step of placing a grid in the proper place, which would have removed the danger to their neighbour's land. They adopted the nuisance, for they continued during all that time to use the artificial contrivance of the conduit for the purpose of getting rid of water from their property without taking the proper means for rendering it safe.

Lord Atkin chimed in as follows:

> In this state of the facts, the legal position is not, I think, difficult to discover. For the purpose of ascertaining whether, as here, the plaintiff can establish a private nuisance, I think that nuisance is sufficiently defined as a wrongful interference with another's enjoyment of his land or premises by the use of land or premises either occupied – or, in some cases, owned – by oneself. The occupier or owner is not an insurer. There must be something more than mere harm done to the neighbour's property to make the party responsible. Deliberate act or negligence is not an essential ingredient, but some degree of personal responsibility is required, which is connoted in my definition by the word 'use'.
>
> This conception is implicit in all the decisions which impose liability only where the defendant has 'caused or continued' the nuisance. We may eliminate, in this case, 'caused'. What is the meaning of 'continued'? In the context in which it is used, 'continued' must indicate mere passive continuance. If a man uses on premises something which he finds there, and which itself causes a nuisance by noise, vibration, smell or fumes, he is himself, in continuing to bring into existence the noise, vibration, smell or fumes, causing a nuisance. Continuing, in this sense, and causing are the same thing. It seems to me clear that, if a man permits an offensive thing on his premises to continue to offend – ie if he knows that it is operating offensively, is able to prevent it, and omits to prevent it – he is permitting the nuisance to continue. In other words, he is continuing it. ...
>
> In the present case ... there is ... sufficient proof of the knowledge of the defendants both of the cause and of its probable effect. What is the legal result of the original cause being due to the act of a trespasser? In my opinion, the defendants clearly continued the nuisance, for they come clearly within the terms

> I have mentioned above. They knew the danger, they were able to prevent it, and they omitted to prevent it.

The other three judges also agreed that the appeal should be allowed on similar grounds.

Continuing or isolated escape?

Normally a nuisance will be a continuing state of affairs for which the plaintiff may want damages for the harm in the past, but, perhaps, more importantly, wants an order preventing its continuance. Generally, where the nuisance is of a continuing nature, foreseeability of consequences is regarded as irrelevant, but where the nuisance is an isolated escape, it is argued that foreseeability is a necessary prerequisite of liability. In *British Celanese v Hunt*, a case we have already considered in the previous chapter, Lawton J discussed the possibility of there being liability in nuisance in relation to the escape of the metal foil strips. He said:

> I turn now to the plaintiff's contention that the re-amended statement of claim discloses a cause of action both in private and public nuisance. As to private nuisance, they say that the defendants' alleged method of storing metal foil resulted, as the defendants knew it would, in an interference with the beneficial enjoyment of their own premises whereby they suffered damage; and as to public nuisance, their case is that the nuisance was one which affected a class of persons, namely those members of the public supplied with electricity from the sub-station, and that as members of that class they suffered special damage.
>
> The defendants made three answers to these contentions: firstly, that an isolated happening such as the plaintiffs relied upon was not enough to found an action in nuisance since this tort can only arise out of a continuing condition; secondly, that if there was a nuisance upon the defendants' premises, it did not affect the plaintiff's premises directly; and thirdly that the re-amended statement of claim did not disclose enough facts to justify a ruling that a class of the public had been injuriously affected by the alleged nuisance.
>
> In my judgment, all three answers are misconceived. Most nuisances do arise from a long continuing condition; and many isolated happenings do not constitute a nuisance. It is, however, clear from the authorities that an isolated happening by itself can create an actionable nuisance. ... I am satisfied that the law is correctly stated in *Winfield on Tort*, 8th edn at p 364: 'When the nuisance is the escape of tangible things which damage the plaintiff in the enjoyment of his property, there is no rule that he cannot sue for the first escape'.

The judge dismissed the second argument of the defendants and, with regard to the third, merely said that this would have to await the evidence at the trial as to whether the class of persons was large enough to make it a public nuisance.

Substantial harm

The extent of the harm caused or likely to be caused is an important factor in deciding whether the defendant's activity is actionable in nuisance. The harm must be substantial and it is accepted that any actual physical damage will normally be regarded as substantial, whereas the courts require more convincing that an intangible harm is actionable. In *St Helen's Smelting Co v Tipping*[9] the defendants smelting operations caused damage to trees and shrubs

9 (1865) 11 HL Cas 642.

on the plaintiff's estate. The following is an extract from the speech of Lord Westbury in the House of Lords:

> My Lords, in matters of this description it appears to me that it is a very desirable thing to mark the difference between an action brought for a nuisance upon the ground that the alleged nuisance produces material injury to the property, and an action brought for a nuisance on the ground that the thing alleged to be a nuisance is productive of sensible personal discomfort. With regard to the latter, namely, the personal inconvenience and interference with one's enjoyment, one's quiet, one's personal freedom, anything that discomposes or injuriously affects the senses or the nerves, whether that may or may not be denominated a nuisance, must undoubtedly depend greatly on the circumstances of the place where the thing complained of actually occurs. If a man lives in a town, it is necessary that he should subject himself to the consequences of those operations of trade which may be carried on in his immediate locality, which are actually necessary for trade and commerce, and also for the enjoyment of property, and for the benefit of the inhabitants of the town and of the public at large. If a man lives in a street where there are numerous shops, and a shop is opened next door to him, which is carried on in a fair and reasonable way, he has no ground for complaint, because to himself individually there may arise much discomfort from the trade carried on in that shop. But when an occupation is carried on by one person in the neighbourhood of another, and the result of that trade, or occupation, or business, is a material injury to property, then there unquestionably arises a very different consideration. I think, my Lords, that in a case of that description, the submission which is required from persons living in society to that amount of discomfort which may be necessary for the legitimate and free exercise of the trade of their neighbours, would not apply to circumstances, the immediate result of which is sensible injury to the value of the property.
>
> ... the whole neighbourhood where these copper smelting works were carried on is a neighbourhood more or less devoted to manufacturing purposes of a similar kind, and therefore it is said, that inasmuch as this copper smelting is carried on in what the appellant contends is a fit place, it may be carried on with impunity, although the result may be the utter destruction, or the very considerable diminution, of the value of the plaintiff's property. My lords, I apprehend that that is not the meaning of the word 'suitable', or the meaning of the word 'convenient', which has been used as applicable to the subject. The word 'suitable' unquestionably cannot carry with it this consequence, that a trade may be carried on in a particular locality, the consequence of which trade may be injury and destruction to the neighbouring property.

Locality

The last case illustrates the point, to some extent at least, that locality may be a factor in deciding whether the plaintiff's complaint is actionable as a nuisance. This is reinforced by the decision in *Adams v Ursell*,[10] in which the plaintiff was complaining about the smell from the defendant's fish and chip shop next door. The High Court judge observed:

> I have no doubt that the plaintiff has proved that having the odour pervading his house is an intolerable inconvenience, and in my judgment he has made out a case of nuisance at common law. It was urged that an injunction would cause

10 [1913] 1 Ch 269.

> great hardship to the defendant and to the poor people who get food at his shop. The answer to that is that it does not follow that the defendant cannot carry on his business in another more suitable place somewhere in the neighbourhood. It by no means follows that, because a fried fish shop is a nuisance in one place, it is a nuisance in another. The evidence shows that the defendant supplies fresh fish and has the most approved appliances; but a case is none the less made out, and I must grant an interlocutory injunction restraining the defendant from carrying on his fried fish business on the premises which he now occupies. It will not extend to the whole street as asked.

It follows from this that the defendant merely had to move a few doors away and he could lawfully ply his trade. A commercial activity is less likely to be actionable in a mixed residential and industrial area as opposed to a mainly residential area.

Social utility

It is sometimes the case that the defendant will argue that to prevent his activity would deprive the community of certain benefits. We have seen this argument before in the context of the general discussion of breach of duty in negligence. It seems to be less successful in nuisance cases. One of the less successful attempts to employ this factor was that of Lord Denning MR in *Miller v Jackson*,[11] in which he launched into a panegyric on the subject of village cricket in his typical staccato style:

> In summer time village cricket is the delight of everyone. Nearly every village has its own cricket field where the young men play and the old men watch. In the village of Lintz in County Durham they have their own ground, where they have played these last 70 years. They tend it well. The wicket area is well rolled and mown. The outfield is kept short. It has a good clubhouse for the players and seats for the onlookers. The village team play there on Saturdays and Sundays. They belong to a league, competing with the neighbouring villages. On other evenings after work they practice while the light lasts. Yet now after these 70 years a judge of the High Court has ordered that they must not play there any more. He has issued an injunction to stop them. He has done it at the instance of a newcomer who is no lover of cricket. ... His wife got so upset about it that they always go out at weekends. They do not go into the garden when cricket is being played. They say that this is intolerable. So they asked the judge to stop the cricket being played. And the judge, much against his will, has felt that he must order the cricket to be stopped; with the consequences, I suppose, that the Lintz Cricket Club will disappear. The cricket ground will be turned to some other use. I expect for more houses or a factory. The young men will turn to other things instead of cricket. The whole village will be much the poorer. ...
>
> This case is new. It should be approached on principles applicable to modern conditions. There is a contest between the interest of the public at large and the interest of the private individual. The *public* interest lies in protecting the environment by preserving our playing field in the face of mounting development, and by enabling our youth to enjoy all the benefits of outdoor games, such as cricket and football. The *private* interest lies in securing the privacy of his home and garden without intrusion or interference by anyone. As between their conflicting interests, I am of opinion that the public interest should prevail over the private interest. ...

11 [1977] 3 All ER 338.

The other two judges were less emotional and less impressed with the social utility argument, Geoffrey Lane LJ being concerned that the type of likely injury was physical in nature. They both held that there was, in addition to negligence, an actionable nuisance. We shall return shortly to this case on the issue of remedies.

Plaintiff's hypersensitivity

If the plaintiff's use of his own premises is hypersensitive or unusual in any way, and he is unable to use his property for that purpose because of what the defendant is doing on his land, the court may decide that there is no actionable nuisance. In a sense, the cause of the harm to the plaintiff is his own unusual use of his own premises rather than the use of those of the defendant. An illustrative case is that of *Robinson v Kilvert*,[12] in which the plaintiff complained that the heat coming from the defendant's premises was damaging the brown paper he was storing on his premises. Cotton LJ in the Court of Appeal discussed the nuisance, speaking in the following terms:

> Now the heat is not excessive, it does not rise above 80° at the floor, and in the room itself it is not nearly so great. If a person does what in itself is noxious, or which interferes with the ordinary use and enjoyment of a neighbour's property, it is a nuisance. But no case has been cited where the doing something not in itself noxious has been held a nuisance, unless it interferes with the ordinary enjoyment of life, or the ordinary use of property for the purposes of residence or business. It would, in my opinion, be wrong to say that the doing something not in itself noxious is a nuisance because it does harm to some particular trade in the adjoining property, although it would not prejudicially affect any ordinary trade carried on there, and does not interfere with the ordinary enjoyment of life. Here it is shown that ordinary paper would not be damaged by what the defendants are doing, but only a particular kind of paper, and it is not shown that there is heat such as to incommode the work people on the plaintiff's premises. I am of opinion, therefore, that the plaintiff is not entitled to relief on the ground that what the defendants are doing is a nuisance.

Lopes LJ commented:

> A man who carries on an exceptionally delicate trade cannot complain because it is injured by his neighbour doing something lawful on his property, if it is something which would not injure anything but an exceptionally delicate trade.

Lindley LJ was of a similar view.

Duration, frequency and intensity

All the above may be relevant in making the decision as to whether the defendant's activity amounts to an actionable nuisance. In *Bolton v Stone*,[13] the infrequency of the escapes of the ball seems to be the reason as to why it was conceded that there was no nuisance, although there is a suggestion that the nuisance claim could only succeed if negligence was established. In *Miller v Jackson*, Geoffrey Lane LJ stated:

> Was there here a use by the defendants of their land involving an unreasonable interference with the plaintiffs' enjoyment of *their* land? There is here in effect no

12 (1889) 41 Ch D 88.

13 [1951] AC 950.

> dispute that there has been, and is likely to be in the future, an interference with the plaintiffs' enjoyment of no 20 Brackenbridge. The only question is whether it is unreasonable. It is a truism to say that this is a matter of degree. What that means is this. A balance has to be maintained between, on the one hand the rights of the individual to enjoy his house and garden without the threat of damage, and on the other hand the rights of the public in general or a neighbour to engage in lawful pastimes.
>
> Difficult questions may sometimes arise when the defendants' activities are offensive to the senses, for example by way of noise. Where, as here, the damage or potential damage is physical the answer is more simple. There is, subject to what appears hereafter, no excuse I can see which exonerates the defendants from liability in nuisance for what they have done or from what they threaten to do. It is true no one has yet been physically injured. That is probably due to a great extent to the fact that the householders in Brackenbridge desert their gardens whilst cricket is in progress. The danger of injury is obvious and is not slight enough to be disregarded. There is here a real risk of serious injury.

Clearly, the frequency of the landing of the ball in the plaintiffs' garden is a factor, as is the seriousness of the harm. In *British Celanese v Hunt* we saw earlier that an isolated escape could be a nuisance, although it should be emphasised that the damage arose from the state of affairs on the land, namely, in that case the storage of the strips on the premises, rather than a single act of negligence.

Motive

The defendant's motive is not normally relevant in tort, however malice or ill-will has been regarded as a factor in some nuisance cases. In particular, *Christie v Davey*[14] shows that malice on the part of the defendant may swing the balance in favour of the plaintiff. The plaintiff in that case complained that the defendant was deliberately banging on the middle walls of the semi-detached property and making other noises to vex his neighbours. North J stated:

> The result is that I think I am bound to interfere for the protection of the plaintiffs. In my opinion the noises which were made in the defendant's house were not of a legitimate kind ... I am satisfied that they were made deliberately and maliciously for the purpose of annoying the plaintiffs. If what has taken place had occurred between two sets of persons both perfectly innocent, I should have taken an entirely different view of the case. But I am persuaded that what was done by the defendant was done only for the purpose of annoyance, and in my opinion it was not a legitimate use of the defendant's house to use it for the purpose of vexing and annoying his neighbours.

In *Hollywood Silver Fox Farm Ltd v Emmett*[15] the defendant deliberately caused his son to fire a gun to disturb the plaintiff's foxes so as to disturb their breeding. After reviewing the various authorities, the judge gave judgment for the plaintiff on the basis that this was an actionable nuisance. It seems clear that the malice of the defendant was the factor which made what would otherwise have been a lawful activity into a nuisance.

14 [1893] 1 Ch 316.

15 [1936] 2 KB 468.

Who can sue

The creator of the nuisance can always be sued, and so may the occupier who may be jointly and severally liable with the creator where the latter was under his control or where he expressly or impliedly authorises the nuisance. In *Tetley v Chitty*[16] the defendant council permitted the use of its land for go-karting purposes. It was held that the noise constituted a nuisance but the issue of the liability of the council was sharply contested. On this point, McNeill J observed:

> In this case the nuisance from noise generated by go-karting racing and practising was, in my view on the facts, an ordinary and necessary consequence of the operation ... or a natural and necessary consequence of the operation. ... There was, in my view ... express or at the least implied consent to do that which on the facts here inevitably would amount to a nuisance. ...
>
> I say at once that there can be no criticism of a local authority making a laudable attempt to increase the recreational facilities of their area. But here, despite all those warnings to which I have referred, they decided to go ahead with full knowledge that noise nuisance was a necessary or ordinary or natural consequence of go-kart racing and practising. If that were not enough, there was a series of complaints, either in the form of letters or recorded telephone messages. ... All that is associated with ... totally inadequate investigation of what was going to happen if the proposal was put into operation. I cannot see any ground on which the council, in the circumstances, can escape liability for the nuisance.

The liability of the occupier for a nuisance created by an independent contractor employed by him needs considering. Normally there is no liability in tort for the activities of such a person, but where the nuisance is an inevitable consequence of the operations on the land, the occupier's duty is regarded as 'non-delegable'. This means that, although the occupier may actually entrust the task to a contractor, he remains personally responsible for the nuisance. In *Matania v National Provincial Bank Ltd*[17] the occupier was held liable for the nuisance caused by an independent contractor during alterations to the building of the occupier, namely, dust and noise which affected neighbouring premises. Slesser LJ, after deciding that there was an actionable interference, turned his attention to the issue of the occupier's liability:

> Here, of course, we are not concerned with danger such as might found an action for negligence. We are concerned with annoyance such as may found an action for nuisance, but the principles in my opinion are the same as regards the liability of a person who employs an independent contractor, that is to say, that if the act done is one which, in its very nature, involves a special danger of nuisance being complained of, then it is one which falls within the exception for which the employer of the contractor will be responsible if there is a failure to take the necessary precautions that the nuisance shall not arise.
>
> Now, what are the facts of the present case? They are these. It is not really in dispute that, as regards the place where this work was to be done, this noise and this dust were inevitable. That is the evidence of both the plaintiff and the defendants, and it is the conclusion of the learned judge. The only question which I see is whether, in that state where the production of noise and dust is

16 [1986] 1 All ER 663.

17 [1936] 2 All ER 633.

> inevitable, sufficient precautions were taken to prevent that noise and dust affecting Mr Matania. In every case, whether it be a case of ordinary employment of a contractor or whether it be a case of a hazardous operation, the problem must arise whether a precaution would or would not prevent the result of an operation.
>
> To say that a precaution will prevent the result of an operation does not, by itself, take the case outside the rule that a person may be responsible, where the act is a hazardous one, for the acts of his contractor. Where the act is hazardous, to presume that every hazardous act would result in the danger or the nuisance would be to say that the act was inevitable in its consequences, regardless of any question of precaution or not, but that is not the right way of looking at it ... [It] was hazardous as regards to the possible nuisance to Mr Matania to bring the noise and dust immediately below his apartment. What is said is, with sufficient and proper precaution the result of that hazardous operation could have been avoided without detriment to him, ... I think that [the occupiers] are responsible for the fact that neither they nor the contractors ... took those reasonable precautions which could have been taken to prevent this injury to the plaintiff.

Romer LJ commented:

> ... where a man employs an independent contractor to do work which, of its very nature, involves a risk of damage being occasioned to a third party, that person is responsible to the third party if such damage be occasioned and cannot shelter himself under the general principle of non-liability for the negligence of an independent contractor.

He came to the same conclusion as Slesser LJ applying this principle to the facts. Finlay LJ also agreed with this outcome. We have also already seen that an occupier may be held liable for the acts of a trespasser in certain circumstances, as illustrated in the *Sedleigh-Denfield* case.

A landlord, who is not in occupation of the premises, is not normally liable for a nuisance emanating from those premises. However, there are a number of exceptions to this rule. As we have observed already, a landlord who authorises a nuisance may be liable (*Tetley v Chitty*). The landlord may also be liable where the state of affairs giving rise to the nuisance existed before s/he gave up possession to the tenant, or where the landlord retains control of any part of the premises and the nuisance is on that part. There are also a number of situations where the landlord may be held liable where s/he is responsible for repairs, or even has a right of access to check whether the tenant has carried out his/her obligation to repair, and moreover as we have seen, where the premises are adjacent to the highway, for example, the liability will be strict (*Wringe v Cohen*).

Remoteness of damage

The usual thorny issue of remoteness of damage arises in relation to nuisance in much the same way as it does in negligence and under the rule in *Rylands v Fletcher*. The facts giving rise to the litigation in *The Wagon Mound (No 1)* were also the source of the litigation in *The Wagon Mound (No 2)*, with the exception that the plaintiff in the latter case was the owner of a vessel moored at the wharf of the plaintiff in the first case. Lord Reid read the opinion of the Privy Council, and the following is a brief extract from it:

> Comparing nuisance with negligence, the main argument for the respondent was that, in negligence, foreseeability is an essential element in determining liability,

and therefore it is logical that foreseeability should also be an essential element in determining the amount of damages; but negligence is not an essential element in determining liability for nuisance, and therefore it is illogical to bring in foreseeability when determining the amount of damages. It is quite true that negligence is not an essential element in nuisance. Nuisance is a term used to cover a wide variety of tortious acts or omissions, and in many, negligence in the narrow sense is not essential. An occupier may incur liability for the emission of noxious fumes or noise, although he has used the utmost care in building and using his premises. The amount of fumes or noise which he can lawfully emit is a question of degree, and he or his advisers may have miscalculated what can be justified. Or he may deliberately obstruct the highway adjoining his premises to a greater degree than is permissible, hoping that no one will object.

On the other hand the emission of fumes or noise or the obstruction of the adjoining highway may often be the result of pure negligence on his part; there are many cases ... where precisely the same facts will establish liability both in nuisance and negligence. And although negligence may not be necessary, fault of some kind is almost always necessary, and fault generally involves foreseeability, eg in cases like *Sedleigh-Denfield v O'Callaghan* the fault is in failing to abate a nuisance of the existence of which the defender is or ought to be aware as likely to cause damage to his neighbour. (Their Lordships express no opinion about cases like *Wringe v Cohen* on which neither counsel relied.) The present case is one of creating a danger to persons or property in navigable waters (equivalent to a highway), and there it is admitted that fault is essential – in this case the negligent discharge of the oil.

But how are we to determine whether a state of affairs in or near a highway is [a] danger? This depends, I think, on whether injury may reasonably be foreseen. If you take all the cases in the books you will find that, if the state of affairs is such that injury may reasonably be anticipated to persons using the highway, it is a public nuisance (*per* Denning LJ, in *Morton v Wheeler* (1956), unreported).

So, in the class of nuisance, which includes this case, foreseeability is an essential element in determining liability.

It could not be right to discriminate between different cases of nuisance so as to make foreseeability a necessary element in determining liability, but not in others. So the choice is between it being a necessary element in all case of nuisance or none. In their Lordships' judgment, the similarities between nuisance and other forms of tort to which *The Wagon v Mound (No 1)* applies, far outweigh any differences, and they must therefore hold that judgment appealed from is wrong on this branch of the case. It is not sufficient that the injury suffered by the respondents' vessels was the direct result of the nuisance, if that injury was in the relevant sense unforeseeable.

Notwithstanding this, the Privy Council found for the respondents on the basis that the type of harm in question, unlike the decision in the first case, was reasonably foreseeable on the evidence.

There has been some uncertainty as to the precise scope of the principle's applicability over the last 30 years. Was it restricted merely to cases of public nuisance as the case itself only involved that kind of action? Did the foreseeability principle extend to cases of nuisance which were considered to be strict liability by their nature? You will notice that no view was expressed on that point in the above extract in relation to cases such as *Wringe v Cohen*.

Lord Goff, in the House of Lords in the *Cambridge Water* case, was plainly aware of the controversy and attempted to deal with it, as the following extract shows:

> It is against this background that it is necessary to consider the question whether foreseeability of harm of the relevant type is an essential element of liability, either in nuisance or under the rule in *Rylands v Fletcher*. I shall take first the case of nuisance. In the present case, as I have said, this is not strictly speaking a live issue. Even so, I propose briefly to address it as part of the analysis of the background to the present case.
>
> It is, of course, axiomatic that, in this field, we must be on our guard when considering liability for damages for nuisance, not to draw inapposite conclusions from cases concerned only with a claim for an injunction. This is because, where an injunction is claimed, its purpose is to restrain further action by the defendant which may interfere with the plaintiff's enjoyment of his land, and *ex hypothesi* the defendant must be aware, if and when an injunction is granted, that such interference may be caused by the act which he is restrained from committing.
>
> It follows that these cases provide no guidance on the question whether foreseeability of harm of the relevant type is a prerequisite of the recovery of damages for causing such harm to the plaintiff. In the present case, we are not concerned with liability in damages in respect of a nuisance which has arisen through natural causes, or by the act of a person for whose actions the defendant is not responsible, in which cases the applicable principles in nuisance have become closely associated with those applicable in negligence: see *Sedleigh-Denfield v O'Callaghan* and *Goldman v Hargrave.*
>
> We are concerned with the liability of a person where a nuisance has been created by one for whose actions he is responsible. Here, as I have said, it is still the law that the fact that the defendant has taken all reasonable care will not of itself exonerate him from liability, the relevant control mechanism being found within the principle of reasonable user. But it by no means follows that the defendant should be held liable for damage of a type which he could not reasonably foresee; and the development of the law of negligence in the past 60 years points strongly towards a requirement that such foreseeability should be a prerequisite of liability in damages in nuisance, as it is of liability in negligence. For, if a plaintiff is, in ordinary circumstances, only able to claim damages in respect of personal injuries where he can prove such foreseeability on the part of the defendant, it is difficult to see why, in common justice, he should be in a stronger position to claim damages for interference with the enjoyment of his land where the defendant is unable to foresee such damage. Moreover, this appears to have been the conclusion of the Privy Council in *The Wagon Mound (No 2).* Lord Reid, who delivered the advice of the Privy Council, considered that, in the class of nuisance which included that before the board, foreseeability is an essential element in determining liability.

Lord Goff quoted a passage included in the extract above from the *Wagon Mound (No 2)*, and continued as follows:

> It is widely accepted that this conclusion, although not essential to the decision of the particular case, has nevertheless settled the law to the effect that foreseeability of harm is, indeed, a prerequisite of the recovery of damages in private nuisance, as in the case of public nuisance. I refer in particular to the opinion expressed by Professor Fleming in his book on *Torts* (8th edn, 1992) pp 443–44. It is unnecessary in the present case to consider the precise nature of

this principle; but it appears from Lord Reid's statement of the law that he regarded it essentially as one relating to remoteness of damage.

It perhaps should be emphasised that this statement by Lord Goff, as even he acknowledges at the beginning of the extract, is not itself a part of the decision in the case in which it appears. It will be recalled, however, that reasonable foreseeability of the type of harm was held to be the principle applicable in respect of claims under the rule in *Rylands v Fletcher* in the *Cambridge Water* case, and it is hardly likely that a court dealing with a nuisance case would be prepared to ignore that point.

Types of damage recoverable

Whilst nuisance is a tort primarily concerned with interferences with land, it would seem that any interference which caused or threatened personal injury to the occupier of the land or to the personal possessions of such a person would constitute an actionable private nuisance. If a person cannot go into his garden for fear of being struck by a cricket ball every Saturday or Sunday afternoon, it cannot seriously be suggested that this is not an unreasonable interference with his use and enjoyment of his back garden. The better view is that claims for damage to the person or personal belongings are within the scope of a nuisance action. It would seem to be the case from what was discussed in the previous section that such harm must, however, be shown to be reasonably foreseeable. There does not appear to have been any serious suggestion that personal injury damages may not be recoverable in private nuisance as there has been in relation to the rule in *Rylands v Fletcher* discussed in the previous chapter. In addition, it may now be the case that the interest in land requirement has been dropped in private nuisance actions, which would extend personal injury claims to persons other than owners or occupiers of premises. We saw this in *Khorasandjian v Bush* at the beginning of the chapter, and recently the Court of Appeal has reaffirmed that this is the position.[18]

It would seem obvious that actual physical damage to land is recoverable, as are damages for the inability to use the land because of intangible harm, such as smell, noise and so on. The usual question now arises as to whether economic loss is recoverable in nuisance. It has been held to be recoverable in public nuisance in the very old case of *Rose v Miles*,[19] where the blocking of a canal involved the plaintiff in extra expenditure to have his goods carried by other means to get round the obstruction, although the position is not free of doubt. There seems to be no reason why, in an appropriate case, a claim for such loss could not succeed in private nuisance where the plaintiff's premises were used for business purposes and the plaintiff could not so use them because of an unreasonable interference. The objections which surface in negligence cases are not germane in nuisance cases as the potential claims are geographically restricted. In a sense it may be argued that such a claim is not for pure economic loss because it is dependent on harm to property of the plaintiff.

---

18 See *Hunter v Canary Wharf Ltd* [1996] 1 All ER 482.

19 (1815) 4 M & S 101.

Defences

Defences available to the plaintiff in a nuisance action in particular are prescription and statutory authority. Prescription can only be set up as a defence where the nuisance has continued for 20 years uninterrupted. Statutory authority will often depend on the wording of the particular statute authorising the setting up of whatever it is that is causing the alleged nuisance, eg an oil refinery. The defendant is not normally liable for interferences which are an inevitable consequence of the setting up of the refinery, but the plaintiff may succeed where s/he can show that the interference goes beyond what is inevitable, in other words, that there has been negligence by the defendant in failing to keep the interference down at the level of what was inevitable.[20]

The argument that the plaintiff came to the nuisance is no defence as far as the issue of liability is concerned, according to the old case of *Sturges v Bridgeman*,[21] although, as we shall see below, it has been used as an argument for refusal of an injunction.

A more recent development which emphasises the role of nuisance as an environmental tort with a role to play still, is that concerning the relationship between planning permission and common law nuisance. This has come up for consideration recently in two cases. In *Gillingham Borough Council v Medway (Chatham) Dock Co Ltd*[22] the plaintiff council had given planning permission to the defendants for the use of part of the old naval dockyard, with certain qualifications about vehicular access, although the council assured them of unrestricted access. The alleged nuisance arose because of lorries operating 24 hours a day along a road through a residential neighbourhood. The council brought an unsuccessful nuisance action against the defendants. After discussing the defence of statutory authority, Buckley J turned his attention to the grant of planning permission as a form of defence to a nuisance action:

> Doubtless one of the reasons for this approach [statutory authority] is that Parliament is presumed to have considered the interests of those who will be affected by the undertaking or works, and decided that the benefits from them should outweigh any necessary adverse side effects. I believe that principle should be utilised in respect of planning permission. Parliament has set up a statutory framework and delegated the task of balancing the interests of the community against those of individuals, and of holding the scales between individuals and the local planning authority. There is the right to object to any proposed grant, provision for appeals and inquiries, and ultimately the minister decides. There is the added safeguard of judicial review. If the planning authority grants permission for a particular construction or use in its area, it is almost certain that some local inhabitants will be prejudiced in the quiet enjoyment of their properties. Can they defeat the scheme simply by bringing an action in nuisance? If not, why not? It has been said, no doubt correctly, that planning permission is not a licence to commit nuisance, and that a planning authority has no jurisdiction to authorise nuisance. However, a planning authority can, through its development plans and decisions, alter the character of

20 See eg *Allen v Gulf Oil Refining Ltd* [1979] 3 All ER 1008.

21 (1879) 11 Ch D 852.

22 [1992] 3 All ER 923.

> a neighbourhood. That may have the effect of rendering innocent activities which, prior to the change, would have been an actionable nuisance.

In the light of the above the judge went on to decide that the alleged interference was not actionable. The issue was explored once again in the recent case of *Wheeler v Saunders*,[23] where the defendants sought to argue that the giving of planning permission conferred immunity on them to continue causing the smell from their pig farm. Staughton LJ stated:

> I do not consider that planning permission necessarily has the same effect as statutory authority. Parliament is sovereign and can abolish or limit the civil rights of individuals. As Sir John May put it in the course of argument, Parliament cannot be irrational just as the Sovereign can do no wrong. The planning authority on the other hand has only the powers delegated to it by Parliament. It is not in my view self-evident that they include the power to abolish or limit civil rights in any or all the circumstances. The process by which planning permission is obtained allows for objections by those who might be adversely affected, but they have no right of appeal if their objections are overruled. It is not for us to say whether the private bill procedure in Parliament is better or worse. It is enough that it is different.
>
> In *Allen v Gulf Oil Refining Ltd* [1980] QB 156, before the Court of Appeal, Cumming Bruce LJ touched on the effect of planning permission on what would otherwise be a nuisance. He said at p 174, 'the planning authority has no jurisdiction to authorise a nuisance save (if at all) in so far as it has statutory power to permit the change of the character of a neighbourhood'.
>
> One can readily appreciate that planning permission will, quite frequently, have unpleasant consequences for some people. The man with a view over open fields from his window may well be displeased if a housing estate is authorised by the planners and built in front of his house; the character of the neighbourhood is changed. But there may be nothing which would qualify as a nuisance and no infringement of his civil rights. What if the development does create what would otherwise be nuisance?
>
> Instead of a housing estate the planners may authorise a factory which would emit noise and smoke to the detriment of neighbouring residents. Does that come within the first proposition of Cumming Bruce LJ, that a planning authority has no jurisdiction to authorise a nuisance? Or is it within the second, that the authority may change the character of a neighbourhood?...
>
> I accept what was said by Cumming Bruce LJ: firstly, that a planning authority has in general no jurisdiction to authorise a nuisance; and, secondly, if it can do so at all, that is only by the exercise of its power to permit a change in the character of a neighbourhood. To the extent that those two propositions feature in the judgment of Buckley J, I agree with his decision, but I would not for the present go any further that that.
>
> It would, in my opinion, be a misuse of language to describe what has happened in the present case as a change in the character of a neighbourhood. It is a change and abuse of a very small piece of land a little over 350 square metres, according to the dimensions on the plan, for the benefit of the applicant and to the detriment of the objectors in the quiet enjoyment of their house. It is not a strategic planning decision affected by considerations of public interest. Unless one is prepared to accept that any planning decision authorises any nuisance

23 [1995] 3 WLR 466.

> which must inevitably come from it, the argument that the nuisance was authorised by planning permission in this case must fail. I am not prepared to accept that premise. It may be – I express no concluded opinion – that some planning decisions will authorise some nuisances. But that is as far as I am prepared to go. There is no immunity from liability for nuisance in the present case.

Peter Gibson LJ was of a similar view, commenting that :

> The court should be slow to acquiesce in the extinction of private rights without compensation as a result of administrative decisions which cannot be appealed and are difficult to challenge.

Sir John May was also of a similar mind, suggesting that any decision of an authority which sanctioned a nuisance in this way would be challengeable by judicial review on ground of irrationality.[24]

Remedies for nuisance

In relation to the torts we have considered in previous chapters, the appropriate remedy has been damages and the principles involved in the assessment of awards in such cases will be discussed in a later chapter. The only comment at this stage on damages, a point to be explored later, is that there can be no claim for exemplary damages in a public nuisance case.[25] However, as mentioned in the introduction to this chapter, there is often a far more desirable alternative remedy in a nuisance case, namely the injunction to prevent any further damage or to ward off any damage at all in the first place. The relationship between these two remedies is far from straightforward in this area, as the subsequent case extracts will amply demonstrate. There is a feeling that, in some recent cases, the courts have departed from well established principles in regard to the award of damages in lieu of an injunction, which must be seen as the primary remedy in this branch of the law. The principles were laid down in the case of *Shelfer v London Electric Lighting Co*,[26] in which the defendants, it was found, were guilty of an actionable nuisance by means of vibrations and noise from their powerful machines. There was evidence of structural damage to the plaintiff's premises. The High Court judge refused to grant an injunction. The plaintiff's appeal was successful. Lord Halsbury commented:

> But it is said, and truly said, that the law has been altered by Lord Cairns' Act, and the question is: what construction is to be placed on that enactment? Undoubtedly, it conferred upon Courts of Equity the jurisdiction to award damages which did not exist before. But the question is: did it mean to interfere with the well settled principles upon which Courts of Equity were in the habit of interfering in such cases as the present?
>
> It seems to me that the defects in the powers of the Equity Courts which were sought to be supplied by that statute gave ample grounds for the provisions of the statute, without supposing that it meant to revolutionise the principles upon which equitable jurisprudence had been administered up to that time. The

24 See also *Hunter v Canary Wharf Ltd* (above) in which Pill LJ confirmed that planning permissions could confer immunity from nuisance.

25 See *AB v Southwest Water Services Ltd* [1993] QB 507.

26 [1895] 1 Ch 287.

> language is, of course, general; the discretion given is necessarily wide enough in terms to authorise a judge to award damages where formerly he would have given an injunction. But there is nothing in this case which, to my mind, can justify the court in refusing to aid the legal rights established, by an injunction preventing the continuance of the nuisance. On the contrary, the effect of such a refusal in a case like the present would necessarily operate to enable a company who could afford it to drive a neighbouring proprietor to sell, whether he would or no, by continuing a nuisance, and simply paying damages for its continuance.

Lindley LJ made similar noises:

> Without denying the jurisdiction to award damages instead of an injunction, even in cases of continuing actionable nuisance, such jurisdiction ought not to be exercised in such cases except under very exceptional circumstances. I will not attempt to specify them, to lay down rules for the exercise of judicial discretion. It is sufficient to refer, by way of example, to trivial and occasional nuisances; cases in which a plaintiff has shown that he only wants money; vexatious and oppressive cases; and cases where the plaintiff has so conducted himself as to render it unjust to give him more than pecuniary relief. In all such cases as these, and in all others where an action for damages is really an adequate remedy – as where the acts complained of are already finished – an injunction can be properly refused. There are no circumstances here which, according to recognised principles, justify the refusal of an injunction; and in my opinion, therefore, an injunction ought to have been granted in the action brought by the tenant.

The leading statement is contained, however, in the judgment of A L Smith LJ as follows:

> In my opinion, it may be stated as a good working rule that:
>
> (1) if the injury to the plaintiff's legal rights is small; and
>
> (2) is one which is capable of being estimated in money; and
>
> (3) is one which can be adequately compensated by a small money payment; and
>
> (4) the case is one in which it would be oppressive to the defendant to grant an injunction;
>
> then damages in substitution for an injunction may be given.
>
> It is impossible to lay down any rule as to what, under the differing circumstances of each case, constitutes either a small injury, or one that can be estimated in money, or what is a small money payment, or an adequate compensation, or what would be oppressive to the defendant. This must be left to the good sense of the tribunal which deals with each case as it comes up for adjudication ... In the present case it appears to me that the injury to the plaintiff is certainly not small, nor is it in my judgment capable of being estimated in money, or of being adequately compensated by a small money payment.

Those are the recognised principles upon which the court is to base its reasons for exercising its discretion to award damages. In a sense, in most cases of nuisance the plaintiff is presumed to be entitled to an injunction. However, in the case of *Miller v Jackson* the principles, it has been argued, were completely ignored when the Court of Appeal, by a majority, refused an injunction to the residents living around the cricket ground. Lord Denning MR was not in favour of granting an injunction because, in his view, there was no actionable nuisance in the first place. Geoffrey Lane LJ commented:

> Given that the defendants are guilty of both negligence and nuisance, is it a case where the court in its discretion should give relief, or should the plaintiffs be left

> to their remedy in damages? There is no doubt that, if cricket is played, damage will be done to the plaintiffs' tiles or windows or both. There is a not inconsiderable danger that, if they or their son or their guests spend any time in the garden during the weekend afternoons in the summer, they may be hit by a cricket ball. So long as this situation exists it seems to me that damages cannot be said to provide an adequate form of relief. Indeed, quite apart from the risk of physical injury, I can see no valid reason why the plaintiffs should have to submit to the inevitable breakage of tiles and/or windows, even though the defendants have expressed their willingness to carry out any repairs at no cost to the plaintiffs. I would accordingly uphold the grant of the injunction to restrain the defendants from committing the nuisance.

Unfortunately for the plaintiffs, Cumming Bruce LJ, although agreeing that there was a nuisance, took a different view as to the appropriate remedy:

> ... on the facts of this case, a court of equity must seek to strike a fair balance between the right of the plaintiffs to have quiet enjoyment of their house and garden without exposure to cricket balls occasionally falling like thunderbolts from the heavens, and the opportunity of the inhabitants of the village in which they live to continue to enjoy the manly sport which constitutes a summer recreation for adults and young persons, including, one would hope and expect, the plaintiffs' son.
>
> It is a relevant circumstance which a court of equity should take into account that the plaintiffs decided to buy a house which, in June 1972 when completion took place, was obviously on the boundary of quite a small cricket ground where cricket was played at weekends and sometimes on evenings during the working week. They selected a house with the benefit of the open space beside it. In February, when they first saw it, they did not think about the use of this open space. But before completion they must have realised that it was the village cricket ground, and that balls would sometimes be knocked from the wicket into their garden, or even against the fabric of the house. If they did not realise it, they should have done. ... It is reasonable to decide that during matches the family must keep out of the garden. The risk of damage to the house can be dealt with in other ways, and is not such as to fortify significantly the case for an injunction stopping play on this ground.

The net result of this decision is that the plaintiffs' rights were being curtailed in exchange for compensation as and when any damage might occur. To put it another way, the defendants were being given leave by the court to go on committing unlawful activity on their land so long as they were willing to pay for the privilege. There was no mention of the *Shelfer* case in the judgments, and very little discussion of the principles.

The case was shortly followed by another in which the injunction issue was central, *Kennaway v Thompson*,[27] in which the plaintiff complained about the noise coming from a nearby lake on which a club held many motorboat and water skiing events. The judge agreed that there was a nuisance but refused an injunction and, on appeal, the Court of Appeal took the view that some form of restraint was appropriate. Lawton LJ gave the judgment of the court as follows:

> We are of the opinion that there is nothing in *Miller v Jackson*, binding on us, which qualifies what was decided in *Shelfer*. Any decisions before *Shelfer's* case ...

27 [1980] 3 All ER 329.

which give support for the proposition that the public interest should prevail over the private interest, must be read subject to the decision in *Shelfer's* case.

It follows that the plaintiff was entitled to an injunction and that the judge misdirected himself in law, adjudging that the appropriate remedy for her was an award of damages under Lord Cairns' Act. But she was only entitled to an injunction restraining the club from activities which caused a nuisance, and not all the activities did. As the judge pointed out, and counsel for the plaintiff accepted in this court, an injunction in general terms would be unworkable.

Our task has been to decide on a form of order which will protect the plaintiff from the noise which the judge found intolerable, but which will not stop the club from organising activities about which she cannot reasonably complain.

When she decided to build a house alongside Mallam Water she knew that some motor boat racing and water skiing was done on the club's water, and she thought that the noise which such activities created was tolerable. She cannot now complain about that kind of noise provided it does not increase in volume by reason of the increase in activities. The intolerable noise is mostly caused by the large boats; it is these which attract the public interest.

Now, nearly all of us living in these islands have to put up with a certain amount of annoyance from our neighbours. Those living in towns may be irritated by their neighbours' noisy radios or incompetent playing of musical instruments; and they in turn may be inconvenienced by the noise caused by our guests slamming car doors and chattering after a late party. Even in the country the lowing of a sick cow or the early morning crowing of a farmyard cock may interfere with sleep and comfort. Intervention by injunction is only justified when the irritating noise causes inconvenience beyond what other occupiers in the neighbourhood can be expected to bear. The question is whether the neighbour is using his property reasonably, having regard to the fact that he has a neighbour. The neighbour who is complaining must remember, too, that the other man can use his property in a reasonable way and there must be a measure of 'give and take, live and let live'.

Understandably the plaintiff finds intolerable the kind of noise which she has had to suffer for such long periods in the past; but if she knew that she would only have to put up with such a noise on a few occasions between the end of March and the beginning of November each year, and she also knew when those occasions were likely to occur, she could make arrangements to be out of her house at the material times. We can see no reason, however, why she should have to absent herself from her house for many days so as to enable club members and others to make noises which are a nuisance.

We consider it probable that those who are interested in motor boat racing are attracted by the international and national events which tend to have the larger and noisier boats. Justice will be done, we think, if the club is allowed to have, each racing season, one international event extending over three days, the first day being given over to practice and the second and third to racing. In addition there can be two national events, each of two days but separated from the international event and from each other by at least four weeks. Finally there can be three club events, each of one day, separated from the international and national events and each other by three weeks. Any international or national event not held can be replaced by a club event of one day. No boats creating a noise of more than 75 decibels are to be used on the club's water at any time other than when there are events as specified in this judgment. If events are held at weekends as they probably will be, six weekends covering a total of ten days will be available for motor boat racing on the club's water. Water skiing, if too

> many boats are used, can cause a nuisance by noise. The club is not to allow more than six motor boats to be used for water skiing at any one time.

Why it should be thought by the court that a general injunction should not be workable and this particular order should be is not immediately clear. How and by whom this order is to be supervised is not at all obvious. Also, what these two cases perhaps illustrate is that the common law is having to clear up the mess made by poor planning decisions. This is particularly true in the *Miller* case.

The final case to be considered in this section is that of *Tetley v Chitty*, in which, it will be recalled, the local authority was held liable for the go-karting nuisance on its land. On the remedy issue, the judge said:

> To my mind damages would be a wholly insufficient remedy here, and the plaintiffs are entitled to an injunction. This case is unlike the *Kennaway* case in that the plaintiffs were already there, and had for some time been there, when the nuisance began, and I have come to the conclusion that, as things stand at present, there should be a permanent injunction. There is here no question of such an injunction being unworkable, as was the case in the *Kennaway* decision and, second, it is not, I think, for this court to work out for defendants at fault the way in which they can continue in operation which, as if it has been continued, was an offending operation. It is not merely that the council ... accept that they would have little, if any, control of what actually went on at the track, but it is also clear from ... evidence the council has not applied itself to any sound barriers or other measures which would reduce the volume and pitch of noise created by the operation, or taken professional advice.
>
> Finally, I regret to say that the council's record in their consideration of the proposal, as it appears from the documents that I have read *in extenso*, prior to the approval of the commencement of go-kart racing, gives me no confidence in their capacity to take proper steps to protect their ratepayers in this regard.

The decision in that case at least pays some regard to the principles, even though they are not expressly mentioned. There is also the impression that the judge thought the council was being a law unto itself, and the only way to bring it to heel was to issue an injunction.

CHAPTER 11

TRESPASS TO THE PERSON

INTRODUCTION

Trespass to the person is comprised of three causes of action, namely assault, battery and false imprisonment. We shall cover all of these in what follows, although it is conventionally accepted that the latter is perhaps more appropriately covered in a civil liberties or constitutional law context. As a series of tort actions, they have played, in a quantitative sense at least, a diminished role in terms of their importance as a means of obtaining compensation for personal injury. This may have been due to the introduction in 1964 of the Criminal Injuries Compensation Scheme, designed to fill a hole into which the victims of criminal attacks often fell by awarding them compensation where their injuries, in broad terms, were brought about as a result of a crime. The truth is that the civil law of trespass had, for a long time before then, been thought to be something of a dead letter, because the victim of an attack would rarely in practice recover any damages, the defendant not being apprehended or worth suing if he or she was caught, hence the need for the scheme.

The scheme itself has recently been under attack from the Home Secretary and is now been covered in statute by the Criminal Injuries Compensation Act 1995. When initially established, compensation was payable on an *ex gratia* basis, and the basis of assessment broadly speaking followed principles applied in tort cases (for which see the next chapter). In 1988 it was put on a statutory basis although the part of the legislation purporting to do this was never in fact activated.[1] They will be repealed without ever having come under starter's orders, as and when the new Act is brought into force. The new legislation will move the assessment of compensation away from the tort model and will have the effect, when the secretary of state finally publishes his tariff, of restricting the levels of compensation. This may make the tort action a slightly more popular option in the future.

As with some of the torts already considered, there is a difficulty in the relationship between assault and battery on the one hand and negligence on the other which will be explored below. It will also become evident that the torts are commonly pursued against police and/or the authorities which employ them, and the tort of battery is sometimes involved in both medical and sporting contexts.

This area of law is one where there is a significant overlap between the civil and criminal law. Historically, the writ of trespass was designed to keep the peace, but gradually the law began to allow civil claims by affected individuals. Many of the cases discussed below are criminal cases in which the points at issue are thought to be important for the civil law. It should also be noted at this stage that, in the criminal law, the word 'assault' includes a battery, whereas in the civil law they are separate and distinct causes of action.

---

1 Sections 108–17 Criminal Justice Act 1988.

In one significant respect, these torts are quite different from the other tort actions that we have considered so far. They are actionable *per se,* which means the plaintiff does not have to prove any actual damage to his person in order to be able to bring an action, whereas we have seen that the gist of negligence is that damage has been caused. This position accords with the view stated above that these actions are concerned with protection of civil liberties, protecting human dignity and freedom from insult.

Before going on to look at the torts of assault and battery individually, there are three major issues which need consideration: firstly, whether the harm must be direct result of the defendant's act; secondly, the much-debated issue of whether trespass is an intentional tort or whether there is such a thing as a negligent trespass; and thirdly, the issue of whether hostility is an essential ingredient of the torts of assault and battery.

DIRECT HARM

The trespass action is only available in circumstances where the plaintiff can show that the harm is a direct consequence of the defendant's voluntary act, as opposed to harm which is said to be consequential only. This is easy to state but often difficult to apply. The usual case discussed at this point is that of *Scott v Shepherd,*[2] in which the defendant threw a lighted squib into a market-house. The squib was picked up by a stallholder who threw it away from himself and another person did the same. The firework exploded in the face of the plaintiff who lost an eye as a result. He brought an action in trespass. The majority of the court found for the plaintiff, two of the judges relying on the unlawfulness of the act as their justification for imposing liability on the defendant. Blackstone J took the dissenting view that the trespass action was not the appropriate one, saying as follows:

> ... where the injury is immediate, an action of trespass will lie; where it is only consequential, it must be an action on the case: *Reynolds and Clarke,* Lord Raym, 1401 Stra 634. ... The lawfulness or unlawfulness of the original act is not the criterion; though something of that sort is put into Lord Raymond's mouth in Stra 635, where it can only mean that if the act then in question, of erecting a spout, had been in itself unlawful, trespass might have lain; but as it was a lawful act (upon the defendant's own ground) and the injury only consequential, it must be an action on the case. But this cannot be the general rule, for it is held by the court in the same case that, if I throw a log of timber into the highway (which is an unlawful act), and another man tumbled over it and is hurt, an action on the case only lies, it being a consequential damage; but if in throwing it I hit another man he may bring trespass, because it is an immediate wrong. ...
>
> The original act was, as against Yates, a trespass; not as against Ryal or Scott. the tortious act was complete when the squib lay at rest upon Yates' stall. He, or any bystander, had, I allow, a right to protect themselves by removing the squib, but should have taken care to do it in such a manner as not to endamage others. But Shepherd, I think, is not answerable in an action of trespass and assault for the mischief done by the squib in the new motion impressed upon it, and the new direction given it by either Willis or Ryal, who were both free agents, and acted upon their own judgment. ...

2 (1770) 2 W Bl 892.

De Grey CJ, siding with the majority, stated:

> This case is one of those wherein the line drawn by the law between actions on the case and actions of trespass is very nice and delicate. Trespass is an injury accompanied with force, for which an action of trespass *vi et armis* lies against the person from whom it is received. The question here is whether the injury received by the plaintiff arises from the force of the original act of the defendant, or from a new force by a third person. I agree with my brother Blackstone as to the principles he has laid down, but not in his application of those principles to the present case. ... I look upon all that was done subsequent to the original throwing as a continuation of the first force and first act, which will continue until the squib was spent by bursting. And I think that any innocent person removing the danger from himself to another is justifiable; the blame lights upon the first thrower. The new direction and new force flow out of the first force, and are not a new trespass. ... It has been urged that the intervention of a free agent will make a difference; but I do not consider Willis and Ryal as free agents in the present case, but acting under a compulsive necessity for their own safety and self-preservation.

The case must be at the outermost edge of what may be encompassed in the meaning of 'direct'. By way of contrast is the case of *Dodwell v Burford*[3] in which the defendant slapped the horse upon which the female plaintiff was sitting, causing it to run off; she was thrown to the ground and another horse ran over her resulting in her losing the use of two fingers. It seems that the injury caused by the second horse was considered consequential only as the court refused to increase the damages to cover that injury.

If the plaintiff cannot show that the harm is direct, then she is outside the scope of the trespass writ and must sue in an action on the case as they used to be called, such as negligence or nuisance.

Nature of liability in trespass to the person

This is an extremely important issue, or so it seems from the amount of time that has been spent discussing it in the cases. It is thought that originally the liability in trespass to the person was strict, although it must be said that this is hardly free from doubt. It was thought that a defendant might escape responsibility in law for the direct harm caused to the plaintiff by his act, if he could show that the harm was an inevitable accident. Whatever was the true position historically, it was clear by the latter part of the 19th century that, in so far as highway accidents were concerned, the situation was that the plaintiff had to plead and prove fault if she was to succeed in a damages claim against the defendant. The case of *Holmes v Mather*[4] is to the point on this issue. The defendant's horses ran out of control as a result of a dog barking at them. The defendant's servant was doing his best to control them but they struck the plaintiff nonetheless. Bramwell B said as follows:

> The driver is absolutely free from all blame in the matter; not only does he not do anything wrong, but he endeavours to do what is best to be done under the circumstances. This misfortune happens through the horses being so startled by

3 (1670) 1 Mod 24.

4 (1875) LR 10 Ex 261.

> the barking of a dog that they run away with the groom and the defendant, who is sitting beside him. Now, if the plaintiff under such circumstances bring an action, I cannot see why she should not bring an action because a splash of mud, in the ordinary course of driving, was thrown upon her dress or got into her eye and so injured it. It seems manifest that, under such circumstances, she could not maintain an action. For the convenience of mankind in carrying on the affairs of life, people as they go along roads must expect, or put up with, such mischief as reasonable care on the part of others cannot avoid. I think the present action not maintainable.

The message here is clear; the plaintiff must prove fault, whether intention or negligence, in order to succeed in the trespass action in relation to a highway accident for the reason given by the judge in the above extract.

The position was initially not so clear in relation to other types of incident. In *Stanley v Powell*[5] the plaintiff was struck by a pellet fired by the defendant which glanced off the bough of a tree. Denman J commented:

> In the present case the plaintiff sued in respect of an injury owing to the defendant's negligence – there was no pretence for saying that it was intentional so far as any injury to the plaintiff was concerned – and the jury negatived such negligence. It was argued that nevertheless, inasmuch as the plaintiff was injured by a shot from the defendant's gun, that was an injury owing to an act of force by the defendant, and therefore an action would lie. I am of the opinion that this is not so, and that against any statement of claim which the plaintiff could suggest, the defendant must succeed if he were to plead the facts sworn to by the witnesses for the defendant in this case, and the jury believing those facts, as they must now be taken by me to have done, found the verdict which they have found as regards negligence.
>
> In other words, I am of opinion that, if the case is regarded as an action on the case for an injury by negligence, the plaintiff has failed to establish that which is the very gist of such an action. If, on the other hand, it is turned into an action for trespass, and the defendant is (as he must be) supposed to have pleaded a plea denying negligence and establishing that the injury was accidental in the sense above explained, the verdict of the jury is equally fatal to the action.

The case suggests that the burden of disproving negligence in a trespass action lay with the defendant, so it would be enough for the plaintiff to establish that he was shot if the defendant was unable to discharge that burden. The later shooting case of *Fowler v Lanning*[6] suggests that the burden is on the plaintiff in trespass to show that the defendant intended or was negligent as to the consequences of his action. The plaintiff was shot during a shooting party and, in his statement of claim, merely stated that he had been shot by the defendant on a particular date at a particular place. The defendant argued that no cause of action was disclosed. Diplock J, as he was at the time, observed as follows:

> If, therefore, it is conceded – as all agree that it must be, at any rate today – that in the case of involuntary trespass to the person on the highway the onus of proving negligence lies on the plaintiff; why should it be otherwise when the involuntary trespass to the person is not committed on a highway?

---

5 [1891] 1 QB 86.

6 [1959] 1 QB 426.

After discussing the cases, including *Stanley v Powell*, the judge continued:

> I can summarise the law as I understand it from my examination of the cases as follows:
>
> (1) Trespass to the person does not lie if the injury to the plaintiff, although the direct consequence of the act of the defendant, was caused unintentionally and without negligence on the defendant's part.
>
> (2) Trespass to the person on the highway does not differ in this respect from trespass to the person committed in any other place.
>
> (3) If it were right to say ... that negligence is a necessary ingredient of unintentional trespass only where the circumstances are such as to show that the plaintiff has taken on himself the risk of inevitable injury (ie injury which is the result of neither intention nor carelessness on the part of the defendant), the plaintiff must today in this crowded world be considered as taking on himself the risk of inevitable injury from any acts of his neighbour which, in the absence of damage to the plaintiff, would not in themselves be unlawful – of which discharging a gun at a shooting party in 1957 or a trained band exercise in 1617 are obvious examples.
>
> (4) The onus of proving negligence, where the trespass is not intentional, lies on the plaintiff, whether the action be framed in trespass or negligence.
>
> If, as I have held, the onus of proof of intention or negligence on the part of the defendant lies on the plaintiff, then, under the modern rules of pleading, he must allege either intention on the part of the defendant; or, if he relies on negligence, he must state the facts which he alleges constitute negligence. Without either of such allegations the bald statement that the defendant shot the plaintiff in unspecified circumstances with an unspecified weapon in my view discloses no cause of action.
>
> This is no academic pleading point. It serves to secure justice between the parties. If it is open to the plaintiff – as counsel for the plaintiff must, I think, contend – on the pleadings as they at present stand, to prove that the defendant shot him deliberately. Failure to allege such intention deprives the defendant of his right to stay the action pending prosecution for the felony. ... I should repeat that there is, of course, in fact no suggestion that the shooting here was intentional, and thus felonious. But if counsel for the plaintiff be right, proof of intention would be open on the pleading in its present form.
>
> Turning next to the alternative of negligent trespass to the person, there is here the bare allegation that, on a particular day at a particular place, 'the defendant shot the plaintiff'. In what circumstances, indeed with what weapon from bow and arrow to atomic warhead, is not stated. So bare an allegation is consistent with the defendant's having exercised reasonable care. It may be – I know not – that, had the circumstances been set out with greater particularity, there would have been disclosed facts which themselves shouted negligence, so that the doctrine of *res ipsa loquitur* would have applied. In such a form the statement of claim might have disclosed a cause of action even though the word 'negligence' itself had not been used, and the plaintiff in that event would have been limited to relying for proof of negligence on the facts which he alleged. But I have today to deal with the pleading as it stands. As it stands, it neither alleges negligence in terms nor alleges facts which, if true, would of themselves constitute negligence; nor, if counsel for the plaintiff is right, would he be bound at any time before the trial to disclose to the defendant what facts he relies on as constituting negligence.

I do not see how the plaintiff will be harmed by alleging now the facts on which he ultimately intends to rely. On the contrary, for him to do so will serve to secure justice between the parties. It offends the underlying purpose of the modern system of pleading that a plaintiff, by calling his grievance 'trespass to the person' instead of 'negligence', should force a defendant to come to trial blindfold; and I am glad to find nothing in the authorities which compels the court in this case to refrain from stripping the bandage from his eyes.

I hold that the statement of claim in its present form discloses no cause of action.

This statement settles the issue that, in order to maintain an action in trespass to the person, the plaintiff must plead and prove some fault, be it intention or negligence, against the defendant. The one issue that the case does not conclusively resolve is that of whether there is such a thing as a negligently inflicted trespass to the person. Clearly, Diplock J did not rule this out. The point came in for consideration in the later case of *Letang v Cooper*,[7] in which the plaintiff was run over by a car negligently driven by the defendant. A writ was issued over three years later alleging negligence, and in the alternative trespass to the person, both based on the same facts. Any claim for personal injuries arising from negligence, nuisance or breach of duty must normally be started within three years. The plaintiff sought to argue that, where the action was based on trespass, the limitation period was the usual six years. Lord Denning in a famous judgment, observed:

> The argument, as was developed before us, became a direct invitation to this court to go back to the old forms of action and to decide this case by reference to them. The statute [of limitation] bars *an action on the case*, it is said, after three years, whereas *trespass to the person* is not barred for six years. ... I must say that if we are, at this distance of time, to revive the distinction between trespass and case, we should get into the most utter confusion. The old common lawyers tied themselves in knots over it, and we should find ourselves doing the same. ...
>
> I must decline therefore, to go back to the old forms of action in order to construe this statute. I know that in the last century Maitland said 'the forms of action we have buried, but they still rule us from their graves', But we have in this century shaken off their trammels. These forms of action have served their day. They did at one time form a guide to substantive rights; but they do so no longer. Lord Atkin told us what to do about them: 'When these ghosts of the past stand in the path of justice, clanking their mediaeval chains, the proper course for the judge is to pass through them undeterred.' See *United Australia Ltd v Barclays Bank Ltd* ([1940] 4 All ER 20 at p 37).
>
> The truth is that the distinction between trespass and case is obsolete. We have a different sub-division altogether. Instead of dividing actions for personal injuries into *trespass* (direct damage) or *case* (consequential damage), we divide the causes of action now according, as the defendant did the injury intentionally or unintentionally. If one man intentionally applies force directly to another, the plaintiff has a cause of action in assault and battery, or, if you so please to describe it, in trespass to the person. 'The least touching of another in anger is a battery.' If he does not inflict injury intentionally, but only unintentionally, the plaintiff has no cause of action today in trespass. His only cause of action is in negligence, and then only on proof of want of reasonable care. If the plaintiff cannot prove want of reasonable care, he may have no cause of action at all.

7 [1965] 1 QB 232.

> Thus, it is not enough nowadays for the plaintiff to plead that 'the defendant shot the plaintiff'. He must also allege that he did it intentionally or negligently. If intentional, it is the tort of assault and battery. If negligent and causing damage, it is the tort of negligence.
>
> The modern law on this subject was well expounded by my brother Diplock J in *Fowler v Lanning*, with which I fully agree. But I would go this one step further; when the injury is not inflicted intentionally, but negligently, I would say that the only cause of action is negligence and not trespass. If it were trespass, it would be actionable without proof of damage; and that is not the law today. In my judgment, therefore, the only cause of action in the present case (because the injury was unintentional) is negligence and is barred by reason of the express provision of the statute.

The Master of the Rolls then went on to say that, if he was wrong about this, he needed to consider the other argument based on the wording of the statute. He continued:

> So we come back to construe the words of the statute with reference to the law of this century and not of past centuries. So construed, they are perfectly intelligible. The tort of 'negligence' is firmly established. So is the tort of 'nuisance'. These are given by the legislature as signposts. Then these are followed by words of the most comprehensive description: 'Actions for breach of duty (whether the duty existed by virtue of a contract or of a provision made by or under a statute or independently of any contract or any such provision).'
>
> Those words seem to me to cover not only a breach of a contractual duty or a statutory duty, but also a breach of any duty under the law of tort. Our whole law of tort today proceeds on the footing that there is a duty owed by every man not to injure his neighbour in a way forbidden by law. Negligence is a breach of such a duty. So is nuisance. So is trespass to the person. So is false imprisonment, malicious prosecution or defamation of character. ...
>
> In my judgment, therefore, the words 'breach of duty' are wide enough to comprehend the cause of action for trespass to the person as well as negligence.
>
> ...
>
> I come, therefore, to the clear conclusion that the plaintiff's cause of action here is barred by the statute of limitation. Her only cause of action here, in my judgment (where the damage was unintentional), was negligence and not trespass to the person. It is therefore barred by the word 'negligence' in the statute; but even if it was trespass to the person, it was an action for 'breach of duty' and is barred on that ground also.

Danckwerts LJ agreed with Lord Denning MR on both the grounds discussed above. Diplock LJ agreed on the construction of the statute of limitation point, but preferred to leave open the issue as to whether there could be a negligently inflicted trespass to the person as shown by the following extract:

> The factual situation on which the plaintiff's action was founded is set out in the statement of claim. It was that the defendant, by failing to exercise reasonable care (of which failure particulars were given), drove his motor car over the plaintiff's legs and so inflicted on her direct personal injuries in respect of which the plaintiff claimed damages. That factual situation was the plaintiff's cause of action. It was the cause of action 'for' which the plaintiff claimed damages in respect of the personal injuries which she sustained. That cause of action or factual situation falls within the description of the tort of 'negligence', and an action founded on it, that is, brought to obtain the remedy to which the existence

of that factual situation entitles the plaintiff, falls within the description of an 'action for negligence'.

The description 'negligence' was in fact used by the plaintiff's pleader; but this cannot be decisive, for we are concerned not with the description applied by the pleader to the factual situation and the action founded on it, but with the description applied to it by Parliament in the enactment to be construed. It is true that the factual situation also falls within the description of the tort of 'trespass to the person'. But that, as I have endeavoured to show, does not mean that there are two causes of action. It merely means that there are two apt descriptions of the same cause of action. It does not cease to be the tort of 'negligence', because it can be called by another name. An action founded on it is none the less an 'action for negligence' because it can also be called an 'action for trespass to the person'.

The above clearly leaves it open, at least in a theoretical sense, for an action to be brought for a negligently inflicted trespass, although in practice, where the plaintiff cannot prove intention, even where the injury is direct, the action will be framed in negligence. However, it should be pointed out that, in *Williams v Humphreys*,[8] the High Court judge seemed to accept that there could be such a cause of action. It might be argued that Lord Denning's discussion on this point was not essential to the decision, and that the decision was based on the narrower ground relating to the construction of the statute on which all three judges in the Court of Appeal were agreed. However, in *Wilson v Pringle*,[9] Croom-Johnson LJ confirmed what was said above by Lord Denning MR in the following terms:

The judgment of Lord Denning MR was widely phrased, but it was delivered in an action where the only contact between the plaintiff and the defendant was unintentional. It has long been the law that claims arising out of an unintentional trespass must be made in negligence.

The position is perhaps not so clear cut as this statement makes out.

Hostility

The final general question relates to the issue of whether hostility is an essential requirement in an action for trespass to the person. There is a tendency at times to confuse this issue with that of intention, with which it may often overlap. It is another point which has occasioned considerable judicial discussion, although it is an argument which only came into the spotlight in the recent case *Wilson v Pringle*. However, perhaps the starting point should be taken as the slightly earlier case of *Collins v Wilcock*,[10] in which the plaintiff successfully sued for battery when she was restrained unlawfully by a police woman by the arm. There is a very useful statement in this case by Robert Goff LJ which is set out below:

The law draws a distinction, in terms more easily understood by philologists than by ordinary citizens, between an assault and a battery. An assault is an act which causes another person to apprehend the infliction of immediate, unlawful force on his person; a battery is the actual infliction of unlawful force on another

8 (1975) Times, 20 February.

9 [1986] 2 All ER 440.

10 [1984] 3 All ER 374.

person. Both assault and battery are forms of trespass to the person. Another form of trespass to the person is false imprisonment, which is the unlawful imposition of constraint on another's freedom of movement from a particular place. The requisite mental element is of no relevance in the present case

We are here primarily concerned with battery. The fundamental principle, plain and incontestable, is that every person's body is inviolate. It has long been established that any touching of another person, however slight, may amount to a battery. So Holt CJ held in 1704 that 'the least touching of another in anger is a battery': see *Cole v Turner* (1704) 6 Mod Rep 149, 90 ER 958. The breadth of the principle reflects the fundamental nature of the interest so protected; as Blackstone wrote in his commentaries, 'the law cannot draw the line between different degrees of violence, and therefore totally prohibits the first and lowest stage of it; every man's person being sacred, and no other having the right to meddle with it, in nay the slightest manner' (see 3 Bl Com 120). The effect is that everybody is protected, not only against physical injury, but against any form of physical molestation.

But so widely drawn a principle must inevitably be subject to exceptions. For example, children may be subjected to reasonable punishment; people may be subjected to the lawful exercise of the power of arrest; and reasonable force may be used in self-defence or for the prevention of crime. But apart from these special instances where the control or constraint is lawful, a broader exception has been created to allow for the exigencies of daily life. Generally speaking, consent is a defence to battery; and most of the physical contacts of ordinary life are not actionable because they are impliedly consented to by all who move in society, and so expose themselves to the risk of bodily contact. So nobody can complain of the jostling which is inevitable from his presence in, for example, a supermarket, an underground station or a busy street; nor can a person who attends a party complain if his hand is seized in friendship, or even if his back is (within reason) slapped (see *Tuberville v Savage* (1669) 1 Mod Rep 3, 86 ER 684).

Although such cases are recorded as examples of implied consent, it is more common nowadays to treat them as falling within a general exception embracing all physical contact which is generally acceptable in the ordinary conduct of daily life. We observe that, although in the past it has sometimes been stated that a battery is only committed where the action is 'angry, or revengeful, or rude, or insolent' (see 1 Hawk PC c 62, s 2), we think that nowadays it is more realistic, and indeed more accurate, to state the broad underlying principle, subject to the broad exception.

Among such forms of conduct, long held to be acceptable, is touching a person for the purpose of engaging his attention, though of course using no greater degree of physical contact than is reasonably necessary in the circumstances for that purpose. So, for example, it was held by the Court of Common Pleas in 1807 that a touch by a constable on the shoulder of a man who had climbed on a gentleman's railing to gain a better view of a mad ox, the touch being only to engage the man's attention, did not amount to a battery (see *Wiffin v Kincard* (1807) 2 Bos & PNR 471, 127 ER 713; for another example see, see *Coward v Baddeley* (1859) 4 H& N 478, 157 ER 927).

But a distinction is drawn between a touch to draw a man's attention, which is generally acceptable, and a physical restraint, which is not. So we find Parke B observing in *Rawlings v Till* (1837) 3 M&W 28 at 29, 150 ER 1042, with reference to *Wiffin v Kincard*, that 'There the touch was merely to engage a man's attention, not to put a restraint on his person'. Furthermore, persistent touching to gain attention in the face of obvious disregard may transcend the norms of acceptable behaviour, and so be outside the exception. We do not say that more than one touch is never permitted; for example, the lost or distressed may surely be permitted a second touch, or possibly even more, on a reluctant or impervious sleeve or shoulder, as may a person who is acting reasonably in the exercise of a duty. In each case, the test must be whether the physical conduct so persisted in has in the circumstances gone beyond generally acceptable standards of conduct; and the answer to that question will depend on the facts of the particular case.

The distinction drawn by Parke B in *Rawlings v Till* is of importance in the case of police officers. Of course, a police officer may subject another to restraint when he lawfully exercises his power of arrest ... but, putting such cases aside, police officers have for present purposes no greater rights than ordinary citizens. It follows that, subject to such cases, physical contact by a police officer with another person may be unlawful as a battery, just as it might be if he was an ordinary member of the public. But a police officer has his rights as a citizen, as well as his duties as a policeman. A police officer may wish to engage a man's attention, for example, if he wishes to question him. If he lays his hand on a man's sleeve or taps his shoulder for that purpose, he commits no wrong. He may even do so more than once; for he is under a duty to prevent and investigate crime, and so his seeking further, in the exercise of that duty, to engage a man's attention in order to speak to him may in the circumstances be regarded as acceptable. ...

But if, taking into account the nature of his duty, his use of physical contact in the face of non-cooperation persists beyond generally acceptable standards of conduct, his action will become unlawful; and if a police officer restrains a man, for example by gripping his arm or his shoulder, then his action will be unlawful, unless he is lawfully exercising his power of arrest. A police officer has no power to require a man to answer him, though he has the advantage of authority, enhanced as it is by the uniform which the state provides and requires him to wear, in seeking a response to his inquiry. What is not permitted, however, is the unlawful use of force or the unlawful threat (actual or implicit) to use force; and, excepting the lawful exercise of his power of arrest, the lawfulness of a police officer's conduct is judged by the same criteria as are applied to the conduct of any ordinary citizen of this country. ...

The fact is that the respondent took hold of the appellant by the left arm to restrain her. In so acting, she was not proceeding to arrest the appellant; and since her action went beyond the generally acceptable conduct of touching a person to engage his or her attention, it must follow, in our judgment, that her action constituted a battery on the appellant, and was therefore unlawful. It follows that the appellant's appeal must be allowed and her conviction quashed.

There is clearly no use of the word 'hostility' in this extract, nonetheless the discussion is germane to the issue. Parts of the above extract were quoted in the leading case on this issue, *Wilson v Pringle.* In this case a schoolboy was involved in what the court called 'horseplay' with another boy who was injured as a result. The defendant argued that there had to be some hostility if the plaintiff was to succeed. Croom-Johnson LJ, after discussing the cases of *Letang v Cooper* and *Fowler v Lanning*, continued:

... for there to be either an assault or a battery there must be something in the nature of hostility. It may be evinced by anger, by words or gesture. Sometimes the very act of battery will speak for itself, as where somebody uses a weapon on another. What, then, turns a friendly touching (which is not actionable) into an unfriendly one (which is)?

The judge then went on to discuss other cases including Robert Goff LJ's statements in *Collins v Wilcock*. He then continued as follows:

> Nevertheless, it still remains to indicate what is to be proved by a plaintiff who brings an action for battery. Robert Goff LJ's judgment is illustrative of the considerations which underlie such an action, but it is not practicable to define a battery as 'physical contact which is not generally acceptable in the ordinary conduct of daily life'.
>
> In our view, the authorities lead to one conclusion that, in a battery, there must be an intentional touching or contact in one form or another of the plaintiff by the defendant. That touching must be proved to be a hostile touching. That still leaves unanswered the question, when is a touching to be called hostile? Hostility cannot be equated with ill-will or malevolence. It cannot be governed by the obvious intention shown in acts like punching, stabbing or shooting. It cannot solely be governed by an expressed intention, although that may be strong evidence. But the element of hostility, in the sense in which it is now to be considered, must be a question of fact for the tribunal of fact. It may be imported from the circumstances.
>
> Take the example of the police officer in *Collins v Wilcock*. She touched the woman deliberately, but without an intention to do more than restrain her temporarily. Nevertheless, she was acting unlawfully and in that way was acting with hostility. She was acting contrary to the woman's legal right not to be physically restrained. We see no more difficulty in establishing what she intended by means of question and answer, or by inference from the surrounding circumstances, than there is in establishing whether an apparently playful blow was struck in anger. The rules of law governing the legality of arrest may require strict application to the facts of appropriate cases, but in the ordinary give and take of everyday life the tribunal of fact should find no difficulty in answering the question 'was this, or was it not, a battery?' Where the immediate act of touching does not itself demonstrate hostility, the plaintiff should plead the facts which are said to do so.

The defendant was given unconditional leave to defend for the court to investigate this point in particular. There has been criticism of the use of the word 'hostility', and Lord Goff in particular responded in the case of *F v West Berkshire Health Authority*,[11] a case concerning the issue of consent to surgical operation by those suffering serious mental disability. Lord Goff took the opportunity to come back on this issue as follows:

> In the old days it used to be said that, for a touching of another's person to amount to a battery, it had to be a touching 'in anger' (see *Cole v Turner* (1704) Holt KB 108, 90 ER 958 *per* Holt CJ); and it has recently been said that the touching must be 'hostile' to have that effect (see *Wilson v Pringle* [1986] 2 All ER 440 at 447, [1987] QB 237 at 253. I respectfully doubt whether that is correct. A prank that gets out of hand, an over-friendly slap on the back, surgical treatment by a surgeon who mistakenly thinks that patient has consented to it, all these things may transcend the bounds of lawfulness, without being characterised as hostile. Indeed, the suggested qualification is difficult to reconcile with the principle that any touching of another's body is, in the absence of lawful excuse, capable of amounting to a battery and a trespass.

11 [1989] 2 All ER 545.

In some cases it seems clear that the word 'hostile' is too strong a word to use to describe what is required to be proved by the plaintiff, and it is argued that in some cases the plaintiff merely has to show that the contact was 'unwanted' or that she did not consent to it. Unfortunately, this approach was of no help in the case of *R v Brown*,[12] where the House of Lords discussed whether consent was a defence to sado-masochistic acts in private. It was clear that all parties freely consented to the acts being performed, but nonetheless the House held that consent could not be a defence. Lord Jauncey, after discussing briefly *Wilson v Pringle* and *Collins v Wilcock* said, even more briefly, 'If the appellants' activities in relation to the receivers were unlawful, they were also hostile and a necessary ingredient of assault was present'. Lord Lowry agreed with him on this point. The argument, however, appears circular. 'Hostility' is regarded by some as an element in assault and battery which helps to decide whether what the defendant has done is unlawful, rather than the other way round. It seems clear that in some cases, such as *Brown*, the word is simply inappropriate as part of the description of the offence.

Assault and battery

There are some specific points that need to be made in respect of these causes of action. In battery, it has been said that there must be a positive act by the defendant. In *Innes v Wylie*[13] a policeman prevented the plaintiff from pushing into a room. Denman CJ, in summing up to the jury, said:

> You will say whether, on the evidence, you think that the policeman committed an assault on the plaintiff, or was merely passive. If the policeman was entirely passive, like a door or a wall put to prevent the plaintiff from entering the room, and simply obstructing the entrance of the plaintiff, no assault has been committed on the plaintiff, and your verdict will be for the defendant. The question is, did the policeman take any active measures to prevent the plaintiff entering the room, or did he stand in the door way passive, and not move at all?

Something of a contrast is provided by the case of *Fagan v Commissioner of Metropolitan Police*,[14] in which the defendant was instructed by a police constable to park his car to answer questions. The defendant drove the vehicle onto the policeman's foot and only after being asked several times to remove it, did he do so. James J gave a judgment with which Lord Parker CJ agreed. He commented as follows:

> In our judgment the question arising, which has been argued on general principles, falls to be decided on the facts of the particular case. An assault is any act which intentionally – or possibly recklessly – causes another person to apprehend immediate and unlawful personal violence. Although 'assault' is an independent crime and is to be treated as such, for practical purposes today 'assault' is generally synonymous with the term 'battery' and is a term used to mean the actual intended use of unlawful force to another person without his consent. On the facts of the present case the 'assault' alleged involved a 'battery'. Where an assault involves a battery, it matters not, in our judgment, whether the

12 [1993] 2 All ER 75.

13 (1844) 1 Car & Kir 257.

14 [1969] 1 QB 439.

> battery is inflicted directly by the body of the offender or through the medium of some weapon or instrument controlled by the action of the offender. An assault may be committed by the laying of a hand upon another, and the action does not cease to be an assault if it is a stick held in the hand itself which is laid on the person of the victim. So for our part we see no difference in principle between the action of stepping on to a person's toe and maintaining that position, and the action of driving a car on to a person's foot and sitting in the car whilst its position on the foot is maintained.
>
> ... On the facts found the action of the appellant may have been initially unintentional, but the time came when, knowing that the wheel was on the officer's foot, the appellant:
>
> (1) remained seated in the car so that his body, through the medium of the car, was in contact with the officer;
>
> (2) switched off the ignition of the car;
>
> (3) maintained the wheel of the car on the foot; and
>
> (4) used words indicating the intention of keeping the wheel in that position. For our part we cannot regard such conduct as mere omission or inactivity.
>
> There was an act constituting a battery which, at its inception, was not criminal because there was no element of intention but which became criminal from the moment the intention was formed to produce the apprehension which was flowing from the continuing act. The fallacy of the appellant's argument is that it seeks to equate the facts of this case with such a case as where a motorist has accidentally run over a person and, that action having been completed, fails to assist the victim with the intent that the victim should suffer.

Bridge J took a different line in his dissent:

> I have no sympathy at all for the appellant, who behaved disgracefully. But I have been unable to find any way of regarding the facts which satisfies me that they amounted to the crime of assault. This has not been for want of trying. But at every attempt I have encountered the inescapable question: after the wheel of the appellant's car had accidentally come to rest on the constable's foot, what was it that the appellant did which constituted the act of assault? However the question is approached, the answer I feel obliged to give is: precisely nothing. The car rested on the foot by its own weight and remained stationary by its own inertia. The appellant's fault was that he omitted to manipulate the controls to set it in motion again.

This looks a harsh decision in view of the law's general reluctance to impose a duty to act positively for the benefit of others.

As to the cause of action of assault in the specific sense of conduct falling short of a battery, there are several points to be considered. It is the effect of the defendant's action on the plaintiff which is important rather than whether the defendant was going to carry out his threat. Fear is not necessary, merely the reasonable apprehension of the infliction of a battery, otherwise, it is said, the brave and courageous would be penalised. This emphasises the point that the tort is actionable *per se* without proof of damage. On this issue of reasonable apprehension there are two conflicting cases concerning loaded guns. In *Blake v Barnard*[15] it was suggested by Abinger CJ that to point an unloaded pistol at the

---

15 (1840) 9 Car & P 626.

plaintiff was not an assault. Parke B seems to have the correct approach in *R v St George*[16] when he said:

> My idea is, that it is an assault to present a pistol at all, whether loaded or not. If you threw the powder out of the pan, or took the percussion cap off, and said to the party 'This is an empty pistol', then that would be no assault; for there the party must see that it was not possible that he should be injured; but if a person presents a pistol which has the appearance of being loaded, and puts the other party into fear and alarm, that is what it is the object of the law to prevent.

This seems to represent the law on this issue.

Another hotly debated area in relation to assault is the question of whether words can constitute an assault. Resort is usually had to the statement in the very old case of *Mead's and Belt's*[17] case where Holroyd J, in addressing the jury, said that '... no words or singing are equivalent to an assault'. However, in *R v Wilson*,[18] in a brief statement Lord Goddard CJ took the view that to shout 'Get out the knives!' would in itself be an assault without more. It would seem to make sense that if a person, for example, was in a dark alley and heard someone close to him shout such a phrase, that this would create a reasonable apprehension of the infliction of a battery; likewise if this was shouted out close to a blind person.

Gestures alone can constitute an assault as raising one's fist in the other's face, but words may also reinforce an action or *vice versa*. In *Read v Coker*[19] the plaintiff was approached by the defendant's employees, rolling up their sleeves and threatening to break his neck if he did not leave. Jervis CJ said:

> If anything short of actual striking will in law constitute an assault, the facts here clearly showed that the defendant was guilty of an assault. There was a threat of violence exhibiting an intention to assault, and a present ability to carry the threat into execution.

On the other hand words may signify that the defendant has no intention of carrying out any threat and, in such circumstances, the plaintiff will not be able to establish that there was a reasonable apprehension of unlawful contact. In *Tuberville v Savage*[20] it was alleged that the defendant put his hand upon his sword and said 'if it were not assize time, I would not take such language from you'. The court held that this was not an assault but, if the words had not been uttered, it would have been. This should be distinguished, however, from the conditional threat situation which may well be assault. If the defendant threatens to break the plaintiff's leg if he does not leave, this could be an assault, as the defendant is forcing the plaintiff to do something under a reasonable apprehension of physical contact.

What about telephone threats, a common enough phenomenon these days. There may be other ways of dealing with these, but do they amount to assault, as the element of immediacy in carrying out the threat seems to be a stumbling

16 (1840) 9 Car & P 483.

17 (1823) 1 Lew CC 184.

18 [1955] 1 WLR 493.

19 (1853) 13 CB 850.

20 (1669) 1 Mod 3.

block. It has been held elsewhere[21] that this may be an assault. However, as we have seen in the case of *Khorasandjian v Bush* discussed in the previous chapter, the court resolved this type of problem to some extent by developing the tort of private nuisance to cover telephone threats to a daughter living in her parents' house. provoking exaggerated suggestions that we now have an new tort of harassment. This may still leave an anomaly where the telephone threats are not made to a person's home.

One final point on assault arose in the old case of *Stephens v Myers*[22] where, in a parish meeting following heated discussion, the defendant advanced towards the plaintiff with fists clenched but was prevented from reaching him by others at the meeting well before he could get anywhere near enough to land a blow. Tindal CJ told the jury as follows:

> It is not every threat, when there is no actual personal violence, that constitutes an assault; there must, in all cases, be the means of carrying the threat into effect. The question I shall leave to you will be, whether the defendant was advancing at the time, in a threatening attitude, to strike the chairman, so that his blow would almost immediately have reached the chairman if he had not been stopped. Then, though he was not near enough at the time to have struck him, yet if he was advancing with intent, I think it amounts to an assault in law. If he was so advancing that, within a second or two of time, he would have reached the plaintiff, it seems to me it is an assault in law.

Intentionally caused harm outside trespass

The inadequacies of the trespass writ were all too obvious and they have been discussed above. The question that arises is whether there is a form of action on the case in respect of harm which is intentionally caused but, for one reason or another, cannot be brought within the scope of the trespass action. The answer would appear to be that there is, but the precise scope of the principle involved is far from clear. The issue arose in *Wilkinson v Downton*,[23] in which the defendant, as a joke, told the plaintiff that her husband had been injured and had broken both his legs. The plaintiff travelled to the scene only to discover that it was not true. She suffered a violent nervous shock. Wright J, finding in her favour in deceit for her wasted expenditure travelling to the scene and on the case for the shock, said:

> The defendant has, as I assume for the moment, wilfully done an act calculated to cause physical harm to the plaintiff – that is to say, to infringe her legal right to personal safety – and has in fact thereby caused physical harm to her. That proposition without more appears to me to state a good cause of action, there being no justification alleged for the act. This wilful *injuria* is in law malicious, although no malicious purpose to cause the harm which was caused, nor any motive of spite, is imputed to the defendant.
>
> It remains to consider whether the assumptions involved in the proposition are made out. One question is whether the defendant's act was so plainly calculated to produce some effect of the kind which was produced, that an intention to

21 See *Barton v Armstrong* [1969] 2 NSWLR 451.

22 (1830) 4 Car & P 349.

23 [1897] 2 QB 57.

> produce it ought to be imputed to the defendant, regard being had to the fact that the effect was produced on a person proved to be in an ordinary state of health and mind. I think that it was. It is difficult to imagine that such a statement, made suddenly and with apparent seriousness, could fail to produce grave effects under the circumstances upon any but an exceptionally indifferent person, and therefore an intention to produce such an effect must be imputed, and it is no answer in law to say that more harm was done than was anticipated, for that is the case commonly with all wrongs.

The rule in *Wilkinson v Downton*, as it is called, was approved of by the Court of Appeal in the case of *Janvier v Sweeney*[24] in which a private detective, by false statements and threats, induced the plaintiff to allow him to see some letters on the premises of her employer. She alleged that, as a result of the statements and threats, she became ill. All three judges found for the plaintiff, holding that the case of *Wilkinson v Downton* had been correctly decided. In particular, Duke LJ had this to say:

> This is a much stronger case than *Wilkinson v Downton*. In that case there was no intention to commit a wrongful act; the defendant merely intended to play a practical joke upon the plaintiff. In the present case there was an intention to terrify the plaintiff for the purpose of attaining an unlawful object in which both the defendants were jointly concerned.

Clearly the rule is not restricted to practical jokes as this last case illustrates, but the question is whether there is some wider principle underlying these two cases. Two final points on this. The judge used the word 'calculated' in *Wilkinson* and went on to emphasise that this did not mean 'intended', but rather something such as 'likely' to cause the harm which was caused. Finally, he also made it clear that the rule could only apply if the plaintiff could show that she was a normally susceptible person, although presumably even a person of abnormal susceptibility could succeed if it could be shown that a normal person would have suffered harm as a result of the defendant's statements.

Defences to assault and battery

There are a number of defences to assault and battery with which we need to deal before turning our attention to the other tort of false imprisonment.

Self-defence

This is a defence of considerable antiquity. It will only be allowed as a defence if the force used is reasonable and not out of proportion to the force offered to the defendant. It can be put forward as a defence to prevent harm to others or to property.[25] In *Cockcroft v Smith*,[26] in a court room scuffle the plaintiff moved his finger as if to poke the defendant in the eye and the latter bit the end of the finger off. Holt CJ said:

> ... if a man strike another, who does not immediately after resent it, but takes his opportunity, and then some time after falls upon him and beats him, in this case, *son assault* is no good plea; neither ought a man, in case of a small assault, give a

24 [1919] 2 KB 316.

25 See s 3 Criminal Law Act 1967.

26 (1705) 11 Mod 43.

> violent or an unsuitable return; but in such case plead what is necessary for a man's defence, and not who struck first; though this ... has been the common practice, but this he wished was altered; for hitting a man a little blow with a little stick on the shoulder, is not a reason for him to draw a sword and cut and hew the other, etc.

It was thought that the defence was only available if the defendant had no option but to defend himself, ie there were no avenues of escape or retreat to avoid a fight. However, this was doubted in *R v Bird*,[27] in which Lord Lane CJ said:

> If the defendant is proved to have been attacking or retaliating or revenging himself, then he was not truly acting in self-defence. Evidence that the defendant tried to retreat or tried to call off the fight may be a cast-iron method of casting doubt on the suggestion that he was the attacker or retaliator or the person trying to revenge himself. But it is not by any means the only method of doing that.

It seems, therefore, that the defendant must show that it was reasonable for him to defend himself, and then use reasonable force to carry out the self-defence.

Provocation

There is some controversy as to whether this is a defence or only goes to mitigate the damages in a fashion similar to the defence of contributory negligence. In *Lane v Holloway*[28] the plaintiff was struck a severe blow to the face after he had made some rude comments about the defendant's woman friend and having pushed the defendant on the shoulder. Lord Denning MR on this point said:

> The defendant has done a civil wrong and should pay compensation for the physical damage done by it. Provocation by the plaintiff can properly be used to take away any element of aggravation; but not to reduce the real damages.

Salmon LJ commented:

> I cannot see how, logically or on any principle of law, the fact that the plaintiff has behaved rather badly and is a cantankerous old man can be even material when considering what is proper compensation for the physical injury he has suffered.

It perhaps should be emphasised that, in this case, the court took the view that what the defendant did to the plaintiff was totally out of proportion to what the plaintiff had inflicted on the defendant, almost trivial by comparison. In Scotland the position is different as, in the case of *Ross v Bryce*,[29] the court did in fact reduce the element of compensatory damages because of provocation by the plaintiff leading to the assault, reference being made to the case of *Lane v Holloway*, so the court was aware of the decision in that case. The English position was reaffirmed in *Barnes v Nayer*[30] where the Court of Appeal was considering a case where the defendant severed the head of the wife of the

---

27 [1985] 1 All ER 513.

28 [1967] 3 All ER 129.

29 1972 SLT 76.

30 (1986) Times, 19 December.

plaintiff. It was alleged that there was provocation by the deceased woman. May LJ observed:

> With regard to provocation, the better view was that, although it could reduce exemplary damages, it could not affect compensatory damages.

This seems to confirm the point made by Lord Denning MR in the earlier case, although he referred to aggravated damages as opposed to exemplary damages. If they are different, which will be discussed in the next chapter, the rule applies to both, it would seem.

Contributory negligence

It is not altogether clear what the difference is, if any, between provocation and the defence of contributory negligence under the Law Reform (Contributory Negligence) Act 1945. It seems that the same facts may be used to support both defences. In both *Lane v Holloway* and *Barnes v Nayer* the Court of Appeal seems to acknowledge that the Act could provide a defence, but in both cases decided that the act of the defendant was completely out of proportion to the conduct of the plaintiff. In *Murphy v Culhane*[31] the defendant had pleaded guilty to the manslaughter of the husband of the plaintiff. In the civil case the defendant pleaded, *inter alia,* contributory negligence on the basis that the deceased was involved in a criminal affray initiated by him with a view to assaulting the defendant. Lord Denning MR, with whom the other two judges in the Court of Appeal agreed, seemed in no doubt that any claim by the plaintiff might be subject to a reduction for contributory fault. However, we shall consider below other defences which may apply to actions for assault and battery and completely rule out a claim. It is difficult to envisage circumstances where they would not apply but contributory negligence would, so there may only be limited circumstances in which it might be a successful plea.

Ex turpi causa *and* volenti

These two defences are treated together, as they have the similar effect of ruling out a claim completely. Lord Denning MR commented on them both in the context of *Lane v Holloway* as follows:

> It has been argued before us that no action lies because this was an unlawful fight; that both of them were concerned in illegality; and that, therefore, there can be no cause of action in respect of it. *Ex turpi causa non oritur actio.* To that I entirely demur. Even if the fight started by being unlawful, I think that one of them can sue the other for damages for a subsequent injury if it was inflicted by a weapon or savage blow out of all proportion to the occasion. I agree that, in an ordinary fight with fists, there is no cause of action to either of them for any injury suffered. The reason is that each of the participants in a fight voluntarily takes on himself the risk of incidental injuries to himself. *Volenti fit injuria.* But he does not take on himself the risk of a savage blow out of all proportion to the occasion. The man who strikes a blow of such severity is liable in damages, unless he can prove accident or self-defence.

31 [1976] 3 All ER 533.

Salmon LJ commented:

> Since the injury was inflicted with the fist alone, the conclusion is inescapable that it must have been a savage blow, that the defendant must have smashed his fist with great force into the eye of this man 40 years older that he was, after coming up to him in a threatening manner and having received no more than a slight punch on the shoulder. To say in these circumstances such as those that *ex turpi causa non oritur* action is a defence seems to me to be quite absurd. Academically, of course, one can see the argument, but one must look at it, I think, from a practical point of view. To say that this gentleman was engaged with the defendant in a criminal venture is a step which, like the learned judge, I feel wholly unable to take.
>
> The defence of *volenti non fit injuria* seems to me to be equally difficult. It is inconceivable that the old man, full of beer as he was, was voluntarily taking the risk of having an injury of this kind inflicted on him. I think that the learned judge was quite right in rejecting the defence of *volenti non fit injuria*.

Winn LJ confirmed in his brief judgment that the entire court was completely out of sympathy with any of the defences raised by the defendant because of the disproportionate nature of the battery in relation to what had gone on before it. A similar approach was taken by the Court of Appeal in *Barnes v Nayer*, where May LJ commented on the pleading of the two defences by the defendant as follows:

> The state of the law as to the effect of those defences in actions for trespass to the person was by no means clear ... if in a claim for damages it was possible on the facts to establish that either maxim applied, it would provide a complete defence to the claim.

The judge held that, like the pleading of contributory fault, bearing in mind the disparity between the defendant's conduct and that of the deceased and her family, neither of the defences was made out on the facts. By way of contrast, however, the Court of Appeal in *Murphy v Culhane,* without deciding on the facts, gave a strong lead to the trial court that the pleas ought to succeed. Lord Denning MR hinted as follows:

> If Murphy was one of a gang which set out to beat up Culhane, it may well be that he could not sue for damages if he got more than he bargained for. A man who takes part in a criminal affray may well be said to have been guilty of such a wicked act as to deprive himself of a cause of action or, alternatively, to have taken on himself the risk. I put the case in the course of argument: suppose that a burglar breaks into a house and the householder, finding him there, picks up a gun and shoots him, using more force maybe than is reasonably necessary. The householder may be guilty of manslaughter and liable to be brought before the criminal courts. But I doubt very much whether the burglar's widow could have an action for damages. The householder might well have a defence either on ground of *ex turpi causa non oritur actio* or *volenti non fit injuria.* So, in the present case it is open to Mr Culhane to raise both of these defences. Such defences would go to the whole claim.

Precisely that happened in the very recent case of *Revill v Newbery*,[32] where the Court of Appeal, subject to a substantial reduction for contributory negligence,

32 [1996] 1 All ER 291.

found for the burglar in both negligence and under the Occupiers' Liability Act 1984. Evans LJ stated:

> ... the underlying principle is that there is a public interest which requires that the wrongdoer should not benefit from his crime or other offence. But [if the rule *ex turpi causa* applied] it would mean that the trespasser who was also a criminal was effectively an outlaw who was debarred by the law from recovering compensation for any injury which he might sustain. This same consideration also prompts the thought that, it is one thing to deny to a plaintiff any fruits from his illegal conduct, but different and more far-reaching to deprive him even of compensation for injury which he suffers and which otherwise he is entitled to recover at law.
>
> It is abundantly clear, in my judgment, that the trespasser/criminal is not an outlaw, and it is noteworthy that even the old common law authorities recognised the existence of some duty towards trespassers, even though the duty was limited and strictly defined, and was much less onerous than the common law duty of care ... it follows that the law recognises that the plaintiff has some rights, however limited, which the law does recognise and protect. ...

The other two judges agreed, and the defendant's appeal was dismissed. There is here a plain contradiction between the *dicta* of Lord Denning MR and the decision in this case. It is, perhaps, still the case that the courts have not quite settled the precise scope of these defences.

Consent

To some extent this has been discussed already in the shape of the *volenti* defence, which is often called, in the alternative, consent. Consent can be express or implied. In sport, it is implied by the plaintiff undertaking the activity in question, particularly in the physical contact sports such as rugby and to a lesser extent football. However, the plaintiff does not consent to force going beyond what is normally expected, even if the conduct is prevalent. In *R v Billinghurst*[33] the defendant punched an opposition player in an off-the-ball incident. It was established in evidence that this was a common occurrence. Nonetheless, the judge directed the jury that there was a distinction between force used in the course of play and force used outside that context. The jury convicted by a majority. In addition, as we have already seen in actions for negligence, the courts consider the consent issue in a broadly similar way.[34]

Consent is a major issue in surgery or medical treatment cases. We saw in Chapter 3 that, if the plaintiff's claim is essentially one concerning a lack of information about, eg, the side effects of treatment, the action would normally be in negligence as in *Sidaway v Bethlem Hospital*.

If an action is brought in trespass, the courts have said that, for consent to be a defence, it must be real. In *Chatterton v Gerson*[35] the plaintiff brought an action in trespass and negligence against a medical practitioner for failing to inform her of the implications of certain operations which she underwent, but did not

33 [1978] Crim LR 553.

34 See *Condon v Basi* (above).

35 [1981] QB 432.

improve her condition. Bristow J, in dealing with the trespass allegation, commented:

> It is clear law that, in any context in which the consent of the injured party is a defence to what would otherwise be a crime or civil wrong, the consent must be real. Where, for example, a woman's consent to sexual intercourse is obtained by fraud, her apparent consent is no defence to a charge of rape. It is not difficult to state the principle or to appreciate its good sense, as so often the problem lies in its application. ...
>
> In my judgment, what the court has to do in each case is to look at all the circumstances and say, 'Was there real consent?' I think justice requires that, in order to vitiate the reality of consent, there must be a greater failure of communication between doctor and patient than that involved in a breach of duty if the claim is based on negligence. When the claim is based on negligence the plaintiff must prove, not only the breach of duty to inform, but that, had the duty not been broken, she would not have chosen to have the operation. Where the claim is based on trespass to the person, once it is shown that the consent is unreal then, what the plaintiff would have decided if she had been given the information which would have prevented vitiation of the reality of her consent, is irrelevant.
>
> In my judgment, once the patient is informed in broad terms of the nature of the procedure which is intended, and gives her consent, that consent is real, and the cause of the action on which to base a claim for failure to go into risks and implications is negligence, not trespass. Of course, if information is withheld in bad faith, the consent will be vitiated by fraud. Of course, if by some accident, as in a case in the 1940s in the Salford Hundred Court, where a boy was admitted to hospital for a tonsillectomy and, due to administrative error, was circumcised instead, trespass would be the appropriate cause of action against the doctor, though he was as much a victim of the error as the boy. But in my judgment it would be very much against the interests of justice if actions, which are really based on a failure by a doctor to perform his duty adequately to inform, were pleaded in trespass.
>
> In this case, in my judgment, even taking Miss Chatterton's evidence at its face value, she was under no illusion as to the general nature of what an intrathecal injection of phenol solution nerve block would be, and in the case of each injection her consent was not unreal. I should add that, getting the patient to sign a *pro forma* expressing consent to undergo the operation, 'the effect and nature of which have been explained to me', as was done here in each case, should be a valuable reminder to everyone of the need for explanation and consent. But it would be no defence to an action based on trespass to the person if no explanation had in fact been given; the consent would have been expressed in form only, not in reality.

The action also failed in negligence.

In the case of *R v Brown* mentioned earlier, despite the fact that the participants all consented to the infliction of the batteries on them, the majority of the House of Lords held that, in the public interest, to protect society form the cult of violence and to protect young men from corruption, the activities were unlawful. Lord Templeman set the tone for the majority when he said:

> In principle there is a difference between violence which is incidental and violence which is inflicted for the indulgence of cruelty. The violence of sado-masochistic encounters involves the indulgence of cruelty by sadists and the degradation of victims. Such violence is injurious to the participants and

> unpredictably dangerous. I am not prepared to invent a defence of consent for sado-masochistic encounters which breed and glorify cruelty and result in offences under ss 47 and 20 of the 1861 Act.

Lord Jauncey was no less emphatic in his rejection of the defendants' arguments when he said:

> ... in considering the public interest it would be wrong to look only at the activities of the appellants alone, there being no suggestion that they and their associates are the only practitioners of homosexual sado-masochism in England and Wales. This House must therefore consider the possibility that these activities are practised by others and by others who are not so controlled or responsible as the appellants claim to be. Without going into details of all the rather curious activities in which the appellants engaged, it would appear to be good luck rather than good judgment which has prevented serious injury from occurring. Wounds can easily become septic if not properly treated, the free flow of blood from a person who is HIV positive or who has Aids can infect another, and an inflicter who is carried away by sexual excitement or by drink or drugs could very easily inflict pain and injury beyond the level to which the receiver had consented. ...
>
> Furthermore, the possibility of proselytisation and corruption of young men is a real danger, even in the case of these appellants, and the taking of video recordings of such activities suggests that secrecy may not be as strict as the appellants claimed to your Lordships. If the only purpose of the activity is the sexual gratification of one or both of the participants, what then is the need of a video recording?

The fact that the decision in this case was by a three to two majority suggests that the judiciary is far from settled in its own mind with the justification of the interference with individual freedom.

FALSE IMPRISONMENT

The third tort we need to consider in this chapter is that of false imprisonment. This was defined for us earlier in *Collins v Wilcock* as 'the unlawful imposition of constraint on another's freedom of movement from a particular place'. In *Bird v Jones*[36] the plaintiff was prevented from proceeding in the direction on which he wished to go, but was free to go back or in any other direction he wished. Coleridge J stated:

> And I am of the opinion that there was no imprisonment. To call it so appears to me to confound partial obstruction and disturbance with total obstruction and detention. A prison may have its boundary, large or narrow, visible and tangible, or, though real, still in the conception only; it may itself be moveable or fixed; but a boundary it must have, and that boundary the party imprisoned must be prevented from passing; he must be prevented from leaving that place, within the ambit of which the party imprisoning would confine him, except by prison-breach. Some confusion seems to me to arise from confounding imprisonment of the body with mere loss of freedom; it is one part of the definition of freedom to be able to go whithersoever one pleases, but imprisonment is something more than the mere loss of this power; it includes the notion of restraint within some limits defined by a will or power exterior to our own. ...

36 (1845) 7 QB 742.

> If it be said that, to hold the present case to amount to an imprisonment would turn every obstruction of the exercise of a right of way into an imprisonment, the answer is, that there must be something like personal menace or force accompanying the act of obstruction, and that, with this, it will amount to imprisonment. I apprehend that is not so. If, in the course of a night, both ends of a street were walled up, and there was no egress from the house but into the street, I should have no difficulty in saying that the inhabitants were thereby imprisoned; but if only one end were walled up, and an armed force stationed outside to prevent any scaling of the wall or passage that way, I should feel equally clear that there was no imprisonment.

Williams J agreed with Patteson J who himself made similar comments to the above. Denman CJ, dissenting, raised some interesting questions when he said:

> It is said that the party here was at liberty to go in another direction. I am not sure that in fact he was, because the same unlawful power which prevented him from taking one course might, in case of acquiescence, have refused him any other. But this liberty to do something else does not appear to me to affect the question of imprisonment. As long as I am prevented from doing what I have a right to do, of what importance is it that I am permitted to do something else? How does the imposition of an unlawful condition shew that I am not restrained? If I am locked in a room, am I not imprisoned because I effect my escape through a window, or because I might find an exit dangerous or inconvenient to myself, as by wading through water or by taking a route so circuitous that my necessary affairs would suffer by delay?
>
> It appears to me that this is a total deprivation of liberty with reference to the purpose for which he lawfully wished to employ his liberty; and, being effected by force, it is not the mere obstruction of a way, but a restraint of the person.

However, the Privy Council in *Robinson v Balmain New Ferry Co Ltd*[37] took a similar line to that of the majority in the previous case. In this case the plaintiff had, in pursuance of a contract, entered the defendants' wharf to get on their boat, but he changed his mind and was prevented from leaving the wharf without paying to go through their turnstile. Lord Loreburn LC delivered the judgment, and said:

> There was no complaint, at all events there was no question left to the jury by the plaintiff's request, of any excessive violence, and in the circumstances admitted it is clear to their lordships that there was no false imprisonment at all. The plaintiff was merely called upon to leave the wharf in the way in which he contracted to leave it. There is no law requiring the defendants to make the exit from their premises gratuitous to people who come there upon a definite contract which involves their leaving the wharf by another way; and the defendants were entitled to resist a forcible passage through their turnstile. ...
>
> When the plaintiff entered the defendants' premises there was nothing agreed as to the terms on which he might go back, because neither party contemplated his going back. When he desired to do so the defendants were entitled to impose a reasonable condition before allowing him to pass through their turnstile from a place to which he had gone of his own free will. The payment of a penny was a quite fair condition, and if he did not choose to comply with it the defendants were not bound to let him through. He could proceed on the journey he contracted for.

37 [1910] AC 295

It might be argued that, to charge him for leaving the wharf, having paid to get on there, was hardly a fair condition. Another controversial and dubious decision is that in *Herd v Weardale Steel, Coal and Coke Co Ltd*[38]. The plaintiff, a miner, wished to leave the mine before his shift was due to finish. The lift was available for 20 minutes before the employers allowed him to leave. The House of Lords rejected his claim. Viscount Haldane LC stated:

> My Lords, by the law off this country no man can be restrained of his liberty without authority in law. That is a proposition the maintenance of which is of great importance; but at the same time it is a proposition which must be read in relation to other propositions which are equally important. If a man chooses to go into a dangerous place at the bottom of a quarry or the bottom of a mine, from which by the nature of physical circumstances he cannot escape, it does not follow from the proposition I have enunciated about liberty that he can compel the owner to bring him up out of it. The owner may or may not be under a duty arising from circumstances, on broad grounds the neglect of which may possibly involve him in a criminal charge or a civil liability. It is unnecessary to discuss the conditions and circumstances which might bring about such a result, because they have, in the view I take, nothing to do with false imprisonment.
>
> My Lords, there is another proposition which has to be borne in mind, and that is the application of the maxim *volenti non fit injuria*. If a man gets into an express train and the doors are locked pending its arrival at its destination, he is not entitled, merely because the train has been stopped by signal, to call for the doors to be opened to let him out. He has entered the train on the terms that he is to be conveyed to a certain station without the opportunity of getting out before that, and he must abide by the terms on which he has entered the train. So, when a man goes down a mine, from which access to the surface does not exist in the absence of special facilities given on the part of the owner of the mine, he is only entitled to the use of these facilities (subject possibly to the exceptional circumstances to which I have alluded) on the terms on which he has entered.

The other Law Lords agreed with this view.

There are one or two interesting points which have cropped up recently in false imprisonment cases. In *Hague v Deputy Governor of Parkhurst Prison*[39] the issue was whether a prisoner, restrained in breach of the prison rules, could bring an action for false imprisonment on the basis that this was an infringement of his residual liberty. Lord Bridge, with whom all the others in the House of Lords agreed, stated:

> In my opinion, to hold a prisoner entitled to damages for false imprisonment on the ground that he has been subject to a restraint upon his movement which was not in accordance with the prison rules would be, in effect, to confer on him, under a different legal label, a cause of action for breach of statutory duty under the rules. Having reached the conclusion that it was not the intention of the rules to confer such a right, I am satisfied that the right cannot properly be asserted in the alternative guise of a claim to damages for false imprisonment.

Lord Jauncey added:

> To say that detention becomes unlawful when the conditions thereof become intolerable is to confuse conditions of confinement with the nature of

38 [1915] AC 67.

39 [1991] 3 All ER 733.

> confinement. ... If, as I believe to be the case, a prisoner at any time has no liberty to be in any place other than where the regime permits, he has no liberty capable of deprivation by the regime so as to constitute the tort of false of imprisonment. An alteration of conditions therefore deprives him of no liberty, because he has none already.

A rather different point came up in *Davidson v Chief Constable of North Wales*,[40] where the plaintiff was arrested by police on suspicion of shoplifting on information supplied by a store detective, but it was a mistake because the item in question had actually been paid for by the plaintiff's friend. The plaintiff sued for false imprisonment against, *inter alia*, the employers of the store detective. The relevant principle is contained in the following brief extract from the judgment of Sir Thomas Bingham MR:

> ... the question which arose for the decision of the learned judge in this case was whether there was information properly to be considered by the jury as to whether what [the store detective] did went beyond laying information before police officers for them to take such action as they thought fit, and amounted to some direction, or procuring, or direct request, or direct encouragement that they should act by way of arresting the defendants. He decided that there was no evidence which went beyond the giving of information. Certainly there was no express request. Certainly there was no encouragement. Certainly there was no discussion of any kind as to what action the police officers should take.

The other two judges agreed with the decision of the Master of the Rolls to dismiss the plaintiff's appeal against the judge's decision to remove the issue from the jury. There seems to be no doubt that a person in the position of a store detective could be liable for false imprisonment, provided that the decision to arrest made by the police could be said to have been encouraged in some way by the detective, as opposed to being an exercise of discretion by the police officers acting on the information supplied by the detective. On the other hand, the detective had made an extremely serious mistake, and it seems somewhat unfair that the plaintiff has no remedy in such a situation.

The final point on the topic of false imprisonment, and one which has been the subject of some considerable controversy, is whether the plaintiff need be aware of the restraint in order to bring an action.

This issue arose most recently in the case of *Murray v Ministry of Defence*,[41] in which the plaintiff was suspected of being involved in the collection of money for the IRA and was arrested, although she was not immediately told for half an hour, whilst her premises were searched. There was some doubt as to whether the plaintiff was aware that she had been arrested, and Lord Griffiths discussed the point as to whether it was a necessary ingredient of the tort that the plaintiff should be so aware. Lord Griffiths gave the only judgment and made the following comments on this issue:

> Although, on the facts of this case, I am sure that the plaintiff was aware of the restraint on her liberty from 7 am, I cannot agree with the Court of Appeal that it is an essential element of the tort of false imprisonment that the victim should be aware of the fact of denial of liberty. The Court of Appeal relied on *Herring v*

40 [1994] 2 All ER 597.

41 [1988] 2 All ER 521.

Boyle (1834) 1 CR M & R 377, 149 ER 1126 for this proposition, which they preferred to the view of Atkin LJ, to the opposite effect in *Meering v Graham-White Aviation Co Ltd* (1919) 122 LT 44.

After considering the first of these cases, His Lordship said that he could not believe that, on the same facts, the case would be decided similarly nowadays. He continued:

In *Meering v Graham-White Aviation Co Ltd*, the plaintiff's employers, who suspected him of theft, sent two of the works' police to bring him in for questioning at the company's offices. He was taken to a waiting-room where he said that, if he was not told why he was there, he would leave. He was told he was wanted for the purpose of making enquiries about things that had been stolen, and he was wanted to give evidence; he then agreed to stay. Unknown to the plaintiff, the works' police had been instructed not to let him leave the waiting-room until the Metropolitan Police arrived. The works' police therefore remained outside the waiting-room and would not have allowed the plaintiff to leave until he was handed over to the Metropolitan Police, who subsequently arrested him. The question for the Court of Appeal was whether, on this evidence, the plaintiff was falsely imprisoned during the hour he was in the waiting room, or whether there could be no 'imprisonment' sufficient to found a civil action unless the plaintiff was aware of the restraint on his liberty.

Atkin LJ said (122 LT 44 at 53–54): 'It appears to me that a person could be imprisoned without his knowing it. I think a person can be imprisoned while he is asleep, while he is in a state of drunkenness, while he is unconscious and while he is a lunatic. Those are cases where it seems to me that the person might properly complain if he were imprisoned, though the imprisonment began and ceased while he was in that state. Of course, the damages might be diminished and would be affected by the question of whether he was conscious or not. So a man might in fact, to my mind, be imprisoned by having the key of a door turned against him so that he is imprisoned in a room in fact, although he does not know that the key has been turned. It may be that he is being detained in that room by persons who are anxious to make him believe that he is not in fact being imprisoned, and at the same time his captors outside that room may be boasting to persons that he is imprisoned; and it seems to me that, if we were to take this case as an instance, supposing it could be proved that Prudence had said while the plaintiff was waiting: "I have got him detained there waiting for the detective to come in and take him to prison," it appears to me that that would be evidence of imprisonment. It is quite unnecessary to go on to show that, in fact, the man knew that he was imprisoned. If a man can be imprisoned by having the key turned upon him without his knowledge, so he can be imprisoned if, instead of a lock and key or bolts and bars, he is prevented from, in fact, exercising his liberty by guards and warders or policemen. They serve the same purpose. Therefore it appears to me a question of fact. It is true that, in all cases of imprisonment, so far as the law of civil liberty is concerned, that "stone walls do not a prison make", in the sense that they are not the only form of imprisonment, but any restraint within defined bounds which is restraint in fact may be an imprisonment.'

I agree with this passage.

It would seem that this issue is now settled and that the decision in *Herring v Boyle* must be treated as effectively overruled on this issue.

CHAPTER 12

DEFAMATION

INTRODUCTION

The tort of defamation is principally designed to protect interests in reputation from untrue statements. It is a difficult tort to understand for a number of reasons. Firstly, it is infected with a mass of procedural rules of pleading which serve to make it both complex and, in places, an extremely turgid subject to study. The cases may often be interesting but the interest disappears amidst a welter of special pleading points which should have long since been laid to rest. Secondly, a further complicating factor is that, unlike most other types of civil trial, defamation cases are heard before a judge and jury. Not only does this result in anomalous and obscene awards of damages by juries, it also often makes for apparently inconsequential discussions about what it is the judge must decide or what must be left to the jury. The sooner this anachronism is put to rights, the more realistic awards of damages will be and the less complex at the same time will be the decision-making in defamation cases.

Another peculiarity is that an action for defamation is normally the preserve of the rich, as actions have, up to the present time, had to be commenced in the High Court and legal aid is not available. Unless the poor plaintiff can allege that his/her action falls within the scope of another tort as well, for which legal aid may be available,[1] his/her interest in his/her reputation goes totally unprotected and is illusory.

There is a bewildering array of common law and statutory defences available to the defendant, some of which are tainted with procedural flavours which once again add to the complexity.

The tort is right on the edge of the line between the individual's right to his reputation remaining intact and the right to freedom of speech. The 'chilling' effect of the tort on freedom of expression has been referred to in recent cases, and it is particularly significant that the courts have begun to refer frequently to Article 10 of the Convention for the Protection of Human Rights and Fundamental Freedoms in an attempt to bring the law in the UK into line with it.

WHO CAN SUE?

An individual's right to sue does not survive for the benefit of his estate, as we have seen in the Law Reform (Miscellaneous Provisions) Act 1934. It seems that a trading corporation can sue to protect its commercial reputation, but nowadays a trade union cannot.[2] The most recent discussion on who can seek protection of the tort arose in the case of *Derbyshire County Council v Times*

---

1 See *Joyce v Sengupta* [1993] 1 All ER 897, a case on malicious falsehood.

2 See *South Hetton Coal Co Ltd v North Eastern News Association Ltd* [1894] 1 QB 133; and *Electrical, Electronic, Telecommunication & Plumbing Union v Times Newspapers Ltd* [1980] QB 585.

Newspapers Ltd,[3] in which the local authority brought an action against the defendant newspaper in relation to articles concerning the authority's management of its superannuation fund. The central issue was whether a local authority was capable of maintaining an action to protect its reputation. In rejecting the authority's argument, Lord Keith stated, after discussing other types of corporation's ability to sue, stated:

> There are, however, features of a local authority which may be regarded as distinguishing it from other types of corporation, whether trading or non-trading. The most important of these features is that it is a governmental body. Further, it is a democratically elected body, the electoral process nowadays being conducted almost exclusively on party political lines. It is of the highest public importance that a democratically elected governmental body, or indeed any governmental body, should be open to uninhibited public criticism. The threat of a civil action for defamation must inevitably have an inhibiting effect on freedom of speech. ...
>
> What has been described as 'the chilling effect' induced by the threat of civil actions for libel is very important. Quite often the facts which would justify a defamatory publication are known to be true, but admissible evidence capable of proving those facts is not available. This may prevent the publication of matters which it is very desirable to make public. ...
>
> I regard it as right for this House to lay down that, not only is there no public interest favouring the right of organs of government, whether central or local, to sue for libel, but that it is contrary to the public interest that they should have it. It is contrary to the public interest because, to admit such actions, would place an undesirable fetter on freedom of speech.

After citing Article 10 of the Convention on Human Rights, His Lordship continued:

> As regards the words 'necessary in a democratic society' in connection with the restrictions on the right to freedom of expression which may properly be prescribed by law, the jurisprudence of the European Court of Human Rights has established that 'necessary' requires the existence of a pressing social need, and that the restrictions should be no more than is proportionate to the legitimate aim pursued. The domestic courts have a 'margin of appreciation' based upon local knowledge of the needs of the society to which they belong. ...
>
> My Lords, I have reached my conclusion upon the common law of England without finding any need to rely upon the European convention. Lord Goff of Chievley in *AG v Guardian Newspapers Ltd (No 2)* [1988] 3 All ER 545 at 660, [1990] 1 AC 109 at 283–84 expressed the opinion that, in the field of freedom of speech, there was no difference in principle between English law on the subject and Article 10 of the Convention. I agree, and can only add that I find it satisfactory to be able to conclude that the common law of England is consistent with the obligations assumed by the Crown under the treaty in this particular field.

Their Lordships were unanimous. It should not be forgotten that any individual member of an organ of government is free to bring an action if the criticism of the government affects that person's reputation, and the freedom of speech argument would not hold sway in such circumstances.

---

3 [1993] 1 All ER 1011.

THE MEANING OF DEFAMATORY?

We can do no better initially than consider the statement of Lord Atkin to discover what is meant by the word 'defamatory' in the case of *Sim v Stretch*.[4] In this case the housemaid of the plaintiff returned to the employment of the defendant, and the latter sent a telegram as follows:

> Edith has resumed her service with us today. Please send her possessions and the money you borrowed, also her wages to Old Barton-Sim.

The plaintiff alleged that the words were defamatory in that they suggested that the plaintiff had money difficulties and had borrowed from a servant. His Lordship commented:

> The question, then, is whether the words in their ordinary signification are capable of being defamatory. Judges and textbook writers alike have found difficulty in defining with precision the word 'defamatory'. The conventional phrase exposing the plaintiff to hatred, ridicule and contempt is probably too narrow. The question is complicated by having to consider the person or class of persons whose reaction to the publication is the test of the wrongful character of the words used. I do not intend to ask your Lordships to lay down a formal definition, but after collating the opinions of many authorities I propose in the present case the test: would the words tend to lower the plaintiff in the estimation of right-thinking members of society generally? Assuming such to be the test of whether words are defamatory or not there is no dispute as to the relative functions of judge and jury, of law and fact. It is well settled that the judge must decide whether the words are capable of a defamatory meaning. That is a question of law: is there evidence of a tort? If they are capable, then the jury is to decide whether they are in fact defamatory.

Turning to the facts of the case, His Lordship went on:

> It was said by the learned judge at the trial, and accepted by the two members of the Court of Appeal who affirmed the judgment, that the words were capable of conveying to anybody that the plaintiff had acted in a mean way, borrowing money from his own maid and not paying her as he was required to, and required to by telegram and also withholding her wages. With the greatest respect, that is imputing to the words a suggestion of meanness both in borrowing and in not repaying which I find it impossible to extract from their ordinary meaning. The sting is said to be in the borrowing ... I am at a loss to understand why a person's character should be lowered in anyone's estimation if he or she has borrowed from a domestic servant.

The other Law Lords agreed with this statement and conclusion.

An another alternative phrase which was mentioned in *Youssoupoff v MGM Ltd*[5] was whether the words caused the plaintiff to be 'shunned and avoided'.

It is clear that the lack of intention to defame is not a defence although, as we shall see, there is a statutory defence of 'innocent' publication. In *Cassidy v Daily Mirror Newspapers Ltd*[6] the newspaper published a photograph of a married man, referring to him by name and as having become engaged to a

4 [1936] 2 All ER 1237.

5 (1934) 50 TLR 581.

6 [1929] All ER Rep 117.

woman also in the photograph. The plaintiff, his wife, brought a successful libel action. Scrutton LJ said on this issue:

> In my view, since *Hulton & Co v Jones* it is impossible for the person publishing a statement which, to those who know certain facts, is capable of a defamatory meaning in regard to A to defend himself by saying, 'I never heard of A and did not mean to injure him'. If he publishes words reasonably capable of being read as relating directly or indirectly to A and to those who know the facts about A capable of a defamatory meaning, he must take the consequences of the defamatory inferences reasonably drawn from his words.
>
> It is said that this decision would seriously interfere with the reasonable conduct of newspapers. I do not agree. If newspapers, who have no more rights than private persons, publish statements which may become defamatory of other people without inquiry as to their truth, in order to make their paper attractive, they must take the consequences if, on subsequent inquiry, their statements are found to be untrue or capable of defamatory and unjustifiable inferences. ... To publish statements first and inquire into their truth afterwards may seem attractive and up to date. Only to publish after inquiry may be slow, but at any rate it would lead to accuracy and reliability.

Russell LJ commented that:

> Liability for libel does not depend on the intention of the defamer, but on the fact of defamation.

Greer LJ dissented, stating that in his view the alleged defamer must be aware of the extrinsic facts which render the word defamatory if he is to be liable.

As the test is related to what right-thinking people generally would understand of the words, it is not defamatory if the plaintiff is carrying out his duty as a citizen. For example, in the famous case of *Byrne v Deane*[7] a person gave information to the police relating to some illegal gambling machines on the premises of a golf club. Shortly after a notice was placed on the club notice board, the last two lines of which read:

> But he who gave the game away/May he byrnn in hell and rue the day.

The plaintiff alleged that this defamed, him suggesting that he was the disloyal informer. The majority of the Court of Appeal decided against the plaintiff, Greer LJ dissenting. Slesser LJ remarked as follows:

> Now, in my view, to say or allege of a man – and for this purpose, as my Lord has said, it does not matter whether the allegation is true or not true – that he has reported certain acts, wrongful in law, to the police, cannot possibly be said to be defamatory of him in the minds of the general public.
>
> We have to consider in this connection the *arbitrium boni*, the view which would be taken by the ordinary good and worthy subject of the King, and I have assigned to myself no other criterion than what a good and worthy subject of the King would think of some person of whom it had been said that he put the law in motion against wrongdoers, in considering that such a good and worthy subject would not consider such an allegation in itself to be defamatory.

Greene LJ was in broad agreement with the above.

7 [1937] 1 KB 818.

In *Lewis v Daily Telegraph Ltd*[8] two newspapers reported that the affairs of the plaintiffs were being investigated by the Fraud Squad. One of the issues raised was whether there was an extended meaning to the words. Lord Reid commented:

> What the ordinary man would infer without special knowledge has generally been called the natural and ordinary meaning of the words. But that expression is rather misleading in that it conceals the fact that there are two elements in it. Sometimes it is not necessary to go beyond the words themselves, as where the plaintiff has been called a thief or a murderer. But more often the sting is not so much in the words themselves as in what the ordinary man will infer from them and that is also regarded as part of their natural and ordinary meaning. Here there would be nothing libellous in saying that an inquiry into the appellants' affairs was proceeding: the inquiry might be by a statistician or other expert. The sting is in inferences drawn from the fact that it is the fraud squad which is making the inquiry.
>
> What the ordinary man, not avid for scandal, would read into the words complained of must be a matter of impression. I can only say that I do not think that he would infer guilt of fraud merely because an inquiry is on foot. And if that is so then it is the duty of the trial judge to direct the jury that it is for them to determine the meaning of the paragraph, but they must not hold it to impute guilt of fraud because as a matter of law the paragraph is not capable of having that meaning. So there was here, in my opinion, misdirection of the two juries sufficiently serious to require that there must be new trials.

Lord Hodson, also in favour of ordering a new trial, stated:

> Whether the words are capable of a defamatory meaning is for the judge, and where the words, whether on the face of them they are or are not innocent in themselves, bear a defamatory or more defamatory meaning because of extraneous facts known to those to whom the libel has been published, it is the duty of the judge to rule whether there is evidence of such extraneous facts fit to be left to the jury.
>
> It is in conjunction with secondary meanings that much of the difficulty surrounding the law of libel exists. These secondary meanings are covered by the word 'innuendo' which signifies pointing out what and who is meant by the words complained of. Who is meant raises no problem here, but what is meant is of necessity divided into two parts much discussed in this case. Libels are of infinite variety and the literal meaning of the words, even of such simple phrases as 'X is a thief', does not carry one very far, for they may have been spoken in play or other circumstances showing that they could not be taken by reasonable persons as imputing an accusation of theft. Conversely, to say that a man is a good advertiser only becomes capable of a defamatory meaning if coupled with proof, for example that he was a professional man whose reputation would suffer if such were believed of him.
>
> The first subdivision of the innuendo has lately been called the false innuendo, as it is no more than an elaboration or embroidering of the words used without proof of extraneous facts. The true innuendo is that which depends on extraneous facts which the plaintiff has to prove in order to give the words the secondary meaning of which he complains.

8 [1963] 2 All ER 151.

Another example of innuendo in the true sense, which must be pleaded and proved, is the case of *Tolley v Fry*[9] where the defendants issued an advertisement of their chocolates containing a caricature of the plaintiff golfer. The plaintiff alleged that this prostituted his reputation as an amateur sportsman in that it was suggested that he had agreed to the advertisement for reward. The majority of the House found for the plaintiff and allowed his appeal. Viscount Dunedin stated:

> I find that the caricature of the plaintiff, innocent itself as a caricature, is so to speak imbedded in the advertisement. It is held out as part of an advertisement, so that its presence there gives rise to speculation as to how it got there, or in other words provokes in the mind of the public an inference as to how and why the plaintiff's picture, caricatured as it was, became associated with a commercial advertisement. The inference that is suggested is that his consent was given either gratuitously or for a consideration to its appearance. Then it is said, and evidence on that point was given and not cross-examined to, that if that were so, the status of the plaintiff as an amateur golfer would be called in question. It seems to me that all this is within the province of a jury to determine. The idea of the inference in the circumstances is not so extravagant as to compel a judge to say it was so beside the mark that no jury ought to be allowed to consider it.

It goes without saying that the extrinsic facts which give the secondary meaning to the words must be known to the person to whom the libel is published.

DEFAMATORY OF THE PLAINTIFF

The plaintiff has to establish that the words in question are defamatory of him. It was held in *Morgan v Odhams Press Ltd*[10] that there need not be any 'key or pointer' or 'peg' in the relevant statement as a means of identifying the plaintiff. In that case an article was published by one of the defendants stating that a key witness in a dog-doping scandal had been forced to hide for safety reasons. It was suggested that she had been kidnapped by the gang involved after making a statement to the police, and had been kept at an address in Finchley but eventually set free. No one was mentioned by name except the witness. The witness had stayed in the plaintiff's flat in Willesden for a short period around the same time as the alleged kidnapping. The House, by a majority, held that there were no grounds for holding that the article could not reasonably be taken to refer to the plaintiff, and the judge had rightly left the issue to the jury. In *Hulton v Jones*[11] the defendant published a defamatory article about a named person who was though to be fictitious. The name was that of the plaintiff, Artemus Jones. Lord Loreburn LC gave the main judgment which was agreed with by his colleagues in the House. He observed:

> Libel is a tortious act. What does the tort consist in? It consists in using language which others, knowing the circumstances, would reasonably think to be defamatory of the person complaining of and injured by it. A person charged with libel cannot defend himself by showing that he intended, in his own breast,

9 [1931] AC 33.

10 [1971] 1 WLR 1239.

11 [1910] AC 21.

> not to defame, or that he intended not to defame the plaintiff, if in fact he did both, he has nonetheless imputed something disgraceful and has none the less injured the plaintiff. A man in good faith may publish a libel believing it to be true, and it may be found by the jury that he acted in good faith believing it to be true, and reasonably believing it to be true, but that in fact the statement was false. Under those circumstances he has no defence to the action, however excellent his intention. If the intention of the writer be immaterial in considering whether the matter written is defamatory, I do not see why it need be relevant in considering whether it is defamatory of the plaintiff.

The problem was ever so slightly different in *Newstead v London Express Newspaper Ltd*[12] where the defendants published a report about a 30 year old man called Harold Newstead being a bigamist. The plaintiff was of the same age and with exactly the same name living in the same area, Camberwell. The other person really did exist but the Court of Appeal still found for the plaintiff. Sir Wilfrid Greene MR stated:

> After giving careful consideration to the matter, I am unable to hold that the fact that the defamatory words are true of A makes it as a matter of law impossible for them to be defamatory of B, which was in substance the main argument on behalf of the appellants. At first sight, this looks as though it would lead to great hardship, but the hardships are in practice not so serious as might appear, at any rate in the case of statements which are *ex facie* defamatory. Persons who make statements of this character may not unreasonably be expected, when describing the person of whom they are made, to identify that person so closely as to make it very unlikely that a judge would hold them to be reasonably capable of referring to someone else, or that a jury would hold that they did so refer. This is particularly so in the case of statements which purport to deal with actual facts. If there is a risk of coincidence, it ought, I think, in reason to be borne, not by the innocent party to whom the words are held to refer, but by the party who puts them into circulation. In matters of fiction, there is no doubt more room for hardship. Even in the cases of matters of fact it is no doubt possible to construct imaginary facts which would lead to hardship. There may also be hardship if words, not on their faces defamatory, are true of A but are reasonably understood by some as referring to B, and, as applied to B, are defamatory. Such cases, however, must be rare.

Defamation of a class is not possible as there is normally nobody identifiable who may sue.

Section 4 Defamation Act 1952 provides a defence in relation to both libel and slander as follows:

> (1) A person who has published words alleged to be defamatory of another person may, if he claims that the words were published by him innocently in relation to that other person, make an offer of amends under this section; and in any such case–
>
> (a) if the offer is accepted by the party aggrieved and is duly performed, no proceedings for libel or slander shall be taken or continued by that party against the person making the offer in respect of the publication in question (but without prejudice to any cause of action against any other person jointly responsible for that publication);

12 [1939] 4 All ER 319.

(b) if the offer is not accepted by the party aggrieved, then, except as otherwise provided by this section, it shall be a defence, in any proceedings by him for libel or slander against the person making the offer in respect of the publication in question, to prove that the words complained of were published by the defendant innocently in relation to the plaintiff and that the offer was made as soon as practicable after the defendant received notice that they were or might be defamatory of the plaintiff, and has not been withdrawn.

(2) An offer of amends under this section must be expressed to be made for the purposes of [this section and must be accompanied by an affidavit specifying] the facts relied upon by the person making it to show that the words in question were published by him innocently in relation to the party aggrieved; and for the purposes of a defence under paragraph (b) of subsection (1) of this section no evidence, other than evidence of facts specified in the affidavit, shall be admissible on behalf of that person to prove that the words were so published.

(3) An offer of amends under this section shall be understood to mean an offer–

(a) in any case, to publish or join in the publication of a suitable correction of the words complained of, and a sufficient apology to the party aggrieved in respect of those words;

(b) where copies of a document or record containing the said words have been distributed by or with the knowledge of the person making the offer, to take such steps as are reasonably practicable on his part for notifying persons to whom copies have been so distributed that the words are alleged to be defamatory of the party aggrieved.

(4) Where an offer of amends under this section is accepted by the party aggrieved–

(a) any question as to the steps to be taken in fulfilment of the offer as so accepted shall in default of agreement between the parties be referred to and determined by the High Court, whose decision thereon shall be final;

(b) the power of the court to make orders as to costs on proceedings by the party aggrieved against the person making the offer in respect of the publication in question, or in proceedings in respect of the offer under paragraph (a) of this subsection, shall include power to order the payment by the person making the offer to the party aggrieved of costs on an indemnity basis and any expenses reasonably incurred or to be incurred by that party in consequence of the publication in question;

and if no such proceedings as aforesaid are taken, the High Court may, upon application made by the party aggrieved, make any such order for the payment of such costs and expenses as aforesaid as could be made in such proceedings.

(5) For the purposes of this section words shall be treated as published by one person (in this subsection referred to as the publisher) innocently in relation to another person if and only if the following conditions are satisfied, that is to say–

(a) that the publisher did not intend to publish them of and concerning that other person, and did not know of circumstances by virtue of which they might be understood to refer to him; or

(b) that the words were not defamatory on the face of them, and the publisher did not know of circumstances by virtue of which they might be understood to be defamatory of that other person;

and in either case that the publisher exercised all reasonable care in relation to the publication; and any reference in this subsection to the publisher shall be construed as including a reference to any servant or agent of his who was concerned with the contents of the publication.

(6) Paragraph (b) of subsection (1) of this section shall not apply in relation to the publication by any person of words of which he is not the author unless he proves that the words were written by the author without malice.

This section is clearly designed to deal with the situations discussed in the above cases, but it should be emphasised that the burden is on the defendant to satisfy the court that he is within the defence, otherwise the apparently harsh rules established in the above cases will apply.

PUBLICATION

The tort of defamation protects the reputation of the plaintiff in the eyes of others and therefore there must be publication of the libel or slander to some person other than the plaintiff. Where the defamatory statement is contained in a letter or in circumstances where it was intended for the eyes or ears of the plaintiff only but it is read or heard by a third party, the test of whether there has been publication is that established in the case of *Theaker v Richarson*,[13] where the defendant wrote a defamatory letter to the plaintiff. The letter was read by the plaintiff's husband who opened it thinking it was an election address. The majority of the Court of Appeal found for the plaintiff in holding that it was a proper question of fact for the jury as to whether there had been publication in these circumstances. Pearson LJ put the question in this way:

> The plaintiff's husband, acting carelessly and thoughtlessly but meaning no harm, picked up and opened and began to read the letter. Was his conduct unusual, out of the ordinary and not reasonably to be anticipated, or was it something which could quite easily and naturally happen in the ordinary course of events? In my judgment that is a fair formulation of the question, and, when so formulated, it is seen to be a question of fact which, in a trial with a jury, who have observed the witnesses giving evidence and have and are expected to use their own common sense and knowledge of the world, and perhaps some particular knowledge (if they have it) of the locality concerned and the ways of its inhabitants ...

For example, as was held in *Huth v Huth*,[14] it would not be reasonably anticipated that a butler would read a letter in such circumstances and there would be no publication in that event. A person other than the author of the statement may of course be liable for publishing the libel. In *Byrne v Deane* it was said that there had been publication by the secretary of the golf club by not removing the unauthorised notice in question from the notice board. It will be recalled that liability, however, was not established in that case because the court held that the statement was not capable of a defamatory meaning.

---

13 [1906] 1 WLR 151.

14 [1915] 2 KB 32.

At common law there is a defence of innocent dissemination for people such as newsagents, libraries and booksellers who are considered to be mere mechanical distributors of the libel. It has been said that they may have a defence if:

(a) they were innocent of any knowledge of the libel contained in the work; and
(b) there was nothing in the work or in the circumstances in which it came to them or was disseminated by them which ought to have led them to suppose it contained a libel; and
(c) that when the work was disseminated by them, it was not by negligence on their part that they were unaware that it contained the libel.[15]

Difference between libel and slander

Slander normally takes the form of the spoken word whereas libel is considered to be defamation in a more permanent form. In *Monson v Tussauds*[16] the placing of a wax model of the plaintiff amongst models of other people, one of whom was a convicted murderer, was said to be capable of being libel. Lopes LJ commented:

> Libels are generally in writing or printing, but this is not necessary; the defamatory matter may be conveyed in some other permanent form. For instance, a statue, a caricature, an effigy, chalk marks upon a wall, signs or pictures may constitute a libel.

In *Youssoupoff v MGM* it was held that a film, accompanied by a sound track containing the defamatory material, was libel. Slesser LJ commented:

> In my view, this action, as I have said, was properly framed in libel. There can be no doubt that, as far as the photographic part of the exhibition is concerned, that is a permanent matter to be seen by the eye, and is the proper subject of an action for libel, if defamatory. I regard the speech which is synchronised with the photographic reproduction and forms part of one complex, common exhibition as an ancillary circumstance part of the surroundings explaining that which is to be seen.

Section 166(1) Broadcasting Act 1990 provides:

> For the purposes of the law of libel and slander (including the law of criminal libel so far as it relates to the publication of defamatory matter) the publication of words in the course of any programme included in a programme service shall be treated as publication in permanent form.

By s 16(1) Defamation Act 1952 it is provided:

> Any reference in this Act to words shall be construed as including a reference to pictures, visual images, gestures and other methods of signifying meaning.

Additionally, by the Theatres Act 1968 it is provided:

> 4(1) For the purposes of the law of libel and slander (including the law of criminal libel so far as it relates to the publication of defamatory matter) the publication of words in the course of a play shall, subject to section 7 of this Act, be treated as a publication in a permanent form.

---

15 See *Vizetelly v Mudie's Select Library Ltd* [1900] 2 QB 170 at 180 *per* Romer LJ.

16 [1891–94] All ER Rep 1051.

4(3) In this section 'words' includes pictures, visual images, gestures and other methods of signifying meaning.

7(1) Nothing in sections 2 to 4 of this Act shall apply in relation to the performance of a play given on a domestic occasion in a private dwelling.

7(2) Nothing in sections 2 to 6 of this Act shall apply in relation to a performance of a play given solely or primarily for one or more of the following purposes, that is to say–

(a) rehearsal; or

(b) to enable:

(i) a record or cinematograph film to be made from or by means of the performance; or

(ii) the performance to be broadcast; or

(iii) the performance to be included in a cable programme service which is or does not require to be licensed; ...

There is some uncertainty about records and tape recordings as to whether they are libel or slander. As there is no communication until they are played there is a reasonable case for saying that they can only amount to slander. On the other hand they are in a more than just transient form thus suggesting libel is the appropriate action. Defamation whilst surfing the Internet is at present a possibility, although at the time of writing there are proposals to exempt the operators of such communications systems from the law of defamation, as well as broadcasters of live programmes in respect of statements on the air made by persons outside the broadcaster's control, eg chat shows.[17]

Arbitrary as some of the distinctions may appear, they are nonetheless important by virtue of the fact that libel is one of those rare torts which is actionable *per se*, whereas the sister tort of slander normally requires proof of damage. However, there are four situations in which slander is actionable *per se*, namely the imputation of a criminal offence punishable by imprisonment, the imputation of unchastity or adultery to any woman or girl (Slander of Women Act 1891), the imputation of an existing contagious disease, including those such as venereal disease, leprosy or plague and, finally, an imputation as to the plaintiff's competence or fitness in any office, profession, calling, trade or business. In the case of this latter exception, it is not now essential since s 2 of the 1952 Act was brought in, that the words should be spoken of the plaintiff in his office, calling etc. The removal of these distinctions was recommended some 20 years ago by the Faulks Committee whose report is still gathering dust.[18]

DEFENCES

It is proposed to look at the four defences of justification, absolute and qualified privilege, and fair comment in a reasonable amount of detail in this section. The defences are a mixture of common law and statutory rules as we shall see. We have already covered the unintentional defamation defence in s 4 of the 1952 Act, and the common law defence of innocent dissemination. It should be

17 See the Defamation Bill 1996.

18 Cmnd 5909, 1975.

noted, however, that there is a defence available to a newspaper which has published a libel without malice or gross negligence, and is prepared to publish an apology and to pay money into court by way of amends. A much under-used defence, it may be replaced by a new proposed defence in the current Defamation Bill (cll 2 to 4).

Justification

It is a compete defence if the defendant proves that the words complained of are true, even if she is actuated by malice. Malice may, however, be relevant where the defendant seeks to rely on a 'spent' conviction to justify his statement. If the plaintiff can prove malice, the defence will be defeated.[19] Section 5 Defamation Act 1952 provides:

> In an action for libel or slander in respect of words containing two or more distinct charges against the plaintiff, a defence of justification shall not fail by reason only that the truth of every charge is not proved if the words not proved to be true do not materially injure the plaintiff's reputation having regard to the truth of the remaining charges.

With regard to allegations concerning criminal convictions, s 13 Civil Evidence Act 1968 provides:

> (1) In an action for libel or slander in which a question whether a person did or did not commit a criminal offence is relevant to an issue arising in the action, proof that, at the time when that issue falls to be determined, that person stands convicted of that offence shall be conclusive evidence that he committed that offence; and his conviction thereof shall be admissible in evidence accordingly.
>
> (2) In any such action as aforesaid in which by virtue of this section a person is proved to have been convicted of an offence, the contents of any document which is admissible as evidence of the conviction, and the contents of the information, complaint, indictment or charge-sheet on which that person was convicted, shall, without prejudice to the reception of any other admissible evidence for the purpose of identifying the facts on which the conviction was based, be admissible in evidence for the purpose of identifying those facts.
>
> (3) For the purposes of this section a person shall be taken to stand convicted of an offence if but only if there subsists against him a conviction of that offence by or before a court in the United Kingdom or by a court-martial there or elsewhere.

Both the above provisions were introduced to circumvent difficulties placed in the defendant's way by the common law. In the case of the first, the defendant had to justify every allegation for his defence to succeed, and in the latter a defendant was required to establish that a conviction was rightly made against the plaintiff if justification was to be upheld as a defence. The defendant need only justify the so-called 'sting' of the libel.[20]

19 See s 8 Rehabilitation of Offenders Act 1974.

20 See *Alexander v North Eastern Rly Co* (1865) 6 B & S 340.

Absolute privilege

A defamatory false statement made on an occasion which is accorded absolute privilege is not actionable, even in cases where the plaintiff can clearly establish ill-will, spite or malice on the part of the defendant. Parliamentary proceedings are privileged, and so members are free from the fetter of defamation proceedings whilst making statements in the Houses in the public interest. Papers, reports, votes or proceedings published by order of either House are the subject of absolute privilege under s 1 Parliamentary Papers Act 1840.

Statements made in judicial proceedings are also absolutely privileged, and this includes those of the judiciary, counsel and witnesses, provided they do have some connection with the case. Communications between solicitor and client are absolutely privileged if they relate to proceedings, but may only attract qualified privilege if not so connected. Section 3 Law of Libel Amendment Act 1888 provides:

> A fair and accurate report in any newspaper of proceedings publicly heard before any court exercising judicial authority shall, if published contemporaneously with such proceedings, be privileged, provided nothing in this section shall authorise the publication of any blasphemous or indecent matter.

This has been extended to broadcast reports by radio or television from a station within the UK by s 9(2) Defamation Act 1952.

Statements by officers of state to each other during the course of their official duties are within the absolute privilege defence. In *Chatterton v Secretary of State for India*[21] it was held that a communication between the defendant and the Parliamentary Under-Secretary for India, which the plaintiff alleged defamed him, was absolutely privileged. The plaintiff's appeal was rejected by all three judges in the Court of Appeal. Lord Esher justified the decision by saying:

> What is the reason for the existence of this law? It does not exist for the benefit of the official. All judges have said that the ground of its existence is the injury to the public good which would result if such an inquiry were allowed as would be necessary if the action were maintainable. An inquiry would take away from the public official his freedom of action in a matter concerning the public welfare, because he would have to appear before a jury and be cross-examined as to his conduct. That would be contrary to the interest of the public, and the privilege is, therefore, absolute in regard to the contents of such a document as that upon which this action is founded.

This immunity extends to internal embassy memoranda of foreign states on the basis that it would be inappropriate to meddle in affairs of foreign states.[22]

Qualified privilege

In the case of *Adams v Ward*,[23] Lord Atkinson stated that a privileged occasion was one:

21 [1895–99] All ER Rep 1035.

22 See *Fayed v Al-Tajir* [1987] 2 All ER 396.

23 [1917] AC 309.

> ... where the person who makes the communication has an interest or a duty, legal, social or moral, to make it to the person to whom it is made, and the person to whom it is so made has a corresponding interest or duty to receive it. This reciprocity is essential.

The case of *Watt v Longsdon*[24] is one in which the issue of duty to communicate arose. The plaintiff was managing director of a company of which the defendant was also a director. The plaintiff was working overseas and one of the company's managers out there with him sent a letter to the defendant containing charges of drunkenness, immorality and dishonesty on the part of the plaintiff. The defendant, without waiting for corroboration, but believing the allegations to be true, showed the letter to the chairman of the board of directors and to the plaintiff's wife whom he knew well. The charges were untrue. Scrutton LJ stated:

> By the law of England there are occasions on which a person may make defamatory statements about another which are untrue without incurring any legal liability for his statements. These occasions are called privileged occasions. A reason frequently given for this privilege is that the allegation that the speaker has 'unlawfully and maliciously published' is displaced by proof that the speaker has either a duty or an interest to publish, and that this duty or interest confers the privilege. But communications made on these occasions may lose their privilege:
>
> (1) they may exceed the privilege of the occasion by going beyond the limits of the duty or interest, or
>
> (2) they may be published with express malice, so that the occasion is not being legitimately used, but abused ...
>
> The question whether the occasion was privileged is for the judge, and so far as 'duty' is concerned, the question is: was there a duty, legal, moral or social, to communicate? As to legal duty, the judge should have no difficulty – the judge should know the law; but as to moral or social duties of imperfect obligation, the task is far more troublesome. The judge has no evidence as to the view the community takes of moral or social duties.

Turning to the facts the judge continued:

> First, as to the communication between Longsdon and Singer, I think the case must proceed on the admission that, at all material times, Watt, Longsdon and Browne were in the employment of the same company, and the evidence afforded by the answer to the interrogatory put in by the plaintiff that Longsdon believed the statements in Browne's letter. In my view, on these facts there was a duty, both from a moral and material point of view, on Longsdon to communicate the letter to Singer, the chairman of his company, who, apart from questions of present employment, might be asked by Watt for a testimonial to a future employer. ...
>
> The communication to Mrs Watt stands on a different footing. I have no intention of writing an exhaustive treatise on the circumstances when a stranger or a friend should communicate to husband or wife information he receives as to the conduct of the other party to the marriage. I am clear that it is impossible to say he is always under a moral or social duty to do so; it is equally impossible to say he is never under such a duty. It must depend on the circumstances of each case, the nature of the information and the relation of the speaker and recipient. It

24 [1930] KB 130.

> cannot, on the one hand, be the duty even of a friend to communicate all the gossip the friend hears at men's clubs or women's bridge parties to one of the spouses affected. ... I have come to the conclusion that there was not a moral or social duty in Longsdon to make this communication to Mrs Watt such as to make the occasion privileged, and that there must be a new trial so far as it relates to the claim for publication of a libel to Mrs Watt.

The other two judges were in agreement with this view of the case.

Another illustration of the operation of the defence is *Beach v Freeson*,[25] in which the defendant Member of Parliament, having received a complaint from a constituent about the plaintiffs, a firm of solicitors practising in the constituency, wrote a letter to the Law Society, having received other complaints in the past about this firm, and also wrote to the Lord Chancellor. It was accepted that the letters were defamatory but the defendant successfully relied on qualified privilege. Geoffrey Lane J stated:

> There is no doubt at all on the evidence which I have heard that ... there has been a remarkable increase in the amount of work done by Members of Parliament outside the House of Commons on behalf of their constituents. The reasons for this increase are not altogether clear, but possibly it is that the private individual feels, increasingly, that he is at the mercy of huge, amorphous and unfeeling organisations who will pay no attention to his feeble cries unless they are amplified by someone in authority. The Member of Parliament in those circumstances is the obvious ally to whom to turn. It is a short step and, in my judgment, a proper one from there to hold that, in general, the Member of Parliament has both an interest and a duty to communicate to the appropriate body at the request of a constituent any substantial complaint from the constituent about a professional man in practice at the service of the public. ...
>
> The reciprocal interest or duty of the Law Society in receiving the complaint cannot, in the circumstances, be in doubt and therefore, so far as this publication to the Law Society was concerned, the occasion was the subject of qualified privilege.

As to the letter being sent to the Lord Chancellor, the judge continued:

> ... the lack of any direct power to discipline or punish does not mean that the Lord Chancellor has no interest in the complaint. It may be that the nature of the interest is difficult to define, but he is sufficiently concerned in the proper behaviour of solicitors; in solicitors as potential holders of judicial office; in the expeditious prosecution of litigation and in ensuring that litigants are honestly and conscientiously advised, to give him the necessary interest to protect the communication on occasions such as this with qualified privilege.

There are a number of different types of reports which attract a qualified privilege; eg s 3 Parliamentary Papers Act 1840 provides:

> In proceedings for printing any extract or abstract of a paper, it may be shown that such extract was *bona fide* made. ... It shall be lawful in any civil or criminal proceeding to be commenced or prosecuted for printing any extract from, or abstract of, such report, paper, votes or proceedings, to give in evidence ... such report, paper, votes, or proceedings, and to show that such extract or abstract was published *bona fide* and without malice; and if such shall be the opinion of the jury, a verdict of not guilty shall be entered for the defendant or defendants.

25 [1972] 1 QB 14.

Section 9(1) Defamation Act 1952 provides:

> Section 3 of the Parliamentary Papers Act 1840 (which confers protection in respect of proceedings for printing extracts from or abstracts of parliamentary papers) shall have effect as if the reference to printing included a reference to broadcasting by means of wireless telegraphy.

At common law, fair and accurate reports of Parliamentary proceedings attract qualified privilege.[26] The same applies to judicial proceedings held in public in the UK.

Section 7 Defamation Act 1952 (as amended by s 166(3) Broadcasting Act 1990 to cover programme services) provides as follows:

> (1) Subject to the provisions of this section, the publication in a newspaper of any such report or other matter as is mentioned in the Schedule to this Act shall be privileged unless the publication is proved to be made with malice.
>
> (2) In an action for libel in respect of the publication of any such report or matter as is mentioned in Part II of the Schedule to this Act, the provisions of this section shall not be a defence if it is proved that the defendant has been requested by the plaintiff to publish in the newspaper in which the original publication was made a reasonable letter or statement by way of explanation or contradiction, and has refused or neglected to do so, or has done so in a manner not adequate or not reasonable having regard to all the circumstances.
>
> (3) Nothing in this section shall be construed as protecting the publication of any matter, the publication of which is prohibited by law, or of any matter which is not of public concern and the publication of which is not for the public benefit.
>
> (4) Nothing in this section shall be construed as limiting or abridging any privilege subsisting (otherwise than by virtue of section 4 of the Law of Libel Amendment Act 1888) immediately before the commencement of this Act.
>
> (5) In this section the expression 'newspaper' means any paper containing public news or observations thereon, or consisting wholly or mainly of advertisements, which is printed for sale and is published in the United Kingdom either periodically or in parts or numbers not exceeding 36 days.
>
> *Schedule*
>
> *Part 1 – Statements privileged without explanation or contradiction*
>
> 1 A fair and accurate report of any proceedings in public of the legislature of any part of Her Majesty's dominions outside Great Britain.
>
> 2 A fair and accurate report of any proceedings in public of an international organisation of which the United Kingdom or Her Majesty's Government in the United Kingdom is a member, or of any international conference to which that Government sends a representative.
>
> 3 A fair and accurate report of any proceedings in public of an international court.
>
> 4 A fair and accurate report of any proceedings before a court exercising jurisdiction throughout any part of Her Majesty's dominions outside the United Kingdom under the Naval Discipline Act 1957, the Army Act 1955 or the Air Force Act 1955.

26 See *Wason v Walter* (1868) LR 4 QB 73.

5 A fair and accurate report of any proceedings in public of a body or person appointed to hold public inquiry by the government or legislature of any part of Her Majesty's dominions outside the United Kingdom.

6 A fair and accurate copy of or extract from any register kept in pursuance of any Act of Parliament which is open to inspection by the public, or of any other document which is required by the law of any part of the United Kingdom to be open to inspection by the public.

7 A notice or advertisement published by or on the authority of any court within the United Kingdom or any judge or officer of such court.

Part II – Statements privileged subject to explanation or contradiction.

8 A fair and accurate report of the findings or decision of any of the following associations, or of any committee or governing body thereof, that is to say–

(a) an association formed in the United Kingdom for the purpose of promoting or encouraging the exercise of or interest in any art, science, religion or learning, and empowered by its constitution to exercise control over or adjudicate upon matters of interest or concern to the association, or the actions or conduct of any persons subject to such control or adjudication;

(b) an association formed in the United Kingdom for the purpose of promoting or safeguarding the interest of any trade, business, industry or profession, or of the persons carrying on or engaged in any trade, business, industry or profession, and empowered by its constitution to exercise control over or adjudicate upon matters connected with the trade, business, industry or profession, or the actions or conduct of those persons;

(c) an association formed in the United Kingdom for the purpose of promoting or safeguarding the interests of any game, sport or pastime to the playing or exercise of which members of the public are invited or admitted, and empowered by its constitution to exercise control over or adjudicate upon persons connected with or taking part in the game, sport or pastime;

being a finding or decision relating to a person who is a member of or is subject by virtue of any contract to the control of the association.

9 A fair and accurate report of the proceedings at any public meeting held in the United Kingdom, that is to say, a meeting *bona fide* and lawfully held for a lawful purpose and for the furtherance or discussion of any matter of public concern, whether the admission to the meeting is general or restricted.

10 A fair and accurate report of the proceedings at any meeting or sitting in any part of the United Kingdom of–

(a) any local authority or committee of a local authority or local authorities;

(b) any justice or justices of the peace acting otherwise than as a court exercising judicial authority;

(c) any commission, tribunal, committee or person appointed for the purposes of any inquiry by Act of Parliament, by Her Majesty or by a Minister of the Crown;

(d) any person appointed by a local authority to hold a local inquiry in pursuance of any Act of Parliament;

(e) any other tribunal, board, committee or body constituted by or under, and exercising functions under, an Act of Parliament;

not being a meeting or sitting admission to which is denied to representatives of newspapers and other members of the public.

11 A fair and accurate report of the proceedings at a general meeting of any company or association constituted, registered or certified by or under any Act of Parliament or incorporated by Royal Charter, not being a private company within the meaning of the Companies Act 1948.

12 A copy or fair and accurate report or summary of any notice or other matter issued for the information of the public by or on behalf of any government department, officer of state, local authority or chief officer of police.

In *Blackshaw v Lord*[27] the issue was whether information obtained by the defendant reporter from an official of a government department over the telephone fell within para 12 above. Stephenson LJ commented on this point as follows:

> It may be right to include in the paragraph's ambit the kind of answers to telephoned interrogatories which Mr Lord, quite properly in the discharge of his duty to his newspaper, administered to [the official]. To exclude them in every case might unduly restrict the freedom of the press, and I did not understand counsel for the plaintiff to submit the contrary. But information which is put out on the initiative of a government department falls more easily within the paragraph than information pulled out of the mouth of an unwilling officer of the department, and I accept the argument of counsel for the plaintiff that not every statement of fact made to a journalist by a press officer of a government department is privileged, and what is certainly outside the privilege is assumption, inference, speculation on the part of the journalist. That is not authorised; that is not official.

The other two judges agreed with Stephenson LJ on this point.

An interesting case on common law privilege is *Watts v Times Newspapers Ltd*,[28] in which the defendants had published an article which suggested that the plaintiff had plagiarised a novel by another writer. The article was accompanied by a photograph meant to be of the plaintiff, but was actually of another person. At the request of the latter an apology was published which repeated the defamatory comment. The defendants argued that the statement in the apology was privileged, as did the solicitors for the other person whose photograph was mistakenly included in the article. It was held that the privilege did cover the solicitors for the third party. As to the defendants, Hirst LJ, with whom the other judges agreed, was of the view that the privilege did not extend to them as perpetrators of the libel in the first place.

Fair comment

The final defence to be considered is that of fair comment. The comment must be one of opinion on a matter of public interest which is honest. As we shall see the defence is negatived by proof of malice on the part of the defendant. In the case of *London Artists v Littler*,[29] the defendant wrote a letter suggesting that there was a plot by the plaintiffs to force the end of a run of a successful play

27 [1983] 2 All ER 311.

28 [1996] 1 All ER 152.

29 [1969] 2 QB 375.

produced by him. On the issue of public interest, Lord Denning MR commented:

> There is no definition in the books as to what is a matter of public interest. All we are given is a list of examples, coupled with the statement that it is for the judge and not the jury. I would not myself confine it within narrow limits. Whenever a matter is such as to affect people at large, so that they may be legitimately interested in, or concerned at, what is going on; or what may happen to them or to others; then it is a matter of public interest on which everyone is entitled to make fair comment. ... Here the public are legitimately *interested*. Many people are interested in what happens in the theatre. The stars welcome publicity. They want it put at the top of the bill. Producers wish it too. They like the house to be full. The comings and goings of performers are noticed everywhere. When three top stars and a satellite all give notice to leave at the same time – thus putting a successful play in peril – it is to my mind a matter of public interest in which everyone, press and all, are entitled to comment freely.

The defence failed, however, because the Court of Appeal came to the conclusion that the comment was not opinion but an assertion of fact in the circumstances.

In *Kemsley v Foot*[30] the defendant published an article critical of the plaintiff's conduct of a newspaper with which he had no connection. The article was published under the title 'Lower than Kemsley'. The defendant argued the defence of fair comment. Lord Porter, with whom their Lordships all agreed, said:

> It is not, as I understand, contended that the words contained in that article are fact and not comment; rather it is alleged that they are comment with no facts to support it. The question for your Lordships' decision is, therefore, whether a plea of fair comment is only permissible where the comment is accompanied by a statement of facts upon which the comment is made and to determine the particularity with which the facts must be stated. ...
>
> Can the defendant point to definite assertions of fact in the alleged libel upon which the comment is made and becomes; is the subject-matter indicated with sufficient clarity to justify comment being made; and was the comment actually made such as an honest, though prejudiced, man might make?
>
> Is there, then, in this case, sufficient subject-matter upon which to make comment? In an article which is concerned with what has been described as 'the Beaverbrook Press' and which is violently critical of Lord Beaverbrook's newspapers, it is, I think, a reasonable construction of the words 'Lower than Kemsley' that the allegation which is made is that the conduct of the Kemsley Press was similar to, but not quite so bad as, that of the press controlled by Lord Beaverbrook, ie it is possibly dishonest, but in any case low. The exact meaning, however, is not, in my opinion, for your Lordships but for the jury. All I desire to say is that there is subject-matter and it is at least arguable that the words directly complained of imply as fact that Lord Kemsley is in control of a number of known newspapers is in question.

30 [1952] AC 345.

MALICE

It has already been said that malice will defeat the defences both of qualified privilege and fair comment.[31] The leading case on malice is *Horrocks v Lowe*,[32] in which the defendant made defamatory statements about the plaintiff at a meeting of the town council, urging the plaintiff's removal from a particular committee. The judge held that the defendant acted out of personal spite and out of gross and unreasoning prejudice. Lord Diplock commented:

> In the instant case Mr Lowe's speech at the meeting of the Bolton Borough Council was on matters which were undoubtedly of local concern with one major exception, the only facts relied on as evidence from which express malice was to be inferred had reference to the contents of the speech itself, the circumstances in which the meeting was held and the material relating to the subject-matter of Mr Lowes' speech which was within his actual knowledge or available to him on enquiry. The one exception was his failure to apologise to Mr Horrocks when asked to do so two days later. A refusal to apologise is at best but tenuous evidence of malice, for it is consistent with a continuing belief in the truth of what he said. Stirling J found it to be so in the case of Mr Lowe.
>
> So the judge was left with no other material on which to found an inference of malice except the contents of the speech itself, the circumstances in which it was made and, of course, Mr Lowe's own evidence in the witness box. Where such is the case, the test of malice is very simple. It was laid down by Lord Esher himself, as Brett LJ in *Clark v Molyneux* (1877) 3 QBD 237. It is: has it been proved that the defendant did not honestly believe that what he said was true, ie was he either aware that it was not true or indifferent to the truth or falsity? ... All Lord Esher was saying was that such indifference to the truth or falsity of what was stated constituted malice even though it resulted from prejudice with regard to the subject-matter of the statement rather than with regard to the particular person defamed. But however gross, however unreasoning the prejudice, it does not destroy the privilege unless it has this result. If what it does is to cause the defendant honestly to believe what a more rational or impractical person would reject or doubt, he does not thereby lose protection of the privilege.

The House dismissed the plaintiff's appeal as it held that the privilege protected the defendant in the absence of any proof of malice.

DAMAGES

We shall see in the chapter on assessment of damages that an award of exemplary damages is possible in defamation cases. Quite apart from the controversy surrounding such awards, there has been considerable criticism of the high awards in libel cases in recent years. In the case of *Sutcliffe v Pressdram*,[33] the case in which *Private Eye* was found guilty of libelling the wife of Peter Sutcliffe, the so-called 'Yorkshire Ripper', the Court of Appeal ordered a new trial on the issue of damages on the basis that the jury's award was so

31 See *Thomas v Bradbury, Agnew & Co Ltd* [1906] 2 KB 627.

32 [1974] 1 All ER 662.

33 [1990] 1 All ER 269.

substantially in excess of what would be considered a reasonably appropriate award. Lord Donaldson MR observed:

> What is, I think, required, is some guidance to juries in terms which will assist them to appreciate the real value of large sums. It is, and must remain, a jury's duty to award lump sums by way of damages, but there is no reason why they should not be invited notionally to 'weigh' any sum which they have in mind to award.
>
> Whether the jury did so, and how it did so, would be a matter for them, but the judge could, I think, properly invite them to consider what the result would be in terms of weekly, monthly or annual income if the money was invested in a building society deposit account without touching the capital sum awarded, or, if they have in mind smaller sums, to consider what they could buy with it. Had that been done in the present case, and I stress that it would have represented a total departure from the existing practice, which he could not be expected to undertake, I think that the result would have been a very large award, but not as high as £600,000, and one with which this court would not have wished to interfere.

Since that case, the Court of Appeal has been given the power to intervene and substitute its own view of an appropriate award instead of ordering a new trial, by virtue of s 8 Courts and Legal Services Act 1990 and r 11(4) RSC Ord 59. This power was used in the case of *Rantzen v Mirror Group Newspapers (1986) Ltd*,[34] but interesting comments were made concerning Article 10 of the Convention mentioned earlier. The plaintiff in this case was awarded £250,000 in relation to articles which accused her of hypocrisy in her establishing 'Childline' to protect children from abuse. The damages were reduced to £110,000 by the appeal court. Neill LJ, giving the judgment of the court, made some interesting observations on what the jury should be told when considering their award. After deciding that the courts should subject 'large awards of damages to a more searching scrutiny than has been customary in the past'. He continued, after discussing the present state of the practice of advising the jury, as follows:

> It is for consideration whether this state of affairs should continue or whether the present practice conflicts with the principle enshrined in para (2) of Article 10 that restrictions on the exercise of freedom of expression should be prescribed by law. As was said in *Sunday Times v UK* (1979) 2 EHRR 245 at 271: 'A norm cannot be regarded as a "law" unless it is formulated with sufficient precision to enable the citizen to regulate his conduct, and to enable him to foresee, if need be with appropriate advice, the consequences which a given action may entail.'
>
> The matter can be approached in three stages:
>
> (a) reference to other jury awards in defamation cases;
>
> (b) references to (what we may call) s 8 awards by the Court of Appeal in defamation cases; and
>
> (c) references to conventional awards in personal injury actions.
>
> We are not persuaded that, at the present time, it would be right to allow references to be made to awards by juries in previous cases. Until very recently it had not been the practice to give juries other than minimal guidance as to how they should approach their task of awarding damages, and in these

34 [1993] 4 All ER 925.

> circumstances previous awards cannot be regarded as establishing a norm or standard to which reference can be made in the future.
>
> Awards made by the Court of Appeal in the exercise of its powers under s 8 of the 1990 Act and Ord 59, r 11(4) stand on a different footing. It seems to us that it must have been the intention of the framers of the 1990 Act that, over a period of time, the awards made by the Court of Appeal would provide a corpus to which reference could be made in subsequent cases. Any risk of over-citation would have to be controlled by the trial judge, but to prevent reference to such awards would seem to us to conflict with the principle that restrictions on freedom of expression should be 'prescribed by law'. The decisions of the Court of Appeal could be relied upon as establishing the prescribed norm.

The judge then turned to the thorny issue of whether reference should be made to awards in personal injury cases when advising the jury on damages in defamation cases. He continued:

> We see the force of the criticism of the present practice whereby a plaintiff in an action for libel may recover a much larger sum by way of damages for an injury to his reputation, which may prove transient in its effect, than the damages awarded for pain and suffering to the victim of an industrial accident who has lost an eye or the use of one or more of his limbs. We have come to the conclusion, however, that there is no satisfactory way in which the conventional awards in actions for damages for personal injuries can be used to provide guidance for an award in an action for defamation. Despite Mr Gray's submissions to the contrary, it seems to us that damages for defamation are intended at least in part as a vindication of the plaintiff to the public. ... We therefore feel bound to reject the proposal that the jury should be referred to awards made in actions involving serious personal injuries.
>
> It is to be hoped that, in the course of time, a series of decisions of the Court of Appeal will establish some standards as to what are, in the terms of s 8 of the 1990 Act, 'proper' awards. In the meantime, the jury should be invited to consider the purchasing power of any award which they make. In addition, they should be asked to ensure that any award they make is proportionate to the damage which the plaintiff has suffered, and is a sum which it is necessary to award him to provide adequate compensation and to re-establish his reputation.

On the facts the court decided that the jury's award to the plaintiff was excessive, bearing in mind that she had maintained a successful career as a television presenter throughout her ordeal.

Some reconsideration of the issue has even more recently taken place, presumably because juries still continue to award excessive amounts to famous people in libel actions. The matter came to the Court of Appeal once again in the case of *John v Mirror Group Newspapers Ltd*,[35] in which the defendants libelled the plaintiff, Elton John, in connection with allegations about his eating habits. The jury awarded £75,000 compensatory damages and £275,000 exemplary damages. The Court of Appeal reduced these to £25,000 and £50,000 respectively. Sir Thomas Bingham, in delivering the judgment of the court, had some interesting observations on what juries should be referred to assist them in making their deliberations. He stated:

> Any legal process should yield a successful plaintiff appropriate compensation, that is, compensation which is neither too much nor too little. That is so whether

35 [1996] 2 All ER 35.

the award is made by a judge or jury. No other result can be accepted as just. But there is continuing evidence of libel awards in sums which appear so large as to bear no relation to the ordinary values of life. ... We are persuaded by the arguments we have heard that the subject should be reconsidered. ...

In considering the criticisms of the present lack of guidance which is given to juries on the issue of compensatory damages, we have examined four possible changes in the present practice:

(a) *Reference to awards by other juries in comparable actions for defamation*

We wholly agree without the ruling in *Rantzen* that juries should not at present be reminded of previous libel awards by juries. Those awards will have been made in the absence of specific guidance by the judge and may themselves be very unreliable markers. ...

(b) *Reference to awards approved or substituted by the Court of Appeal*

We agree with the ruling in *Rantzen* that reference may be made to awards approved or made by the Court of Appeal. As and when a framework of awards is established, this will provide a valuable pointer to the appropriate level of award in the particular case. But it is plain that such a framework will not be established quickly ... if used with discretion, awards which have been subjected to scrutiny in the Court of Appeal should be able to provide *some* guidance to a jury called upon to fix an award in a later case.

(c) *Reference to damages in actions for personal injuries*

It has often and rightly been said that there can be no precise correlation between a personal injury and a sum of money. The same is true, perhaps even more true, of injury to reputation. There is force in the argument that to permit reference in libel cases to conventional levels of award in personal injury cases is simply to admit yet another incommensurable into the field of consideration. There is also weight in the argument, often heard, that conventional levels of award in personal injury cases are too low, and therefore provide an uncertain guide. But these awards would not be relied on as any exact guide, and of course there can be no precise correlation between a loss of a limb or of sight, or quadriplegia, and damage to reputation. But if these personal injuries respectively command conventional awards of, at most, about £52,000, £90,000 and £125,000 for pain and suffering and loss of amenity (of course excluding claims based on loss of earnings, the cost of care and other specific financial claims), juries may properly be asked to consider whether the injury to his reputation of which the plaintiff complains should fairly justify any greater compensation. The conventional compensatory scales in personal injury cases must be taken to represent fair compensation in such cases, unless and until those scales are amended by the courts or by Parliament.

It is, in our view, offensive to public opinion, and rightly so, that a defamation plaintiff should recover damages for injury to reputation greater, perhaps by a significant factor, than if that same plaintiff had been rendered a helpless cripple or an insensate vegetable. The time in our view has come when judges, and counsel, should be free to draw attention of juries to these comparisons.

(d) *Reference to an appropriate award and an appropriate bracket*

It has been the invariable practice in the past that neither counsel nor the judge may make any suggestion to the jury as what would be an appropriate award. ... We have come to the conclusion, however, that the reasons which have been given for prohibiting any reference to figures are unconvincing. Indeed, far from devaluing into an auction (and we do not see how it could) the process of mentioning figures would in our view induce a mood of realism on both sides.

On the issue of exemplary damages, the Master of the Rolls, after discussing the meaning of 'recklessness' in the context of defamation and employing the meaning attributed to that word in *Derry v Peek*, stated:

> It seems to us ... that the phrase 'not caring whether the publication be true or false', though an accurate formulation of the test of recklessness, is capable of leading to confusion because the words 'not caring' may be equated in the jury's minds with 'mere carelessness'. We therefore consider that, where exemplary damages are claimed, the jury should in future receive some additional guidance to make it clear that, before such damages can be awarded, the jury must be satisfied that the publisher had no genuine belief in the truth of what he published. The publisher must have suspected that the words were untrue and have deliberately refrained from taking obvious steps which, if taken, would have turned suspicion into certainty.

The Court of Appeal seems at great pains in this case to counteract the so-called 'chilling effect' that high awards of compensatory and exemplary damages have on the right to freedom of expression. In addition, there is the impression that large awards of damages to celebrities in respect of their reputation is obscene, and merely transfers more wealth to those already well off. The impact of the above measures will take some time to come through, if they do at all.

CHAPTER 13

DEFENCES

INTRODUCTION

In this chapter we shall look at two of the most important defences which have not been considered, in depth at least, in the previous chapters in the context of the specific torts, namely contributory negligence and *volenti non fit injuria*. Some defences have been discussed in context, as it makes obvious sense to deal with defences such as justification, fair comment and privilege in the defamation chapter. We have also discussed defences such as *ex turpi causa*, provocation and contributory negligence in the chapter on trespass to the person. The *volenti* defence has featured in a number of contexts already in the earlier chapters; in particular it was discussed in the context of sporting competitions and the requisite standard of care and the chapters including the discussion on occupier's liability and liability for animals. Nonetheless there was little opportunity in those contexts to discuss the detail of the defences.

In an important way there is a relationship between the two defences in that, although *volenti*, if successfully pleaded, amounts to a complete defence while contributory negligence is normally only a partial defence, both may be pleaded on similar facts. Bearing in mind that a conclusion of *volenti*, namely assent to the risk, is a complete rejection of the plaintiff's claim, it is perhaps not surprising that the defence has become increasingly of less value to defendants in circumstances where the judge can employ contributory negligence, thus not refusing the plaintiff any compensation at all.

VOLENTI NON FIT INJURIA

This defence is sometimes expressed as 'voluntary assumption of risk' and, as explained above, if successful prevents the plaintiff from recovering at all for the defendant's breach of duty. At the outset, it must be stressed that knowledge of the risk alone is not likely to be sufficient to establish the defence; there must also be, it is said, agreement by the plaintiff to accept that risk willingly. It has sometimes been explained in terms of the plaintiff agreeing to waive her rights in respect of the defendant's breach of duty, but this may lead to confusion with attempts to exclude liability, which is covered by different rules both at common law and statute as we saw in the chapter on occupier's liability. We shall look at cases in three areas below, namely, the application of the principle in the workplace, in relation to drunken drivers and, finally, in the context of rescuers.

In the workplace, the courts have generally shown themselves to be reluctant to allow the maxim to apply, bearing in mind the employer and employee relationship. A classic illustration of this reluctance is to be found in the House of Lords' case of *Smith v Baker*,[1] in which the plaintiff was employed by the defendants drilling holes in rock in the vicinity of a crane carrying stones

1 [1891] AC 325.

above his head. The plaintiff was very aware of the danger. He was injured when a stone fell and he sued his employers, who amongst others, raised the *volenti* defence. Lord Halsbury was of the following view:

> My Lords, I am of the opinion that the application of the maxim '*volenti non fit injuria*' is not warranted by these facts. I do not think that the plaintiff consented at all. His attention was fixed upon a drill, and while, therefore, he was unable to take precautions himself, a stone was negligently slung over his head without due precautions against its being permitted to fall. My Lords, I emphasise the word 'negligently' here because, with all respect, some of the judgments below appear to me to alternate between the question whether the plaintiff consented to the risk, and the question of whether there was any evidence of negligence to go to the jury, without definitely relying on either proposition. ...
>
> It appears to me that the proposition upon which the defendants must rely must be a far wider one than is involved in the maxim, '*volenti non fit injuria*'. I think they must go to the extent of saying that wherever a person knows there is a risk of injury to himself, he debars himself from any right of complaint if an injury should happen to him in doing anything which involves that risk. For this purpose, and in order to test this proposition, we have nothing to do with the relation of employer and employed. The maxim in its application in the law is not so limited; but where it applies, it applies equally to a stranger as to anyone else; and if applicable to the extent that is now insisted on, no person ever ought to have been awarded damages for being run over in London streets; for no one (at all events some years ago, before the admirable police regulations of later years) could have crossed London streets without knowing that there was a risk of being run over. ...
>
> I am of opinion myself that, in order to defeat the plaintiff's right by the application of the maxim relied on, who would otherwise be entitled to recover, the jury ought to be able to affirm that he consented to the particular thing being done which would involve the risk, and consented to take the risk upon himself. It is manifest that, if the proposition which I have just enunciated, be applied to this case, the maxim could here have no application. So far from consenting, the plaintiff did not even know of the particular operation that was being performed over his head until the injury happened to him, and consent, therefore, was out of the question.

Lord Watson commented:

> The maxim, '*volenti non fit injuria*', originally borrowed from the civil law, has lost much of its literal significance. A free citizen of Rome who, in concert with another, permitted himself to be sold as a slave in order that he might share in the price, suffered a serious injury; but he was in the strictest sense of the term *volens*. The same can hardly be said of a slater who is injured by a fall from the roof of a house, although he too may be *volens* in the sense of English law. In its application to questions between the employer and the employed, the maxim as now used generally imports that the workman had either expressly or by implication agreed to take upon himself the risks attendant upon the particular work which he was engaged to perform, and from which he has suffered injury. The question which has most frequently to be considered is not, whether he voluntarily and rashly exposed himself to injury, but whether he agreed that, if injury should befall him, the risk was to be his and not his masters. When, as is commonly the case, his acceptance or non-acceptance of the risk is left to implication, the workman cannot reasonably be held to have undertaken it unless he knew of its existence, and appreciated or had the means of appreciating its danger. But assuming that he did so, I am unable to accede to the suggestion that

> the mere fact of his continuing at his work, with such knowledge and appreciation, will in every case necessarily imply his acceptance. Whether it will have that effect or not depends, in my opinion, to a considerable extent upon the nature of the risk and the workman's connection with it, as well as upon other considerations which must vary according to the circumstances of each case.

By a majority of four to one the House held that the maxim did not apply to the facts of the case.

The principle's application in the employment context was further elaborated upon in the case of *Bowater v Rowley Regis Corpn*[2] in which the plaintiff, a carter employed by the defendants, was ordered to take out a horse which was known to have a tendency to run away. The plaintiff expressed his unhappiness at the time of the order. A few weeks later he was injured when the horse ran off and he was thrown from the cart. The Court of Appeal rejected the defence of *volenti*. Goddard LJ delivered the following statement:

> The maxim '*volenti non fit injuria*' is one which, in the case of master and servant, is to be applied with extreme caution. Indeed, I would say that it can hardly ever be applicable where the act to which the servant is said to be '*volens*' arises out of his ordinary duty, unless the work for which he is engaged is one in which danger is necessarily involved. Thus, a man in an explosives factory must take the risk of an explosion occurring in spite of the observance and provision of all statutory regulations and safeguards. A horse-breaker must take the risk of being thrown or injured by a restive or unbroken horse. It is an ordinary risk of his employment.
>
> A man, however, whose occupation is not one of a nature inherently dangerous but who is asked or required to undertake a risky operation, is in a different position. To rely on this doctrine the master must show that the servant undertook that the risk should be on him. It is not enough that, whether under protest or not, he obeyed an order or complied with a request which he might have declined as one which he was not bound either to obey or to comply with. It must be shown that he agreed that, what risk there was should lie on him. I do not mean that it must necessarily be shown that he contracted to take the risk, as that would involve consideration, though a simple way of showing that a servant did undertake a risk on himself would be that he was paid extra for so doing, and in some occupations '*danger money*' is often paid.

Scott LJ echoed the above comments in his judgment and Du Parcq LJ agreed also.

However, for an employment case in which the maxim did apply, there is the case of *ICI v Shatwell*,[3] in which the plaintiff and his brother were employed by the defendants as shot-firers. In spite of knowing of earlier accidents and being warned by their employers against a dangerous procedure, they proceeded to test a shot-firing circuit whilst standing in the open, not being prepared to wait for a colleague to return with some longer wires with which to carry out the test from a position of safety. An explosion occurred which injured the brothers. The plaintiff brought an action against the defendants as being vicariously liable for the breach of duty by his brother and fellow employee.

2 [1944] 1 KB 476.

3 [1964] 2 All ER 999.

The House of Lords decided that the *volenti* principle could be successfully relied upon by the defendants. Lord Reid observed:

> I think that most people would say, without stopping to think of the reason, that there is a world of difference between two fellow servants collaborating carelessly, so that the acts of both contribute to cause injury to one of them, and two fellow servants combining to disobey an order deliberately, though they know the risk involved. It seems reasonable that the injured man should recover some compensation in the former case, but not in the latter. If the law treats both as merely cases of negligence, it cannot draw a distinction. In my view the law does and should draw a distinction. In the first case only the partial defence of contributory negligence is available. In the second *volenti non fit injuria* is a complete defence, if the employer is not himself at fault and is only liable vicariously for the acts of the fellow servant. If the plaintiff invited or freely aided and abetted his fellow servant's disobedience, then he was *volens* in the fullest sense. He cannot complain of the resulting injury, either against the fellow servant or against the master, on the ground of his vicarious responsibility for his fellow servant's conduct.

Turning to the second category of cases in which the defence has commonly been raised, namely those involving the drivers of vehicles and their passengers, the first case to consider is that of *Dann v Hamilton*.[4] The plaintiff had allowed herself to be driven by the deceased knowing that the latter had been drinking alcohol which influenced his driving. She claimed damages for personal injuries sustained in the accident in which the deceased was killed. Asquith J in the High Court held in favour of the plaintiff. On the issue of the defence, he observed:

> The question is whether ... the rule or maxim '*volenti non fit injuria*' applies so as to defeat the plaintiff's claim. It has often been pointed out that the maxim says *volenti*, not *scienti*. A complete knowledge of the danger is in any event necessary, but such knowledge does not necessarily import consent. It is evidence of consent, weak or strong, according to circumstances. The question whether the plaintiff was *volens* is one of fact, to be determined on this amongst other evidence. ...
>
> I find it difficult to believe, although I know of no authority directly in point, that a person who voluntarily travels as passenger in a vehicle who is known by the passenger to have driven negligently in the past is *volens* as to future negligent acts of such driver, even though he could have chosen some other form of transport if he had wished. Then, to take the last step, suppose that such a driver is likely to drive negligently on the material occasion, not because he is known to the plaintiff to have driven negligently in the past, but because he is known to the plaintiff to be under the influence of drink. That is the present case. Ought the result to be any different? After much debate I have come to the conclusion that it should not, and that the plaintiff, by embarking in the car or re-entering it, with knowledge that through drink the driver had materially reduced his capacity for driving safely, did not impliedly consent to, or absolve the driver from, liability for any subsequent negligence on his part whereby she might suffer harm.
>
> There may be cases in which the drunkenness of the driver at the material time is so extreme and so glaring that, to accept a lift from him is like engaging in an intrinsically and obviously dangerous occupation, intermeddling with an

4 [1939] 1 KB 509.

> unexploded bomb or walking on the edge of an unfenced cliff. It is not necessary to decide whether, in such a case, the maxim *'volenti non fit injuria'* would apply, for in the present case I find as a fact that the driver's intoxication fell short of this degree.

The decision has not been without its critics and, in the light of the perceived changes in public attitudes to drunken driving, a different result might occur nowadays, although as we shall see below it has been held more recently that it might be contributory negligence to do what the plaintiff did in the above case.

The defence was raised and rejected in *Nettleship v Weston*,[5] in which, it will be recalled, the learner driver was held to be negligent towards her driving instructor. On the *volenti* defence, Lord Denning MR commented:

> Knowledge of the risk of injury is not enough. Nor is a willingness to take the risk of injury. Nothing will suffice short of an agreement to waive any claim for negligence. The plaintiff must agree, expressly or impliedly, to waive any claim for any injury that may befall him due to the lack of reasonable care by the defendant; or more accurately, due to the failure of the defendant to measure up to the standard of care that the law requires of him. ...
>
> Applying the doctrine in this case, it is clear that Mr Nettleship did not agree to waive any claim for injury that might befall him. Quite the contrary. He enquired about the insurance policy so as to make sure he was covered.

Megaw LJ emphasised the same point when rejecting the defence. Lord Denning and the other judge, Salmon LJ, held, however, that the instructor plaintiff was contributorily negligent and reduced his damages by 50% (Megaw LJ dissenting on this point).

It should be noted at this juncture that the *volenti* defence cannot be employed in relation to a passenger in a motor vehicle in circumstances where insurance cover for passengers is compulsory. This, it seems, applies not only to express agreements, eg the notice on the dashboard informing passengers ride at their own risk, but also to implied agreements.[6]

No such problems are encountered in circumstances where the road traffic legislation is inoperable, as is evidenced by the tragic case of *Morris v Murray*,[7] in which the plaintiff climbed aboard a plane belonging to the deceased. Both had been drinking heavily in the hours before the short and disastrous flight which killed the owner of the plane and seriously injured the plaintiff. The defence was successfully pleaded in this case. Fox LJ was quite forthright in his condemnation of the plaintiff's behaviour as follows:

> If he was capable of understanding what he was doing, then the fact is that he knowingly and willingly embarked on a flight with a drunken pilot. The flight served no useful purpose at all; there was no need or compulsion to join it; it was just entertainment. The plaintiff co-operated fully in the joint activity and did what he could to assist it. He agreed in evidence that he was anxious to start the engine and to fly. A clearer source of danger could hardly be imagined. The sort of errors of judgment which an intoxicated pilot may make are likely to have a disastrous result. The high probability was that Mr Murray was simply not fit to

5 [1971] 3 All ER 581.

6 See *Pitts v Hunt* [1990] 3 All ER 344 and s 149 Road Traffic Act 1988. It is likely, however, that a plea of *ex turpi causa* might succeed in such circumstances.

7 [1990] 3 All ER 801.

> fly an aircraft. Nothing that happened on the flight itself suggests otherwise, from the take-off down wind to the violence of the manoeuvres in flight.

The judge felt that the case fell squarely within the exception stated by Asquith J above. He continued, mentioning the possibility of reducing damages for contributory negligence:

> The judge held that the plaintiff was only 20% to blame (which seems to me to be too low) but, if that were increased to 50% so that the plaintiff's damages were reduced by half, both sides would be substantially penalised for their conduct. It seems to me, however, that the wild irresponsibility of the venture is such that the law should not intervene to award damages and should leave the loss where it falls. Flying is intrinsically dangerous and flying with a drunken pilot is great folly. The situation is very different from what has arisen in motoring cases.

Stocker LJ used similar language to convey the stupidity of the plaintiff's behaviour, but there seems no doubt that the decision of the Court of Appeal is designed to punish the plaintiff and deter others like him from becoming involved in such situations. However, the deceased was thought to be equally guilty but his estate is not penalised in any way by this decision. One other issue in the case was whether the plaintiff, in his drunken state, could appreciate the risk. In the end the court was of the view that he could, but it seems ironic that if the plaintiff was so drunk as to be unable to appreciate the danger involved, the maxim could not apply. Discussion on that is left, perhaps, for another day.

The other categories of cases in which the *volenti* defence appeared are the so-called rescue cases. In *Cutler v United Dairies (London) Ltd*[8] the plaintiff was injured whilst trying to help pacify the defendant's horse in a field adjoining his garden. The *volenti* defence succeeded. In the Court of Appeal, Scrutton LJ stated:

> I start with this: a horse bolts along a highway and a spectator runs out to stop it and is injured. Is the owner of the horse under any legal liability in those circumstances? On those facts it seems to me that he is not. The damage is the result of the accident. The man who was injured, in running out to stop the horse, must be presumed to know the ordinary consequences of his action, and the ordinary and natural consequence of a man trying to stop a runaway horse is that he may be knocked down and injured. A man is under no duty to run out and stop another person's horse, and, if he chooses to do an act, the ordinary consequence of which is that damage may ensue, the damage must be on his own head and not on that of the owner of the horse. This is sometimes put on the legal maxim *volenti non fit injuria*; sometimes it is put that a new cause has intervened between the original liability, if any, of the owner of the horse which has run away. That new cause is the action of the injured person, and that new cause intervening prevents liability attaching to the owner of the horse.

This may seem to be a far too sweeping statement in relation to the runaway horse situation. Slesser LJ was a little more circumspect than his fellow judge when he said:

> There may be cases, where, for example, a man sees his child in great peril in the street and, moved by paternal affection, dashes out and holds a runaway horse's head in order to save his child, and is injured; there is no *novus actus interveniens*.

8 [1933] 2 KB 297.

> Certainly a man is entitled, in order to save himself, to attempt to arrest a runaway horse. But in the present case the respondent of his own motion gets over a hedge in response to the words 'help, help!' and imperils his life or limbs by trying to hold the horse. However heroic and laudable may have been his act, it cannot properly be said that it was not in the legal sense the cause of the accident.

It is perhaps more appropriate to restrict the decision in this case to the fact that there was no immediate emergency as there might have been if the horse had been loose in a busy street, for example. In *Haynes v Harwood*[9] the Court of Appeal had occasion to reconsider the issue of the runaway horse within two years or so of *Cutler*. In the later case a policeman was injured in attempting to stop a horse out of control in the street. The court rejected the *volenti* defence categorically. After brief mention of some American cases, Greer LJ continued:

> The effect of the American cases is, I think, accurately stated in Professor Goodhart's article to which we have been referred on 'Rescue and Voluntary Assumption of Risk' in *Cambridge Law Journal*, vol v, p 192. In accurately summing up the American authorities ... the learned author says this (p 196): 'The American rule is that the doctrine of the assumption of risk does not apply where the plaintiff has, under an exigency caused by the defendant's wrongful misconduct, consciously and deliberately faced a risk, even of death, to rescue another from imminent danger of personal injury or death, whether the person endangered is one to whom he owes a duty of protection, as a member of his family, or is a mere stranger to whom he owes no such special duty.' In my judgment that passage not only represents the law of the United States, but I think it also accurately represents the law of this country. It is, of course, all the more applicable to this case because the man injured was a policeman who might readily be anticipated to do the very thing which he did, whereas the intervention of a mere passer-by is not so probable.

The judge observed that the decision in *Cutler* on the facts was right, but expressed reservations about Scrutton LJ's runaway horse example in that case. On the further issue of whether the act was impulsive or deliberate, the judge continued:

> I have considered the matter from the point of view of principle, and from that point of view I think it is quite immaterial whether the policeman acted on impulse or whether he acted from a sense of moral duty to do his best to prevent injury to people lawfully using the highway. If it were necessary to find that he acted on impulse, there is ample evidence of that in his own evidence that he did it on the spur of the moment, but I do not think that is essential. I think it would be absurd to say that, if a man deliberately incurs a risk, he is entitled to less protection than if he acts on a sudden impulse without thinking whether he should do so or not.

Maugham LJ added:

> In my opinion the police constable was not in any true sense a volunteer.

Roche LJ agreed with the views of his fellow judges. The rescuer, as was said earlier in the chapter on duty, is one of the law's favourite plaintiffs and has been since the case of *Haynes v Harwood*, although it has been held that a rescuer may be guilty of contributory negligence.[10]

---

9 [1935] 1 KB 146.

10 See *Harrison v BRB* [1981] 3 All ER 679.

CONTRIBUTORY NEGLIGENCE

Where the plaintiff's harm is brought about partly by the defendant's negligence and partly the plaintiff's own fault, the defence of contributory negligence may come into operation. It is now a partial defence since the enactment of the Law Reform (Contributory Negligence) Act 1945, but at common law it was considered to be a full defence. The result of this at common law was that the courts developed doctrines to avoid the severity of the rule that it was a full defence, such as 'the last clear opportunity rule' which applied where the evidence showed that the defendant had the last real chance to avoid the damage to the plaintiff. If applied, such a rule enabled the plaintiff to claim all his damage, but the 1945 Act would now mean that, in a similar situation, the court would apportion the responsibility for the harm as between the plaintiff and the defendant and reduce the damages to the plaintiff. Section 1(1) of the 1945 Act provides:

> Where any person suffers damage as the result partly of his own fault and partly of the fault of any other person or persons, a claim in respect of that damage shall not be defeated by reason of the fault of the person suffering the damages, but the damages recoverable in respect thereof shall be reduced to such extent as the court thinks just and equitable having regard to the claimant's share in the responsibility for the damages.

We are concerned in this chapter with the issue as to the scope of the defence in negligence actions.

Essentially, the question is one of causation. In *Jones v Livox Quarries Ltd*[11] the plaintiff, contrary to orders, jumped upon the back of a slow-moving tracked vehicle in the quarry. A dumper truck driven by an employee of the defendants negligently crashed into the rear of the vehicle on which the plaintiff was travelling and caused injury to the plaintiff. Denning LJ stated in his usual style:

> It can now safely be asserted that the doctrine of last opportunity is obsolete; and also that contributory negligence does not depend on the existence of a duty. But the troublesome problem of causation still remains to be solved.
>
> Although contributory negligence does not depend on a duty of care, it does depend on foreseeability. Just as actionable negligence requires the foreseeability of harm to others, so contributory negligence requires the foreseeability of harm to oneself. A person is guilty of contributory negligence if he ought reasonably the have foreseen that, if he did not act as a reasonable, prudent man, he might be hurt himself; and in his reckonings he must take into account the possibility of others being careless.
>
> Once negligence is proved, then no matter whether it is actionable negligence or contributory negligence, the person who is guilty of it must bear his proper share of responsibility for the consequences. The consequences do not depend on foreseeability, but on causation. The question in every case is: What faults were there which caused the damage? Was his fault one of them? The necessity of causation is shown by the word 'result' in section 1(1) of the Act of 1945. ...
>
> There is no clear guidance to be found in the books about causation. All that can be said is that causes are different from the circumstances in which, or on which,

11 [1952] 2 QB 608.

> they operate. The line between the two depends on the facts of each case. It is a matter of common sense more than anything else. In the present case, as the argument of Mr Arthian Davies proceeded, it seemed to me that he sought to make foreseeability the decisive test of causation. He relied on the trial judge's statement that a man who rode on the tow-bar of the traxcavator 'ran the risk of being thrown off and no other risk'. That is, I think, equivalent to saying that such a man could reasonably foresee that he might be thrown off the traxcavator, but not that he might be crushed between it and another vehicle.
>
> In my opinion, however, foreseeability is not the decisive test of causation. It is often a relevant factor, but it is not decisive. Even though the plaintiff did not foresee the possibility of being crushed, nevertheless in the ordinary plain common sense of this business the injury suffered by the plaintiff was due in part to the fact that he chose to ride on the tow-bar to lunch, instead of walking down on his feet. If he had been thrown off in the collision, Mr Arthian Davies admits that his injury would be partly due to his own negligence in riding on the tow-bar; but he says that, because he was crushed, and not thrown off, his injury is in no way due to it. That is too fine a distinction for me. I cannot believe that the purely fortuitous circumstance can make all the difference to the case.
>
> In order to illustrate this question of causation, I may say that if the plaintiff, whilst he was riding on the tow-bar, had been hit in the eye by a shot from a negligent sportsman, I should have thought that the plaintiff's negligence would in no way be a cause of his injury. It would only be the circumstance in which the cause operated; it would only be part of the history. But I cannot say that in the present case. The man's negligence here was so mixed up with his injury that it cannot be dismissed as mere history. His dangerous position on the vehicle was one of the causes of his damage. ...
>
> It all comes to this: if a man carelessly rides on a vehicle in a dangerous position, and subsequently there is a collision in which his injuries are made worse by reason of his position than they otherwise would have been, then his damage is partly the result of his own fault, and the damages recoverable by him fall to be reduced accordingly.

The other two judges in the Court of Appeal were of the same view and the plaintiff's damages were reduced by one-fifth.

The difficulties that can arise in applying the defence came to the fore in *Stapley v Gypsum Mines Ltd*,[12] in which the husband of the plaintiff was employed as a miner in the defendant's mine. He and another employee were ordered to bring down a part of the roof as it was unsafe. They could not do so, and decided to carry on working. The husband was killed when part of the roof caved in on him. A majority of the House of Lords found in favour of the plaintiff's widow on the basis that the fault of the other employee was attributable to the defendants, but that there was considerable contributory negligence.

Lord Reid, one of the majority, commented:

> The question must be determined by applying common sense to the facts of each particular case. One may find that, as a matter of history, several people have been at fault and that, if any one of them had acted properly, the accident would not have happened, but that does not mean that the accident must be regarded as having been caused by the faults of all of them. One must discriminate between

12 [1953] 2 All ER 478.

> those faults which must be discarded as being too remote and those which must not. Sometimes it is proper to discard all but one and to regard that one as the sole cause, but in other cases it is proper to regard two or more as having jointly caused the accident. I doubt whether any test can be applied generally.

His Lordship went on to ask:

> Was Dale's fault 'so much mixed up with the state of things brought about' by Stapley that 'in the ordinary plain common sense of this business' it must be regarded as having contributed to the accident? I can only say that I think it was, and that there was no 'sufficient separation of time, place or circumstance' between them to justify its being excluded. Dale's fault was one of omission rather than commission and it may often be impossible to say that, if a man had done what he omitted to do, the accident would certainly have been prevented. It is enough, in my judgment, if there is a sufficiently high degree of probability that the accident would have been prevented. I have already stated my view of the probabilities in this case and I think that it must lead to the conclusion that Dale's fault ought to be regarded as having contributed to the accident.

On the question of apportionment the House interfered with the judge's fifty-fifty split and decided that the deceased was more blameworthy than his colleague Dale by entering the danger area and continuing to work. The plaintiff's damages were reduced by 80% to reflect this.

The plaintiff may not contribute at all to the cause of the accident, but may nonetheless suffer a reduction in his damages if it can be shown that he has contributed to his damage. This is the issue which was raised in the crash helmet and seat belt cases in the 1970s. In *O'Connell v Jackson*[13] the plaintiff was penalised by his failure to wear a crash helmet in that his damages were reduced. Edmund Davies LJ delivered the judgment of the court, saying:

> It must be borne in mind that, for so much of the injuries and damage as would have resulted from the accident even if a crash helmet had been worn, the defendant is wholly to blame, and the plaintiff not at all. For the additional injuries and damage which would not have occurred if a crash helmet had been worn, the defendant, as solely responsible for the accident, must continue in substantial measure to be held liable, and it is only in that last field of additional injuries and damage that the contributory negligence has any relevance. It is not possible on the evidence to measure the extent of that field and then apportion that measure between the blameworthiness and causative potency of the acts and omissions of the parties. We can only cover the two stages in one stride and express the responsibility of the plaintiff in terms of a percentage of the whole. Giving the best consideration that we can to the whole matter, we assess the responsibility of the plaintiff in terms of 15% of the whole, and allow the appeal to the extent of reducing the damages to that extent.

In *Froom v Butcher*,[14] the Court of Appeal had a similar issue to decide in the case of failure to wear a seat belt by the plaintiff out of fear of being trapped in the car if involved in an accident. Lord Denning MR stated:

> The question is not what was the cause of the accident. It is rather what was the cause of the damage. In most accidents on the road the bad driving, which causes the accident, also causes the ensuing damage. But in seat belt cases the cause of

13 [1971] 3 All ER 129.

14 [1975] 3 All ER 520.

> the accident is one thing; the cause of the damage is another. The *accident* is caused by the bad driving. The *damage* is caused in part by the bad driving of the defendant, and in part by the failure of the plaintiff to wear a seat belt. If the plaintiff was to blame in not wearing a seat belt, the damage is in part the result of his own fault. He must bear some share in the responsibility for the damage and his damages fall to be reduced to such extent as the court thinks just and equitable. ...
>
> Sometimes the evidence will show that the failure made no difference. The damages would have been the same, even if a seat belt had been worn. In such cases the damages should not be reduced at all. At other times the evidence will show that the failure made all the difference. The damage would have been prevented altogether if a seat belt had been worn. In such cases I would suggest that the damages should be reduced by 25%. But often enough, the evidence will only show that the failure made a considerable difference. Some injuries to the head, for instance, would have been a good deal less severe if a seat belt had been worn, but there would still have been some injury to the head. In such a case I would suggest that the damages attributable to the failure to wear a seat belt should be reduced by 15%.

The other two appeal judges agreed with this statement.

In *Capps v Miller*[15] the Court of Appeal had to consider the apportionment for contributory negligence for failure to fasten securely the chin strap on a crash helmet. The three judges were of the view that this was not a similar degree of blameworthiness as is involved in not wearing one at all, and only reduced the damages by 10%.

We have already discussed the issue of whether the entering of a vehicle in the knowledge that the driver is intoxicated amounts to *volenti*. In *Owens v Brimmell*[16] the High Court judge, Tasker Watkins J, observed:

> Thus, it appears to me that there is widespread and weighty authority abroad for the proposition that a passenger may be guilty of contributory negligence if he rides with the driver of a car whom he knows has consumed alcohol in such quantity as is likely to impair to a dangerous degree that driver's capacity to drive properly and safely. So, also, may a passenger be guilty of contributory negligence if he, knowing that he is going to be driven in a car by his companion later, accompanies him on a bout of drinking which has the effect, eventually, of robbing the passenger of clear thought and perception and diminishes the driver's capacity to drive properly and carefully. Whether this principle can be relied on successfully is a question of fact and degree to be determined in the circumstances out of which the issue is said to arise. ...
>
> I think this is a clear case on the facts of contributory negligence, either on the basis that the minds of the plaintiff and the defendant, behaving recklessly, were equally befuddled by drink so as to rid them of clear thought and perception; or, as seems less likely, the plaintiff remained able to, and should have if, he actually did not, foresee the risk of being hurt by riding with the defendant as passenger. In such a case as this the degree of blameworthiness is not, in my opinion, equal. The driver, who alone controls the car and has it in him, therefore, to do whilst in drink great damage, must bear by far the greater responsibility. I, therefore, adjudge the plaintiff's contribution to be 20%.

15 [1989] 2 All ER 333.

16 [1976] 3 All ER 765.

The final issue is that of the standard of care expected of the plaintiff. In *Jones v Livox Quarries Ltd* Denning LJ, in the extract above, referred to the standard as that of a 'reasonable, prudent man'. What of children and others such as the old and the infirm? In *Gough v Thorne*[17] the plaintiff, a 13 year old girl waiting to cross the road with her brothers, was waved across the road by a stationary lorry. As she was crossing she was struck by a bubble car being driven at excessive speed. The judge found that she was guilty of contributory negligence. Lord Denning MR said:

> I am afraid that I cannot agree with the judge. A very young child cannot be guilty of contributory negligence. An older child may be; but it all depends on the circumstances. A judge should only find a child guilty of contributory negligence if he or she is of such an age as reasonably to be expected to take precautions for his or her own safety; and then he or she is only to be found guilty if blame should be attached to him or her. A child has not the road sense or the experience of his or her elders. He or she is not to be found guilty unless he or she is blameworthy.
>
> In this particular case I have no doubt that there was no blameworthiness to be attributed to the plaintiff at all. Here she was with her elder brother crossing a road. They had been beckoned on by the iorry driver. What more could you expect the child to do than to cross in pursuance of the beckoning? It is said by the judge that she ought to have leant forward and looked to see whether anything was coming. That indeed might be reasonably expected of a grown-up person with a fully developed road sense, but not a child of thirteen and a half.

The other two judges were plainly in sympathy with this approach and the appeal by the plaintiff was allowed.

Presumably, a similar approach would be taken in respect of the elderly or the infirm, in that one could not expect them in all circumstances to achieve a standard expected of the average fit person. In addition, it may be argued that the defendant driver has to make allowances for the fact that there are many children and infirm or elderly persons on our streets who may not be so careful for themselves as an ordinary adult might be. It should also be emphasised that, where the defendant's negligence places the plaintiff in a dilemma about taking evasive action, he is not allowed to be too critical about the fact that the plaintiff may have made a wrong choice in the circumstances.[18]

17 [1966] 3 All ER 398.

18 See *Jones v Boyce* (1816) 1 Stark 493.

CHAPTER 14

VICARIOUS LIABILITY

INTRODUCTION

The doctrine of vicarious liability is concerned with the legal responsibility of a person for the torts of another. The most important area in which the principle operates is that of employer and employee, where the former is considered liable for the torts of the latter committed during the course of his employment. There are also one or two other areas in which the principle is relevant, and these will also be considered below. We need to consider, albeit briefly, the justifications for the imposition of liability in such circumstances as the decision to place responsibility in law on a person, eg the employer of the acts of an employee. This is clearly an illustration of strict liability which is generally something, as we have already seen, the judiciary is reluctant to impose. It is has been said that the doctrine is based on considerations of 'social convenience and rough justice' as opposed to any legal principle.[1] Common justifications include the idea that the doctrine represents a response to the development of business organisations, as legal organisations in their own right as distinct from the human beings through whom they function. Another view is that the employer who takes the benefit of the activity of the employee must also shoulder the burden when things go wrong, a form of enterprise theory. Further, it is suggested that, even if there is no or little benefit to the employer in what the employee has done, the employer has a moral responsibility to any one harmed by the tort of the employee, having placed him/her in a position whereby s/he can exploit the third party plaintiff. None of these are completely satisfactory. The final justification is recognition for the point that, often, the employee is not worth suing and therefore the employer, having the deepest pocket, is in a better position to meet any claim. This loss distribution theory is hardly a principle of law, rather it is a description of what is happening if a court does employ a doctrine of vicarious liability in the employer/employee and other relationships.

We need to distinguish between direct liability of an employer and vicarious liability. Direct or primary liability arises where the duty in question is imposed personally on the employer and, although in practice the employer delegates the task of performing the duty to another, the duty is said in law to be 'non-delegable'. This explains why, in some circumstances, an employer, contrary to the general rule, is held liable for the work of an independent contractor. In the chapters on nuisance and strict liability we saw that there were certain duties involving extra-hazardous activities which fall into this category. Under the Occupiers' Liability Act 1957, as we have also already seen, the occupier may be held liable for the activities of an independent contractor in certain circumstances in relation to the selection of the contractor and the duty to supervise non-technical work. In these situations the distinction between employees and independent contractors is not crucial. However, generally this

1 See Lord Pearce in *ICI Ltd v Shatwell* [1965] 656 at 686.

is of major importance because of the general rule that an employer is not liable for the torts of his/her independent contractor. The first issue to consider, therefore, is who is an employee?

TEST FOR DECIDING WHO IS AN EMPLOYEE

There are a number of different contexts in which it is important to decide who is an employee, the doctrine of vicarious liability being only one. For example, it may be important to decide this issue for tax and social security reasons or for resolving issues of ownership of copyright. The extracts below are taken from a small selection of the many cases on this question of who is an employee.

One of the tests used is to assess the degree of control of the employer over the work carried out by the tortfeasor. In *Collins v Hertfordshire County Council*,[2] a final year medical student was employed as a resident junior house surgeon on a temporary basis and a surgeon was appointed to the staff to work two days a week for a fixed number of hours and to be on call at other times. Both were on the pay list of the hospital run by the defendant. Both were found guilty of negligence. In an action by the widow of the patient who died as a result of the negligence, one of the issues was whether the defendant authority was liable vicariously for the negligence. Hilbery J observed that:

> ... the distinction between the contract for services and the contract of service can be summarised in this way: in the one case the master can order or require what is to be done, while in the other case he can not only order or require what is to be done but how it shall be done.

Later, he said:

> Here, as part of the amenities of the hospital offered to a person resorting to it for treatment and accommodation, was the presence at all times on the premises of a resident medical officer. Treatment was given by a resident medical officer, and her acts done in the course of treatment of the patient are, in my view, acts for which the hospital is responsible.

On the issue of whether the defendant authority was liable for what the surgeon had or had not done, he continued:

> On the whole ... I think that [his] position was one where, if the test to be applied is whether the authorities could in any way control how he was to perform his duties, they certainly could not. I do not think that they could even say what he should or should not do. I think that he had only to say 'I will not do this operation', for them to have to put up with it. I do not think they could possibly have said that they could order him to do an operation which he said he would not do. I do not think that they could say what he was to do, and I am certain that they could not say how he should do it.

The judge concluded that he did not consider that the authority was vicariously liable for the negligence of the surgeon. A somewhat different approach was taken in *Cassidy v Ministry of Health*,[3] in which both Somervell LJ and Denning LJ were doubtful about Hilbery J's decision on the lack of liability of the surgeon. The plaintiff in this case had a problem with two fingers of the left

2 [1947] KB 598.

3 [1957] 1 All ER 574.

hand and had an operation done to remedy it. After the operation, the hand was bandaged and remained so for 14 days. The plaintiff complained of pain during this time but nothing was done. When the bandage was removed he was found to have four stiff fingers and the hand was almost useless. All three judges in the Court of Appeal found the hospital authorities liable for the post-operational treatment of the plaintiff. In his usual forthright manner, Denning LJ commented:

> In my opinion, authorities who run a hospital, be they local authorities, government boards or any other corporation, are in law under the self-same duty as the humblest doctor. Whenever they accept a patient for treatment, they must use reasonable care and skill to cure him of his ailment. The hospital authorities cannot, of course, do it by themselves. They have no ears to listen through the stethoscope, and no hands to hold the knife. They must do it by the staff they employ, and, if their staff are negligent in giving the treatment, they are just as liable for that negligence as is anyone one else who employs others to do his duties for him. ... It is no answer for them to say that their staff are professional men and women who do not tolerate any interference by their lay masters in the way they do their work. ... The reason why employers are liable in such cases is not because they can control the way in which the work is done – they often have insufficient knowledge to do so – but because they employ the staff and have chosen them for the task, and have in their hands the ultimate sanction for good conduct – the power of dismissal. ...
>
> The truth is that, in cases of negligence, the distinction between a contract of service and a contract for services only becomes of importance when it is sought to make the employer liable, not for breach of his own duty of care, but for some collateral act of negligence by those whom he employs. He cannot escape the consequences of a breach of his own duty, but he can escape responsibility for collateral or casual acts of negligence if he can show that the negligent person was employed, not under a contract of service, but only under a contract for services.
>
> Turning now to the facts in the present case, this is the position. The hospital authorities accepted the plaintiff as a patient for treatment, and it was their duty to treat him with reasonable care. They selected, employed and paid all the surgeons and nurses who looked after him. He had no say in their selection at all. If those surgeons and nurses did not treat him with proper care and skill, then the hospital authorities must answer for it, for it means that they themselves did not perform their duty to him. I decline to enter into the question of whether any of the surgeons were employed only under a contract for services, as distinct from a contract of service. The evidence is meagre enough in all conscience on that point, but the liability of the hospital authorities should not, and does not, depend on nice considerations of that sort. The plaintiff knew nothing of the terms on which they employed their staff. All that he knew was that he was treated in the hospital by people whom the hospital authorities appointed, and the hospital authorities must be answerable for the way in which he was treated.
>
> This conclusion has an important bearing on the question of evidence. If the plaintiff has to prove that some particular doctor or nurse was negligent, he would not be able to do it, but he was not put to that impossible task. He says: 'I went in to the hospital to be cured of two stiff fingers. I have come out with four stiff fingers, and my hand is useless. That should not have happened if due care had been used. Explain it if you can.' I am quite clearly of the opinion that that raises a *prima facie* case against the hospital authorities.

It seems from this case that the test to be applied had moved on from the straightforward 'control' test to an 'integration within the business' test. Denning LJ had already promoted this test in the earlier case of *Stevenson Jordan and Harrison Ltd v Macdonald and Evans*,[4] in which the Court of Appeal became involved in an ownership of copyright case. An accountant employed by the plaintiffs wrote a book based on his working experiences whilst under contract to them. The book also contained information covered by him in a series of public lectures prepared and given by him during his employment, as well as a chapter relating to material prepared by him for a special assignment in Manchester. The plaintiffs sought an injunction on the basis that they owned the copyright. The Court of Appeal only continued the injunction in relation to that part of the book based on the Manchester work.

Denning LJ observed as follows:

> It is often easy to recognise a contract of service when you see it, but difficult to say wherein the difference lies. A ship's master, a chauffeur and a reporter on the staff of a newspaper are all employed under a contract of service; but a ship's pilot, a taxi-man and a newspaper contributor are employed under a contract for services. One feature which seems to run through the instances is that, under a contract of service, a man is employed as part of the business, and his work is done as an integral part of the business; whereas, under a contract for services, his work, although done for the business, is not integrated into to it but is only accessory to it.
>
> It must be remembered, however, that a man who is employed under a contract of service may sometimes perform services outside the contract. A good illustration is *Byrne v Statist Co*,[5] where a man on the regular staff of a newspaper made a translation for the newspaper in his spare time. It was held that the translation was not made under a contract of service but under a contract for services. Other instances occur, as when a doctor on the staff of a hospital or a master on the staff of a school is employed under a contract of service to give lectures or lessons orally to students. If, for his own convenience, he puts the lectures into writing, then his written work is not done under the contract of service. It is most useful as an accessory to his contracted work, but it is not really part of it. The copyright is in him and not in his employers.
>
> The present case affords a good example of a mixed contract which is partly a contract of service and partly a contract for services. In so far as Mr Evans-Hemming prepared and wrote manuals for the use of a particular client of the company, he was doing it as part of his work as a servant of the company under a contract of service; but in so far as he prepared and wrote lectures for delivery to universities and to learned and professional societies, he was doing so as an accessory to the contract of service and not as part of it. The giving of lectures was no doubt very helpful to the company, in that it might serve directly as an advertisement for the company, and on that account the company paid Mr Evans-Hemming the expenses he incurred. The lectures were, in a sense, part of the services rendered by Mr Evans-Hemming for the benefit of the company. But they were in no sense part of his service. It follows that the copyright in the lectures was in Mr Evans-Hemming. The foreword or 'Manchester section' stands on a different footing, ... It was prepared and written as an integral part of

4 [1952] 1 TLR 101.

5 [1914] 1 KB 622.

> the business of the company and not merely as an accessory to it. The copyright in it, therefore, belonged to the company.

This approach is not without its critics, and in the next case we shall consider, *Ready Mixed Concrete (South East) Ltd v Minister of Pensions and National Insurance*,[6] MacKenna J commented that it raised more questions than he could answer. In this case the issue was whether a man was an employee for national insurance purposes. He had entered into a contract for the carriage of concrete with his employer which involved him taking, on hire-purchase, a lorry with an associated finance company. The essential detail of this contract is contained in one of the extracts from the judge's judgment. MacKenna J laid down the requirements for a contract of service to exist as follows:

> A contract of service exists if the following three conditions are fulfilled:
>
> (i) The servant agrees that, in consideration of a wage or other remuneration, he will provide his own work and skill in the performance of some service for his master.
>
> (ii) He agrees, expressly or impliedly, that in the performance of that service he will be subject to the other's control in a sufficient degree to make that other master.
>
> (iii) The other provisions of the contract are consistent with its being a contract of service. ...

In applying these to the contract in question, only (iii) needed any discussion as follows:

> I have shown earlier that Mr Latimer must make the vehicle available throughout the contract period. He must maintain it (and also the mixing unit) in working order, repairing and replacing worn parts when necessary. He must hire a competent driver to take his place if he should be, for any reason, unable to drive at any time when the company requires the services of the vehicle. He must do whatever is needed to make the vehicle (with a driver) available throughout the contract period. He must do all this, at his own expense, being paid a rate per mile for the quantity which he delivers. Theses are obligations more consistent, I think, with a contract of carriage than with one of service. The ownership of the assets, the chance of profit and the risk of loss in the business of carriage are his and not the company's. ...
>
> It is true that the company are given special powers to ensure that he runs his business efficiently, keeps proper accounts and pay his bills. I find nothing in these or any other provisions of the contract inconsistent with the company's contention that he is running a business of his own. A man does not cease to run a business on his own account because he agrees to run it efficiently or to accept another's superintendence.

The test applied here seems to be more concerned with the allocation of the financial risks in the venture than anything discussed in the previous cases.

The intention of the parties is clearly a factor but not a conclusive necessarily. In *Ferguson v John Dawson & Partners*[7] the plaintiff was injured whilst working as a general labourer for the defendants, and the issue was whether he was an employee so as to enable him to take the benefit of

6 [1968] 1 All ER 433.

7 [1976] 3 All ER 817.

regulations for the safety of employees. He was paid an hourly rate but no deductions were made by the employer, and it was stated that he was to be part of the 'lump labour force' as it was called. After discussing the issues of control and other aspects of the relationship, and concluding that it was one of employer and employee in reality, Megaw LJ turned to the issue of the intention of the parties:

> My own view would have been that a declaration by the parties, even if it be incorporated, in the contract, that the workman is to be, or is deemed to be, self-employed, an independent contractor ought to be wholly disregarded – not merely treated as not being conclusive – if the remainder of the contractual terms, governing the realities of the relationship, show the relationship of employer and employee. The Roman soldier would not have been a self-employed labourer, only sub-contractor, because of any verbal exchange between him and the centurion when he enlisted. I find difficulty in accepting that the parties, by a mere expression of intention as to what the legal relationship should be, can in any way influence the conclusion of law as to what the relationship is. I think that it would be contrary to the public interest if that were so; for it would mean that the parties, by their own whim, by the use of a verbal formula, unrelated to the reality of the relationship, could influence the decision on whom the responsibility for the safety of workmen, as imposed by statutory regulations, should rest. But, as I shall indicate later, I am prepared for the purposes of this appeal to accept a less stringent view of the law on this point, and my decision is therefore not based on that view.

Browne LJ sided with Megaw LJ with Lawton LJ dissenting. It would seem that the intention of the parties may be considered as a factor nonetheless in appropriate cases.

The question of who is, in law, responsible for the negligence of a worker, assumes major importance where the services of a worker are lent to another by his normal employer. The point arose before the House of Lords in *Mersey Docks and Harbour Board v Coggins and Griffith (Liverpool) Ltd*,[8] where the harbour authority lent a crane and a driver to a firm of stevedores for loading a ship. A third party was injured as a result of the negligence of the crane driver. Lord Macmillan commented:

> *Prima facie*, therefore, it was as the servant of the appellant board that [the driver] was driving the crane when it struck the plaintiff. But it is always open to an employer to show, if he can, that he has for a particular purpose or on a particular occasion temporarily transferred the services of one of his general servants to another party, so as to constitute him *pro hac vice* the servant of that other party with consequent liability for his negligent acts. The burden is on the general employer to establish that such a transference has been effected. Agreeing, as I do, with the trial judge and the Court of Appeal, I am of opinion that, on the facts of the present case, [the driver] was never so transferred from the service and control of the appellant board to the service and control of the stevedores as to render the stevedores answerable for the manner in which he carried on his work of driving the crane. The stevedores were entitled to tell him where to go, what parcels to lift and where to take them; that is to say, they could direct him as to what they wanted him to do; but they had no authority to tell him how he was to handle the crane in doing his work. In driving the crane,

8 [1947] AC 1.

> which was the appellant board's property confided to his charge, he was acting as the servant of the appellant board, not as the servant of the stevedores. It was not in consequence of any order of the stevedores that he negligently ran down the plaintiff; it was in consequence of his negligence in driving the crane, that is to say, in performing the work which he was employed by the appellant board to do.

Lord Porter was in agreement with the above and added:

> In the present case, if the appellants' contentions were to prevail, the crane driver would change his employer each time he embarked on the discharge of a fresh ship. Indeed, he might change it from day to day, without any say as to who his master should be, and with all the concomitant disadvantages of uncertainty as to who should be responsible for his insurance in respect of health, unemployment and accident. I cannot think that such a conclusion is to be drawn from the facts established.

The three remaining Law Lords agreed that the appeal should be dismissed.

Once it has been decided that a workman is an employee, the next issue is whether what he or she has done falls within the course of employment, so as to enable the victim of the tort to sue the employer.

COURSE OF EMPLOYMENT

There are a number of factors which must be considered in any decision on this issue, none of which by itself is regarded as conclusive. A distinction is drawn in the cases between the situation in which an employee does an unauthorised act where the employer is not thought to be liable, and one in which the employee does an authorised act in an unauthorised manner, where the employer is considered liable.

Time

The court will consider whether the tort was committed during working hours. In *Ruddiman v Smith*[9] the defendants sublet the lower floor of a building to the plaintiffs. The defendants' employees were allowed to use a toilet on the upper floor. Their foreman used the room some 10 minutes after his work for the day finished and negligently left the tap on, with the result that the plaintiffs' property was damaged. Lord Coleridge, finding for the plaintiff, stated:

> I agree that it is not for every act of negligence by a servant that a master is liable; but the master is liable if the act of negligence was done by the servant, either within the scope of his authority or as an incident to his employment. I say with some doubt, on the variety of cases decided, that it might have been within the scope of his employment to wash his hands; I should say it was, though I do not desire to place my judgment upon that, as I am clearly of opinion that it was an incident to his employment. In such houses there is generally some place for the clerks to hang up their hats, and a lavatory and so on; all these things are incident to the employment.

9 (1889) 60 LT 708.

By way of contrast, in *Stevens v Woodward*[10] the court decided in favour of the defendant employer. In this case a solicitor's clerk used the toilet solely for the use of the solicitors with similar consequences for the plaintiffs as in the previous case. Grove J stated:

> Although a definition is difficult, I should say that the act for which the master is to be held liable must be something incident to the employment for which the servant is hired, and which it is his duty to perform.
>
> ... what possible part of the clerk' employment could it be for him to go into his master's room to use his master's lavatory, and not only the water but probably his soap and towels solely for his, the clerk's, own purposes? What is there in any way incident to his employment as a clerk? I see nothing. The case seems to me the same as if he had gone up two or three flights of stairs and washed his hands in his master's bedroom. It is a voluntary trespass on the portion of the house private to his master. I do not use the word trespass in the sense of anything seriously wrong, but he had no business there at all. In doing that which his employment did not in any way authorise him to do, he negligently left the stop-cock open and the water escaped and did damage. I think there was nothing in this within the scope of his authority or incident to the ordinary duties of his employment.

Place

The place where the tort was committed may have some significance. In *Staton v National Coal Board*[11] the plaintiff's husband was employed by the defendants, and he was killed as a result of the negligence of another employee. The latter had completed his work for the day and was on his way to the pay office when the accident occurred. Finnemore J said:

> One has to approach questions of this sort in a common sense and realistic way. I confess that, apart from authority, I should have said that a man is still in the course of his employment when he goes to collect his wages on his master's premises. It seems to me to be wholly unrealistic to say that a man who has finished the manual work he was employed to do, and is walking across his master's premises to collect the wages which the master had contracted to pay him and for which he has done the work, has ceased to be in the course of his employment. There has been nothing to break the course of his employment. He has not gone off on any frolic of his own; he has not begun to do something for his own interest, for I think it is in the interest of the employer as well as the employee that a workman should receive his wages and receive them at a convenient place and at a convenient time.

The judge found for the plaintiff on that basis.

What was the employee employed to do?

This may often be a crucial question, as in *Poland v Parr and Sons*,[12] in which the employee saw a boy following his employer's cart loaded with sugar and thought the boy was pilfering. He gave the boy a blow with his hand on the

10 (1881) 16 QBD 318.

11 [1957] 1 WLR 893.

12 [1927] 1 KB 236.

back of his neck and the boy fell under the wheels of the cart. All members of the Court of Appeal found for the plaintiff. Atkin LJ commented as follows:

> The learned judge has not given enough weight to the consideration that a servant may be impliedly authorised, in an emergency, to do an act different in kind from the class of acts which he is expressly authorised or employed to do. Any servant is, as a general rule, authorised to do acts which are for the protection of his master's property. I say 'authorised' for, though there are acts which he is bound to do and for which therefore his master is responsible, it does not follow that the servant must be bound to do an act in order to make his master responsible for it. For example, a servant may be authorised to stop a runaway horse, but it would be hard to say that every servant was bound to do this, or that a servant commits a breach of his duty who refrains from doing so, or from extinguishing a fire. Some men may have the necessary courage to encounter such dangers, others may shrink from facing them. It cannot be said that all are bound to encounter them. Thus there is a class of acts which, in an emergency, a servant, though not bound, is authorised to do. And then the question is not whether the act of the servant was for the master's benefit, but whether it is an act of this class. I agree that, where the servant does more than the emergency requires, the excess may be so great as to take the act out of the class. For example, if Hall had fired a shot at the boy, the act might have been in the interest of his employers, but that is not the test. The question is whether the act is one of the class of acts which the servant is authorised to do in an emergency. In the present case the man Hall was doing an act of this class-namely, protecting his master's property, which was, or which he reasonably and honestly thought was, being pillaged. His mode of doing it was not, in my opinion, such as to take it out of the class. He was therefore doing an authorised act for which the respondents are responsible.

A contrasting case is that of *Warren v Henlys Ltd*,[13] in which the plaintiff was assaulted by the defendants' employee after the latter had mistakenly thought that the plaintiff was leaving a garage without paying for petrol. The defendant had been rude to the plaintiff who then threatened to report him to his employers, and the assault then took place. The High Court held that the employer was not liable. Hilbery J discussed the issue as follows:

> It seems to me that it was an act entirely of personal vengeance. He was personally inflicting punishment, and intentionally inflicting punishment, on the plaintiff because the plaintiff proposed to take a step which might affect [the employee] in his own personal affairs. It had no connection whatever with the discharge of any duty for the defendants. The act of assault by [the employee] was done by him in relation to a personal matter affecting his personal interests, and there is no evidence that it is otherwise.

Benefit of employer

The fact that the employee may not be acting for the benefit of the employer does not necessarily mean that s/he is acting outside the course of his/her employment. A clear illustration of an act obviously not for the benefit of the employer, or anyone else for that matter, is afforded by the case of *Century Insurance Co Ltd v Northern Ireland Transport Board*,[14] in which the employee was

13 [1948] 2 All ER 935.

14 [1942] 1 All ER 491.

delivering petrol when he threw a lighted match away and caused an explosion. All of their Lordships found against the employer. Lord Wright expressed his view as follows:

> The act of a workman in lighting his pipe or cigarette is an act done for his own comfort and convenience and at least, generally speaking, not for his employers' benefit. That last condition, however, is no longer essential to fix liability on the employer (*Lloyd v Grace Smith & Co*). Nor is such an act *prima facie* negligent. It is in itself both innocent and harmless. The negligence is to be found by considering the time when and the circumstances in which the match is struck and thrown down. The duty of the workman to his employer is so to conduct himself in doing his work as not negligently to cause damage either to the employer himself or his property or to third persons or their property, and thus to impose the same liability on the employer as if he had been doing the work himself and committed the negligent act.

In *Lloyd v Grace Smith & Co*[15] the employee, a solicitor's clerk, fraudulently persuaded a client of his employer's firm to transfer the deeds to her property to him, and he disposed of the property for his own benefit. The firm was held liable by the House of Lords. After lengthy discussion of the cases, Lord Macnaugthen stated:

> The only difference in my opinion between the case where the principal receives the benefit of the fraud, and the case where he does not, is that in the latter case the principal is liable for the wrong done to the person defrauded by his agent acting within the scope of his agency; in the former case he is liable on that ground and also on the ground that, by taking the benefit, he has adopted the act of his agent; he cannot approbate and reprobate.
>
> So much for the case as it stands upon the authorities. But putting aside the authorities altogether, I must say that it would be absolutely shocking to my mind if Mr Smith were not held liable for the fraud of his agent in the present case. When Mrs Lloyd put herself in the hands of the firm, how was she to know what the exact position of [the employee] was? Mr Smith carries on business under a style or firm which implies that unnamed persons are, or may be, included in its members. [The employee] speaks and acts as if he were one of the firm. He points to the deed boxes in the room and tells her that the deeds are quite safe in 'our' hands. Naturally enough she signs the documents he puts before her without trying to understand what they were. Who is to suffer for this man's fraud? The person who relied upon Mr Smith's accredited representative, or Mr Smith who put this rogue in his own place and clothed him with his own authority?
>
> If [the employee] had been a partner in fact, Mr Smith would have been liable for the fraud of [the employee] as his agent. it is a hardship to be liable for the fraud of your partner. But that is the law under the Partnership Act. It is less hardship for a principal to be held liable for the fraud of his agent or confidential servant. You can hardly ask your partner for a guarantee of his honesty; but there are such things as fidelity policies. You can insure the honesty of the person you employ; in a confidential situation you can make your confidential agent obtain a fidelity policy.

15 [1912] AC 716.

The basis for this principle appears to be the doctrine of apparent authority in agency law, and this is evident in the above extract when His Lordship talks of 'clothed him his own authority'.

The principle was also applied to cases of bailment where goods were entrusted to the employer who had a duty to keep them safe, and an employee made off with the goods. In *Morris v C W Martin & Sons Ltd*[16] the plaintiff's mink stole was sent to the defendants for cleaning. It was stolen by an employee. One of the issues before the Court of Appeal was that of vicarious liability. Lord Denning MR, after discussing the cases, concluded:

> From all these instances we may deduce the general proposition that, where a principal has in his charge the goods or belongings of another in such circumstances, that he is under a duty to take all reasonable precautions to protect them from theft or depredation, then if he entrusts that duty to a servant or agent, he is answerable for the manner in which that servant or agent carries out his duty. If the servant or agent is careless so that they are stolen by a stranger, the master is liable. So also if the servant or agent himself steals or makes away with them.

Salmon LJ expressed his view as follows:

> A bailee for reward is not answerable for a theft by any of his servants, but only for a theft by such of them as are deputed by him to discharge some part of his duty of taking reasonable care. A theft by any servant, who is not employed to do anything in relation to the goods bailed, is entirely outside the scope of his employment and cannot make the master liable. So in this case, if someone employed by the defendants in another depot had broken in and stolen the fur, the defendants would not have been liable. Similarly, in my view, if a clerk employed in the same depot has seized the opportunity of entering the room where the fur was kept and had stolen it, the defendants would not have been liable. The mere fact that the master, by employing a rogue, gives him the opportunity to steal or defraud does not make the master liable for his depredations. It might be otherwise if the master knew or ought to have known that his servant was dishonest, because then the master could be liable in negligence for employing him.

Diplock LJ held similar views.

Express prohibitions by employer

Even where the employer expressly forbids the employee to do a certain act, it may still be regarded as in the course of employment, provided the act does benefit the employer. A good illustration of this is the case of *Rose v Plenty*,[17] in which the employer expressly prohibited its milkmen from allowing children to help them on their rounds. Contrary to this instruction, the plaintiff was allowed to help and was injured by the negligent driving of the employee. The majority of the Court of Appeal found for the plaintiff. Lord Denning MR put it this way:

> In considering whether a prohibited act was within the course of the employment, it depends very much on the purpose for which it is done. If it is

16 [1965] 2 All ER 725.

17 [1976] 1 All ER 97.

> done for his employers' business, it is usually done in the course of his employment, even though it is a prohibited act. ... But if it is done for some purpose other than his master's business, as, for instance, giving a lift to a hitchhiker, such an act, if prohibited, may not be within the course of his employment. ... In the present case it seems to me that the course of Mr Plenty's employment was to distribute the milk, collect the money and to bring back bottles to the van. He got, or allowed this young boy, Leslie Rose, to do part of that business which was the employers' business. It seems to me that, although prohibited, it was conduct which was within the course of the employment; and on this ground I think that the judge was in error. I agree it is a nice point in these cases on which side of the line the case falls; but, as I understand the authorities, this case falls within those in which the prohibition affects only the conduct within the sphere of the employment, and did not take the conduct outside the sphere altogether.

Scarman LJ was of a similar view (Lawton LJ dissenting). It must be said that the case must have been very close to that line referred to by the Master of the Rolls.

Where there are no express instructions to employees about what they can and cannot do, nonetheless the act in question may be so far removed from what the employee is employed to do, that it cannot be regarded as in the course of employment. An illustration is the case of *Beard v London General Omnibus Co*,[18] in which the conductor of a bus drove the vehicle in an attempt to turn it round to get ready for the return journey. There was no evidence as to what the conductor could or could not do, and the plaintiff, injured by the negligent driving of the conductor, was held not to have established that the driving fell within the course of the employment.

AL Smith LJ was of the following view:

> I agree that, on a plaintiff giving evidence that the driver of an omnibus of the defendants was guilty of negligence, there would be a *prima facie* case that the omnibus was being driven by an authorised servant of the company within the scope of his employment. But that is not this case, for it was expressly opened to the jury as a case in which the omnibus was not being driven by the driver who was employed to drive it, but by the conductor. When a case is so opened, that negatives the presumption that the omnibus was being driven by the unauthorised agent of the company, because *prima facie* it is not the duty of the conductor to drive any more than it is the duty of the driver to take fares.

Vaughan Williams LJ thought that it was 'not necessarily beyond the functions of a conductor to take charge of an omnibus in the absence of the driver'. Nonetheless, he considered that the plaintiff had not discharged the burden on him to show authority for the driving by the conductor. Romer LJ agreed with his two fellow judges.

If the act of the employee is considered to be outside the course of employment, the employer may be liable directly for a failure to select suitable employees. In *Hudson v Ridge Manufacturing Co Ltd*[19] the plaintiff was injured when a prank by a fellow employee went wrong. The tendency of the errant

18 [1900] QB 530.

19 [1957] 2 All ER 229.

employee was known to the employers, and he had been frequently reprimanded for his behaviour. In finding for the plaintiff, Streatfield J said:

> As it seems to me, the matter is covered not by authority so much as principle. It is the duty of employers, for the safety of their employees, to have reasonably safe plant and machinery. It is their duty to have premises which are similarly reasonably safe. It is their duty to have a reasonably safe system of work. It is their duty to employ reasonably competent workmen. All of those duties exist at common law for the safety of the workmen, and if, for instance, it is found that a piece of plant or part of the premises is not reasonably safe, it is the duty of the employers to cure it, to make it safe and to remove that source of danger. In the same way, if the system of working is found, in practice, to be beset with dangers, it is the duty of the employers to evolve a reasonably safe system of working so as to obviate those dangers, and, on principle, it seems to me that if, in fact, a fellow workman is not merely incompetent but, by his habitual conduct, is likely to prove a source of danger to his fellow employees, a duty lies fairly and squarely on the employers to remove that source of danger. ...
>
> It is really unarguable that here is a case where there did exist, as it were in the system of work, a source of danger, through the conduct of one of the employers' workmen, of which the employers knew; repeated conduct which went on over a long space of time, and which they did nothing whatever to remove, except to reprimand and go on reprimanding to no effect whatever.

Lending of vehicles

Where the owner of a chattel, usually a motor vehicle, lends it to another to complete a journey, the issue, if anything goes wrong on that journey as a result of the negligence of the borrower, of whether the owner is vicariously liable, arises. In *Ormrod v Crosville Motor Services Ltd*[20] the owner of a vehicle was attending the Monte Carlo rally, and it was agreed that a friend would drive the owner's car to Monte Carlo carrying a suitcase for the owner, but that the friend would travel via Bayeux to see friends of his there. On the way to the coast to France the car negligently collided with a bus belonging to the defendants who were counter-claiming for the damage to their bus in the action. The issue was whether the friend was an agent of the owner. The Court of Appeal unanimously held that he was. Singleton LJ said:

> It has been said more than once that a driver of a motor car must be doing something for the owner of the car in order to become an agent of the owner. The mere fact of consent by the owner to the use of a chattel is not proof of agency, but the purpose for which this car was being taken down the road on the morning of the accident was either that it should be used by the owner, the third party, or that it should be used for the joint purposes of the male plaintiff and the third party when it reached Monte Carlo. In those circumstances it appears to me that the judgment of Devlin J, that at the time of the accident the male plaintiff was the agent of the third party, was right.

Denning LJ agreed in very similar terms with the above. Morris LJ agreed also.

In the celebrated case of *Morgans v Launchberry*,[21] the House of Lords had this problem to deal with. However, they distinguished the decision in the

20 [1953] 2 All ER 753.

21 [1972] 2 All ER 606.

previous case. The owner in this case had allowed her husband to use the car to get to and from work. Occasionally he would stay late for a drink, promising his wife that, if he was unfit to drive, he would get a friend to drive him home. On one occasion this happened and, as result of the negligence of the friend, a collision occurred. On the issue of agency, the House decided in favour of the owner wife. In the Court of Appeal Denning MR had used the concept of a 'family car' to fix liability on the owner. This was rejected by the House. Lord Wilberforce also denied any agency:

> I must now consider the special circumstances upon which the judge relied – the understanding between the appellant and her husband. What does it amount to? In my opinion, it is nothing more than the kind of assurance that any responsible citizen would give to his friends, any child would give to his parent, any responsible husband would give to his wife; that he intends to do what is his legal and moral duty, not to drive if in doubt as to his sobriety. The evidence is that this assurance originated from the husband and no doubt it was welcomed by the wife. But it falls short of any authority by the wife to drive on her behalf, or of any delegation by her of the task of driving. If the husband was, as he clearly was, using the car for his own purposes, I am unable to understand how his undertaking to delegate his right to drive to another can turn the driver into the wife's agent in any sense of the word. The husband remains the user, the purposes remain his.

The other Law Lords were in accord with this view. There may be scope for extending the agency principle to other personal possessions which are lent, but so far the cases have concerned, understandably, motor vehicles. It is a somewhat limited principle in any event.

CHAPTER 15

ASSESSMENT OF DAMAGES

INTRODUCTION

Damages, it stands to reason, is the most sought after remedy in tort law. This is particularly true since most actions are for personal injuries arising either from accidents on the road or work-related incidents. In the main, in this chapter we shall be looking at the way in which the law attempts to assess damages for personal injury and death following a tort, but the principles are the same whether the liability is classed as tortious or contractual. The rules on death are special statutory rules, as the common law uncharitably refused to allow claims to continue by or against the estate of the deceased following an accident causing the death.

The basic principle is that the plaintiff should be fully compensated for loss as far as this can be done by an award of money, and therein lies the difficulty as we shall discover. In some instances, the courts may be prepared to award aggravated or exemplary (punitive) damages which are designed to teach a defendant that tort does not pay. These are only awarded in restricted circumstances and are often highly controversial, in practice as well as at a theoretical level.

The system of assessment is under review and the Law Commission is particularly busy at present in a number of relevant areas. It is currently awaiting responses to a consultation paper on non-pecuniary loss,[1] having issued a final report on structured settlements, interim and provisional damages recently,[2] and a further report dealing with, in the main, the level of damages in personal injury cases.[3] There will be a discussion of some of the main proposals in the conclusion, but the studies tend to suggest that plaintiffs feel badly let down by the system, both in terms of the levels of compensation and the way they are treated procedurally by the system of awards.

Many of the difficulties in personal injury cases stem from the fact that, in the more serious cases, the future of the victim post-accident is uncertain. The courts have to predict on the basis of the medical evidence whether the plaintiff is going to recover from the injuries, or to what extent there will be any improvement or deterioration in her condition. In addition, the court has to guess, where claims for loss of future earnings are involved, as to what would have happened to the plaintiff if the accident had not occurred. Some of these difficulties arise because of the nature of the payment to the plaintiff, which is a lump sum in nearly all cases, and in addition a further complication occurs because of the problems of deciding what must be deducted from the plaintiff's damages so that he only gets compensation for his actual loss; eg the deduction of state benefits is a nightmare and has not been helped by the government's

1 Paper no 140.

2 1994 no 224.

3 Genn, *Personal Injury Compensation: how much is enough?*, 1994.

attempts to claw back some of the payments made to accident victims. In some cases plaintiffs are blatantly over-compensated, in others they may go under-compensated.

It should be pointed out that some torts are actionable *per se*. Indeed we saw that this was the case in actions for trespass to the person. The court, in such circumstances, may award only nominal damages, a small sum merely to vindicate the rights interfered with. However, it should be recalled that, in negligence cases, damage is an essential part of the liability rules in the first instance.

GENERAL AND SPECIAL DAMAGES

Losses which are capable of being calculated more or less precisely are 'special damages', eg in a personal injury action the plaintiff may have suffered a loss of earnings either until she returns to work or, in the case of serious incapacity, up to the date of trial or earlier settlement. There may be a claim for damage to clothes, equipment, medical expenses, transport costs and so on. These will form part of the special damages claim and must be specifically pleaded by the plaintiff. General damages must be asked for in the pleadings, but because of their very nature they are incapable of precise calculation, and the plaintiff is not expected to state how much she is claiming under this head in specific terms, eg for pain and suffering, or loss of amenity. Future earnings may be amenable to a fairly precise calculation, but they are considered as part of the general damages claim.

AGGRAVATED AND EXEMPLARY DAMAGES

As was mentioned in the introduction to this chapter, the courts may infrequently award damages which seem to go beyond the purely compensatory. This is a confused and controversial area and is the subject of review by the Law Commission.[4] It is confused because, in the past, courts have tended to confuse aggravated and exemplary damages. It is thought that aggravated damages are really compensatory in nature, but are higher than the normal compensatory award to reflect greater injury to the plaintiff through loss of dignity, pride or humiliation by the defendant's conduct. Aggravated damages are often awarded in assault and battery cases, but rarely, if ever, in negligence cases.

Exemplary damages are designed to punish the defendant and teach him that it does not pay to commit torts. The damages are payable to the plaintiff over and above the compensatory element and thus are regarded as a windfall, and herein lies much of the controversy as we shall see. The conduct of the defendant must be considered outrageous and shocking to the court, not just to the plaintiff. But this of itself is not enough, according to the House of Lords in the famous case of *Rookes v Barnard*,[5] a case concerning the tort of intimidation

4 Consultation Paper no 132 (1993).

5 [1964] 1 All ER 3676.

with which we need not be concerned here. The case is important for the comments of Lord Devlin on the circumstances in which a court should award exemplary damages. The other judges all agreed with him on this issue without indulging in any detailed discussion. After examining some of the cases in which it appeared that the courts had gone past the compensatory point in awarding damages, he continued:

> These authorities convince me of two things. First, that your Lordships could not, without a complete disregard of precedent and indeed of statute, now arrive at a determination that refused altogether the exemplary principle. Secondly, that there are certain categories of cases in which an award of exemplary damages can serve a useful purpose in vindicating the strength of the law, and thus affording a practical justification for admitting into the civil law a principle which ought logically to belong to the criminal. I propose to state what these two categories are; and I propose also to state three general considerations which, in my opinion, should always be borne in mind when awards of exemplary damages are being made. I am well aware that what I am about to say will, if accepted, impose limits not hitherto expressed on such awards, and that there is powerful, though not compelling, authority for allowing them a wider range. ...
>
> The first category is oppressive, arbitrary or unconstitutional action by the servants of the government. I should not extend this category – I say this with particular reference to the facts of this case – to oppressive action by private corporations or individuals. Where one man is more powerful than another, it is inevitable that he will try to use his power to gain his ends; and if his power is much greater than the other's, he might perhaps be said to be using it oppressively. If he uses his power illegally, he must pay for his illegality in the ordinary way; but he is not to be punished simply because he is more powerful. In the case of the government it is different, for the servants of the government are also the servants of the people, and the use of their power must always be subordinate to their duty of service. It is true there is something repugnant about a big man bullying a small man, and very likely the bullying will be a source of humiliation that makes the case one for aggravated damages, but it is not in my opinion punishable by damages.
>
> Cases in the second category are those in which the defendant's conduct has been calculated by him to make a profit for himself which may well exceed the compensation payable to the plaintiff ... it is a factor also that is taken into account in damages for libel; one man should not be allowed to sell another man's reputation for profit. Where a defendant with a cynical disregard for a plaintiff's rights has calculated that the money to be made out of his wrongdoing will probably exceed the damages at risk, it is necessary for the law to show that it cannot be broken with impunity. This category is not confined to moneymaking in the strict sense. It extends to cases in which the defendant is seeking to gain at the expense of the plaintiff some object –perhaps some property which he covets – which either he could not obtain at all or not obtain at a price greater than he wants to put down. Exemplary damages can properly be awarded whenever it is necessary to teach a wrongdoer that tort does not pay.
>
> To these two categories, which are established as part of the common law, there must of course be added any category in which exemplary damages are awarded by statute.
>
> I wish now to express three considerations which I think should always be borne in mind when awards of exemplary damages are being considered. Firstly, the plaintiff cannot recover exemplary damages unless he is a victim of the punishable behaviour. The anomaly inherent in exemplary damages would

> become an absurdity if a plaintiff, totally unaffected by some oppressive conduct which the jury wished to punish, obtained a windfall in consequence. Secondly, the power to award exemplary damages constitutes a weapon that, while it can be used in defence of liberty ... can also be used against liberty. Some of the awards that juries have made in the past seem to me to amount to a greater punishment than would likely to be incurred if the conduct were criminal; and moreover a punishment imposed without the safeguard which the criminal law gives to an offender. I should not allow the respect which is traditionally paid to an assessment of damages by a jury to prevent me from seeing that the weapon is used with restraint. It may even be that the House may find it necessary to ... place some arbitrary limit on awards of damages that are made by way of punishment. Exhortations to be moderate may not be enough. Thirdly, the means of the parties, irrelevant in the assessment of compensation, are material in the assessment of exemplary damages. Everything which aggravates or mitigates the defendant's conduct is relevant.

His Lordship went on to consider the case in hand. He was of the opinion that this was not a case for exemplary damages, and was also doubtful whether it was one falling into the aggravated damages area. The matter was not for their Lordships to decide as it was ordered that there should be a new trial as to damages. As His Lordship indicated, he did not like the concept of exemplary damages and he did his best to curtail their application. Some would say that he went too far, others not far enough. The comments of Lord Devlin were the focus of much attention in the case, some eight years later, of *Cassell & Co Ltd v Broome*.[6] This was a libel case in which substantial damages were awarded by the jury under the heading of exemplary damages to the defamed commander of naval ships escorting the PQ 17 convoy on a mission which went disastrously wrong.

It was clear that the case fell into Lord Devlin's second category of case. The majority of the House found for the plaintiff (5–2) but much was said on the topic of exemplary damages. The majority endorsed the principles laid down by Lord Devlin above. Some refinements, however, were suggested by some of their Lordships. Lord Hailsham commented on the first of Lord Devlin's categories as follows:

> The only category exhaustively discussed before us was the second, since the first could obviously have no application to the instant case. But I desire to say of the first that I would be surprised if it included only servants of the government in the strict sense of the word. It would, in my view, obviously apply to the police ... and almost as certainly to local and other officials exercising improperly rights of search or arrest without warrant, and it may be that, in the future, it will be held to include other abuses of power without warrant by persons purporting to exercise legal authority. What it will not include is the simple bully, not because the bully ought not to be punished in damages, for he manifestly ought, but because an adequate award of compensatory damages by way of *solatium* will necessarily have punished him.

Three others amongst the seven Law Lords assembled for this case went along with this point.[7] Whilst not necessary for the decision, it has been generally accepted since that the category is not solely restricted to servants of the

6 [1972] 1 All ER 801.

7 Lords Reid, Diplock and Kilbrandon.

government in the narrow sense. As to category two in Lord Devlin's speech, Lord Hailsham observed that the reference to 'a cynical disregard for a plaintiff's rights', and the defendant's calculation as to 'the money to be made out of his wrongdoing will probably exceed the damages at risk' was not meant 'to be exhaustive but illustrative, and is not intended to be limited to the kind of mathematical calculations to be found on a balance sheet.'[8]

One other important issue was discussed by the Lord Chancellor in this case, and his view was endorsed by Lord Diplock. This concerned the question of which torts were considered to be the ones in which it was thought appropriate to award exemplary damages. Of Lord Devlin's attempt to rationalise the law on the topic of exemplary damages, Lord Hailsham said:

> I do not think that he was under the impression either that he had completely rationalised the law of exemplary damages, nor by listing the 'categories' was he intending, I would think, to add to the number of torts for which exemplary damages can be awarded. Thus I disagree with the *dictum* of Widgery LJ in *Mafo v Adams*[9] (which, for this purpose, can be treated as an action for deceit) when he said: 'As I understand Lord Devlin's speech, the circumstances in which exemplary damages may be obtained have been drastically reduced, but the range of offences in respect of which they may be granted has been increased, and I see no reason since *Rookes v Barnard* why, when considering a claim for exemplary damages, one should regard the nature of the tort as excluding the claim.'
>
> This would be a perfectly logical inference if Lord Devlin imagined that he was substituting a completely rational code by enumerating the categories and stating the considerations. It is true, of course, that actions for deceit could well come within the purview of the second category. But I can see no reason for thinking that Lord Devlin intended to extend the category to deceit, and counsel on both sides before us were constrained to say that, although it may be paradoxical, they were unable to find a single case where either exemplary or aggravated damages had been awarded for deceit, despite the fact that contumelious, outrageous, oppressive or dishonest conduct on the part of the defendant is almost inherently associated with it. The explanation may lie in the close connection that the action has always had with breach of contract.

Whilst this point was not essential to the decision before the House, which was concerned with defamation, about which there was no issue as to the award of exemplary damages, the statement by the Lord Chancellor has been treated as definitive on this issue. In *AB v South West Water Services Ltd*[10] the defendants' water supply became accidentally contaminated, and the plaintiffs were some of their customers who were made ill as a result of drinking the contaminated water. They brought actions in nuisance, negligence and breach of statutory duty against the defendants, and sought aggravated and exemplary damages on the basis of the behaviour of the defendants after the contamination was discovered. It was alleged that, for some weeks after the discovery, the defendants' employees had acted in an arrogant and high-handed manner by ignoring complaints from consumers; had deliberately misrepresented the

8 Lords Reid, Morris and Kilbrandon agreed with him on this issue.

9 [1969] 3 All ER at 1410.

10 [1993] QB 507.

position in a circular letter to customers saying the water was safe to drink; had failed to give details of precautionary measures; and failed to give information to the plaintiffs' medical advisers to enable the plaintiffs to be treated appropriately. The High Court judge, on the defendants' summons to strike out the exemplary and aggravated damages claims, held that the only arguable basis for such a claim was in nuisance. In a unanimous rejection of the claim for exemplary damages, Stuart-Smith LJ gave the leading judgment. After discussing the cases above, he stated:

> ... accordingly I would hold that, before an award of exemplary damages can be made by any court or tribunal, the tort must be one in respect of which such an award was made prior to 1964. ...
>
> I am quite satisfied that, if exemplary damages are to be awarded for nuisance, such awards should be confined to those cases of private nuisance where there is deliberate or wilful interference with the plaintiff's rights of enjoyment of land, where the defendant has calculated that the profit or benefit for him will exceed the damages he may have to pay. ... Where there has been a public nuisance, a plaintiff who can show particular damage can sue in tort. But it is an entirely different class of case; there is no conduct deliberately and wilfully aimed at the plaintiffs as individuals. There is no case prior to 1964 of exemplary damages being awarded to a plaintiff who proved particular damage resulting from a public nuisance; and I would not extend the remedy to such a case. ...
>
> If I am wrong in concluding that exemplary damages cannot be awarded where the claim is based on particular damage flowing from public nuisance, does the case fall within either of Lord Devlin's two categories? It is not clear from the judge's judgment into which of the two categories he thought this case fell, or whether he thought it fell into both, since he does not expressly deal with the point. By implication he must have held that it was in one or other or both.
>
> The first category is 'oppressive, arbitrary or unconstitutional actions by the servants of government'. It is common ground that this category of persons is not limited to the servants of central government, but includes servants of local government and the police. ...
>
> In the court below Mr Symons had conceded that the defendants' servants might be within the first category. However, before us he sought and was granted leave to withdraw the concession. At the time of these events the defendants were a nationalised body set up under statute for a commercial purpose, namely the supply of water. They have since been privatised, but carry on essentially the same functions. Although it is conceivable that governmental functions could be delegated or entrusted to a nationalised industry with appropriate powers to carry out such functions, perhaps for example with powers of entry and search, I do not think it can possibly be argued that the defendants' servants or agents were performing such a function in this case. A serious mishap had occurred in the course of the defendants' commercial operations, their reaction to it was open to criticism if the allegations in the statement of claim are true, as they must be assumed to be for the purpose of this case. But their conduct was not an exercise of executive power derived from government, central or local, and no amount of rhetoric describing it as arbitrary, oppressive, unconstitutional, arrogant or high-handed makes it so. It would have been no different if the defendants had already been privatised and their servants answerable to a board of directors and the shareholders, rather than a board set up under statute.
>
> Mr Melville Williams sought to argue that, since the defendants could properly be regarded as an 'emanation of the state' for the purpose of direct enforcement

> of EEC Directives, it followed that the defendants' servants were exercising executive power as government servants when performing their function of supplying water, the subject matter of the Directive.
>
> I hope I do no injustice to the argument, which I found difficult to follow. There seems to me to be no logical nexus between the premise and the conclusion. I cannot see that it is arguable that the case falls within the first category.

The judge gave less time to the argument that the case fell within the second category, stating that the allegation was lacking 'in particularity and is little more than an incantation of Lord Devlin's second category'. He continued:

> The essence of the second category is that the tort is knowingly committed for the purpose of gaining some pecuniary or other advantage. The award is to show that tort does not pay. It cannot possibly be said that the defendants continued the nuisance for this purpose. In my judgment, what the allegation amounts to is an attempt by the defendants to cover up the fact that they had committed a tort. That may be reprehensible but not uncommon conduct. The object of such conduct may well be to limit the amount of damages payable to the victim, but that is an entirely different concept from that involved in the second category. In my judgment the case does not fall within either of the two categories for which exemplary damages are awarded.

On the issue of aggravated damages, he said:

> In my judgment, if the plaintiffs experienced greater or more prolonged pain and suffering because the nuisance continued for longer than it should have done, or they drank more contaminated water with ill effect, that is a matter for which they are entitled to be compensated by way of general damages.
>
> Likewise, if uncertainty as to the true position caused by the defendants' lack of frankness following the initial incident led to real anxiety and distress, that is an element for which they are entitled to compensation under general damages for suffering. But anger and indignation is not a proper subject for compensation; it is neither pain nor suffering.

On this basis the judge threw out the claim for aggravated damages also. Simon Brown LJ agreed without delivering a speech and Sir Thomas Bingham MR agreed in his short speech with the approach in the above extracts.

It is difficult to imagine circumstances more appropriate to an award of at least aggravated damages as the ones before the court. The court's view on the issue of exemplary damages attracts criticism as it effectively freezes arbitrarily the right to claim exemplary damages as at 1964, for which there is no justification to be found in Lord Devlin's speech in that year.

The two main reasons for the civil courts' dislike of exemplary damages are the possible confusion of the roles of civil and criminal law and the fact that an award is an unexpected windfall or bonus for the plaintiff. It seems that an extension to claims brought in negligence is extremely unlikely for the foreseeable future.

LUMP SUM

Damages are only recoverable once and are paid normally by means of a lump sum. It is therefore essential for the plaintiff to ensure that any future losses are considered and claimed for in the proceedings. This is the usual position in respect of negligence where the tort comprises a one-off situation. Where the tort is frequently of a continuing type, eg nuisance, there is a fresh cause of action whenever there is a recurrence which causes new damage.

The court has no power to make the defendant pay by periodical payments. If the estimate of the loss is incorrect, therefore, there is no power to review it once the appeal, if any, has been dealt with or the time for lodging an appeal has passed. New evidence, eg such as an improvement or deterioration in the plaintiff's condition, appearing between trial and appeal will normally be admitted, because the court should not ignore what little it has by way of fact, as opposed to predictions about an uncertain future facing the plaintiff. In *Lim Poh Choo v Camden and Islington Area Health Authority*,[11] a case involving serious injuries to a woman psychiatric registrar following a normally straightforward operation, Lord Scarman commented:

> The course of the litigation illustrates, with devastating clarity, the insuperable problems implicit in a system of compensation for personal injuries which (unless the parties agree otherwise) can only yield a lump sum assessed by the court at the time of judgment. Sooner or later, and too often later rather than sooner, if the parties do not settle, a court (once liability is admitted or proved), has to make an award of damages. The award, which covers past, present and future injury and loss, must, under our law, be a lump sum assessed at the conclusion of the legal process. The award is final; it is not susceptible to review as the future unfolds, substituting fact for estimate. Knowledge of the future being denied to mankind, so much of the award as is to be attributed to future loss and suffering (in many cases the major part of the award) will almost surely be wrong. There is only one certainty; the future will prove the award to be too high or too low. ...
>
> The device of granting the parties leave to adduce fresh evidence at the appellate stages of litigation can, as in the present case, mitigate the injustices of a lump sum system by enabling the appellate courts to bring the award into line with what has happened since trial. But it is an unsatisfactory makeshift, and of dubious value in any case where the new facts are themselves in issue.

One of the problems in personal injuries cases stems from the fact that, in the more serious cases, the medical prognosis may be uncertain. The court is in such circumstances involved in a process of guesswork. There are three ways round this at present, in the absence of a general power vested in the court to award periodical payments with the ability to review at intervals so as to take into account any relevant changes in the plaintiff's condition.

Firstly, s 32A Supreme Court Act 1981[12] provides for an award of provisional damages where there is a chance that the plaintiff will suffer some serious disease or serious deterioration in condition. Initially, this will be done on the basis that it has not and will not occur. If the event occurs at some later date, the plaintiff may make a further application for more compensation. This power can only be used in relation to the event which was foreseen in the original action. Any unforeseen development or a general deterioration in the plaintiff's condition cannot be dealt with under this provision. So, if in the original proceedings it is noted that the plaintiff might suffer from epilepsy in

11 [1979] 2 All ER 910.

12 Inserted by s 6 Administration of Justice Act 1982.

the future but at that time it has not shown itself, this is something for which a provisional award might be made. However, if the plaintiff is suffering from osteo-arthritis at the time of the original proceedings and this merely worsens at a later stage, this is not covered by the provision. It seems that there must be a clear cut event which triggers the right of the plaintiff to return to court for a reassessment. It is difficult to assess the value of this power but it is anticipated that it will make only a small impact. The Pearson Commission would have had all compensation awarded in relation to future losses paid by periodical payments with reviews at fixed intervals.[13] This would be objectionable on the ground that it would be more expensive to administer than a lump sum system, but it would remove some of the guesswork in the present method of assessing such losses.

Secondly, and of even less value, is the possibility of split trials in which the trial of liability is held and, if there is a finding in favour of the plaintiff, the court may make an interim award and postpone for a while the final assessment of the award. This could be useful where the plaintiff's medical state had not yet stabilised but was expected to fairly soon. This has the effect of prolonging the litigation which normally is against the interests of the plaintiff. Insurance companies also seem to prefer the finality of the once and for all payment.

Thirdly, we need to consider the phenomenon of the structured settlement. The following is a brief extract from one of the many articles written by Lewis on this topic, although it must be stressed that the literature in general terms is extremely limited in this country. Lewis writes:[14]

> Structured settlements have radically affected the way that damages are negotiated and paid in cases of personal injury. They substitute a pension for part of the lump sum traditionally obtained as compensation. The pension is usually derived from an annuity bought by the insurer covering the liability involved, and held for the benefit of the injured person. Unlike the lump sum, the amount of the pension can be varied, and its payments 'structured' over a period of time; they may last for as long as the plaintiff lives, or longer if there is still a need to support dependants. The pension can be protected against inflation. It can also be tailored to allow for the release of larger amounts in the future if it is expected that the plaintiff's needs or expenses will be greater than now. Lump sums can then be made available (eg to replace a car) provided that a specific date is set for the release of such money. However, such contingencies must be planned in advance, because a structure cannot be revised once it has been formed; there is no easy way of unlocking the capital in the structure if unforeseen circumstances arise which increase the plaintiff's needs. This is the major disadvantage of a structure.
>
> By contrast, one of the advantages of a structure is that it may provide a plaintiff with a higher income from the damages, whilst at the same time saving money for the insurer. Both sides are said to win. These financial benefits arise from the favourable tax treatment now given to structures by the revenue authorities on both sides of the Atlantic. Whereas formerly the income from the investment of the damages award was subject to tax in the plaintiff's hands, it has now been

13 Pearson Commission, 1978, vol 1, para 573; compare the Law Commission, 1973, no 56, para 328.

14 (1993) 42 Int and Comp LQ 780.

agreed that this tax can be avoided if the damages are structured. The periodic payments to the plaintiff are considered to be capital and not income, and are therefore free from income tax. Insurers may now be able to pay out less, and yet fund a higher income for the plaintiff than if the damages were invested directly by the plaintiff.

Apart from its financial attractions, structuring offers plaintiffs freedom from the responsibilities of investment. They can also be protected from the vagaries of the financial world. The income from the structure can be tied to a prices index, so that a plaintiff need not worry about the potential ravages of inflation. ... The income from the structure will not be affected by falls in the stock exchange, or by the revision of tax or interest rates. At the same time there is relief from the burden of having to manage a capital sum often in excess of anything normally encountered in the lifetime of the average person. If the plaintiff lives longer than the period envisaged when the structure was agreed, there is no fear of the money running out. Of course, this is a real fear when a lump sum made for it is often based upon little more than a guess as to the plaintiff's life expectancy. Finally, the plaintiff is protected form his own fecklessness (and that of his investment advisers), and from the depredations of spendthrift friends or relatives. The capital is locked away and cannot be dissipated. In short, structuring not only offers plaintiffs an opportunity to protect the sum awarded for their future, but can also relieve them of the worry and cost of the continued management of the fund. Overall, it can be argued that the development is the most important reform of tort in over 40 years.

Lewis, with some justification, makes out a strong case for this form of settlement. However, it must be pointed out that it is still necessary to calculate the lump sum in the first place before setting up the structure. Also, the setting up of a structure is a private arrangement between the parties; the court has no power to impose such a settlement or to interfere at any stage. It seems evident that the structured settlement can only be used where the claim for future losses is a substantial element in the award. It comes out plainly in the extract above that the structure must be meticulously planned in advance, any variation being provided for in the original agreement between the parties. Structures can also be criticised from the viewpoint of the ordinary taxpayer who may feel that he is subsidising insurance companies in view of the tax advantages provided by structuring.

Pecuniary and non-pecuniary losses

Pecuniary losses are those in which the damages are capable of being worked directly in money terms, eg loss of earnings, past or future, but also items such as medical, travelling expenses, expenditure on necessary equipment, alterations to premises or vehicles and the cost of employing specialist care. Non-pecuniary losses cover pain and suffering and loss of amenity. These payments are arbitrary in relation to injuries such as the loss of a limb, loss of ability to play sport, musical instruments and so on. They are said to be an attempt to soften the blow to the plaintiff, to cover hidden expenses or enable e plaintiff to find some alternative satisfaction from another activity of which still capable. The courts usually adopt some form of unofficial tariff for types of injury. Good sources of information are: *Guidelines of the Judicial* ard, *Current Law*; and Kemp and Kemp, *The Quantum of Damages*.

Non-pecuniary loss is the single biggest component of most personal injury claims. In addition, most small claims are made up entirely of this kind of loss. The Pearson Commission[15] would have abolished claims for such loss for the first three months after the accident, which would have involved tremendous savings on administration but this, like nearly all their proposals, fell by the wayside.

Medical expenses

These are recoverable if reasonably incurred. Future expenses are part of general damages, whereas past expenses are special damages. The plaintiff can insist on private medical treatment, but if s/he uses the NHS s/he cannot recover what s/he would have paid for private treatment. Section 2(4) Law Reform (Personal injuries) Act 1948 states:

> In an action for damages for personal injuries (including any such action arising out of a contract), there shall be disregarded, in determining the reasonableness of any expenses, the possibility of avoiding those expenses or part of them by taking advantage of facilities under the National Health Service Act 1977 or the National Health Service (Scotland) Act 1978, or of any corresponding facilities in Northern Ireland.

The plaintiff is entitled to claim expenses for private treatment for the future even if s/he does not eventually use private facilities. There is no obligation to repay the money in such circumstances.

Section 5 Administration of Justice Act 1982 provides:

> In an action under the law of England and Wales or the law of Northern Ireland for damages for personal injuries (including any such action arising out of a contract), any saving to the injured person which is attributable to his maintenance wholly or partly at public expense in a hospital, nursing home or other institution shall be set off against any income lost by him as a result of his injuries.

However, the plaintiff is entitled to the reasonable costs of a private nursing home or of attendance at home. The cost of adapting the home, subject to a deduction for any increase in the capital value of the home, is recoverable. If the plaintiff has to spend money on special accommodation, the additional expenditure this entails over and above the normal cost of running his/her home, is recoverable.

A non-earner obviously cannot claim for loss of earnings, but is entitled to be compensated for the fact that he or she cannot do household tasks, even if these tasks are undertaken by others in the household. The claim can include the cost of future help even if a housekeeper is not to be employed. Where care has or is to be provided by a third party, whether a relative of a friend who gives up paid employment to carry out the task, it was thought at first that the plaintiff could not be compensated for this unless there was a legal, or possibly a moral, obligation to pay for that assistance. This was because it was argued that the loss was that of the provider of the care rather than that of the plaintiff. However, it came to be recognised that the loss was that of the plaintiff because

15 *Op cit* vol 1, para 388.

of the need for the provision of the service, rather than the expending of the money. It is not normal, however, to pay the commercial rate for the services.

One unresolved difficulty was whether the plaintiff, who was paid the money as part of his award, was required to hand the money over to the third party provider. It had been suggested that the money was to be held on trust for the latter. The issue, amongst others, came up in the case of *Hunt v Severs*,[16] in which the plaintiff was seriously injured in an accident caused by the defendant's negligence. She was a pillion passenger on the defendant's motor cycle. When she left hospital she went to live with the defendant and they eventually married. The care for which the plaintiff was claiming was that provided by the defendant himself. In allowing the defendant's appeal, Lord Bridge gave the only judgment with which the others all agreed. He stated:

> My Lords, a plaintiff who establishes a claim for damages for personal injury is entitled in English law to recover, as part of those damages, the reasonable value of services rendered to him gratuitously by a relative or friend in the provision of nursing care, or domestic assistance of the kind rendered necessary by the injuries the plaintiff has suffered. The major issue which arises for determination in this appeal is whether the law will sustain such a claim in respect of gratuitous services in the case where the voluntary carer is the tortfeasor himself. ...
>
> The starting point for any inquiry into the measure of damages which an injured plaintiff is entitled to recover is the recognition that damages in the tort of negligence are purely compensatory. He should recover from the tortfeasor no more and no less than he has lost. Difficult questions may arise when the plaintiff's injuries attract benefits from third parties. According to their nature, they may or may not be taken into account as reducing the tortfeasor's liability. The two well-established categories of receipt which are to be ignored in assessing damages are the fruits of insurance which the plaintiff himself has provided against the contingency causing his injuries (which may or may not lead to a claim by the insurer as subrogated to the rights of the plaintiff) and the fruits of the benevolence of third parties motivated by sympathy for the plaintiff's misfortune. The policy considerations which underly these two apparent exceptions to the rule against double recovery are, I think, well understood. ... But I find it difficult to see what considerations of public policy can justify a requirement that the tortfeasor himself should compensate the plaintiff twice over for the self same loss. If the loss in question is a direct pecuniary loss (eg loss of wages) [there] is clear authority that the defendant employer, as the tortfeasor who makes good the loss either voluntarily or contractually, thereby mitigates his liability in damages *pro tanto*. ...
>
> I accept that the basis of a plaintiff's claim for damages may consist in his need for services, but I cannot accept that the question from what source that need has been met is irrelevant. If an injured plaintiff is treated in hospital as a private patient he is entitled to recover the cost of that treatment. But if he receives free treatment under the National Health Service, his need has been met without cost to him and he cannot claim the cost of the treatment from the tortfeasor. So it cannot, I think, be right to say that in all cases the plaintiff's loss is 'for the purpose of damages ... the proper and reasonable cost of supplying [his] needs'.

16 [1994] 2 All ER 385.

His Lordship proceeded to discuss the different way in which the law developed in Scotland on this point, and that statutory intervention was felt necessary to bring Scottish law into line with that in England. He continued:

> Thus, in both England and Scotland the law now ensures that an injured plaintiff may recover the reasonable value of gratuitous services rendered to him by way of voluntary care by a member of his family. Differences between the English common law route and the Scottish statutory route to this conclusion are, I think, rarely likely to be of practical importance, since in most cases the sum recovered will simply go to swell the family income. But it is nevertheless important to recognise that the underlying rationale of the English law ... is to enable the voluntary carer to receive proper recompense for his or her services, and I would think it appropriate for the House to take this opportunity so far as possible to bring the law of the two countries into accord by adopting the view ... that in England, the injured plaintiff who recovers damages under this head should hold them on trust for the voluntary carer.

In relation to the final point in the above extract, whilst it was not essential to the decision, it was a point agreed by all their Lordships.

Loss of earnings

The plaintiff's actual loss of earnings is calculated from the date of the injury up to the date of assessment, ie trial or earlier settlement. The appropriate figure on which to base the calculation is the plaintiff's net income, after deduction of tax and contributions. This then forms an item in the special damages claim.

As to future loss, immense difficulty faces the court. The starting point is the plaintiff's net annual loss of earnings. This is then multiplied by a figure ('the multiplier') which is the number of years the plaintiff might have carried on working less a discount for the 'vicissitudes of life', the uncertainties inherent in the future, eg illness, redundancy and so on. The fact that the plaintiff receives the money in advance of receiving it if he had carried on working and can invest it is also a factor in reducing the multiplier. The maximum is said to be 18, with 14 being the more normal figure. The process is unscientific and the courts have generally refused to rely upon actuarial evidence to decide the appropriate multiplier. There is much criticism of this approach taken by the judiciary.[17]

Two points are worth emphasising about this process: the effect of inflation and the incidence of taxation. As to inflation, the trial judge in *Lim's* case had made an allowance for future inflation in the multiplier for cost of future care and loss of earnings. Lord Scarman commented:

> The law appears to me to be now settled that, only in exceptional cases where justice can be shown to require it, will the risk of future inflation be brought into account in the assessment of damages for future loss. ... It is perhaps incorrect to call this rule a rule of law. It is better described as a sensible rule of practice, a matter of common sense. Lump sum compensation cannot be a perfect compensation for the future. An attempt to build into it a protection against future inflation is seeking after a perfection which is beyond the inherent

17 Section 10 Civil Evidence Act 1995 permits the use of the Ogden Tables (Actuarial Tables published by HMSO).

> limitations of the system ... the better course in the great majority of cases is to disregard it. And this for several reasons. First, it is pure speculation whether inflation will continue at present, or higher, rates, or even disappear. The only sure comment one may make on any financial prediction is that it is as likely to be falsified as to be borne out by the event ... inflation is best left to be dealt with by investment policy. It is not unrealistic in modern social conditions, nor is it unjust, to assume that the recipient of a large capital sum by way of damages will take advice as to its investment and use. Thirdly, it is inherent in a system of compensation by way of a lump sum immediately payable, and, I would think, just, that the sum be calculated at current money values, leaving the recipient in the same position as others who have to rely on capital for their support to face the future.
>
> The correct approach should be, therefore, in the first place to assess damages without regard to the risk of future inflation. If it can be demonstrated that, on the particular facts of a case, such an assessment would not result in a fair compensation (bearing in mind the investment opportunity that a lump sum award offers), some increase is permissible. But the victims of tort who receive a lump sum award are entitled to no better protection against inflation than others who have to rely on capital for their future support. To attempt such protection would be to put them into a privileged position at the expense of the tortfeasor, and so to impose on him an excessive burden, which might go far beyond compensation for loss.

The taxation issue cropped up in the case of *Hodgson v Trapp*,[18] in which the plaintiff received severe injuries in a car accident as a result of the negligence of the defendant. The judge, when considering the appropriate multipliers, increased the figures to take into account the fact that, on investing the large amount of damages, the plaintiff might pay higher rate tax on the income realised. Lord Oliver stated:

> Essentially what the court has to do is to calculate as best it can the sum of money which will on the one hand be adequate, by its capital and income, to provide annually for the injured person a sum equal to his estimated annual loss over the whole of the period during which that loss is likely to continue, but which, on the other hand, will not, at the end of that period, leave him in a better financial position than he would have been apart from the accident. Hence the conventional approach is to assess the amount notionally required to be laid out in the purchase of an annuity which will provide the annual amount needed for the whole period of the loss.

On the issue of higher rate taxation and whether allowance should be made for it, His Lordship continued:

> There are, I think, four considerations which have to be borne in mind at the outset. First and foremost is the fact that the exercise on which the court has to embark is one which is inherently unscientific and in which expert evidence can be of only the most limited assistance. Average life expectations can be actuarially ascertained, but to assess the probabilities of future political, economic and fiscal policies requires not the services of an actuary or an accountant, but those of a prophet. Second, the question is not whether the impact of taxation is a factor legitimately to be taken into account at all, but to what extent, if at all, it is right to treat it as a separate, individual and independent consideration which justifies the making of additional provision

18 [1988] 3 All ER 870.

> conditioned not by the loss sustained but by the way in which the provision made for that loss is assumed to be dealt with by the recipient. Third, what the court is concerned with is the adequacy of a fund of damages specifically designed to meet the loss of future earnings and the cost of future care. It cannot, I think, be right in assessing the adequacy of that fund to take into account what the plaintiff may choose to do with other resources at his command, including any sums which he may receive by way of compensation for other loss or injury. If he chooses, for instance, to retain other sums awarded to him for, for example, loss of amenity or pain and suffering, and to supplement his income by investing them so as, incidentally, to put himself into a higher tax bracket, that cannot, in my judgment, constitute a legitimate ground for increasing the compensatory fund for loss of future earnings and care. That fund must, in my judgment, be treated as a fund on its own for the purposes of assessing its adequacy. Fourth, it must not be assumed that there is only one way in which a plaintiff can deal with the award. ... In practice, of course, the probability is that the plaintiff who receives a high award will treat the fund as a capital fund to be retained and invested in the most advantageous way. But the award has been calculated by reference to the cost of purchasing an appropriate annuity; and since the fund is at his complete disposal it is open to the plaintiff actually so to apply it either in whole or in part. If that were done, the capital proportion of each annual payment, calculated by dividing the cost of the annuity by the life expectation of the annuitant at the date of purchase, would be free from tax and the balance alone would be taxable. It is, I suppose, conceivable that that proportion could attract tax at the higher rate, but it would require a very large annuity before a significant additional fiscal burden was attracted. ...
>
> That tax will be levied is, no doubt, as Benjamin Franklin observed, one of the two certainties of life, but the extent and manner of its exaction in the future can only be guessed at. It is as much an imponderable as any of the other uncertainties which are embraced in the exercise of making a just assessment of damages for future loss. The system of multipliers and multiplicands conventionally employed in the assessment takes account of a variety of factors, none of which is, or indeed is capable of being, worked out scientifically, but which are catered for by allowing a reasonably generous margin in the assumed rate of interest on which the multiplier is based. There is, in my judgment, no self-evident justification for singling out this particular factor and making for it an allowance which is not to be made for the equally imponderable factor of inflation.

The remainder of their Lordships agreed with this view.

THE LOST YEARS

In situations where the plaintiff's life expectancy is reduced as a result of the accident, there is the issue of whether the plaintiff could include a claim for the amount of money that s/he would have earned during those years which would now be lost to him/her. Initially, the courts took the harsh line that a person could not suffer a loss when s/he was dead. This approach entailed a severe problem for any dependants of the plaintiff. It was thought that once the plaintiff, whilst alive, had successfully brought his/her claim, on his/her death the dependants could not then bring an action for their loss of dependency under the fatal accidents legislation. The approach penalised the dependants who might have expected to receive support from the plaintiff during those lost years. It seems that, ironically, it would have been better for the plaintiff and all concerned if s/he had died more or less straight away.

In *Pickett v British Rail Engineering Ltd*[19] the plaintiff was a 53 year old with dependants. As a result of negligent exposure to asbestos dust over a period of years his life expectancy was reduced to one year. The judge allowed a claim for the lost years but this was reversed by the Court of Appeal. In the meantime the plaintiff had died and his widow was substituted for him and appealed to the House of Lords. The majority (Lord Russell dissenting) decided in favour of the plaintiff. Lord Wilberforce, after discussing the previous cases, commented:

> My Lords, in the case of the adult wage earner with or without dependants who sues for damages during his lifetime, I am convinced that a rule which enables the 'lost years' to be taken account of comes closer to the ordinary man's expectations than one which limits his interest to his shortened span of life. The interest which such a man has in the earnings he might hope to make over a normal life, if not saleable in a market, has a value which can be assessed. A man who receives that assessed value would surely consider himself and be considered compensated; a man denied it would not. And I do not think that, to act in this way, creates insoluble problems of assessment in other cases. In that of a young child ... neither present nor future earnings could enter into the matter; in the more difficult case of adolescents just embarking on the process of earning ... the value of 'lost' earnings might be real but would probably be assessable as small.
>
> There will remain some difficulties. In cases, probably the normal, where a man's actual dependants coincide with those for whom he provides out of the damages he receives, whatever they obtain by inheritance will simply be set off against their own claim. If on the other hand this coincidence is lacking, there might be duplication of recovery. To that extent injustice may be caused to the wrongdoer. But if there is a choice between taking a view of the law which mitigates a clear and recognised injustice in cases of normal occurrence, at the cost of the possibility in fewer cases of excess payments being made, or leaving the law as it is, I think that our duty is clear. We should carry the judicial process of seeking a just principle as far as we can, confident that a wise legislator will correct resultant anomalies.
>
> ... the amount to be recovered in respect of earnings in the 'lost' years should be that amount after deduction of an estimated sum to represent the victim's probable living expenses during those years. I think that this is right because the basis, in principle, for recovery lies in the interest which he has in making provision for dependants and others, and this he would do out of his surplus. There is the additional merit of bringing awards under this head into line with what could be recovered under the Fatal Accidents Acts.

The major criticism of this approach is that there is no mechanism for ensuring that the dependants do receive the money which the plaintiff gets during his lifetime. There is no suggestion, as with the amounts for future care discussed above, of the money being held on trust for the dependants. The better solution would seem to have been to amend the fatal accidents legislation to allow a claim by dependants for the lost years, even though the plaintiff is still alive.

19 [1979] 1 All ER 774.

Deductions from damages

The issue of whether the receipt of moneys by the plaintiff, as a result of being injured, are to be deducted from the damages is a minefield. In theory, anything that the plaintiff receives ought to be taken into account when assessing damages, if the compensatory principle is to be followed. We have seen already that some items, eg private insurance taken out by the plaintiff and charitable donation, are not considered by the courts. The position with regard to state benefits is unnecessarily complex, a complexity heightened by the attempted claw-back by the government mentioned below. In a series of cases up to 1988 the courts had decided that several types of benefit were deductible in full from the plaintiff's compensation.[20] Some benefits covered by s 2(1) Law Reform (Personal Injuries) Act 1948 were to be 50% deductible for the period lasting five years from the date of the accident. These benefits included sickness benefit, invalidity benefit, severe disablement allowance and disablement benefit. Statutory sick pay replaced sickness benefit and this was to be deducted in full. This was the position until 1 January 1989 when s 22 Social Security Act 1989 came into force. The purpose of this provision is to ensure that the government recoups the benefits payable by the state to the plaintiff from the defendant. There are further provisions now to be found in ss 81 and 82 Social Security Administration Act 1992 as follows:

Section 81

(1) In this part of this Act–

'benefit' means any benefit under the Contributions and Benefits Act except child benefit and, subject to regulations under subsection (2) below, the 'relevant benefits' are such of those benefits as may be prescribed for the purposes of this Act;

'certificate of deduction' means a certificate given by the compensator specifying how much he has deducted and paid to the Secretary of State in pursuance of section 82(1) below;

'certificate of total benefit' means a certificate given by the Secretary of State in accordance with this part of this Act;

'compensation payment' means any payment falling to be made (whether voluntarily, or in pursuance of a court order or an agreement, or otherwise)–

(a) to or in respect of the victim in consequence of the accident, injury or disease in question; and

(b) either–

(i) by or on behalf of a person who is, or is alleged to be, liable to any extent in respect of that accident, injury or disease; or

(ii) in pursuance of a compensation scheme for motor accidents;

but does not include benefit or an exempt payment or so much of any payment as is referable to costs incurred by any person;

'compensation scheme for motor accidents' means any scheme or arrangement under which funds are available for the payment of compensation in respect of motor accidents caused, or alleged to have been caused, by uninsured or unidentified persons;

20 See *Hodgson v Trapp* (above) in relation to mobility and attendance allowance.

'compensator', 'victim' and 'intended recipient' shall be construed in accordance with section 82(1) below;

'payment' means payment in money or money's worth, and cognate expressions shall be construed accordingly;

'relevant deduction' means the deduction required to be made from the compensation payment in question by virtue of this Part of this Act;

'relevant payment' means the payment required to be made to the Secretary of State by virtue of this Part of this Act;

'relevant period' means–

(a) in the case of a disease, the period of five years beginning with the date on which the victim first claims a relevant benefit in consequence of the disease; or

(b) in any other case, the period of five years immediately following the day on which the accident or injury in question occurred;

but where before the end of that period the compensator makes a compensation payment in final discharge of any claim made by or in respect of the victim and arising out of the accident, injury or disease, the relevant period shall end on the date on which that payment is made; and

'total benefit' means the gross amount referred to in section 82(1)(a) below.

(2) If statutory sick pay is prescribed as a relevant benefit, the amount of that benefit for the purposes of this Part of this Act shall be a reduced amount determined in accordance with regulations by reference to the percentage from time to time specified in section 158(1)(a) of the Contributions and Benefits Act (percentage of statutory sick pay recoverable by employers by deduction from contributions).

(3) For the purposes of this Part of this Act the following are the 'exempt payments'–

(a) any small payment, as defined in section 85 below;

(b) any payment made to or for the victim under section 35 of the Powers of Criminal Courts Act 1973 or section 58 of the Criminal Justice (Scotland) Act 1980;

(c) any payment to the extent that it is made–

(i) in consequence of an action under the Fatal Accidents Act 1976; or

(ii) in circumstances where, had an action been brought, it would have been brought under that Act;

(d) any payment to the extent that it is made in respect of a liability arising by virtue of section 1 of the Damages (Scotland) Act 1976;

(e) without prejudice to section 6(4) of the Vaccine Damage Payments Act 1979 (which provides for the deduction of any such payment in the assessment of any award of damages), any payment made under that Act to or in respect of the victim;

(f) any award of compensation made to or in respect of the victim by the Criminal Injuries Compensation Board under section 111 of the Criminal Justice Act 1988;

(g) any payment made in the exercise of a discretion out of property held subject to a trust in a case where no more than 50% by value of the capital contributed to the trust was directly or indirectly provided by persons who are, or are alleged to be, liable in respect of–

(i) the accident, injury or disease suffered by the victim in question;

(ii) the same or any connected accident, injury or disease suffered by another;

(h) any payment made out of property held for the purposes of any prescribed trust (whether the payment also falls within paragraph (g) above or not);

(i) any payment made to the victim by an insurance company within the meaning of the Insurance Companies Act 1982 under the terms of any contract of insurance entered into between the victim and the company before–

(i) the date on which the victim first claims a relevant benefit in consequence of the disease in question; or

(ii) the occurrence of the accident or injury in question;

(j) any redundancy payment falling to be taken into account in the assessment of damages in respect of an accident, injury or disease.

(4) Regulations may provide that any prescribed payment shall be an exempt payment for the purposes of this Part of this Act.

(5) Except as provided by any other enactment, in the assessment of damages in respect of an accident, injury or disease the amount of any relevant benefits paid or likely to be paid shall be disregarded.

(6) If, after making the relevant deduction from the compensation payment, there would be no balance remaining for payment to the intended recipient, any reference in this Part to the making of the compensation payment shall be construed in accordance with regulations.

Section 82

(1) A person (the 'compensator') making a compensation payment, whether on behalf of himself or another, in consequence of an accident, injury or disease suffered by any another person (the 'victim') shall not do so until the Secretary of State has furnished him with a certificate of total benefit and shall then–

(a) deduct from the payment an amount, determined in accordance with the certificate of total benefit, equal to the gross amount of any relevant benefits paid or likely to be paid to or for the victim during the relevant period in respect of that accident, injury or disease;

(b) pay to the Secretary of State an amount equal to that which is required to be deducted; and

(c) furnish the person to whom the compensation payment is or, apart from this section, would have been made (the 'intended recipient') with a certificate of deduction.

(2) Any right of the intended recipient to receive the compensation payment in question shall be regarded as satisfied to the extent of the amount certified in the certificate of deduction.

Small payments are those which do not exceed £2,500 at the present time. It would seem that the common law and statutory rules in s 2(1) of the 1948 Act will apply to such payments, namely that some benefits will be deducted in full and in respect of others, only 50%. It should be noted that the recoupment provisions do not extend to prospective payments which go beyond the five year period. No deduction is to be made for any such payments by the court either, so the plaintiff gets over-compensated to that extent. Some benefits are not included in the provisions in any event, and it is presumed that the common law rules will apply to these.[21]

Other issues have covered the deduction of collateral benefits, eg occupational sick pay schemes. In *Hussain v New Taplow Paper Mills Ltd*[22] the plaintiff was injured in an accident arising during the course of his employment. His employers had taken out a policy of insurance to cover their contractual obligation to pay him, after the first 13 weeks, 50% of his earnings. The terms made it clear that this was meant to be a continuation of his earnings and was taxable. In an action for damages against the employer the issue was whether this had to be brought into account. The House of Lords held that it was. Lord Bridge, with whom all their Lordships agreed, stated:

> The question whether the scheme payments are, or are not, deductible in assessing damages for loss of earnings must be answered in the same way whether, after the first 13 weeks of incapacity, the payments fall to be made for a few weeks or for the rest of an employee's working life. Looking at the payments made under the scheme by the defendants in the first weeks after the expiry of the period of 13 weeks of continuous incapacity, they seem to me indistinguishable in character from the sick pay which the employee receives during the first 13 weeks. They are payable under a term of the employee's contract by the defendants to the employee *qua* employee as a partial substitute for earnings, and are the very antithesis of a pension, which is payable after employment ceases. The fact that the defendants happen to have insured their liability to meet these contractual commitments as they arise cannot affect the issue in any way. ...
>
> It positively offends my sense of justice that a plaintiff, who has certainly paid no insurance premiums as such, should receive full wages during a period of incapacity to work from two different sources, her employer and the tortfeasor. It would seem to me still more unjust and anomalous where, as here, the employer and the tortfeasor are one and the same. I would accordingly dismiss the appeal.

However, in *McCamley v Cammell Laird Shipbuilders Ltd*[23] the plaintiff brought an action against his employers, and the outstanding issue was whether the proceeds of a policy he received which the employers had taken out should be deducted from any award of damages. The proceeds were paid in a lump sum and he did not contribute towards the policy. The judge said that the policy proceeds should be left out of the calculation and the Court of Appeal agreed with him, distinguishing *Hussain*'s case. O'Connor LJ read the judgment of the court and on this point said:

> The reason why the judge came to the correct decision on this matter is that the payment to the plaintiff was a payment by way of benevolence, even though the mechanics required the use of an insurance policy. The payment was not an *ex*

21 See reg 2 Social Security (Recoupment) Regulations 1990 (SI 1990/322) for a list of those included within the provisions of the 1992 Act.

22 [1988] 1 All ER 541.

23 [1990] 1 All ER 854.

> *gratia* act where the accident had already happened, but the whole idea of the policy, covering all the many employees of British Shipbuilders and its subsidiary companies, was clearly to make the benefit payable as an act of benevolence whenever a qualifying injury took place. It was a lump sum payable regardless of fault or whether the employers or anyone else were liable, and it was not a method of advancing sick pay covered by a contractual scheme such as existed in *Hussain*'s case. ... That the arrangement was made before the accident is immaterial. The act of benevolence was to happen contingently on an event and was prepared for in advance. ...
>
> The point was well made on behalf of the plaintiff that this sum was not to be payable in respect of any particular head of damage suffered by him, and was not an advance in respect of anything at all. To say that does not mean that, in an appropriate case, there may not be a general payment or advance to cover a number of different heads of damage. The importance in the present case is that the sum was quantified before there had been an accident at all, and when it could not have been foreseen what damages might be sustained when one did take place.

Whilst it can be seen what the judge was driving at in the above extract, it does not seem an adequate reason for departing from the principle in *Hussain*'s case. There is no analogy with an occupational pension scheme of any kind at all. The compensatory principle appears to be under threat from decisions such as this.

Loss of earning capacity

This may seem to overlap with the issue of loss of future earnings, but there may be situations where the plaintiff is kept on by his/her employer and is paid at the same rate as before. However, if s/he was to lose that job, there may be a loss of earning capacity because the plaintiff's ability to find an equivalent job may be significantly reduced. This ought to be reflected in the damages. Where the plaintiff is a young child, only moderate sums are awarded under this head.

Pain and suffering

Actual and prospective pain and suffering constitutes a head of damages. This includes a neurosis and any pain and suffering relating to necessary medical treatment. The courts also include an element to cover mental anguish at the knowledge of the loss of life expectancy. There used to be a head of damage known as 'loss of expectation of life', for which a conventional damage award of a small amount only would given. This was abolished by s 1(1)(a) Administration of Justice Act 1982. a person who is incapacitated and capable of appreciating her condition is to be compensated for the anguish. In *West v Shephard*[24] the House of Lords considered the plight of a plaintiff who suffered serious injuries which rendered her bedridden and in need of constant nursing attention in hospital. She could appreciate some food and could recognise relatives and the nurses and communicate by signs to a limited extent. Lord Morris commented as follows:

> Certain particular questions have been raised. How are general damages affected, if at all, by the fact that the sufferer is unconscious? How are they

24 [1963] 2 All ER 625.

affected, if at all, if it be the fact that the sufferer will not be able to make use of any money which is awarded?

The first of these questions may be largely answered if it is remembered that damages are designed to compensate for such results as have actually been caused. If someone has been caused pain then damages to compensate for the enduring of it may be awarded. If, however, by reason of an injury someone is made unconscious for a short or for a prolonged period with the result that he does not feel pain, then he needs no monetary compensation in respect of pain because he will not have suffered it. Apart from actual physical pain, it may often be that some physical injury causes distress or fear or anxiety. If, for example, personal injuries include the loss of a leg, there may be much physical suffering, there will be the actual loss of the leg (a loss the gravity of which will depend on the particular circumstances of the particular case) and there may be (depending on particular circumstances) elements of consequential worry and anxiety.

One part of the affliction (again depending on particular circumstances) may be an inevitable and constant awareness of the deprivations which the loss of the leg entails. These are all matters which judges take into account. In this connection also the length of the period of life during which the deprivations will continue will be a relevant factor. ... To the extent to which any of these last-mentioned matters depend for their existence on an awareness in the victim, it must follow that they will not exist and will not call for compensation if the victim is unconscious. An unconscious person will be spared pain and suffering and will not experience the mental anguish which may result from the knowledge of what has in life been lost, or from knowledge that life has been shortened. The fact of unconsciousness is therefore relevant in respect of, and will eliminate, those heads or elements of damages which can only exist by being felt or thought or experienced. The fact of unconsciousness does not, however, eliminate the actuality of the deprivations of the ordinary experiences and amenities of life which may be the inevitable result of some physical injury.

If damages are awarded to a plaintiff on a correct basis, it seems to me that it can be of no concern to the court to consider any question as to the use that will thereafter be made of the money awarded. It follows that, if damages are assessed on a correct basis, there should not then be a paring down of the award because of some thought that a particular plaintiff will not be able to use the money. In assessing damages there may be items which will only be awarded if certain needs of a plaintiff are established. A particular plaintiff may have provision made for some future form of transport; a particular plaintiff may have to have provision made for some special future attention or some special treatment or medication. If, however, some reasonable sum is awarded to a plaintiff as compensation for pain endured or for the loss of past or future earnings or for ruined years of life or lost years of life, the use to which a plaintiff puts such sum is a matter for the plaintiff alone. A rich man, merely because he is rich and is not in need, is not to denied proper compensation; nor is a thrifty man merely because he may keep and not spend.

Loss of amenity

This is regarded as a separate head of damages. In the case of *Wise v Kay*[25] the plaintiff's injuries were so severe that she was, and would remain, in a coma.

25 [1962] 1 All ER 257.

The majority of the Court of Appeal refused to reduce the general damages in respect of loss of amenity because of her unconscious state. Sellers LJ observed:

> At common law, in assessing damages for physical injuries, consideration has also been given, expressly in recent times and perhaps at all times, to what has been called loss of amenities. This is separate and distinct from pain and suffering, and, in my opinion, means something different from loss of happiness or even enjoyment. Physical incapacity may restrict activity in one form or another or alter the conduct of life, the manner or the extent of living. The inquiry may be taken as far as that, to ascertain the limitations and variations which a physical injury has imposed, or may impose, so as to compensate for that, but I see no reason for inquiring further how, in any given case, it has affected the happiness of the victim. ...
>
> It was further submitted that, because the plaintiff has been, throughout, unconscious and has so far no knowledge of her condition and, as far as can be foreseen, never will have any knowledge of the wreck that she is, no damages, or very limited damages, should be awarded. In these circumstances there is no room for an award for pain and suffering, but otherwise I regard it as an untenable submission. The court is, in effect, asked to treat the injured party as if she were dead, and to award compensation for loss of expectation of life and nothing else by way of general damages. I refuse to do so. I am not apprised of any branch of our law which permits a person who is known or believed to be alive to be treated as if he or she were dead. This is a most exceptional case but, as long as the plaintiff lives, her damages, in my view, fall to be considered as damages to be awarded to a living person, and no living person could have lost more of the use of limbs and faculties.

This case was approved by the House of Lords in *West v Shephard.* Nonetheless it is from one point of view difficult to justify. If the provision of money for this head of damage is to enable the plaintiff to obtain alternative sources of pleasure, this can hardly be said to be the position in the case of *Wise v Kay*, where there was no realistic prospect of the plaintiff doing this. The so-called objective loss approach in this area seems to ignore this important question.

Damages on death

There are two possible causes of action: one by the estate of the deceased and the other by his/her dependants. As to the estate itself, it was mentioned earlier that the cause of action died with the deceased at common law. Section 1 Law Reform (Miscellaneous Provisions) Act 1934 provided as follows:

> (1) Subject to the provisions of this section, on the death of any person after the commencement of this Act all causes of action subsisting against or vested in him shall survive against, or, as the case may be, for the benefit, his estate. Provided that this subsection shall not apply to causes of action for defamation ...
>
> (a) The right of a person to claim under section 1(a) of the Fatal Accidents Act 1976 (bereavement) shall not survive for the benefit of his estate on his death.
>
> (2) Where a cause of action survives as aforesaid for the benefit of the estate of a deceased person, the damages recoverable for the benefit of the estate of that person–

(a) shall not include–

(i) any exemplary damages;

(ii) any damage for loss of income in respect of any period after that person's death; ...

(c) where the death of that person has been caused by the act or omission which gives rise to the cause of action, shall be calculated without reference to any loss or gain to his estate consequent on his death, except that a sum in respect of funeral expenses may be included.

(4) Where damage has been suffered by reason of any act or omission in respect of which a cause of action would have subsisted against any person if that person had not died before or at the same time as the damage was suffered, there shall be deemed for the purposes of this Act, to have been subsisting against him before his death such cause of action in respect of that act or omission as would have subsisted if he had died after the damage was suffered.

(5) The rights conferred by this Act for the benefit of the estates of deceased persons shall be in addition to and not in derogation of any rights conferred on the dependants of deceased persons by the Fatal Accidents Act 1976, and so much of this Act as relates to causes of action against the estates of deceased persons shall apply in relation to causes of action under the said Act as it applies in relation to other causes of action not expressly excepted from the operation of subsection (1) of this section.

The claim under this provision by the estate is likely to be a modest one, being made up of damages for pain and suffering from the accident up to the date of death (if any), loss of earnings up to that time also. There is no award for the lost years for the benefit of the estate. In another case arising from the tragic events at Hillsborough, *Hicks v Chief Constable of South Yorkshire*[26] the two deceased were crushed to death and a claim was brought on behalf of their estates for damages for suffering from the awareness of impending death. Their Lordships all agreed that the claim should be rejected. Lord Bridge gave the only speech and said:

> It is perfectly clear law that fear by itself, of whatever degree, is a normal humane motion for which no damages can be awarded. Those trapped in the crush at Hillsborough who were fortunate enough to escape without injury have no claim in respect of the distress they suffered in what must have been a truly terrifying experience. It follows that fear of impending death felt by the victim of a fatal injury before that injury is inflicted, cannot by itself give rise to a cause of action which survives for the benefit of the victim's estate.

The Fatal Accidents Act 1976 provides:

1(1) If death is caused by any wrongful act, neglect or default which is such as would (if death had not ensued) have entitled the person injured to maintain an action and recover damages in respect thereof, the person who would have been liable if death had not ensued shall be liable to an action for damages, notwithstanding the death of the person injured.

(2) Subject to section 1A(2) below, every such action shall be for the benefit of the dependants of the person ('the deceased') whose death has been so caused.

26 [1992] 2 All ER 65.

(3) In this Act, 'dependant' means–

(a) the wife or husband or former wife or husband of the deceased;

(b) any person who–

(i) was living with the deceased in the same household immediately before the date of the death; and

(ii) had been living with the deceased in the same household for at least two years before that date; and

(iii) was living during the whole of that period as the husband or wife of the deceased;

(c) any parent or other ascendant of the deceased;

(d) any person who was treated by the deceased as his parent;

(e) any child or other descendant of the deceased;

(f) any person (not being a child of the deceased) who, in the case of any marriage to which the deceased was at any time a party, was treated by the deceased as a child of the family in relation to that marriage;

(g) any person who is, or is the issue of, a brother, sister, uncle or aunt of the deceased.

(4) The reference to the former wife or husband of the deceased in subsection (3)(a) above includes a reference to a person whose marriage to the deceased has been annulled or declared void as well as a person whose marriage to the deceased has been dissolved.

(5) In deducing any relationship for the purposes of subsection (3) above–

(a) any relationship by affinity shall be treated as a relationship by consanguinity, any relationship of the half blood as a relationship of the whole blood, and the stepchild of any person as his child; and

(b) an illegitimate person shall be treated as the legitimate child of his mother and his reputed father.

(6) Any reference in this Act to injury includes any disease and any impairment of a person's physical or mental condition.

1A(1) An action under this Act may consist of or include a claim for damages for bereavement.

(2) A claim for damages for bereavement shall only be for the benefit:

(a) of the wife or husband of the deceased; and

(b) where the deceased was a minor who was never married:

(i) of his parents, if he was legitimate; and

(ii) of his mother, if he was illegitimate.

(3) Subject to subsection (5) below, the sum to be awarded as damages under this section shall be [£7,500].

(4) Where there is a claim for damages under this section for the benefit of both the parents of the deceased, the sum awarded shall be divided equally between them (subject to any deduction falling to be made in respect of costs not recovered from the defendant).

(5) The Lord Chancellor may by order made by statutory instrument, subject to annulment in pursuance of a resolution of either House of Parliament, amend this section by varying the amount for the time being specified in subsection (3) above.

2(1) The action shall be brought by and in the name of the executor or administrator of the deceased.

(2) If–

(a) there is no executor or administrator of the deceased; or

(b) no action is brought within six months after the death by and in the name of an executor or administrator of the deceased;

the action may be brought by and in the name of all or any of the persons for whose benefit an executor or administrator could have brought it.

(3) Not more than one action shall lie for and in respect of the same subject matter of complaint.

(4) The plaintiff in the action shall be required to deliver to the defendant or his solicitor full particulars of the persons for whom and on whose behalf the action is brought and of the nature of the claim in respect of which damages are sought to be recovered.

3(1) In the action such damages, other than damages for bereavement, may be awarded as are proportioned to the injury resulting from the death to the dependants respectively.

(2) After deducting the costs not recovered from the defendant any amount recovered otherwise than as damages for bereavement shall be divided among the dependants in such shares as may be directed.

(3) In an action under this Act where there fall to be assessed damages payable to a widow in respect of the death of her husband there shall not be taken into account the re-marriage of the widow or her prospects of re-marriage.

(4) In an action under this Act where there fall to be assessed damages payable to a person who is a dependent by virtue of section 1(3)(b) above in respect of the death of the person with whom the dependant was living as husband or wife there shall be taken into account (together with any other matter that appears to the court to be relevant to the action) the fact that the dependant had no enforceable right to financial support by the deceased as a result of their living together.

(5) If the dependants have incurred funeral expenses in respect of the deceased, damages may be awarded in respect of those expenses.

(6) Money paid into court in satisfaction of a cause of action under this Act may be in one sum without specifying any person's share.

4 In assessing damages in respect of a person's death in an action under this Act, benefits which have accrued or will or may accrue to any person from his estate or otherwise as a result of his death shall be disregarded.

5 Where any person dies as the result partly of his own fault and partly the fault of any other person or persons, and accordingly if an action were brought for the benefit of the estate under the Law Reform (Miscellaneous Provisions) Act 1934 the damages recoverable would be reduced under section 1(1) of the Law Reform (Contributory Negligence) Act 1945, any damages recoverable in an action under this Act shall be reduced to a proportionate extent.

The provisions relating to bereavement loss were inserted by s 3 Administration of Justice Act 1982. The figure was originally £3,500 but has been increased under the power in s 1A(5) above. There is no need to prove any dependency but the claim is limited to a small number of persons, compared to the main action under the legislation. Bereavement loss claims were meant to replace loss of expectation of life claims.

Both types of claim under the 1976 Act are derivative, in that only if the deceased would have had a cause of action can the dependent have one. The claims are clearly for economic loss in so far as they relate to the dependency. In *Mallett v McMonagle*,[27] Lord Diplock gave an account of the function of an award in dependency cases. He stated:

> My Lords, the purpose of an award of damages under the Fatal Accidents Acts is to provide the widow and other dependants of the deceased with a capital sum which with prudent management will be sufficient to supply them with material benefits of the same standard and duration as would have been provided for them out of the earnings of the deceased had he not been killed by the tortious act of the respondents, credit being given for the value of any material benefits which will accrue to them (otherwise than as fruits of insurance) as a result of his death.
>
> To assess the damages it is necessary to form a view on three matters each of which is in greater or less degree one of speculation:
>
> (i) the value of the material benefits which the deceased would have provided out of his earnings for each year in the future during which he would have provided them had he not been killed;
>
> (ii) the value of any material benefits which the dependants will be able to obtain each such year from sources (other than insurance) which would not have been available to them had the deceased lived but which will become available to them as a result of his death;
>
> (iii) the amount of the capital sum which with prudent management will produce annual amounts equal to the difference between (i) and (ii) (ie 'the dependency') for each of the years during which the deceased would have provided benefits for the dependants had he not been killed.
>
> Since the essential arithmetical character of this assessment is the calculation of the present value of an annuity, it has become usual both in England and in Northern Ireland to arrive at the total award by multiplying a figure assessed as the annual 'dependency' by a number of 'years' purchase'. If the figure of the annual 'dependency' remained constant and could be assessed with certainty, it would be possible in times of stable currency, interest rates and taxation to calculate with certainty the number of years' purchase of the dependency which would provide a capital sum sufficient to produce an annuity, equal in amount to the dependency for the number of years for which it would have continued. If the estimated 'dependency' did not remain constant, but altered at intervals during the period of its enjoyment, an accurate assessment of the appropriate award would involve calculating the present value of a series of annuities for fixed periods progressively deferred ... this is seldom ever done. Anticipated future variations in the 'dependency' are normally dealt with by an adjustment in the multiplicand to be multiplied by the single multiplier – the number of years' purchase.

27 [1969] 2 All ER 178.

Inflation and the incidence of higher rate taxation are to be left out of account in assessing the multiplier in the same way as with cases brought by living plaintiffs.[28]

The widow's actual re-marriage or her prospects in that regard are to be ignored, so as to avoid distasteful episodes in the courtroom in which the judge would have to consider the widow in the witness box to enable him to assess the damages based on the dependency. However, this produces the ludicrous situation of a judge knowing full well that the widow has remarried and[29] having to do her best to ignore this fact.

Finally, a dependant's claim is not affected in any way by any benefit she receives from the deceased's estate, including any claim under s 1 of the 1934 Act. The provisions as to recoupment of benefits in the 1992 Act do not apply to claims under the 1976 Act.

CONCLUSION

The Law Commission is currently reviewing some of the areas discussed in this chapter, hardly surprising in view of the many anomalies occurring in this area. Because of the conflicting approaches to the deductions of state and collateral benefits, there is much scope for over-compensation of some plaintiffs, whereas the present lack of use of actuarial tables may result in some plaintiffs being under-compensated. Some changes are on the horizon; more may follow.

28 See *Taylor v O'Connor* [1970] 1 All ER 365.

29 See *Thompson v Price* [1973] 2 All ER 846 and *Howitt v Heads* [1972] 1 All ER 491. It should be noted that, when assessing the dependency of children, the widow's re-marriage prospects may be considered by the judge, which seems to defeat the object of s 3(3) of the 1976 Act.

INDEX

E